The Revised & Expanded
TEACHINGS OF THE PROPHET JOSEPH SMITH

The Revised & Expanded

TEACHINGS OF THE PROPHET JOSEPH SMITH

Compared with the Earliest Known Manuscripts

Compiled by Alonzo L. Gaskill and Richard G. Moore

Greg Kofford Books
Salt Lake City, 2024

Copyright © 2024 Alonzo L. Gaskill and Richard G. Moore.
Cover design copyright © 2024 Greg Kofford Books, Inc.
Cover design by Loyd Isao Ericson.

Published in the USA.

All rights reserved. No part of this volume may be reproduced in any form without written permission from the publisher, Greg Kofford Books. The views expressed herein are the responsibility of the authors and do not necessarily represent the position of Greg Kofford Books.

ISBN: 978-1-58958-815-8 (paperback)
Also available in pdf ebook.

Greg Kofford Books
P. O. Box 1362
Draper, UT 84020
www.gregkofford.com
facebook.com/gkbooks
twitter.com/gkbooks

Library of Congress Control Number: 2024950762

In memory of Dr. Robert J. Matthews (1926–2009)

CONTENTS

Acknowledgements	ix
Introduction	xi
Abbreviations	xix
Editorial Notes	xxv
Section One: 1830–1834	1
Section Two: 1834–1837	53
Section Three: 1838–1839	145
Section Four: 1839–1842	195
Section Five: 1842–1843	303
Section Six: 1843–1844	365
Appendix A: Joseph Smith Sermon, April 8, 1843	529
Appendix B: Joseph Smith Sermon, June 11, 1843	535
Appendix C: King Follett Discourse, April 7, 1844	539
Appendix D: Joseph Smith's Potential Ghostwriters	561
Index	569

ACKNOWLEDGEMENTS

We wish to express our sincere appreciation to a number of students who have helped with the research on this project, including Michael Duval, Hannah Lyons, Sam Spice, Taylor Wanket, and Paige H. Murphy. Each served as a research assistant at various stages of the project, and each made much needed contributions.

We express our sincere thanks to our formative reviewers, Andy Skelton and Andrew Hedges, both affiliates of the Joseph Smith Papers project. Their reviews of the manuscript, and their helpful suggestions, have greatly improved the final product. In addition to our formative reviewers, we also express appreciation to those who served as summative reviewers—who took the time to examine the manuscript and offer their expert opinions.

We are indebted to numerous employees at the Church Historians Office and the Joseph Smith Papers project who regularly responded to questions posed about sources and the provenance of various documents, and who provided us with access to much needed texts. They have been most helpful. The significant work done by the various scholars of the Joseph Smith Papers project has provided researchers and authors invaluable access to primary sources and has markedly changed the landscape of research and writing in early Latter-day Saint history. One cannot say enough about the important contributions made by affiliates of the Joseph Smith Papers project.

Finally, we acknowledge the generosity and support of Jeff Franco, whose magnanimous backing made this project possible and whose consecrated support will ever be appreciated.

INTRODUCTION

On the very day on which the then "Church of Christ" was officially organized, the Lord gave this command: "Behold, there shall be a record kept among you; and in it [Joseph Smith shall] be called a seer, a translator, a prophet, an apostle of Jesus Christ, an elder of the church through the will of God the Father, and the grace of your Lord Jesus Christ, Being inspired of the Holy Ghost to lay the foundation thereof, and to build it up unto the most holy faith" (D&C 21:1–2). While the Church certainly struggled in its early years to faithfully fulfill this command, thousands of documents, letters, sermon summaries, and journal entries have nevertheless survived as a testament to the reality that those who knew the Prophet firmly believed in his prophetic and divinely ordained call. For example, Brigham Young said of his mentor and predecessor in the Presidency:

> The excellency of the glory of the character of brother Joseph Smith was that he could reduce heavenly things to the understanding of the finite. When he preached to the people—revealed the things of God, the will of God, the plan of salvation, the purposes of Jehovah, the relation in which we stand to him and all the heavenly beings, he reduced his teachings to the capacity of every man, woman, and child, making them as plain as a well-defined pathway. This should have convinced every person that ever heard of him of his divine authority and power, for no other man was able to teach as he could, and no person can reveal the things of God, but by the revelation of Jesus Christ. When we hear a man that can speak of heavenly things, and present them to the people in a way that they can be understood, you may know that to that man the avenue is open, and that he, by some power, has communication with heavenly beings.[1]

In a separate sermon, Young added: "It was decreed in the counsels of eternity, long before the foundations of the earth were laid, that [Joseph Smith] should be the man, in the last dispensation of this world, to bring forth the word of God to the people, and receive the fullness of the keys and power of the Priesthood of the Son of God. The Lord had his eye upon him. . . . He was foreordained in eternity to preside over this last dispensation."[2]

Like Young, others have seen in Joseph Smith's life and ministry evidence of the hand of God working in and through him. After the Prophet's martyrdom, the following was included at the end of the 1844 Doctrine and Covenants—which was nearly ready for publication when Joseph was slain:

> Joseph Smith, the Prophet and Seer of the Lord, has done more, save Jesus only, for the salvation of men in this world, than any other man that ever lived in it. In the short space of twenty years, he has . . . sent the fulness of the everlasting gospel . . . to the four quarters of the earth; has brought forth . . . revelations and commandments . . . and many other wise documents and instructions for the benefit of the children of men. (D&C 135:3)

While there is unquestionably power and inspiration in the Book of Mormon and the Doctrine and Covenants, Joseph's personal teachings and instructions hold a sacred place in the hearts and minds of the Church and its membership.

Noting the depth and breadth of the Prophet's teachings, one of his biographers recorded:

> Nothing was too trivial or too big to occupy his thoughts. He talked about tea, coffee, and tobacco; about the hours one should sleep and work; about whether the human epidermis changes every

---

1. Brigham Young, "Remarks," *Deseret News* 10, no. 39 (28 November 1860): 305.
2. Brigham Young, in *The Complete Discourses of Brigham Young*, ed. Richard S. Van Wagoner, 5 vols. (Smith-Pettit Foundation, 2009), 3:1521.

seven years; about laying out a city that would give a town and a country effect in one; about how to eliminate both poverty and riches from our present economic system; about the arrogance of those who come into power too soon; about the "planet that is nearest the throne of God"; about the much mooted question of his day as to whether the earth and man were created out of nothing or out of pre-existing matter; about the freedom of the will; about heaven and hell and whether there is a devil; about God and the true immorality of the soul.[3]

Though so much more could be said, these three testimonies highlight why a fascination with Joseph's public teachings is both appropriate and important. As Dean C. Jessee once noted, "His teachings, eagerly sought, are often read with scriptural reverence."[4] Indeed, from early in the history of the Church, members and nonmembers alike wished to know what Joseph thought and said on a variety of subjects. That fascination with the founder of the faith has led to the production of numerous texts highlighting heaven's declarations through its divinely appointed prophet. For example, in 1912, Edwin F. Parry, a Latter-day Saint composer and publisher, compiled the book *Joseph Smith's Teachings*—which was the forerunner to, and inspiration behind, the 1938 *Teachings of the Prophet Joseph Smith*.[5] Joseph Fielding Smith (who was the chief compiler of the latter of these two works) wrote:

> Elder Edwin F. Parry compiled and published a classified arrangement of excerpts from doctrinal sermons and writings of the Prophet Joseph Smith. . . . That little work filled an important mission, but left in the hearts and minds of all who were interested in the sayings of the great latter-day Prophet, a longing for more of his sayings, which longing was not satisfied. Many faithful members of the Church have expressed the desire that a more extensive work of this kind be published. The members of the Church quite generally desire to know what the Prophet Joseph Smith may have said on important subjects, for they look upon his utterance as coming through divine inspiration. . . .
>
> In accordance with the many calls that have been made that there be a more extensive compilation of these discourses and sayings, the matter was taken up in the Historians Office[6] and such a compilation has been prepared, submitted to the First Presidency and passed by them for publication.[7]

The resulting volume, *Teachings of the Prophet Joseph Smith*, supplanted Parry's 1912 work and has become a standard in Mormon literature ever since.[8]

---

3. John Henry Evans, *Joseph Smith—An American Prophet* (Deseret Book, 1966), 9–10.

4. Dean C. Jessee, "Priceless Words and Fallible Memories: Joseph Smith as Seen in the Effort to Preserve His Discourses," in *BYU Studies* 31, no. 2 (Spring 1991): 22.

5. Among others, Parry composed the music to hymns "Hail to the Brightness of Zion's Glad Morning!" and "Oh, Holy Words of Truth and Love." Parry was also a member of the Mormon Tabernacle Choir. In addition, he worked as an editor and typesetter for the *Juvenile Instructor*.

6. Joseph Fielding Smith was at that time the Church Historian—a position he served in from 1921 until 1970. He also served as Assistant Church Historian from 1906 until 1921. Including his four-and-a-half years in a non-administrative role (October 1901–April 1906), Elder Smith served some sixty-nine years in the Church Historian's Office.

7. Joseph Fielding Smith, "Introduction," in *Teachings of the Prophet Joseph Smith*, comp. Joseph Fielding Smith (Deseret Book, 1976), 3.

8. While Edwin Parry's work was clearly the inspiration behind Joseph Fielding Smith's 1938 compilation, even before Parry published *Joseph Smith's Teachings*, Elder Franklin D. Richards (of the Twelve) compiled "Gems from the History of Joseph Smith"—which appeared in the book *A Compendium of the Doctrines of the Gospel* (Deseret Book, 1882), 266–289. Richards wrote this book along with Elder James A. Little, and it consisted of statements by the Prophet Joseph, as recorded in the manuscript history of the Church and elsewhere.

Nearly four decades later, Deseret Book released a new edition of the *Teachings of the Prophet Joseph Smith*. This 1976 version included, for the first time, a concordance compiled by Brigham Young University's Robert J. Matthews.[9] Then, in 1993, Deseret Book released an additional revision of the classic, under the title *Scriptural Teachings of the Prophet Joseph Smith*. This version of the popular compilation utilized the traditional text, but included the additional study aid of extensive footnotes, directing readers to scriptures that supported the Prophet's doctrinal teachings. Compiled by BYU's Richard C. Galbraith, *Scriptural Teachings* seemed like a marked improvement on the older text—and many had hoped it would permanently replace the original. However, such was not to be the case. The 1993 version never caught on and is today out of print.[10]

In his introduction to the original edition of *Teachings*, Joseph Fielding Smith cautioned his readers: "It should be remembered that this compilation contains some discourses and statements from the minutes of council and priesthood meetings, which are not verbatim reports of the Prophet's remarks."[11] He further noted that "many of these discourses and writings" were drawn from "the Documentary History of the Church."[12] This last point is important to understand, as it emphasizes the fact that much of the underlying text that *Teachings* relied on was drawn from words ascribed to the Prophet but not written by Joseph. George A. Smith, who was heavily instrumental in the editing and publishing Joseph Smith's *History of the Church* (which was the basis for the *Documentary History of the Church*[13]), made this clarifying and important

---

9. Matthew's concordance expanded the index from fourteen pages (in the 1938 edition) to forty-one pages (in the 1976 edition).

10. Galbraith's edition is available in e-book, but no longer in print in hard copy.

11. See Smith, "Introduction," 3.

12. See Smith, 3.

13. Willard Richards, George A. Smith, and others compiled Joseph Smith's *History* between 1838 and 1856 (vols. A-1 through F1). Of course, most of the text of Joseph Smith's *History* was written by scribes rather than by the Prophet. Dean C. Jessee explained, "Joseph Smith did little of the actual writing of his history. According to his journal, he seldom used the pen himself, dictating all of his communications to a scribe. Shortly before his death he wrote: 'For the last three years I have ... kept several good, faithful, and efficient clerks in constant employ: they have accompanied me everywhere, and carefully kept my history, and they have written down what I have done, where I have been, and what I have said.' The number of scribes engaged in writing for Joseph Smith during the final fourteen years of his life reflect his continued concern for his history." [See Dean C. Jessee, *The Writing of Joseph Smith's History* (Mormon Miscellaneous, 1984), 2.] Thus, the various parts of the work attributed to Joseph were traditionally either dictated by him to one of his scribes, or they consisted of a secretary/historian independently describing his activities, whereabouts, and teachings during a given time period. Jessee's "The Writing of Joseph Smith's History" suggests that much of the writing of the official history occurred after the Prophet's 1844 death. (See Jessee, particularly 28–35.) Jessee lists the following men as the primary scribal authors of the work during the time periods listed: Oliver Cowdery (1829–38); John Whitmer (1829–38); Sidney Rigdon (1830–38); Frederick G. Williams (1832–39); Orson Hyde (1833–36); W. W. Phelps (circa 1831–44); Warren Parrish (1835–37); Sylvester Smith (1834–36); Warren A. Cowdery (1836–38); George W. Robinson (1836–40); James Mulholland (1838–39); Robert B. Thompson (1839–41); Howard Coray (1840–41); James Sloan (1840–43); Willard Richards (1841–54); William Clayton (1842–44); Thomas Bullock (circa 1843–56); Robert Lang Campbell (1845–50, 1854–56); Leo Hawkins (1853–56); and Jonathan Grimshaw (1853–56) [Jessee, 2–20, 22]. As noted above, in addition to the Prophet's personal scribes, others participated in the compilation of the history. For example, Wilford Woodruff's personal journals were an important source of information, and he

statement concerning how the various quotes attributed to the Prophet and subsequently used in Joseph Fielding Smith's *Teachings of the Prophet Joseph Smith* were acquired:

> I have filled up all the reports of sermons by Prest. Joseph Smith . . . from minutes or sketches taken at the time in long hand by Dr. Willard Richards, Wilford Woodruff, Thomas Bullock, William Clayton, Miss Eliza R. Snow &c., which was an immense labor, requiring the deepest thought and the closest application, as *there were mostly only two or three words (about half written) to a sentence. The greatest care has been taken to convey the ideas in the prophet's style as near as possible*; and in no case has the sentiment been varied that I know of; as I heard . . . most of his discourses myself, was on the most intimate terms with him, have retained a most vivid recollection of his teachings, and was well acquainted with his principles and motives.[14]

Thus, rather than being direct quotations, a significant number of the statements in the *History of the Church*—and, thus, many of the words attributed to the Prophet in *Teachings*—were summary statements developed by Willard Richards, George A. Smith, and others after looking at very cursory notes taken by individuals who attended Joseph's sermons, as well as from George A. Smith's personal memory. While George A. Smith stressed his attempt to be accurate and not "vary the sentiment" of Joseph's words in any way, it is nevertheless evident that such a process would have tremendous limitations. As Andrew F. Ehat and Lyndon W. Cook note: "Because there were no mechanical devices for recording the Prophet's sermons, verbatim accounts of his words do not exist. Therefore, contemporary reports (almost always in the form of private notes and diaries) constitute the closest approximation of Joseph Smith's actual

---

was engaged in review of the history during its final stages (circa 1855). While Willard Richards was the chief editor per se, upon his death George A. Smith took over as editor until the project's completion in 1856. The completed manuscript is said to have been read by and revised by Brigham Young before it was published in 1858 (Jessee, 20, 32, 35). At the turn of the twentieth century, Elder Francis M. Lyman (of the Twelve) suggested to the First Presidency that Elder B. H. Roberts (of the Seventy) revise the *History of Joseph Smith*. Though this suggestion was initially rejected because of costs, eventually Roberts was appointed to revamp the history. In the process, he corrected known errors, sought to improve the flow of the narrative, and provided some commentary and additional source material—particularly in his extensive footnotes. Elder Anthon H. Lund (of the Twelve) and President Joseph F. Smith reviewed Roberts's work prior to its 1902–1912 publication. Elder Roberts's revision of the history was published as the seven-volume *History of the Church of Jesus Christ of Latter-day Saints* or *Documentary History of the Church*. [See Matthew O. Richardson, "History of the Church," in *Encyclopedia of Latter-day Saint History*, ed. Arnold K. Garr, Donald Q. Cannon, and Richard O. Cowan (Deseret Book, 2000), 504–5.] Joseph Fielding Smith relied heavily on this revised history as a source for his *Teachings of the Prophet Joseph Smith*.

14. George A. Smith letter to Wilford Woodruff, 21 April 1856, cited in Jessee, "The Writing of Joseph Smith's History," 32, 34, emphasis added. See also Andrew F. Ehat and Lyndon W. Cook, comp., *The Words of Joseph Smith: The Contemporary Accounts of the Nauvoo Discourses of the Prophet Joseph* (Religious Studies Center, Brigham Young University, 1980), xvi. As the official Church Historian, Willard Richards sent out a request (on November 16, 1845) for any documents of any kind that would be useful in his work of compiling the history. In part, that request stated: "All those who have letters, or documents of any kind in their possession, which in any way related to the History of the Church of Jesus Christ of Latter Day Saints, are requested to leave them with the Historian. . . . Every individual who may be in possession of any fact, circumstance[,] incident, event, or transaction . . . will report it in writing. . . . The Historian wants all . . . papers, documents, of every kind[,] name[,] and nature, and all information that may relate to, or have a bearing in any wise upon the History of the Church . . ." See Willard Richards, in Brigham Young, *Manuscript History of the Church*, 16 November 1845, cited in Jessee, "The Writing of Joseph Smith's History," 32.

words."¹⁵ Ehat and Cook continue: "George A. Smith . . . amalgamated the various versions of Joseph Smith's discourses in preparing them for publication."¹⁶ Highlighting the circumstances of the times, and their influence upon recording what Joseph taught and all that happened in those early days, *The Joseph Smith Papers* project reports:

> The turbulent conditions of Joseph Smith's life hindered his attempts to write and oversee the creation of a history. Violent opposition threatened the Saints from without and dissension divided them from within. Lawsuits and financial problems were a constant distraction. Smith's history identifies the factors that complicated his literary efforts, describing "long imprisonments, vexatious and long continued Law Suits[;] The treachery of some of my clerks; the death of others; and the poverty of myself and brethren from continued plunder and driving." Record keeping and history writing did not thrive in these unsettled and sometimes bloody years, and the documents that were produced are fragmentary, recording only a fraction of Smith's activities and teachings. For example, the written record carries only traces of the vigorous oral tradition of preaching, debate, and the sharing of beliefs that existed from the earliest days of the church.¹⁷

They continue:

> Joseph Smith's sermons, in particular, were a vital part of the experience of the early Saints, but Smith left no notes or texts of his preaching, and those who attended his sermons in the early years made no attempt to capture his words. Smith's early histories are all but silent regarding his sermons, but other documents of the time often allude to oral transmission of doctrine and instruction. For example, in a June 1835 letter to his wife, William W. Phelps reported hearing Joseph Smith speak on the subject "This is my beloved son; hear ye him," which likely included an account of his first visionary experience. Phelps reported: "He preached one of the greatest sermons I ever heard—it was about 3½ hours long—and unfolded more mysteries than I can write at this time." Even when official church record keeping improved in the 1840s, only a fraction of Smith's sermons were recorded in detail. By Dean C. Jessee's count, fewer than one-fifth of Smith's known sermons were captured in any text (very few of them adequately), and the majority of those texts date from the last few years of Smith's life.¹⁸

---

15. Ehat and Cook, *The Words of Joseph Smith*, xvi.

16. Ehat and Cook, xvi. Dean Jessee recorded: "Using procedures typical of the literary world of their day, the editors inserted words, phrases, and sometimes even a paragraph, to smooth out or bridge gaps in the reported text of a speech without indicating that the added material was an editorial expansion of the original report. . . . Repeatedly in the months from November 1854 to July 1856, George A. Smith, Wilford Woodruff, Robert Campbell, John L. Smith, Jonathan Grimshaw, Leo Hawkins, and Thomas Bullock 'amalgamated' reports of Joseph Smith's speeches, read them to the President, and copied them into the history. . . . To assure the greatest accuracy, they read their work to Church leaders who had heard the original discourses in some instances and were in a position to insure [*sic*] the doctrinal integrity of what was said." Jessee, "Priceless Words and Fallible Memories," 28–29.

17. *The Joseph Smith Papers—Histories Volume 1: Joseph Smith Histories 1832–1844*, ed. Karen Lynn Davidson, David J. Whittaker, Mark Ashurst-McGee and Richard L. Jensen (Church Historians Press, 2012), xiv.

18. Davidson et al., xiv, note 4. See also Jessee, "Priceless Words and Fallible Memories," 23. It should be noted that the Nauvoo era had the best records of what Joseph publicly taught. Whereas accounts of Joseph's earliest discourses are often drawn from a singular source, during the Nauvoo era the Prophet's public comments were frequently referenced or partially recorded by two or, in some rare cases, three attendees.

The sad reality is that so much of what the Prophet of the Restoration taught went unrecorded.[19] And while circumstances of the times limited the ability to get a verbatim address, much more could have been done to preserve what Joseph taught the early Saints—but few saw the importance at the time.[20] Consequently, men like George A. Smith did their best to capture from the collective memory all that they could of the Prophet's divinely inspired teachings.[21] Though imperfect, what George A. Smith and Joseph Fielding Smith offered us were important contributions—sufficient for their day, and helpful in the cause.[22]

That being said, with the invaluable flow of information coming forth today through The Joseph Smith Papers Project, the classic *Teachings of the Prophet Joseph Smith* may be losing its place in the Latter-day Saint library. Knowing that many of the quotations therein attributed to the Prophet are but post-martyrdom summaries of the notes of those who heard him speak, scholars and members alike have become a bit reticent to be dogmatic about the content of

---

19. Dean Jessee noted: "Since Joseph Smith almost always spoke extemporaneously, without a prepared text, there are no drafts to help document his discourses. In 1843 he told an audience, 'I am not like other men, my mind is continually occupied with the business of the day, and I have to depend entirely upon the living God for everything I say on such occasions as these.' This was his common practice, a practice suggested by revelation in 1830: 'It shall be given thee in the very moment what thou shalt speak and write'" (Jessee, 26).

20. Jessee also noted: "in addition to the inability of clerks to report verbatim all that Joseph Smith said, years elapsed between the delivery and the editing of most of the discourses.... Most of the reports of Joseph Smith's discourses were not incorporated into the history until labor resumed on that work several years after the arrival of the Saints in the Salt Lake Valley; the boxes containing the contents of the Historian's Office were not unpacked until 7 June 1853. Even then, more than a year elapsed before work recommenced on the Prophet's speeches" (Jessee, 28).

21. "In comparing the published discourses of the Prophet with original reports of what he said, one finds elements of harshness, hypercriticism, egotism, ill humor, boasting, etc., cropping up at the points of heaviest editing—traits that have filtered into the record during the reporting and editing process and that appear to be more characteristic of the reporters and editors than of Joseph Smith. Thus the editing process has superimposed the personality of others over that of the Prophet.... Like the bones concealed in the wrappings of an ancient mummy, the sharp outlines of the Prophet lie hidden beneath the personalities of clerks, editors, and ghostwriters. None of those who recorded Joseph Smith's speeches realized that their efforts to preserve what he said would partially obscure the very greatness and individuality they sought to make immortal" (Jessee, 31, 37).

22. One source suggests: "In recent years anti-Mormon critics have charged that the written history of Joseph Smith published in the six volume *History of the Church* was produced by men whose tools were 'falsification,' 'deceit,' and "forgery."" [See unsigned foreword to Dean C. Jessee, *The Writing of Joseph Smith's History* (Mormon Miscellaneous, 1984).] Elsewhere we read: "In recent years a greater sense of 'getting to the sources' has marked Mormon historical writing.... However, some have argued that the sources of official Church writings were altered to create faithful, but inaccurate history. Some have even argued that Joseph Smith's public teachings were not actually his but were created after his death—that Church historians took a free hand in creating or amplifying nonexistent or cryptic notes into full-blown discourses" (Ehat and Cook, *The Words of Joseph Smith*, xv). Ehat and Cook add that in their research, they have found that "all of the Prophet's teachings during the Nauvoo period"—the era when we have the most detailed accounts of what he said—"can be documented from original sources. Admittedly the reports of his discourses were incomplete, but having multiple accounts of many of the sermons allows one to compare and contrast what each reporter recorded of the Prophet's ideas. Thus, there is no evidence that Church historians who prepared Joseph Smith's discourses for publication went beyond a reasonable interpretation of the original recorded statements" (Ehat and Cook, xv–xvi).

the summary quotations in that once-treasured volume. Indeed, in a recent policy announced by the Religious Studies Center at Brigham Young University, authors were counseled, "Avoid quoting from this book in Church publications because the scholarship is no longer current. For example, some of the statements attributed to Joseph Smith in the book were not actually made by him."[23] *Teachings* has been a mainstay source for Latter-day Saints for nearly eighty years, and many Latter-day Saint scholars and laymen alike have much of that traditional text committed to memory. But advancements in scholarship require us to say "goodbye" to that old friend, even if the passing of this classic has brought a measure of sadness to those of us who loved it. Therefore, in attempt to preserve one of the standard texts in Mormon literature, we offer this updated version: a parallel-column revised edition of *The Teachings of the Prophet Joseph Smith*.

Placing Joseph Fielding Smith's compilation in a side-by-side comparison with the original sources will enable readers to readily look up well-known and much-loved statements traditionally attributed to the Prophet, while providing readers with the original, more cryptic summaries of his sermons—as given by those who heard him deliver them.[24] In this way, it is our hope that *The Teachings of the Prophet Joseph Smith* will not be shelved as a forgotten classic, but will instead remain one of the important works of Latter-day Saint literature. *"Praise to the Man!"*

---

23. *Religious Studies Center Style Guide*, 7 February 2017, 67, s.v., 14:30.

24. It is worth noting that the original pagination in the 1938 edition of *Teachings of the Prophet Joseph Smith* was retained in subsequent editions of that text, with the sole exception of Richard Galbraith's *Scriptural Teachings of the Prophet Joseph Smith* (1993), which inserted the original pagination in brackets in the body of the text.

ABBREVIATIONS

D&C—Doctrine and Covenants

A collection of revelations and declarations received primarily through Joseph Smith Jr. Originally, it was to be published in Missouri as the Book of Commandments; however, mob violence destroyed the press and prevented its publication. Additional revelations were subsequently added, and the first edition of the Doctrine and Covenants was published at Kirtland, Ohio, in August 1835.[1]

E&MS—*Evening and Morning Star*

The *Evening and the Morning Star* was the first Latter-day Saint newspaper. It was published in Independence, Missouri, from June 1832 through July 1833, when the press was destroyed by mobocrats. Publication of the *Evening and the Morning Star* began again five months later in Kirtland, Ohio. The September 1834 issue was the last one printed. It was replaced in Kirtland by *The Latter Day Saints' Messenger and Advocate*.[2]

DHC—Documentary History of the Church

Joseph Smith, *History of the Church of Jesus Christ of Latter-day Saints*, 7 vols., edited by B. H. Roberts (The Church of Jesus Christ of Latter-day Saints, 1932–1951). The Documentary History of the Church is commonly known as *History of the Church*. (The official title of the first six of this seven-volume series is *History of the Church of Jesus Christ of Latter-day Saints, Period I: History of Joseph Smith, the Prophet, by Himself*. In actuality, many of the documents in the *History of the Church* are not from the Prophet himself. One of the weaknesses of this history is its failure to distinguish between the Prophet's writings and those of others which are often presented as his own. Beginning in 1902, assistant Church Historian B. H. Roberts began to compile and edit the "History of Joseph Smith" previously published in the *Times and Seasons* and other periodicals from the Manuscript History of the Church. The final product was the [Documentary] *History of the Church*.)[3]

History, A-1 through F-1—Manuscript History

During the summer of 1839, Joseph Smith began dictating to scribes his "history." Eventually, this history would fill six volumes with over 2,400 pages, consisting of volumes A-1 through F-1 of the Joseph Smith Papers Project. It became known as the "Manuscript History of the Church."[4] The Joseph Smith Papers refers to it as "History,

---

1. See H. Dean Garrett, "Doctrine and Covenants," in Arnold K. Garr, Donald Q. Cannon, and Richard O. Cowan, *Encyclopedia of Latter-day Saint History* (Deseret Book, 2000), 300–302.

2. Clark V. Johnson, "Evening and the Morning Star, The" in Garr, Cannon, and Cowan, *Encyclopedia of Latter-day Saint History*, 347–48; Andrew H. Hedges, "Messenger and Advocate, Latter-day Saints'," in in Garr, Cannon, and Cowan, *Encyclopedia of Latter-day Saint History*, 738–39.

3. See Matthew O. Richardson, "History of the Church," in Garr, Cannon, and Cowan, *Encyclopedia of Latter-day Saint History*, 504–5; Karen Lynn Davidson, David J. Whittaker, Mark Ashurst-McGee, and Richard L. Jensen, eds., *Histories Volume 1: Joseph Smith Histories, 1832–1844* (Church Historian's Press, 2012), xxxi–xxxii.

4. See Howard C. Searle, "History of the Church (History of Joseph Smith)," in *Encyclopedia of Mormonism*, 4 vols., Daniel H. Ludlow, ed. (Macmillian Publishers, 1992), 2:647.

1838–1856."[5] Portions of the Manuscript History of the Church were published in serial form in the Nauvoo *Times and Seasons* and Utah's *Deseret News* under the title "History of Joseph Smith."[6] Some of this history was also published in England's *Millennial Star*. The published versions in various periodicals are not as complete or accurate as the actual manuscripts from which they were drawn.[7] An overview of Manuscript History is as follows:

Volume	Period Covered	Pages
A-1	Dec. 1805–Aug. 1834	1–553
B-1	1 Sept. 1834–2 Nov. 1838	554–849
C-1	2 Nov. 1838–31 July 1842	850–1361
D-1	1 Aug. 1842–1 July 1843	1362–1636
E-1	1 July 1843–30 April 1844	1637–2029
F-1	1 May 1844–8 Aug. 1844	1–304[8]

The above histories can be found online at josephsmithpapers.org.

JSP, AR—*Joseph Smith Papers, Administrative Records, Council of Fifty Minutes, March 1844–January 1846*

Matthew J. Grow, Ronald K. Esplin, Mark Ashurst-McGee, Gerrit J. Dirkmaat, and Jeffrey D. Mahas, eds. *Council of Fifty, Minutes, March 1844–January 1846*. This first volume of the Administrative Records series of *The Joseph Smith Papers*, edited by Ronald K. Esplin, Matthew J. Grow, and Matthew C. Godfrey (Church Historian's Press, 2016) is the only one of the series to be published in print.

JSP, D2—*Joseph Smith Papers, Documents volume 2*

Matthew C. Godfrey, Mark Ashurst-McGee, Grant Underwood, Robert J. Woodford, and William G. Hartley, eds. *Documents, Volume 2: July 1831–January 1833*. Vol. 2 of the Documents series of *The Joseph Smith Papers*, edited by Dean C. Jessee, Ronald K. Esplin, Richard Lyman Bushman, and Matthew J. Grow (Church Historian's Press, 2013).

JSP, D3—*Joseph Smith Papers, Documents volume 3*

Gerrit J. Dirkmaat, Brent M. Rogers, Grant Underwood, Robert J. Woodford, and William G. Hartley, eds. *Documents, Volume 3: February 1833–March 1834*. Vol. 3 of the Documents series of *The Joseph Smith Papers*, edited by Ronald K. Esplin and Matthew J. Grow (Church Historian's Press, 2014).

---

5. See "Introduction to History, 1838–1856 (Manuscript History of the Church)," The Joseph Smith Papers, josephsmithpapers.org.

6. See Searle, "History," 2:647.

7. See "Introduction to History, 1838–1856 (Manuscript History of the Church)," The Joseph Smith Papers josephsmithpapers.org.

8. This chart has been reproduced from josephsmithpapers.org/doc/introduction-to-history-1838-1856-manuscript-history-of-the-church.

JSP, D4—*Joseph Smith Papers, Documents volume 4*

    Matthew C. Godfrey, Brenden W. Rensink, Alex D. Smith, Max H. Parkin, and Alexander L. Baugh, eds. *Documents, Volume 4: April 1834–September 1835*. Vol. 4 of the Documents series of *The Joseph Smith Papers*, edited by Ronald K. Esplin and Matthew J. Grow (Church Historian's Press, 2016).

JSP, D5—*Joseph Smith Papers, Documents volume 5*

    Brent M. Rogers, Elizabeth A. Kuehn, Christian K. Heimburger, Max H. Parkin, Alexander L. Baugh, and Steven C. Harper, eds. *Documents, Volume 5: October 1835–January 1838*. Vol. 5 of the Documents series of *The Joseph Smith Papers*, edited by Ronald K. Esplin, Matthew J. Grow, and Matthew C. Godfrey (Church Historian's Press, 2017).

JSP, D6—*Joseph Smith Papers, Documents volume 6*

    Mark Ashurst-McGee, David W. Grua, Elizabeth A. Kuehn, Brenden W. Rensink, and Alexander L. Baugh, eds. *Documents, Volume 6: February 1838–August 1839*. Vol. 6 of the Documents series of *The Joseph Smith Papers*, edited by Ronald K. Esplin, Matthew J. Grow, and Matthew C. Godfrey (Church Historian's Press, 2017).

JSP, D7—*Joseph Smith Papers, Documents volume 7*

    Matthew C. Godfrey, Spencer W. McBride, Alex D. Smith, and Christopher James Blythe, eds. *Documents, Volume 7: September 1839–January 1841*. Vol. 7 of the Documents series of *The Joseph Smith Papers*, edited by Ronald K. Esplin, Matthew J. Grow, and Matthew C. Godfrey (Church Historian's Press, 2018).

JSP, D8—*Joseph Smith Papers, Documents volume 8*

    Brent M. Rogers, Mason K. Allred, Gerrit J. Dirkmaat, and Brett D. Dowdle, eds. *Documents, Volume 8: February–November 1841*. Vol. 8 of the Documents series of *The Joseph Smith Papers*, edited by Ronald K. Esplin, Matthew J. Grow, Matthew C. Godfrey, and R. Eric Smith (Church Historian's Press, 2019).

JSP, D9—*Joseph Smith Papers, Documents volume 9*

    Matthew C. Godfrey, R. Eric Smith, Matthew J. Grow, and Ronald K. Esplin, eds. *Documents, Volume 9: December 1841–April 1842*. Vol. 9 of the Documents series of *The Joseph Smith Papers*, edited by Alex D. Smith, Christian K. Heimburger, and Christopher James Blythe (Church Historian's Press, 2019).

JSP, D11—*Joseph Smith Papers, Documents volume 11*

    Spencer W. McBride, Jeffrey D. Mahas, Brett D. Dowdle, and Tyson Reeder, eds. *Documents, Volume 11: September 1842–February 1843*. Vol. 11 of the Documents series of *The Joseph Smith Papers*, edited by Ronald K. Esplin, Matthew J. Grow, Matthew C. Godfrey, and R. Eric Smith (Church Historian's Press, 2020).

JSP, D12—*Joseph Smith Papers, Documents volume 12*

    David W. Grua, Brent M. Rogers, Matthew C. Godfrey, Robin Scott Jensen, Christopher James Blythe, and Jessica M. Nelson, eds. *Documents, Volume 12: March–July 1843*. Vol. 12 of the Documents series of *The Joseph Smith Papers*, edited by Matthew C. Godfrey, R. Eric Smith, Matthew J. Grow, and Ronald K. Esplin (Church Historian's Press, 2020).

JSP, D13—Joseph Smith Papers, Documents volume 13

    Christian K. Heimburger, Jeffrey D. Mahas, Brent M. Rogers, Mason K. Allred, J. Chase Kirkham, and Matthew S. McBride, eds. *Documents, Volume 13: August–December 1843*. Vol. 13 of the Document series of *The Joseph Smith Papers*, edited by Matthew C. Godfrey, R. Eric Smith, Matthew J. Grow, and Ronald K. Esplin. Salt Lake City: Church Historian's Press, 2022.

JSP, D14—Joseph Smith Papers, Documents volume 14

    Alex D. Smith, Adam H. Petty, Jessican M. Nelson, and Spencer W. McBride, eds. *Documents, Volume 14: 1 January–15 May 1844*. Vol. 14 of the Documents series of *The Joseph Smith Papers*, edited by Matthew C. Godfrey, R. Eric Smith, Matthew J. Grow, and Ronald K. Esplin (Church Historian's Press, 2023).

JSP, H1—Joseph Smith Papers, Histories volume 1

    Karen Lynn Davidson, David J. Whittaker, Mark Ashurst-McGee, and Richard L. Jensen, eds. *Histories, Volume 1: Joseph Smith Histories, 1832–1844*. Vol. 1 of the Histories series of *The Joseph Smith Papers*, edited by Dean C. Jessee, Ronald K. Esplin, and Richard Lyman Bushman (Church Historian's Press, 2012).

JSP, H2—Joseph Smith Papers, Histories volume 2

    Karen Lynn Davidson, Richard L. Jensen, and David J. Whittaker, eds. *Histories, Volume 2: Assigned Historical Writings, 1831–1847*. Vol. 2 of the Histories series of *The Joseph Smith Papers*, edited by Dean C. Jessee, Ronald K. Esplin, and Richard Lyman Bushman. (Church Historian's Press, 2012).

JSP, J1—Joseph Smith Papers, Journals volume 1

    Dean C. Jessee, Mark Ashurst-McGee, and Richard L. Jensen, eds. *Journals, Volume 1: 1832–1839*. Vol. 1 of the Journals series of *The Joseph Smith Papers*, edited by Dean C. Jessee, Ronald K. Esplin, and Richard Lyman Bushman (Church Historian's Press, 2008).

JSP, J2—Joseph Smith Papers, Journals volume 2

    Andrew H. Hedges, Alex D. Smith, and Richard Lloyd Anderson, eds. *Journals, Volume 2: December 1841–April 1843*. Vol. 2 of the Journals series of *The Joseph Smith Papers*, edited by Dean C. Jessee, Ronald K. Esplin, and Richard Lyman Bushman (Church Historian's Press, 2011).

JSP, J3—Joseph Smith Papers, Journals volume 3

    Andrew H. Hedges, Alex D. Smith, and Brent M. Rogers, eds. *Journals, Volume 3: May 1843–June 1844*. Vol. 3 of the Journals series of *The Joseph Smith Papers*, edited by Ronald K. Esplin and Matthew J. Grow (Church Historian's Press, 2015).

JSP, MB2—Joseph Smith Papers, Minute Book 2

    Minute Book 2 is sometimes known as the Far West Record. A volume entitled *Far West Record: Minutes of The Church of Jesus Christ of Latter-day Saints, 1830–1844*, edited by Donald Q. Cannon and Lyndon W. Cook, was published in 1983 by Deseret Book Company. However, the online Joseph Smith Papers version of Minute Book 2 is the version we have relied upon in this compilation. At present, there is no plan to print hard copies of the volume.

JSP, R2—Revelations and Translations volume 2

>Robin Scott Jensen, Richard E. Turley Jr., and Riley M. Lorimer, eds. *Revelations and Translations, Volume 2: Published Revelations*. Vol. 2 of the Revelations and Translations series of *The Joseph Smith Papers*, edited by Dean C. Jessee, Ronald K. Esplin, and Richard Lyman Bushman (Church Historian's Press, 2011).

M&A—Latter Day Saints' Messenger and Advocate

>*The Latter Day Saints' Messenger and Advocate* was a periodical published in Kirtland, Ohio, by the "Church of the Latter Day Saints" from October 1834 to September 1837. During that time, it served as the Church's "official monthly newspaper."[9] Editors included Oliver Cowdery and his brother Warren Cowdery.[10]

PWJS—The Personal Writings of Joseph Smith

>Dean C. Jesse, ed., *Personal Writings of Joseph Smith*, revised edition (Deseret Book and Brigham Young University, 2002). This volume was a precursor to the Joseph Smith Papers Project and contains holograph writings of Joseph Smith, documents in the handwriting of clerks of the Prophet that indicate that they were dictated by him, and non-holographic documents that appear (because of style and content) to have been authored by him.[11]

RSM—Minutes from Relief Society meetings

>Jill Mulvay Derr, Carol Cornwall Madsen, Kate Holbrook, and Matthew J. Grow, eds., *The First Fifty Years of Relief Society: Key Documents in Latter-day Saint Women's History* (The Church Historian's Press, 2016).

T&S—Times and Seasons

>The *Times and Seasons* was a periodical published in Nauvoo, Illinois, from November 1839 through February 1846. It was first issued in pamphlet form—as a "monthly religious paper." However, starting in 1840, it became a semimonthly sixteen-page newspaper. Initially privately published, the Church purchased the periodical from Ebenezer Robinson in 1841. The paper was "a major source of information on early Latter-day Saint thought." Editors included Don Carlos Smith, Ebenezer Robinson, Robert B. Thompson, Joseph Smith Jr., and John Taylor.[12]

TPJS—Teachings of the Prophet Joseph Smith

>Joseph Fielding Smith, comp., *Teachings of the Prophet Joseph Smith* (Deseret News Press, 1938). A collection of Joseph Smith's "discourses and sayings" compiled by the Historian's Office under the direction of Joseph Fielding Smith (during his tenure as head of the Church's Historian's Office). First published in 1938, after approval from the First Presidency, the volume always acknowledged that much of its con-

---

9. Hedges, "Messenger and Advocate," 738.

10. See Richard G. Moore, "A History of Mormon Periodicals From 1830–1838" (master's thesis, Brigham Young University, 1983), 40, 51, 67.

11. See Dean C. Jesse, ed. *Personal Writings of Joseph Smith*, revised edition (Deseret Book and Brigham Young University, 2002), xvii.

12. See Richard D. McClellan, "Times and Seasons," in Garr, Cannon, and Cowan, *Encyclopedia of Latter-day Saint History*, 1248–49.

tent was not "verbatim reports of the Prophet's remarks." Drawing heavily on the Documentary History of the Church and other published works from the early days of the restoration, *TPJS* served as the most drawn upon resource for the Prophet's teachings for more than 80 years.

WCJ—William Clayton Journal

William Clayton Journals, 1842–1845.[13] Clayton joined the Church in England in 1837. He migrated to America in 1840 and, in June of 1842, succeeded Willard Richards as the Joseph Smith's clerk. He was one of the Prophet's closest associates and a meticulous record keeper—helping to prepare the official history of Joseph Smith.[14]

WJS—The Words of Joseph Smith

Andrew F. Ehat and Lyndon W. Cook, eds., *The Words of Joseph Smith* (Grandin Book Company, 1991). This volume is a compilation of the various extant accounts of 173 of Joseph Smith's Nauvoo discourses. It draws from private journals and official records (kept by the Prophet's personal secretaries/clerks).[15]

WWJ—The Wilford Woodruff Journals

Dan Vogel, ed., *The Wilford Woodruff Journals*, 7 vols. (Benchmark Books, 2020). Wilford Woodruff was, by all accounts, the most prolific of journal keepers among early nineteenth century members of the restoration movement. Of Woodruff's work as a record keeper, one compiler noted, "The 1833–1898 journals of Wilford Woodruff . . . rank among the most significant documents of Mormonism and the American West. . . . [T]heir seven thousand manuscript pages 'are for Mormon history what the Thomas Jefferson papers are for American history: bedrock—primary source material for the men and ideas that shaped their respective institutions. From New York to Ohio, Missouri, Illinois, and Utah, this remarkable man of faith recorded virtually the entire spectrum of nineteenth-century Mormonism.'"[16] Woodruff's journals, which record nearly sixty-five years of Church history, are perhaps the single most important record of the events of the early Church.[17]

---

13. Selections of this journal are available at josephsmithpapers.org. See also George D. Smith, ed., *An Intimate Chronicle: The Journals of William Clayton* (Signature Books and Smith Research Associates, 1991). George Smith divides Clayton's journal into six sections: Journal 1—England and Emigration (1840–1842), Journal 2—Nauvoo (1842–1846), Journal 3—Nauvoo Temple (1845–1846), Journal 4—The Trek West (1846–1847), Journal 5—Visit to Utah Settlements (1853), and Journal 6—Mission to England (1853). See Smith, xii.

14. See James B. Allen, "William Clayton," in Garr, Cannon, and Cowan, *Encyclopedia of Latter-day Saint History*, 218–19.

15. Ehat and Cook, *The Words of Joseph Smith*, xv–xx.

16. Scott G. Kenney, ed., *Wilford Woodruff's Journal*, 9 vols. (Signature Books, 1983–1985), 1:ix.

17. See B. H. Roberts, *A Comprehensive History of the Church*, 6 vols. (Sonos Publishing, 1991), 6:354–55.

EDITORIAL NOTES

The pagination of Joseph Fielding Smith's *Teachings of the Prophet Joseph Smith* has been retained in this volume as bracketed inserts. For example, the beginning of page 43 in the original *Teachings* is indicated as **[p.43]** in the left-hand column of this book. These bracketed page numbers were included in this revised and expanded edition of *Teachings* in order to enable readers to locate passages found in the original version of the text. (Corresponding bracketed numbers have also been added to the top of each page to assist in quickly locating the original *Teachings* page numbers.) Similarly, where a given section of the right-hand column covers multiple pages (in a *JSP* document or other primary source), a bolded, bracketed number has been inserted into the text as well.

The Prophet Joseph Smith was often listed as "editor" of Church periodicals, such as the *Times & Seasons*, even though there is some evidence that he was not always the actual author of entries attributed to the volume's editor. (For a discussion of potential ghost authors, see Appendix D herein.) Consequently, in some cases, we simply do not know if Joseph penned the words attributed to him.

The subheadings Joseph Fielding Smith included in his version of *Teachings of the Prophet Joseph Smith* did not appear in the original discourses and documents from which he drew the Prophet's words. Elder Smith inserted them in order to give the Prophet's words a more topical feel. While they artificially break up the discourses in which they have been inserted, they have been retained herein for continuity with the original version of *Teachings*.

In order to reduce confusion, we have essentially employed the same type of transcription symbols used in the production of the *Joseph Smith Papers*. Punctuation, case, and spelling errors in the original sources have been retained in the right-hand column of this volume. Thus, sentences sometimes end with a comma (rather than a period) or begin with a lowercase letter, and words are often misspelled. These are not typos in this updated text, but they have been retained in order to give the reader an accurate sense of the original (or earliest available) texts from which each of these quotes attributed to the Prophet have been drawn.[1] In addition to spelling and punctuation errors in the original documents, we have also retained (in the text of the right-hand column) insertions of letters, words, and sentences, as well as letters, words, and sentences that have been crossed out or corrected in the original documents. Each of these are noted with the use of the following transcription symbols:

> [*illegible*] A bracket with the word [*illegible*] is the symbol employed to denote indecipherable handwriting in the original document.
>
> [clarification] A bracket with a word or letter enclosed has been used in order to correct or clarify the text found in the original manuscript. For example, exorcise [exercise]; passge pass[a]ge; etc.

---

1. The reader should be aware that, in many cases, the original sources no longer exist. For example, certain original letters have been lost, but hand-written copies were made in Joseph's "letterbook." In numerous situations, therefore, these copies are the earliest known sources we can draw upon.

[word?] A bracket with a word followed by a question mark represents the editor's interpretation of a word that the original author may have meant, or words that may have been accidentally omitted. For example, through [throw?]; we say unto [you?] that; etc.

<inserted> Angled brackets are used to denote letters and words that were inserted into the text or margins of the original manuscript for correction or clarification. For example, their ~~grate~~ <great> anxiety; walls and <iron> doors; etc.

~~cross outs~~ A word or words crossed out indicates that these words were crossed out, canceled, or replaced in the original document. For example, who will not ~~return~~ repent and return; provide ~~bread~~ <food> for them; etc.

<u>underlined</u> Words that are underlined in the text indicate underlining in the original text. For example, "Oliver Cowdery, <u>Clerk and Recorder;</u> conduct which we <u>highly disapprobate</u>"; etc.

◊ A letter that appears in the original document but is illegible. For example, he prepared the way d◊◊ before the Savior; the Lord ◊◊◊ gave me; etc.

SECTION ONE

1830–1834

SECTION ONE

Title Page of the Book of Mormon

Joseph Smith's History

[p.7]¹ Meantime our translation drawing to a close, we went to Palmyra, Wayne County, New York, secured the copyright, and agreed with Mr. Egbert B. Grandin to print five thousand copies for the sum of three thousand dollars.

Mean time our translation drawing to a close, we went to Palmyra, Wayne County, N. Y: secured the Copyright; and agreed with Mr Egbert Grandon [Grandin] to print five thousand Copies, for the sum of three thousand dollars.³

I wish to mention here, that the title-page of the Book of Mormon is a literal translation, taken from the very last leaf, on the left hand side of the collection or book of plates, which contained the record which has been translated, the language of the whole running the same as all Hebrew writing in general; and that said title-page is not by any means a modern composition, either of mine or of any other man who has lived or does live in this generation. Therefore, in order to correct an error which generally exists concerning it, I give below² that part of the title-page of the English version of the Book of Mormon, which is a genuine and literal translation of the title-page of the original Book of Mormon, as recorded on the plates.—DHC 1;71. (1830.)

I would mention here also in order to correct a misunderstanding, which has gone abroad concerning the title page of the Book of Mormon, that it is not a composition of mine or of any other man's who has lived or does live in this generation, but that it is a literal translation taken from the last leaf of the plates, on the left hand side of the collection of plates, the language running same as ~~the~~ <all> Hebrew <wr[i]ting> ~~language~~ <in general>. And that no error can henceforth possibly exist I give here the Title so far as it is a translation.⁴

Value of the Revelations and Commandments

Joseph Smith's History

My time was occupied closely in reviewing the commandments and sitting in conference, for nearly two weeks, for from the first to the twelfth of November [1831] we held four special conferences. In the last which was held at

My time was occupied closely in reviewing the commandments and sitting in conference for nearly two weeks; for we held from the first to the twelfth of November, four special conferences. In the last, which was held at Brother

---

1. The bracketed numbers in bold in the left-hand column's text—e.g., **[p.7]**—refer to the pagination of the original *TPJS*.
2. The original *TPJS* footnote reads: "See the title-page of the Book of Mormon, the two paragraphs mentioned."
3. This paragraph was taken from *JSP, H1*, draft 2, 352.
4. *JSP, H1*, draft 1, 352, 354.

Brother Johnson's, in Hiram, after deliberate consideration, in consequence of the book of revelations, now to be printed,[5] being **[p.8]** the foundation of the Church in these last days, and a benefit to the world, showing that the keys of the mysteries of the kingdom of our Savior are again entrusted to man; and the riches of eternity within the compass of those who are willing to live by every word that proceedeth out of the mouth of God—therefore the conference voted that they prize the revelations to be worth to the Church the riches of the whole earth, speaking temporally. The great benefits to the world which result from the Book of Mormon and the revelations, which the Lord has seen fit in His infinite wisdom to grant unto us for our salvation, and for the salvation of all that will believe, were	[John] Johnson's in Hiram, after deliberate consideration, in consequence of the book of Revelations, now to be printed, being the foundation of the church in these last days; and a benefit to the world, showing that the keys of the mysteries of the Kingdom of our Savior, are again entrusted to man, and the riches of eternity within the compass of those who are willing to live by every word that proceedeth out of the mouth of God: ~~therefore~~ the conference priced the Revelations to be worth to the church, the riches of the whole earth, speaking temporally. The great benefits to the world, which result from the Book of Mormon and the Revelations, which the Lord has seen fit, in his infinite wisdom, to grant unto us for our salvation, and for the salvation of all that will

---

5. The original *TPJS* footnote reads: "At a conference of the Church held in November, 1831, the Prophet received the revelation known as Section One, or the Preface to the Book of Commandments. At this conference the Elders considered the question of publishing the revelations which had been given up to that time as the Book of Commandments. This action the Lord approved by revelation. It was decided that 10,000 copies should be published, but later this was changed to 3,000 copies. A number of the brethren, at this conference, arose and stated that they were willing to testify to the world that they knew that the revelations received by the Prophet were of the Lord. In due time the revelations were compiled by the Prophet, and at a conference held November 12, 1831, the revelations were received with thanksgiving. Oliver Cowdery, John Whitmer and William W. Phelps, were appointed to review the revelations for printing, and Oliver Cowdery and John Whitmer were appointed to carry them to Missouri where the printing was to be done. These brethren were 'dedicated and consecrated with the sacred writings and all they have entrusted to their care to the Lord.' The publication was commenced by William W. Phelps and Co. in Jackson County, Missouri, but before the work was completed the press and type were destroyed by a mob, July 20, 1833, and only a few of the printed forms were preserved; these were bound and used by those fortunate enough to secure them in the uncompleted condition as the Book of Commandments. Later, in the year 1835, the revelations, now greatly increased in number, were again compiled and ordered printed as The Doctrine and Covenants. This first edition, prepared under the care of the Prophet Joseph Smith, contained 254 pages and was printed by Frederick G. Williams and Co. in Kirtland, Ohio. The revelations ranged over a period from 1828 to 1834. Seven Lectures on Faith, which had been given before the School of the Elders in Kirtland were also added to the volume, not as revelations, but as stated by the brethren at that time 'as profitable for doctrine.' In this book there also appeared two articles written by Oliver Cowdery, one on Marriage, and the other on Governments and Laws in General. These were ordered printed in the volume with the revelations, but it should be remembered this was done in the absence and without the approval of the Prophet Joseph Smith, who with President Frederick G. Williams was in Michigan at the time this action was taken. Hence these articles are not, as some have supposed, revelations and were not so considered by the Church. It was on the occasion of the acceptance of the revelations for publication, November 12, 1831, when the Prophet wrote in his journal the comment on the value of the revelations."

duly appreciated; and in answer to an inquiry, I received the following.[6] (Nov., 1831) DHC 1:235–236.

believe, were duly appreciated: and in answer to an enquiry, I received the following.[7]

Parting the Veil Through Perfect Faith

Minute Book 2[10]

Brother Joseph Smith, Jr. said: We have assembled together to do the business of the Lord and it is through the great [p.9] mercy of our God that we are spared to assemble together, many of us have gone at the command of the Lord in defiance of everything evil, and obtained blessings unspeakable, in consequence of which our names are sealed in the Lamb's book of life, for the Lord has spoken it. It is the privilege of every Elder to speak of the things of God; and could we all come together with one heart and one mind in perfect faith the veil might as well be rent today as next week, or any other time, and if we will but cleanse ourselves and covenant before God, to serve Him, it is our privilege to have an assurance that God will protect us at all times.[8]— FWR,[9] pp. 13-14. (Oct. 25, 1831.)

Br Joseph Smith Jr said we have assembled together to do the business of the Lord and it is through the great mercy of our God that we are spared to assemble together, many of us have went at the command of the Lord in defiance of every thing evil, and obtained blessings unspeakable in consequence of which, our names are sealed in the Lambs' Book of life, for the Lord has spoken it. It is the privilege of every Elder to speak of the things of God &c, And could we all come together with one heart and one mind in perfect faith the vail might as well be rent to day as next week or any other time and if we will but cleanse ourselves and covenant before God, to serve him, it is our privilege to have an assurance that God will protect us at all times.[11]

Perfect Love a Safeguard Against Falling from Grace

Minute Book 2

Brother Joseph Smith, Jr. said: That he intended to do his duty before the Lord and hoped that the brethren would be patient as they had a considerable distance (to go). Also said that the promise of God was that the greatest blessings which God had to bestow should be given to those who contributed to the support of his family while he was translating the fulness of the scriptures. Until we have perfect love we are

Br Joseph Smith Jr said that he intended to do his duty before the Lord and hoped that the brethren would be patient, as they had a considerable distance. also said that the promise of God was that the greatest blessings which God had to bestow should be given to those who contributed to the support of his family while translating the fulness of the Scriptures; also said until we have perfect love we are li-

---

6. The original *TPJS* footnote reads: "D&C, Sec. 70."
7. November 1831, History, A-1, 173–74.
8. The original *TPJS* footnote reads: "This is not a verbatim statement, but report in the minutes of the meeting of the conference held on that day."
9. Far West Record.
10. JSP, MB2.
11. 25–26 October 1831, JSP, MB2, 11.

liable to fall and when we have a testimony that our names are sealed in the Lamb's book of life we have perfect love and then it is impossible for false Christs to deceive us; also said, that the Lord held the Church bound to provide for families of the absent Elders while proclaiming the gospel; further, that God had often sealed up the heavens because of covetousness in the Church. The Lord would cut short his work in righteousness and except the Church receive the fulness of the scriptures that they would yet fail.[12]—FWR,[13] p. 16. (Oct. 25, 1831.)

able to fall and when we have a testimony that our names are sealed in the Lamb's Book of life we have perfect love & then it is impossible for false Christ's to decieve us. also said that the Lord held the Church bound to provide for the families of the absent Elders while proclaiming the Gospel: further said that the God had often sealed up the heavens because of covetousness in the Church. Said that the Lord would cut his work short in righteousness and except the church recieve the fulness of the Scriptures that they would yet fall.[14]

Comment on Revision of the Scriptures

Joseph Smith's History

Upon my return from Amherst Conference, I resumed the translation of the Scriptures.[15] From sundry revelations which **[p.10]** had been received, it was apparent that many important points touching the salvation of men, had been taken from the Bible, or lost before it was compiled. It appeared from what truths were left, that if God rewarded every one according to the deeds **[p.11]** done in the body the term "Heaven" as intended for the Saints' eternal home, must include more kingdoms than one.

Upon my return from Amherst conference, I resumed the translation of the scriptures, From sundry revelations which had been received, it was apparent that many important points, touching the Salvation of man, had been taken from the Bible, or lost before it was compiled. It appeared self evident from what truths were left, that if God rewarded every one according to the deeds done in the body, the term "heaven", as intended for the Saints eternal home, must include more kingdoms than one. Accordingly on the 16th of

---

12. The original *TPJS* footnote reads: "This is also a statement from the minutes of the Prophet's remarks as recorded by the scribe, not a verbatim report but a synopsis."

13. Far West Record.

14. 25–26 October 1831, JSP, MB2, 13.

15. The original *TPJS* footnote reads:

> Shortly after the organization of the Church the Lord commanded Joseph Smith to make a translation of the Book of Mormon that because of iniquity 'many plain and precious things' were 'taken away from the book, which is the book of the Lamb of God.' (1 Nephi 13:28.) Moreover, because of the 'many plain and precious things which have been taken out of the book, which were plain unto the understanding of the children of men, according to the plainness which is in the Lamb of God—because of these things which are taken away out of the gospel of the Lamb, an exceeding great many do stumble, yea, insomuch that Satan hath great power over them.' (1 Nephi 13:29.)
>
> As early as April, 1829, the Lord declared that many of these plain and precious sayings were to be restored, not only through the Book of Mormon, but through a revision of the Bible. When Oliver Cowdery came to the Prophet Joseph Smith and commenced to write at the Prophet's dictation in the translation of the Book of Mormon, the Lord said unto him: 'Verily verily, I say unto you, that there are records which contain much of my gospel, which have been kept back because of the wickedness of the people. And now I command you, that if you have good desires—a desire to lay up treasures for yourself in heaven—then shall you assist in bringing to light, with your gift, those parts

Accordingly, on the 16th of February, 1832, while translating St. John's Gospel, myself and Elder Rigdon saw the following vision.[16] — DHC 1:245. (Feb. 16, 1832.)

February, 1832. while translating St John's Gospel, myself and Elder [Sidney] Rigdon Saw the following.[17]

The Prophet's Views on the Vision

Nothing could be more pleasing to the Saints upon the order of the Kingdom of the Lord, than the light which burst upon the world through the foregoing vision. Every law, every

Joseph Smith's History

Nothing could be more pleasing to the Saint, upon the order of the kingdom of the Lord, than the light which burst upon the world, through the foregoing vision. Every law, every

---

of my scriptures which have been hidden because of iniquity.' (D. and C. 6:26–27. A few days later, in the same month of April, 1829, the Lord again referred to the coming forth of these scriptures in the following words: 'I would that ye should continue until you have finished this record [i.e., the Book of Mormon], which I have entrusted unto him [Joseph Smith]. And then, behold, other records have I, that I will give unto you power that you may assist to translate.' (D. and C. 9:1–2.) The earliest manuscripts of the Bible translation are in the handwriting of Oliver Cowdery. These bear the beginning date of June, 1830, and continue until October 21, the same year. This was done in Harmony, Pennsylvania, and Fayette, New York. Brother Cowdery then departed for Ohio and Missouri in response to a call from the Lord for missionary service among the Lamanites. (D. and C. 32:1–2.) At this juncture, John Whitmer served as scribe to the Prophet as the translation continued. In December, 1830, having recently joined the Church, Sidney Rigdon came to Fayette to see the Prophet Joseph and was called by revelation to do this writing in the following words: 'And a commandment I give unto thee—that thou shalt write for him; and the scriptures shall be given, even as they are in mine own bosom, to the salvation of mine own elect.' (D. and C. 35:20.) In February, 1831, the Lord spoke again, saying: 'Thou shalt ask, and my scriptures shall be given as I have appointed, and they shall be preserved in safety; and it is expedient that thou shouldst hold thy peace concerning them, and not teach them until ye have received them in full. And I give unto you a commandment that then ye shall teach them unto all men; for they shall be taught unto all nations, kindreds, tongues and people.' (D. and C. 42:56–58.)

From June, 1830, until March 7, 1831, the Brethren labored with the revision of the early chapters of Genesis. However, on the latter date they were instructed to begin a translation of the New Testament also. (D. and C. 45:60–61.) This they began the next day, March 8. The work continued through both the Old and New Testaments until July 2, 1833, when the Prophet finished the work as far as the Lord required of him at that time. In the remaining eleven years of his life the Prophet further revised some passages and attempted to prepare the manuscript for publication. However, because of persecution and a lack of financial means, this was not accomplished before his death. The original manuscripts came into the hands of his widow, Emma Smith, who refused to give them to the Church, although a request was made to her for them. The manuscripts subsequently came into the possession of the Reorganized Church and were used for the publication of the 'Inspired Version' of the Bible in 1867.

A partial copy of the manuscripts was made in the spring of 1845 by Dr. John M. Bernhisel and is now in the archives of the Church in Salt Lake City. Although it is an incomplete copy, it served to corroborate the accuracy of the printed editions insofar as its limited scope permits. The Prophet Joseph Smith's translation of the Bible is one of the greatest tangible evidences of his spiritual insight and divine calling.

16. The original *TPJS* footnote reads: "Section 76, D. and C."
17. 16 February 1832, History, A-1, 183.

commandment, every promise, every truth, and every point touching the destiny of man, from Genesis to Revelation, where the purity of the Scriptures remain unsullied by the folly of men, go to show the perfection of the theory (of different degrees of glory in the future life) and witness the fact that the document is a transcript from the records of the eternal world. The sublimity of the ideas; the purity of the language; the scope for action; the continued duration for completion, in order that the heirs of salvation may confess the Lord and bow the knee; the rewards for faithfulness, and the punishments for sins, are so much beyond the narrow-mindedness of men, that every man is constrained to exclaim: "It came from God." (Feb., 1832.) DHC 1:252-253.

commandment, every promise, every truth, and every point, touching the destiny of man, from Genesis to Revelation, where the purity of either remains unsullied from the wisdom of men, goes to shew the perfection of the theory, and witnesses the fact that that document is a transcript from the Records of the eternal world. The sublimity of the ideas; the purity of the language; the scope for action; the continued duration for completion, in order that the heirs of salvation, may confess the Lord and bow the knee; The rewards for faithfulnes & the punishments for sins, are so much beyond the narrow mindedness of men, that every honest man is constrained to exclaim; <u>It came from God</u>.[18]

Search the Revelations of God

The following excerpts are taken from the second number of the Evening and Morning Star, published in August, 1832. The article from which these thoughts are taken was prepared by the Prophet and published in this issue of the Star.[19]

Search the scriptures—search the revelations which we publish, and ask your Heavenly Father, in the name of His Son Jesus Christ, to manifest the truth unto you, and if you do it with an eye single to his glory nothing doubting, He will answer you by the power of His Holy Spirit. You will then know for yourselves and not for another. You will not then be dependent on man for the knowledge of God; nor will there **[p.12]** be any room for speculation. No; for when men receive their instruction from Him that made them, they know how He will save and learn what portion of them belongs to you and the people of the nineteenth century.

The Evening and the Morning Star
Search the Scriptures—search the revelations which we publish, and ask your heavenly Father, in the name of his Son Jesus Christ, to manifest the truth unto you, and if you do it with an eye single to his glory, [nothing doubting], he will answer you by the power of his Holy Spirit: You will then know for yourselves and not for another: You will not then be dependent on man for the knowledge of God; nor will there be any room for speculation. No: for, when men receive their instruction from him that made them, they know how he will save them. Then again we say, Search the Scriptures; search the prophets, and learn what portion of them belongs to you, and the people of the nineteenth century.

---

18. 16 February 1832, History, A-1, 192.
19. This introductory paragraph was authored by Joseph Fielding Smith.

You, no doubt, will agree with us, and say, that you have no right to claim the promises of the inhabitants before the flood; that you cannot found your hopes of salvation upon the obedience of the children of Israel when journeying in the wilderness, nor can you expect that the blessings which the apostles pronounced upon the churches of Christ eighteen hundred years ago, were intended for you. Again, if others' blessings are not your blessings, others' curses are not your curses; you stand then in these last days, as all have stood before you, agents unto yourselves, to be judged according to your works.

You, no doubt, will agree with us, and say, that you have no right to claim the promises of the inhabitants before the flood; that you cannot found your hopes of salvation upon the obedience of the children of Israel, when journeying in the wilderness; nor can you expect that the blessings which the apostles pronounced upon the churches of Christ, eighteen hundred years ago, were intended for you: Again, if others' blessings are not your blessings, other's curses are not your curses; you stand then in these last days, as all have stood before you, agents unto yourselves, to be judged according to your works.[20]

Every Man an Agent for Himself

Every man lives for himself. Adam was made to open the way of the world, and for dressing the garden. Noah was born to save seed of everything, when the earth was washed of its wickedness by the flood; and the Son of God came into the world to redeem it from the fall. But except a man be born again, he cannot see the kingdom of God. This eternal truth settles the question of all men's religion. A man may be saved, after the judgment, in the terrestrial kingdom, or in the telestial kingdom, but he can never see the celestial kingdom of God, without being born of water and the Spirit. He may receive a glory like unto the moon, [i.e., of which the light of the moon is typical], or a star, [i.e., of which the light of the stars is typical], but he can never come unto Mount Zion, and unto the city of the living

The Evening and the Morning Star

Every man lives for himself. Adam was made to open the ways of the world, and for dressing the garden. Noah was born to save seed of every thing, when the earth was washed of its wickedness by the flood; and the Son of God came [into the world] to redeem it from the fall. But except a man be born again, he cannot see the kingdom of God. This eternal truth settles the question of all man's religion. A man may be saved, after the judgment, in the Terrestrial kingdom, or in the Telestial kingdom, but he can never see the Celestial kingdom of God, without being born of water and the Spirit. He may receive a glory like unto the Moon, or a star, but he can never come unto mount Zion, and unto the city of the living God, the heavenly Jerusalem, and to an innumerable company of angels; to the

---

20. *E&MS* 1, no. 3 (August 1832): 6. This quotation comes from page 6 of that particular issue. The original *TPJS* mistakenly cited this as vol. 1, no. 2. Volume 1 of *The Evening and the Morning Star* did not have page numbers. *The Evening and Morning Star* didn't begin numbering its pages until volume 2 on page 97, which was the total number of pages (up to that point) of both volumes combined. Page numbers cited herein for volume 1 will be the pages of that issue. Beginning with volume 2, the page numbers cited will be those actually printed on the page. Although attributed to Joseph Smith by Joseph Fielding Smith (in *TPJS*), this quotation is not included in the Joseph Smith Papers, Documents, because it is likely the work of W. W. Phelps. The reader needs to be aware that even at times when Joseph Smith was listed as the editor of a newspaper, others often wrote the editorials. Consequently, without further evidence, those editorials cannot definitively be considered to be the words of Joseph Smith.

God, the heavenly Jerusalem, and to an innumerable company of angels; to the general assembly and church of the Firstborn, which are written in heaven, and to God the judge of all, and to the spirits of just men made perfect, and to Jesus the Mediator of the new covenant, unless he becomes as a little child, and is taught by the Spirit of God. Wherefore, we again say, search the revelations of God; study the prophecies, and rejoice that God grants unto the world Seers and Prophets. They are they who saw the mysteries of godliness; they saw the flood before it came; they saw angels ascending and descending upon a ladder that [p.13] reached from earth to heaven; they saw the stone cut out of the mountain, which filled the whole earth; they saw the Son of God come from the regions of bliss and dwell with men on earth; they saw the deliverer come out of Zion, and turn away ungodliness from Jacob; they saw the glory of the Lord when he showed the transfiguration of the earth on the mount; they saw every mountain laid low and every valley exalted when the Lord was taking vengeance upon the wicked; they saw truth spring out of the earth, and righteousness look down from heaven in the last days, before the Lord came the second time to gather his elect; they saw the end of wickedness on earth, and the Sabbath of creation crowned with peace; they saw the end of the glorious thousand years, when Satan was loosed for a little season; they saw the day of judgment when all men received according to their works, and they saw the heaven and the earth flee away to make room for the city of God, when the righteous receive an inheritance in eternity. And, fellow sojourners upon earth, it is your privilege to purify yourselves and come up to the same glory, and see for yourselves, and know for yourselves. Ask, and it shall be given you; seek and ye shall find; knock, and it shall be opened unto you.—*E&MS* August, 1832. DHC 1:282-284.

general assembly and church of the first-born, which are written in heaven, and to God the Judge of all, and to the spirits of just men made perfect, and to Jesus the Mediator of the new covenant, unless he becomes as a little child, and is taught by the Spirit of God. Wherefore, we again say, Search the revelations of God: study the prophecies, and rejoice that god grants unto the world seers and prophets: They are they who saw the mystery of godliness; they saw the flood before it came; they saw angels ascending and descending upon a ladder that reached from earth to heaven; they saw the stone cut out of the mountain, that filled the whole earth: they say the Son of God come from the regions of bliss and dwell with men on earth; they saw the Deliverer come out of Zion, and turn away ungodliness from Jacob; they saw the glory of the Lord when he shewed the transfiguration of the earth on the Mount; they saw every mountain laid low and every valley exalted when the Lord was taking vengeance upon the wicked; they saw truth spring out of the earth, and righteousness look down from heaven in the last days, before the Lord came the second time, to gather his elect; they saw the end of wickedness on earth, & the sabbath of creation crowned with peace; they saw the end of the glorious thousand years, when Satan was loosed for a little season; they saw the day of judgment when all men received according to their works, and they saw the heaven and earth flee away to make room for the city of God, when the righteous receive an inheritance in eternity: And, fellow sojourners upon earth, it is your privilege to purify yourselves and come up to the same glory, and see for yourselves, and know for yourselves: Ask, and it shall be given you; seek, and ye shall find; knock, and it shall be opened unto you.[21]

---

21. *E&MS* 1, no. 3 (August 1832): 6.

Letter to Editor Seaton

January 4, 1833, the Prophet wrote to Mr. N. E. Seaton, an editor of a newspaper, the following words of counsel and warning concerning the state of the world and the purpose of the Lord in the restoration spoken of [p.14] by the ancient prophets.[22]

Kirtland, January 4th, 1833.

Mr. Editor:—Sir, Considering the liberal principles upon which your interesting and valuable paper is published, myself being a subscriber, and feeling a deep interest in the cause of Zion, and in the happiness of my brethren of mankind, I cheerfully take up my pen to contribute my mite at this very interesting and important period.

For some length of time I have been carefully viewing the state of things, as it now appears, throughout our Christian land; and have looked at it with feelings of the most painful anxiety. While upon one hand I behold the manifest withdrawal of God's Holy Spirit, and the veil of stupidity which seems to be drawn over the hearts of the people; upon the other hand, I behold the judgments of God that have swept, and are still sweeping hundreds and thousands of our race, and I fear unprepared, down to the shades of death. With this solemn and alarming fact before me, I am led to exclaim, "O that my head were waters, and mine eyes a fountain of tears, that I might weep day and night."

Joseph Smith Letter
Kirtland 4th. Jany. 1833—
Mr. Editor Sir,
Considering the Liberal priscples [principles] upon which your interesting and valuable paper is published and myself being a subscriber and feeling a deep intrist in the cause of Zion and in the happiness of my brethren of mankind I cheerfully take up my pen to contribute my mite at this every [very] interesting and important period

For some length of time I have been car[e]fully viewing the state of things as now appear throug[h]out our christian Land and have looked at it with feelings of the most painful anxiety while upon the one hand beholding the manifested withdrawal of Gods holy Spirit and the vail of stupidity which seems to be drawn over the hearts of the people and upon the other hand beholding the [p.351] Judgments of God that have swept and are still sweeping hundreds and thousands of our race (and I fear unprepared) down to the shades of death with this solemn and alarming fact before me I am led to exclaim ["]O that my head were waters and mine ey[e]s a fountain of tears that I might weep day and night &c,"[23]

---

22. This introductory paragraph was authored by Joseph Fielding Smith.
23. 4 January 1833, *JSP, D2*, 350–51. A portion of this letter was published in *The American Revivalist, and Rochester Observer* 7, no. 6, (2 February 1833). *TPJS* lists the editor's name as N. E. Sexton. The Joseph Smith Papers lists the name of the editor as Noah C. Saxton.

A Sleeping Christianity

Joseph Smith Letter

I think that it is high time for a Christian world to awake out of sleep, and cry mightily to that God, day and night, whose anger we have justly incurred. Are not these things a sufficient stimulant to arouse the faculties, and call forth the energies of every man, woman or child that possesses feelings of sympathy for their fellows, or that is in any degree endeared to the budding cause of our glorious Lord? I leave an intelligent community to answer this important question, with a confession, that this is what has caused me to overlook my own inability, and expose my weakness to a learned world; but, trusting in that God who has said that these things are hid from the wise and prudent and revealed unto babes, I step forth into the field to tell you what the Lord is doing, and what you must do, to enjoy the smiles of your Savior in these last days.	I think that it is high time for a christian world to awake out of sleep and cry mightely to that God day and night whose anger we have Justly incured. Are not these things a sufficient stimulant to arouse the faculties and call forth the energies of evry man woman and child that poseses feeling of sympathy for his fellow[s] or that is in any degree endeared to the bud[d]ing cause of our glorious Lord; I leave an inteligent community to answer this important question with a confession that this is what has caused me to overlook my own inability and expose my weakness to a learned world but trusting in that God. who has said these things are hid from the wise and prudent and reve[a]led unto babes I step forth into the field to tell you what the Lord is doing and what you must do to enjoy the smiles of your saviour in these last day[s]——[24]

The Covenant with Israel

Joseph Smith Letter

The time has at last arrived when the God of Abraham, of Isaac, and of Jacob, has set his hand again the second time to recover the remnants of his people, which have been left from Assyria, and from Egypt, and from Pathros, and from Cush, and from Elam, and from Shinar, and from Hamath, and from the islands of the sea, and with them to bring in the fulness of the Gentiles, and establish that covenant with them, which was promised when their sins should be taken away. See Isaiah 11; Romans 11:25, 26 and 27, and also Jeremiah 31:31, 32 and 33. This covenant has never been established with the house of Israel, nor with the house of Judah, for it requires two parties to make a covenant, and those two parties must be agreed, or no covenant can be made.	The time has at last come arived when the Gods of Abraham of Isaac and of Jacob has set his hand again the seccond time to recover the remnants of his people which have been left from Assyria, and from Egypt and from Pathros &.c. and from the Islands of the sea and with them to bring in the fulness of the Gentiles and establish that covenant with them which was promised when their sins should be taken away. See Romans 11, 25, 26, & 27 and also Jeremiah 31. 31, 32, & 33, This covenant has never been established with the house of Isreal nor with th[e] house of Judah for it requires two parties to make a covenant and those two parties must be agreed or no covenant can be made.

---

24. 4 January 1833, *JSP, D2*, 351.

Christ, in the days of His flesh, proposed to make a covenant with them, but they rejected Him and His proposals, and [p.15] in consequence thereof, they were broken off, and no covenant was made with them at that time. But their unbelief has not rendered the promise of God of none effect: no, for there was another day limited in David, which was the day of His power; and then His people, Israel, should be a willing people;—and He would write His law in their hearts, and print it in their thoughts; their sins and their iniquities He would remember no more.

Christ in the days of his flesh proposed to make a covenant with them but they rejected him and his proposals [p.352] and in consequence thereof they were broken off and no covenant was made with them at that time but their unbelief has not rendered the promise of God of none effect; no, for there was another day limited in David which was the day of his power and then his people Isreal, should be a willing people and he would write his laws in their hearts and print them in their thoughts their sins and their eniquities he would remember no more,[25]

The Covenant to the Gentiles

Joseph Smith Letter

Thus after this chosen family had rejected Christ and His proposals, the heralds of salvation said to them, "Lo we turn unto the Gentiles;" and the Gentiles received the covenant, and were grafted in from whence the chosen family were broken off: but the Gentiles have not continued in the goodness of God, but have departed from the faith that was once delivered to the Saints, and have broken the covenant in which their fathers were established (see Isaiah 24:5); and have become high-minded, and have not feared; therefore, but few of them will be gathered with the chosen family. Have not the pride, high-mindedness, and unbelief of the Gentiles, provoked the Holy One of Israel to withdraw His Holy Spirit from them, and send forth His judgments to scourge them for their wickedness? This is certainly the case.

Thus after this chosen family had rejected Christ and his proposals the heralds of salvation said to them. "lo I we turn <un>to the gentiles," and the gentiles received the covenant and were grafted in from whence the chosen family were broken off but the Gentiles have not continued in the goodness of God but have departed from the faith that was once delivered to the saints and have broken the ~~everlasting~~ covenant in which their fathers were established see Isaiah 24th 5th. and have become high minded and have not feared therefore but few of them will be gathered with the chosen family Has not the pride highmindedness and unbelief of the Gentiles provoked the holy one of Israel to withdraw his holy spirit from them and send forth his Judgments to scourge them for their wickedness; this is certianly the case,[26]

The Earth Defiled

Joseph Smith Letter

Christ said to His disciples (Mark 16:17 and 18), that these signs should follow them that believe:—"In my name shall they cast out devils; they shall speak with new tongues;

Christ said to his deciples Mark 16, 17 & 18 that these signs should followthem that believe; In my name shall they cast out Devils they shall speap [speak] with new tongues

---

25. 4 January 1833, *JSP, D2*, 351–52.
26. 4 January 1833, *JSP, D2*, 352.

they shall take up serpents; and if they drink any deadly thing, it shall not hurt them; they shall lay hands on the sick, and they shall recover;" and also, in connection with this, read 1st Corinthians, 12th chapter. By the foregoing testimonies we may look at the Christian world and see the apostasy there has been from the apostolic platform; and who can look at this and not exclaim, in the language of Isaiah, "The earth also is defiled under the inhabitants thereof; because they have transgressed the laws, changed the ordinances, and broken the everlasting covenant?"

The plain fact is this, the power of God begins to fall [p.16] upon the nations, and the light of the latter-day glory begins to break forth through the dark atmosphere of sectarian wickedness, and their iniquity rolls up into view, and the nations of the Gentiles are like the waves of the sea, casting up mire and dirt, or all in commotion, and they are hastily preparing to act the part allotted them, when the Lord rebukes the nations, when He shall rule them with a rod of iron, and break them in pieces like a potter's vessel. The Lord declared to His servants, some eighteen months since, that He was then withdrawing His Spirit from the earth; and we can see that such is the fact, for not only the churches are dwindling away, but there are no conversions, or but very few: and this is not all, the governments of the earth are thrown into confusion and division; and Destruction, to the eye of the spiritual beholder, seems to be written by the finger of an invisible hand, in large capitals, upon almost every thing we behold.

they shall take up serpants and if they drink any deadly thing it shall not hurt them they shall lay hands on the sick and they shall recover, and also in connection with this read 1 Corinthians 12 Chapt, By the foregoing testamonies or through the glass of the foregoing testamonies we may look at the Christian world and see the apostacy there has been from the Apostolic platform, and who can look at this, and and not exclaim in the language of Isaiah, ["]the earth is defiled under the inhabitants thereof because they have transgressed the Laws; changed the ordinances and broken the everlasting covenant"

The plain fact is this, the power of God begins to fall upon the Nations, and the light of the latter day glory begins to break forth through the dark atmosphere of sectarian wickedness and their iniquity rools [rolls] up into [p,353] view and the Nations of the Gentiles are like the waves of the sea casting up mire and dirt or all in commotion and they hastily are preparing to act the part allotted them when the Lord rebukes the nations, when he shall rule them with a rod of iron & break them in peaces like a potters vessel, The Lord has declared to his servants some Eighteen months since that he was then withdrawing his spirit from the earth, and we can see that such is the fact for not only the churches are dwindling away, but there are no convers[i]ons, or but very few, and this is not all, the governments of the earth are thrown into confusion & division, and distruction to the eye of the spiritual beholder seemes to be writen by the finger of an invisable hand in Large capitals upon almost evry thing we behold——[27]

How to Escape Judgments

Joseph Smith Letter

And now what remains to be done, under circumstances like these? I will proceed to tell you what the Lord requires of all people, high and

And now what remains to be done under circumstan[c]es like these, I will proce[e]d to tell you what the Lord requires of all people

---

27. 4 January 1833, *JSP, D2*, 352–53.

low, rich and poor, male and female, ministers and people, professors of religion and non-professors, in order that they may enjoy the Holy Spirit of God to a fullness, and escape the judgments of God, which are almost ready to burst upon the nations of the earth. Repent of all your sins, and be baptized in water for the remission of them, in the name of the Father, and of the Son, and of the Holy Ghost, and receive the ordinance of the laying on of the hands of him who is ordained and sealed unto this power, that ye may receive the Holy Spirit of God; and this is according to the Holy Scriptures, and the Book of Mormon; and the only way that man can enter into the celestial kingdom. These are the requirements of the new covenant, or first principles of the Gospel of Christ: then "Add to your faith, virtue; and to virtue, knowledge; and to knowledge, temperance; and to temperance, patience; and to patience, godliness; and to godliness, brotherly kindness; and to brotherly kindness, charity [or love]; for if these things be in you, and abound, they make you that ye shall neither be barren nor unfruitful, in the knowledge of our Lord Jesus Christ."

high and Low, rich and poor, male and female, ministers & people professors of religeon, and non-proffessors in order that they may enjoy the holy spirit of God to a fulness, and escape the Judgments of God which are almost ready to burst upon the nations of the earth— Repent of all your sins and be baptized in water for the remis**[p.354]** sion of them, in the name of the father, and of the son, and of the Holy Ghost, and receive the ordinance of the laying on of the hands of him who is ordained and sealed unto this power, that ye may receive the holy spirit of God, and this according to the holy scriptures, and of the Book of Mormon; and the only way that man can enter into the Celestial kingdom. These are the requisitions of the new Covenant or first principles of of the Gospel of Christ; then add to you[r] faith virtue and to virtue knowledge and to knowledge temperance, and to temperance patience, and to patitence, brotherly kindness and to brotherly kindness charity (or Love) and if these things be in you and abound, they make you to be neither baran nor unfruitful in the knowledge of our Lord Jesus Christ——[28]

Zion and Jerusalem

Joseph Smith Letter

[p.17] The Book of Mormon is a record of the forefathers of our western tribes of Indians; having been found through the ministration of an holy angel, and translated into our own language by the gift and power of God, after having been hid up in the earth for the last fourteen hundred years, containing the word of God which was delivered unto them. By it we learn that our western tribes of Indians are descendants from that Joseph who was sold into Egypt, and that the land of America is a promised land unto them, and unto it all the tribes of Israel will come, with as many of the Gentiles as shall comply with the requisitions of the new covenant. But the tribe of Judah

The Book of Mormon is a reccord of the forefathers of our western Tribes of Indians, having been found through the ministration of an holy Angel translated into our own Language by the gift and power of God, after having been hid up in the earth for the last fourteen hundred years containing the word of God, which was delivered unto them, By it we learn that our western tribes of Indians are desendants from that Joseph that was sold into Egypt, and that the Land of America is a promised land unto them, and unto it all the tribes of Israel will come. With as many of the gentiles as shall comply with the requesitions of the new co[v]enant. But the tribe of

---

28. 4 January 1833, *JSP, D2*, 353–54.

will return to old Jerusalem. The city of Zion spoken of by David, in the one hundred and second Psalm, will be built upon the land of America, "And the ransomed of the Lord shall return, and come to Zion with songs and everlasting joy upon their heads." (Isaiah 35:10); and then they will be delivered from the overflowing scourge that shall pass through the land. But Judah shall obtain deliverance at Jerusalem. See Joel 2:32; Isaiah 26:20 and 21; Jeremiah 31:12; Psalms 1:5; Ezekiel 34:11, 12 and 13. These are testimonies that the Good Shepherd will put forth His own sheep, and lead them out from all nations where they have been scattered in a cloudy and dark day, to Zion, and to Jerusalem; besides many more testimonies which might be brought.

And now I am prepared to say by the authority of Jesus Christ, that not many years shall pass away before the United States shall present such a scene of bloodshed as has not a parallel in the history of our nation; pestilence, hail, famine, and earthquake will sweep the wicked of this generation from off the face of the land, to open and prepare the way for the return of the lost tribes of Israel from the north country. The people of the Lord, those who have complied with the requirements of the new covenant, have already commenced gathering together to Zion, which is in the state of Missouri; therefore I declare unto you the warning which the Lord has commanded me to declare unto this generation, remembering that the eyes of my Maker are upon me, and that to Him I am accountable for every word I say, wishing nothing worse to my fellowmen than their eternal salvation; therefore, "Fear God, and give **[p.18]** glory to Him, for the hour of His judgment is come." Repent ye, repent ye, and embrace the everlasting covenant, and flee to Zion, before the overflowing scourge overtake you, for there are those now living upon the earth whose eyes shall not be closed in death until they see all these things, which I have spoken, fulfilled. Remember

Judah will return to old Jerusalem, The City, of Zion, spoken of by David in the 102 Psalm will be built upon the Land of America and the ransomed of the Lord shall return **[p.355]** and come to it with songs and everlasting joy upon their heads, and then they will be delivered from the overflowing scourge that shall pass through the Land But Judah shall obtain deliverence at Jerusalem see Joel 2. 32. Isaiah 26, 20 & 21, Jer. 31, 12, Psalm 50. 5, Ezekiel 34, 11, 12 & 13, These are testamonies that the good Shepherd will put forth his own sheep and Lead them out from all nations where they have been scattered in a cloudy and dark day, to Zion and to Jerusalem beside many more testamonies which might be brought——

And now I am prepared to say by the authority of Jesus Christ, that not many years shall pass away before the United States shall present such a scene of <u>bloodshed</u> as has not a parallel in the hystory of our nation pestalence hail famine and earthquake will sweep the wicked off this generation from off the face of this Land to open and prepare the way for the return of the lost tribes of Israel from the north country— The people of the Lord, those who have complied with the requsitions of the new covenant have already commenced gathering togethe[r] to Zion which is in the State of Missouri. Therefore I declare unto you the warning which the lord has commanded me to declare unto this generation, rembring [remembering] that the eyes of my maker are upon me and that to him I am accountabl for evry word I say wishing nothing worse to my fellow men then their eternal salvation therefore fear God, and give glory to him for the hour of his Judgment is come, <Repent ye> Repent, ye and imbrace the everlasting Covenant and flee to Zion before the over flowing scourge overtake you, For there are those now living upon the earth whose eyes shall not be closed in death until they see all these things which I have spoken

these things; call upon the Lord while He is near, and seek Him while He may be found, is the exhortation of your unworthy servant. (Signed) JOSEPH SMITH, JUN.
—DHC 1:312-316.

fulfilled Rem[em]ber these things, call upon the Lord while he is near and seek him while he may be found is the exhortation of your unworthy servant.
Joseph Smith Jr
<To N. E. Sextan [Noah C. Saxton] Rochester N Y.>[29]

Important Correspondence with the Brethren in Zion

The "Olive Leaf" is the name given by the Prophet to the wonderful revelation known as Sec. 88, in the Doctrine and Covenants. There are few, if any, revelations given to the Church—and to the world if the world will receive them—greater than this "Olive Leaf, plucked from the Tree of Paradise." In this letter to W. W. Phelps, one of the presiding brethren in Missouri, the Prophet raises a warning voice based upon the word of the Lord as revealed in the revelation and correspondence from Missouri.[30]

Joseph Smith Letter

Kirtland, January 14, 1833.

Kirtland January 11— 1833[31]

Brother William W. Phelps:
I send you the "olive leaf" which we have plucked from the tree of Paradise, the Lord's message of peace to us; for though our brethren in Zion indulge in feelings towards us, which are not according to the requirements of the new covenant, yet, we have the satisfaction of knowing that the Lord approves of us, and has accepted us, and established His name in Kirtland for the salvation of the nations; for the Lord will have a place whence His word will go forth, in these last days, in purity; for if Zion will not purify herself, so as to be approved of in all things, in His sight, He will seek another people; for His work will

Brother William [W. Phelps]
I Send you the Olieve leaf which we have plucked from the tree of Paradise, the Lords message of peace to us, for though our Brethren in Zion, [p.367] indulge in feelings towards us, which is are not according to the requirements of the new covenant yet we have the satisfaction of knowing that the Lord approves of us & has accepted us, & established his name in kirtland for the salvation of the nations, for the Lord will have a place for from whence his word will go forth in these last days in purity, for if Zion, will not purify herself so as to be approved of in all things in his sight he will seek— another people for his

---

29. 4 January 1833, *JSP, D2*, 354-55.
30. This introductory paragraph was authored by Joseph Fielding Smith.
31. *TPJS* has this document dated 14 January 1833. The original document is dated 11 January 1833. *JSP, D2*, 365.

go on until Israel is gathered, and they who will not hear His voice, must expect to feel His wrath. Let me say unto you, seek to purify yourselves, and also the inhabitants of Zion, lest the Lord's anger be kindled to fierceness.

A Warning to Zion

Repent, repent, is the voice of God to Zion; and strange as it may appear, yet it is true, mankind will persist in self-justification until all their iniquity is exposed, and their character past being redeemed, and that which is treasured up in their hearts be exposed to the gaze of mankind. I say to you (and what I say to you I say to all), hear the warning voice of God, lest Zion fall, and the Lord swear in His wrath the inhabitants of Zion shall not enter into His rest.

The brethren in Kirtland pray for you unceasingly, for, knowing the terrors of the Lord, they greatly fear for you. You will see that the Lord commanded us, in Kirtland, to build a house of God, and establish a school for the Prophets, this is the word of the Lord to us, and we must, yea, the Lord helping us, we will obey: as on conditions of our obedience He has promised us great things; yea, even a visit from the heavens to honor us with His own presence. We greatly fear before the Lord lest we should fail of this great honor, which our Master proposes to confer on us; we are seeking for humility and great faith lest we be ashamed in His presence. Our hearts are greatly grieved at the spirit which is breathed both in your letter and that of Brother Gilbert's, the very spirit which is wasting the strength of Zion like a pestilence; and if it is not detected and driven from you, it will ripen Zion for the threatened judgments of God. Remember God sees the secret springs of human action, and knows the hearts of all living.

---

work will go on untill Isreal is gathered & they who will not hear his voice must expect to feel his wrath, Let me say unto you, seek to purefy yourselves, & also all the inhabitants of Zion lest the Lords anger be kindled to fierceness,[32]

repent, repent, is the voice of God, to Zion, & yet strange as it may appear, yet it is true mankind will presist in self Justification until all their eniquity is exposed & their character past being redeemed, & that which is treasured up in their hearts be exposed to the gaze of mankind, I say to you— (& what I say to you, I say to all) hear the <warning.> voice of God lest Zion fall, & the Lord swore swear in his wrath the inhabiteints of Zion shall not enter into my rest,

The Brethren in Kirtland pray for you unceasingly, for knowing the terrors of the Lord, they greatly fear for you; you will see that the Lord commanded us in Kirtland to build an house of God, & establish a school for the Prophets, this is the word of the Lord to us, & we must— yea the Lord helping us we will obey, as on conditions of our obedience, he has promised <us> great things, yea <even> a visit from the heavens to honor us with his own presence, we greatly fear before the Lord lest we should fail of this great honor which our master proposes to confer on us, we are seeking for humility & great faith lest we be ashamed in his presence, our hearts are greatly greaved at the spirit which is breathed both in your letter & that of Bro G—s [Sidney Gilbert] the wery spirit which is wasting the strength of Zion like a pestalence, and if it is not detected & driven from you it will ripen Zion for the threatened Judgments of God, remember God sees the secret springs of human action, & knows the hearts of all living,

---

32. 11 January 1833, *JSP, D2*, 365, 367.

Brother, suffer us to speak plainly, for God has respect to the feelings of His Saints, and He will not suffer them to be tantalized with impunity. * * * All we can say by way of conclusion is, if the fountain of our tears be not dried up, we will still weep for Zion. This from your brother who trembles for Zion, and for the wrath of heaven, which awaits her if she repents not.
(Signed) JOSEPH SMITH, JUN.
—DHC 1:316.

Br suffer **[p.368]** us to speak plainly for God has respect to the feelings of his saints & he will not let them be tantalized with impunity tell Br. G—t [Gilbert] that low insinuations God hates, but he rejoices in an honest heart and knows better who is guilty than he does, we send him this worning [warning] voice & let him fear greatly for himself lest a worse thing overtake him, all we can say by way of conclusion is, if the fountain of our tears are not dried up we will <still> weep for zion, this from your brother who trembles greatly for Zion,— and for the wrath of heaven which awaits her if she repent not,— —[33]

An Epistle

Of the First Presidency, to the Church of Christ in Thompson, Geauga County, Ohio.

Kirtland, February 6th, 1833.

Dear Brethren:

We salute you, by this our epistle, in the bonds of love, rejoicing in your steadfastness in the faith which is in Christ Jesus our Lord; and we desire your prosperity in the ways of truth and righteousness, praying for you continually, that your **[p.20]** faith fail not, and that you may overcome all the evils with which you are surrounded, and become pure and holy before God, even our Father, to whom be glory for ever and ever. Amen.

Joseph Smith Letter
An Epistle to the Church in Thompson Kirtland February 6th 1833——
To the Church of Christ in Thompson Geauga County Ohio

Dear Brethren

We salute you by this our Epistle in the bonds of Love rejoicing in your steadfastness in the faith which is in Christ Jesus our Lord and we desire your prosperity in the ways of truth and righteousness in the bowels of Jesus Christ praying for you continually that your faith fail not and that you may overcome all the evils with which you are surrounded and become pure and holy before God even our father to whom be glory for and ever and ever Amen

---

33. 11 January 1833, *JSP, D2*, 367–68. At this point in the original text, Joseph added the following post script: "PS. I am not in the habit of crying peace, when there is no peace, and knowing the th[r]eatened Judgments of God, I say Wo,— unto them who are at ease in zion fearfulnes will speedily lay hold of the hypocrite, I did not expect that you had lost Commandments, but thought from your letters you had neglected to read them, otherwise you would not have writen as you did, it is in vain to try to hide a bad spirit from the eyes of them who are spiritual for it will shewe itself in speaking & in writing as well as all our other conduct, it is also useless to mak[e] great pretentions when the heart is not right before God, for God looks at the heart, and where the heart is not right the Lord will expose it to the view of his faithful saints, we wish you to render the Star as interesting as possable by setting forth the rise progress and faith of the church, as well as the doctrine for if you do not render it more interesting than at present it will fall, and the church suffer a great Loss thereby——" *JSP, D2*, 368.

It has seemed good unto the Holy Spirit and unto us, to send this our epistle to you by the hand of our beloved Brother Salmon Gee, your messenger, who has been ordained by us, in obedience to the commandments of God, to the office of Elder to preside over the Church in Thompson, taking the oversight thereof, to lead you and to teach the things which are according to godliness; in whom we have great confidence, as we presume also you have, we therefore say to you, yea, not us only, but the Lord also, receive him as such, knowing that the Lord has appointed him to this office for your good, holding him up by your prayers, praying for him continually that he may be endowed with wisdom and understanding in the knowledge of the Lord, that through him you may be kept from evil spirits, and all strifes and dissensions, and grow in grace and in the knowledge of our Lord and Savior Jesus Christ.

Brethren beloved, continue in brotherly love, walk in meekness, watching unto prayer, that you be not overcome. Follow after peace, as said our beloved brother Paul, that you may be the children of our Heavenly Father, and not give occasion for stumbling, to Saint or sinner. Finally, brethren, pray for us, that we may be enabled to do the work whereunto we are called, that you may enjoy the mysteries of God, even a fullness; and may the grace of our Lord Jesus Christ be with you all. Amen.

JOSEPH SMITH, JUN.
SIDNEY RIGDON,
FREDERICK G. WILLIAMS.
—DHC 1:324, 325.

It has seemed good unto the holy spirit and unto us to send this our epistle to you by the hand of our beloved broth[e]r Salmon [Gee] your messenger who has been ordained by us in obedience to the commandment of God to the **[p.6]** office of Elder to preside over the Church in Thompson taking the oversight thereof to Lead you & to teach the thing[s] which are according to Godliness in whom we have great confidence as we presume also you we therefore say to you yea not us only but the Lord also receive you him as such knowing that the lord has appointed him to this office for your good holding him up by your prayers praying for him continually that he may be endued with wisdom and understanding in the knowledge of the Lord that through him you may be kept from evil spirits and all strifes and discensions and grow in grace and in the know[l]edge of our Lord and Saviour Jesus Christ

Brethren beloved continue in brotherly Love walking in meekness watching unto prayer that you be not overcome Follow after peace as said our beloved brothe[r] Paul that you may be the children of our heavenly Father and <not> give occasion <of> for stumbling to saint or sinner— finely [finally] brethren pray for us that we may be enabled to do the work whereunto we are called that you may enjoy the mysteries of God even a fulness and may the grace of our Lord Jesus Christ be with you all amen.

Joseph Smith Jr—
Sidney Rigdon
F. G. William [Frederick G. Williams]——[34]

---

34. 6 February 1833, *JSP, D3*, 5–6.

Order for Instruction in the Church

Joseph Smith Letter

Kirtland, April 13, 1833 | Kirtlan[d] 13th April 1833

Dear Brother Carter:—Your letter to Brother Jared is just put into my hand, and I have carefully perused its contents, and embrace this opportunity to answer it. We proceed to answer your questions: first concerning your labor in the region where you live; we acquiesce in your feelings on this subject **[p.21]** until the mouth of the Lord shall name. Respecting the vision you speak of we do not consider ourselves bound to receive any revelation from any one man or woman without his being legally constituted and ordained to that authority, and giving sufficient proof of it.

Dear Broth[er] [John S.] Carter your Letter to Broth Jared [Carter] is just put into my hand and I have carefully purrused its contents and imbrace this oppertunity to answer it, we proceed to answer your questions first concerning your labour in the region where you live we acquiesce in your feelings on this subject until the the mouth of the Lord shall name and as it respects the vision you speak of we do not consider ourselves bound to receive any revelation forom [from] any one man or woman without being legally constituted and ordained to that authority and given sufficien[t] proof of it,[35]

Order by Which Revelation Comes

I will inform you that it is contrary to the economy of God for any member of the Church, or any one, to receive instruction for those in authority, higher than themselves; therefore you will see the impropriety of giving heed to them; but if any person have a vision or a visitation from a heavenly messenger, it must be for his own benefit and instruction; for the fundamental principles, government, and doctrine of the Church are vested in the keys of the kingdom. Respecting an apostate, or one who has been cut off from the Church, and who wishes to come in again, the law of our Church expressly says that such shall repent, and be baptized, and be admitted as at the first.

[p.59] I will inform you that it is contrary to the economy of God for any member of the Church or any <one> any one to receive instruction for those in authority hig[h]er than themselves, therefore you **[p.61**[36]**]** will see the impropriety of giving <heed> to them, but if any <have a vision> ~~heavenly~~ or a visitation from an hevenaly [heavenly] messenger it must be for their own benefit and instruction, for the fundimental principals, government and doctrine of the church is invested in the keys of the kingdom as it respects an apostate or one who has been cut off from the Church and wishes to come in again the law of our church expresly says that such shall repent, and be babtised and be admited the same as at the first,

The duty of a High Priest is to administer in spiritual and holy things, and to hold communion with God; but not to exercise monarchial government, or to appoint meetings for

the duty of a high priest is to administer spriitual and holy things and to hold Communeion <with> God but not to exorcise [exercise] ~~monarchy~~ monarchal government

---

35. 13 April 1833, *JSP, D3*, 59.
36. Page 60 contains a photograph instead of printed text.

the Elders without their consent. And again, it is the High Priests' duty to be better qualified to teach principles and doctrines, than the Elders; for the office of Elder is an appendage to the High Priesthood, and it concentrates and centers in one. And again, the process of laboring with members: We are to deal with them precisely as the Scriptures direct. If thy brother trespass against thee, take him between him and thee alone; and, if he make thee satisfaction, thou hast saved thy brother; and if not, proceed to take another with thee, etc., and when there is no Bishop, they are to be tried by the voice of the Church; and if an Elder, or a High Priest be present, he is to take the lead in managing the business; but if not, such as have the highest authority should preside.

With respect to preparing to go to Zion:— First it would be pleasing to the Lord that the church or churches going to Zion should be organized, and a suitable person appointed who is well acquainted with the condition of the church, and he be sent to Kirtland to inform the Bishop, and procure a license [p.22] from him agreeable to the revelation: by so doing you will prevent confusion and disorder, and escape many difficulties that attend an unorganized band in journeying in the last days.

And again, those in debt, should in all cases pay their debts; and the rich are in no wise to cast out the poor, or leave them behind, for it is said that the poor shall inherit the earth.

You quoted a passage in Jeremiah, with regard to journeying to Zion; the word of the Lord stands sure, so let it be done.

There are two paragraphs in your letter which I do not commend, as they are written blindly. Speaking of the Elders being sent like lightning from the bow of Judah; the second, no secret in the councils of Zion. You mention

or to appoint meetings for the Elders without their concent and again it is the high priests duty to be bet[t]er qualifide to teach principles and doctrines than the Elder for the office of Elders is an appendege to the high priesthood and it <centers &> concentrates in one, and again the ~~proper~~ <process> ~~way~~ of Labouring with a member we are to deal with them percisely as the scripturs direct if thy brother trespass against the[e] take him betwen him and thee alone and if he maketh the satisfaction thou hast saved thy brother and if not proce[e]d to take another with the[e] & [illegible] when there is no bishop they are to be tried by the voice of the Church and if an Elder or an high priest be presant they are to take the lead in managing the business if not by such that have the highest authority,

with respect to preparing to go to Zion first it would be pleasing to the lord that ~~that~~ the Church or Churches going to Zion should be organised, and appointed a suitable [p.62] person who is well acquainted with the Conditions of the Church & and be sent to Kirtland to inform the Bishop and procure licence from him agreeable to ~~the~~ revelation so doing you will prevent confusion and disorder and escape many difficulties that attend an unorganised band in Journey[ing] ~~to~~ in the last days

and again those in debt should in all cases pay their debts and the rich ~~in~~ are in no wise to cast out the poor or leave them behind for it is said that the poor shall inherit the earth

you quoted a pass[a]ge in Jeremiah with regard to Journey to Zion the word of God stands sure so let it be done

There are two paragraphs in your letter which I do not commend as they are writen blind speaking of the Elder being sent like lightning from the bow of Judah the second, no secret in the councils of Zion you mention this as if these as if fear rested upon your mind, otherwise we cannot understand it. And again we never inquire at the hand of God for special revelation only in case of there being no previous revelation to suit the case; and that in a council of High Priests.

* * *

it is a great thing to inquire at the hands of God, or to come into His presence; and we feel fearful to approach Him on subjects that are of little or no consequence, to satisfy the queries of individuals, especially about things the knowledge of which men ought to obtain in all sincerity, before God, for themselves, in humility by the prayer of faith; and more especially a teacher or a High Priest in the Church. I speak these things not by way of reproach, but by way of instruction; and I speak as if acquainted with you, whereas we are strangers to each other in the flesh.

I love your soul, and the souls of the children of men, and pray and do all I can for the salvation of all.

I now close by sending you a salutation of peace in the name of the Lord Jesus Christ. Amen.

The blessing of our Lord Jesus Christ be and abide with you all. Amen.
JOSEPH SMITH, JUN.
—DHC 1:338, 339.

fear rested upon your mind otherwise we cannot understand it and again we never enquire of at the hand of ~~the Lord~~ God for special revelation only in case of ther being no previous revelation to suit the case and that in a court of high Priests...

* * *

[p.63] it <is> a great thing to enquire at the hand of God or to come into his presence and we feel fearful to appro[a]ch him upon subject[s] that are of little or no consequen[ce] to satisfy the enqueries of individuals especially <about> things the knowledge of which men aught to obtain in all cencerity before God for themselves in humility by the prayer of faith, and more especially a teacher or a high Priest in the Church of Christ I speak these things not by way of reproach but by way of instruction and I speak as being acquainted whereas we are strangers to each other in the flesh

I love your soul and the souls of the Children of men and pray and do all I can for the salvation of all

I now close by sending you a salutation of peace in the name of the Lord Jesus Christ Amen the blessings of our Lord Jesus Christ be and abide with you all Amen——
Joseph Smith Jr
F[rederick] G Williams[37]

Items of Instruction Concerning the Consecration of Property

Brother Edward Partridge:

Sir:—I proceed to answer your questions, concerning the consecration of property:—First, it is not right to condescend to very great particulars in taking inventories. The fact is this, [p.23] a man is bound by the law

Joseph Smith Letter
Bro Edward

Sir, I proceed to answer your [p.153] question concerning the consecration of Property. First, it is not right to condescend to verry great particulars in takeing inventories. the fact is this, that a man is bound by the law of the

---

37. 13 April 1833, *JSP, D3,* 59, 61–63.

of the Church, to consecrate to the Bishop, before he can be considered a legal heir to the kingdom of Zion; and this, too, without constraint; and unless he does this, he cannot be acknowledged before the Lord on the Church Book; therefore, to condescend to particulars, I will tell you that every man must be his own judge how much he should receive, and how much he should suffer to remain in the hands of the Bishop. I speak of those who consecrate more than they need for the support of themselves and their families.

church to consecrate to the Bishop before he can be considered a legal heir to the Kingdom of Zion, and this too, without constraint, and unless he does this, he cannot be acknowledged before the Lord on the Church Book. Therefore, to condescend to particulars, I will tell you that every man must be his own judge how much he should receive, and how much he should suffer to remain in the hands of the Bishop. I speak of those who consecrate more than they need for the support of themselves and family[38]

By Mutual Consent

Joseph Smith Letter

The matter of consecration must be done by the mutual consent of both parties; for to give the Bishop power to say how much every man shall have, and he be obliged to comply with the Bishop's judgment, is giving to the Bishop more power than a king has; and, upon the other hand, to let every man say how much he needs, and the Bishop be obliged to comply with his judgment, is to throw Zion into confusion, and make a slave of the Bishop. The fact is, there must be a balance or equilibrium of power, between the Bishop and the people; and thus harmony and good-will may be preserved among you.

The matter of consecration must be done by the mutual consent of both parties— For, to give the Bishop power to say how much every man shall have and he be obliged to comply with the Bishops judgment, is giveing to the Bishop more power than a King has and upon the other hand, to let every man say how much he needs and the Bishop obliged to comply with his judgment, is to throw Zion into confusion and make a Slave of the Bishop. The fact is, there must be a balance or equalibrium of power between the bishop and the people, and thus harmony and good will may be preserved among you.

Therefore, those persons consecrating property to the Bishop in Zion, and then receiving an inheritance back, must reasonably show to the Bishop that they need as much as they claim. But in case the two parties cannot come to a mutual agreement, the Bishop is to have nothing to do about receiving such consecrations; and the case must be laid before a council of twelve High Priests, the Bishop not being one of the council, but he is to lay the case before them.

Therefore, those persons consecrating property to the Bishop in Zion, and then receiveing an inheritance back, must show reasonably to the Bishop that he wants as much as he claims. but in case the two parties can<not> come to a mutual agreement, the Bishop is to have nothing to do about receiveing their consecations and the case must be laid before a council of twelve high Priests, **[p.154]** the Bishop not being one of the council, but he is to lay the case before them.

* * *

We were not a little surprised to hear that some of our letters of a public nature, which

* * *

We were not a little surprised to hear that some of our letters of a public nature which

---

38. 25 June 1833, *JSP, D3*, 152–53.

we sent for the good of Zion, have been kept back from the Bishop. This is conduct which we highly disapprobate.

we sent for the good of Zion <have been> kept back from the Bishop, this is conduct which we highly disapprobate,[39]

Answers to Queries to Brother Phelps' Letter of June 4th

Joseph Smith Letter

First, in relation to the poor: When the Bishops are appointed according to our recommendation, it will devolve upon them to see to the poor, according to the laws of the Church.

First in relation to the poor, when the Bishops are appointed according to our reccommendation, it will involve upon them to see to the poor according to the laws of the church.

* * *

[p.24] Say to the brothers Hulet and to all others, that the Lord never authorized them to say that the devil, his angels, or the sons of perdition, should ever be restored; for their state of destiny was not revealed to man, is not revealed, nor ever shall be revealed, save to those who are made partakers thereof: consequently those who teach this doctrine have not received it of the Spirit of the Lord. Truly Brother Oliver declared it to be the doctrine of devils. We, therefore, command that this doctrine be taught no more in Zion. We sanction the decision of the Bishop and his council, in relation to this doctrine being a bar to communion.

[p.155] Say to the Brethren Hulits and to all others that the Lord never authorized them to say that the Devil nor his angels nor the Sons of perdition should ever be restored, for their state of destiny was not revealed to man, is not revealed, nor ever shall be revealed save to those who are made partakers thereof, consequently, those who teach this doctrine have not received it of the Spirit of the Lord, Truly, Bro Oliver [Cowdery] declared it to be the doctrine of devils. We therefore, command that this doctrine be taught no more in Zion— We sanction the decission of the Bishop and his council in relation to this doctrine being a bar of communion

* * *

We conclude our letter by the usual salutation, in token of the new and everlasting covenant. We hasten to close, because the mail is just going.

[p.156] We conclude our letter by the usual salutation in token of the new and everlasting covenant We hasten to a close because the mail is just going

JOSEPH SMITH, JUN.,
SIDNEY RIGDON,
F. G. WILLIAMS.

Joseph Smith Jr
Sidney Rigdon
F, G, Williams
Martin Harris
Orson Hyde Clk ~~of~~ for the presidency

P.S.—We feel gratified with the way in which Brother William W. Phelps is conducting the *Star* at present, we hope he will seek to render it more and more interesting. In relation

[p.157] P.S. We feel gratified with the way in which Bro William is conducting the Star at present we hope he will seek to render it more and more interesting. In [re]lation to the

---

39. 25 June 1833, *JSP, D3*, 153–54.

to the size of Bishoprics: When Zion is once properly regulated there will be a Bishop to each square of the size of the one we send you with this; but at present it must be done according to wisdom. It is needful, brethren, that you should be all of one heart, and of one mind, in doing the will of the Lord.

There should exist the greatest freedom and familiarity among the rulers in Zion.

We were exceedingly sorry to hear the complaint that was made in Brother Edward Partridge's letter, that the letters attending the Olive Leaf had been kept from him, as it is meet that he should know all things in relation to Zion, as the Lord has appointed him to be a judge in Zion. We hope, dear brethren, that the like occurrence will not take place again. When we direct letters to Zion to any of the High Priests, which pertain to the regulation of her affairs, we always design that they should be laid before the Bishop, so as to enable him to perform his duty. We say so much hoping it will be received in kindness; and our brethren will be careful of one another's [p.25] feelings, and walk in love, honoring one another more than themselves, as is required by the Lord.

    Yours as ever,
J. S.,
S. R.,
F. G. W.
—DHC 1:364-368.

size of Bishopricks when Zion is once properly regulated there will be a Bishop to each square of the size of the one we send you with this; but at present it must be done according to wisdom. It is needful Brethren that you should be all of one heart and of one mind in doing the will of the Lord.

there should exist the greatest freedom and familiarity among the Rulers in Zion.

We were exceeding sorry to hear the complaint which was made in Bro Edwards letter that the letters attending the olive leaf had been kept from him as it is meet that he should know all thing[s] in relation to Zion as the Lord has appointed him to be a judge in Zion. We hope dear Brethren that the like circumstance will not take place again— When we direct letters to Zion to any of the High Priests which pertains to the regulation thereof, we always design that they Should be laid before the Bishop so as to enable him to perform his duty, we say say so much hopeing that it will be received in Kindness and our Brethren be careful about each others feelings and walk in love honoring one another more than themselves as is required of the Lord You[r]s as ever[40]

Excerpts from the Second Communication to the Brethren in Zion

Kirtland, July 2nd, 1833.

To the Brethren in Zion:

* * *

Joseph Smith Letter
Kirtland July 2d— 1833–

Brethren—

* * *

---

40. 25 June 1833, *JSP, D3*, 154-57.

The Gift of Tongues

We are engaged in writing a letter to Eugene [branch] respecting the two Smiths, as we have received two letters from them; one from John Smith, the other from the Elder of the Church [Eden Smith]. As to the gift of tongues, all we can say is, that in this place we have received it as the ancients did: we wish you, however, to be careful, lest in this you be deceived. Guard against evils which may arise from any accounts given by women, or otherwise; be careful in all things lest any root of bitterness spring up among you, and thereby many be defiled. Satan will no doubt trouble you about the gift of tongues, unless you are careful; you cannot watch him too closely, nor pray too much. May the Lord give you wisdom in all things. In a letter mailed last week, you will doubtless, before you receive this, have obtained information about the New Translation. Consign the box of the Book of Commandments to N. K. Whitney & Co., Kirtland, Geauga county, Ohio, care of Kelly and Walworth, Cleveland, Cuyahoga county, Ohio.

* * *

We conclude by giving our heartiest approbation to every measure calculated for the spread of the truth, in these last days; and our strongest desires, and sincerest prayers for the prosperity of Zion. Say to all the brethren and sisters in Zion, that they have our hearts, our best wishes, and the strongest desires of our spirits for their welfare, temporal, spiritual, and [p.26] eternal. As ever, we salute you in the name of the Lord Jesus. Amen.
JOSEPH SMITH, JUN.,
SIDNEY RIGDON,
F. G. WILLIAMS.
—DHC 1:368-370.

we are engaged in writing a letter to Eugine respecting the two Smith[s] as we have received two from them one from John Smith the other [p.167] from the Elders of the Church. As to the gift of tongues, all we can say is that in this place we have received it as the ancients did we wish you however to be careful lest in this you be deceived guard against evils which may arise from any accounts given of women or otherwise be careful in all things lest any root of bitterness spring up among you and thereby many be defiled. Satan will no doubt trouble you about the Gift of tongues unless you are careful you cannot watch him too closly nor pray to[o] much may the Lord give you wisdom in all things, in a letter mailed last week you will doubtless see before you receive this <have> obtained information about the new translation. Consign the Box of the book of the Commandments to NK Whitney & Co Kirtland Geauga Co Ohio care of Killy and Walworth Cleaveland Cuyahoga County Ohio,

* * *

[p.168] We conclude by giving our heartiest approbation to evry measure calculated for the spread of <the> truth in these last days and our strongest desires and sincerest prayers for the prosperity of Zion— Say to all the brethren and sisters in Zion that they have our hearts our best wishes and the strongest desires of our spirits for their welfare Temporal Spiritual, and Eternal.
As ever we salute you in the name of the Lord Jesus Amen
Sidney Rigdon
Joseph Smith Jr
F. G. Williams—[41]

---

41. 2 July 1833, *JSP, D3*, 166–68.

Minor Events in Zion and Kirtland—An Appeal to the Governor of Missouri
* * *
Letter to Vienna Jaques

| | **Joseph Smith Letter** |

September 4.—I wrote as follows to Sister Vienna Jaques, at Independence, Missouri:

Sept. 4. 1833 I wrote as follows to Sister "Vienna Jaquish [Jaques] at Independence Miss⁰.[42]

Dear Sister:—Having a few leisure moments, I sit down to communicate to you a few words, which I know I am under obligation to improve for your satisfaction, if it should be a satisfaction for you to receive a few words from your unworthy brother in Christ. I received your letter some time since, containing a history of your journey and your safe arrival, for which I bless the Lord; I have often felt a whispering since I received your letter, like this: "Joseph, thou art indebted to thy God for the offering of thy Sister Vienna, which proved a savor of life as pertaining to thy pecuniary concerns. Therefore she should not be forgotten of thee, for the Lord hath done this, and thou shouldst remember her in all thy prayers and also by letter, for she oftentimes calleth on the Lord, saying, O Lord, inspire thy servant Joseph to communicate by letter some word to thine unworthy handmaiden, and say all my sins are forgiven, and art thou not content with the chastisement wherewith thou hast chastised thy handmaiden?" Yes, sister, this seems to be the whispering of a spirit, and judge ye what spirit it is. I was aware when you left Kirtland that the Lord would chasten you, but I prayed fervently in the name of Jesus that you might live to receive your inheritance, agreeable to the commandment which was given concerning you. I am not at all astonished at what has happened to you, neither to what has happened to Zion, and I could tell all they whys and wherefore of all these calamities. But alas, it is in vain to warn

Dear Siste[r] Having a few Leisur moments I sit down to communicate to you a few wordes which I know I am under obligation to improve ~~for~~ to your Satisfaction if it should be a satisfaction for you to receive a few words from your unworthy brother in Christ, I received your Letter some time since containing a history of your Journey and your safe arival for which I bless the Lord I have often **[p.292]** felt a whispering since I received your letter like this Joseph thou art indebted to thy God for the offering of thy Sister Viana [Vienna Jaques] which proved a Savior of life as pertaining to thy pecunary concern therefor she should not be forgotten of thee for the Lord hath done this and thou shouldst remember her in all thy prayers and also by letter for she oftentimes calleth on the Lord saying O Lord inspire thy Servant Joseph to communicate by letter some word to thine unworthy handmaid canst thou not speak peaciably unto thine handmaid and say all my sins are forgiven and art thou not content with the chastisement wherewith thou hast chastised thy handmaid yea siste[r] this seams to be the whisperings of a spirit and Judge ye what spirit it is I was sensable, when you left Kirtland that the Lord would chasten you but I pray<ed> fervantly in the name of Jesus that you might live to receive your inheritance agreeable to the commandm[e]nt which was given concerning you I am not at all astonished at what has happened to you neithe[r] to what has happened to Zion and

---

42. See 9 September 1833, History A-1, Addenda, 1.

and give precepts, for all men are naturally disposed to walk in their own paths as they are pointed out by their own fingers, and are not [p.27] willing to consider and walk in the path which is pointed out by another, saying, This is the way, walk ye in it, although he should be an unerring director, and the Lord his God sent him. Nevertheless I do not feel disposed to cast any reflections, but I feel to cry mightily unto the Lord that all things which have happened may work together for good; yea, I feel to say, O Lord, let Zion be comforted, let her waste places be built up and established an hundred fold; let Thy Saints come unto Zion out of every nation; let her be exalted to the third heavens, and let Thy judgment be sent forth unto victory; and after this great tribulation, let Thy blessing fall upon Thy people, and let Thy handmaid live till her soul shall be satisfied in beholding the glory of Zion; for notwithstanding her present affliction, she shall yet arise and put on her beautiful garments, and be the joy and glory of the whole earth. Therefore let you heart be comforted; live in strict obedience to the commandments of God, and walk humbly before Him, and He will exalt thee in His own due time.

I could tell all the why's & wherefores of all there calamities but alas it is in vain to warn and give precepts for all men are naturally disposed to walk in their own paths as they are pointed out by their own fingers and are not willing to considder and walk in the path which is pointed out by another saying this is the way walk ye in it altho he should be [p.293] an uner[r]ing director and the Lord his God sent him nevertheless I do not feel disposed to cast any reflections but I feel to cry mightily unto the Lord that all things might work together for good which has happened yea I feel to say O Lord let Zion be comforted let her waste places be built up and established an hundred fold let thy saints come unto Zion out of every nation let her be exalted to the third heavens and let thy Judgments be sent forth unto victory and after this great tribulation let thy blessings fall upon thy people and let thy handmaid live till her soul shall be satisfied in beholding the glory of Zion notwithstanding her present affliction she shall yet arise and put on her beautiful garments and be the Joy and ~~praise~~ <glory> of the whole earth therefore let your heart be comferted live in strict obedience to the commandments of God and walk humble before him and he will exalt thee in his own due time

* * *

I will assure you that the Lord has respect unto the offering you made. Brother David W. Patten has just returned from his tour to the east, and gives us great satisfaction as to his ministry. He has raised up a church of about eighty-three members in that part of the country where his friends live—in the state of New York. Many were healed through his instrumentality, several cripples were restored. As many as twelve that were afflicted came at a time from a distance to be healed; he and others administered in the name of Jesus, and they were made whole. Thus you see that the laborers in the Lord's vineyard are laboring

[p.295] I will assure you that the Lord has respect unto the offering you made he is a God that changes not and and his word cannot fail remember what he has said in the book of mormon respecting those who should assist in bringing this work forth we frequently have inteligenc from our elder abroad that are proclaiming the word that God is working with them for they have attained to great faith insomuch that signs do follow them that believe Brothe[r] David Pettin [David W. Patten] has Just returned from his tour ~~from~~ <to> the east and gives us great satisfaction as to his ministry he has raised up a church of

with their might, while the day lasts, knowing "the night soon cometh when no man can work."
(Signed) JOSEPH SMITH.
--DHC 1:407-409

about Eighty <three> members in that part of the country where his friends live in the state of New York many were healed ~~by~~ through his instrumantality several criples were restored as many as twelve that were afflicted came at ~~at~~ a time from a distanc[e] to be healed he <and others> administered in the name of Jesus and they were made whole thus you see that the Laborers in the Lords vineyard are Labouring with their mights while the day **[p.296]** lasts knowing the night soon cometh wherein no man can work

* * *

[Joseph Smith Jr.]⁴³

Remembrance of Canada Saints—
Correspondence and Petition Relative to Missouri Affairs

Joseph Smith Letter

November 19—I wrote as follows, from Kirtland, to Moses C. Nickerson, Mount Pleasant, Upper Canada:

Kirtland Mills, Geauga County, Ohio, Nov. 19, 1833

Anxiety for Afflicted Saints

Brother Moses:—We arrived at this place on the fourth ultimo, after a fatiguing journey, during which we were blessed **[p.28]** with usual health. We parted with Father and Mother Nickerson at Buffalo, in good health, and they expressed a degree of satisfaction for the prosperity and blessings of their journey.

Since our arrival here, Brother Sidney has been afflicted with sore eyes, which is probably the reason why you have not previously heard from us, as he was calculating to write you immediately. But though I expect he will undoubtedly write you soon, as his eyes are evidently better, yet lest you should be impatient to learn something concerning us, I have thought that perhaps a few lines from me, though there may be a lack of fluency according to the literati of the age, might be received with a degree of satisfaction on your

Brother Moses [Nickerson], We arrived at this place on the 4th ult. after a fateagueing journey, during which time we were blessed with health as usual. We parted with father and mother Nickerson at Buffalo, they were both in good health, and expressed a degree of satisfaction for the prosperity and blessings of their journey.

Since our arrival here, bro. Sidney [Rigdon] has been afflicted with sore eyes, which is probably the reason why you have not previously heard from us, as he was calculating to write you immediately. But, though I expect that he will undoubtedly write you soon, as his eyes are considerably better, yet lest you should be impatient to learn something concerning us, I have thought that perhaps a few lines from me, though there may be a lack of fluency in address according to the literati of the age, may be received with a degree of

---

43. 4 September 1833, *JSP, D3*, 291–96.

part, at least, when you call to mind the near relation with which we are united by the everlasting ties of the Gospel of our Lord Jesus Christ.

We found our families and the Church in this place well, generally. Nothing of consequence happened while we were absent, except the death of one of our brethren—David Johnson—a young man of great worth as a private citizen among us, the loss of whom we justly mourn.

We are favored with frequent intelligence from different sections of our country, respecting the progress of the Gospel, and our prayers are daily to our Father, that it may greatly spread, even till all nations shall hear the glorious news and come to a knowledge of the truth.

We have received letters from our brethren in Missouri of late, but we cannot tell, from their contents, the probable extent to which those persons who are desirous to expel them from that country will carry their unlawful and unrighteous purposes. Our brethren have applied to the executive of the state, who has promised them all the assistance that the civil law can give; and in all probability a suit has been commenced ere this.

We are informed, however, that those persons are very violent, and threaten immediate extermination upon all those who profess our doctrine. How far they will be suffered to execute their threats, we know not, but we trust in the Lord, and leave the event with Him to govern in His own wise providence.

I shall expect a communication from you on receipt of [p.29] this, and hope you will give me information concerning the brethren, their health, faith, etc., also inform me concerning our friends with whom we formed acquaintance.

satisfaction on your part, at least, when you call to mind the near relation with which we are united by the everlasting ties of the gospel of our Lord Jesus Christ.

[p.357] We found our families, and the church in this place, well, generally: nothing of consequence transpires while we were abscent, except the death of one of our brethren, a young man of great worth as a private citizen among us, the loss of whom we justly mourn.

We are favored with frequent intelligence from different sections of our country, respecting the progress of the gospel, and our prayers are daily to our Father, that it may greatly prevail <spread>, even till all nations shall hear the glorious news and come to a knowledge of the truth.

We have received letters from our breth[r]en in Missouri of late, but we cannot tell from their contents the probable extent that those persons who are desirous to expel them from that country, will carry their unlawful and unrighteous purposes. Our breth[r]en have applied to the Executive of that State, [p.358] who has promised them all the assistance that the civil law can give; and in all probability with us, a suit has been commenced ere this.

We are informed, however, that those persons are very violent, and threaten immediate excision upon all those who profess this faith doctrine. How far they will be suffered to execute their threats we know not, but we trust in the Lord, and leave the event with him to govern in his own wise providence.

I shall expect a communication from you on the reception of this, and hope you will give me information concerning the brethren, their health, faith, &c. Also inform me concerning our friends with whom we formed acquaintance.

You are aware, no doubt, dear brother, that anxieties inexpressible crowd themselves continually upon my mind for the Saints, when I consider the many temptations to which we are subject, from the cunning and flattery of the great adversary of our souls: and I can truly say, with much fervency have I called upon the Lord for our brethren in Canada. And when I call to mind with what readiness they received the word of truth by the ministry of Brother Sidney and myself, I am truly under great obligations to humble myself before Him.	You are aware, no doubt, dear brother, that anxieties inexpresible croud themselves continually upon my mind for the saints, when I consider the many temptations with which we are subject from the cunning and flattery of the great adversary of our souls. And I can truely say, that with much fervency I have called upon the Lord in behalf of our brethren in Canada. And when I call to mind with what rediness they received the word of truth by the ministry of bro. Sidney and myself, I am truely under great obligation to humble myself in thankfulness before him.[44]

Coming of the Son of Man

	Joseph Smith Letter
When I contemplate the rapidity with which the great and glorious day of the coming of the Son of Man advances, when He shall come to receive His Saints unto Himself, where they shall dwell in His presence, and be crowned with glory and immortality: when I consider that soon the heavens are to be shaken, and the earth tremble and reel to and fro; and that the heavens are to be unfolded as a scroll when it is rolled up; and that every mountain and island are to flee away, I cry out in my heart, What manner of persons ought we to be in all holy conversation and godliness!	When I contemplate the rapidity with which the great and glorious day of the coming of the Son of Man advances, when he shall come to receive his saints unto himself where they shall dwell in his presence and be crowned with glory & immortality; when I consider that soon the heavens are to be shaken, and the earth tremble and reel to and fro; and <that> the heavens are to be unfolded as a scroll when it is ~~folded~~ <rolled> up, that every mountain and island are to flee ~~away~~ <away> I cry out in my heart, What manner of person ought I to be in all holy conversasion and godliness!
You remember the testimony which I bore in the name of the Lord Jesus, concerning the great work which He has brought forth in the last days. You know my manner of communication, how that in weakness and simplicity, I declared to you what the Lord had brought forth by the ministering of His holy angels to me for this generation. I pray that the Lord may enable you to treasure these things in your mind, for I know that His Spirit will bear testimony to all who seek diligently after knowledge from Him. I hope you will search the Scriptures to see whether these things are	You remember the testimony which I bore in the name of the Lord Jesus, concerning the great work which he has brought forth in the last days. You know my manner of communication, how that in weakness and simpleness I declared to you what the Lord had brought forth by the ministering of his holy angels to me, for this generation. I pray that the Lord may enable you to treasure these things up in your mind; for I know that his Spirit will bear testimony to all who seek diligently after knowledge from him. I hope you will search the scriptures, to see whether these things are

---

44. 19 November 1833, *JSP, D3*, 356–58.

not also consistent with those things which the ancient Prophets and Apostles have written.

I remember Brother Freeman and wife, Ransom also, and Sister Lydia, and little Charles, with all the brethren and sisters. I entreat for an interest in all your prayers before the throne of mercy, in the name of Jesus. I hope the Lord will grant **[p.30]** that I may see you all again, and above all that we may overcome, and sit down together in the kingdom of our Father.
Your brother, etc.
JOSEPH SMITH
—DHC 1:441-443.

not also consistant with those things that the ancient prophets and apostles have written.

I remember brother Freeman [Eleazer Freeman Nickerson] and Wife, Ranson also, and sister Lydia [Goldthwaite Bailey], and little Charles, with all the brethren and sisters. I intreat for an interest in all your prayers before the throne of mercy in the name of Jesus. I hope that the Lord will grant that I **[p.360]** may see you all again, and above all that we may overcome and set down together in the Kingdom of our Father...

(Signed)   Joseph Smith Jr.[45]

The Prophet's Reflections Concerning Sidney Rigdon

The character of Sidney Rigdon is here vividly portrayed, followed by an earnest prayer for his salvation and a prophecy concerning his posterity. It is true that his generations have been hunted for, and some of them found. His son, John W., joined the Church many years ago after wandering in the wilderness of darkness. More recently one of his grandsons, now an old man, joined the Church and another grandson has expressed himself favorably towards the Church. In this way, in part at least, we see the fulfilment of this earnest plea by the Prophet Joseph Smith.[46]

Nothing of note occurred from the falling of the stars on the 13th, to this date, November 19th, when my heart is somewhat sorrowful, but I feel to trust in the Lord, the God of Jacob. I have learned in my travels that man is treacherous and selfish, but few excepted.

Joseph Smith's Journal
November 19th from the 13th u[n]till this date of nothing of note has transpired since the great sign in the heavins this day my \<hart\> is somewhat sorrowfull but feel to trust in the Lord the god of Jacob I̶ I have learned in my travels that man is trecheous [treacherous] and selfish but few excepted[47]

---

45. 19 November 1833, *JSP, D3*, 359–60.
46. This introductory paragraph was authored by Joseph Fielding Smith.
47. 19 November 1833, *JSP, J1*, 18.

Sidney Rigdon

Brother Sidney is a man whom I love, but he is not capable of that pure and steadfast love for those who are his benefactors that should characterize a President of the Church of Christ. This, with some other little things, such as a selfishness and independence of mind, which too often manifested destroy the confidence of those who would lay down their lives for him—these are his faults. But notwithstanding these things, he is a very great and good man; a man of great power of words, and can gain the friendship of his hearers very quickly. He is a man whom God will uphold, if he will continue faithful to his calling. O God, grant that he may, for the Lord's sake. Amen.

And again, blessed be Brother Sidney: notwithstanding he shall be high and lifted up, yet he shall bow down under the yoke like unto an ass that croucheth beneath his burden, that learneth his master's will by the stroke of the rod; thus saith the Lord: yet, the Lord will have mercy on him, and he shall bring forth much fruit, even as the vine of the choice grape, when her clusters are ripe, before the time of the gleaning [p.31] of the vintage; and the Lord shall make his heart merry as with sweet wine, because of Him who putteth forth His hand, and lifteth him up out of deep mire, and pointeth him out the way, and guideth his feet when he stumbles, and humbleth him in his pride. Blessed are his generations: nevertheless one shall hunt after them as a man hunteth after an ass that has strayed in the wilderness, and straightway findeth him and bringeth him into the fold. Thus shall the Lord watch over his generation, that they may be saved. Even so, Amen.

Joseph Smith's Journal

Brother <Sidney [Rigdon]> is a man whom I love but is not capab[le] of that pure and stedfast love for those who are his benefactors as should posess possess the breast of an man a Presedent of the chu[r]ch of Christ this with some other little things such as a selfish and indipendance of mind which to[o] often manifest distroys the confidence of those who would lay down their lives for him but notwithstanding these things he is <a> very great and good man a man of great power of words and can <gain> the friendship of his hearrers very quick he is a man whom god will uphold if he will continue faithful to his calling O God grant that he may for the Lords sake Amen[48]

And again, blessed be brother Sidney, also, not withstanding he shall be high and lifted up, yet he shall bow down under the yoke like unto an ass that couchett beneath his burthen; that learneth his master's <will> by the stroke of the rod: thus saith the Lord. Yet the Lord will have mercy on him, and he shall bring forth much fruit; even as the vin vine of the choice grape when her clusters are <is> ripe, before the time of the gleaning of the vintage: and the Lord shall make his heart merry as with sweet wine because of him who putteth forth his hand and lifteth him up from <out of> deep mire, and pointeth him out the way, and guideth his feet when he stumbles; and humbleth him in his pride, Blessed are his generations. Nevertheless, one shall hunt after them as a man hunteth after an ass that hath strayed in the wilderness, & straitway findeth him and bringeth him into the fold. Thus shall the Lord watch over his generation that they may be saved: even so; Amen.[49]

---

48. 19 November 1833, *JSP, J1*, 18.
49. 19 November 1833, *JSP, J1*, 19.

The Prophet's Maxims

Joseph Smith's Journal

The man who willeth to do well, we should extol his virtues, and speak not of his faults behind his back. A man who wilfully turneth away from his friend without a cause, is not easily forgiven. The kindness of a man should never be forgotten. That person who never forsaketh his trust, should ever have the highest place of regard in our hearts, and our love should never fail, but increase more and more, and this is my disposition and these my sentiments.
--DHC 1:443-444.

the man who willeth to do well we should extall his virtues and speak not of his faults behind his back a man who willfuly turneth away from his friend without a cause is not ~~lightly~~ <easily> ~~to be fogiven~~ <forgiven.> the kindness of a man <should> ~~is~~ never ~~to~~ be forgotten that person who never forsaketh his trust should ever have the highest place for regard in our hearts and our love should never fail but increase more and more and this my disposition and sentiment &c Amen[50]

Instructions on Sale of Land in Zion

The following is an excerpt taken from a communication to the Saints in Zion, who had been driven from their homes and basely persecuted by a mob in Jackson County, Missouri.[51]

Kirtland, December 5, 1833
* * *

Joseph Smith Letter

I wish, when you receive this letter, that you would collect every particular, concerning the mob, from the beginning, and send us a correct statement of facts, as they occurred from time to time, that we may be enabled to give the public correct information on the subject; and inform us also of the situation of the brethren, with respect to their means of sustenance.

I wish when you receive this letter that you would collect every particular concerning the Mob from the begining and send us a correct statement of fact as they transpired from time to time that we may be enabled to give the public correct information on the subject and inform us also of the situation of the brethren with respect to their means of sustinance &c

---

50. 19 November 1833, *JSP, J1*, 18–19. A related journal entry for 13 November records: "nothing of of note transpired from the 4th of Noveber u[n]til this day in the morning at 4 Oh clock I was awoke by Brother Davis knocking at <my> door saying Brother Joseph come git <up> and see the signs in the heavens and I arrose and beheld to my great Joy the stars fall from heaven yea they fell like hail stones a litteral fullfillment of the word of God as recorded in the holy scriptures and a sure sign that the coming of Christ is clost at hand Oh how marvellous are thy works Oh Lord and I thank thee for thy me[r]cy unto me thy servent Oh Lord save me in thy kingdom for Christ sake Amen." *JSP, J1*, 16, 18.

51. This introductory paragraph was authored by Joseph Fielding Smith.

I would inform you that it is not the will of the Lord for you to sell your lands in Zion, if means can possibly be procured for your sustenance without. Every exertion should be made to maintain the cause you have espoused, and to contribute to the necessities of one another, as much as possible, in this your great calamity, and remember not to murmur at [p.32] the dealings of God with his creatures. You are not as yet brought into as trying circumstances as were the ancient Prophets and Apostles. Call to mind Daniel, the three Hebrew children, Jeremiah, Paul, Stephen, and many others, too numerous to mention, who were stoned, sawn asunder, tempted, slain with the sword, and wandered about in sheep skins and goat skins, being destitute, afflicted, tormented, of whom the world was not worthy. They wandered in deserts and in mountains, and hid in dens, and caves of the earth; yet they all obtained a good report through faith; and amidst all their afflictions they rejoiced that they were counted worthy to receive persecution for Christ's sake.

We know not what we shall be called to pass through before Zion is delivered and established; therefore, we have great need to live near to God, and always be in strict obedience to all His commandments, that we may have a conscience void of offense toward God and man. It is your privilege to use every lawful means in your power to seek redress for your grievances from your enemies, and prosecute them to the extent of the law; but it will be impossible for us to render you any temporal assistance, as our means are already exhausted, and we are deeply in debt, and know of no means whereby we shall be able to extricate ourselves. The inhabitants of this county threaten our destruction, and we know not how soon they may be permitted to follow the example of the Missourians; but our trust is in God, and we are determined, His grace assisting us, to maintain the cause and hold out faithful unto the end, that we may be crowned with crowns of celestial

I would inform you that it is not the will of the Lord for you to sell your Lands in Zion if means can possably be procured for their sustenance without, evry exertion [p.372] should be to maintain the cause you have espoused and to contribute to the necessities of one another as much as possable in this your great calamity and remember not to murmur at the dealings of God with his creature you are not as yet brought into as trying circumstances as were the ancient Prophets & apostles Call to mind a Daniel the three Hebrew Children, Jeremiah Paul Stephen and many more too numerous to mention who were stoned sawn asunder tempted slain with the sword and wandered about in sheep skins & goat skins being destitute afflicted tormented of whom the world was not worthy. they wandered in deserts and in mountains and in dens and caves of the earth yet they all obtained a good report through faith and amidst all their afflictions they rejoiced that they were <counted> worthy to receive persecution for Christs sake

we know not what we shall be called to pass through before Zion is delivered and established therefore we have great need to live near to God and always be in strict obedience to all his commandments that we may have a concience void of offense towards God and man, It is your privelege to use every lawful means in your power to seek redress for your grievances of your enemies and prosecute them to the extent of the Law but it will be impossible for us to render you any assistance in a temporal point of view as our means are already exhausted and are deeply in debt and know no means whereby we shall be able to extricate ourselves; The inhabitants of this county threaten our distruction and we know not how soon they may be permitted to follow the examples of the Missourians but our trust is in [p.373] God and we are determined by his grace assisting us to maintain the cause and hold out faithful to the end that we may be crowned with crowns of celestial glory and glory, and enter into the rest that is prepared for the children of God.

We are now distributing the type, and intend to commence setting today, and issue a paper the last of this week, or beginning of next. We wrote to Elder Phelps some time since, and also sent by Elder Hyde, for the list of names of subscribers to the Star, which we have not yet received; and, until we receive it, the most of the subscribers will be deprived of the paper; and when you receive this, if you have not sent the list, I wish you to attend to it immediately, as much inconvenience will follow a delay.

* * *

We learn by Elder Phelps, that the brethren have sur[p.33]rendered their arms to the Missourians, and are fleeing across the river. If that is the case, it is not meet that they should recommence hostilities with them; but, if not, you should maintain the ground as long as there is a man left, as the spot of ground upon which you were located, is the place appointed of the Lord for your inheritance, and it is right in the sight of God that you contend for it to the last.

You will recollect that the Lord has said, that Zion should not be removed out of her place; therefore the land should not be sold, but be held by the Saints, until the Lord in His wisdom shall open a way for your return; and until that time, if you can purchase a tract of land in Clay county, for present emergencies, it is right you should do so, if you can do it, and not sell your land in Jackson county. It is not safe for us to send you a written revelation on the subject, but what is stated above is according to wisdom. I haste to a close to give room for Brother Oliver, and remain yours in the bonds of the everlasting covenant,
Joseph Smith, Jun.

enter into that rest that is prepared for the children of God,

we are now distributing the tipe and calculate to commence setting to day and issue a paper the Last of this week or beginning of next, we wrote to bro Phelps some time since and also sent by bro Orson for the names of the subscribe[r]s for the star which we have not yet received and until we receive them the most of the brethren will be deprived of them and when you receive this if you have not sent them I wish you to attend to it immediately as much inconvenience will attend a delay,

* * *

We Learn by Bro Phelps that the brethren have surrendered their [p.374] arms to the enemy and are fleeing across the river if that is the case it is not meet that they should recommence hostilities with them but if not you should maintain the ground as Long as there is a man Left. as the spot of ground upon which you were located is the place appointed of the Lord for your inheritance and it was right in the sight of God that you contend for it to the last,

you will recollect that the Lord has said that Zion should not be moved out of her place therefore the land should not be sold but held by the brethren until the Lord ~~of~~ in his wisdom opens a way for your return and until that time if you can purchase a tract of Land in Clay for present imergenes it is right you should do so if you can do it and not sell your Land in Jackson county it is not safe for us to send you a writen revelation on the subject but what is writen above is according to wisdom, I haste to a close to give room for Bro Oliver [Cowdery] and remain yours in the bonds of the new and everlasting covenant

Joseph Smith J[52]

---

52. 5 December 1833, *JSP, D3*, 371–74.

A Letter from the Prophet Joseph Smith to the Exiled Saints in Missouri

—DHC 1:448–451 This letter depicts the tenderness and sympathy of the Prophet towards the Saints in Missouri, and his desire to encourage and strengthen them by faith and hope in this great hour of their deep affliction.

Kirtland Mills, Ohio
December 10, 1833.

Edward Partridge, W. W. Phelps, John Whitmer, A. S. Gilbert, John Corrill, Isaac Morley, and all the Saints whom it may concern:

Beloved Brethren:—This morning's mail brought letters from Bishop Partridge, and Elders Corrill and Phelps, all mailed at Liberty, November 19th, which gave us the melancholy intelligence of your flight from the land of your inheritance, having been driven before the face of your enemies in that place.

From previous letters we learned that a number of our brethren had been slain, but we could not learn from the letters referred to above, that there had been more than one killed, and that one Brother Barber; and that Brother Dibble was **[p.34]** wounded in the bowels. We were thankful to learn that no more had been slain, and our daily prayers are that the Lord will not suffer his Saints, who have gone up to His land to keep His commandments, to stain His holy mountain with their blood.

I cannot learn from any communication by the Spirit to me, that Zion has forfeited her claim to a celestial crown, notwithstanding the Lord has caused her to be thus afflicted, except

Joseph Smith Letter
Kirtland Mills Ohio December 10th 1833

Beloved brethren E[dward] Partridge, W[illiam] W. Phelps J[ohn] Whitmer A S[idney] Gilbert J Corril [John Corrill] I[saac] Morley, and all the saints whom it may concern.

This morning the mail brought bros Partridge & Corrils letters & also bro Williams, all mailed at Liberty Nov. 19th which gave us the melancholy inteligence of your flight from the land of your inheritance having been driven before the face of your enemies in that place

From previous letters we had learned that a number of our brethren have been slain, but we could not learn from those refered to above as there had been but one, that was bro [Andrew] Barber and bro [Philo] Dibble wounded in the bowels, we were thankful to learn that no more were slain, and our daily prayers are, that the Lord will not suffer his saints who have gone up to his land to keep his commandments, to stain his holy mountain with their blood.[53]

Zion to Suffer Affliction

Joseph Smith Letter

I cannot learn from any communication by the spirit to me that Zion has forfeited her claim to a celestial crown not withstanding the Lord has caused her to be thus afflicted; except it may it

---

53. 10 December 1833, *JSP, D3*, 376.

it may be some individuals, who have walked in disobedience, and forsaken the new covenant; all such will be made manifest by their works in due time. I have always expected that Zion would suffer some affliction, from what I could learn from the commandments which have been given. But I would remind you of a certain clause in one which says, that after much tribulation cometh the blessing. By this, and also others, and also one received of late, I know that Zion, in the due time of the lord, will be redeemed; but how many will be the days of purification, tribulation, and affliction, the Lord has kept hid from my eyes; and when I inquire concerning this subject, the voice of the Lord is: Be still, and know that I am God; all those who suffer for my name shall reign with me, and he that layeth down his life for my sake shall find it again.

Now, there are two things of which I am ignorant; and the Lord will not show them unto me, perhaps for a wise purpose in Himself—I mean in some respects—and they are these: Why God has suffered so great a calamity to come upon Zion, and what the great moving cause of this great affliction is; and again, by what means he will return her back to her inheritance, with songs of everlasting joy upon her head. These two things, brethren, are in part kept back that they are not plainly shown unto me; but there are some things that are plainly manifest which have incurred the displeasure of the Almighty.

may be some individuals who have walked in disobedience and forsaken the new covenants; all such will be made manifest by their works in due time. I have always expected that Zion would suffer sore affliction from what I could learn from the commandments which have been given. but I would remind you of a certain clause in one which says that after much tribulation cometh the blessing. by this and [p.377] also others, and also one received of late, I know that Zion, in the own due time of the Lord will be redeemed, but how many will be the days of her purification, tribulation and affliction, the Lord has kept hid from my eyes; and when I enquire concerning this subject the voice of the Lord is, Be still, and know that I am God! all those who suffer for my name shall reign with me, and he that layeth down his life for my sake shall find it again.

Now there are two things of which I am ignorant and the Lord will not show me— perhaps for a wise purpose in himself. I mean in some respects, and they are these, Why God hath suffered so great calamity to come upon Zion; or what the great moving cause of this great affliction is. These two things and again by what means he will return her back to her inheritance with songs of everlasting Joy upon her head. These two things brethren, are in part kept back that they are not plainly <shewn unto me. but there are some things that are plainly> manifest, that has incured <th[e]> displeasure of displeasure the Almighty.[54]

The Righteous Suffer with the Guilty

Joseph Smith Letter

When I contemplate upon all things that have been manifested, I am aware that I ought not to murmur, and do not murmur, only in this, that those who are innocent are compelled to suffer for the iniquities of the guilty; and I cannot account [p.35] for this, only on this wise, that the saying of the Savior has not

when I contemplate upon all things that have been manifested, I am sensable that I aught not to murmer and do not murmer only in this, but that those who are innocent are compelled to suffer for the iniquities of the guilty; and I cannot account for this, only on this wise, that the saying of the savior has not been

---

54. 10 December 1833, *JSP, D3*, 376–77.

been strictly observed: "If thy right eye offend thee, pluck it out, and cast it from thee; or if thy right arm offend thee, cut it off, and cast it from thee." Now the fact is, if any of the members of our body is disordered, the rest of our body will be affected with it, and then all are brought into bondage together; and yet, notwithstanding all this, it is with difficulty that I can restrain my feelings when I know that you, my brethren, with whom I have had so many happy hours—sitting, as it were, in heavenly places in Christ Jesus; and also, having the witness which I feel, and ever have felt, of the purity of your motives—are cast out, and are as strangers and pilgrims on the earth, exposed to hunger, cold, nakedness, peril, sword—I say when I contemplate this, it is with difficulty that I can keep from complaining and murmuring against this dispensation; but I am sensible that this is not right, and may God grant that notwithstanding your great afflictions and sufferings, there may not anything separate us from the love of Christ.

Brethren, when we learn your sufferings, it awakens every sympathy of our hearts; it weighs us down; we cannot refrain from tears, yet, we are not able to realize, only in part, your sufferings: and I often hear the brethren saying, they wish they were with you, that they might bear a part of your sufferings; and I myself should have been with you, had not God prevented it in the order of His provident, that the yoke of affliction might be less grievous upon you, God having forewarned me, concerning these things, for your sake; and also, Elder Cowdery could not lighten your afflictions by tarrying longer with you, for his presence would have so much the more enraged your enemies; therefore God hath dealt mercifully with us. O brethren, let us be thankful that it is as well with us as it is, and we are yet alive and peradventure, God hath laid up in store great good for us in this generation, and may grant that we may yet glorify His name.

strictly observed: If thy right eye offend thee pluck it out. and cast it from thee <or if thy right arm offend thee pluck it of[f] and cast it from thee>. Now the fact is, if any of the members of our body are disordered, the rest of our body will be effected with them and then all is brought into bondage together. And yet notwithstanding all this, it is with difficulty that I can restrain my feelings; when I know that you my brethren with whom I have had so many happy [p.378] hours, sitting as it were in heavenly places in Christ Jesus. and also haveing the witness which I feel, and even have felt, of the purity of your motives— are cast out, and are as strangers and pilgrims on the earth, exposed to hunger, cold, nakedness peril, sword &c I say when I contemplate this, it is with difficulty that I can keep from complaining and murmerings against this dispensation; but I am sensible that this is not right and may God grant that notwithstanding your great afflictions and sufferings there may not any thing sepperate us from the Love of Christ.

Brethren, when we learn your sufferings it awakens evry sympathy of our hearts; it weighs us us down; we cannot refrain from tears [*illegible*] yet we are not able to realize only in part your sufferings. And I often hear the brethren saying they wish they were with you that they might bear a part of your sufferings; and I myself should have been with you had not God prevented it in the order of his providence, that the yoke of affliction might be less grievous upon you; God having forewarned me concerning these things for your sakes; and also bro Oliver [Cowdery], could not lighten your afflictions by tarrying longer with you, for his presence would have so much the more enraged your enemies; therefore, God hath deals dealt mercifully with us. O brethren, let us be thankful that it is as well with us as it is, and we are yet alive that peradvent[u]re, God hath Laid up in store great good for us in this generation, and grant that we may yet glorify his name,[55]

---

55. 10 December 1833, *JSP, D3*, 377–78.

The Value of an Inheritance

	Joseph Smith Letter
I feel thankful that there have no more denied the faith; I pray God in the name of Jesus that you all may be kept in the faith unto the end: let your sufferings be what they may, it is better in the eyes of God that you should die, than that **[p.36]** you should give up the land of Zion, the inheritances which you have purchased with your moneys; for every man that giveth not up his inheritance, though he should die, yet, when the Lord shall come, he shall stand upon it, and with Job, in his flesh he shall see God. Therefore, this is my counsel, that you retain your lands, even unto the uttermost, and employ every lawful means to seek redress of your enemies; and pray to God, day and night, to return you in peace and in safety to the lands of your inheritance: and when the judge fail you, appeal unto the executive; and when the executive fail you, appeal unto the president; and when the president fail you, and all laws fail you, and the humanity of the people fail you, and all things else fail you but God alone, and you continue to weary Him with your importunings, as the poor woman did the unjust judge, He will not fail to execute judgment upon your enemies, and to avenge His own elect that cry unto Him day and night.	I feel thankful that there have no more denied the faith; I pray God, in the name of Jesus that you all may be kept in the faith, unto the end, let your sufferings be what they may, it is better that you should die in the ey[e]s of God, then that you **[p.379]** should give up the Land of Zion, the ~~inhabitant~~ inheritances which you have purchased with your monies; for evry man that giveth not up his inheritances, though he should die yet when the Lord shall come, he shall stand upon it, and with Job in his flesh he shall see God. Therefore this is my council that you retain your lands even unto the uttermost, and seeking <evry> lawful means to obtain redress of your enemies &c &c and pray to God day and night to return you in peace and in safety to the Lands of your in heritance and, ~~and~~ when the Judge fails you, appeal unto the Executive, and when the Executive fails you, appeal unto the President, and when the President fails you, and all Laws fail you and the humanity of the people fails you, and all things else fails you but God alone, and you continue to weary him with your importunings, as the poor woman the unjust Judge, he will not fail to exicute Judgment upon your enemies and to avenge his own elect that cry unto him day and night—
Behold, He will not fail you! He will come with ten thousand of His Saints, and all His adversaries shall be destroyed with the breath of His lips! All those who keep their inheritances, notwithstanding they should be beaten and driven, shall be likened unto the wise virgins who took oil in their lamps. But all those who are unbelieving and fearful, will be likened unto the foolish virgins, who took no oil in their lamps: and when they shall return and say unto the Saints, Give us of your lands—behold, there will be no room found for them. As respects giving deeds, I would advise you to	Behold he will not fail you! he will come with ten thousand of his saints and all his advisaries shall be distroyed by the breath of his lips! all those that keep their inheritances not withstanding they should be pealed and driven shall be likened unto the wise virgins who took oil in their lamps, But all those who are unbelieving and fearful, will be likened unto the foolish virgins, who took no oil in their Lamps; and when they shall return, and say unto the saints, give us of your lands, behold there will be no room found for them. As respects giving <u>deeds</u> I would advise to give

give deeds as far as the brethren have legal and just claims for them, and then let every man answer to God for the disposal of them.	deeds as far as the brethren have legal and Just claims for ~~their~~ them and then let evry man answer to God for the disposal of them.

***

But, perhaps, the people in Liberty may feel willing, God having power to soften the hearts of all men, to have a press established there; and if not, in some other place; any place where it can be the most convenient, and it is possible to get to it; God will be willing to have it in any place where it can be established in safety. We must be wise as serpents and **[p.37]** harmless as doves. Again, I desire that Elder Phelps should collect all the information, and give us a true history of the beginning and rise of Zion, and her calamities.	**[p.380]** But purhaps, the people in Liberty may feel willing, God having power to soften the hearts of all men, to have a press established there; and if not, in some other place; any place where it can be the most convenient and it is possable to get to it: God will be willing to have it in any place where it can be practiculer and safe. we must be <u>wise</u> as serpents and harmless as doves. Again I desire that bro William would collect all the information, and give us a true history of the begining and rise of Zion, and her calamities &c[56]

A Prayer for the Afflicted Saints

	Joseph Smith Letter
Now hear the prayer of your unworthy brother in the new and everlasting covenant:—O my God! Thou who hast called and chosen a few, through Thy weak instrument by commandment, and sent them to Missouri, a place which Thou didst call Zion, and commanded Thy servants to consecrate it unto Thyself for a place of refuge and safety for the gathering of Thy Saints, to be built up a holy city unto Thyself; and as thou hast said that no other place should be appointed like unto this, therefore, I ask Thee in the name of Jesus Christ, to return Thy people unto their houses and their inheritances, to enjoy the fruit of their labors; that all the waste places may be built up; that all the enemies of Thy people, who will not repent and turn unto Thee, may be destroyed from off the face of the land; and let a house be built and established unto Thy name; and let all the losses that Thy people have sustained, be rewarded unto them, even more than four-fold, that the borders of Zion may be enlarged forever; and let her be established no more to be thrown down; and let all Thy Saints, when they are scattered as	Now hear the prayer of your unworthy Brothe[r] in the bonds of the new and everlasting covenant: O my God! thou who has called and chosen a few through thy weak instrument by commandment and sent them to Missouri a place which thou didst call <u>Zion</u> and commanded thy servants to consecrate unto thyself for a place of a refuge, and of safety for the gathering of thy saints, to be built up a holy city unto thyself and as thou hast said that none other place should be **[p.381]** appointed like unto this therefore I ask thee in the name of Jesus Christ, to return thy people unto their homes, & there inheritances, to enjoy the fruit of their Labors; that all the waste places may be built up; that all the enemies of thy people, who will not ~~return~~ repent and ~~return~~ unto thee be distroyed from off the face of that Land; and let an house be built and established unto thy name, and let all the losses that thy people have sustained be rewarded unto them, even more than fourfold; that the borders of Zion be enlarged forever, and let her be established no more to be thrown down; and let all thy saints when they are scattered as sheep, and

---

56. 10 December 1833, *JSP, D3*, 378–80.

sheep, and are persecuted, flee unto Zion, and be established in the midst of her; and let her be organized according to Thy law; and let this prayer ever be recorded before Thy face. Give Thy Holy Spirit unto my brethren, unto whom I write; send Thine angels to guard them, and deliver them from all evil; and when they turn their faces toward Zion, and bow down before Thee and pray, may their sins never come up before Thy face; neither have place in the book of Thy remembrance; and may they depart from all their iniquities. Provide food for them as Thou doest for the ravens; provide clothing to cover their nakedness, and houses that they may dwell therein; give unto them friends in abundance, and let their names be recorded in the Lamb's book of life, eternally before Thy face. Amen.

Finally, brethren, the grace of our Lord Jesus Christ be with you all until His coming in His kingdom. Amen.
JOSEPH SMITH, JUN.
—DHC 1:453-456.

are persecuted, ~~and~~ flee unto Zion, and be established in the midst of her, and let her be organized according to thy law and let this prayer even ~~before~~ be recorded before thy face; give thy holy spirit unto my brethren: unto whom I write: send thy angels to guard them and to deliver them from all evil; and when they turn there faces towards Zion and bow down before thee and pray may their sins never com[e] up before thy face neithe[r] have place in the book of thy remembrance and may they depart from all their eniquities. provide ~~bread~~ <food> for them as thou doest for the ravens, provide clothing to cover there nakedness, and <houses that they may> ~~cause that they~~ dwell therein give unto them friends in abundance, and let their names be recorded in the Lambs book of Life eternally before thy face Amen

finely [finally], brethren, the grace of our Lord Jesus Christ be with you all unto his coming and Kingdom, Amen
<u>Joseph Smith J</u>[57]

[p.38] Blessings Given to Oliver Cowdery and the Prophet's Family

On the eighteenth day of December, 1833, the Prophet and a number of the leading Elders of the Church assembled in the printing office which had just been built and that office was dedicated by the Prophet Joseph Smith. Following this ceremony the Prophet proceeded to bless Oliver Cowdery and several members of the Smith family, after having conferred upon Joseph Smith, Sen., the office and Priesthood of Patriarch of the Church. The blessings follow.[58]

---

57. 10 December 1833, *JSP, D3*, 380–81.
58. This introduction was written by Joseph Fielding Smith. "The blessings [that] follow" appear to have been given (to Oliver Cowdery, Joseph Smith Sr., Hyrum Smith, etc.) in December 1833, but they were not recorded until September 1835. See *JSP, J1*, 24n60.

Blessing of Oliver Cowdery

	Joseph Smith's Journal
Blessed of the Lord is Brother Cowdery, nevertheless there are two evils in him that he must needs forsake, or he cannot altogether escape the buffetings of the adversary. If he forsake these evils he shall be forgiven, and shall be made like unto the bow which the Lord hath set in the heavens; and shall be a sign and an ensign unto the nations. Behold, he is blessed of the Lord for his constancy and steadfastness in the work of the Lord; wherefore, he shall be blessed in his generation, and they shall never be cut off, and he shall be helped out of many troubles; and if he keep the commandments, and hearken unto the counsel of the Lord, his rest shall be glorious.	blessed of the Lord is bro Oliver nevertheless there are are two evils in him that he must needs forsake or he cannot altogeth[er] escape the buffettings of the advers[ar]y if he shall forsak these evils he shall be forgiven and shall be made like unto the bow which the Lord hath set in the heavens he shall be a sign and an ensign unto the nations behold he is blessed of the Lord for his constancy and steadfastness in the work of the Lord wherefore he shall be blessed in his generation and they shall never be cut off and he shall be helped out of many troubles and if he keep the ~~commandmend~~ <commandments> and harken unto the <council of the> Lord ~~his and~~ his rest shall be glorious[59]

The Prophet's Blessing to His Father and Mother

Thus spoke the Seer, and these are the words which fell from his lips whole the visions of the Almighty were open to his view, saying:[60]

	Patriarchal Blessing Book 1
Blessed of the Lord is my father, for he shall stand in the midst of his posterity and shall be comforted by their blessings when he is old and bowed down with years, and shall be called a prince over them, and shall be numbered among those who hold the right of Patriarchal Priesthood, even the keys of that ministry: for he shall assemble together his posterity like unto Adam; and the assembly which he called shall be an example for my father, for thus it is written of him:	Blessed of the Lord is my father, for he shall stand in the midst of his posterity and shall be comforted by their blessings when he is old and bowed down with years, and shall be called a prince over them, and shall be numbered among those who hold the right of patriarchal priesthood, even the keys of that ministry: for he shall assemble together his posterity like unto Adam; and the assembly which he called shall be an ensample for my father, for this it is written of him:
Three years previous to the death of Adam, he called Seth, Enos, Cainan, Mahalaleel, Jared,	Three years previous to the death of Adam, he called Seth, Enos, Cainan, Mahalaleel,

---

59. 18 December 1833, *JSP, J1*, 21, 23. See also Patriarchal Blessing Book 1:12, cited in H. Michael Marquardt, comp., *Early Patriarchal Blessings of The Church of Jesus Christ of Latter-day Saints* (The Smith-Pettit Foundation, 2007), 7–9.

60. This introductory paragraph, and the blessings that follow, are in the handwriting of Oliver Cowdery. See *JSP, D4*, 487.

Enoch and Methuselah, who were High Priests, with the residue of his posterity, who were righteous, into the valley of Adam-ondi-Ahman, and there bestowed upon them his last blessing. And the Lord appeared unto them, and they rose up and blessed Adam, and called **[p.39]** him Michael, the Prince, the Archangel. And the Lord administered comfort unto Adam, and said unto him, I have set thee to be at the head: a multitude of nations shall come of thee, and thou art a Prince over them forever.

So shall it be with my father: he shall be called a prince over his posterity, holding the keys of the patriarchal Priesthood over the kingdom of God on earth, even the Church of the Latter-day Saints, and he shall sit in the general assembly of Patriarchs, even in council with the Ancient of Days when he shall sit and all the Patriarchs with him and shall enjoy his right and authority under the direction of the Ancient of Days.

And blessed also, is my mother, for she is a mother in Israel, and shall be a partaker with my father in all his patriarchal blessings.

And blessed, also, are my brothers and my sisters, for they shall yet find redemption in the house of the Lord, and their offsprings shall be a blessing, a joy and a comfort unto them.

Blessed is my mother, for her soul is ever filled with benevolence and philanthropy; and notwithstanding her age, she shall yet receive strength and be comforted in the midst of her house: and thus saith the Lord. She shall have eternal life.

And again, blessed is my father, for the hand of the Lord shall be over him, and he shall be full of the Holy Ghost; for he shall predict whatsoever shall befall his posterity unto the latest generation, and shall see the affliction of his children pass away, and their enemies under their feet: and when his head is fully ripe

Jared, Enoch and Methuselah, who were high priests, with the residue of his posterity, who were righteous, into the valley of Adam-ondi-ahman, and there bestowed upon them his last blessing. And the Lord appeared unto them, and they rose up and blessed Adam, and called him Michael, the Prince, the Arch angel. And the Lord administered comfort unto Adam, and said unto him, I have set thee to be at the head: a multitude of nations shall come of thee, and thou art a Prince over them forever.

So shall it be with my father: he shall be called a prince over his posterity, holding the keys of the patriarchal priesthood over the kingdom of God on earth, even the Church of the Latter Day Saints; and he shall sit in the general assembly of patriarchs, even in council with the Ancient of Days when he shall sit and all the patriarchs with him—and shall enjoy his right and authority under the direction of the Ancient of Days.

And blessed, also, is my mother, for she is a mother in Israel, and shall be a partaker with my father in all his patriarchal blessings.

And blessed, also, are my ~~fathers~~ <brothers> and my sisters, for they shall yet find redemption in the house of the Lord, and their offsprings shall be a blessing, a joy and a comfort unto them.

[p.489] Blessed is my mother, for her soul is ever filled <with> benevolence and philanthropy; and notwithstanding her age, she shall yet receive strength and be comforted in the midst of her house: and thus saith the Lord, She shall have eternal life.

And again, blessed is my father, for the hand of the Lord shall be over him, and he shall be full of the Holy Ghost; for he shall predict whatsoever shall befal[l] his posterity unto the latest generation, and shall see the affliction of his children pass away, and their enemies under their feet: and when his head is fully ripe he shall behold himself as an olive tree whose branches are bowed down with much fruit. Behold, the blessings of Joseph by the hand of his progenitor, shall come upon the head of my father and his seed after him, to the uttermost, even he shall be a fruitful bough; he shall be as a fruitful bough, even a fruitful bough by a well whose branches run over the wall, and his seed shall abide in strength, and the arms of their hands shall be made strong by the hands of the mighty God of Jacob, and the God of his fathers: even the God of Abraham, Isaac and Jacob, shall help him and his seed after him: even the Almighty shall bless him with blessings of heaven above and his seed after him, and the blessings of the deep that lieth under: and his seed shall rise up and call him blessed. He shall be as the vine of the choice grape when her clusters are fully **[p.40]** ripe: and he shall also possess a mansion on high, even in the Celestial Kingdom. His counsel shall be sought for by thousands, and he shall have place in the house of the Lord; for he shall be mighty in the council of the elders, and his days shall yet be lengthened out: and when he shall go hence he shall go in peace, and his rest shall be glorious; and his name shall be had in remembrance to the end. Amen.

   Oliver Cowdery, Clerk and Recorder —MSS, Dec. 18, 1833.

he shall behold himself as an olive tree whose branches are bowed down with much fruit. Behold the blessings of Joseph by the hand of his progenitor, shall come upon ~~him~~ <the> head of my father and his seed after him, to the uttermost; even he shall be a fruitful bough: he shall be as a fruitful bough, even a fruitful bough by a well whose branches run over the wall, and his seed shall abide in strength, and the arms of their hands shall be made strong by the hands of the mighty God of Jacob, and the God of his fathers: Even <the God> of Abraham, Isaac and Jacob, shall help him and his seed after him: even the Almighty shall bless him with blessings of heaven above and his seed after him, and the blessings of the deep that lieth under: and his seed shall rise up and call him blessed. He shall be as the vine of the choice grape when her clusters are fully ripe: and he shall also possess a mansion on high, even in the Celestial Kingdom. His counsel shall be sought for by thousands, and he shall have place in the house of the Lord; for he shall be mighty in the council of the elders, and his days shall yet be lengthened out: and when he shall go hence he shall go in peace, and his rest shall be glorious: and his name shall be had in remembrance to the end. Amen.

{Oliver Cowdery, <u>Clerk and Recorder</u>.[61]

The Prophet's Blessing to His Brother Hyrum

Blessed of the Lord is my brother Hyrum for the integrity of his heart; he shall be girt about with strength, truth and faithfulness shall be the strength of his loins. From generation to generation he shall be a shaft in the hand of his God to execute judgment upon his enemies: and he shall be hid by the hand of the Lord that none of his secret parts shall be discovered unto his enemies, unto his hurt. His name shall be called

Patriarchal Blessing Book 1

Blessed of the Lord is my brother Hyrum [Smith] for the integrity of his heart: he shall be girt about with <truth> strength and faithfulness shall be the strength of his loins. From generation to generation he shall be a shaft in the hand of his God to execute judgment upon his enemies: and he shall be hid by the hand of the Lord that none of his secret parts shall be discovered unto his enemies, unto his hurt. His name shall be

---

61. 18 December 1833, *JSP, D4*, 488–89. See also Marquardt, *Early Patriarchal Blessings of The Church of Jesus Christ of Latter-day Saints*, 4–5.

a blessing among men. His acquaintance shall be among kings, and he shall be sought for that he may sit in council, by nations and kings that are afar off; and thousands of souls shall he be an instrument in the hand of his God in bringing unto salvation. And when he is in trouble, and great tribulation has come upon him, he shall remember the God of Jacob, and he shall shield him from the power of Satan. He shall receive counsel in the house of the Most High that he may be strengthened in hope. He shall be as a cooling spring that breaketh forth at the foot of the mountain, overshadowed with choice trees bowed down with ripe fruit, that yieldeth both nourishment to the appetite and quencheth the thirst, thereby yielding refreshment to the weary traveller: and the goings of his feet shall ever be by streams of living water. He shall not fail nor want for knowledge, for the Lord his God shall put forth his hand and lift him up and shall call upon him with his voice in the way wherein he is travelling, that he may be established forever. He shall stand in the tracks of his father and be numbered among those who hold the right of Patriarchal Priesthood, even the Evangelical Priesthood and power shall be upon him, that in his old age his name may be magnified on the earth. Behold he shall be blessed with an abundance of riches of the earth—gold, **[p.41]** silver, and treasures of precious stones, of diamonds and platina. His chariots shall be numerous, and his cattle shall multiply abundantly: horses, mules, asses, camels, dromedaries, and swift beasts, that he may magnify the name of the Lord and benefit the poor. Yea, this shall be the desire of his soul, to comfort the needy and bind up the broken in heart. His children shall be many and his posterity numerous, and they shall rise up and call him blessed. And he shall have eternal life. Amen.

Oliver Cowdery, Clerk and Recorder
Given in Kirtland, December 18, 1833.

called a blessing among men. His acquaintance shall be among kings, and he shall be sought for that he may sit in council, by nations and kings that are afar off; and thousands of souls, shall be he be an instrument in the hand of his God in bringing unto salvation. And when he is in trouble, and great tribulation has come upon him, he shall remember the God of Jacob, and he shall shield him from the power **[p.491]** of satan. He shall receive counsel in the house of the Most high that he may be strengthened in hope. He shall be as a cooling spring that breaketh forth at the foot of the mountain, overshadowed with choice trees bowed down with rip[e] fruit, that yieldeth both nourishment to the appetite and quencheth the thirst, thereby yielding refreshment to the weary traveller: and the goings of his feet shall ever be by streams of living water. He shall not fail nor want for knowledge, for the Lord his God shall put forth his hand and lift him up and shall call upon him with his voice in the way wherein he is travelling, that he may be established forever. He shal[l] stand in the tracts of his father and be numbered among those who hold the right of patriarchal priesthood, even the evangelical priesthood and power shall be upon him, that in his old age, his name may be magnified on the earth. Behold he shall be blessed with an abundance of riches of the earth: gold, silver, and treasures of precious stones, of diamonds and platina [platinum]. His chariots shall be numerous, and his cattle shall multiply abundantly: horses, mules, asses, camels, dromedaries, and swift beasts, that he may magnify the name of the Lord and benefit the poor. Yea, this shall be the desire of his soul, to comfort the needy and bind up the broken in heart. His children shall be many and his posterity numerous, and they shall rise up and call him blessed. And he shall have eternal life. Amen.

Oliver Cowdery, <u>Clerk and Recorder.</u>
Given in Kirtland, December 18, 1833, and recorded September, 1835.[62]

---

62. 18 December 1833, *JSP, D4*, 490–91. See also Patriarchal Blessing Book 1:9–10, cited in Marquardt, *Early Patriarchal Blessings of The Church of Jesus Christ of Latter-day Saints*, 5.

Blessing to Samuel and William Smith

Blessed of the Lord is my brother Samuel, because the Lord shall say unto him, Samuel, Samuel; therefore he shall be made a teacher in the house of the Lord, and the Lord shall mature his mind in judgment, and thereby he shall obtain the esteem and fellowship of his brethren, and his soul shall be established and he shall benefit the house of the Lord, because he shall obtain answer to prayer in his faithfulness.

Patriarchal Blessing Book 1

Blessed of the Lord is brother Samuel [Smith], because the Lord shall say unto him, Samuel, Samuel: therefore, he shall be made a teacher in the house of the Lord, among the school of the prophets; and the Lord shall mature his mind and correct his judgment, and he shall have a sound mind, and shall be correct in his understanding; and he shall be like unto Abraham, of old, because of his faithfulness and the integrity of his soul, and thereby he shall obtain the esteem and fellowship of his brethren; and his soul shall be established and he shall benefit the house of the Lord, and also be an instrument in the hands of his God, in spreading abroad upon the mountains, and among all nations, the fulness of of the everlasting gospel, because he shall obtain answer to prayer, in his faithfulness. His name shall be choice, and he shall be held in everlasting honor, and shall prove a blessing unto his posterity after him, from generation to generation, forever. He shall have an abundance of ~~wealth~~ <the> good things of the earth, for he shall possess great wealth, while he lives, and in the liberality of his soul he shall benefit the poor. He shall be likened unto the sun, that sheddeth forth his rays upon the mountains, and causeth vegetation to bloom forth in all its splendor, and the earth to bring forth in her glorious apparel, yielding her strength for the sustinance of man, by his warming influence;— so shall the voice of Samuel be to the hearts of those that shall seek counsel at his hand in his old age. And his testimony shall shine forth to the ends of the earth, and shall never be blotted out nor brought down [p.493] from among men. And when the Lord of glory shall descend [he] shall be able to endure the brightness of his glory and dwell in the presence of God. Amen. Oliver Cowdery, Clerk and Recorder.[63]

---

63. 18 December 1833, *JSP, D4*, 492–93. See also Patriarchal Blessing Book 1:10, cited in Marquardt, *Early Patriarchal Blessings of The Church of Jesus Christ of Latter-day Saints*, 5–6.

Brother William is as the fierce lion, which divideth not the spoil because of his strength; and in the pride of his heart he will neglect the more weighty matters until his soul is bowed down in sorrow; and then he shall return and call on the name of his God, and shall find forgiveness, and shall wax valiant, therefore, he shall be saved unto the uttermost; and as the roaring lion of the forest in the midst of his prey, so shall the hand of his generation be lifted up against those who are set on high, that fight against the God of Israel; fearless and undaunted shall they be in battle, in avenging the wrongs of the innocent, and relieving the oppressed; therefore, the blessings of the God of Jacob shall be in the midst of his house, notwithstanding his rebellious heart.

Brother William [Smith] is as the fierce lion which divideth not the spoil because of his much strength; and in the pride of his heart he will neglect the more weighty matters until his soul is bowed down in sorrow, and then he shall return and call on the name of his God and shall find forgiveness, and shall wax valiant in the cause of truth: therefore, he shall be saved unto the uttermost and shall be endowed with power from on high. At his rebuke, **[p.494]** in the name of the Lord, the eyes of the blind shall be opened, the ears of the deaf shall be unstopped, the tongue of the dumb shall be made to speak, and the lame man shall leap as a heart [hart]; and his adversaries shall not have power to withstand his words. Hell shall tremble because of him, and satan shall flee from before his face; and he shall be as a roaring lion of the forest, in the midst of his pray [prey]— so shall his hand be in the midst of his enemies, among those who know not the Lord, but seek the injury of the righteous: and the hand of his generation shall be lifted up also against those who are set on high, that fight the God of Israel: fearless and unda[u]nted shall they be in battle, in avenging the wrongs of the innocent and relieving the oppressed. Therefore, the blessings of the God of Jacob shall be upon him to the uttermost, and in the midst of his house, from generation to generation, forever; and he shall be lifted up at the last day and shall come up before the Lord like as <a full> shock of corn, laden with his tens of thousands, as a reward of his labors, with songs of everlasting joy, with hozannahs upon his lips, to God and to the Lamb, to go no more out. Amen.[64]

And now, O God, let the residue of my father's house ever come up in remembrance before Thee, that Thou mayest save them from the hand of the oppressor, and establish their feet upon the Rock of Ages, that they may have place in Thy house, and be saved in Thy

A prayer — O God, let the residue of my father's house, with the residue of those whom thou hast blessed, ever come up in remembrance before thee and stand virtuous and pure in thy presence, that thou mayest save them from the hand of the oppressor, and establish their feet upon the rock of ages, that they may have place

---

64. 18 December 1833, *JSP, D4*, 493–94. See also Patriarchal Blessing Book 1:10–11, cited in Marquardt, *Early Patriarchal Blessings of The Church of Jesus Christ of Latter-day Saints*, 6.

kingdom; and let all things be even as I have said, for Christ's sake. Amen.
—DHC 1:466–467

in thy house and be saved in thy kingdom, even where God and Christ is: and let all these things be as I have said, for Christ's sake. Amen. Oliver Cowdery, Clerk and Recorder. Given in Kirtland, Geauga County, Ohio, December 18th, 1833, and recorded in this book by me, October 1, 1835. Oliver Cowdery.[65]

Counsel and Admonition

Dear Brethren in Christ, and Companions in Tribulation:—It seemeth good unto us to drop a few lines to you giving you some instruction relative to conducting the affairs of the kingdom of God, which has been committed unto us in these latter times, by the will and testament of our Mediator, whose intercessions in our behalf are lodged in the bosom of the Eternal Father, and ere long will burst with blessings upon the heads of all the faithful.

We have all been children, and are too much so at the present time; but we hope in the Lord that we may grow in grace and be prepared for all things which the bosom of futurity may disclose unto us. Time is rapidly rolling on, and the prophecies must be fulfilled. The days of tribulation are fast approaching, and the time to test the fidelity of the Saints has come. Rumor with her ten thousand tongues is diffusing her uncertain sounds in almost every ear; but in these times of sore trial, let the Saints be patient and see the salvation of God. Those who cannot endure persecution, and stand in the day of affliction, cannot stand in the day when the Son of God shall burst the veil, and appear in all the glory of His Father, with all the holy angels.

The Evening and the Morning Star

Dear Brethren in Christ, and companions in tribulation: It seemeth good unto us, to drop a few lines to you, giving you some instruction relative to conducting the affairs of the kingdom of God, which has been committed unto us in these later times, by the will and testament of our Mediator, whose intersessions in our behalf, are lodged in the bosom of the Eternal Father, and ere long will burst with blessings upon the heads of all the faithful:

We have all been children, and are too mutch so at the present time; but we hope in the Lord, that we may grow in grace and be prepared for all things which the bosom of futurity may disclose unto us. Time is rapidly rolling on, and the prophecies must be fulfilled. The days of tribulation are fast approaching, and the time to test the fidelity of the Saints, has come.—Rumor with her ten thousand tongues is diffusing her uncertain sounds in almost every ear: but in these times of sore trial, let the saints be patient and see the salvation of God. Those who cannot endure persecution and stand in the day of affliction, cannot stand in the day when the Son of God shall burst the veil, and appear in all the glory of his Father with the holy angels.[66]

---

65. Patriarchal Blessing Book 1:11, cited in Marquardt, *Early Patriarchal Blessings of The Church of Jesus Christ of Latter-day Saints*, 7. This prayer was given by the Prophet Joseph, apparently just after Don Carlos Smith received a patriarchal blessing from his father, Joseph Smith Sr.

66. *E&MS* 2, no. 15 (December 1833): 120. Although Joseph Fielding Smith attributed this quote to the Prophet Joseph, the author of this published letter is unidentified.

The Evils of Hasty Ordinations

The Evening and the Morning Star

On the subject of ordination, a few words are necessary. In many instances there has been too much haste in this thing, and the admonition of Paul has been too slightingly passed over, which says, "Lay hands suddenly upon no man." Some have been ordained to the ministry, and have never acted in that capacity, or magnified their calling at all. Such may expect to lose their appointment, except they awake and magnify their office. Let the Elders abroad be exceedingly careful upon this subject, and when they ordain a man to the holy ministry, let him be a faithful man, who is able to teach others also; that the cause of Christ suffer not. It is not the multitude of preachers that is to bring about the glorious millennium! but it is those who are "called, and chosen, and faithful."

On the subject of ordination, a few words are necessary: In many in stances there has been too much haste in this thing, and the admonition of Paul has been too slightingly passed over, which says, "Lay hands suddenly upon no man." Some have been ordained to the ministry, and have never acted in that capacity, or magnified their calling, at all: Such may expect to lose their calling, except they awake and magnify their office. Let the elders abroad be exceedingly careful upon this subject, and when they ordain a man to the holy ministry, let it be a faithful man, who is able to teach others also; that the cause of Christ suffer not. It is not the multitude of preachers that is to bring about the glorious Millenium! but it is those who are "called, and chosen, and faithful."[67]

[p.43] Avoiding Disputes

The Evening and the Morning Star

Let the Elders be exceedingly careful about unnecessarily disturbing and harrowing up the feelings of the people. Remember that your business is to preach the Gospel in all humility and meekness, and warn sinners to repent and come to Christ.

Let the elders be exceedingly careful about unnecessarily disturbing and harrowing up the feelings of the people. Remember, that your business is, to preach the gospel in all humility and meekness, and warn sinners to re pent and come to Christ.

Avoid contentions and vain disputes with men of corrupt minds, who do not desire to know the truth. Remember that "it is a day of warning, and not a day of many words." If they receive not your testimony in one place, flee to another, remembering to cast no reflections, nor throw out any bitter sayings. If you do your duty, it will be just as well with you, as though all men embraced the Gospel.

Avoid contentions and vain disputes with men of corrupt minds, who do not desire to know the truth. Remember that "it is a day of warning, and not a day of many words." If they receive not your testimony in one place, flee to another, remembering, to cast no re flections, nor throw out any bitter sayings. If you do your duty, it will be just as well with you, as though all men embraced the gospel.

---

67. *E&MS* 2, no. 15 (December 1833): 120. Although Joseph Fielding Smith attributed this quote to the Prophet Joseph, the author of this published letter is unidentified.

Be careful about sending boys to preach the Gospel to the world; if they go let them be accompanied by some one who is able to guide them in the proper channel, lest they become puffed up, and fall under condemnation, and into the snare of the devil. Finally, in these critical times, be careful; call on the Lord day and night; beware of pride; beware of false brethren, who will creep in among you to spy out your liberties. Awake to righteousness, and sin not; let your light shine, and show yourselves workmen that need not be ashamed, rightly dividing the word of truth. Apply yourselves diligently to study, that your minds may be stored with all necessary information.

We remain your brethren in Christ, anxiously praying for the day of redemption to come, when iniquity shall be swept from the earth, and everlasting righteousness brought in. Farewell. (Dec., 1833.) DHC 1:467-469.

Be careful about sending boys to preach the gospel to the world; if they go, let them be accompanied by some one who is able to guide them in the proper channel, lest they become puffed up, and fall under condemnation and into the snare of the devil: finally, in these critical times, be careful; call on the Lord day and night. Beware of pride: Beware of false brethren, who will creep in among you to spy out your liberties, &c. Awake to righteousness and sin not; let your light shine, and show yourselves workmen that need not be ashamed, rightly dividing the word of truth. Apply yourselves diligently to study, that your minds may be stored with all necessary information.

We remain your brethren in Christ, anxiously praying for the day of redemption to come, when iniquity shall be swept from the earth; and ever lasting righteousness brought in: Farewell.[68]

---

68. *E&MS* 2, no. 15 (December 1833): 120. Although Joseph Fielding Smith attributed this quote to the Prophet Joseph, the author of this published letter is unidentified.

SECTION TWO

1834–1837

SECTION TWO

Excerpts from an Epistle of the Elders of the Church in Kirtland to Their Brethren Abroad

[p.47] Dear Brethren in Christ, and Companions in Tribulation:

* * *

The Evening and the Morning Star

Dear brethren in Christ, and companions in tribulation:

Spiritual Darkness

Consider for a moment, brethren, the fulfillment of the words of the prophet; for we behold that darkness covers the earth, and gross darkness the minds of the inhabitants thereof—that crimes of every description are increasing among men—vices of great enormity are practiced—the rising generation growing up in the fullness of pride and arrogance—the aged losing every sense of conviction, and seemingly banishing every thought of a day of retribution—intemperance, immorality, extravagance, pride, blindness of heart, idolatry, the loss of natural affection; the love of this world, and indifference toward the things of eternity increasing among those who profess a belief in the religion of heaven, and infidelity spreading to commit acts of the foulest kind, and deeds of the blackest dye, blaspheming, defrauding, blasting the reputation of neighbors, stealing, robbing, murdering; advocating error and opposing the truth, forsaking the covenant of heaven, and denying the faith of Jesus—and in the midst of all this, the day of the Lord fast approaching when none except those who have won the wedding garment will be permitted to eat and drink in the presence of the Bridegroom, the Prince of Peace!

Consider for a moment, brethren, the fulfillment of the words of the prophet; for we behold that darkness covers the earth, and gross darkness the minds of the inhabitants thereof—that crimes of every discription are increasing among men—vices of every enormity are practiced—the rising generation growing up in the fulness of pride and arrogance—the aged losing every sense of conviction, and seemingly banishing every thought of a day of retribution—intemperence, immorality, extravagance, pride, blindness of heart, idolatry, the loss of natural affection, the love of this world, and indifference toward the things of eternity increasing among those who profess a belief in the religion of heaven, and infidelity spreading itself in consequence of the same—men giving themselves up to commit acts of the foulest kind, and deeds of the blackest dye; lying, blaspheming, stealing, robbing, murdering, defaming, defrauding, blasting the reputation of neighbors, advocating error and opposing the truth, forsaking the covenant of heaven, and denying the faith of Jesus—and in the midst of all this, the day of the Lord fast approaching when none except those who have on the wedding garment will be permitted to eat and drink in the presence of the Bridegroom, the Prince of peace![1]

---

1. *E&MS* 2, no. 17 (February 1834): 135.

The World's Deplorable Condition

	The Evening and the Morning Star
Impressed with the truth of these facts what can be the feelings of those who have been partakers of the heavenly gift and have tasted the good word of God, and the powers of the world to come? Who but those that can see the awful precipice **[p.48]** upon which the world of mankind stands in this generation, can labor in the vineyard of the Lord without feeling a sense of the world's deplorable situation? Who but those who have duly considered the condescension of the Father of our spirits, in providing a sacrifice for His creatures, a plan of redemption, a power of atonement, a scheme of salvation, having as its great objects, the bringing of men back into the presence of the King of heaven, crowning them in the celestial glory, and making them heirs with the Son to that inheritance which is incorruptible, undefiled, and which fadeth not away—who but such can realize the importance of a perfect walk before all men, and a diligence in calling upon all men to partake of these blessings? How indescribably glorious are these things to mankind! Of a truth they may be considered tidings of great joy to all people; and tidings, too, that ought to fill the earth and cheer the heart of every one when sounded in his ears. The reflection that everyone is to receive according to his own diligence and perseverance while in the vineyard, ought to inspire everyone who is called to be a minister of these glad tidings, to so improve his talent that he may gain other talents, that when the Master sits down to take an account of the conduct of His servants, it may be said, Well done, good and faithful servant: thou hast been faithful over a few things; I will now make thee ruler over many things: enter thou into the joy of thy Lord.	Impressed with the truth of these facts, what can be the feelings of those who have been made partakers of the heavenly gift, and have tested the good word of God, and the powers of the world to come? Who but those who can see the awful precipice upon which the world of mankind stand in this generation, can labor in the vineyard of the Lord with a feeling sense of their deplorable situation? Who but those who have duly considered the condesention of the Father of our spirits, in providing a sacrifice for his creatures, a plan of redemption, a power of atonement, a scheme of salvation, having as one of its great objects, to bring men back into the presence of the King of heaven; crown them in the celestial glory, and make them heirs with his Son to that inheritance which is incorruptible, undefiled, and which fadeth not away—can realize the importance of a perfect walk before all men, and a diligence in calling upon all men to partake of these blessings! How indescribably glorious are these tidings to mankind! Of a truth they may be considered tidings of great joy to all people; and tidings too that ought to fill the earth and cheer the heart of every one when sounded in his ears.—And the reflection, that every one is to receive according to his own diligence and perseverance while in the vineyard, ought to inspire every one who is called to be a minister of these glad tidings, to so improve upon their talent that they may gain other talents, that when the Master sits down to take an account of the conduct of his servants, that it may be said, Well done, good and faithful servant: thou hast been faithful over a few things; I will now make thee ruler over many things: enter thou into the joy of thy Lord.
Some may pretend to say that the world in this age is fast increasing in righteousness; that the	Some may presume to say, that the world in this age is fast increasing in righteousness;

dark ages of superstition and blindness have passed, when the faith of Christ was known and held only by a few, when ecclesiastical power had an almost universal control over Christendom, and the consciences of men were bound by the strong chains of priestly power: but now, the gloomy cloud is burst, and the Gospel is shining with all the resplendent glory of an apostolic day; and that the kingdom of the Messiah is greatly spreading, that the Gospel of our Lord is carried to divers nations of the earth, the Scriptures translating into different tongues; the ministers of truth crossing the vast deep to proclaim to men in darkness a risen Savior, and to erect the standard of Emmanuel where light has never shone; and that the idol is destroyed, the temple of images forsaken; and those who but a short time previous followed the traditions of their fathers and sacrificed their own flesh to **[p.49]** appease the wrath of some imaginary god, are now raising their voices in the worship of the Most High, and are lifting their thoughts up to Him with the full expectation that one day they will meet with a joyful reception in His everlasting kingdom!

that the dark ages of superstition and blindness have passed over, when the faith of Christ was known and practiced only by a few, when ecclesiastic power held an almost universal control over christendom, and when the consciences of men were held bound by the strong chains of priestly power; but now, the gloomy cloud is burst, and the gospel is shining with all the resplendent glory of an apostolic day; and that the kingdom of the Messiah is greatly spreading, that the gospel of our Lord is carried to divers nations of the earth, the scriptures translating into different tongues, the ministers of truth crossing the vast deep to proclaim to men in darkness a risen Savior, and to erect the standard of Emmanuel where light has never shone, and that the idol is destroyed, the temple of images forsaken; and those who but a short time previous followed the traditions of their fathers and sacrificed their own flesh to appease the wrath of some imaginary god, are now raising their voices in the worship of the Most High, and are lifting their thoughts up to him with the full expectation, that one day they will meet with a joyful reception into his everlasting kingdom![2]

The Law of Free Agency

But a moment's candid reflection upon the principles of these systems, the manner in which they are conducted, the individuals employed, the apparent object held out as an inducement to cause them to act, we think, is sufficient for every candid man to draw a conclusion in his own mind whether this is the order of heaven or not. We deem it a just principle, and it is one of the force of which we believe ought to be duly considered by every individual, that all men are created equal, and that all have the privilege of thinking for themselves upon all matters relative to conscience. Consequently, then, we are not disposed, had we the power, to deprive any one

The Evening and the Morning Star

But, a moment's candid reflection upon the principles of these systems, the manner they are conducted, the individuals employed, the apparent object held out as an inducement to cause them to act, we think, is sufficient for every candid man to draw a conclusion in his own bosom, whether this is the order of heaven or not. We deem it a just principle, and it is one the force of which we believe ought to be duly considered by every individual, that all men are created *equal*, and that all have the privilege of thinking for themselves upon all matters relative to conscience. Consequently, then we are not disposed, had we the power, to deprive any one from exercising that free

---

2. *E&MS* 2, no. 17 (February 1834): 135.

of exercising that free independence of mind which heaven has so graciously bestowed upon the human family as one of its choicest gifts; but we take the liberty (and this we have a right to do) of looking at this order of things a few moments, and contrasting it with the order of God as we find it in the sacred Scriptures. In this review, however, we shall present the points as we consider they were really designed by the great Giver to be understood, and the happy results arising from a performance of the requirements of heaven as revealed to every one who obeys them; and the consequence attending a false construction, a misrepresentation, or a forced meaning that was never designed in the mind of the Lord when He condescended to speak from the heavens to men for their salvation.

* * *

independence of mind which heaven has so graciously bestowed upon the human family as one of its choicest gifts, but we take the liberty, (and this we have a right to do,) of looking at this order of things a few moments, and contrasting it with the order of God as we find it in the sacred scriptures. In this review, however, we shall present the points as we consider they were really designed by the great Giver to be understood, and the happy result arising from a performance of the requirements of heaven, as therein revealed, to every one who obeys them; and the consequence attending a false construction, a misrepresentation, or a forced meaning that was never designed in the mind of the Lord when he condescended to speak from the heavens to men for their salvation.[3]

Obedience to Governments Necessary

The Evening and the Morning Star

Previous to entering upon a subject of so great a moment to the human family, there is a prominent item which suggests itself to our minds which, here, in few words we wish to discuss: All regularly organized and well established governments, have certain laws by which, more or less, the innocent are protected and the guilty punished. The fact admitted, that certain laws are good, equitable and just, ought to be binding upon the individual who admits this fact, to observe in the strictest manner an obedience to those laws. These laws when violated, or broken by that individual, must, in justice convict his mind with a double force, if possible, of the extent and magnitude of his crime; because he could have no plea of ignorance to produce; and his act of transgression was openly committed against light and knowledge. But the individual who may be ignorant, and imperceptibly transgresses or violates these laws, though the voice of the country requires that he should

All regularly organized and well established governments have certain laws by which, more or less, the innocent are protected and the guilty punished. The fact admitted that certain laws are good, equitable and just, ought to be binding upon the individual who admits this, and lead him to observe in the strictest manner an obedience to those laws. These laws when **[p.50]** violated, or broken by the individual, must, in justice, convict his mind with a double force, if possible, of the extent and magnitude of his crime; because he could have no plea of ignorance to produce; and his act of transgression was openly committed against light and knowledge. But the individual who may be ignorant and imperceptibly transgresses or violates laws, though the voice of the country requires that he should suffer, yet he

---

3. E&MS 2, no. 17 (February 1834): 135.

will never feel that remorse of conscience that the other will, and that keen, cutting reflection will never rise in his breast that otherwise would, had he done the deed, or committed the offense in full conviction that he was braking the law of his country, and having previously acknowledged the same to be just. It is not our intention by these remarks, to attempt to place the law of man on a parallel with the law of heaven; because we do not consider that it is formed in the same wisdom and propriety; neither do we consider that it is sufficient in itself to bestow anything on man in comparison with the law of heaven, even should it promise it. The laws of men may guarantee to a people protection in the honorable pursuits of this life, and the temporal happiness arising from a protection against unjust insults and injuries; and when this is said, all is said, that can be in truth, of the power, extent, and influence of the laws of men, exclusive of the law of God. The law of heaven is presented to man, and as such guarantees to all who obey it a reward far beyond any earthly consideration; though it does not promise that the believer in every age should be exempt from the afflictions and troubles arising from different sources in consequence of the acts of wicked men on earth. Still in the midst of all this there is a promise predicated upon the fact that it is the law of heaven, which transcends the law of man, as far as eternal life the temporal; and as the blessings which God is able to give, are greater than those which can be given by man. Then, certainly, if the law of man is binding upon man when acknowledged, how much more must the law of heaven be! And as much as the law of heaven is more perfect than the law of man, so much greater must be the reward if obeyed. The law of man promises safety in temporal life; but the law of God promises that life which is eternal, even an inheritance at God's own right hand, secure from all the powers of the wicked one.

suffer, yet he will never feel that remorse of conscience that the other will, and that keen-cutting reflection will never rise in his brest that otherwise would, had he done the deed, or committed the offence in full conviction that he was breaking the law of his country, and having previously acknowledged the same to be just. It is not our intention by these remarks, to attempt to place the law of man on a parallel with the law of heaven; because we do not consider that it is formed in that wisdom and propriety; neither do we consider that it is sufficient in itself to bestow any thing in comparison to the law of heaven, even should it promise it. The law of men may guarantee to a people protection in the honorable pursuits of this life and the temporal happiness arising from a protection against unjust insults and injuries; and when this is said, all is said, that can be in truth, of the power, extent, and influence of the law of men, exclusive of the law of God. The law of heaven is presented to man, and as such guarantees to all who obey it a reward far beyond any earthly consideration: it does not promise that the believer in every age should be exempt from the afflictions and troubles arising from different sources in consequence of wicked men on earth; though in the midst of all this there is a promise predicated upon the fact that it is the law of heaven, which transcends the law of man, as far as eternal life is prefferable to temporal; and the blessings which God is able to give, greater than those which can be given by man! Then, certainly, if the law of man is binding upon man when acknowledged, much more must the law of heaven be. And as much as the law of heaven is perfect, more than the law of man, so much greater must be the reward if obeyed. The law of man promises safety in temporal life; but the law of God promises that life which is eternal, even an inheritance at his own right hand, secure from all the powers of the wicked one.[4]

---

4. *E&MS* 2, no. 17 (February 1834): 135.

As Man Approaches God He Is Enlightened

The Evening and the Morning Star

[p.51] We consider that God has created man with a mind capable of instruction, and a faculty which may be enlarged in proportion to the heed and diligence given to the light communicated from heaven to the intellect; and that the nearer man approaches perfection, the clearer are his views, and the greater his enjoyments, till he has overcome the evils of his life and lost every desire for sin; and like the ancients, arrives at that point of faith where he is wrapped in the power and glory of his Maker and is caught up to dwell with Him. But we consider that this is a station to which no man ever arrived in a moment: he must have been instructed in the government and laws of that kingdom by proper degrees, until his mind is capable in some measure of comprehending the propriety, justice, equality, and consistency of the same. For further instruction we refer you to Deut. 32, where the Lord says, that Jacob is the lot of His inheritance. He found him in a desert land, and in the waste, howling wilderness; He led him about, He instructed him, He kept him as the apple of His eye, etc.; which will show the force of the last item advanced, that it is necessary for men to receive an understanding concerning the laws of the heavenly kingdom, before they are permitted to enter it: we mean the celestial glory. So dissimilar are the governments of men, and so divers are their laws, from the government and laws of heaven, that a man, for instance, hearing that there was a country on this globe called the United States of North America, could take his journey to this place without first learning the laws of governments; but the conditions of God's kingdom are such, that all who are made partakers of that glory, are under the necessity of learning something respecting it previous to their entering into it. But the foreigner can come to this country without knowing a syllable of its laws, or

We consider that God has created man with a mind capable of instruction, and a faculty which may be enlarged in proportion to the heed and diligence given to the light communicated from heaven to the intellect; and that the nearer man approaches perfection, the more conspicuous are his views, & the greater his enjoyments, until he has overcome the evils of this life and lost every desire of sin; and like the ancients, arrives to that point of faith that he is wrapped in the glory and power of his Maker and is caught up to dwell with him. But we consider that this is a station to which no man ever arrived in a moment: he must have been instructed into the government and laws of that kingdom by proper degrees, till his mind was capable in some measure of comprehending the propriety, justice equity, and consistency of the same. For further instruction we refer you to Deut. XXXII. where the Lord says, that Jacob is the lot of his inheritance. He found him in a desert land, and in the waste howling wilderness; he led him about, he instructed him, he kept him as the apple of his eye, &c. which will show the force of the last item advanced, that it is necessary for men to receive an understanding concerning the laws of the heavenly kingdom, before they are permitted to enter it: we mean the celestial glory. So dissimilar are the governments of men, and so divers are their laws, from the government and laws of heaven, that a man, for instance, hearing that there was a country on this globe called the United States of North America, could take his journey to this place without first learning the laws of this government; but the conditions of God's kingdom are such, that all who are made partakers of that glory, are under the necessity of first learning something respeting it previous to their entering into it. But the foreignor can come to this country without knowing a syllable of

even subscribing to obey them after he arrives. Why? Because the government of the United States does not require it: it only requires an obedience to its laws after the individual has arrived within its jurisdiction.

Laws of Man Not on Parallel with Laws of Heaven

As we previously remarked, we do not attempt to place the law of man on a parallel with the law of heaven; but we will [p.52] bring forward another item, to further urge the propriety of yielding obedience to the law of heaven, after the fact is admitted, that the laws of man are binding upon man. Were a king to extend his dominion over the habitable earth, and send forth his laws which were the most perfect kind, and command his subjects one and all to yield obedience to the same, and add as a reward to those who obeyed them, that at a certain period they should be called to attend the marriage of his son, who in due time was to receive the kingdom, and they should be made equal with him in the same; and fix as a penalty for disobedience that every individual guilty of it should be cast out at the marriage feast, and have no part nor portion with his government, what rational mind could for a moment accuse the king with injustice for punishing such rebellious subjects? In the first place his laws were just, easy to be complied with, and perfect: nothing of a tyrannical nature was required of them; but the very construction of the laws was equity and beauty; and when obeyed would produce the happiest condition possible to all who adhered to them, beside the last great benefit of sitting down with a royal robe in the presence of the king at the great, grand marriage supper of his son, and be made equal with him in all affairs of the kingdom.

The Evening and the Morning Star

As we previously remarked, we do not attempt to place the law of man on a parallel with the law of heaven; but we will bring forward another item, to futher urge the propriety of yielding obedience to the law of heaven, after the fact is admitted, that the laws of man are binding upon man. Were a king to extend his dominion over the habitable earth, and send forth his laws which were of the most perfect kind, and command his subjects one and all to yield obedience to the same; and annex as a reward to those who obeyed them, that at a certain period they should be called to attend the marriage of his son, who in due time was to receive the kingdom, and they should be made equal with him in the same and annex as a penalty for disobedience that every individual should [p.136] be cast out at the marriage feast, and have no part nor portion with his government; and what rational mind could for a moment accuse the king with injustice for punishing such rebellious subjects? In the first place his laws were just, easy and perfect: nothing was required in them of a tyranical nature; but their very construction was equity and beauty; and when obeyed would produce the happiest situation possible to all who adheard to them, beside the last great benefit of sitting down with a royal robe in the presence of the king at the great grand marriage supper of his son, and be made equal with him in all the affairs of the kingdom.⁶

---

5. *E&MS* 2, no. 17 (February 1834): 135.
6. *E&MS* 2, no. 17 (February 1834): 135–36.

"Thus Saith the King"

	The Evening and the Morning Star

When these royal laws were issued, and promulgated throughout the vast dominion, every subject, when interrogated whether he believed them to be from his sovereign or not, answered, Yes; I know they are, I am acquainted with the signature, for it is as usual. Thus saith the King! This admitted, the subject is bound by every consideration of honor to his country, his king, and his own personal character, to observe in the strictest sense every requisition in the royal edict. Should any escape the search of the ambassadors of the king, and never hear these last laws, giving his subjects such exalted privileges, an excuse might be urged in their behalf, and they escape the censure of the king. But for those who had heard, who had admitted, and who had promised obedience to these just laws no excuse could be urged, and when brought into the presence of the king certainly, justice would require that they should suffer a penalty. Could that king be just in admitting these rebellious individuals into the full enjoyment and priv[p.53]ileges with his son, and those who had been obedient to his commandments? Certainly not. Because they disregarded the voice of their lawful king; they had no regard for his virtuous laws, for his dignity, nor for the honor of his name; neither for the honor of their country, nor their private virtue. They regarded not his authority enough to obey him, neither did they regard the immediate advantages and blessings arising from these laws if kept, so destitute were they of virtue and goodness; and above all, they regarded so little the joy and satisfaction of a legal seat in the presence of the king's only son, and to be made equal with him all the blessings, honors, comforts, and felicities of his kingdom, that they turned away from a participation in them, and considered that they were beneath their present notice, though they had no doubt as to the real authenticity of the royal edict.

When these royal laws were issued, and promulgated throughout the vast dominion, every subject, when interrogated whether he believed them to be from his sovereign answered, Yes, I know they are, I am acquainted with the signature, for it is as usual, THUS SAITH THE KING! This admitted, the subject is bound by every consideration of honor to his country, his king, and his own personal character, to observe in the strictest sense every requisition in the royal edict. Should any escape the search of the embassadors of the king, and never hear these last laws, giving his subjects such exalted privileges, an excuse might be urged in their behalf, and they escape the censure of the king. But for those who had heard, who had admitted, and who had promised obedience to these just laws no excuse could be urged, and when brought into the presence of the king, certainly, justice would require that they should suffer a penalty! Could that king be just in admitting these rebellious individuals into the full enjoyment and privileges with his son, and those who had been obedient to his commandments? Certainly not. Because they disregarded the voice of their lawful king; they had no regard for his virtuous laws, for his dignity, nor for the honor of his name; neither for their own country's sake, nor their private virtue! They neither regarded his authority enough to obey him, neither did they regard the immediate advantages and blessings arising from these laws if kept, to observe them, so destitute were they of virtue and goodness; and above all, they regarded so little the joy and satisfaction of a legal seat in the presence of the king's only son, and to be made equal with him in all the blessings, honors, comforts, and felicities of his kingdom, that they turned away from an anticipation of them, and considered that they were beneath their present notice, though they had no doubt as to the real authenticity of the royal edict.

***

How could a government be conducted with harmony if its administrators were possessed with such different dispositions and different principles? Could it prosper? Could it flourish?

Would harmony prevail? Would order be established, and could justice be executed in righteousness in all branches of its department? No! In it were two classes of men as dissimilar as light and darkness, virtue and vice, justice and injustice, truth and falsehood, holiness and sin. One class were perfectly harmless and virtuous: they knew what virtue was for they had lived in the fullest enjoyment of it, and their fidelity to truth had been fairly tested by a series of years of faithful obedience to all its heavenly precepts. They knew what good order was, for they had been orderly and obedient to the laws imposed on them by their wise sovereign, and had experienced the benefits arising from a life spent in his government till he has now seen proper to make them equal with his son. Such individuals would indeed adorn any court where perfection was one of its main springs of action, and shine far more fair then the riches gem in the diadem of the prince.

***

God Speaks from Heaven

We take the sacred writings into our hands, and admit that they were given by direct inspiration for the good of man. We believe that God condescended to speak from the heavens [p.54] and declare His will concerning the human family, to give them just and holy laws, to regulate their conduct, and guide them in a direct way, that in due time He might take them to Himself, and make them joint heirs with His Son. But when this fact is admitted, that the immediate will of heaven is contained in the Scriptures, are we not bound as rational creatures to live in accordance to all its

***

How could a government be conducted with harmony if its administrators were possessed with such different dispositions and different principles? Could it prosper? Could it flourish?

Would harmony prevail? Would order be established, and could justice be executed in righteousness in all branches of its department? No! In it were two classes of men as discimilar as light is from darkness, virtue from vice, justice from injustice, truth from falsehood, and holiness from sin! One class were perfectly harmless and virtuous; they knew what virtue was for they had lived in the fullest enjoyment of it, and their fidelity to truth fairly tested by a series of years of faithful obedience to all its heavenly precepts. They knew what good order was, for they had been orderly and obedient to the laws imposed on them by their wise sovereign, and had experienced the benefits arising from a life spent in his government till he had now seen proper to make them equal with his son—Such individuals would indeed adorn any court where perfection was one of its main springs of action, and shine far more brilliant than the richest gem in the diadem of the prince.[7]

***

The Evening and the Morning Star

We take the sacred writings into our hands, and admit that they were given by direct inspiration for the good of man. We believe that God condescended to speak from the heavens and declare his will concerning the human family: give to them just and holy laws to regulate their conduct, and guide them in a direct way, that in due time he might take them to himself, and make them joint heirs with his Son. But when this fact is admitted, that the immediate will of heaven in here contained, are we not bound as rational creatures to live in accordance to all its precepts? Will

---

7. *E&MS* 2, no. 17 (February 1834): 136.

precepts? Will the mere admission, that this is the will of heaven ever benefit us if we do not comply with all its teachings? Do we not offer violence to the Supreme Intelligence of heaven, when we admit the truth of its teachings, and do not obey them? Do we not descend below our own knowledge, and the better wisdom which heaven has endowed us with, by such a course of conduct? For these reasons, if we have direct revelations given us from heaven, surely those revelations were never given to be trifled with, without the trifler's incurring displeasure and vengeance upon his own head, if there is any justice in heaven; and that there is must be admitted by every individual who admits the truth and force of God's teachings, His blessings and cursings, as contained in the sacred volume.

the mere admission that this is the will of heaven ever benefit us if we do not comply with all its teaching? Do we not offer violence to the Supreme Intelligence of heaven, when we admit the truth of its teachings, and do not obey them? Do we not condescend beneath our own character, and the better wisdom which heaven has endowed us with, by such a course of conduct? For these reasons, if we have direct revelations given us from heaven, surely those revelations were never given to be trifled with, without the triflers incurring displeasure, and assuring vengeance upon their own heads, if there is any justice in heaven; and that there is, must be admitted by every individual who admits the truth and force of its teachings; its blessings and cursings, as contained in the sacred volume.[8]

The Faithful to Receive Celestial Rest

Here, then, we have this part of our subject immediately before us for consideration: God has in reserve a time, or period appointed in His own bosom, when He will bring all His subjects, who have obeyed His voice and kept His commandments, into His celestial rest. This rest is of such perfection and glory, that man has need of a preparation before he can, according to the laws of that kingdom, enter it and enjoy its blessings. This being the fact, God has given certain laws to the human family, which, if observed, are sufficient to prepare them to inherit this rest. This, then, we conclude, was the purpose of God in giving His laws to us: If not, why, or for what were they given? If the whole family of man were as well off without them as they might be with them, for what purpose or intent were they ever given? Was it that God wanted to merely show that He could talk? It would be nonsense to suppose that He would condescend to talk in vain: for it would be in vain, and to no purpose whatever (if the law of God were of no benefit to man): because,

The Evening and the Morning Star

Here, then, we have this part of our subject immediately before us for consideration: God has in reserve a time, or period appointed in his own bosom, when he will bring all his subjects, who have obeyed his voice and kept his commandments, into his celestial rest. This rest is of such perfection and glory, that man has need of a preparation before he can, according to the laws of that kingdom enter it and enjoy its blessings.—This being the fact, God has given certain laws to the human family, which, if observed, are sufficient to prepare them to inherit this rest. This, then, we conclude, was the purpose of God in giving his laws to us: if not, why, or for what were they given? If the whole family of man were as well off without them as they might be with them, for what purpose or intent were they ever given? Was it that God wanted to merely show that he could talk? This would be nonsense, to suppose that he would condescend to talk in vain; for it would be in vain, and to no purpose whatever: because,

---

8. *E&MS* 2, no. 17 (February 1834): 136.

all the commandments contained in the law of the Lord, have the sure promise annexed of a [p.55] reward to all who obey, predicated upon the fact that they are really the promises of a Being who cannot lie, One who is abundantly able to fulfill every tittle of His word: and if man were as well prepared, or could be as well prepared, to meet God without their ever having been given in the first instance, why were they ever given? for certainly, in that case they can now do him no good.

all the commandments contained in the law of the Lord, have the sure promise annexed of a reward to all who obey; predicated upon the fact, that they are really the promises of a Being who cannot lie, and who is abundantly able to fulfil every tittle of his word: and if man were as well prepared, or could be as well prepared, to meet God without their ever having been given in the first instance, why were they ever given? for certainly, in that case they can now do him no good.[9]

All Governments Have Laws

The Evening and the Morning Star

As we previously remarked, all well established and properly organized governments have certain fixed and prominent laws for the regulation and management of the same. If man has grown to wisdom and is capable of discerning the propriety of laws to govern nations, what less can be expected from the Ruler and Upholder of the universe? Can we suppose that He has a kingdom without laws? Or do we believe that it is composed of an innumerable company of beings who are entirely beyond all law? Consequently have need of nothing to govern or regulate them? Would not such ideas be a reproach to our Great Parent, and at variance with his glorious intelligence? Would it not be asserting that man had found out a secret beyond Deity? That he had learned that it was good to have laws, while God after existing from eternity and having power to create man, had not found out that it was proper to have laws for His government? We admit that God is the great source and fountain from whence proceeds all good; that He is perfect intelligence, and that His wisdom is alone sufficient to govern and regulate the mighty creations and worlds which shine and blaze with such magnificence and splendor over our heads, as though touched with His finger and moved by His Almighty word. And if so, it is done and regulated by law; for

As we previously remarked, all well established and properly organized government have certain fixed and prominent laws for the regulation and management of the same.—If man has grown to wisdom and is capable of discerning the propriety of laws to govern nations, what less can we expect from the Ruler and Upholder of the universe? Can we suppose that he has a kingdom without laws? Or do we believe that it is composed of an innumerable company of beings who are entirely beyond all law? Consequently have need of nothing to govern or regulate them? Would not such ideas be reproachful to our Great parent, and an attempt to cast a stigma upon his glorious character? Would it not be asserting, that we had found out a secret beyond Deity? that we had learned that it was good to have laws, and yet He, after existing from eternity, and having power to create man, had not found out the fact, that it was proper to have laws for his government! We admit that God is the great source and fountain from whence proceeds all good; that he is perfect intelligence, and that *his* wisdom is alone sufficient to govern and regulate the mighty creations and worlds which shine and blaze with such magnificence and splendor over our heads, as though touched with his finger and moved by his Almighty word. And if so, it is done and regulated by law; for

---

9. *E&MS* 2, no. 17 (February 1834): 136.

without law all must certainly fall into chaos. If, then, we admit that God is the source of all wisdom and understanding, we must admit that by His direct inspiration He has taught man that law is necessary in order to govern and regulate His own immediate interest and welfare; for this reason, that law is beneficial to promote peace and happiness among men.

And as before remarked, God is the source from whence proceeds all good; and if man is benefited by law, then certainly, law is good; and if law is good, then law, or the principle of it emanated from God; for God is the source of all good; **[p.56]** consequently, then, he was the first Author of law, or the principle of it, to mankind.

* * *

What Is the Purpose of Existence?

The Evening and the Morning Star

Think for a moment, of the greatness of the Being who created the Universe; and ask, could He be so inconsistent with His own character, as to leave man without a law or rule by which to regulate his conduct, after placing him here, where, according to the formation of his nature he must in a short period sink into the dust? Is there nothing further; is there no existence beyond this veil of death which is so suddenly to be cast over all of us? If there is, why not that Being who had power to place us here, inform us something of the hereafter? If we had power to place ourselves in this present existence, why not have power to know what shall follow when that dark veil is cast over our bodies? If in this life we receive our all; if when we crumble back to dust we are no more, from what source did we emanate, and what was the purpose of our existence? If this life were all, we should be led to query, whether or not there was really any substance

Think for a moment, of the greatness of the Being who created the universe; and ask, Could he be so inconsistant with his own character, as to leave man without a law or rule to regulate his conduct, after placing him here, where, according to the formation of his nature he must in a short period sink into the dust? Is there nothing further; is there no existence beyond this vail of death which is so suddenly to be cast over all of us? If there is, why not that Being who had power to place us here, inform us something concerning hereafter? If we had power to place ourselves in this present existence, why not have power to know what shall follow when that dark vail is cast over our bodies? If in this life we receive our all; if when we crumble back to dust we are no more, from what source did we emanate, and what was the purpose in our existence? If this were all, we should be led to query, whether there was really any substance

---

10. *E&MS* 2, no. 17 (February 1834): 136. This article was written as an epistle from Joseph Smith and other leaders in Kirtland, Ohio. Although attributed to Joseph Smith in the original *TPJS*, the author of this published letter is unidentified.

in existence, and we might with propriety say, "Let us eat, drink, and be merry, for tomorrow we die!" But if this life is all, then why this constant toiling, why this continual warfare, and why this unceasing trouble? But this life is not all; the voice of reason, the language of inspiration, and the Spirit of the living God, our Creator, teaches us, as we hold the record of truth in our hands, that this is not the case, that this is not so; for, the heavens declare the glory of a God, and the firmament showeth His handiwork; and a moment's reflection is sufficient to teach every man of common intelligence, that all these are not the mere productions of chance, nor could they be supported by any power less than an Almighty hand; and He that can mark the power of Omnipotence, inscribed upon the heavens, can also see God's own handwriting in the sacred volume: and he who reads it oftenest will like it best, and he who is acquainted with it, will know the hand wherever he can see it; and when once discovered, it will not only receive an acknowledgment, but an obedience to all its heavenly precepts. For a moment reflect: what could have been the purpose of our Father in giving [p.57] to us a law? Was it that it might be obeyed, or disobeyed? And think further, too, not only of the propriety, but of the importance of attending to His laws in every particular. If, then, there is an importance in this respect, is there not a responsibility of great weight resting upon those who are called to declare these truths to men? Were we capable of laying any thing before you as a just comparison, we would cheerfully do it; but in this our ability fails, and we are inclined to think that man is unable, without assistance beyond what has been given to those before, of expressing in words the greatness of this important subject. We can only say, that if an anticipation of the joys of the celestial glory, as witnessed to the hearts of the humble is not sufficient, we will leave to yourselves the result of your own diligence; for God ere long, will call all His servants before Him, and there

in existence: and we might with propriety say, "Let us eat and drink; for tomorrow we die!" If this were really so, then why this constant toiling, why this continual warfare, and why this unceasing trouble? But this is not the case, the voice of REASON, the language of INSPIRATION, and the Spirit of the living GOD, our Creator, teaches us, as we hold the record of truth in our hands, that this is not the case; that this is not so; for, the heavens declare the glory of a GOD, and the firmament shows his handy work; and a moment's reflection, is sufficient to teach every man of common intellect, that all these are not the mere production of *chance*, nor could they be supported by any power less than by an Almighty hand: and he that can mark the power of Omnipotence inscribed upon the heavens, can also see His own hand-writing in the sacred volume; and he who reads it oftenest will like it best, and he who is acquainted with it, will know the hand wherever he can see it; and when once discovered, it will not only receive an acknowledgment, but an obedience to all its heavenly precepts. For a moment reflect, what could have been the purpose in our Father in giving to us a law? Was it that it might be obeyed, or disobeyed? And think [p.143] further too, not only the propriety, but the importance of attending to his laws in every particular. If, then, there is an importance in this respect, is there not a responsibility of great weight resting upon those who are called to declare these truths to men? Could we, or were we capable of laying any thing before you as a just comparison, we would cheerfully do it; but in this our capacity fails, and we are inclined to think, that man is unable, without an assistance beyond what has been given to those before us, of expressing in words the greatness of this important office. We can only say, that if an anticipation of the joys of the celestial glory, as witnessed to the hearts of the humble is not sufficient, we will leave with yourselves the result of your own diligence; for God ere long, will call *all*

Man Departed from the Lord's Government

It is reasonable to suppose that man departed from the first teachings, or instructions which he received from heaven in the first age, and refused by his disobedience to be governed by them. Consequently, he formed such laws as best suited his own mind, or as he supposed, were best adapted to his situation. But that God has influenced man more or less since that time in the formation of law for His benefit we have no hesitancy in believing; for, as before remarked, being the source of all good, every just and equitable law was in a greater or less degree influenced by Him. And though man in his own supposed wisdom would not admit the influence of a power superior to his own, yet for wise and great purposes, for the good and happiness of His creatures, God has instructed man to form wise and wholesome laws, since he had departed from Him and refused to be governed by those laws which God had given by His own voice from on high in the beginning. But notwithstanding the transgression, by which man had cut himself off from an immediate intercourse with his Maker without a Mediator, it appears that the great and glorious plan of His redemption was previously provided; the sacrifice prepared; [p.58] the atonement wrought out in the mind and purpose of God, even in the person of the Son, through whom man was now to look for acceptance and through whose merits he was now taught that he alone could find redemption, since the word had been pronounced, Unto dust thou shalt return.

The Evening and the Morning Star

From these facts, in short, and the further knowledge contained in the scriptures, it is reasonable to suppose, that man departed from the first teachings, or instructions which he received from heaven in the first age, and refused by his disobedience to be governed by them. Consequently, he formed such laws as best suited his own mind, or as he supposed, best adapted to his situation. But that God has influenced man more or less since that time in the formation of law for his benefit we have no hesitancy in believing; for, as before remarked, he being the source of all good, every just and equitable law was in a greater or less degree influenced by him. And though man in his own supposed wisdom would not admit the influence of a power superior to his own, yet for wise and great purposes, for the good and happiness of his creatures, God has instructed man to form wise and wholesome laws, since he had departed from him and refused to be governed by those laws which he had given by his own voice from on high in the beginning. But notwithstanding this transgression, by which man had cut himself off from an immediate intercourse with his Maker without a Mediator, it appears that the great and glorious plan of his redemption was previously meditated; the sacrifice prepared; the atonement wrought out in the mind and purpose of God, even in the person of the Son, through whom man was now to look for acceptance, and through whose merits he was now taught that he alone could find redemption, since the word had been pronounced, Unto dust thou shalt return![12]

---

11. *E&MS* 2, no. 18 (March 1834): 142–43.
12. *E&MS* 2, no. 18 (March 1834): 143.

The Law of Sacrifice

The Evening and the Morning Star

But that man was not able himself to erect a system, or plan with power sufficient to free him from a destruction which awaited him is evident from the fact that God, as before remarked, prepared a sacrifice in the gift of His own Son who should be sent in due time, to prepare a way, or open a door through which man might enter into the Lord's presence, whence he had been cast out for disobedience. From time to time these glad tidings were sounded in the ears of men in different ages of the world down to the time of Messiah's coming. By faith in this atonement or plan of redemption, Abel offered to God a sacrifice that was accepted, which was the firstlings of the flock. Cain offered of the fruit of the ground, and was not accepted, because he could not do it in faith, he could have no faith, or could not exercise faith contrary to the plan of heaven. It must be shedding the blood of the Only Begotten to atone for man; for this was the plan of redemption; and without the shedding of blood was no remission; and as the sacrifice was instituted for a type, by which man was to discern the great Sacrifice which God had prepared; to offer a sacrifice contrary to that, no faith could be exercised, because redemption was not purchased in that way, nor the power of atonement instituted after that order; consequently Cain could have no faith; and whatsoever is not of faith, is sin. But Abel offered an acceptable sacrifice, by which he obtained witness that he was righteous, God Himself testifying of his gifts. Certainly, the shedding of the blood of a beast could be beneficial to no man, except it was done in imitation, or as a type, or explanation of what was to be offered through the gift of God Himself; and this performance done with an eye looking forward in faith on the power of that great Sacrifice for a remission of sins. But however various may have been, and may be at the present time,

But that man was not sufficient of himself to erect a system, or plan with power sufficient to free him from a destruction which awaited him, is evident from the fact, that God, as before remarked, prepared a sacrifice in the gift of his own Son which should be sent in due time, in his own wisdom, to prepare a way, or open a door through which man might enter into his presence, from whence he had been cast for disobedience.—From time to time these glad tidings were sounded in the ears of men in different ages of the world down to the time of his coming. By faith in this atonement or plan of redemption, Abel offered to God a sacrifice that was accepted, which was the firstlings of the flock. Cain offered of the fruit of the ground, and was not accepted, because he could not do it in faith: he could have no faith, or could not exercise faith contrary to the plan of heaven. It must be the shedding of the blood of the Only Begotten to atone for man; for this was the plan of redemption; and without the shedding of blood was no remission; and as the sacrifice was instituted for a type, by which man was to discern the great Sacrifice which God had prepared; to offer a sacrifice contrary to that, no faith could be exercised, because redemption was not purchased in that way, nor the power of atonement instituted after that order; consequently, Cain could have no faith: and whatsoever is not of faith is sin. But Abel offered an acceptable sacrifice, by which he obtained witness that he was righteous, God himself testifying of his gifts. Certainly, the shedding of the blood of a beast could be beneficial to no man, except it was done in imitation, or as a type, or explanation of what was to be offered through the gift of God himself; and this performance done with an eye looking forward in faith on the power of that great Sacrifice for a remission of sins. But however various may have been, and may be at the

the opinions of men respecting the conduct of Abel, and the knowledge which he had on the subject of atonement, it is evident in our minds, that he was instructed more fully in the plan than what the Bible speaks of, for how could he offer a sacrifice in faith, looking to God for a remission of his sins in the power of the great atonement, without having been previously instructed in that plan? And further, if he was accepted of God, what were the ordinances performed further than the offering of the firstlings of the flock?

present time the opinions of men respecting the conduct of Abel, and the knowledge which he had on the subject of atonement, it is evident in our minds, that he was instructed more fully into the plan than what the bible speaks; for how could he offer a sacrifice in faith, looking to God for a remission of his sins in the power of the great Atonement, without having been previously instructed into that plan? And further, if he was accepted of God, what were the ordinances performed further than the offering of the firstlings of the flock?[13]

The Lord Spake to Abel

The Evening and the Morning Star

It is said by Paul in his letter to the Hebrew brethren, that Abel obtained witness that he was righteous, God testifying of his gifts. To whom did God testify of the gifts of Abel, was it to Paul? We have very little on this important subject in the forepart of the Bible. But it is said that Abel himself obtained witness that he was righteous. Then certainly God spoke to him: indeed, it is said that God talked with him; and if He did, would He not, seeing that Able was righteous deliver to him the whole plan of the Gospel? And is not the Gospel the news of the redemption? How could Abel offer a sacrifice and look forward with faith on the Son of God for a remission of his sins, and not understand the Gospel? The mere shedding of the blood of beasts or offering anything else in sacrifice, could not procure a remission of sins, except it were performed in faith of something to come; if it could, Cain's offering must have been as good as Abel's. And if Abel was taught of the coming of the Son of God, was he not taught also of His ordinances? We all admit that the Gospel has ordinances, and if so, had it not always ordinances, and were not its ordinances always the same?

It is said by Paul in his letter to his Hebrew brethren, that Abel obtained witness that he was righteous, God testifying of his gifts. To whom did God testify of the gifts of Abel, was it to Paul? We have very little on this important subject in the fore part of the bible. But it is said, that Abel himself obtained witness that he was righteous. Then certainly God spoke to him: indeed, it is said that God talked with him; and if he did, would he not, seeing he was righteous, deliver to him the whole plan of the gospel? And is not the gospel the news of redemption? How could Abel offer a sacrifice and look forward with faith on the Son of God for a remission of his sins, and not understand the gospel? The mere shedding the blood of beasts or offering any thing else in sacrifice, could not procure a remission of sins, except it were performed in faith of something to come, if it could, Cain's offering must have been as good as Abel's. And if Abel was taught of the coming of the Son of God, was he not taught of his ordinances? We all admit that the gospel has ordinances, and if so, had it not always ordinances, and were not its ordinances always the same?[14]

---

13. *E&MS* 2, no. 18 (March 1834): 143.
14. *E&MS* 2, no. 18 (March 1834): 143.

Gospel Ordinances from the Beginning

	The Evening and the Morning Star
Perhaps our friends will say that the Gospel and its ordinances were not known till the days of John, the son of Zacharias, in the days of Herod, the king of Judea. But we will here look at this point: For our own part we cannot believe that the ancients in all ages were so ignorant of the system of heaven as many suppose, since all that were ever saved, were saved through the power of this great plan of redemption, as much before the coming of Christ as since; if not, God has had **[p.60]** different plans in operation (if we may so express it), to bring men back to dwell with Himself; and this we cannot believe, since there has been no change in the constitution of man since he fell; and the ordinance or institution of offering blood in sacrifice, was only designed to be performed till Christ was offered up and shed His blood—as said before—that man might look forward in faith to that time. It will be noticed that, according to Paul, (see Gal. 3:8) the Gospel was preached to Abraham. We would like to be informed in what name the Gospel was then preached, whether it was in the name of Christ or some other name. If in any other name, was it the Gospel? And if it was the Gospel, and that preached in the name of Christ, had it any ordinances? If not, was it the Gospel? And if it has ordinances what were they? Our friends may say, perhaps, that there were never any ordinances except those of offering sacrifices before the coming of Christ, and that it could not be possible before the Gospel to have been administered while the law of sacrifices of blood was in force. But we will recollect that Abraham offered sacrifice, and notwithstanding this, had the Gospel preached to him. That the offering of sacrifice was only to point the mind forward to Christ, we infer from these remarkable words of Jesus to the Jews: "Your Father Abraham rejoiced to see my day: and he saw it, and was glad" (John 8:56). So, then, because	Perhaps, our friends will say, that the gospel and its ordinances were not known till the days of John the son of Zecharias, in the days of Herod the king of Judea. But we will here look at this point: For our own part, we cannot believe, that the ancients in all ages were so ignorant of the system of heaven as many suppose, since all that were ever saved, were saved through the power of this great plan of redemption, as much so before the coming of Christ as since; if not, God has had different plans in operation, (if we may so express it,) to bring men back to dwell with himself; and this we cannot believe, since there has been no change in the constitution of man since he fell; and the ordinance or institution of offering blood in sacrifice, was only designed to be performed till Christ was offered up and shed his blood, as said before, that man might look forward with faith to that time. It will be noticed that according to Paul, [see Gal. III 8.] the gospel was preached to Abraham. We would like to be informed in what name the gospel was then preached, whether it was in the name of Christ or some other name? If in any other name, was it the gospel? And if it was the gospel, and that preached in the name of Christ, had it any ordinances? If not, was it the gospel? And if it had, what were they? Our friends may say, perhaps, that there were never any ordinances except those of offering sacrifices, before the coming of Christ, and that it could not be possible for the gospel to have been administered while the sacrifices of blood were. But we will recollect, that Abraham offered sacrifice, and notwithstanding this, had the gospel preached to him. That the offering of sacrifice was only to point the mind forward to Christ, we infer from these remarkable words of his to the Jews, Your father Abraham rejoiced to see my day: and he saw it and was glad. [See John VIII 56.] So, then, because

the ancients offered sacrifice it did not hinder their hearing the Gospel; but served, as we said before, to open their eyes, and enable them to look forward to the time of the coming of the Savior, and rejoice in His redemption. We find also, that when the Israelites came out of Egypt they had the Gospel preached to them, according to Paul in his letter to the Hebrews, which says: "For unto us was the Gospel preached, as well as unto them: but the word preached did not profit them, not being mixed with faith in them that heard it" (see Heb. 4:2). It is said again, in Gal. 3:19, that the law (of Moses, or the Levitical law) was "added" because of transgression. What, we ask, was this law added to, if it was not added to the Gospel? It must be plain that it was added to the Gospel, since we learn that they had the Gospel preached to them. From these few facts, we conclude that whenever the Lord revealed Himself to men in ancient days, and commanded them to offer sacrifice to Him, that it was done that they might look forward in faith to the **[p.61]** time of His coming, and rely upon the power of that atonement for a remission of their sins. And this they have done, thousands who have gone before us, whose garments are spotless, and who are, like Job, waiting with an assurance like his, that they will see Him in the latter day upon the earth, even in their flesh.

We may conclude, that though there were different dispensations, yet all things which God communicated to His people were calculated to draw their minds to the great object, and to teach them to rely upon God alone as the author it their salvation, as contained in His law.

the ancients offered sacrifice it did not hinder their hearing the gospel; but served, as we said before, to open their eyes, and enabled them to look forward to the time of the coming of the Savior, and to rejoice in his redemption. We find also, that when the Israelites came out of Egypt they had the gospel preached to them, according to Paul in his letter to the Hebrews, which says, For unto us was the gospel preached, as well as unto them: but the word preached did not profit them, not being mixed with faith in them that heard it. [See Heb. IV 2.] It is said again, in Gal. III 19, that the law [of Moses, or the Levitical law] was added because of transgression. What, we ask, was this law added to, if it was not added to the gospel? It must be plain that it was added to the gospel, since we learn that they had the gospel preached to them. From these few facts, we conclude, that whenever the Lord revealed himself to men in ancient days, and commanded them to offer sacrifice to him, that it was done that they might look forward in faith to the time of his coming, and rely upon the power of that atonement for a remission of their sins. And this they have done, thousands who have gone before us, whose garments are spotless, and who are, like Job, waiting with an assurance like his, that they will see him in the *latter day* upon the earth, even in their flesh.

We may conclude, that though there were different dispensations, yet all things which God communicated to his people, were calculated to draw their minds to the great object, and to teach them to rely upon him alone as the Author of their salvation, as contained in his law.[15]

Not All Revelation Is in the Bible

From what we can draw from the Scriptures relative to the teaching of heaven, we are induced to think that much instruction has been given to man since the beginning which we do

The Evening and the Morning Star
From what we can draw from the scriptures relative to the teachings of heaven we are induced to think, that much instruction has been given to man since the beginning which

---

15. *E&MS* 2, no. 18 (March 1834): 143.

not possess now. This may not agree with the opinions of some of our friends who are bold to say that we have everything written in the Bible which God ever spoke to man since the world began, and that if He had ever said anything more we should certainly receive it. But we ask, does it remain for a people who never had faith enough to call down one scrap of revelation from heaven, and for all they have now are indebted to the faith of another people who lived hundreds and thousands of years before them, does it remain for them to say how much God has spoken and how much He has not spoken? We have what we have, and the Bible contains what it does contain: but to say that God never said anything more to man than is there recorded, would be saying at once that we have at last received a revelation: for it must require one to advance thus far, because it is nowhere said in that volume by the mouth of God, that He would not, after giving what is there contained, speak again; and if any man has found out for a fact that the Bible contains all that God ever revealed to man he has ascertained it by an immediate revelation, other than has been previously written by the prophets and apostles. But through the kind providence of our Father a portion of His word which he delivered to His ancient saints, has fallen into our hands, is presented to us with a promise of a reward if obeyed, and with a penalty if disobeyed. That all are deeply **[p.62]** interested in these laws or teachings, must be admitted by all who acknowledge their divine authenticity.

we have not. This may not agree with the opinions of some of our friends, who are bold to say, that we have every thing written in the bible which God ever spake to men since the world began, and that if he had ever said any thing more we should certainly have received it. But we ask, does it remain for a people who never had faith enough to call down one scrap of revelation from heaven, and for all they have now, are indebted to the faith of another people who lived hundreds and thousands of years before them, to say how much God has spoken and how much he has not spoken? We have what we have, and the bible contains what it does **[p.144]** contain; but to say that God never said any thing more to man than is there recorded, would be saying at once, that we have at last received a revelation; for it must be one to advance thus far, because it is no where said in that volume by the mouth of God, that he would not, after giving what is there contained, speak again; and if any man has found out that for a fact, he has ascertained it by an immediate revelation, other than has been previously written by the prophets and apostles. But through the kind providence of our Father a portion of his word which he delivered to his ancient saints, has fallen into our hands, and they are presented to us with a promise of a reward if obeyed, and with a penalty if disobeyed; and that all are deeply interested in these laws, or teachings, must be admitted by all who acknowledge their divine authenticity.[16]

Blessings for the Faithful—The Resurrection

The Evening and the Morning Star

It may be proper for us to notice in this place a few of the many blessings held out in this law of heaven as a reward to those who obey its teachings. God has appointed a day in which He will judge the world, and this He has given an assurance of in that He raised up His Son Jesus Christ from the dead—the point on

It may be proper for us to notice in this place, a few of the many blessings held out in this law of heaven as a reward to those who obey its teachings. God has appointed a day in which he will judge the world, and this he has given an assurance of in that he raised up his Son Jesus Christ from the dead; the point on which the

---

16. *E&MS* 2, no. 18 (March 1834): 143–44.

which the hope of all who believe the inspired record is found for their future happiness and enjoyment; because, "If Christ be not raised," said Paul to the Corinthians, "your faith is vain; ye are yet in your sins. Then they also which are fallen asleep in Christ are perished" (see 1 Cor. 15). If the resurrection from the dead be not an important point, or item in our faith, we must confess that we know nothing about it; for if there be no resurrection from the dead, then Christ has not risen; and if Christ has not risen He was not the Son of God; and if He was not the Son of God, there is not nor cannot be a Son of God, if the present book called the Scriptures is true; because the time has gone by when, according to that book, He was to make His appearance. On this subject, however, we are reminded of the words of Peter to the Jewish Sanhedrin, when speaking of Christ, he says that God raised Him from the dead, and we (the apostles) are His witnesses of these things, and so is the Holy Ghost, whom God had given to them that obey Him (see Acts 5). So that after the testimony of the Scriptures on this point, the assurance is given by the Holy Ghost, bearing witness to those who obey Him, that Christ Himself has assuredly risen from the dead; and if He has risen from the dead, He will by His power, bring all men to stand before Him; for if He has risen from the dead the bands of the temporal death are broken that the grave has no victory. If then, the grave has no victory, those who keep the sayings of Jesus and obey His teachings have not only a promise of a resurrection from the dead, but an assurance of being admitted into His glorious kingdom; for, He Himself says, "Where I am, there shall also my servant be" (see John 12).

hope of all who believe the inspired record is founded for their future happiness and enjoyment: because, if Christ is not risen, said Paul to the Corinthians, your faith is vain; ye are yet in your sins: and those who have fallen asleep in him have perished. [See 1 Cor. xv.] If the resurrection from the dead is not an important point, or item in our faith, we must confess that we know nothing about it; for if there is no resurrection from the dead, then Christ has not risen; and if Christ has not risen he was not the Son of God; and if he was not the Son of God there is not nor cannot be a Son of God, if the present book called the scriptures is true; because the time has gone by when, according to that book he was to make his appearance. On this subject, however, we are reminded of the words of Peter to the Jewish Sanhedrim, when speaking of Christ, he says, that God raised him from the dead, and we [the apostles] are his witnesses of these things, and so is also the Holy Ghost, whom God hath given to them that obey him. [See Acts v.] So that after the testimony of the scriptures on this point, the assurance is given by the Holy Ghost, bearing witness to those who obey him, that Christ himself has assuredly risen from the dead; and if he has risen from the dead, he will, by his power, bring all men to stand before him; for if *he* has risen from the dead the bands of the temporal death are broken that the grave has no victory. If then, the grave has no victory, those who keep the sayings of Jesus and obey his teachings have, not only a promise of a resurrection from the dead; but an assurance of being admitted into his glorious kingdom; for, he himself says, Where I am, there shall also my servant be. [see John XII,].[17]

The Marriage Supper

The Evening and the Morning Star

[p.63] In the 22nd chapter of Matthew's account of the Messiah, we find the kingdom of heaven likened unto a king who made a mar-

In the twenty second chapter of Luke's account of the Messiah, we find the kingdom of heaven likened unto a king who made a marriage for

---

17. *E&MS* 2, no. 18 (March 1834): 144.

riage for his son. That this son was the Messiah will not be disputed, since it was the kingdom of heaven that was represented in the parable; and that the Saints, or those who are found faithful to the Lord, are the individuals who will be found worthy to inherit a seat at the marriage supper, is evident from the sayings of John in the Revelation where he represents the sound which he heard in heaven to be like a great multitude, or like the voice of mighty thunderings, saying, the Lord God Omnipotent reigneth. Let us be glad and rejoice, and give honor to Him; for the marriage of the Lamb is come, and His wife hath made herself ready. And to her was granted that she should be arrayed in fine linen, clean and white: For the fine linen is the righteousness of Saints (Rev. 19).

his son. That this son was the Messiah will not be disputed, since it was the *kingdom of heaven* that was represented in the parable; and that the saints, or those who are found faithful to the Lord, are the individuals who will be found worthy to inherit a seat at the marriage-supper, is evident from the sayings of John in the Revelations, where he represents the sound which he heard in heaven to be like a great multitude, or like the voice of mighty thunderings, saying, The Lord God Omnipotent reigneth. Let us be glad and rejoice, and give honor to him; for the marriage of the Lamb is come, and his wife hath made herself ready. And to her was granted that she should be arrayed in fine linen, clean and while for the fine linen is the righteousness of saints. [Rev. XIX.][18]

They Who Endure to the End

That those who keep the commandments of the Lord and walk in His statutes to the end, are the only individuals permitted to sit at this glorious feast, is evident from the following items in Paul's last letter to Timothy, which was written just previous to his death,—he says: "I have fought a good fight, I have finished my course, I have kept the faith: henceforth there is laid up for me a crown of righteousness, which the Lord, the righteous Judge, shall give me at that day: and not to me only, but unto all them also that love His appearing." No one who believes the account, will doubt for a moment this assertion of Paul which was made, as he knew, just before he was to take his leave of this world. Though he once, according to his own word, persecuted the Church of God and wasted it, yet after embracing the faith, his labors were unceasing to spread the glorious news: and like a faithful soldier, when called to give his life in the cause which he had espoused, he laid it down, as he says, with an assurance of an eternal crown. Follow the labors of this Apostle from the time of his conversion to

The Evening and the Morning Star

That those only are the individuals who keep the commandments of the Lord and walk in his statutes to the end, that are permitted to set at this glorious feast, is evident from the following items: In Paul's last letter to Timothy, which was written just previous to his death, he says, I have fought a good fight, I have finished my course, I have kept the faith: henceforth there is laid up for me a crown of righteousness which the Lord, the righteous Judge shall give me at that day: and not to me only, but unto all them also that love his appearing. No one who believes the account, will doubt for a moment this assertion of Paul which was made, as he knew, just before he was to take his leave of this world. Though he once, according to his own word, persecuted the church of God and wasted it, yet after embracing the faith, his labors were unceasing to spread the glorious news; and like a faithful soldier, when called to give his life in the cause which he had espoused, he laid it down, as he says, with an assurance of an eternal crown. Follow the labors of this apostle from the time of his conversion

---

18. E&MS 2, no. 18 (March 1834): 144.

the time of his death, and you will have a fair sample of industry and patience in promulgating the Gospel of Christ. Derided, whipped, and stoned, the moment he escaped **[p.64]** the hands of his persecutors he as zealously as ever proclaimed the doctrine of the Savior. And all may know that he did not embrace the faith for honor in this life, nor for the gain of earthly goods. What, then, could have induced him to undergo all this toil? It was, as he said, that he might obtain the crown of righteousness from the hand of God. No one, we presume, will doubt the faithfulness of Paul to the end. None will say that he did not keep the faith, that he did not fight the good fight, that he did not preach and persuade to the last. And what was he to receive? A crown of righteousness. And what shall others receive who do not labor faithfully, and continue to the end? We leave such to search out their own promises if any they have; and if they have any they are welcome to them, on our part, for the Lord says that every man is to receive according to his works. Reflect for a moment, brethren, and enquire, whether you would consider yourselves worthy a seat at the marriage feast with Paul and others like him, if you had been unfaithful? Had you not fought the good fight, and kept the faith, could you expect to receive? Have you a promise of receiving a crown of righteousness from the hand of the Lord, with the Church of the Firstborn? Here then, we understand, that Paul rested his hope in Christ, because he had kept the faith, and loved His appearing and from His hand he had a promise of receiving a crown of righteousness.

to the time of his death, and you will have a fair sample of industry and patience in promulgating the gospel of Christ: Whipped, stoned, and derided, the moment he escaped the hands of his persecutors, he, as zealously as ever, proclaimed the doctrine of the Savior. And all may know, that he did not embrace the faith for the honor of this life, nor for the gain of earthly goods. What then could have induced him to undergo all this toil? It was, as he said, that he might obtain that crown of righteousness from the hand of God. No one, we presume, will doubt the faithfulness of Paul to the end: None will say, that he did not keep the faith, that he did not fight the good fight, that he did not preach and persuade to the last: And what was he to receive? A crown of righteousness. And what shall others receive who do not labor faithfully, and continue to the end? We leave such to search out their own promises if any they have; and if they have any they are welcome to them, on our part, for the Lord says, that every man is to recive according to his works. Reflect for a moment, brethren, and enquire, whether you would consider yourselves worthy a seat at the marriage feast with Paul and others like him, if you had been unfaithful? Had you not fought the good fight, and kept the faith, could you expect to receive; have you a promise of receiving a crown of righteousness from the hand of the Lord, with the church of the first born? Here then, we understand, that Paul rested his hope in Christ because he had kept the faith, and loved his appearing: and from his hand he had a promise of receiving a crown of righteousness.[19]

A Crown for the Righteous

The Evening and the Morning Star

If the Saints are not to reign, for what purpose are they crowned? In an exhortation of the Lord to a certain Church in Asia, which was built up in the days of the Apostles, unto whom He communicated His word on

If the saints are not to reign, for what purpose are they crowned? In an exhortation of the Lord to a certain church in Asia, which was built up in the days of the apostles, unto whom he communicated his word on that occasion by his

---

19. *E&MS* 2, no. 18 (March 1834): 144.

that occasion by His servant John, He says, "Behold, I come quickly: hold that fast which thou hast, that no man take thy crown." And again, "To him that overcometh will I grant to sit with Me in My throne, even as I also overcame, and am set down with My Father in His Throne" (see Rev. 3). And again, it is written, "Beloved, now are we the sons of God, and it doth not yet appear what we shall be: but we know that, when He shall appear, we shall be like Him; for we shall see Him as He is. And every man that hath this hope in him purifieth himself, even as He is pure" (1 John 3:2, 3). How is it that these old Apostles [p.65] should say so much on the subject of the coming of Christ? He certainly had once come; but Paul says, To all who love His appearing, shall be given the crown: and John says, When He shall appear, we shall be like Him; for we shall see Him as He is. Can we mistake such language as this? Do we not offer violence to our own good judgment when we deny the second coming of the Messiah? When has He partaken of the fruit of the vine new with His ancient Apostles in His Father's kingdom, as He promised He would just before he was crucified? In Paul's epistle to the Philippians (3:20, 21) he says: "For our conversation is in heaven; from whence also we look for the Savior, the Lord Jesus Christ: who shall change our vile body, that it may be fashioned like unto His glorious body, according to the working whereby He is able even to subdue all things unto Himself." We find another promise to individuals living in the church at Sardis who had not defiled their garments: "And they shall walk with me in white: for they are worthy. He that overcometh, the same shall be clothed in white raiment; and I will not blot out his name out of the book of life, but I will confess his name before my Father, and before His angels." John represents the sound which he heard from heaven, as giving thanks and glory to God, saying that the Lamb was worthy to take the book and to open its seals; because he was slain, and had made them kings and priests unto God; and they should reign on the earth (see Rev. 5). In the 20th chapter we find a length of time specified, during which Satan is to be confined in his own place, and the Saints reign in peace, all these promises and blessings we find contained in the law of the Lord, which the righteous are to enjoy: and we might enumerate many more places where the same or similar promises are made to the faithful, but we do not deem it of importance to rehearse them here, as this epistle is now lengthy; and our brethren, no doubt, are familiar with them all.

its seals; because he was slain, and had by his blood redeemed them out of every kindred and tongue, and people, and nation; and had made them kings and priests unto God: and they should reign on the earth. [see Rev. V.] In the twentieth chapter we find a length of time specified, during which Satan is to be confined in his own place, and the saints reign in peace. All these promises and blessings we find contained in the law of the Lord, which the righteous are to enjoy; and we might enumerate many more places where the same or similar promises are made to the faithful, but we do not deem it of importance to rehearse them here, as this letter is now lengthy; and our brethren no doubt, are familiar with them all.[20]

The Ancient Saints Obtained Promises

The Evening and the Morning Star

Most assuredly it is, however, that the ancients, though persecuted and afflicted by men, obtained from God promises of such weight and glory, that our hearts are often filled with gratitude that we are even permitted to look upon them while **[p.66]** we contemplate that there is no respect of persons in His sight, and that in every nation, he that feareth God and worketh righteousness, is acceptable with Him. But from the few items previously quoted we can draw the conclusion that there is to be a day when all will be judged of their works, and rewarded according to the same; that those who have kept the faith will be crowned with a crown of righteousness; be clothed in white raiment; be admitted to the marriage feast; be free from every affliction, and reign with Christ on the earth, where, according to the ancient promise, they will partake of the fruit of the vine new in the glorious kingdom with Him; at least we find that such promises were made to the ancient Saints. And though we cannot claim these promises which were made to the ancients for they are not our property, merely because they were made to the ancient

Most assuredly it is, however, that the ancients, though persecuted and afflicted by men, obtained from God promises of such weight and glory, that our hearts are often filled with gratitude, that we are even permitted to look upon them, while we contemplate that there is no respect of persons in HIS sight, and that in every nation, he that feareth him and worketh righteousness, is accepted with him. But from the few items previously quoted, we can draw a conclusion, that there is to be a day when all will be judged of their works, and rewarded according to the same; that those who have kept the faith will be crowned with a crown of righteousness; be clothed in white raiment; be admitted to the marriage-feast; be free from every affliction, and reign with Christ on the earth, where, according to the ancient promise, they will partake of the fruit of the vine new in the glorious kingdom with him: at least we find that such promises were made to the ancient saints. And though we cannot claim these promises which were made to the ancients, or that they are not our property merely because they were made to them, yet if we are the children of the

---

20. *E&MS* 2, no. 18 (March 1834): 144.

Saints, yet if we are the children of the Most High, and are called with the same calling with which they were called, and embrace the same covenant that they embraced, and are faithful to the testimony of our Lord as they were, we can approach the Father in the name of Christ as they approached Him, and for ourselves obtain the same promises. These promises, when obtained, if ever by us, will not be because Peter, John, and the other Apostles, with the churches at Sardis, Pergamos, Philadelphia, and elsewhere, walked in the fear of God, and had power and faith to reveal and obtain them; but it will be because we, ourselves, have faith and approach God in the name of His Son Jesus Christ, even as they did; and when these promises are obtained, they will be promises directly to us, or they will do us no good. They will be commandments and walking uprightly before Him. If not, to what end serves the Gospel of our Lord Jesus Christ, and why was it ever communicated to us?

* * *

most High, and are called with the same calling with which they were called, and embrace the same covenant that they embraced, and are faithful to the testimony of our Lord as they were, we can approach the Father in the name of Christ as they approached him, and for ourselves obtain the same promises. These promises, when obtained, if ever by us, will not be because Peter, John, and the other apostles, with the churches at Sardis, Purgamos, Philadelphia, and elsewhere, walked in the fear of God and had power and faith to prevail and obtain them; but it will be because *we, ourselves,* have faith and approach him in the name of his Son Jesus Christ, even as they did; and when these promises are obtained, they will be promises directly to us, or they will do us no good: communicated for *our* benefit; being our own property, (through the gift of God,) earned by our own diligence in keeping his commandments, and walking uprightly before him. If not, to what end serves the gospel of our Lord Jesus Christ, and why was it ever communicated to us?[21]

Apostates Excluded from Fellowship

The Messiah's kingdom on earth is of that kind of government, that there has always been numerous apostates, for the reason that it admits of no sins unrepented of without [p.67] excluding the individual from its fellowship. Our Lord said, "Strive to enter in at the strait gate: for many, I say unto you, will seek to enter in, and shall not be able." And again, many are called, but few are chosen. Paul said to the elders of the Church at Ephesus, after he had labored three years with them, that he knew that some of their own number would turn away from the faith, and seek to lead away disciples after them. None, we presume, in this generation will pretend that he has the experience of Paul in building up the Church of Christ and

The Evening and the Morning Star
The Messiah's kingdom on earth is of that kind of government, that there has always been numerous apostates, for this very fact, that it admits of no sins unrepented of without excluding the individual from its fellowship. Our Lord said, Strive to enter in at the strait gate: for many, I say unto you, will seek to enter in, and shall not be able. And again, many are called, but few chosen. Paul said to the elders of the church at Ephesus, after he had labored three years with them, that he knew, that some of their own number would turn away from the faith, and seek to lead away disciples after them. None, we presume, in this generation will pretend that they have the experience of Paul, in building up the church of Christ; and

---

21. *E&MS* 2, no. 18 (March 1834): 144. This article was written as an epistle from Joseph Smith and other leaders in Kirtland, Ohio. Although attributed to Joseph Smith in the original *TPJS*, the author of this published letter is unidentified.

yet, after his departure from the Church at Ephesus, many, even of the elders turned away from the truth; and what is almost always the case, sought to lead away disciples after them. Strange as it may appear at first thought, yet it is no less strange than true, that notwithstanding all the professed determination to live godly, apostates after turning from the faith of Christ, unless they have speedily repented, have sooner or later fallen into the snares of the wicked one, and have been left destitute of the Spirit of God, to manifest their wickedness in the eyes of multitudes. From apostates the faithful have received the severest persecutions. Judas was rebuked and immediately betrayed his Lord into the hands of His enemies, because Satan entered into him. There is a superior intelligence bestowed upon such as obey the Gospel with full purpose of heart, which, if sinned against, the apostate is left naked and destitute of the Spirit of God, and he is, in truth, nigh unto cursing, and his end is to be burned. When once that light which was in them is taken from them, they become as much darkened as they were previously enlightened, and then, no marvel, if all their power should be enlisted against the truth, and they, Judas like, seek the destruction of those who were their greatest benefactors. What nearer friend on earth, or in heaven, had Judas than the Savior? And his first object was to destroy Him. Who, among all the Saints in these last days can consider himself as good as our Lord? Who is as perfect? Who is as pure? Who is as holy as He was? Are they to be found? He never transgressed or broke a commandment or law of heaven—no deceit was in His mouth, neither was guile found in His heart. And yet one that ate with Him who had often drunk of the same cup, was the first to lift up his heel against Him. Where is one like Christ? He cannot be found on earth. Then why should His followers complain, if from **[p.68]** those whom they once called brethren, and considered as standing in the nearest relation in the everlasting covenant they should receive

yet, after his departure from the church at Ephesus, many, even of the elders, turned away from the truth; and what is almost always the case, sought to lead away disciples after them. Strange as it may appear, at first thought, yet it is no less so than true, that with all the professed determination to live godly, after turning from the faith of Christ, apostates have, unless they have speedily repented, sooner or later, fallen into the snares of the wicked one and been left destitute of the Spirit of God, to manifest their wickedness in the eyes of multitudes. From apostates the faithful have received the severest persecutions: Judas was rebuked, and immediately betrayed his Lord into the hands of his enemies, because *satan* entered into him. There is a supreme intelligence bestowed upon such as obey the gospel with full purpose of heart, which, if sinned against, the apostate is left *naked* and destitute of the Spirit of God, and they are in truth, nigh unto cursing, and their end is to be burned. When once that light which was in them is taken from them, they become as much darkened as they were previously enlightened. And then, no marvel, if all their power should be enlisted against the truth, and they, Judas like, seek the destruction of those who were their greatest benefactors! What nearer friend on earth, or in heaven, had Judas, than the Savior? and his first object was to destroy him! Who, among all the saints in these last days, can consider himself as good as our Lord? Who is as perfect, who is as pure, and who as holy as he was? Are they to be found? He never transgressed or broke a commandment or law of heaven—no deceit was in his mouth, neither was guile found in his heart! and yet one that ate with him, who had often supped of the same cup, was the first to lift up his heel against him! Where is there one like him? He cannot be found on earth. Then why should his followers complain, if from those whom they once called brethren, and considered in the nearest relation in the everlasting covenant, they should receive persecution? From what source persecution? From what source emanated the principle which has ever been manifest by apostates from the true Church to persecute with double diligence, and seek with double perseverance, to destroy those whom they once professed to love, with whom they once communed, and with whom they once covenanted to strive with every power in righteousness to obtain the rest of God? Perhaps our brethren will say the same that caused Satan to seek to overthrow the kingdom of God, because he himself was evil, and God's kingdom is holy.

* * *

emanated the principle which has ever been manifested by apostates from the true church, to persecute with double diligence, and seek with double perseverance, to destroy those whom they once professed to love, with whom they once communed, and with whom they once covenanted to strive, with every power, in righteousness, to obtain the rest of God? Perhaps, our brethren will say, The same that caused satan to seek to overthrow the kindom of God, because he himself was evil, and God's kingdom is holy.[22]

Gift of Salvation

The great plan of salvation is a theme which ought to occupy our strict attention, and be regarded as one of heaven's best gifts to mankind. No consideration whatever ought to deter us from showing ourselves approved in the sight of God, according to His divine requirement. Men not infrequently forget that they are dependent upon heaven for every blessing which they are permitted to enjoy, and that for every opportunity granted them they are to give an account. You know, brethren, that when the Master in the Savior's parable of the stewards called his servants before him he gave them several talents to improve on while he should tarry abroad for a little season, and at the end of it He will call each to render an account; and where the five talents were bestowed, ten will be required; and he that has made no improvement will be cast out as an unprofitable servant, while the faithful will enjoy everlasting honors. Therefore we earnestly implore the grace of our Father to rest upon you, through Jesus Christ His Son, that you may not faint in the hour of temptation, nor be overcome in the time of persecution. (January 22, 1834) DHC 2:4-24.

The Evening and the Morning Star

The great plan of salvation is a theme which ought to occupy our strictest attention, and be regarded as one of heaven's best gifts to mankind. No consideration whatever ought to deter us from approving ourselves in the sight of God, according to his divine requirement. Men not unfrequently forget, that they are dependent upon heaven for every blessing which they are permitted to enjoy, and that for every opportunity, granted them, they are to give an account. You know, brethren, that when the Master called his servants, he gave them their several benefits to improve only while he should tarry for a little season, and then he will call each to render his account; and where five tallents were bestowed, ten will be required, and he that has made no improvement will be cast out as an unprofitable servant, and the faithful are to enjoy everlasting honors.—Therefore, we earnestly emplore the grace of our Father to rest upon you, through Jesus Christ his Son, that you may not faint in the hour of temptation, nor be overcome in the time of persecution.[23]

---

22. E&MS 2, no. 19 (April 1834): 152.

23. E&MS 2, no. 19 (April 1834): 152. This article was written as an epistle from Joseph Smith and other leaders in Kirtland, Ohio. Although attributed to Joseph Smith by Joseph Fielding Smith in the original TPJS, the author of this published letter is unidentified.

Duties of Seventies

Joseph Smith's History

<Council began to ordain the Seventies> On the 28th. the Church in council assembled, commenced selecting certain individuals from the number of those who went up to Zion, with me, in the camp; & the following are some the names of those who were ordained and blessed at that time to begin the organization of the first Quorum of the Seventies according to the visions and revelations which I had received;—

The Seventies are to constitute traveling quorums, to go into all the earth, whithersoever the Twelve Apostles shall call them. (Feb. 8, 1834.) DHC 2:202.

The seventies to constitute travelling Quorums, to go into all the earth, whither-soever the twelve Apostles should call them.[24]

Orders in Councils

Minute Book 1

Thursday Evening, February 12. 1834. This evening the high Priests and Elders of the Church in Kirtland at the house of bro. Joseph Smith Jun. in Council for Church business. The Council was opened organized, and opened [p.429] by bro. Joseph Smith Ju[nior] in prayer. Bro. Joseph then rose and said: I shall now endeavour to set forth before this Council, the dignity of the office which has been conferred upon me by the ministering of the Angel of God, by his own voice and by the voice of this Church. I have never set before any council in all the order in which a Council ought to be conducted, which, prehaps, has deprived the Councils of some, or many blessings.

[p.69] At a council of the High Priests and Elders, (Orson Hyde, clerk), at my house in Kirtland, on the evening of the 12th of February (1834), I remarked that I should endeavor to set before the council the dignity of the office which had been conferred on me by the ministering of the angel of God, by His own voice, and by the voice of this Church; that I had never set before any council in all the order in which it ought to be conducted, which, perhaps, has deprived the councils of some or many blessings.

And I continued and said, no man is capable of judging a matter, in council, unless his own heart is pure; and that we frequently are so filled with prejudice, or have a beam in our own eye, that we are not capable of passing right decisions.

He said, that no man was capable of judging a matter in council without his own heart was pure; and that we frequently, are so filled with prejudice, or have a beam in our own eye, that we are not capable of passing right descissions, &c.

---

24. 28 February–1 March 1834, History, B-1, 577.

But to return to the subject of order; in ancient days councils were conducted with such strict propriety, that no one was allowed to whisper, be weary, leave the room, or get uneasy in the least, until the voice of the Lord, by revelation, or the voice of the council by the Spirit, was obtained, which has not been observed in this Church to the present time. It was understood in ancient days, that if one man could stay in council, another could; and if the president could spend his time, the members could also; but in our councils, generally, one will be uneasy, another asleep; one praying, another not; one's mind on the business of the council, and another thinking on something else.

But to return to the subject of the order: In ancient days councils were conducted with such strict propriety, that no one was allowed to whisper, be weary, leave the room, or get uneasy in the least, until the voice of the Lord, by revelation, or by the voice of the Council by the spirit was obtained: which has not been observed in this church to the present. It was understood in ancient days, that if one man could stay in Council another Could, and if the president could spend his time, the members could also. But in our Councils, generally, one would be uneasy, another asleep, one praying another not; one's mind on the business of the Council and another thinking on something else &c.[25]

Our Acts Are Recorded

Minute Book 1

Our acts are recorded, and at a future day they will be laid before us, and if we should fail to judge right and injure our fellow-beings, they may there, perhaps, condemn us; there they are of great consequence, and to me the consequence appears to be of force, beyond anything which I am able to express. Ask yourselves, brethren, how much you have exercised yourselves in prayer since you heard of this council; and if you are now prepared to sit in council upon the soul of your brother.

Our acts are recorded, and at a future day they will be laid before us, and if we should fail to judge right and injure our fellow beings, they may there prehaps condemn us; then, they are of great Consequence: and to me the Consequence appears to be of force beyond any thing which I am able to **[p.430]** express &c. Ask yourselves, brethrn, how much you have exercised yourselves in prayer since you heard of this Council; and if you are now prepared to sit in judgment upon the soul of your brother.—

I then gave a relation of my situation at the time I obtained the record [Book of Mormon], the persecutions I met with, and prophesied that I would stand and shine like the sun in the **[p.70]** firmament, when my enemies and the gainsayers of my testimony shall be put down and cut off, and their names blotted out from among men.—DHC 2:25-26.

Bro Joseph then went on to give us a relation of his situation at the time he obtained the record, the persecution he met with &C. He also told us of his transgressing at the time he was translateing the Book of Mormon. He also prophecied that he should stand and shine like the sun in the firmament when his enemies and the gainsayers of his testimony should be put down and Cut off and their names blotted out from among men.[26]

---

25. 12 February 1834, *JSP, D3*, 428–29.
26. 12 February 1834, *JSP, D3*, 429–30.

Covenant of Tithing

On the evening of the 29th of November, I united in prayer with Brother Oliver for the continuance of blessings. After giving thanks for the relief which the Lord had lately sent us by opening the hearts of the brethren from the east, to loan us $430; after commencing and rejoicing before the Lord on this occasion, we agreed to enter into the following covenant with the Lord, viz:

That if the Lord will prosper us in our business and open the way before us that we may obtain means to pay our debts, that we be not troubled nor brought into disrepute before the world, nor His people; after that, of all that He shall give unto us, we will give a tenth to be bestowed upon the poor in His Church, or as He shall command; and that we will be faithful over that which he has entrusted to our care, that we may obtain much; and that our children after us shall remember to observe this sacred and holy covenant; and that our children, and our children's children, may know of the same, we have subscribed our names with our own hands. (March 29, 1834.) DHC 2:174-175. (Signed) JOSEPH SMITH, JUN., OLIVER COWDERY.

Joseph Smith's Journal

November 29. 1834. This evening Joseph and Oliver [Cowdery] united in prayer for the continuance of blessings, after giving thanks for the relief which the Lord had lately sent us by opening the hearts of certain brethren from the east to loan us $430. After conversing and rejoicing before the Lord on this occasion we agreed to enter into the following covenant with the Lord, viz:=

That if the Lord will prosper us in our business, and open the way before <us> that we may obtain means to pay our debts, that we be not troubled nor brought into disrepute before the world nor his people, that after that of all that he shall give us we will give a tenth, to be bestowed upon the poor in his church, or as he shall command, and that we will be faithful over that which he has entrusted to our care and that we may obtain much: and that our children after us shall remember to observe this sacred and holy covenant: after us. And [p.47] that our children and our children's may know of the same we here subscribe our names with our own hands before the Lord:

Joseph Smith Jr
Oliver Cowdery.[27]

Importance of Revelation

At a conference of the Elders of the Church held at the home of Jared Carter, April 21, 1834, the Prophet read the second chapter of Joel and then made the following remarks:[28]

It is very difficult for us to communicate to the churches all that God has revealed to us, in consequence of tradition; for we are differently situated from any other people that ever existed upon this earth; consequently those former

Minute Book 1

It is very difficult for us to communicate to the churches all that God has revealed to us, in consequence of tradition; for we are differently situated from any other people that ever existed upon this earth: Consequently

---

27. 29 November 1834, *JSP, J1*, 46–47.
28. This introductory paragraph was authored by Joseph Fielding Smith.

revelations cannot be suited to our conditions; they were given to other people, who were before us; but in the last days, God was to call a remnant, in which was to be deliverance, as well as in Jerusalem and Zion. Now if God should give no more revela[p.71]tions, where will we find Zion and this remnant? The time is near when desolation is to cover the earth, and then God will have a place of deliverance in his remnant, and in Zion,

* * *

Take away the Book of Mormon and the revelations, and where is our religion? We have none; for without Zion, and a place of deliverance, we must fall; because the time is near when the sun will be darkened, and the moon turn to blood, and the stars fall from the heaven, and the earth reel to and fro. Then, if this is the case, and if we are not sanctified and gathered to the places God has appointed, with all our former professions and our great love for the Bible, we must fall; we cannot stand; we cannot be saved; for God will gather out his Saints from the Gentiles, and then comes desolation and destruction, and none can escape except the pure in heart who are gathered.—DHC 2:52.

those former revelations cannot be suited to our condition, because they were given to other people who were before us; but in the last days, God was to call a remnant, in which was to be deliverance, as well as in Jerusalem, and Zion. Now, if God should give no more revelations, where will we find Zion and this remnant? He said that the time was near when desolation was to cover the Earth, and then God would have a place of deliverance in his remnant, and in Zion, &c.

He then gave a relation of obtaining and translating the Book of Mormon, the revelation of the priesthood of Aaron, the organization of the Church in the year 1830, the revelation of the high priesthood, and the gift of the Holy Spirit poured out upon the church, &c.

Take away the book of Mormon, and the revelations, and where is our religion? We have none; for without a Zion and a place of deliverance, we must fall, because the time is near when the sun will be darkened, the moon turn to blood, the stars fall from heaven and the earth reel to and fro; then if this is the case, if we are not sanctified and gathered to the places where God has appointed, our former professions and our great love [p.16] for the bible, we must fall, we cannot stand, we cannot be saved; for God will gather out his saints from the gentiles and then comes desolations or destruction and none can escape except the pure in heart who are gathered, &c.[29]

Kindness to Animals Required of Man

The following incidents occurred while Zion's Camp was on the march from Kirtland to Missouri.[30]

In pitching my tent we found three massasaugas or prairie rattlesnakes, which the

Joseph Smith's History

in pitching my tent we found three Massasaugers or Prairie Rattle Snakes which

---

29. 21 April 1834, *JSP, D4*, 15–16.
30. This introductory paragraph was authored by Joseph Fielding Smith.

brethren were about to kill, but I said, "Let them alone—don't hurt them! How will the serpent ever lose its venom, while the servants of God possess the same disposition, and continue to make war upon it? Men must become harmless before the brute creation, and when men lose their vicious dispositions and cease to destroy the animal race, the lion and the lamb can dwell together, and the sucking child can play with the serpent in safety." The brethren took the serpents carefully on sticks and carried them across the creek. I exhorted the brethren not to kill a serpent, bird, or an animal of any kind during our journey unless it became necessary in order to preserve ourselves from hunger. (May 26, 1834.) DHC 2:71.

the brethren were about to kill, but I said let them alone, don't hurt them, how will the serpent ever lose its venom, while the servants of God possess the same disposition, and continue to make war upon them, men must become harmless before the brute creation, and when men lose their vicious dispositions and cease to destroy the animal race, the lion and the lamb can dwell together, and the sucking child play with the serpent with safety; the brethren took the serpents carefully on sticks, and carried them across the creek—I exhorted the brethren not to kill a serpent, bird, or ~~and~~ any animal of any kind, during our journey unless it—were necessary to preserve ourselves from hunger[31]

Never Trifle with Promises of God

Joseph Smith's History

Martin Harris having boasted to the brethren that he could handle snakes with perfect safety, while fooling with a black snake with his bare feet, he received a bite on his left **[p.72]** foot. The fact was communicated to me, and I took occasion to reprove him, and exhort the brethren never to trifle with the promises of God. I told them it was presumption for any one to provoke a serpent to bite him, but if a man of God was accidentally bitten by a poisonous serpent, he might have faith, or his brethren might have faith for him, so that the Lord would hear his prayer and he might be healed; but when a man designedly provokes a serpent to bite him, the principle is the same as when a man drinks deadly poison knowing it to be such. In that case no man has any claim on the promises of God to be healed. (June 16, 1834.) DHC 2:95–96.

Martin Harris having boasted to the brethren that he could handle snakes with perfect safety, while fooling with a black snake with his bare feet, he received a bite on his left foot, it was communicated to me, and I took occasion to reprove him, and exhort the brethren never to trifle with the promises of God—I told them it was presumption for any one to provoke a serpent to bite him, but if a man of God was accidentally bitten by a poisonous serpent, he might have faith, or his brethren might have faith for him, so that the Lord would hear his prayer and he might be healed—but when a man designedly provokes a serpent to bite him, the principle is the same, as when a man drinks deadly poison knowing it to be such—in that case no man has any claim on the promises of God to be healed[32]

---

31. 26 May 1834, History, A-1, Addenda, 8.
32. 16 June 1834, History, A-1, Addenda, 14.

Important Items of Instruction to the Twelve

	Joseph Smith's History
Kirtland, February 27, 1835	Kirtland February 27th

This evening, nine of the Twelve, viz., Lyman Johnson, Brigham Young, Heber C. Kimball, Orson Hyde, David W. Patten, Luke Johnson, William E. M'Lellin, John F. Boynton, and William Smith, assembled at the house of President Joseph Smith, Jun., who was present, with Frederick G. Williams, Sidney Rigdon, Bishop Whitney, and three Elders. Parley P. Pratt had gone to New Portage, and Orson Pratt and Thomas B. Marsh had not yet arrived to receive their ordination.

This evening, nine of the twelve, viz. Lyman Johnson, Brigham Young, Heber C. Kimball, Orson Hyde, David W. Patten, Luke Johnson, William E. McLellin, John F. Boynton and William Smith assembled at the house of President Josep Smith Jn., who was present, with Frederick G. Williams, Sidney Rigdon, Bishop [Newel K.] Whitney and three elders. Parley P. Pratt had gone to New Portage, and, Orson Pratt and Thomas B. Marsh had not yet arrived to receive their ordination.[33]

Importance of Records

Record of the Twelve[34]

After prayer by President Joseph Smith, Jun., he said, if we heard patiently, he could lay before the council an item which would be of importance. He had for himself, learned a fact by experience, which, on recollection, always gave him deep sorrow. It is a fact, if I now had in my possession, every decision which had been had upon important items of doctrine and duties since the commencement of this work, I would not part with them for any sum of money; but we have neglected to take minutes of such things, thinking, perhaps, that they would never benefit us afterwards; which, if we had them now, would decide almost every point of doctrine which might be agitated.

After the council was opened by prayer, he arose and made the following observations, (Viz) "I have something to lay before this council, an item which they will find to be of great importance to them. I have for myself learned a fact by experience which on reflection gives me deep sorrow. It is a truth that if I now had in my possession every decision which has been given had upon important items of doctrine and duties since the rise of this church, they would be of incalculable worth to the saints, but we have neglected to keep record of such things, thinking that prehaps that they would never benefit us afterwards, wh[i]ch had we now, would decide almost any point that might be agitated;

---

33. 27 February 1835, History, B-1, 575.

34. The Record of the Twelve is a document (created by William E. McLellin and Orson Hyde) containing minutes of the 1835 meeting in which the Twelve Apostles (i.e., Thomas B. Marsh, David W. Patten, Brigham Young, Heber C. Kimball, Orson Hyde, William E. McLellin, Parley P. Pratt, Luke Johnson, William Smith, Orson Pratt, John F. Boynton, and Lyman E. Johnson) were called. As a result of that meeting, in the summer of 1835, the Twelve were then sent on missions to conduct conferences with branches of the Church in New York and New England—preaching and baptizing along the way. The Record of the Twelve tells of their trials and accomplishments during that mission. Joseph Fielding Smith used the Minute Book version of this address by Joseph Smith, which is a somewhat later version of the Record of the Twelve. For the Minute Book 1 version, see *JSP, D4*, 252–54.

But this has been neglected, and now we cannot bear record to the Church and to the world, of the great and glorious manifestations which have been made to us with that degree of power and authority we otherwise could, if we now had these things to publish abroad.

[p.73] Since the Twelve are now chosen, I wish to tell them a course which they may pursue, and be benefited thereafter, in a point of light of which they are not now aware. If they will, every time they assemble, appoint a person to preside over them during the meeting, and one or more to keep a record of their proceedings, and on the decision of every question or item, be it what it may, let such decision be written, and such decision will forever remain upon record, and appear an item of covenant or doctrine. An item thus decided may appear, at the time, of little or no worth, but should it be published, and one of you lay hands on it after, you will find it of infinite worth, not only to your brethren, but it will be a feast to your own souls.

and now we cannot bear record to the church nor unto the world of the great and glorious manifestations that have been made to us with that degree of power and authority whi[c]h we otherwise could if we had those decisions to publish abroad.

Since the twelve are now chosen, I wish to tell them a course which they may pursue and be benefitted hereafter in a point of light of which they, prehaps, are not now aware. At all times when you assemble in the capacity of a [p.251[35]] council to transact business let the oldest of your number preside, and let one or more be appointed to keep a record of your proceedings and on the decision of every important item, be it what it may, let such decision be noted down, and they will ever after remain upon record as law, covenants and doctrine. ~~Any~~ Questions thus decided might at the time appear unimportant, but should they be recorded and one of you lay hands upon them afterward you might find them of infinite worth not only to your brethren but a feast als[o] to your own souls.[36]

Records a Protection Against Evil

Here is another important item. If you assemble from time to time, and proceed to discuss important questions, and pass decisions upon the same, and fail to note them down, by and by you will be driven to straits from which you will not be able to extricate yourselves, because you may be in a situation not to bring your faith to bear with sufficient perfection or power to obtain the desired information; or, perhaps, for neglecting to write these things when God had revealed them, not esteeming them of sufficient worth, the Spirit may withdraw, and God may be angry; and there is, or

Record of the Twelve[37]
Should you assemble from time to time and proceed to discuss important questions and pass decisions upon them and omit to record such decisions, by and by, you will be driven to straits from which you will not be able to extricate yourselves— not being in a ~~sufficient~~ situation to bring your faith to bare with sufficient perfection or power to obtain the desired information. Now in consequence of a neglect to write these things when God reveals them, not esteeming them of sufficient worth the spirit may withdraw and God may be angry, and here is a fountain of intelligence

---

35. Page 250 consists of an image rather than text.
36. 27 February 1835, *JSP, D4*, 249, 251.
37. Joseph Fielding Smith used the Minute Book version of this address by Joseph Smith, which is a somewhat later version of the Record of the Twelve. For the Minute Book 1 version, see *JSP, D4*, 252–54.

was, a vast knowledge, of infinite importance, which is now lost. What was the cause of this? It came in consequence of slothfulness, or a neglect to appoint a man to occupy a few moments in writing all these decisions.

Here let me prophesy. The time will come, when, if you neglect to do this thing, you will fall by the hands of unrighteous men. Were you to be brought before the authorities, and be accused of any crime or misdemeanor, and be as innocent as the angels of God, unless you can prove yourselves to have been somewhere else, your enemies will prevail against you; but if you can bring twelve men to testify that you were in a certain place, at that time, you will escape their hands. Now, if you will be careful to keep minutes of these things, as I have said, it will be one of the most important records ever seen: for all such decisions will ever after remain as items of **[p.74]** doctrine and covenants. (From minutes of Instruction to the Council of the Twelve, Feb. 27, 1835. DHC 2:198-199.)

or knowledge of infinite importance which is lost. What was the cause of this? The answer is slothfulness or a neglect to appoint a man to occupy a few moments in writing.

Here let me prophecy the time will come when if you neglect to do this, you will fall by the hands of unrighteous men. Were you to be brought before the authorities and accused of any crime or misdemeanor and be as innocent as the angels of God unless you can prove that you were somewhere else, your enemies will prevail against you: but if you can bring twelve men to testify that you were in some other place at that time you will escape their hands. Now if you will be careful to keep minutes of these things as I have said, it will be one of the most important and interesting records ever seen. I have now laid these things before you for your consideration and you are left to act according to your own judgments."[38]

Calling of the Apostles

President Smith proposed the following question: What importance is there attached to the calling of the Twelve Apostles, different from the other callings or officers of the Church?

After the question was discussed by Councilors Patten, Young, Smith, and M'Lellin, President Joseph Smith, Jun., gave the following decision:

They are the Twelve Apostles, who are called to the office of the Traveling High Council, who are to preside over the churches of the Saints, among the Gentiles, where there is no presidency established; and they are to travel and preach among the Gentiles, until the

Record of the Twelve

The following question was then proposed by president J Smith Jun. (viz) What importance is attached to the callings of these twelve apostles differrent from the other callings and offices of the chu[r]ch.

After some discussion by Elders [David W.] Patten, [Brigham] Young, M'cLellin and W[illiam] Smith, the following decision was given by President Smith, the Prophet of God.

[p.252] "They are the twelve apostles who are called to a travelling high council to preside over all the churches of the saints among the gentiles when there is no presidency established. They are to travel and preach among the Gentiles until the Lord shall shall command them to go to

---

38. 27 February 1835, *JSP, D4*, 251.

Lord shall command them to go to the Jews. They are to hold the keys of this ministry, to unlock the door of the Kingdom of heaven unto all nations, and to preach the Gospel to every creature. This is the power, authority, and virtue of their apostleship.
OLIVER COWDERY, Clerk
(Feb. 27, 1835. DHC 2:200.)

the Jews. They are to hold ~~this~~ the keys of this ministry— to unlock the door of the kingdom of heaven unto all nations and preach the Gospel unto every creation. This is the virtue powr and authority of their Apostleship— Amen. It is all important that the twelve should understand the power and authority of the priesthoods, for without this knowledge they can do nothing to profit. In the first place God manifested himself to me and gave me authority to establish his church, and you have received your authority from God through me; and now it is your duty to go and unlock the kingdom of heaven to foreign nations, for no man can do that thing but yourselves. Neither has any man authority or a right to go to other nations before you; and you, twelve, stand in the same relation to those nations that I stand in to you, that is, as a minister; and you have each the same authority in other nations that I have in this nation.["]³⁹

Items of Instruction to the Twelve and the Seventy

Order of Councils

President Joseph Smith stated that the Twelve will have no right to go into Zion, or any of the stakes, and there undertake to regulate the affairs thereof, where there is a standing high council; but it is their duty to go abroad and regulate all matters relative to the different branches of the Church. When the Twelve are together, or a quorum of them, in any church, they will have authority to act independently, and make decisions, and those decisions will be valid. But where there is not a quorum, they will have to do business by the voice of the Church. No standing High Council has authority to go into the churches abroad, and regulate the matters thereof, for this belongs to the Twelve. No standing High Council will ever be established only in Zion, or one of her stakes. When the Twelve pass a decision, it is in the name of the Church, therefore it is valid.

Minute Book 1

The president then stated that the Twelve will have no right to go into Zion or any of its stakes and there undertake to regulate the affairs thereof where there is a standing High Council. But it is their **[p.302]** duty to go abroad and regulate all matters relative to the different branches of the Church. When the Twelve are together, or a quorum of them in any Church, they will have authority to act independently and make decisions, and those decisions, and those decissions are valid. But where there is not a quorum they will have to do business by the voice of the Church. No standing high council has authority ~~his~~ to go into the churches abroad and regulate the matters thereof, for this belongs to the Twelve. No High Council will ever be established only in Zion or one of its Stakes. When the twelve pass a decision it is in the name of the church, Therefore, it is valid.

---

39. 27 February 1835, *JSP, D4*, 251–52.

[p.75] No official member of the Church has authority to go into any branch thereof, and ordain any minister for that church, unless it is by the voice of that branch. No Elder has authority to go into any branch of the Church, and appoint meetings, or attempt to regulate the affairs of the Church, without the advice and consent of the presiding Elder of that branch.

No individual has a right to go into any church and ordain any minister for the Church, unless it is by the Voice of the Church. No Elder has a right to go into any branch of the church and appoint meetings or regulate the Church without the consent or advice[e] of the presiding Elder of said branch.[40]

Calling of Seventies

Minute Book 1

If the first Seventy are all employed, and there is a call for more laborers, it will be the duty of the seven presidents of the first Seventy to call and ordain other Seventy and send them forth to labor in the vineyard, until, if needs be, they set apart seven times seventy, and even until there are one hundred and forty-four thousand thus set apart for the ministry.

[p.302] If the first Seventy are all occupied, and there is a call for more laborers it will be the duty of the seven presidents of the first seventy to call and ordain other Seventy and send them forth to labor, in the vineyard until if need be they set a part apart seven times Seventy, even until there shall be one hundred & forty and four thousand.

The Seventy are not to attend the conferences of the Twelve, unless they are called upon or requested so to do by the Twelve. The Twelve and the Seventy have particularly to depend upon their ministry for their support, and that of their families; and they have a right, by virtue of their offices, to call upon the churches to assist them.

The Seventy are not to attend the conferences of the Twelve unless they are called upon or requested to by the Twelve. The twelve and the Seventy have particularly to depend upon their Ministry for their support and that of their families, and they have a right by virtue of their offices to call upon the Church to assist them.

* * *

The circumstances of the presidents of the Seventy were severally considered, relative to their traveling in the vineyard: and it was unanimously agreed that they should hold themselves in readiness to go, at the call of the Twelve when the Lord opens the way. Twenty-seven of the Seventy were also considered, and it was decided they should hold themselves in readiness to travel in the ministry, at the call of the president of the Seventy, as the Lord opens the way.

[p.305] These men's circumstances and cases were considered and they were disposed of as the council directed. The Elders of Kirtland and its vicinity were next called upon, or their circumstances were considered. Their names being enrolled. President J. Smith Junr arose with the list in his hand and made some very appropriate remarks, relative to the deliverance of Zion and so much of the Authority being present, he moved that we never give up the struggle for Zion, even until Death. or until Zion is Redeemed. The vote was unanimous and with apparent deep feeling.

* * *

---

40. 2 May 1835, *JSP, D4*, 301–2.

Voted, that all the Elders of the Church are bound to travel in the world to preach the Gospel, with all their might, mind, and strength, when their circumstances will admit of it; and that the door is now opened.

Voted, that Elders Brigham Young, John P. Greene, and Amos Orton be appointed to go and preach the Gospel to the remnants of Joseph, the door to be opened by Elder Brigham Young; and this will open the door to the whole house of Joseph. Voted, that when another Seventy is required, the presidency of the first Seventy shall choose, ordain, and set [p.76] them apart from among the most experienced of the Elders of the Church.—From the Minutes of a General Priesthood Meeting held May 2, 1835.—DHC 2:220-222.

Voted that all the Elders of the Church are bound to travel in the World to preach the gospel with all their might mind & Strength when their circumstances will admit of it, and that the door is now opened.

Motioned, seconded & voted that Elder Brigham Youngs, John P. Green[e] & Amos Orton are appointed to go and preach the gospel to the remnants of Joseph. <the door to be opened by> ~~Motioned, seconded & voted~~ Elder B. Young and this will open a door to all the house of Joseph. [p.306] Motioned, seconded & voted. that when another Seventy is required, the presidency of the first Seventy, shall choose ordain and set them apart from among the most experienced Elders of the Church.[41]

Epistle to the Saints Scattered Abroad

Love for One Another

Messenger and Advocate

Dear Brethren:—It is a duty which every Saint ought to render to his brethren freely—to always love them, and ever succor them. To be justified before God we must love one another: we must overcome evil; we must visit the fatherless and the widow in their affliction, and we must keep ourselves unspotted from the world: for such virtues flow from the great fountain of pure religion, strengthening our faith by adding every good quality that adorns the children of the blessed Jesus, we can pray in the season of prayer; we can love our neighbor as ourselves, and be faithful in tribulation, knowing that the reward of such is greater in the kingdom of heaven. What a consolation! What a joy! Let me live the life of the righteous, and let my reward be like his!

Dear Brethren:—It is a duty which every saint ought to render to his brethren freely—to always love them, and ever succor them. To be justified be fore God we must love one another: we must overcome evil; we must visit the fatherless and the widow in their affliction, and we must keep ourselves unspotted from the world: for such virtues flow from the great fountain of pure religion. Strengthening our faith by adding every good quality that adorns the children of the blessed Jesus, we can pray in the season of prayer; we can love our neighbor as ourselves, & be faithful in tribulation, knowing that the reward of such is greater in the kingdom of heaven. What a consolation! What a joy! Let me live the life of the righteous, and let my reward be like his![42]

---

41. 2 May 1835, *JSP, D4*, 302, 305–6.
42. *M&A* 1, no. 9 (June 1835): 137. This letter published in the *Messenger and Advocate* was based on a letter previously sent to John Burke (1 June 1835) in the handwriting of W. W. Phelps, and signed by Joseph Smith Jr., Oliver Cowdery, W. W. Phelps, and John Whitmer. Included with this letter was a letter written to Phelps's wife, Sally Waterman Phelps (2 June 1835), and a note from Joseph Smith

Duty of the High Council and Elders

Letter from Joseph Smith

According to the order of the kingdom begun in the last days, to prepare men for the rest of the Lord, the Elders in Zion, or in her immediate region, have no authority or right to meddle with her spiritual affairs, to regulate her concerns, or hold councils for the expulsion of members in her unorganized condition. the High Council has been expressly organized to administer in all her spiritual affairs; and the Bishop and his council, are set over her temporal matters: so that the Elders' acts are null and void. Now the Lord wants the tares and wheat to grow together: for Zion must be redeemed with judgment, and her converts with righteousness. Every Elder that can, after providing for his family (if he has any) and paying his debts, must go forth and clear his skirts from the blood of this generation. While they are in that region instead of trying members for transgressions, or offenses, let every one labor to prepare himself for the vineyard, sparing a little time to comfort the mourners; to bind up the broken-hearted; to reclaim the backslider; to bring back the wanderer; to re-invite **[p.77]** into the kingdom such as have been cut off, by encouraging them to lay to while the day lasts, and to work righteousness, and, with one heart and one mind, prepare to help redeem Zion, that goodly land of promise, where the willing and the obedient shall be blessed. Souls are as precious in the sight of God as they ever were; and the Elders were never called to drive any down to hell, but to persuade and invite all men every where to repent, that they

According to the order of the kingdom begun in the last days, to prepare men for the rest of the Lord, the elders in Zion or <in> her immediate region have no **[p.330]** authority, nor right to medelle [meddle] with her affairs to regulate, or <u>even hold any courts</u>. The high council has been organized expressly <to> administer ~~over~~ <in> all her spiritual affairs; And the bishop and his council are set over her temporal matters: so thus the elders' acts are null and void: Now the Lord wants the tares and wheat to grow to gether <while ~~and~~ in an organized states,>; Zion must be redeemed with Judgments and her Converts by righteousness: Every elder that can, after he has provided for his family (if any he has) and paid his debts must go forth and clear his skirts from the blood of this generation: while they are there, instead of holding courts to stop communion, or any thing <else,> let every one laber to bind up the broken hearted; reclaim the wanderer, and persuade back into the Kingdom, such as have been cut off. by encouraging <them> to lay to and work rightousness, and prepare with one heart and one mind to redeem Zion, that goodly land of promise, where the willing and the obedient shall be blessed. Souls are as precious in the sight of God as they ever were, and the elders were never called to drive any down to hell, but ~~entice~~ <invite> and persuade men every where to repent—

---

to his cousin Almira Mack Scobey. See *JSP, D4*, 326–39. Modifications and additions to the letter were made by Phelps for the *Messenger and Advocate* version, entitled "To the Saints Scattered Abroad." The published letter is the version Joseph Fielding Smith used in compiling *TPJS*. The published letter is attributed to "P." The "P" likely refers to Phelps, because he signed several of his hymns with "P." It may be that Joseph Fielding Smith thought the "P" stood for Prophet or President (Joseph Smith). Or it may be that Joseph Smith authorized the letter and the changes, and that is why the compiler of *TPJS* attributed this letter to Joseph Smith.

may become the hears of salvation. It is the acceptable year of the Lord: liberate the captives that they may sing hosanna. the Priests, too, should not be idle; their duties are plain, and unless they do them diligently, they cannot expect to be approved. Righteousness must be the aim of the Saints in all things, and when the covenants are published, they will learn that great things must be expected from them. Do good and work righteousness with an eye single to the glory of God, and you shall reap your reward when the Lord recompenses every one according to his work. the Teachers and Deacons are the standing ministers of the Church, and in the absence of other officers, great things and holy walk are required of them. They must strengthen the members' faith; persuade such as are out of the way to repent, and turn to God and live; meekly persuade and urge every one to forgive one another all their trespasses, offenses and sins, that they may work out their own salvation with fear and trembling.

It is the acceptable year of the Lord. The priests too, should not be **[p.331]** <idle> their duties are plain and unless <they> do them, they can not expect to be approved. Righteousness must govern the saints in all things, and <when> the new covenants come forth the priests will learn that great <things> may be expected <at> their hands.⁴³

Do good and work righteousness with an eye single to the glory of God, and you shall reap your reward when the Lord recompenses every one according to his work.⁴⁴

The Teachers and Deacons are the standing ministers of the church, and in the absence of other officers, they will have great things required at their hands— They must strengthen the members;— persuade such as are out of the way to repent, and meekly urge and persuade every one to forgive each other all their trespasses, offences, and sins; Bear and forbear one with another, brethren, for so God does with us. Cease to find fault and learn to do well:⁴⁵

Seek to Save Souls

Letter from Joseph Smith

Brethren, bear and forbear one with another, for so the Lord does with us. Pray for your enemies in the Church and curse not your foes without: for vengeance is mine, saith the Lord, and I will repay. To every ordained member, and to all, we say, be merciful and you shall find mercy. Seek to help save souls, not to destroy them: for verily you know, that "there is over ninety and nine just persons that need no repentance." Strive not about the mysteries of the kingdom; cast not your pearls before swine, give not the bread of the children to dogs, lest you and the children should suffer, and you thereby offend your righteous Judge. Your brethren who leave their families, with

Pray <for> your enemies in the church, and curse not <your> foes <with>out: for vengence belongs to God. Know you not, that "there is more Joy in heaven over <u>One</u> sinner that repents, than ~~over~~ there is never <ninety> nine Just persons, that need no repentance!" Strive not about the mysteries of the kingdom; to one is given the word of <u>wisdom</u>; to another the power of healing difficulties: To every officer we say be <u>merciful</u> and you shall find mercy. Your Brethren, who leave their families and go forth to warn the present generation of the great things to <come>, expect great things of those who enjoy the society of the sain[ts] and their families— They pray that they may be

---

43. 1 June 1835, *JSP, D4*, 329–31.

44. This sentence is not included in the handwritten letter but is part of the published letter in *M&A* 1, no. 9 (June 1835): 138.

45. 1 June 1835, *JSP, D4*, 331.

whom they have enjoyed an earthly measure of peace and joy, to carry glad tidings around the world, expect **[p.78]** great things of you, while you are privileged to enjoy the blessing of the Saints' society. They pray our heavenly Father that you may be very prayerful, very humble, and very charitable; working diligently, spiritually and temporally for the redemption of Zion, that the pure in heart may return with songs of everlasting joy to build up her waste places, and meet the Lord when He comes in His glory. Brethren, in the name of Jesus Christ, we entreat you to live worthy of the blessings that shall follow, after much tribulation, to satiate the souls of them that hold out faithful to the end—M&A 1:137–138.

very prayerful and very humble, ~~will~~ working diligently ~~for~~ spiritually <&> temporally for the redemption of Zion, when all the pure in heart can return with songs, of everlasting Joy, to enjoy the good of the land of Zion: Brethren, in the name of Jesus we entreat you to live worthy of the blessing which shall <be> heired [inherited] by the faithful after Zion is redeemed.[46]

The substance of the foregoing article from the Messenger and Advocate is also contained, according to John Whitmer's history (manuscript, page 52) in a letter to Hezekiah Peck, signed by Joseph Smith, Jun., Oliver Cowdery, Sidney Rigdon, Frederick G. Williams, W. W. Phelps and John Whitmer; the opening paragraph of which is as follows:

Officers in Transgression

Letter from Joseph Smith
Kirtland Aug. 31, 1835.

"The Presidency of Kirtland and Zion say that the Lord has manifested by revelation of His Spirit, that the High Priests, Teachers, Priests, and Deacons, or in other words, all the officers in the land of Clay County, Missouri, belonging to the Church, are more or less in transgression, because they have not enjoyed the Spirit of God sufficiently to be able to comprehend their duties respecting themselves and the welfare of Zion; thereby having been left to act in a manner that is detrimental to the interest, and also a hindrance to the redemption of Zion.

The Presidency of Kirtland and Zion say that the Lord has manifested by revelation of his spirit: that the high preeist, teachers, Priests and deacons, or in other words all the officers in the land of Clay Co. Mo. belonging to the church are more or less in transgression, because they have not enjoyed the Spirit of God sufficiently to be able to comprehend their duties respecting themselves, and the welfare of Zion. Thereby having been left to act, in a manner that is detrimental to the interest, and also a hindrance, to the redemption of Zion.

---

46. 1 June 1835, *JSP, D4,* 331. The handwritten letter is somewhat different from the version used in the original *TPJS*. Joseph Fielding Smith used the published version found in *M&A* 1, no. 9 (June 1835): 138.

Now if they will be wise, they will humble themselves in a peculiar manner that God may open the eyes of their understanding.	Now if they will be wise, they will humble themselves in a peculiar manner that God may open the eyes of their understanding,
It will be clearly manifested what the design and purposes of the Almighty are with regard to them, and the children of Zion, that they should let the High Council, which is appointed of God and ordained for that purpose, make and regulate all the affairs of Zion, and that it is the will of God that her children should stand still and see the salvation of redemption."	It will be clearly manifest that the design and purposes of the Almighty; are with regard to them and the children of Zion: that they should let the high counsel which is appointed of God, and ordained for that purpose, <make and> regulate all the affairs of Zion: and that it is the will of God, that her children should stand still, and see the salvation of her redemption; and the officers of the church should go forth, inasmuch as they can leave their families in comfortable circumstances; and gather up the saints, even the strength of the Lords house. And those who cannot go forth consistently with the will of God their circumstances prevnting them; remain in deep humility: and in as much [as], th[e]y do any thing confine themselves to teaching the first principles of the Gospel: not endeavoring to institute regulations or laws for Zion, without having been appointed of God.[48]
Then follows the substance of the Messenger and Advocate article. This letter has the following postscript written personally by the Prophet, to Brother Peck, and is a gem which manifests the profound sympathy of the Prophet for the faithful in Israel:[47]	
[p.79] P.S.—Brother Hezekiah Peck: We remember your family with all the first families of the Church who first embraced the truth. We remember your losses and sorrows; our first ties are not broken; we participate with you in the evil as well as the good, in the sorrows as well as the joys; our union, we trust, is stronger than death, and shall never be severed. Remember us unto all who believe in the fulness of the Gospel of our Lord and Savior Jesus Christ. We hereby authorize you, Hezekiah Peck, our beloved brother, to read	[p.89] P.S. Br Hesekiah [Hezekiah] Peck We remember your familly, with all the fi[r]st families of the church, who first embraced the truth, we remember your losses and [p.90] sorrows our first ties are not broken, we participate with you in the evil as well as the good, in the sorrows as well as the Joys, our union we trust is stronger than death, and shall never be severed. Remember us unto all who believe in the fulness of the gospel of our Lord and Saviour Jesus Christ. We hereby authorize you Hezekiah Peck, our beloved brother to read

---

47. This introductory paragraph was authored by Joseph Fielding Smith.
48. 31 August 1835, *JSP, H2*, 87.

this epistle and communicate it unto all the brotherhood in that region of country. Dictated by me, your unworthy brother, and fellow laborer in the testimony of the Book of Mormon, Signed by my own hand in the token of the everlasting covenant. JOSEPH SMITH, JUN. —M&A, June, 1835, also DHC 2:229–231.	this epistle and ~~communication~~ communicate it unto all the brotherhood in all that region of Country, Dictated by me your unworthy brother, and fellow laborer in the testimony of the book of Mormon. Signed by my own hand in the token of the everlasting covenant. Joseph Smith Jr.[49]

Excerpts from an Epistle to the Elders of the Church of Latter-day Saints

	Messenger and Advocate
After so long a time, and after so many things have been said, I feel it my duty to drop a few hints, that perhaps the Elders traveling through the world, to warn the inhabitants of the earth to flee the wrath to come, and save themselves from this untoward generation—may be aided in a measure, in doctrine, and in the way of their duty. I have been laboring in this cause for eight years, during which time I have traveled much, and have had much experience. I removed from Seneca County, New York, to Geauga County, Ohio, in February, 1831.	After so long a time, and after so many things having been said, I feel it my duty to drop a few hints, that, perhaps, the elders, traveling through the world to warn the inhabitants of the earth to flee the wrath to come, and save themselves from this untoward generation, may be aided in a measure, in doctrine, and in the way of their duty. I have been laboring in this cause for eight years, during which time I have traveled much, and have had much experience. I removed from Seneca county, N. Y. to Geauga county, Ohio, in February, 1831.[50]

The Prophet's Commandment to Go to Missouri

	Messenger and Advocate
I received, by a heavenly vision, a commandment in June following, to take my journey to the western boundaries of the State of Missouri, and there designate the very spot which was to be the central place for the commencement of the gathering together of those who embrace the fullness of the everlasting Gospel. Accordingly I undertook the journey, with certain ones of my brethren, and after a long and tedious journey, suffering many privations and hardships, arrived in Jackson County, Missouri, and after viewing the country, seeking diligently at the hand of God, He manifested Himself unto us, and designated,	Having received, by an heavenly vision, a commandment, in June following, to take my journey to the western boundaries of the State of Missouri, and there designate the very spot, which was to be the central spot, for the commencement of the gathering together of those who embrace the fulness of the everlasting gospel—I accordingly undertook the journey with certain ones of my brethren, and, after a long and tedious journey, suffering many privations and hardships, I arrived in Jackson county Missouri; and, after viewing the country, seeking diligently at the hand of God, he manifested himself unto me, and designated to me and others, the very

---

49. 31 August 1835, *JSP, H2*, 89–90. This postscript to Hezekiah Peck is not found in the *Messenger and Advocate* version (which Joseph Fielding Smith relied upon as his source) but comes from a letter found in the history kept by John Whitmer—which is the earlier of the two sources for this statement.

50. *M&A* 1, no. 12 (September 1835): 179.

to me and others, the very spot upon which [p.80] he designed to commence the work of the gathering, and the upbuilding of an "holy city," which should be called Zion—Zion, because it is a place of righteousness, and all who build thereon are to worship the true and living God, and all believe in one doctrine, even the doctrine of our Lord and Savior Jesus Christ. "Thy watchmen shall lift up the voice; with the voice together shall they sing: for they shall bring again Zion" (Isaiah 52:8).

spot upon which he designed to commence the work of the gathering, and the upbuilding of an holy city, which should be called Zion:—Zion because it is to be a place of righteousness, and all who build thereon, are to worship the true and living God—and all believe in one doctrine even the doctrine of our Lord and Savior Jesus Christ. [p.180] "Thy watchmen shall lift up the voice; with the voice together shall they sing: for they shall see eye to eye, when the Lord shall bring again Zion."—Isaiah 52:8.[51]

* * *

Location of Zion

Messenger and Advocate

After having ascertained the very spot, and having the happiness of seeing quite a number of the families of my brethren comfortably situated upon the land, I took leave of them and journeyed back to Ohio, and used every influence and argument that lay in my power to get those who believed in the everlasting covenant, whose circumstances would admit, and whose families were willing to remove to the place which I had designated to be the land of Zion; and thus the sound of the gathering, and of the doctrine, went abroad into the world; and many, having a zeal not according to knowledge, and not understanding the pure principles of the doctrine of the Church, have, no doubt, in the heat of enthusiasm, taught and said many things which are derogatory to the genuine character and principles of the Church; and for these things we are heartily sorry, and would apologize, if apology would do any good.

after having ascertained the very spot, and having the happiness of seeing quite a number of the families of my brethren, comfortably situated upon the land, I took leave of them, and journeyed back to Ohio, and used every influence and argument, that lay in my power, to get those who believe in the everlasting covenant, whose circumstances would admit, and whose families were willing to remove to the place which I now designated to be the land of Zion: And thus the sound of the gathering, and of the doctrine, went abroad into the world; and many we have reason to fear, having a zeal not according to knowledge, not understanding the pure principles of the doctrine of the church, have no doubt, in the heat of enthusiasm, taught and said many things which are derogatory to the genuine character and principles of the church, and for these things we are heartily sorry, and would apologize if an apology would do any good.[52]

Principles of the Gospel

Messenger and Advocate

But we pause here, and offer a remark upon the saying which we learn has gone abroad, and has been handled in a manner detrimental

But we pause here and offer a remark upon the saying which we learn has gone abroad, and has been handled in a manner detrimental to

---

51. *M&A* 1, no. 12 (September 1835): 179–80.
52. *M&A* 1, no. 12 (September 1835): 180.

to the cause of truth, by saying, "that in preaching the doctrine of gathering, we break up families, and give license for men to leave their families, women their husbands, children their parents and slaves their masters, thereby deranging the order and breaking up the harmony and peace of society." We shall here show our faith, and thereby, misrepresentations, which have caused, we have every reason to believe, thousands to think they were doing God's service, when they were persecuting the children of God; whereas, if they could have enjoyed the true light, and had a just under[**p.81**]standing of our principles, they would have embraced them with all their hearts, and been rejoicing in the love of the truth. And now to show our doctrine on this subject, we shall commence with the first principles of the Gospel, which are faith, repentance, and baptism for the remission of sins, and the gift of the Holy Ghost by the laying on of the hands. This we believe to be our duty—to teach to all mankind the doctrine of repentance, which we shall endeavor to show from the following quotations:

"Then opened He their understanding, that they might understand the scriptures, and said unto them, Thus it is written, and thus it behooved Christ to suffer, and to rise from the dead the third day: and that repentance and remission of sins should be preached in His name among all nations, beginning at Jerusalem" (Luke 24:45, 46, 47).

By this we learn that it behooved Christ to suffer, and to be crucified, and rise again on the third day for the express purpose that repentance and remission of sins should be preached to all nations.

the cause of truth, by saying, "that in preaching the doctrine of gathering, we break up families, and give license for men to leave their families; women their husbands; children their parents, and slaves their masters, thereby deranging the order, and breaking up the harmony and peace of society." We shall here show our faith, and thereby, as we humbly trust, put an end to these faults [false], and wicked misrepresentations, which have caused, we have every reason to believe, thousands to think they were doing God's service, when they were persecuting the children of God: where as, if they could have enjoyed the true light, and had a just understanding of our principles, they would have embraced them with all their hearts, and been rejoicing in the love of the truth. And now to show our doctrine on this subject, we shall commence with the first principles of the gospel, which are repentance, and baptism for the remission of sins, and the gift of the Holy Ghost by the laying on of the hands. This we believe to be our duty, to teach to all mankind the doctrine of repentance, which we shall endeavor to show from the following quotations:

"Then opened he their understanding, that they might understand the scriptures, and said unto them, thus it is written, and thus it behoved Christ to suffer, and to rise from the dead, the third day; and that repentance and remission of sins should be preached in his name among all nations, beginning at Jerusalem."—Luke 24:45,46,47.

By this we learn, that it behoved Christ to suffer, and to be crucified, and rise again on the third day, for the express purpose that repentance and [**p.181**] remission of sins should be preached unto all nations.[53]

---

53. *M&A* 1, no. 12 (September 1835): 180–81.

Repentance

	Messenger and Advocate
"Then Peter said unto them, Repent, and be baptized every one of you in the name of Jesus Christ for the remission of sins, and ye shall receive the gift of the Holy Ghost. For the promise is unto you, and to your children, and to all that are afar off, even as many as the Lord our God shall call" (Acts 2:38, 39).	"Then Peter said unto them, repent, and be baptized every one of you, in the name of Jesus Christ, for the remission of sins, and ye shall receive the gift of the Holy Ghost. For the promise is unto you, and to your children, and to all that are afar off, even as many as the Lord our God shall call."—Acts 2:38,39.
By this we learn that the promise of the Holy Ghost is made unto as many as those to whom the doctrine of repentance was to be preached, which was unto all nations. And we discover also, that the promise was to extend by lineage; for Peter says, not only unto you, but "to your children, and to all that are afar off." From this we infer, that the promise was to continue unto their children's children, and even unto as many as the Lord their God should call. We discover here that we are blending two principles together in these quotations. The first is the principle of repentance, and the second is the principle of the remission of sins; and we learn from Peter that remission of sins is to be obtained by baptism in the name of the Lord Jesus Christ; and the gift of the Holy Ghost follows inevitably, for, says Peter, "you shall receive the Holy Ghost."	By this we learn, that the promise of the Holy Ghost, is unto as many as the doctrine of repentance was to be preached, which was unto all nations. And we discover also, that the promise was to extend by lineage: for Peter says, "not only unto you, but unto your children, and unto all that are afar off." From this we infer that it was to continue unto their children's children, and even unto as many generations as should come after, even as many as the Lord their God should call.—We discover here that we are blending two principles together, in these quotations. The first is the principle of repentance, and the second is the principle of remission of sins. And we learn from Peter, that remission of sins is obtained by baptism in the name of the Lord Jesus Christ; and the gift of the Holy Ghost follows inevitably: for, says Peter, "you shall receive the gift of the Holy Ghost."
[p.82] Therefore we believe in preaching the doctrine of repentance in all the world, both to old and young, rich and poor, bond and free, as we shall endeavor to show hereafter how, and in what manner, and how far, it is binding on the consciences of mankind, making proper distinctions between old and young, men, women, children and servants. But we discover, in order to be benefited by the doctrine of repentance, we must believe in obtaining the remission of sins. And in order to obtain the remission of sins, we must believe in the doctrine of baptism in the name of the Lord Jesus Christ. And if we believe in baptism for	Therefore we believe in preaching the doctrine of repentance in all the world, both to old and young, rich and poor, bond and free, as we shall endeavor to show hereafter—how and in what manner, and how far it is binding upon the consciences of mankind, making proper distinctions between old and young men, women and children, and servants. But we discover, in order to be benefitted by the doctrine of repentance, we must believe in obtaining the remission of sins. And in order to obtain the remission of sins, we must believe in the doctrine of baptism, in the name of the Lord Jesus Christ. And if we believe in baptism for

the remission of sins, we may expect a fulfillment of the promise of the Holy Ghost, for the promise extends to all whom the Lord our God shall call; and hath He not surely said, as you will find in the last chapter of Revelation—"And the Spirit and the bride say, Come. And let him that heareth say, Come. And let him that is athirst come. And whosoever will let him take the water of life freely" (Rev. 22:17).

Again, the Savior says, "Come unto me, all ye that labor, and are heavy laden, and I will give you rest. Take my yoke upon you, and learn of me; for I am meek and lowly in heart: and ye shall find rest unto your souls. For my yoke is easy, and my burden is light" (Matt. 11:28, 29, 30).

Again, Isaiah says, "Look unto me, and be ye saved, all the ends of the earth: for I am God, and there is none else. I have sworn by myself, the word is gone out of my mouth in righteousness, and shall not return. That unto me every knee shall bow, every tongue shall swear. Surely shall one say, in the Lord have I righteousness and strength: even to Him shall men come; and all that are incensed against Him shall be ashamed" (Isaiah 45:22–24).

* * *

the remission of sins, we may expect a fulfilment of the promise of the Holy Ghost: for the promise extends to all whom the Lord our God shall call. And hath he not surely said, as you will find in the last chapter of Revelations: "And the Spirit and the bride say, Come. And let him that heareth, say, Come. And let him that is athirst, come. And whosoever will, let him take the water of life freely." Rev. 22:17.

Again the Savior says: "Come unto me, all ye that labor, and are heavy laden, and I will give you rest. Take my yoke upon you, and learn of me; for I am meek and lowly in heart; and ye shall find rest unto your souls. For my yoke is easy, and my burden is light."—Math. 11:28,29,30.

Again Isaiah says: "Look unto me, and be ye saved, all the ends of the earth: for I am God, and there is none else. I have sworn by myself, the word is gone out of my mouth in righteousness, and shall not return, that unto me every knee shall bow, every tongue shall swear. Surely, shall one say, in the Lord have I righteous ness and strength: even to him shall men come; and all that are incensed against him shall be ashamed."—Isaiah 45:22,23,24.[54]

* * *

Not Leaving the First Principles

Messenger and Advocate

"Therefore, leaving the principles of the doctrine of Christ, let us go on unto perfection; not laying again the foundation of repentance from dead works, and of faith toward God, of the doctrine of baptisms, and of laying on of hands, and of resurrection of the dead, and of eternal judgment. And this will we do, if God permit. For it is impossible for those who were once enlightened, and have tasted of the heavenly gift, and were made partakers of the Holy Ghost, and have tasted the **[p.83]** good word of God, and the powers of the world to

"Therefore, leaving the principles of the doctrine of Christ, let us go on unto perfection; not laying again the foundation of repentance from dead works, and of faith towards God, of the doctrine of baptisms, and of laying on of hands, and of resurrection of the dead, and of eternal judgment. And this will we do, if God permit. For it is impossible for those who were once enlightened, and have tasted of the heavenly gift, and were made partakers of the Holy Ghost, and have tasted the good word of God, and the powers of the world to come, if

---

54. *M&A* 1, no. 12 (September 1835): 181.

come, if they shall fall away, to renew them again unto repentance, seeing they crucify to themselves the Son of God afresh, and put Him to an open shame." (Heb. 6:1–6).

* * *

JOSEPH SMITH, JUN.
M&A, Sept. 1, 1835[55], also DHC 2:253-259.

they shall fall away, to renew them again unto repentance; seeing they crucify to themselves the Son of God afresh, and put him to an open shame.— Heb. 6:1,2,3,4,5,6.

These quotations are so plain, in proving the doctrine of repentance and baptism for the remission of sins, I deem it unnecessary to enlarge this letter with comments upon them— but I shall continue the subject in my next.
In the bonds of the new and everlasting covenant,

JOSEPH SMITH, jr.
John Whitmer, Esq.[56]

To the Elders of the Church of the Latter-day Saints

Messenger and Advocate

At the close of my letter in the September number of the Messenger and Advocate I promised to continue the subject there commenced. I do so with a hope that it may be a benefit and a means of assistance in the labors of the Elders, while they are combating the prejudices of a crooked and perverse generation, my having in their possession the facts of my religious principles, which are misrepresented by almost all those whose crafts are in danger by the same; and also, to aid those who are anxiously inquiring, and have been excited to do so from rumor, to ascertain correctly what my principles are. I have been drawn into this course of proceeding by persecution, that is brought upon us from false rumors and misrepresentations concerning my sentiments.

At the close of my letter in the September No. of the "Messenger and Advocate," I promised to continue the subject there commenced: I do so with a hope that it may be a benefit and a means of assistance to the elders in their labors, while they are combatting the prejudices of a crooked and perverse generation, by having in their possession, the facts of my religious principles, which are misrepresented by almost all those whose crafts are in danger by the same; and also to aid those who are anxiously inquiring, and have been excited to do so from rumor, in accertaining correctly, what my principles are. I have been drawn into this course of proceeding, by persecution, that is brought upon us from false rumor, and misrepresentations concerning my sentiments.[57]

---

55. It is unclear why the original *TPJS* gives the date of this document as 1 September 1835. The *Messenger and Advocate* is the September issue, but no particular date is given therein. Josephsmithpapers.org gives October 2 as the date. (It is unclear if the October 2 date has reference to the date on which the letter was written or to the date on which the September issue of the *Messenger and Advocate* was released.)

56. *M&A* 1, no. 12 (September 1835): 182. "To-day wrote a letter to be published in the *Messenger and Advocate*." 2 October 1835, *JSP, J1*, 67. This letter was the first in a series of three letters written by Joseph and published in the September, November, and December issues of the *Messenger and Advocate*.

57. *M&A* 2, no. 2 (November 1835): 209.

Righteousness to Sweep the Earth

But to proceed. In the letter alluded to, the principles of repentance and baptism for the remission of sins were not only set forth, but many passages of scripture were quoted, clearly elucidating the subject; let me add, I do positively rely upon the truth of those principles inculcated in the New Testament, and then pass on from the above-named items, to the item or subject of the gathering, and show my views upon this point. It is a principle I esteem to be of the greatest importance to those who are looking for salvation in this generation, or in these, that may be called, "the latter times." All that the prophets that have written, from the days of righteous Abel, down to the last man that has left any testimony on record for our consideration, in speaking of the salvation of Israel in the last days, goes directly to show that it consists in the work of the gathering.

First, I shall begin by quoting from the prophecy of Enoch, speaking of the last days: "Righteousness will I send down out [p.84] of heaven, and truth will I send forth out of the earth, to bear testimony of mine Only Begotten, His resurrection from the dead (this resurrection I understand to be the corporeal body); yea, and also the resurrection of all men; righteousness and truth will I cause to sweep the earth as with a flood, to gather out mine own elect from the four quarters of the earth, unto a place which I shall prepare, a Holy City, that my people may gird up their loins, and be looking forth for the time of my coming, for there shall be my tabernacle, and it shall be called Zion a New Jerusalem." (Moses 7:62, 1902 edition.)

Messenger and Advocate

But to proceed, in the letter alluded to. The principles of repentance and baptism for the remission of sins, are not only set forth, but many passages of scripture, were quoted, clearly illucidating the subject; let me add, that I do positively rely upon the truth and veracity of those principles inculcated in the new testament; and then pass from the above named items, on to the item or subject of the gathering, and show my views upon this point: which is an item which I esteem to be of the greatest importance to those who are looking for salvation in this generation, or in these what may be called "the latter times," as all the prophets that have written, from the days of righteous Abel down to the last man, that has left any testimony on record, for our consideration, in speaking of the salvation of Israel in the last days, goes directly to show, that it consists in the work of the gathering.

Firstly, I shall begin by quoting from the prophecy of Enoch, speaking of the last days: "Righteousness will I send down out of heaven, and truth will I send forth out of the earth, to bear testimony of mine Only Begotten, his resurrection from the dead, -[this resurrection I understand to be the corporeal body]-yea, and also the resurrection of all men, righteousness and truth will I cause to sweep the earth as with a flood, to gather out mine own elect from the four quarters of the earth, unto a place which I shall pre pare; a holy city, that my people may gird up their loins, and be looking forth for the time of my coming: for there shall be my tabernacle; and it shall be called Zion, a New Jerusalem."[58]

---

58. *M&A* 2, no. 2 (November 1835): 209.

The Glorious Resurrection

Now I understand by this quotation, that God clearly manifested to Enoch the redemption which He prepared, by offering the Messiah as a Lamb slain from before the foundation of the world; and by virtue of the same, the glorious resurrection of the Savior, and the resurrection of all the human family, even a resurrection of their corporeal bodies, is brought to pass; and also righteousness and truth are to sweep the earth as with a flood. And now, I ask, how righteousness and truth are going to sweep the earth as with a flood? I will answer. Men and angels are to be co-workers in bringing to pass this great work, and Zion is to be prepared, even a new Jerusalem, for the elect that are to be gathered from the four quarters of the earth, and to be established an holy city, for the tabernacle of the Lord shall be with them.

Messenger and Advocate

Now I understand by this quotation, that God clearly manifested to Enoch, the redemption which he prepared, by offering the Messiah as a Lamb slain from before the foundation of the world: by virtue of the same, the glorious resurrection of the Savior, and the resurrection of all the human family,—even a resurrection of their corporeal bodies: and also righteousness and truth to sweep the earth as with a flood. Now I ask how righteousness and truth are agoing to sweep the earth as with a flood? I will answer:—Men and angels are to be co-workers in bringing to pass this great work: and a Zion is to be prepared; even a New Jerusalem, for the elect that are to be gathered from the four quarters of the earth, and to be established an holy city: for the tabernacle of the Lord shall be with them.[59]

The Elect Must Be Gathered

Now Enoch was in good company in his views upon this subject: "And I heard a great voice out of heaven, saying, Behold, the tabernacle of God is with men, and He will dwell with them, and they shall be His people and God Himself shall be with them, and be their God" (Revelation xxi:3).

I discover by this quotation, that John upon the isle of Patmos, saw the same things concerning the last days, which Enoch saw. But before the tabernacle can be with men, the elect must be gathered from the four quarters of the earth. And to show further upon this subject of the gathering, Moses, after having pronounced the blessing and cursing upon the children of Israel, for their obedience or disobedience, says thus:

Messenger and Advocate

Now Enoch was in good company in his views upon this subject. See Revelations, 23:3.— "And I heard a great voice out of heaven saying, Behold the tabernacle of God is with men, and he will dwell with them, and they shall be his people, and God himself shall be with them, and be their God."

I discover by this quotation, that John upon the isle of Patmos, saw the same things concerning the last days, which Enoch saw. But before the tabernacle can be with men, the elect must be gathered from the four quarters of the earth. And to show further upon this subject of the gathering: Moses, after having pronounced the blessing and the cursing upon the children of Israel, for their obedience or disobedience, says thus:—

---

59. *M&A* 2, no. 2 (November 1835): 209.

[p.85] "And it shall come to pass, when all these things are come upon thee, the blessing and the curse which I have set before thee, and thou shalt call them to mind, among all the nations whither the Lord thy God hath driven thee, and shalt return unto the Lord thy God, and shalt obey His voice, according to all that I command thee, this day, thou and thy children, with all thine heart, and with all thy soul, that then the Lord thy God will turn thy captivity, and have compassion upon thee, and will return and gather thee from all the nations whither the Lord thy God hath scattered thee. If any of thine be driven out unto the outmost parts of heaven, from thence will the Lord thy God gather thee, and from thence will He fetch thee (Deut. 30:1-4).

"And it shall come to pass, when all these things are come upon thee, the blessing and the curse which I have set before thee; and thou shalt [p.210] call them to mind, among all the nations whither the Lord thy God hath driven thee, and shalt return unto the Lord thy God, and shalt obey his voice, according to all that I command thee, this day, thou and thy children, with all thine heart, and with all thy soul, that then the Lord thy God, will turn thy captivity, and have compassion upon thee, and will return and gather thee from all the nations whither the Lord thy God hath scattered thee; and if any of thine be driven out unto the utmost parts of heaven; from thence will the Lord thy God gather thee; and from thence will he fetch thee."[60]

The New Jerusalem

Messenger and Advocate

It has been said by many of the learned and wise men, or historians, that the Indians or aborigines of this continent, are of the scattered tribes of Israel. It has been conjectured by many others, that the aborigines of this continent are not of the tribes of Israel, but the ten tribes have been led away into some unknown regions of the north. Let this be as it may, the prophecy I have just quoted "will fetch them," in the last days, and place them in the land which their fathers possessed. And you will find in the 7th verse of the 30th chapter, quoted, "And the Lord thy God will put all these curses upon thine enemies, and on them that hate thee, which persecuted thee."

It has been said by many of the learned, and wise men, or historians, that the Indians, or aboriginees of this continent, are of the scattered tribes of Israel. It has been conjectured by many others, that the aboriginees of this continent, are not of the tribes of Israel; but the ten tribes have been led away into some unknown regions of the north. Let this be as it may, the prophesy I have just quoted, "will fetch them" in the last days, and place them, in the land which their fathers possessed: and you will find in the 7th verse of the 30th chapt. [of Deuteronomy] quoted:—"And the Lord thy God will put all these curses upon thine enemies and on them that hate thee, which persecuted thee."

Many may say that this scripture is fulfilled, but let them mark carefully what the prophet says: "If any are driven out unto the outmost parts of heaven," (Which must mean the breadth of the earth). Now this promise is good to any, if there should be such, that are driven out, even in the last days, therefore, the children

Many may say that this scripture is fulfilled, but let them mark carefully what the prophet says: "If any are driven out unto the utmost parts of heaven;" (which must mean the breadths of the earth.) Now this promise is good to any, if there should be such, that are driven out, even in the last days: therefore, the

---

60. *M&A* 2, no. 2 (November 1835): 209–10.

of the fathers have claim unto this day. And if these curses are to be laid over on the heads of their enemies, wo be unto the Gentiles. (See Book of Mormon, 3 Nephi, Chap. 16, current edition). "Wo unto the unbelieving of the Gentiles, saith the Father." And again (see Book of Mormon, 3 Nephi 20:22, current edition, which says), "Behold this people will I establish in this land, unto the fulfilling of the covenant which I made with your father Jacob, and it shall be a New Jerusalem." Now we learn from the Book of Mormon the very identical continent and spot of land upon which the New Jerusalem is to stand, and it must be caught up according to the vision of John upon the isle of Patmos.

Now many will feel disposed to say, that this New Jerusalem spoken of, is the Jerusalem that was built by the Jews on the eastern continent. But you will see, from Revelation 21:2, there was a New Jerusalem coming down from God out of heaven, adorned as a bride for her husband; that after this, the Revelator was caught away in the Spirit, to a great and high mountain, and saw the great and holy city descending out of heaven from God. Now there are two cites spoken of here. As everything cannot be had in so narrow a compass as a letter, I shall say with brevity, that there is a New Jerusalem to be established on this continent, and also Jerusalem shall be rebuilt on the eastern continent (see Book of Mormon, Ether 13:1-12). "Behold, Ether saw the days of Christ, and he spake also concerning the house of Israel, and the Jerusalem from whence Lehi should come; after it should be destroyed, it should be built up again, a holy city unto the Lord, wherefore it could not be a New Jerusalem, for it had been in a time of old." This may suffice, upon the subject of gathering, until my next.[61]

---

61. *M&A* 2, no. 2 (November 1835): 210.

Duties of Elders

	Messenger and Advocate
I now proceed, at the close of my letter, to make a few remarks on the duty of elders with regard to their teaching parents and children, husbands and wives, masters and slaves, or servants, as I said I would in my former letter.	I now proceed, at the close of my letter, to make a few remarks on the duty of elders with regard to their teaching parents and children, husbands and wives, masters and slaves, or servants, &c. as I said I would in my former letter.
And first, it becomes an Elder when he is traveling through the world, warning the inhabitants of the earth to gather together, that they may be built up an holy city unto the Lord instead of commencing with children, or those who look up to parents or guardians to influence their minds, thereby drawing them from their duties, which they rightfully owe these legal guardians, they should commence their labors with parents, or guardians; and their teachings should be such as are calculated to turn the hearts of the fathers to the children, and the hearts of children to the fathers; and no influence should be used with children contrary to the consent of their parents or guardians; but all such as can be persuaded in a lawful and righteous manner, and with common consent, we should feel **[p.87]** it our duty to influence them to gather with the people of God. But otherwise let the responsibility rest upon the heads of parents or guardians, and all condemnation or consequences be upon their heads, according to the dispensation which he hath committed unto us; for God hath so ordained, that His work shall be cut short in righteousness, in the last days; therefore, first teach the parents, and then, with their consent, persuade the children to embrace the Gospel also. And if children embrace the Gospel, and their parents or guardians are unbelievers, teach them to stay at home and be obedient to their parents or guardians, if they require it; but if they consent to let them gather with the people of God, let them do so, and there shall be no wrong; and let all things be done carefully	And firstly, it becomes an elder when he is travelling through the world, warning the inhabitants of the earth to gather together, that they may be built up an holy city unto the Lord, instead of commencing with children, or those who look up to parents or guardians, to influence their minds, thereby drawing them from their duties, which they rightfully owe to such, they should commence their labors with parents, or guardians, and their teachings should be such as are calculated to turn the hearts of the fathers to the children, and the hearts of the children to the fathers. And no influence should be used, with children contrary to the consent of their parents or guardians.— But all such as can be persuaded in a lawful and righteous manner, and with common consent, we should feel it our duty to influence them to gather with the people of God. But otherwise let the responsibility rest upon the heads of parents or guardians, and all condemnation or consequences, be upon **[p.211]** their heads, according to the dispensation which he hath committed unto us: for God has so ordained, that his work shall be cut short in righteousness, in the last days: therefore, first teach the parents, and then, with their consent, let him persuade the children to embrace the gospel also. And if children embrace the gospel, and their parents or guardians are unbelievers, teach them to stay at home and be obedient to their parents or guardians, if they require it; but if they consent to let them gather with the people of God let them do so and there shall be no wrong and let all things be done

and righteously and God will extend to all such His guardian care.

And secondly, it is the duty of Elders, when they enter into any house, to let their labors and warning voice be unto the master of that house; and if he receive the Gospel, then he may extend his influence to his wife also, with consent, that peradventure she may receive the Gospel: but if a man receive not the Gospel, but gives his consent that his wife may receive it, and she believes, then let her receive it. But if a man forbid his wife, or his children, before they are of age, to receive the Gospel, then it should be the duty of the Elder to go his way, and use no influence against him, and let the responsibility be upon his head; shake off the dust of thy feet as a testimony against him, and thy skirts shall then be clear of their souls. Their sins are not to be answered upon such as God hath sent to warn them to flee the wrath to come, and save themselves from this untoward generation. The servants of God will not have gone over the nations of the Gentiles, with a warning voice, until the destroying angel will commence to waste the inhabitants of the earth, and as the prophet hath said, "It shall be a vexation to hear the report." I speak thus because I feel for my fellow men; I do it in then name of the Lord, being moved upon by the Holy Spirit. Oh, that I could snatch them from the vortex of misery, into which I behold them plunging themselves, by their sins; that I might be enabled by the warning voice, to be an instrument of bringing them to unfeigned repentance, that they might have faith to stand in the evil day!

Thirdly, it should be the duty of an Elder, when he enters into a house, to salute the master of that house, and if he gain **[p.88]** his consent, then he may preach to all that are in that house, but if he gain not his consent, let him not go unto his slaves or servants, but let the responsibility be upon the head of the master of that house, and the consequences thereof, and the

carefully, and righteously, and God will extend his guardian care to all such.

And secondly, it should be the duty of elders, when they enter into any house, to let their labors and warning voice, be unto the master of that house: and if he receive the gospel, then he may extend his influence to his wife also, with consent, that peradventure she may receive the gospel; but if a man receive not the gospel, but gives his consent that his wife may receive it, and she believes, then let her receive it. But if the man forbid his wife, or his children before they are of age, to receive the gospel, then it should be the duty of the elder to go his way and use no influence against him: and let the responsibility be upon his head—shake off the dust of thy feet as a testimony against him, and thy skirts shall then be clear of their souls. Their sins are not to be answered upon such as God hath sent to warn them to flee the wrath to come, and save themselves from this untoward generation. The servants of God will not have gone over the nations of the Gentiles, with a warnning voice, until the destroying angel will commence to waste the inhabitants of the earth; and as the prophet hath said, "It shall be a vexation to hear the report." I speak because I feel for my fellow-men: I do it in the name of the Lord, being moved upon by the Holy Spirit. O that I could snatch them from the vortex of misery, into which I behold them plunging themselves, by their sins, that I may be en abled, by the warning voice, to be an instrument of bringing them to unfeigned repentance, that they may have faith to stand in the evil day.

Thirdly, it should be the duty of an elder, when he enters into a house to salute the master of that house, and if he gain his consent, then he may preach to all that are in that house, but if he gain not his consent, let him go not unto his slaves or servants, but let the responsibility be upon the head of the master of that house, and the consequences thereof; and the guilt of guilt of that house is no longer upon his skirts, he is free; therefore, let him shake off the dust of his feet, and go his way. But if the master of that house give consent, the Elder may preach to his family, his wife, his children and his servants, his man-servants, or his maid-servants, or his slaves; then it should be the duty of the elder to stand up boldly for the cause of Christ, and warn that people with one accord to repent and be baptized for the remission of sins, and for the Holy Ghost, always commanding them in the name of the Lord, in the spirit of meekness, to be kindly affectionate one toward another, that the fathers should be kind to their children, husbands to their wives, masters to their slaves or servants, children obedient to their parents, wives to their husbands, and slaves or servants to their masters.

that house is no longer upon thy skirts: Thou art free; therefore, shake off the dust of thy feet, and go thy way. But if the master of that house give consent, that thou mayest preach to his family, his wife, his children, and his servants, his man-servants, or his maid-servants, or his slaves, then it should be the duty of the elder to stand up boldly for the cause of Christ, and warn that people with one accord, to repent and be baptized for the remission of sins, and for the Holy Ghost, always commanding them in the name of the Lord, in the spirit of meekness to be kindly affected one towards another; that the fathers should be kind to their children, husbands to their wives; masters to their slaves or servants; children obedient to their parents, wives to their husbands, and slaves or servants to their masters.[62]

Love of Husbands and Wives

"Wives, submit yourselves unto your own husbands, as unto the Lord, for the husband is the head of the wife, even as Christ is the head of the Church; and He is the Savior of the body. Therefore, as the Church is subject unto Christ, so let the wives be to their own husbands, in everything. Husbands, love your wives, even as Christ also loved the Church and gave Himself for it, that He might sanctify and cleanse it with the washing of water by the Word, that He might present it to Himself a glorious Church, not having spot or wrinkle, or any such thing, but that it should be holy and without blemish, so ought men to love their own wives as their own bodies. He that loveth his wife, loveth himself, for no man every yet hated his own flesh, but nourisheth and cherisheth it, even as the Lord the Church, for we are members of His body, of His flesh, and His bones. For this cause shall a man leave his father and mother, and shall be joined unto his wife, and they two shall be one flesh" (Ephesians 5:22-31).

Messenger and Advocate

"Wives submit youselves unto your own husbands, as unto the Lord. For the husband is the head of the wife, even as Christ is the head of the church: and he is the Savior of the body. Therefore as the church is subject unto Christ, so let the wives be to their own husbands in everything. Husbands, love your wives even as Christ also loved the church and gave himself for it; that he might sanctify and cleanse it with the washing of by the word, that he might present it to himself a glorious church, not having spot, or wrinkle, or any such thing; but that it should be holy and without blemish. So ought men to love their wives as their own bodies. He that loveth his wife loveth himself. For no man ever yet hated his own flesh; but nourisheth and cherisheth it, even as the Lord the church: for we are members of his body, of his flesh, and of his bones.— For this cause shall a man leave his father and mother, and shall be joined unto his wife, and they two shall be one flesh."—Ephesians, Chapt. V. from the 22d to the end of the 21st [31st] verse.

---

62. *M&A* 2, no. 2 (November 1835): 210–11.

"Wives, submit yourselves unto your own husbands, as it is fit in the Lord. Husbands, love your wives, and be not bitter against them. Children, obey your parents in all things, for [p.89] this is well pleasing unto the Lord. Fathers, provoke not your children to anger, lest they be discouraged. Servants, obey in all things your masters, according to the flesh, not with eye-service, as men-pleasers, but in singleness of heart, fearing God" (Colossians 3:18-22).

But I must close this letter, and resume the subject in another number.

In the bonds of the New and Everlasting Covenant,
JOSEPH SMITH, JUN.
M&A, November, 1835; also DHC 2:259-264.

"Wives submit yourselves unto your own husbands, as it is fit in the Lord. Husbands, love your wives, and be not bitter against them. Children, obey your parents in all things: for this is well pleasing unto the Lord. Fathers, provoke not your children to anger, lest they be discouraged. Servants, obey in all things your masters according to the flesh: not with eye service as menpleasers; but in singleness of heart, fearing God." —Colocians, Chapt. III. from the 18th to the end of the 22d verse.
[p.212] But I must close this letter and resume the subject in another number.

In the bonds of the new and everlasting covenant
JOSEPH SMITH, jr.
To J[OHN] WHITMER, ESQ.[63]

Reflections

Joseph Smith's Journal

Friday, November 6.—At home. Attended school during school hours, returned and spent the evening at home. I was this morning introduced to a man from the east. After hearing his name, he remarked that I was nothing but a man, indicating by this expression, that he had supposed that a person to whom the Lord should see fit to reveal His will, must be something more than a man. He seemed to have forgotten the saying that fell from the lips of St. James, that Elias was a man subject to like passions as we are, yet he had such power with God, that He, in answer to his prayers, shut the heavens that they gave no rain for the space of three years and six months; and again, in answer to his prayer, the heavens gave forth rain, and the earth gave forth fruit. Indeed, such is the darkness and ignorance of this generation, that they look upon it as incredible that a man should have any intercourse with his Maker. (Nov. 6, 1835). DHC, Vol. 2:302.

Friday morning 6th at home. attended School during the school hours returned and spent the evening at home I was this morning introduced to a man from the east, after hearing my name he replied remarked that I was nothing but a man: indicating by this expression that he had supposed that a person, <to> who<m> the Lord should see fit to reveal his will, must be something more than a man, he seems to have forgotten the saying that fell from the lips of St. James, that Elias was a man of like passions like unto us, yet he had such power with God that He in answer to his prayer, shut the heavens that they gave no rain for the space of three years and six months, and again in answer to his prayer the heavens gave forth rain and the earth brought forth fruit; and indeed such is the darkness & ignorance of this generation that they look upon it as incredible that a man should have any intercourse with his Maker.[64]

---

63. *M&A* 2, no. 2 (November 1835): 212. This letter was the second in a series of three letters written by Joseph and published in the September, November, and December issues of the *Messenger and Advocate*.
64. 6 November 1835, *JSP, J1*, 85.

The Prophet's Remarks to the Twelve

At six o'clock, Nov. 12, 1835, the Apostles met with the First Presidency in council and on this occasion the Prophet made the following remarks:

Joseph Smith's Journal

This evening viz the 12th at 6 oclock meet with the council of 12. by their request, 9 of them were present council opened by singing & prayer, and I made some remarks as follows;—

I am happy in the enjoyment of this opportunity of meeting with this Council on this occasion. I am satisfied that the Spirit of the Lord is here, and I am satisfied with all the brethren present; and I need not say that you have my utmost confidence, and that I intend to uphold you to the uttermost, for I am well aware that you have to sustain my character against the vile calumnies and reproaches of this ungodly generation, and that you delight in so doing.

I am happy in the enjoyment of this opportunity of meeting with this council on this occasion, I am satisfyed that the spirit of the Lord is here, and I am satisfied with all the breth[r]en present, and I need not say that you have my utmost confidence, and that I intend to uphold, you to the uttermost, for I am well aware that you ~~do and delight in so doing~~ have to sustain my character ~~my charcter~~ against the vile calumnies and reproaches of this ungodly generation and that you delight in so doing:—

[p.90] Darkness prevails at this time as it did at the time Jesus Christ was about to be crucified. The powers of darkness strove to obscure the glorious Sun of righteousness, that began to dawn upon the world, and was soon to burst in great blessings upon the heads of the faithful; and let me tell you, brethren, that great blessings await us at this time, and will soon be poured out upon us, if we are faithful in all things, for we are even entitled to greater spiritual blessings than they were, because they had Christ in person with them, to instruct them in the great plan of salvation. His personal presence we have not, therefore we have need of greater faith, on account of our peculiar circumstances; and I am determined to do all that I can to uphold you, although I may do many things inadvertently that are not right in the sight of God.

darkness prevails, at this time as it was, at the time Jesus Christ was about to be crucified, the powers of darkness strove to obscure the glorious sun of righteousness that began to dawn upon the world, and was soon to burst in great blessings upon the heads of the faithful, and let me tell you brethren that great blessings awate us at this time and will soon be poured out upon us if we are faithful in all things, for we are [p.97] even entitled to greater blessings than they were, because the[y] had the person of Christ with them, to instruct them in the great plan of salvation, his personal presence we have not, therefore we need great faith on account of our peculiar circumstances and I am determined to do all that I can to uphold you, although I may do many things <invertaintly [inadvertently]> that are not right in the sight of God;[65]

---

65. 12 November 1835, *JSP, J1*, 96–97. See also *JSP, D5*, 48–49.

Special Ordinances

You want to know many things that are before you, that you may know how to prepare yourselves for the great things that God is about to bring to pass. But there is one great deficiency or obstruction in the way, that deprives us of the greater blessings; and in order to make the foundation of this Church complete and permanent, we must remove this obstruction, which is, to attend to certain duties that we have not as yet attended to. I suppose I had established this Church on a permanent foundation when I went to Missouri, and indeed I did so, for if I had been taken away, it would have been enough, but I yet live, and therefore God requires more at my hands. The item to which I wish the more particularly to call your attention tonight, is the ordinance of washing of feet. This we have not done as yet, but it is necessary now, as much as it was in the days of the Savior; and we must have a place prepared, that we may attend to this ordinance aside from the world.

We have not desired as much from the hand of the Lord through faith and obedience, as we ought to have done, yet we have enjoyed great blessings, and we are not so sensible of this as we should be. When or where has God suffered one of the witnesses or first Elders of this Church to fall? Never, and nowhere. Amidst all the calamities and judgments that have befallen the inhabitants of the earth, His almighty arm has sustained us, men and devils have raged and spent their malice **[p.91]** in vain. We must have all things prepared, and call our solemn assembly as the Lord has commanded us, that we may be able to accomplish His great work, and it must be done in God's own way. The house of the Lord must be prepared, and the solemn assembly called and organized in it, according to the order of the house of God; and in it we must attend to

Joseph Smith's Journal

you want to know many things that are before you, that you may know how ~~how~~ to prepare your selves for the great things that God is about to bring to pass; but there is on[e] great deficiency or obstruction, in the way that deprives us of the greater blessings, and in order to make the foundation of this church complete and permanent, we must remove this obstruction, which is to attend to certain duties that we have not as yet attended to; I supposed I had established this church on a permanent foundation when I went to the Missourie and indeed I did so, for if I had been taken away it would have been enough, but I yet live, and therefore God requires more at my hands:— The item to which I wish the more particularly to call your attention to night is the ordinance of washing of feet, this we have not done as yet but it is necessary now as much as it was in the days of the Saviour, and we must have a place prepared, that we may attend to this ordinance, aside from the world;

we have not desired much from the hand of the Lord, with that faith and obedience that we ought, yet we have enjoyed great blessings, and we are not so sensible of this as we should be; When or wher has God suffered one of the witnesses or first Elders of this church <to> fall? never nor nowhere amidst all the calamities and judgments that have befallen the inhabitants of the earth his almighty arm has sustained us, men and Devils have raged and spent the malice in vain. we must have all things prepared and call our solem assembly as the Lord has commanded us, that we may be able to accomplish his great work: and it must be done in Gods own way, the house of the Lord must be prepared, and the solem assembly called and organized in it according to the order of the house of God and in it **[p.98]** we must attend to the ordinance of washing of

Order in House of God Always the Same

The endowment you are so anxious about, you cannot comprehend now, nor could Gabriel explain it to the understanding of your dark minds; but strive to be prepared in your hearts, be faithful in all things, that when we meet in the solemn assembly, that is, when such as God shall name out of all the official members shall meet, we must be clean every whit. Let us be faithful and silent, brethren, and if God gives you a manifestation, keep it to yourselves; be watchful and prayerful, and you shall have a prelude of those joys that God will pour out on that day. Do not watch for iniquity in each other, if you do you will not get an endowment, for God will not bestow it on such. But if we are faithful, and live by every word that proceeds forth from the mouth of God, I will venture to prophesy that we shall get a blessing that will be worth remembering, if we should live as long as John the Revelator; our blessings will be such as we have not realized before, nor received in this generation. The order of the house of God as been, and ever will be, the same, even after Christ comes; and after the termination of the thousand years it will be the same; and we shall finally enter into the celestial kingdom of God, and enjoy it forever.

Joseph Smith's Journal

the endowment you are so anxious about you cannot comprehend now, nor could Gabriel explain it to the understanding of your dark minds, but strive to be prepared in your hearts, be faithful in all things that when we meet in the solem assembly that is such as God shall name out of all the official members, will meet, and we must be clean evry whit, let us be faithful and silent brethren, <and> if God gives you a manifestation, keep it to yourselves, be watchful and prayerful, and you shall have a prelude of those joys that God will pour out on that day, do not watch for iniquity in each other if you do you will not get an endowment for God will not bestow it on such; but if we are faithful and live by every word that procedes forth from the mouth of God I will venture to prophesy that we shall get a blessing that will be worth remembering if we should live as long as John the Revelator, our blessings will be such as we have not realized before, nor in this generation. The order of the house of God has and ever will be the same, even after Christ comes, and after the termination of the thousand years it will be the same, and we shall finally roll into the celestial kingdom of God and enjoy it forever;—⁶⁷

Endowment Necessary

Joseph Smith's Journal

You need an endowment, brethren, in order that you may be prepared and able to overcome all things; and those that reject your

you need an endowment brethren in order that you may be prepared and able to overcome all things, and those that reject your testimony

---

66. 12 November 1835, *JSP, J1*, 97–98. See also *JSP, D5*, 49–50.
67. 12 November 1835, *JSP, J1*, 98. See also *JSP, D5*, 50.

testimony will be damned. The sick will be healed, the lame made to walk, the deaf to hear, and the blind to see, through your instrumentality. But let me tell you, that you will [p.92] not have power, after the endowment to heal those that have not faith, nor to benefit them, for you might as well expect to benefit a devil in hell as such as are possessed of his spirit, and are willing to keep it: for they are habitations for devils, and only fit for his society. But when you are endowed and prepared to preach the Gospel to all nations, kindreds, and tongues, in their own languages, you must faithfully warn all, and bind up the testimony, and seal up the law, and the destroying angel will follow close at your heels, and exercise his tremendous mission upon the children of disobedience; and destroy the workers of iniquity, while the Saints will be gathered out from among them, and stand in holy places ready to meet the Bridegroom when he comes.

I feel disposed to speak a few words more to you, my brethren, concerning the endowment: All who are prepared, and are sufficiently pure to abide the presence of the Savior will see Him in the solemn assembly.

The brethren expressed their gratification for the instruction I had given them. We then closed by prayer, when I returned home and retired to rest.—DHC 2:308-310.

will be damned the sick will be healed the lame made to walk the deaf to hear and the blind to see through your instrumentality; But let me tell you that you will not have power after the endowment to heal those who have not faith, nor to benifit them, for you might as well expect to benefit a devil in hell as such a<n> one, who is possessed of his spirit and are willing to keep it for they are habitations for devils and only fit for his society but when you are endowed and prepared to preach the gospel to all nations kindred and toungs in there own languages you must faithfully warn all and bind up the testimony and seal up the law and the destroying angel will follow close at your heels and execute his tremendeous mission upon the children of disobediance, and destroy the workers of iniquity, while the saints [p.99] will be gathered out from among them and stand in holy places ready to meet the bridegroom when he comes.—

I feel disposed to speak a few words more to you my brethren concerning the endowment, all who are prepared and are sufficiently pure to abide the presence of the Saviour will see him in the solem assembly.[68]

The brethren expressed their gratifycation for the instruction I had given them, we then closed by prayer,— I then returned home and retired to rest[69]

High Councils and the Twelve

Joseph Smith's History

I decided that the High Council had nothing to do with the Twelve, or the decisions of the Twelve. But if the Twelve erred they were accountable only to the General Council of the authorities of the whole Church, according to the revelations. (Sept. 26, 1835). DHC, Vol. 2:285.

I decided that the High Council had nothing to do with the Twelve, or the decisions of the Twelve, but if the Twelve erred they were accountable only to the General Council of the Authorities of the whole Church, according to the Revelation.[70]

---

68. 12 November 1835, *JSP, D5*, 50–51. See also *JSP, J1*, 98–99.
69. 12 November 1835, *JSP, J1*, 98–99. See also *JSP, D5*, 50–51.
70. 28 September 1835, History, B-1, Addenda, 621. Joseph Fielding Smith dates this statement to 26 September 1835. In History B-1, the statement is dated 28 September 1835. Neither the minutes of

Indians of Israel

Remarks by the Prophet at a meeting of the High Council at Kirtland.

Gathering of Israel

Much has been said and done of late by the general government in relation to the Indians (Lamanites) within the territorial limits of the United States.[71] One of the most important points in the faith of the Church of the Latter-day Saints, through the fullness of the everlasting Gospel, is the gathering of Israel (of whom the Lamanites constitute a part)[72] that happy time when Jacob shall go up to the house of the Lord, to worship Him in spirit and in truth, to live in holiness; when the Lord [p.93] will restore His judges as at the first, and His counselors as at the beginning; when every man may sit under his own vine and fig tree, and there will be none to molest or make afraid; when He will turn to them a pure language, and the earth will be filled with sacred knowledge, as the waters cover the great deep; when it shall no longer be said, the Lord lives that brought up the children of Israel out of the land of Egypt, but the Lord lives that brought up the children of Israel from the land of the north, and from all the lands whither He has driven them. That day is one, all important to all men.

In view of its importance, together with all that the prophets have said about it before us, we feel like dropping a few ideas in connection with the official statements from the government concerning the Indians. In speaking of the gathering, we mean to be understood as

Messenger and Advocate

One of the most important points in the faith of the church of the Latter Day Saints, is, through the fulness of the everlasting Gospel, the gathering of Israel;— the happy time when Jacob shall go up to the house of the Lord, to worship him in spirit and in truth; to live in holiness, when the Lord will restore his judges as at the first, and his counsellors as at the beginning; when every man may sit under his own vine and fig-tree, and there will be none to molest or make afraid; when he will turn to them a pure language, and the earth will be filled with sacred knowledge, as the waters cover the great deep; when it shall no longer be said, The Lord lives that brought up the children of Israel out of the land of Egypt, but the Lord lives that brought up the children of Israel from the land of the North, and from all the lands whither he had driven them; yea, that day is one all-important to all men!

And in view of it, with all the prophets have said, before us, we feel like dropping a few ideas in connexion with the official statements concerning the indians, from the General Government. In speaking of the gathering. we mean to be understood, according to scripture,

---

September 26 nor those of September 28 contain this statement. Thus, it was likely added to the history at a later date.

71. This first sentence is not found in the *Messenger and Advocate* article, but comes from History, B-1, 680, which is a later document.

72. This parenthetical clause is not in the *Messenger and Advocate* article; instead it comes from History, B-1, 680.

speaking of it according to scripture, the gathering of the elect of the Lord out of every nation on earth, and bringing them to the place of the Lord of Hosts, when the city of righteousness shall be built, and where the people shall be of one heart and one mind, when the Savior comes: yea, where the people shall walk with God like Enoch, and be free from sin. The word of the Lord is precious; and when we read that the veil spread over all nations will be destroyed, and the pure in heart see God, and reign with Him a thousand years on earth, we want all honest men to have a chance to gather and build up a city of righteousness, where even upon the bells of the horses shall be written "Holiness to the Lord."

The Book of Mormon has made known who Israel is, upon this continent. And while we behold the government of the United States gathering the Indians, and locating them upon lands to be their own, how sweet it is to think that they may one day be gathered by the Gospel! (Jan. 6, 1836). DHC 2:357.

the gathering of the elect of the Lord, out of every nation on earth; and bringing them to the place of the Lord of Hosts, where the city of righteousness, shall be built, and where the people shall be of one heart and one mind when the Savior comes; yea, where the people shall walk with God like Enoch, and be free from sin. The word of the Lord is precious, and when we read that the vail spread over all nations, will be destroyed, and the pure in heart see God, and live with him a thousand years on earth, we want all honest men, should have a chance to gather, and build up a city of righteousness, where even the bells on the horses, shall be *holiness to the Lord.*

The book of Mormon has made known who Israel is, upon this continent, and while we behold the government of the United States gathering the Indians, and locating them upon lands to be their own, how sweet it is to think that, they may one day, be gathered by the gospel.[73]

Orders in Councils

From the minutes of a Priesthood meeting in Kirtland Temple.

In the investigation of the subject [i.e., The Government of the House of the Lord], it was found that many who had deliberated upon it, were darkened in their minds, which drew forth some remarks from President Smith respecting the privileges of the authorities of the Church, that each should **[p.94]** speak in his turn and in his place, and in his time and season, that there may be perfect order in all things; and that every man, before he makes an objection to any item that is brought before a council for consideration, should be sure that he can throw light upon the subject rather than spread darkness, and that his

Joseph Smith's Journal
In the investigated of this subject, I found that many who had deliberated upon this subject were darkened in their minds, which drewforth, some remarks from me, respecting the privileges of the authorities of the church, that they should, each speak in his turn, and in his place, and in his time and season, that their may be perfect order in all things, and that every man, before he, makes an objection to any, item, that is thrown before them for their concideration, should be sure that they can throw light upon the subject rather than spread darkness, and that his objections be founded in righteousness which may be done

---

73. *M&A* 2, no. 4 (January 1836): 245.

objection be founded in righteousness, which may be done by men applying themselves closely to study the mind and will of the Lord, whose spirit always makes manifest and demonstrates the truth to the understanding of all who are in possession of the Spirit. (Jan. 15, 1836). DHC, Vol. 2:370.

by applying ourselves closely to study the, mind and will of the Lord, whose Spirit always makes manifest, and demonstrates to the understanding of all who are in possession, of his Spirit—[74]

To the Elders of the Church of Latter-day Saints

Parable of the Sower

Messenger and Advocate
To the Elders of the Church of the Latter Day Saints.

I have shown unto you, in my last, that there are two Jerusalems spoken of in holy writ, in a manner I think satisfactory to your minds; at any rate I have given my views upon the subject, I shall now proceed to make some remarks from the sayings of the Savior, recorded in the 13th chapter of His Gospel according to St. Matthew, which, in my mind, afforded us as clear an understanding upon the important subject of the gathering, as anything recorded in the Bible. At the time the Savior spoke these beautiful sayings and parables contained in the chapter above quoted, we find Him seated in a ship on account of the multitude that pressed upon Him to hear His words; and He commenced teaching them, saying:

I have shown unto you, in my last, that there are two Jerusalems spoken of in holy writ, in a manner I think satisfactorily to your minds: At any rate I have given my views upon the subject. I shall now proceed to make some remarks from the sayings of the Savior, recorded in the 13th chapter of his gospel according to St Matthew, which in my mind affords us as clear an understanding, upon the important subject of the gathering, as anything recorded in the bible. At the time the Savior spoke these beautiful sayings and parables, contained in the chapter above quoted, we find him seated in a ship, on the account of the multitude that pressed upon him to hear his words, and he commenced teaching them by saying:

"Behold, a sower went forth to sow, and when he sowed, some seeds fell by the way side, and the fowls came and devoured them up: some fell upon stony places, where they had not much earth; and forthwith they sprang up because they had no deepness of earth: and when the sun was up they were scorched: and because they had no root they withered away. And some fell among thorns; and the thorns sprung up and choked them: but other fell in good ground, and brought forth good fruit, some an hundred fold, some sixty fold, some thirty fold. Who hath ears to hear, let him hear.

"Behold a sower went forth to sow, and when he sowed, some seeds fell by the way side, and the fowls came and devoured them up; some fell upon stony places, where they had not much earth, and forthwith they sprang up because they had no deepness of earth, and when the sun was up, they were scorched, and because they had not root they withered away; and some fell among thorns and the thorns sprang up and choked them; but other, fell into good ground and brought forth fruit, some an hundred fold, some sixty fold, some thirty fold: who hath ears to hear let him hear.[75]

---

74. 15 January 1836, *JSP, J1*, 154.
75. *M&A* 2, no. 3 (December 1835): 225.

He Who Will Not Receive Light Shall Lose Light

"And the disciples came and said unto Him, Why speakest thou unto them in parables? [I would here remark, that the 'them' made use of in this interrogation, is a personal pronoun, **[p.95]** and refers to the multitude.] He answered and said unto them, [that is unto the disciples] because it is given unto you, to know the mysteries of the Kingdom of Heaven, but to them, [that is, unbelievers] it is not given; for whosoever hath, to him shall be given, and he shall have more abundance; but whosoever hath not, from him shall be taken away even that he hath."

We understand from this saying, that those who had been previously looking for a Messiah to come, according to the testimony of the prophets, and were then, at that time looking for a Messiah, but had not sufficient light, on account of their unbelief, to discern Him to be their Savior; and He being the true Messiah, consequently they must be disappointed, and lose even all the knowledge, or have taken away from them all the light, understanding, and faith which they had upon this subject; therefore he that will not receive the greater light, must have taken away from him all the light which he hath; and if the light which is in you become darkness, behold, how great is that darkness! "Therefore," says the Savior, "speak I unto them in parables because they, seeing, see not, and hearing, they hear not, neither do they understand; and in them is fulfilled the prophecy of Esaias, which saith, By hearing ye shall hear, and shall not understand; and seeing ye shall see, and not perceive."

Now we discover that the very reason assigned by this prophet, why they would not receive the Messiah, was, because they did not or would not understand; and seeing, they did not perceive; "for this people's heart is waxed

Messenger and Advocate

And the disciples came and said unto him, why speakest thou unto them in parables, (I would remark here, that the "*them*," made use of, in this interrogation, is a personal pronoun and refers to the multitude,) he answered and said unto them, (that is the disciples,) it is given unto *you* to know the mysteries of the kingdom of heaven, but unto *them* (that is unbelievers) it is not given, for whosoever hath, to him shall be given, and he shall have more abundance; but whosoever hath not, shall be taken away, even that he hath."

We understand from this saying, that those who had previously been looking for a Messiah to come, according to the testimony of the Prophets, and were then, at that time, looking for a Messiah, but had not sufficient light on the account of their unbelief, to discern him to be their Savior; and he being the true Messiah, consequently they must be disappointed and lose even all the knowledge, or have taken away from them, all the light, understanding and faith, which they had upon this subject: therefore he that will not receive the greater light, must have taken away from him, all the light which he hath. And if the light which is in you, become darkness, behold how great is that darkness? Therefore says the Savior, speak I unto them in parables, because they, seeing, see not; and hearing, they hear not; neither do they understand: and in them is fulfilled the prophecy of Esaias, which saith: by hearing ye shall hear and shall not understand; and seeing ye shall see and not perceive.

Now we discover, that the very reasons assigned by this prophet, why they would not receive the Messiah, was, because they did or would not understand; and seeing they did not perceive: for this people's heart is waxed gross, and their ears are dull of hearing, and their eyes they have closed, lest at any time they should see with their eyes, and hear with their ears, and understand with their heart, and should be converted, and I should heal them." But what saith He to His disciples? "Blessed are your eyes for they see, and your ears for they hear; for verily I say unto you, that many prophets and righteous men have desired to see those things which ye see, and have not seen them; and to hear those things which ye hear, and have not heard them."

Darkness the Condemnation of the World

We again make remark here—for we find that the very principle upon which the disciples were accounted blessed, was [p.96] because they were permitted to see with their eyes and hear with their ears—that the condemnation which rested upon the multitude that received not His saying, was because they were not willing to see with their eyes, and hear with their ears; not because they could not, and were not privileged to see an hear, but because their hearts were full of iniquity and abominations; "as your fathers did, so do ye." The prophet, foreseeing that they would thus harden their hearts, plainly declared it; and herein is the condemnation of the world; that light hath come into the world, and men choose darkness rather than light, because their deeds are evil. This is so plainly taught by the Savior, that a wayfaring man need not mistake it.

And again—hear ye the parable of the sower. Men are in the habit, when the truth is exhibited by the servants of God, of saying, All is mystery; they have spoken in parables, and, therefore, are not to be understood. It is true they have eyes to see, and see not, but none are so blind as those who will not see; and, although the Savior spoke this to such characters, yet unto His disciples he expounded it

gross; their ears are dull of hearing; their eyes they have closed, lest at any time, they should see with their eyes, and hear with their ears, and understand with their hearts, and should be converted and I should heal them. But what saith he to his disciples: Blessed are your eyes, for they see, and your ears, for they hear; for verily I say unto you, that many prophets and righteous men have desired to see those things which ye see, and have not seen them; and to hear those things which ye hear, and have not heard them.[76]

Messenger and Advocate

We again make a remark here, for we find that the very principles upon which the disciples were accounted blessed, was because they were permitted to see with their eyes, and hear with their ears, and the condemnation which rested upon the multitude, which received not his saying, was because they were not willing to see with their eyes and hear with their ears; not because they could not and were not privileged to see, and hear, but because their hearts were full of iniquity and abomi[p.226]nation: as your fathers did so do ye.— The prophet foreseeing that they would thus harden their hearts plainly declared it; and herein is the condemnation of the world, that light hath come into the world, and men choose darkness rather than light because their deeds are evil: This is so plainly taught by the Savior, that a wayfaring man need not mistake it.

And again hear ye the parable of the sower: Men are in the habit, when the truth is exhibited by the servants of God, of saying, all is mystery, they are spoken in parables, and, therefore, are not to be understood, it is true they have eyes to see, and see not; but none are so blind as those who will not see: And although the Savior spoke this parable to such characters, yet unto his disciples he expounded

---

76. *M&A* 2, no. 3 (December 1835): 225.

plainly; and we have reason to be truly humble before the God of our fathers, that He hath left these things on record for us, so plain, that notwithstanding the exertions and combined influence of the priests of Baal, they have not power to blind our eyes, and darken our understanding, if we will but open our eyes, and read with candor, for a moment.

Explanation of the Parable of the Sower

But listen to the explanation of the parable of the Sower: "When any one heareth the word of the Kingdom, and understandeth it not, then cometh the wicked one, and catcheth away that which was sown in his heart." Now mark the expression—that which was sown in his heart. This is he which receiveth seed by the way side. Men who have no principle of truth, do not understand the word of truth when they hear it. The devil taketh away the word of truth out of their hearts, because there is no desire for righteousness in them. "But he that receiveth seed in stony places, the same is he that heareth the word, and anon, with joy receiveth it; yet hath he not root in himself, but dureth for a while; for when tribulation or persecution ariseth because of the [p.97] word, by and by, he is offended. He also that receiveth seed among the thorns, is he that heareth the word; and the care of this world, and the deceitfulness of riches choke the word, and he becometh unfruitful. But he that received seed into the good ground, is he that heareth the word, and understandeth it, which also beareth fruit, and bringeth forth, some an hundred fold, some sixty, some thirty." Thus the Savior Himself explains unto His disciples the parable which He put forth, and left no mystery or darkness upon the minds of those who firmly believe on His words.

Messenger and Advocate

But listen to the explanation of the parable: when any one heareth the word of the kingdom, and understandeth it not, then cometh the wicked one and catcheth away that which was sown in his heart. Now mark the expression; that which was before sown in his heart; this is he which received seed by the way side; men who have no principle of righteousness in themselves, and whose hearts are full of iniquity, and who have no desire for the principles of truth, do not understand the word of truth, when they hear it.— The devil taketh away the word of truth out of their hearts, because there is no desire for righteousness in them. But he that received the seed into stony places the same is he that heareth the word and, anon, with joy receiveth it, yet hath he not root in himself, but dureth for awhile; for when tribulation or persecution ariseth because of the word, by and by he is offended. He also that received seed among the thorns is he that receiveth the word, and the cares of this world, and the deceitfulness of riches choke the word, and he becometh unfruitful: but he that received seed into the good ground, is he that heareth the word and understandeth it which also beareth fruit and bringeth forth some an hundred fold, some sixty, some thirty. Thus the Savior himself explains unto his disciples the parable, which he put forth and left no mystery or darkness upon the minds of those who firmly believe on his words.

---

77. *M&A* 2, no. 3 (December 1835): 225–26.

We draw the conclusion, then, that the very reason why the multitude, or the world, as they were designated by the Savior, did not receive an explanation upon His parables, was because of unbelief. To you, He says (speaking to His disciples) it is given to know the mysteries of the Kingdom of God. And why? Because of the faith and confidence they had in Him. This parable was spoken to demonstrate the effects that are produced by the preaching of the word; and we believe that it has an allusion directly, to the commencement, or the setting up of the Kingdom in that age; therefore we shall continue to trace His sayings concerning this Kingdom from that time forth, even unto the end of the world.

We draw the conclusion then, that the very reason why the multitude, or the world, as they were designated by the Savior, did not receive an explanation upon his parables, was, because of unbelief. To you, he says, (speaking to his disciples) it is given to know the mysteries of the kingdom of God: and why? because of the faith and confidence which they had in him. This parable was spoken to demonstrate the effects that are produced by the preaching of the word; and we believe that it has an allusion directly, to the commencement, or the setting up of the kingdom in that age: therefore, we shall continue to trace his sayings concerning this kingdom from that time forth, even unto the end of the world.[78]

Parable of the Tares

Messenger and Advocate

"Another parable put He forth unto them, saying, [which parable has an allusion to the setting up of the Kingdom, in that age of the world also], The Kingdom of Heaven is likened unto a man which sowed good seed in his field, but while men slept, his enemy came and sowed tares among the wheat, and went his way. But when the blade was sprung up, and brought forth fruit, then appeared the tares also; so the servants of the householder came and said unto him, Sir, didst not thou sow good seed in thy field? From whence, then, hath it tares? He said unto them, An enemy hath done this. The servants said unto him, Wilt thou then that we go and gather them up? But he said, Nay; lest while ye gather up the tares, ye root up also the wheat with them. Let both grow together until the harvest: and in the time of harvest I will say to the reapers, Gather ye together first the tares, and bind them in bundles to burn them, but gather the wheat into my barn."

Another parable put he forth unto them, saying, (which parable has an allusion to the setting up of the kingdom, in that age of the world also) the kingdom of Heaven is likened unto a man which sowed good seed in his field, but while men slept an enemy came and sowed tares among the wheat and went his way; but when the blade was sprung up, and brought forth fruit, then appeared the tares also; so the servants of the householder came and said unto him, sir, didst not thou sow good seed in thy field? from whence then hath it tares? He said unto them, an enemy hath done this. The servants said unto him wilt thou then that we go and gather them up; but he said nay, lest while ye gather up the tares, ye root up also the wheat with them.— Let both grow together until the harvest, and in the time of the harvest, I will say to the reapers, gather ye together first the tares, and bind them in bundles, to burn them; but gather the wheat into my barn.

Now we learn by this parable, not only the setting up of **[p.98]** the Kingdom in the days of

Now we learn by this parable, not only the setting up of the kingdom in the days of the

---

78. *M&A* 2, no. 3 (December 1835): 226.

the Savior, which is represented by the good seed, which produced fruit, but also the corruptions of the Church, which are represented by the tares, which were sown by the enemy, which His disciples would fain have plucked up, or cleansed the Church of, if their views had been favored by the Savior. But He, knowing all things, says, Not so, as much as to say, your views are not correct, the Church is in its infancy, and if you take this rash step, you will destroy the wheat, or the Church, with the tares; therefore it is better to let them grow together until the harvest, or the end of the world, which means the destruction of the wicked, which is not yet fulfilled, as we shall show hereafter, in the Savior's explanation of the parable, which is so plain that there is no room left for dubiety upon the mind, notwithstanding the cry of the priests—"parables, parables! figures, figures! mystery, mystery! all is mystery!" But we find no room for doubt here, as the parables were all plainly elucidated.

Savior, which is represented by the good seed, which produced fruit, but also the corruptions of the church, which is represented by the tares, which were sown by the enemy, which his disciples would fain [p.227] have plucked up, or cleansed the church of, if their views had been favored by the Savior; but he, knowing all things, says not so; as much as to say, your views are not correct, the church is in its infancy, and if you take this rash step, you will destroy the wheat or the church with the tares: therefore it is better to let them grow together until the harvest, or the end of the world, which means the destruction of the wicked; which is not yet fulfilled; as we shall show hereafter, in the Savior's explanation of the parable, which is so plain, that there is no room left for dubiety upon the mind, notwithstanding the cry of the priests, parables, parables! figures, figures! mystery, mystery! all is mystery! but we find no room for doubt here, as the parables were all plainly elucidated.[79]

Parable of the Church in Last Days

Messenger and Advocate

And again, another parable put He forth unto them, having an allusion to the Kingdom that should be set up, just previous to or at the time of the harvest, which reads as follows—"The Kingdom of Heaven is like a grain of mustard seed, which a man took and sowed in his field: which indeed is the least of all seeds: but, when it is grown, it is the greatest among herbs, and becometh a tree, so that the birds of the air come and lodge in the branches thereof." Now we can discover plainly that this figure is given to represent the Church as it shall come forth in the last days. Behold, the kingdom of Heaven is likened unto it. Now, what is like unto it?

And again, another parable put he forth unto them, having an allusion to the kingdom which should be set up, just previous or at the time of harvest, which reads as follows:—The kingdom of heaven is like to a grain of mustard seed, which a man took and sowed in his field, which indeed is the least of all seeds, but when it is grown it is the greatest among herbs, and becometh a tree, so that the birds of the air come and lodge in the branches thereof. Now we can discover plainly, that this figure is given to represent the church as it shall come forth in the last days. Behold the kingdom of heaven is likened unto it. Now what is like unto it?

Let us take the Book of Mormon, which a man took and hid in his field, securing it by his faith, to spring up in the last days, or in due time; let us behold it coming forth out

Let us take the book of Mormon, which a man took and hid in his field; securing it by his faith, to spring up in the last days, or in due time: let us be hold it coming forth out of the

---

79. *M&A* 2, no. 3 (December 1835): 226–27.

of the ground, which is indeed accounted the least of all seeds, but behold it branching forth, yea, even towering, with lofty branches, and God-like majesty, until it, like the mustard seed, becomes the greatest of all herbs. And it is truth, and it has sprouted and come forth out of the earth, and righteousness begins to look down from heaven, and God is sending down His powers, gifts and angels, to lodge in the branches thereof.

The Kingdom of Heaven is like unto a mustard seed. Be[p.99]hold, then is not this the Kingdom of Heaven that is raising its head in the last days in the majesty of its God, even the Church of the Latter-day Saints, like an impenetrable, immovable rock in the midst of the mighty deep, exposed to the storms and tempests of Satan, but has, thus far, remained steadfast, and is still braving the mountain waves of opposition, which are driven by the tempestuous winds of sinking crafts, which have [dashed] and are still dashing with tremendous foam across its triumphant brow; urged onward with redoubled fury by the enemy of righteousness, with his pitchfork of lies, as you will see fairly represented in a cut contained in Mr. Howe's Mormonism Unveiled? And we hope that this adversary of truth will continue to stir up the sink of iniquity, that the people may the more readily discern between the righteous and the wicked.

ground, which is indeed accounted the least of all seeds, but behold it branching forth; yea, even towering, with lofty branches, and God-like majesty, until it becomes the greatest of all herbs: and it is truth, and it has sprouted and come forth out of the earth; and righteousness begins to look down from heaven; and God is sending down his powers, gifts and angels, to lodge in the branches thereof:

The kingdom of heaven is like unto a mustard seed. Behold, then, is not this the kingdom of heaven that is raising its head in the last days, in the majesty of its God; even the church of the Latter day saints,—like an impenetrable, immovable rock in the midst of the mighty deep, exposed to storms and tempests of satan, but has, thus far, remained steadfast and is still braving the mountain waves of opposition, which are driven by the tempestuous winds of sinking crafts, have and are still dashing with tremendous foam, across its triumphing brow, urged onward with redoubled fury by the enemy of righteousness, with his pitchfork of lies, as you will see fairly represented in a cut, contained in Mr. [Eber] Howe's "Mormonism Unveiled?" And we hope that this adversary of truth will continue to stir up the sink of iniquity, that people may the more readily discern between the righteous and wicked.[80]

Modern Sons of Sceva

Messenger and Advocate

We also would notice one of the modern sons of Sceva, who would fain have made people believe that he could cast out devils, by a certain pamphlet, the Millennial Harbringer, that went the rounds through our country; who felt so fully authorized to brand "Jo" Smith with the appellation of Elymas the sorcerer, and to say with Paul, "O full of all subtlety, and all mischief, thou child of the

We also would notice one of the modern sons of Sceva, who would fain have made people believe that he could cast out devils, by a certain pamphlet (viz. the "Millenial Harbinger,") that went the rounds through our country, who felt so fully authorized to brand Jo Smith, with the appellation of Elymus the sorcerer, and to say with Paul, O full of all subtilty and all mischief, thou child

---

80. *M&A* 2, no. 3 (December 1835): 227.

devil, thou enemy of all righteousness, wilt thou not cease to pervert the right ways of the Lord?" We should reply to this gentleman, Paul we know, and Christ we know, but who are ye? And with the best of feeling would say to him, in the language of Paul to those who said they were John's disciples, but had not so much as heard there was a Holy Ghost—to repent and be baptized for the remission of sins, by those who have legal authority, and under their hands you shall receive the Holy Ghost, according to the Scriptures:	of the devil, thou enemy of all righteousness, wilt thou not cease to pervert the right ways of the Lord! We would reply to this gentleman—Paul we know, and Christ we know, but who are ye? And with the best of feelings, we would say to him, in the language of Paul to those who said they were John's disciples, but had not so much as heard there was a Holy Ghost, to repent and be baptised for the remission of sins by those who have legal authority, and under their hands you shall receive the Holy Ghost, according to the scriptures.
"Then laid they their hands upon them, and they received the Holy Ghost" (Acts 8:17). "And when Paul had laid his hands upon them the Holy Ghost came on them and they spake with tongues and prophesied" (Acts 19:6). "Of the doctrine of baptism, and of laying on of hands, and of resurrection of the dead and of eternal judgment" (Hebrews 6:2). "How, then, shall they call on him in whom they have not believed? And how shall they believe in him of whom they have not **[p.100]** heard? And how shall they hear without a preacher? And how shall they preach, except they be sent? As it is written, How beautiful are the feet of them that preach the Gospel of peace, and bring glad tidings of good things" (Romans 10:14, 15). But if this man will not take our admonition, but will persist in his wicked course, we hope that he will continue trying to cast out devils, that we may have the clearer proof that the kingdom of Satan is divided against itself, and consequently cannot stand; for a kingdom divided against itself, speedily hath an end.	Then laid they their hands on them, and they received the Holy Ghost.—Acts: ch. 8, v. 17. And, when Paul had laid his hands upon them, the Holy Ghost came on them: and they spake with tongues, and prophesied.— Acts: ch. 19, v. 6. Of the doctrine of baptisms, and of laying on of hands, and of resurrection of the dead, and of eternal judgment.—Heb. ch. 6, v.2. How then shall they call on him in whom they have not believed? and how shall they believe in him of whom they have not heard? and how shall they hear without a preacher? And how shall they preach except they be sent? as it is written, How beautiful are the feet of them that preach the gospel of peace, and bring glad tidings of good things!—Rom. ch. 10, v. 14-15. But if this man will not take our admonition, but will persist in his wicked course, we hope that he will continue trying to cast out devils, that we may **[p.228]** have the clearer proof that the kingdom of satan is divided against itself, and consequently cannot stand: for a kingdom divided against itself, speedily hath an end.[81]

* * *

Parable of the Leaven

Messenger and Advocate

"And another parable spake He unto them. The Kingdom of Heaven is like unto leaven which a woman took and hid in three	And another parable spake he unto them: The kingdom of heaven is like unto leaven which a woman took the hid in three measures of

---

81. *M&A* 2, no. 3 (December 1835): 227–28.

measures of meal till the whole was leavened." It may be understood that the Church of the Latter-day Saints has taken its rise from a little leaven that was put into three witnesses. Behold, how much this is like the parable! It is fast leavening the lump, and will soon leaven the whole. But let us pass on.

"All these things spake Jesus unto the multitude in parables; and without a parable spake He not unto them: that it might be fulfilled which was spoken by the prophet, saying, I will open my mouth in parables; I will utter things which have been kept secret from the foundation of the world. Then Jesus sent the multitude away, and went into the house: and His disciples came unto Him, saying, Declare unto us the parable of the tares of the field. He answered and said unto them, He that soweth the good seed is the Son of Man; the field is the world; the good seed are the children of the Kingdom; but the tares are the children of the wicked one." Now let our readers mark the expression—"the field is the world, the tares are the children of the wicked one, the enemy that sowed them is the devil, the harvest is the end of the world, [let them carefully mark this expression—the end of the world] and the reapers are the angels."

meal, until the whole was leavened. It may be understood that the church of the Latter Day Saints, has taken its rise from a little leaven that was put into three witnesses. Behold, how much this is like the parable: it is fast leavening the lump, and will soon leaven the whole. But let us pass on.

All these things spake Jesus unto the multitudes, in parables, and without a parable spake he not unto them, that it might be fulfilled which was spoken by the prophet, saying: I will open my mouth in parables: I will utter things which have been kept secret from the foundation of the world: Then Jesus sent the multitude away and went into the house, and his disciples came unto him, saying, declare unto us the parable of the tares of the field. He answered and said unto them, he that soweth the good seed is the son of man; the field is the world; the good seed are the children of the kingdom, but the tares are the children of the wicked one. Now let our readers mark the expression, the field is the world; the tares are the children of the wicked one: the enemy that sowed them is the devil; the harvest is the end of the world. Let them carefully mark **[p.229]** this expression also, the end of the world, and the reapers are the angels.[82]

Destruction of the Wicked the End of the World

Messenger and Advocate

Now men cannot have any possible grounds to say that this is figurative, or that it does not mean what it says: for He **[p.101]** is now explaining what He had previously spoken in parables; and according to this language, the end of the world is the destruction of the wicked, the harvest and the end of the world have no allusion directly to the human family in the last days, instead of the earth, as many have imagined; and that which shall precede the coming of the Son of Man, and the restitution of all things spoken of by the mouth of all the

Now men cannot have any possible grounds to say that this is figurative, or that it does not mean what it says; for he is now explaining what he had previously spoken in parables; and according to this language, the end of the world is the destruction of the wicked; the harvest and the end of the world have an allusion directly to the human family in the last days, instead of the earth, as many have imagined, and that which shall precede the coming of the Son of man, and the restitution of all things spoken of by the mouth of all the holy

---

82. *M&A* 2, no. 3 (December 1835): 228–29.

holy prophets since the world began; and the angels are to have something to do in this great work, for they are the reapers. As, therefore, the tares are gathered and burned in the fire, so shall it be in the end of the world; that is, as the servants of God go forth warning the nations, both priests and people, and as they harden their hearts and reject the light of truth, these first being delivered over to the buffetings of Satan, and the law and the testimony being closed up, as it was in the case of the Jews, they are left in darkness, and delivered over unto the day of burning; thus being bound up by their creeds, and their bands being made strong by their priests, are prepared for the fulfilment of the saying of the Savior—"The Son of Man shall send forth His angels, and gather out of His Kingdom all things that offend, and them which do iniquity, and shall cast them into a furnace of fire, there shall be wailing and gnashing of teeth." We understand that the work of gathering together of the wheat into barns, or garners, is to take place while the tares are being bound over, and preparing for the day of burning; that after the day of burnings, the righteous shall shine forth like the sun, in the Kingdom of their Father. Who hath ears to hear, let him hear.

prophets since the world began; and the angels are to have something to do in this great work, for they are the reapers: as therefore the tares are gathered and burned in the fire, so shall it be in the end of this world; that is, as the servants of God go forth warning the nations, both priests and people, and as they harden their hearts and reject the light of the truth, these first being delivered over unto the buffetings of satan, and the law and the testimony being closed up, as it was with the Jews, they are left in darkness, and delivered over unto the day of burning: thus being bound up by their creeds and their bands made strong by their *priests*, are prepared for the fulfilment of the saying of the Savior: the Son of man shall send forth his angels, and gather out of his kingdom all things that of fend, and them which do iniquity, and shall cast them into a furnace of fire and there shall be wailing and gnashing of teeth. We understand, that the work of the gathering together of the wheat into barns, or garners, is to take place while the tares are being bound over, and preparing for the day of burning: that after the day of burnings, the righteous shall shine forth like the sun, in the kingdom of their Father: who hath ears to hear let him hear.[83]

The Treasure Hid in a Field

Messenger and Advocate

But to illustrate more clearly this gathering: We have another parable—"Again, the Kingdom of Heaven is like a treasure hid in a field, the which, when a man hath found, he hideth, and for joy thereof, goeth and selleth all that he hath, and buyeth that field!" The Saints work after this pattern. See the Church of the Latter-day Saints, selling all that they have, and gathering themselves together unto a place that they may purchase for an inheritance, that they may be together and bear each other's afflictions in the day of calamity.

But to illustrate more clearly upon this gathering, we have another parable. Again the kingdom of heaven is like a treasure hid in a field, the which when a man hath found, he hideth and for joy thereof, goeth and selleth all that he hath and buyeth that field; for the work after this pattern, see the church of the Latter Day Saints, selling all that they have and gathering themselves together unto a place tha[t] they may purchase for an inheritance, that they may be together and bear each other's afflictions in the day of calamity.

---

83. *M&A* 2, no. 3 (December 1835): 229.

"Again, the Kingdom of Heaven is like unto a merchantman seeking goodly pearls, who, when he had found one pearl of [p.102] great price, went and sold all that he had, and bought it." The Saints again work after this example. See men traveling to find places for Zion and her stakes or remnants, who, when they find the place for Zion, or the pearl of great price, straightway sell that they have, and buy it.

Again the kingdom of heaven is like unto a merchant man seeking goodly pearls, who when he had found one pearl of great price, went and sold all that he had, and bought it. For the work of this example, see men travelling to find places for Zion, and her stakes or remnants, who when they find the place for Zion, or the pearl of great price; straitway sell all that they have and buy it.[84]

The Net Cast in the Sea

Messenger and Advocate

"Again, the Kingdom of Heaven is like unto a net that was cast into the sea, and gathered of every kind, which when it was full they drew to shore, and sat down, and gathered the good into vessels, but cast the bad away." For the work of this pattern, behold the seed of Joseph, spreading forth the Gospel net upon the face of the earth, gathering of every kind, that the good may be saved in vessels prepared for that purpose, and the angels will take care of the bad. So shall it be at the end of the world—the angels shall come forth and sever the wicked from among the just, and cast them into the furnace of fire, and there shall be wailing and gnashing of teeth.

Again the kingdom of heaven is like unto a net that was cast into the sea, and gathered of every kind, which when it was full they drew to shore, and sat down and gathered the good into vessels, and cast the bad away.— For the work of this pattern, behold the seed of Joseph, spreading forth the gospel net, upon the face of the earth, gathering of every kind, that the good may be saved in vessels prepared for that purpose, and the angels will take care of the bad: so shall it be at the end of the world, the angels shall come forth, and sever the wicked from among the just, and cast them into the furnace of fire, and there shall be wailing and gnashing of teeth.

"Jesus saith unto them, Have ye understood all these things? They say unto Him, Yea, Lord." And we say, yea, so plain and so glorious, that every Saint in that last days must respond with a hearty Amen to them.

Jesus saith unto them, have you understood all these things? they say unto him yea Lord: and we say yea Lord, and well might they say yea Lord, for these things are so plain and so glorious, that every Saint in the last days must respond with a hearty amen to them.

"Then said He unto them, therefore every scribe which is instructed in the kingdom of heaven, is like unto a man that is an householder, which bringeth forth out of his treasure things that are new and old."

Then said he unto them, therefore every scribe which is instructed into the kingdom of heaven, is like unto a man that is an house holder; which bringeth forth out of his treasure things that are new and old.

For the works of this example, see the Book of Mormon coming forth out of the treasure

For the work of this example, see the book of Mormon, coming forth out of the treasure

---

84. *M&A* 2, no. 3 (December 1835): 229.

of the heart. Also the covenants given to the Latter-day Saints, also the translation of the Bible—thus bringing forth out of the heart things new and old, thus answering to three measures of meal undergoing the purifying touch by a revelation of Jesus Christ, and the ministering of angels, who have already commenced this work in the last days, which will answer to the leaven which leavened the whole lump. Amen

So I close, but shall continue the subject in another number.

In the bonds of the New and Everlasting Covenant,
JOSEPH SMITH, JUN.
—Messenger and Advocate, Dec. 1835, also DHC 2:264-272.

of the heart; also the covenants given to the Latter Day Saints: also the translation of the bible: thus bringing forth out of the heart, things new and old: thus answering to three measures of meal, undergoing the purifying touch by a revelation of Jesus Christ, and the ministering of angels, who have already commenced this work in the last days, which will answer to the leaven which leavened the whole lump. Amen

[p.230] So I close but shall continue the subject in another number.

In the bonds of the new and everlasting covenant.
JOSEPH SMITH, jr.
To J[OHN] WHITMER Esq.[85]

False Doctrines of Joshua the Jewish Minister

[p.103] While sitting in my house, between ten and eleven this morning, a man came in and introduced himself to me by the name of "Joshua, the Jewish Minister." His appearance was something singular, having a beard about three inches in length, quite grey; also his hair was long and considerably silvered with age; I thought him about fifty or fifty-five years old; tall, straight, slender built, of thin visage, blue eyes, and fair complexion; wore a sea-green frock coat and pantaloons, black fur hat with narrow brim; and, while speaking, frequently shut his eyes, with a scowl on his countenance. I made some inquiry after his name, but received no definite answer. We soon commenced talking on the subject of religion, and, after I had made some remarks concerning the Bible, I commenced giving him a relation of the circumstances connected with

Joseph Smith's Journal

while setting in my house between the hours of nine <ten> and 10 11 this morning a man came in, and introduced himself to me, calling <himself> self <by the name of> Joshua the Jewish minister, his appearance was some what <thing> singular, having a beard about 3 inches in length which is quite grey, also his hair is long and considerably silvered with age I should think he is about 50 or 55 years old, tall and strait slender built of thin visage blue eyes, and fair complexion, he wears a sea green frock coat, & pantaloons of the same, black fur hat with narrow brim, and while speaking frequently shuts his eyes, with a scowl on his countinance; I made some enquiry after his name but received no definite answer; we soon commenced talking upon the subject of religion and after I had made some remarks concerning the bible I commenced giving him a relation of

---

85. *M&A* 2, no. 3 (December 1835): 229–30. This letter was the third in a series of three letters written by Joseph and published in the September, November, and December issues of the *Messenger and Advocate*.

the coming forth of the Book of Mormon, as recorded in the former part of this history.

While I was relating a brief history of the establishment of the Church of Christ in the last days, Joshua seemed to be highly entertained. When I had closed my narration, I observed that the hour of worship and dinner had arrived, and invited him to tarry, to which he consented. After dinner, the conversation was resumed, and Joshua proceeded to make some remarks on the prophecies, as follows—he observed that he was aware that I could bear stronger meat than many others, therefore he should open his mind the more freely:

Daniel has told us that he is to stand in his proper lot, in the latter days; according to his vision he had a right to shut it up, and also to open it again after many days, or in latter times. Daniel's image, whose head was gold, and body, arms, legs and feet, were composed of the different materials described in his vision, represents different governments. The golden head was to represent Nebuchadnezzar, King of Babylon; the other parts, other kings and forms of governments which I shall not now mention in detail, but confine my remarks more particularly to the feet of the image. The policy of the wicked spirit is to separate what God has joined together, and unite what He has separated, which the devil has succeeded in doing to admiration in the present society, which is like unto iron and clay.

[p.104] There is confusion in all things, both political and religious; and notwithstanding all the efforts that are made to bring about a union, society remains disunited, and all attempts to unite it are as fruitless as to attempt to unite iron and clay. The feet of the image are the government of these United States. Other nations and kingdoms are looking up to her for an example of union, freedom, and

the circumstances connected with the coming forth of the book of Mormon, as follows—[86]

[p.92] While I was relating this brief history of the establishment of the Church of Christ in these last days, Joshua seemed to be highly entertained after I had got through I observed that, the hour of worship & time to dine had now arived and invited him to tarry, which he concented to, After dinner the conversation was resumed and Joshua proceded to make some remarks on the prophesies, as follows: He observed that he was aware that I could bear stronger meat than many others, therefore he should open his mind the more freely;—

Daniel has told us that he is to stand in his proper lot, in the latter days according to his vision he had a right to shut it up and also to open it again after many days, or in the latter times; Daniels Image whose head was gold, and body, armes, legs and feet was composed of the different materials described in his vision represents different governments, the golden head was <to represent> Nebuchodnazer King of Babylon, the other parts other kings & forms of government, which I shall not now mention in detail, but confine my remarks, more particularly to the feet of the Image; The policy of the wicked spirit, is to separate what God has joined togather and unite what He has separated, which he has succeded in doing to admiration, in the present state of society, which is like unto Iron and clay,

there is confusion in all things, both both Political and religious, and notwithstanding all the efforts that are made to bring about a union, society is remains disunited, and all attempts to <unite her> are as fruitless, as to attemp to unite Iron & Clay. The feet of the Image, is the government of these united States, other Nations & kingdoms are looking up to her for an example, of union fredom and equal rights,

---

86. 9–11 November 1835, *JSP, J1*, 87. See also See also *JSP, D5*, 42. At this point in the journal, an account of the First Vision and the visitation of Moroni are recorded.

equal rights, and therefore worship her as Daniel saw in the vision; although they are beginning to lose confidence in her, seeing the broils and discord that rise on her political and religious horizon. The image is characteristic of all governments.

We should leave Babylon. Twenty-four hours of improvement now, are worth as much as a year a hundred years ago. The spirits of the fathers that were cut down, or those that were under the altar, are now rising; this is the first resurrection. The Elder that falls first will rise last. We should not form any opinion only for the present, and leave the result of futurity with God. I have risen up out of obscurity, but was looked up to in temporal things when but a youth. It is not necessary that God should give us all things in His first commission to us, but in His second. John saw the angel deliver the Gospel in the last days. The small lights that God has given are sufficient to lead us out of Babylon; when we get out, we shall have the greater light.

and therefore worship her, like as Daniel saw in the vision, although they are beginning to loose confidence in her, seeing the broils and discord that distract, her political & religious horizon this Image is characteristic of all governments and institutions or most of them; as they begin with a head of gold and terminate in the contemptible feet of Iron & clay: making a splendid appearance at first, proposing to do much more than the[y] can perform, and finally end in degradation and sink, in infamy; we should not only **[p.93]** start to come out of Babylon but leav it entirely lest we are overthrown in her ruins, we should keep improving and reforming, twenty-fours hours for improvement now is worth as much as a year a hundred years ago; the spirit of the Fathers that was cut down, or those that were under the altar, are now rising this is the first resurection the Elder that fall's first will rise last; we should not form any opinion only for the present, and leave the result of futurity with God: I have risen up out of obscurity, but was look^d. up to when but a youth, in temporal things: It is not necessary that God should give us all things at first or in his first commission to us, but in his second. John saw the angel deliver the gospel in the last days, which would not be necessary if it was already in the world this expression would be inconsistent, the small lights that God has given, is sufficient to lead us out of babylon, when we get out we shall have the greater light.[87]

Transmigration a Doctrine of the Devil

Joseph Smith's Journal

I told Joshua I did not understand his remarks on the resurrection, and wished him to explain. He replied that he did not feel impressed by the Spirit to unfold it further at present, but perhaps he might at some future time.

[p.93] I told Johua that I did not understand him concerning the resurection and wishd him to be more explanitory on the subject; he replied that he did not feell impressed by the spirit to unfold it further at present, but perhaps he might at some other time.

---

87. 9–11 November 1835, *JSP, J1*, 92–93. See also *JSP, D5*, 44–46.

I then withdrew to transact some business with a gentleman who had called to see me, when Joshua informed my scribe that he was born in Cambridge, Washington County, New York. He says that all the railroads, canals, and other improvements are projected by the spirits of the resurrection. The silence spoken of by John the Revelator, which is to be in heaven for the space of half an hour, is between 1830 and 1851, during which time the judgments of God will be poured out, after that time there will be peace.

* * *

Suspicions were entertained that the said Joshua was the noted Matthias of New York, spoken so much of in the public **[p.105]** prints, on account of the trials he endured in that place, before a court of justice, for murder, man-slaughter, contempt of court, whipping his daughter, etc.; for that last two crimes he was imprisoned and came out about four months since. After some equivocating, he confessed that he really was Matthias.

After supper I proposed that he should deliver a lecture to us. He did so, sitting in his chair.

He commenced by saying, God said, let there by light, and there was light, which he dwelt upon throughout his discourse. He made some very excellent remarks, but his mind was evidently filled with darkness.

* * *

I resumed conversation with Matthias, and desired him to enlighten my mind more on his views respecting the resurrection.

He said that he possessed the spirit of his fathers, that he was a literal descendant of Matthias, the Apostle, who was chosen in the place of Judas that fell; that his spirit was

I then withdrew to do some buisness with another gentleman that called to see me. He [Robert Matthews] informed my Scribe that he was born in Washington County Town of Cambridge New York. he says that all the railroads canals and other improvements are performed by spirits of the resurecion. The silence spoken of by John the Revelator which is to be in heaven for the space of half an hour, is between 1830 & 1851, during which time the judgments of God will be poured out after that time there will be peace.

Curiosity to see a man that was reputed to be a jew caused many to call during the day and more particularly at evening suspicions were entertained that said Joshua was the noted Mathias of New York, spoken so much of in the public prints on account of the trials he underwent in that place before a court of justice, for murder manslaughter comtempt of court whiping his Daughter [p.95[88]] &c for the two last crimes he was imprisoned, and came out about 4, months since, after some, equivocating he confessed that he was realy Mathias:

after supper I proposed that he should deliver a lecture to us, he did so sitting in his chair;

he commenced by saying God said let there be light and there was light, which he dwelt upon through his discource, he made some verry exelent remarks but his mind was evidently filled with darkness,

* * *

the next morning Tuesday 10th I resumed the conversation and desired him to enlighten my mind more on his views respecting the resuretion,

he says that he poss[ess]es the spirit of his fathers, that he is a litteral decendant of Mathias the Apostle that was chosen in the place of Judas that fell and that his spirit is resurected

---

88. Page 94 contains an image.

resurrected in him; and that this was the way or scheme of eternal life—this transmigration of soul or spirit from father to son.

I told him that his doctrine was of the devil, that he was in reality in possession of a wicked and depraved spirit, although he professed to be the Spirit of truth itself; and he said also that he possessed the soul of Christ.

He tarried until Wednesday, 11th, when, after breakfast, I told him, that my God told me, that his god was the devil, and I could not keep him any longer, and he must depart. And so I, for once, cast out the devil in bodily shape, and I believe a murderer. (Nov. 9, 1835.) DHC 2:304-307.

in him, and that this is the way or scheme of eternal life, this transmigration of soul or spirit from Father to Son:

I told him that his doctrine was of the Devil that he was in reality in possession of wicked and depraved spirit, although he professed to be the spirit of truth, it self, also that he possesses the soul of Christ;

he tarried until Wednesday 11.th, after breckfast I told him, that my God told me that his God is the Devil, and I could not keep him any longer, and he must depart, and so I for once cast out the Devil in bodily shape, & I believe a murderer[89]

Authority of the Twelve

From the minutes of a special meeting with the Twelve Apostles.
President Smith next proceeded to explain the duty of the Twelve, and their authority, which is next to the present Presidency, and that the arrangement of the assembly in this place, on the 15th instant, in placing the High Councils of Kirtland next the Presidency, was because the business to be transacted, was business relating to that body in particular, which was to fill the several quorums in Kirtland, not because they were first in office, and that the arrangements were the most judicious that could be made on the occasion; also the **[p.106]** Twelve are not subject to any other than the First Presidency, viz., "myself," said the Prophet, "Sidney Rigdon, and Frederick G. Williams, who are now my Counselors, and where I am not, there is no First Presidency over the Twelve."[90]

The Prophet also stated to the Twelve that he did not countenance the harsh language of the President Cowdery to them, neither would

Joseph Smith's Journal
I next proceeded to explain the subject of the duty of the twelve; and their authority which is next to the present presidency, and that the arangement of the assembly in this place on the 15 inst / in placing the high councils of Kirtland ~~and~~ next [to] the presidency was because the buisness to be transacted was buisness that related to that body in particular which was to fill the several quorum's in Kirtland; not beca[u]se they were first in office, and that the arangement was most Judicious that could be made on the occasion also the 12, are not subject to any other than the first presidency; viz. myself S. Rigdon and F G. Williams—

I also stated to the 12, that I do not ~~continue~~ countinance the harsh language of President Cowdery to them neither in myself nor any

---

89. 9–11 November 1835, *JSP, J1*, 93, 95. See also *JSP, D5*, 46–47.

90. The statement "where I am not, there is no First Presidency over the Twelve" is not in the journal entry, but appears to have been added later in History, B-1, 691.

he countenance it in himself nor in any other man, "although," said he, "I have sometimes spoken too harshly from the impulse of the moment, and inasmuch as I have wounded your feelings, brethren, I ask your forgiveness, for I love you and will hold you up with all my heart in all righteousness, before the Lord, and before all men; for be assured, brethren, I am willing to stem the torrent of all opposition, in storms and in tempests, in thunders and in lightnings, by sea and by land, in the wilderness or among false brethren, or mobs, or wherever God in His providence may call us. And I am determined that neither heights nor depths, principalities nor powers, things present or things to come, or any other creature, shall separate me from you. And I will now covenant with you before God, that I will not listen to or credit any derogatory report against any of you, nor condemn you upon any testimony beneath the heavens, short of that testimony which is infallible, until I can see you face to face, and know of a surety; and I do place unremitted confidence in your word, for I believe you to be men of truth. And I ask the same of you, when I tell you anything, that you place equal confidence in my word, for I will not tell you I know anything that I do not know. But I have already consumed more time than I intended when I commenced, and I will now give way to my colleagues." (January 16, 1836.) DHC 2:373-374.

other man, although I have sometimes spoken to[o] harsh from the impulse of the moment and inasmuch as I have wounded your feelings **[p.159]** brethren I ask your forgivness, for I love you and will hold you up with all my heart in all righteousness before the Lord, and before all men, for be assured brethren I am willing to stem the torrent of all opposition; in storms in tempests in thunders and lightning by sea and by land in the wilderness or among fals brethren, or mobs or wherever God in his providence may call us and I am determined that neither hights nor depths principalities nor powers things present or to come nor any other creature shall separate me from you; and I will now covenant with you before God that I will not listen too nor credit, any derogatory report against any of you nor condemn you upon any testimony beneath the heavens, short of that testimony which is infalible, untill I can see you face to face and know of a surity and I do place unlimited confidence in your word for I believe you to be men of truth, and I ask the same of you, when I tell you any thing that you place equal confidence in my word for I will not tell you I know anything which I do not know— but I have already consumed more time than I intended to when I commenced and I will now give way to my colleagues.[91]

Vision of the Celestial Kingdom

On the twenty-first day of January, 1836, the First Presidency, and a number of the presiding brethren in the Church, assembled in the Kirtland Temple where they engaged in the ordinances of the endowment, as far as it had at that time been revealed. After this was done the Prophet states that

Joseph Smith's Journal

At about 3, oclock P.M I dismissed the School and the presidency; retired to the loft of the printing office, where we attended to the ordinance of washing our bodies in pure water, we also perfumed our bodies and our heads, in **[p.167]** the name of the Lord at early candle-light, I meet with the presidency, at the west school room in the Chapel to attend to the ordinance of annointing our heads with holy

---

91. 16 January 1836, *JSP, J1*, 158–59. See also *JSP, D5*, 152–53.

oil— also the councils of ~~Zion~~ Kirtland and Zion, meet in the two adjoining rooms, who waited in prayer while we attended to the ordinance,— I took the oil in my <left> ~~right~~ hand, father Smith being seated before me and the rest of the presidency encircled him round about,— we then streched our right hands to heaven and blessed the oil and concecrated it in the name of Jesus Christ— we then laid our hands on, our aged fath[er] Smith, and invoked, the blessings of heaven,— I then annointed his head with the concecrated oil, and sealed many blessings upon ~~his~~ <him,> ~~head,~~ the presidency then in turn, laid their hands upon his head, beginning at the eldest, untill they had all laid their hands on him, and pronounced such blessings, upon his head as the Lord put into their hearts— all blessing him to be our patraark [patriarch], ~~and~~ <to> annoint our heads, and attend to all duties that pertain to ~~this~~ <that> office.— I then took the seat, and father annoint[ed] my head, and sealed upon me, the blessings, of Moses, to lead Israel in the latter days, even as moses led ~~them~~ <him> in days of old,— also the blessings of Abraham Isaac and Jacob,—[92]

"All of the Presidency laid their hands upon me, and pronounced upon my head many prophecies and blessings, many of which I shall not notice at this time." "All of the Presidency" included Oliver Cowdery and Father Joseph Smith as well as the two counselors, Sidney Rigdon and Frederick G. Williams. Following this ordinance the following vision and revelation were given to the Prophet, making known to him and through him to the [p.107] Church one of the most important principles pertaining to the salvation of men.

all of the presidency laid their hands upon me and pronounced upon my head many prophecies, and blessings, many of which I shall not notice at this time, but as Paul said, so say I, let us come to vissions and revelations, ~~the~~—

The heavens were opened upon us, and I beheld the celestial kingdom of God, and the glory thereof, whether in the body or out I cannot tell. I saw the transcendent beauty of

The heavens were opened upon us and I beheld the celestial kingdom of God, and the glory thereof, whether in the body or out I cannot tell,— I saw the transcendant beauty of

---

92. Joseph Fielding Smith appears to have taken the portion of this entry dealing with washing and anointing to create the introduction to this section.

the gate through which the heirs of that kingdom will enter, which was like unto circling flames of fire; also the blazing throne of God, whereon was seated the Father and the Son. I saw the beautiful streets of that kingdom, which had the appearance of being paved with gold. I saw Father Adam and Abraham, and my father and my mother, my brother, Alvin, that has long since slept, and marvelled how it was that he had obtained an inheritance in that kingdom, seeing that he had departed this life before the Lord had set his hand to gather Israel the second time, and had not been baptized for the remission of sins.

the gate that enters, through which the heirs of that kingdom will enter, which was like unto circling flames of fire, also the blasing throne of God, whereon was seated the Father and the Son,— I saw the beautiful streets of that kingdom, which had the appearance of being paved with gold— I saw father Adam, and Abraham and Michael [**p.168**] and my father and mother, my brother Alvin [Smith] that has long since slept, and marvled how it was that he had obtained this an inheritance <in> this <that> kingdom, seeing that he had departed this life, before the Lord <had> set his hand to gather Israel <the second time> and had not been baptized for the remission of sins—

Thus came the voice of the Lord unto me, saying–

Thus said came the voice <of the Lord un>to me saying[93]

Revelation

Joseph Smith's Journal

All who have died without a knowledge of this Gospel, who would have received it if they had been permitted to tarry, shall be heirs of the celestial kingdom of God; also all that shall die henceforth without a knowledge of it, who would have received it with all their hearts, shall be heirs of that kingdom, for I, the Lord, will judge all men according to their works, according to the desire of their hearts. And I also behold that all children who die before they arrive at the years of accountability are saved in the celestial kingdom of heaven.— DHC 2:380-381.

all who have died with[out] a knowledge of this gospel, who would have received it, if they had been permited to tarry, shall be heirs of the celestial kingdom of God— also all that shall die henseforth, with<out> a knowledge of it, who would have received it, with all their hearts, shall be heirs of that kingdom, for I the Lord <will> judge all men according to their works according to the desires of their hearts— and again I also beheld the Terrestial kingdom I also beheld that all children who die before they arive to the years of accountability, are saved in the celestial kingdom of heaven—[94]

Vision of the Apostles

Joseph Smith's Journal

I saw the Twelve Apostles of the Lamb, who are now upon the earth, who hold the keys of this last ministry, in foreign lands, standing together in a circle, much fatigued, with

I saw the 12, apostles of the Lamb, who are now upon the earth who hold the keys of this last ministry, in foreign lands, standing together in a circle much fatiegued, with their

---

93. 21 January 1836, *JSP, J1*, 166–68. See also *JSP, D5*, 158–59.

94. 21 January 1836, *JSP, J1*, 168. A portion of this revelation is now found in section 137 of the Doctrine and Covenants. See also *JSP, D5*, 159.

their clothes tattered and feet swollen, with their eyes cast downward, and Jesus standing in their midst, and they did not behold Him. The Savior looked upon them and wept. (January 21, 1836.) DHC 2:381.

clothes tattered and feet swolen, with their eyes cast downward, and Jesus <standing> in their midst, and they did not behold him, ~~he~~ the Saviour looked upon them and wept—[95]

The Prophet's Vision of the Twelve

Joseph Smith's Journal

[p.108] I also behold Elder M'Lellin in the south, standing upon a hill, surrounded by a vast multitude, preaching to them, and a lame man standing before him supported by his crutches; he threw them down at his word and leaped as a hart, by the mighty power of God. Also, I saw Elder Brigham Young standing in a strange land, in the far south and west, in a desert place, upon a rock in the midst of about a dozen men of color, who appeared hostile. He was preaching to them in their own tongue, and the angel of God standing above his head, with a drawn sword in his hand, protecting him, but he did not see it. And I finally saw the Twelve in the celestial kingdom of God. I also beheld the redemption of Zion, and many things which the tongue of men cannot describe in full. (Jan. 21, 1836.) DHC 2:381.

I also beheld Elder McLellen [William E. McLellin] in the south, standing upon a hill surrounded with a vast multitude, preaching to them, and a lame man standing before him, supported by his crutches, he threw them down at his word, and leaped as an heart [hart] by the mighty power of God Also Eldr Brigham Young standing in a strange land, in the far south west, in a desert place, upon a rock in the midst of about a dozen men of colour, who, appeared hostile He was preaching to them in their own toung, and the angel of God standing above his head with a drawn sword in his hand protecting him, but he did not see it,— and I finally saw the 12 in the celestial kingdom of God,— I also beheld the redemption of Zion, and many things which the toung of man, cannot discribe in full,—[96]

The Prophet's Draft of Resolutions

Joseph Smith's Journal

First. Resolved—That no one be ordained to any office in the Church in this stake of Zion, at Kirtland, without the unanimous voice of the several bodies that constitute this quorum, who are appointed to do Church business in the name of said Church, viz., the Presidency of the Church; the Twelve Apostles of the Lamb; the twelve High Councilors of Zion; the Bishop of Kirtland and his counselors; the Bishop of Zion and his counselors; and the seven presidents of Seventies; until otherwise ordered by said quorums.

1st— Resolved. that no one be ordained to any office in the church in this stake of Zion at Kirtland without the unanimous voice of the several ~~quorums~~ bodies that constitute this quorum who are appointed to do church buisness in the name of the said church— viz the presidency of the church & council the 12, apostles of the Lamb the 12 high counsellors of Kirtland the 12, high counsellors of Zion, the Bishop of Kirtland & his counsellors the Bishop of Zion and his counsellors— the 7. presidents of Seventies; untill otherwise ordered by the said quorums.—

---

95. 21 January 1836, *JSP, J1*, 168. See also *JSP, D5*, 159.
96. 21 January 1836, *JSP, J1*, 168. See also *JSP, D5*, 159.

Section Two: 1834–1837 [*TPJS* 109] 137

Second. And further Resolved—That no one be ordained in the branches of said Church abroad, unless they are recommended by the voice of the respective branches of the Church to which they belong, to a general conference appointed by the heads of the Church, and from that conference receive their ordination. The foregoing resolutions were concurred in by the presidents of the Seventies. (Feb. 12, 1836.) DHC 2:394.

2ond— and further resolved that no one be ordained in the branches of said church abroad unless they are recommended by the ~~church~~ voice of ~~that~~ <the> respective branches of the church to which they belong, to a general conference appointed by the heads of the church, and from that conference receive their ordination.—[97]

Evils of Intemperance

Joseph Smith's Journal

I was informed today that a man by the name of Clark, who was under the influence of ardent spirits froze to death last night, near this place. How long, O Lord, will this monster intemperance find its victims on the earth! I fear until the [p.109] earth is swept with the wrath and indignation of God, and Christ's kingdom becomes universal. O, come, Lord Jesus, and cut short Thy work in righteousness. (March 12, 1836.) DHC 2:406.

I was informed to day that a man by the name of Clark froze to death, last night near this place, who was under the influenc of ardent spirits; O my God how long will this monster intemperance find it's victims on the earth, me thinks until the earth is swept with the wrath ~~of~~ and indignation of God, and christ's kingdom becomes universal. O come Lord Jesus and cut short thy work in rightieousness.[98]

The Twelve as Revelators

Joseph Smith's Journal

I then called upon the quorums and congregation of Saints to acknowledge the Twelve Apostles, who were present, as Prophets, Seers, Revelators, and special witnesses to all the nations of the earth, holding the keys of the kingdom, to unlock it, or cause it to be done, among them, and uphold them by their prayers, which they assented to by rising. (March 27, 1836.) DHC 2:417.

I then called upon the quorums and congregation of saints to acknowledge the 12 Apostles who were present as Prophets and Seers and special witnesses to all the nations of the earth, holding the keys of the kingdom, to unlock it or cause it to be done among ~~all nations~~ them; and uphold them by their prayers, which they assented to by rising,[99]

Priesthood and Church Organization

Joseph Smith's Journal

While waiting, [i.e., for preparations for the observance of the Sacrament] I made the

while waiting ~~for the wine~~ I made the following remarks, that the time that we were

---

97. 12 February 1836, *JSP, J1*, 185. See also JPS, D5, 172.
98. 12 March 1836, *JSP, J1*, 196.
99. 27 March 1836, *JSP, J1*, 204.

following remarks: that the time that we were required to tarry in Kirtland to be endowed, would be fulfilled in a few days, and then the Elders would go forth, and each must stand for himself, as it was not necessary for them to be sent out, two by two, as in former times, but to go in all meekness, in sobriety, and preach Jesus Christ and Him crucified; not to contend with others on account of their faith, or systems of religion, but pursue a steady course. This I delivered by way of commandment; and all who observe it not, will pull down persecution upon their heads, while those who do, shall always be filled with the Holy Ghost; this I pronounced as a prophecy, and sealed with hosanna and amen. Also that the Seventies are not called to serve tables, or preside over churches, to settle difficulties, but are to preach the Gospel and build them up, and set others, who do not belong to these quorums, to preside over them, who are High Priests. The Twelve also are not to serve tables, but to bear the keys of the Kingdom to all nations, and unlock the door of the Gospel to them, and call upon the Seventies to follow after them, and assist them. The Twelve are at liberty to go wheresoever they will, and if any one will say, I wish to go to such a place, let all the rest say amen.

required to tarry in Kirtland to be endued would be fulfilled in a few days, and then the Elders would go forth and each must stand for himself, that it was not necessary for them to be sent out two by two as in former times; but to go in all meekness in sobriety and preach Jesus Christ & him crucified not to contend with others on the account [p.215] of their faith or systems of religion but pursue a steady course, this I delivered by way of commandment, and all that observe them not will pull down persecution upon your <thier> heads, while those who do shall always be filled with the Holy Ghost, this I pronounced as a prophesy, sealed with a Hosanna & amen. Also that the seventies are not called to serve tables or preside over churches to settle difficulties, but to preach the gospel and build them up, and set others who do not belong to these quorums to preside over them who are high priests— the twelve also are not to serve tables, but to bear the keys of the kingdom to all nations, and unlock them and call upon the seventies to follow after them and assist them. The 12 are at liberty to go wheresoever they will and if one shall say, I wish to go to such a place let all the rest say Amen.[100]

Revelation of Necessary Ceremonies

Joseph Smith's Journal

The Seventies are at liberty to go to Zion if they please, or go wheresoever they will, and preach the Gospel; and let [p.110] the redemption of Zion be our object, and strive to effect it by sending up all the strength of the Lord's house, wherever we find them; and I want to enter into the following covenant, that if any more of our brethren are slain or driven from their lands in Missouri, by the mob, we will give ourselves no rest, until we are avenged of our enemies to the uttermost. This covenant was sealed unanimously, with hosanna and and amen.

The seventies are at liberty to go to Zion if they please or go wheresoever they will and preach the gospel and let the redemtion of Zion be our object, and strive to affect it by sending up all the strength of the Lords house whereever we find them, and I want to enter into the following covenant, that if any more of our brethren are slain or driven from their lands in Missouri by the mob that we will give ourselves no rest until we are avenged of our enimies to the uttermost, this covenant was sealed unaminously by a hosanna and Amen.—

---

100. 30 March 1836, *JSP, J1*, 214–15. See also *JSP, D5*, 219–20.

I then observed to the quorums, that I had now completed the organization of the Church, and we had passed through all the necessary ceremonies,[101] that I had given them all the instruction they needed, and that they now were at liberty, after obtaining their licenses, to go forth and build up the Kingdom of God, and that it was expedient for me and the Presidency to retire, having spent the night previously in waiting upon the Lord in His Temple, and having to attend another dedication on the morrow, or conclude the one commenced on the last Sabbath, for the benefit of these of my brethren and sisters who could not get into the house on the former occasion, but that it was expedient for the brethren to tarry all night and worship before the Lord in His house. (March 29, 1836.) DHC 2:431–432.

I then observed to the quorums— quorum<s> that I had now completed their organization of the church and we had passed through all the necessary ceremonies, that I had given them all the instruction they needed and that they now were at liberty after obtaining their lisences to go forth and build up the kingdom of God, and that it was expedient for me and the presidency to retire, having spent the night previous in waiting upon the Lord in his temple, and having to attend another dedication on the morrow, or conclude the one commenced on the last sabbath for the benifit of those of my brethren and sisters who could not get into the house on the former occasion but that it was expedient for the brethren to tarry all night and worship before the Lord in his house[102]

High Priests Not to Be Seventies

Messenger and Advocate

At an early hour on Thursday, the 6th of April, the official members assembled in the House of the Lord, when **[p.111]** the time for the first two or three hours was spent by the different quorums in washing of feet, singing, praying,

At an early hour on Thursday, the sixth, the official members assembled in the house of the Lord, where the time, for the first two or three hours was spent by the different quorums in washing of feet, singing, praying and prepar-

---

101. The original *TPJS* footnote reads:

> In speaking here of the completion of the organization of the Church, the Prophet had reference to the organizations of the Priesthood quorums; and the reference to the bestowal of 'all the necessary ceremonies,' and that he had given the brethren 'all the instruction they needed,' had reference to their setting apart and the receiving of all the necessary blessings to enable them to go forth and preach the Gospel in all the world. They were now prepared by instruction and endowment sufficiently to carry the message acceptably to the world. This remark by the Prophet did not have any reference to other ceremonies which were revealed later, as set forth in the Doctrine and Covenants, Section 124, 127, 128 and 132.
>
> In 1834 (see D. and C. 105:33) the Elders who had been preaching the Gospel were instructed to gather at Kirtland and there they were to be endowed. This is the commandment: 'Verily I say unto you, it is expedient in me that the first elders of my church should receive their endowment from on high in my house, which I have commanded to be built unto my name in the land of Kirtland.' In the month of March, 1836, these endowment ceremonies were given. These ceremonies were not as complete as are the endowment ceremonies given in the Church today, but they were sufficient for the needs of that time and in keeping with the commandment of the Lord herein stated.

102. 30 March 1836, *JSP, J1*, 215. See also *JSP, D5*, 220–21. *TPJS* has this entry dated 29 March 1836, but the Joseph Smith Papers dates this journal entry to 30 March 1836. Although not included in the original *TPJS* this journal entry records "the Saviour made his appearance to some, while angels minestered unto others, and it was a penticost and enduement indeed, long to be remembered."

and preparing to receive instructions from the Presidency. The Presidents, together with the Seventies and their presidents, repaired to the west room in the attic story, where, for want of time the preceding evening, it became necessary to seal the anointing of those who had recently been anointed and not sealed.

Another subject of vital importance to the Church, was the establishing of the grades of the different quorums. It was ascertained that all but one or two of the presidents of the Seventies were High Priests, and when they had ordained and set apart any from the quorum of Elders, into the quorum of Seventies, they had conferred upon them the High Priesthood also. This was declared to be wrong, and not according to the order of heaven. New presidents of the Seventies were accordingly ordained to fill the places of such of them as were High Priests, and the ex-officio presidents, and such of the Seventies as had been legally ordained to be High Priests, were directed to unite with the High Priests' quorum. (April 6, 1837.) DHC 2:475-476.

ing to receive instruction from the Presidents of the church. The Presidents, together with the Seventies and their presidents repaired to the west room in the attic story, where, for want of time the preceding evening, it be came necessary to seal the anointing of those who had recently been anointed and not sealed.

Another subject of vital importance to the church, was the establshing of the grades of the different quorums.— It was ascertained that all but one, of the presidents of the seventies, were high priests and when they had ordained and set apart from the quorum of elders, into the quorum of seventies, they had confered upon them the high-priesthood also: this was declared to be wrong, and not according to the order of heaven. New presidents of the sev[p.487]enties were accordingly ordained to fill the place of such of them as were high priests, and the *ex officio* presidents and such of the seventies as had been legally ordained to the high priesthood, were directed to unite with the quorum of high priests.[103]

Instruction on Priesthood

A solemn assembly of the official members of the Church was held in the Kirtland Temple commencing Monday, April 3rd, and continuing each day until Thursday the 6th. On the latter day, after these official members had received their endowment as far as it was revealed in the Kirtland Temple, the Prophet addressed them on many subjects, a synopsis of which in relation to the Priesthood he recorded in his journal as follows—[104]

How and By Whom Revelation Comes

Messenger and Advocate

President Joseph Smith, Jun., addressed the assembly and said, the Melchizedek High

Joseph Smith jr. rose and spoke on the subject of the Priesthood. The Melchisidec High

---

103. *M&A* 3, no. 7 (April 1837): 486–87.
104. This introductory paragraph was authored by Joseph Fielding Smith.

Priesthood was no other than the Priesthood of the Son of God; that there are certain ordinances which belong to the Priesthood, from which flow certain results; and the Presidents or Presidency are over the Church; and revelations of the mind and will of God to the Church, are to come through the Presidency. This is the order of heaven, and the power and privilege of this Priesthood. It is also the privilege of any officer in this Church to obtain revelations, so far as relates to his particular calling and duty in the Church.

All are bound by the principles of virtue and happiness, but one great privilege of the Priesthood is to obtain revelations of the [p.112] mind and will of God. It is also the privilege of the Melchizedek Priesthood, to reprove, rebuke, and admonish, as well as to receive revelation. If the Church knew all the commandments, one-half they would condemn through prejudice and ignorance.

priesthood, he said was no other than the priesthood of the son of God. There are certain ordinances which belong to the priesthood, and certain results flow from it. The presidents, or presidency are over the church, and revelations of the mind and will of God to the church are to come through the presidency. This is the order of heaven and the power and privilege of this priesthood. It is also the privilege of any officer in this church, to obtain revelations so far as relates to his particular calling or duty in the church.

All are bound by the principles of virtue and happiness, but one great privilege of this priesthood is to obtain revelations, as before observed, of the mind and will of God. It is also the privilege of the Melchisedec priesthood, to reprove, rebuke and admonish, as well as to receive revelations. Here he remarked something con-concerning the will of God, and said, that what God commanded, the one half of the church would condemn.[105]

<If the church knew all the commandments they would condemn> What commands, one half the Church will condemn, through ignorance and prejudice.[106]

Offices in the Priesthood

Messenger and Advocate

A High Priest is a member of the same Melchizedek Priesthood with the Presidency, but not of the same power or authority in the Church. The Seventies are also members of the same priesthood, [i.e., the High Priesthood], are a sort of traveling council or Priesthood, and may preside over a church or churches, until a High Priest can be had. The Seventies are to be taken from the quorum of Elders, and are not to be High Priests. They are subject to the direction and dictation of

A high Priest, is a member of the same Melchisedec priesthood, with the presidency, but not of the same power or authority in the church. The seventies are also members of the same priesthood, are a sort of travelling council, or priesthood, and may preside over a church or churches until a high priest can be had. The seventies are to be taken from the quorum of elders and are not to be high priests. They are subjebt to the direction and dictation of, the twelve, who have the keys of

---

105. *M&A* 3, no. 7 (April 1837): 487.
106. This sentence is not in the *Messenger and Advocate* article, but appears to have been added to History, B-1, 756.

the Twelve, who have the keys of the ministry. All are to preach the Gospel, by the power and influence of the Holy Ghost; and no man can preach the Gospel without the Holy Ghost.

The Bishop is a High Priest, and necessarily so, because he is to preside over that particular branch of Church affairs, that is denominated the Lesser Priesthood, and because we have no direct lineal descendant of Aaron, to whom it would of right belong. This is the same, or a branch of the same, Priesthood, which may be illustrated by the figure of the human body, which has different members, which have different offices to perform; all are necessary in their place, and the body is not complete without all the members.

From a retrospect of the requirements of the servants of God to preach the Gospel, we find few qualified even to be Priest, and if a Priest understands his duty, his calling, and ministry, and preaches by the Holy Ghost, his enjoyment is as great as if he were one of the Presidency; and his services are necessary in the body, as are also those of Teachers and Deacons. Therefore, in viewing the Church as a whole, we may strictly denominate it one Priesthood. President Smith also said:

Value of a Righteous Rebuke

"I frequently rebuke and admonish my brethren, and that because I love them, not because I wish to incur their displeasure, or mar their happiness. Such a course of conduct is **[p.113]** not calculated to gain the good will of all, but rather the ill will of many; therefore, the situation in which I stand is an important one; so, you see, brethren, the higher the authority, the greater the difficulty of the station; but these rebukes and admonitions become necessary, from the perverseness of the brethren, for their temporal as well as spiritual welfare.

the ministry. All are to preach the gospel, by the power and influence of the Holy Ghost, and no man can preach the gospel without the Holy Ghost.

The Bishop was a high priest, and necessarily so, because he is to preside over that particular branch of church affairs that are denominated the lesser priesthood, and because we have no direct lineal descendant of Aaron to whom it would of right belong. He remarked that this is the same, or a branch of the same priesthood; which may be illustrated his position by the figure of the human body, which has different members, which have different offices to perform: all are necessary in their place, and the body is not complete without all the members.

From a view of the requirements of the servants of God to preach the gospel, he remarked that few were qualified even to be priests, and if a priest understood his duty, his calling and ministry and preached by the Holy Ghost, his enjoyment is as great as if he were one of the presidency; and his services are necessary in the body, as are also those of teachers and deacons. Therefore in viewing the church as whole, we may strictly denominate it one priesthood.[107]

Messenger and Advocate

He remarked that he rebuked and admonished his brethren frequently, and that because he loved them; not because he wished to incur their displeasure or mar their happiness. Such a course of conduct was not calculated to gain the good will of all, but rather the ill will of many, and thejeby the situation in which he stood was an important one. So you see, brethren the higher the authority, the greater the difficulty of the station. But these rebukes and admonitions became nccssary from the perverseness of brethren, for their temporal as well as spiritual

---

107. *M&A* 3, no. 7 (April 1837): 487.

They actually constitute a part of the duties of my station and calling. Others have other duties to perform, that are important, and far more enviable, and may be just as good, like the feet and hands, in their relation to the human body—neither can claim priority, or say to the other, I have no need of you. After all that has been said, the greatest and most important duty is to preach the Gospel.

"There are many causes of embarrassment, of a pecuniary nature, now pressing upon the heads of the Church. They began poor; were needy, destitute, and were truly afflicted by their enemies; yet the Lord commanded them to go forth and preach the Gospel, to sacrifice their time, their talents, their good name, and jeopardize their lives; and in addition to this, they were to build a house for the Lord, and prepare for the gathering of the Saints. Thus it is easy to see this must [have] involved them [in financial difficulties]. They had no temporal means in the beginning commensurate with such an undertaking; but this work must be done; this place [Kirtland] had to be built up. Large contracts have been entered into for lands on all sides, where our enemies have signed away their rights. We are indebted to them but our brethren from abroad have only to come with their money, take these contracts, relieve their brethren from the pecuniary embarrassments under which they now labor, and procure for themselves a peaceable place of rest among us. This place must and will be built up, and every brother that will take hold and help secure and discharge those contracts that have been made, shall be rich." (April 6, 1837.) DHC 2:477-479.

welfare. They actually constituted a part of the duties of his station and calling. Others had other duties to perform that were important and far less enviable, and might be just as good, like the feet or hands in their relation to the human body, neither could claim priority, or say to the other I have no need of you. After all that has been said the greatest duty and the most important is, to preach the gospel.

He then alluded to the temporal affairs of the church in this place, stating the causes of the embarrassments of a pecuniary nature that were now pressing upon the heads of the church. lie observed they began poor, were needy destitutute, and were truly afflicted by their enemies; yet the Lord commanded them to go forth and preach the **[p.488]** gospel, to sacirfice their time, their talents, their good name and jeopardize their lives, and in addition to this, they were to build a house for the Lord, and prepare for the gathering of the saints. Thus it was easy to see this must involve them. They had no temporal means in the beginning commensurate with such an undertaking, but this work must be done, this place had to be built up. He further remarked that it must yet be built up, that more houses must be built. He observed that large contracts had been entered into for land on all sides where our enemies had signed away their right. We are indebted to them to be sure, but our brethren abroad have only to crme with their money, take these contracts, relieve their brethren of the pecuniary embarrassments under which they now labor, and procure for themselves a peaceable place of rest among us. He then closed at about 4 P. M. by uttering a prophesy saying this place must be built up, and would be built up, and that every brother that would take hold and help secure and discharge those contracts that had been made, should be rich.[108]

---

108. *M&A* 3, no. 7 (April 1837), 487–88. See also 6 April 1837, *JSP, D5*, 354–57.

SECTION THREE

1838–1839

SECTION THREE

The Political Motto of the Church of Latter-day Saints

Joseph Smith's Journal

Motto of the Church of Christ of <u>Latterday</u> <u>Saints</u>.

[p.117] The Constitution of our country formed by the Fathers of liberty. Peace and good order in society. Love to God, and good will to man. All good and wholesome laws, virtue and truth above all things, and aristarchy, live forever! But woe to tyrants, mobs, aristocracy, anarchy, and toryism, and all those who invent or seek out unrighteous and vexatious law suits, under the pretext and color of law, or office, either religious or political. Exalt the standard of Democracy! Down with that of priestcraft, and let all the people say Amen! that the blood of our fathers may not cry from the ground against us. Sacred is the memory of that blood which bought for us our liberty.

JOSEPH SMITH, JUN.,
THOMAS B. MARSH,
DAVID W. PATTEN,
BRIGHAM YOUNG,
SAMUEL H. SMITH,
GEORGE M. HINKLE,
JOHN CORRILL,
GEORGE W. ROBINSON
(March, 1838).
—DHC 3:9.

The Constitution of our country formed by the Fathers of Liberty. Peace and good order in society Love to God and good will to man. [p.238] All good and wholesome Law's; And virtue and truth above all things And Aristarchy live forever!!! But Wo to tyrants, Mobs, Aristocracy, Anarchy and Toryism: And all those who invent or seek out unrighteous and vexatious lawsuits under the pretext or color of law or office, either religious or political. Exalt the standard of Democracy! Down with that of Priestcraft, and let all the people say Amen! that the blood of our Fathers may not cry from the ground against us. Sacred is the Memory of that Blood which baught for us our liberty.

Signed

<u>Geo. W. Robinson</u>

Joseph Smith J^{r.}
Thomas B. Marsh
D[avid] W. Patten
Brigham Youngs [Young]
Samuel H. Smith
George M. Hinkle
<u>John Corrill</u>.—[1]

---

1. 13–29 March 1838, *JSP, J1*, 237–38.

The Word of Wisdom

Elders' Journal

President Joseph Smith, Jr., next made a few remarks on the Word of Wisdom, giving the reason of its coming forth, saying it should be observed.[2] (April 7, 1838.) FWR,[3] p. 111.

President Joseph Smith jr. next made a few remarks on the word of wisdom, giving the reason of its coming forth, saying it should be observed.[4]

Revelation Given to Brigham Young at Far West

Joseph Smith's Journal

[p.118] Verily, thus saith the Lord, let my servant Brigham Young go unto the place which he has bought, on Mill Creek, and there provide for his family until an effectual door is opened for the support of his family, until I shall command him to go hence, and not to leave his family until they are amply provided for. Amen. (April 17, 1838.) DHC 3:23.

Revelation given to Brigham Young at Far West April 17th 1838. Verrily [p.258] thus Saith the Lord, Let my Servant Brigham Young go unto the place which he has baught on Mill Creek and there provide for his family until an effectual door is op[e]ned for the suport of his family untill I shall command [him] to go hence, and not to leave his family untill they are amply provided for Amen.———[5]

Evils of Hasty Judgment

Joseph Smith's Journal

Sunday, May 6, 1838—I preached to the Saints, setting forth the evils that existed, and that would exist, by reason of hasty judgment, or decisions upon any subject given by any people, or in judging before they had heard both sides of a question. I also cautioned the Saints against men who came amongst them whining and growling about their money, because they had kept the Saints, and borne

Sunday 6th This day, President Smith. delivered a discourse. to the people. Showing, or setting forth the evils that existed, and would exist, by reason of hasty Judgement or dessisions upon any subject, given by any people. or in judgeing before they hear both sides of the question, He also cautioned them against men men, who should come here whining and grouling about their money, because they had helpt the saints

---

2. The original *TPJS* footnote reads: "This statement by the Prophet is in accord with the action of the High Council of the Church shortly after its organization in February, 1834. At one of the earliest meetings of this council over which the Presidency of the Church presided, the following action was taken: The question was asked: 'Whether disobedience to the word of wisdom was a transgression sufficient to deprive an official member from holding office in the Church, after having it sufficiently taught him?' After a free and full discussion, Joseph Smith the Prophet gave the following decision which was unanimously accepted by the council: 'No official member in this Church is worthy to hold an office after having the word of wisdom properly taught him; and he, the official member, neglecting to comply with and obey it.'"

3. Far West Record.

4. *Elders' Journal* 1, no. 3 (July 1838): 47. The *Elders' Journal* was a Latter-day Saint periodical (1837–1838). Only four issues were ever published: two in Kirtland, Ohio, and two issues in Far West, Missouri. Most of the *Elders' Journal* consisted of conference minutes and letters from missionaries..

5. 17 April 1838, *JSP, J1*, 257–58.

some of the burden with others, and thus thinking that other, who are still poorer, and have borne greater burdens than they themselves, ought to make up their losses. I cautioned the Saints to beware of such, for they were throwing out insinuations here and there, to level a dart at the best interests of the Church, and if possible destroy the character of its Presidency. I also gave some instructions in the mysteries of the kingdom of God; such as the history of the planets, Abraham's writings upon the planetary systems, etc.[6]

[p.119] In the afternoon I spoke again on different subjects: the principle of wisdom, and the Word of Wisdom. (May 6, 1838.) DHC 3:27.

and bore some of the burden with others. and thus thinking that others, (who are still poorer and who have still bore greater burden than themselves) aught to make up their loss &c. And thus he cautioned them to beware of them for here and there they through [throw?] out foul insinuations, to level as it were a dart to <the> best interests of the Church, & if possible to destroy the Characters of its Presidency He also instructed the Church, in the mistories of the Kingdom of God; giving them a history of the Plannets &c. and of Abrahams writings upon the Plannettary System &c. In the after part of the day Pres.^t Smith spoke upon on different subjects he dwelt some upon the Subject of Wisdom, & upon the word of Wisdom. &c.———[7]

The Prophet's Answer to Sundry Questions

Elders' Journal

I answered the questions which were frequently asked me, while on my last journey but one from Kirtland to Missouri, as printed in the Elders' Journal, Vol. 1, Number 2, pages 28 and 29, as follows:

I answered the questions which were frequently asked me while on my last Journey but one from Kirtland to Missouri, as printed in the Elders Journal <Questions & Answers.> Vol 1st, No 2.^d, Pages 28th and 29th, As follows,—

First—"Do you believe the Bible?"

Question 1st. Do you believe the bible?

---

6. The original *TPJS* footnote reads:

>There is a prevalent notion in the world today that before the time of Columbus, Galileo, and Copernicus, all ancient people believed that the earth was flat and the center of the universe. From the writings of the Scriptures, and more especially those which have come to us in this dispensation, we know that the ancient peoples, when they were guided by the Spirit of the Lord, had the true conception of the universe. The Lord revealed to Abraham great truths about the heavenly bodies, their revolutions, times and seasons, and these were published by the Prophet Joseph Smith before modern astronomers were familiar with these facts. From the writings of Abraham we learn that the Egyptians understood the nature of the planets. Moses also recorded much about this and other worlds, but because of the unbelief and apostasy from truth, these writings were eliminated from his writings. In the Book of Abraham we find the following:
>
>"But the records of the fathers, even the patriarchs concerning, the right of Priesthood the Lord my God preserved in mine own hands; therefore a knowledge of the beginning of the creation, and also of the planets, and of the stars, as they were made known unto the fathers, have I kept even unto this day, and I shall endeavor to write some of these things upon this record, for the benefit of my posterity that shall come after me."
>
>We learn from the Book of Mormon (Helaman 12:13–15) that the Nephites understood the nature of the planets. It was not until apostasy and rebellion against the things of God that the true knowledge of the universe, as well as the knowledge of other truths, became lost among men.

7. 6 May 1838, *JSP, J1*, 266.

If we do, we are the only people under heaven that does, for there are none of the religious sects of the day that do.	Answer. If we do, we are the only people under heaven that does. For there are none of the religious sects of the day that do.
Second—"Wherein do you differ from other sects?"	Question 2nd. Wherein do you differ from other sects?
In that we believe the Bible, and all other sects profess to believe their interpretations of the Bible, and their creeds.	Answer. Because we believe the bible, and all other sects profess to believe their interpretations of the bible, and their creeds.
Third—"Will everybody be damned, but Mormons?"	Question 3rd. Will every body be damned but Mormons?
Yes, and a great portion of them, unless they repent, and work righteousness.	Answer. Yes, and a great portion of them, unless they repent and work righteousness.
Fourth—"How and where did you obtain the Book of Mormon?"	Question 4th. How, and where did you obtain the book of Mormon?
Moroni, who deposited the plates in a hill in Manchester, Ontario County, New York, being dead and raised again therefrom, appeared unto me, and told me where they were, and gave me directions how to obtain them. I obtained them, and the Urim and Thummim with them, by the means of which I translated the plates; and thus came the Book of Mormon.	Answer. Moroni, the person who deposited the plates, from whence the book of Mormon [p.43] was translated, in a hill in Manchester, Ontario County New York, being dead, and raised again therefrom, appeared unto me, and told me where they were; and gave me directions how to obtain them. I obtained them, and the Urim and Thummim with them; by the means of which, I translated the plates; and thus came the book of Mormon.
Fifth—"Do you believe Joseph Smith, Jun., to be a Prophet?"	Question 5th. Do you believe Joseph Smith Jr. to be a prophet?
Yes, and every other man who has the testimony of Jesus. For the testimony of Jesus is the spirit of prophecy.—Revelation, 19:10th verse.	Answer. Yes, and every other man who has the testimony of Jesus. "For the testimony of Jesus, is the spirit of prophecy."— Rev. 19: 10.
Sixth—"Do the Mormons believe in having all things in common?"	Question 6th. Do the Mormons believe in having all things common?
No.	Answer. No.
Seventh—"Do the Mormons believe in having more wives than one?"	Question 7th. Do the Mormons believe in having more wives than one.

No, not at the same time. But they believe that if their companion dies, they have a right to marry again. But we do [p.120] disapprove of the custom, which has gained in the world, and has been practiced among us, to our great mortification, in marrying in five or six weeks, or even in two or three months, after the death of their companion. We believe that due respect ought to be had to the memory of the dead, and the feelings of both friends and children.[8]

Eight—"Can they [the Mormons] raise the dead?"

No, nor can any other people that now lives, or ever did live. But God can raise the dead, through man as an instrument.

Ninth—"What signs does Joseph Smith give of his divine mission?"

The signs which God is pleased to let him give, according as His wisdom thinks best, in order that He may judge the world agreeably to His own plan.

Tenth—"Was not Joseph Smith a money digger?"

Yes, but it was never a very profitable job for him, as he only got fourteen dollars a month for it.

Eleventh—"Did not Joseph Smith steal his wife?"

Answer. No, not at the same time. But they believe, that if their companion dies, they have a right to marry again. But we do disapprove of the custom which has gained in the world, and has been practised among us, to our great mortification, of marrying in five or six weeks, or even in two or three months after the death of their companion. We believe that due respect ought to be had, to the memory of the dead, and the feelings of both friends and children.

Question 8th. Can they raise the dead.

Answer. No. nor any other people that now lives or ever did live. But God can raise the dead through man, as an instrument.

Question 9th What signs do Jo Smith give of his divine mission.

Answer. The signs which God is pleased to let him give; according as his wisdom thinks best: in order t'nat he may judge the world agreably to his own plan.

Question 10. Was not Jo Smith a money digger.

Answer. Yes, but it was never a very profitable job to him, as he only got fourteen dollars a month for it.

Question 11th. Did not Jo Smith steal his wife.

---

8. The original *TPJS* footnote reads: "Notwithstanding this remark about due respect for both the living and the dead, the Prophet varied from this view in counseling his brother Hyrum. Hyrum Smith's wife Jerusha, died in October, 1837, leaving an infant daughter and a large family of small children. The Prophet told his brother Hyrum that it was the will of the Lord that he should marry without delay and take as a wife a young English girl, named Mary Fielding, who had joined the Church through the preaching of Elder Parley P. Pratt in Toronto, Canada. Hyrum accepted this counsel from the Prophet and Mary Fielding became his wife and the mother of President Joseph F. Smith, who was born November 13, 1838."

Ask her, she was of age, she can answer for herself."

Twelfth—"Do the people have to give up their money when they join his Church?"

No other requirement than to bear their proportion of the expenses of the Church, and support the poor.

Thirteenth—"Are the Mormons Abolitionists?"

No, unless delivering the people from priest-craft, and the priests from the power of Satan, should be considered abolition. But we do not believe in setting the negroes free.

Fourteen—"Do they not stir up the Indians to war, and to commit depredations?"

No, and they who reported the story knew it was false when they put it in circulation. These and similar reports are [p.121] palmed upon the people by the priest, and this is the only reason why we ever thought of answering them.

Fifteenth—"Do the Mormons baptize in the name of 'Joe' Smith?"

No, but if they did, it would be as valid as the baptism administered by the sectarian priests.

Sixteenth—"If the Mormon doctrine is true, what has become of all those who died since the days of the Apostles?"

All those who have not had an opportunity of hearing the Gospel, and being administered unto by an inspired man in the flesh, must have it hereafter, before they can be finally judged.

Seventeenth—"Does not 'Joe' Smith profess to be Jesus Christ?"

Answer. Ask her; she was of age, she can answer for herself.

Question 12th. Do the people have to give up their money, when they join his church.

Answer. No other requirement than to bear their proportion of the expenses of the church, and support the poor.

Question 13th. Are the Mormons abolitionists.

Answer. No, unless delivering the people from priest-craft, and the priests from the prower[9] of satan, should be considered such.— But we do not believe in setting the Negroes free.

Question 14th. Do they not stir up the Indians to war and to commit depredations.

Answer. No, and those who reported the story, knew it was false when they put it into circulation. These and similar reports, are pawned upon the people by the priests, and this is the reason why we ever thought of answering them.

Question 15th. Do the Mormons baptize in the name of Jo Smith.

Answer. No, but if they did, it would be as valid as the baptism administered by the sectarian priests.

Question 16th. If the Mormon doctrine is true what has become of all those who have died since the days of the apostles.

Answer. All those who have not had an opportunity of hearing the gospel, and being administered to by an inspired man in the flesh, must have it hereafter, before they can be finally judged.

Question 17th. Does not Jo Smith profess to be Jesus Christ.

---

9. "Power" is misspelled in the publication.

No, but he professes to be His brother, as all other Saints have done and now do: Matt. 12:49, 50, "And He stretched forth His hand toward His disciples and said, Behold my mother and my brethren; for whosoever shall do the will of my Father, which is in heaven, the same is my brother, and sister, and mother."

Eighteenth—"Is there anything in the Bible which licenses you to believe in revelation now-a-days?"

Is there anything that does not authorize us to believe so? If there is, we have, as yet, not been able to find it.

Nineteenth—"Is not the canon of the Scriptures full?"

If it is, there is a great defect in the book, or else it would have said so.

Twentieth—"What are the fundamental principles of your religion?"

The fundamental principles of our religion are the testimony of the Apostles and Prophets, concerning Jesus Christ, that He died, was buried, and rose again the third day, and ascended into heaven; and all other things which pertain to our religion are only appendages to it. But in connection with these, we believe in the gift of the Holy Ghost, the power of faith, the enjoyment of the spiritual gifts according to the will of God, the restoration of the house of Israel, and the final triumph of truth.

I published the foregoing answers to save myself the trouble of repeating the same a thousand times over and over again. (May 8, 1838.) DHC 3:28-30.

Answer. No, but he professes to be his brother, as all other saints have done, and now do.— Matthew, 12: 49, 50— And he stretched forth his hand toward his disciples and said, Behold my mother and my brethren: For whosoever shall do the will of my father which is in heaven, the same is my brother, and sister, and mother.

Question 18th. Is there any thing in the Bible which lisences you to believe in revelation now a days.

Answer. Is there any thing that does not authorize us to believe so; if there is, we have, as yet, not been able to find it.

Question 19th. Is not the cannon of the Scriptures full.

[p.44] Answer. If it is, there is a great defect in the book, or else it would have said so.

Question 20th. What are the fundamental principles of your religion.

Answer. The fundamental principles of our religion is the testimony of the apostles and prophets concerning Jesus Christ, "that he died, was buried, and rose again the third day, and ascended up into heaven;" and all other things are only appendages to these, which pertain to our religion. But in connection with these, we believe in the gift of the Holy Ghost, the power of faith, the enjoyment of the spiritual gifts according to the will of God, the restoration of the house of Israel, and the final triumph of truth.[10]

I published the foregoing answers to save myself the trouble of repeating the same <x> a thousand times over, and over again.[11]

---

10. *Elders' Journal* 1, no. 3 (July 1838): 42–44.

11. The sentence "I published the foregoing answers to save myself the trouble of repeating the same <x> a thousand times over, and over again." was not published in the *Elders' Journal*, but was added in History, B-1, 796.

The Prophet and Party at Tower Hill or Adam-ondi-Ahman

Joseph Smith's Journal

[p.122] Saturday, 19—This morning we struck our tents and formed a line of march, crossing Grand River at the mouth of Honey Creek and Nelson's Ferry. Grand River is a large, beautiful, deep and rapid stream, during the high waters of Spring, and will undoubtedly admit of navigation by steamboat and other water craft, At the mouth of Honey Creek is a good landing. We pursued our course up the river, mostly through timber, for about eighteen miles, when we arrived at Colonel Lyman Wight's home. He lives at the foot of Tower Hill (a name I gave the place in consequence of the remains of an old Nephite altar or tower that stood thee), where we camped for the Sabbath.

<19 sat> The next morning we struck our tents, and marched crossed Grand river at the mouth of Honey Creek at a place called Nelsons ferry, Grand River is as large beautifull deep and rapid stream and will undoubtedly admit of steam Boat and other water craft navigation, and at the mouth of honey creek is a splendid harbour for the safety of such crafts, and also for landing freight We next kept up the river mostly in the timber for ten miles, untill we came to Col. Lyman Wight's who lives at the foot of Tower Hill, a name appropriated by Pres^t smith, in consequence of the remains of an old Nephitish Alter an Tower, ~~In the after~~ where we camped for the sabath,

In the afternoon I went up the river about half a mile to Wight's Ferry, accompanied by President Rigdon, and my clerk, George W. Robinson, for the purpose of selecting and laying claim to a city plat near said ferry in Daviess County, township 60, ranges 27 and 28, and sections 25, 36, 31, and 30, which the brethren called "Spring Hill," but by the mouth of the Lord it was named Adam-ondi-Ahman, because, said He, it is the place where Adam shall come to visit his people, or the Ancient of Days shall sit, as spoken of by Daniel the Prophet. (May 19, 1938.) DHC 3:34-35.

In the after part of the day, Prest<s> smith and Rigdon and myself, went to Wights. Ferry about a half mile from this place up the river, for the purpose of selecting and laying claims to city plott near said Ferry, in Davis [Daviess] County Township 60, Range 27 & 28, and Sections 25, 36, 31, 30, which was called Spring Hill a name appropriated by the bretheren present, But after wards named by the mouth of [the] Lord and was called Adam Ondi Awmen [Adam-ondi-Ahman], because said he it is the place where Adam shall come to visit his people, or the Ancient of days shall sit as spoken of by Daniel the Prophet,[12]

The Prophet's Letter to the Church Written from Liberty Jail

December 16, 1838

Joseph Smith Letter

To the Church of Jesus Christ of Latter-day Saints in Caldwell county, and all the Saints who are scattered abroad, who are persecuted, and made desolate, and who are afflicted in divers manners for Christ's sake and the

To the church of latter day saints in Caldwell county and the saints scattered abroad and are persecuted and made desolate and are afflicted in divers manners for christ's sake and the gospel's, and whose perils are greatly [p.299]

---

12. 19 May 1838, *JSP, J1*, 271.

Gospel's, by the hands of a cruel mob and the tyrannical disposition of the authorities of this state; and whose perils are greatly augmented by the wickedness and corruption of false brethren, greeting:

augmented by the wickedness and corruption of false brethren.

May grace, mercy, and the peace of God be and abide with you; and notwithstanding all your sufferings, we assure you that you have our prayers and fervent desires for your welfare, day and night. We believe that that God who seeth us in this solitary place, will hear our prayers, and reward you openly.

May grace, mercy, and peace, be and abide with you and notwithstanding all your sufferings we assure you that you have our prayers and fervent desires for your welfare both day and night. We believe that, that God who sees us in this solitary place will hear our prayers & reward you openly.[13]

In Bonds for the Testimony of Jesus

Joseph Smith Letter

[p.123] Know assuredly, dear brethren, that it is for the testimony of Jesus that we are in bonds and in prison. But we say unto you, that we consider that our condition is better (notwithstanding our sufferings) than that of those who have persecuted us, and smitten us, and borne false witness against us; and we most assuredly believe that those who do bear false witness against us, do seem to have a great triumph over us for the present. But we want you to remember Haman and Mordecai: you know that Haman could not be satisfied so long as he saw Mordecai at the king's gate, and he sought the life of Mordecai and the destruction of the people of the Jews. But the Lord so ordered it, that Haman was hanged upon his own gallows.

Know assuredly dear brethren that it is for the testimony of Jesus that we are in bonds and in prison. But we say unto you that we consider our condition better, (notwithstanding our suffering) than those who have persecuted us and smitten us and <borne> bear false witness against us, and we most assuredly believe that those who bear false witness against us <do> seem to have a great triumph over us for the present. But we want you to remember Haman and Mordecai you know that Haman could not be satisfied so long as he saw Mordecai at the king's gate, and he sought the life of Mordecai and the people of the jews. But the Lord so ordered that Haman was hanged upon his own gallows.

So shall it come to pass with poor Haman in the last days, and those who have sought by unbelief and wickedness and by the principle of mobocracy to destroy us and the people of God, by killing and scattering them abroad, and wilfully and maliciously delivering us into the hands of murderers, desiring us to be put to death, thereby having us dragged about in chains and cast into prison. And for what

So shall it come to pass with poor Haman in the last days. Those who have sought by their unbelief and wickedness and by the principle of mobocracy to destroy us and the people of God by killing and scattering them abroad and wilfully and maliciously delivering us into the hands of murderers desiring us to be put to death thereby having us dragged about in chains and cast into prison, and for what

---

13. 16 December 1838, Letter to the Church in Caldwell County, Missouri, *JSP, D6*, 298–99. See also *PWJS*, 415.

cause? It is because we were honest men, and were determined to defend the lives of the Saints at the expense of our own. I say unto you, that those who have thus vilely treated us, like Haman, shall be hanged upon their own gallows; or, in other words, shall fall into their own gin, and snare, and ditch and trap, which they have prepared for us, and shall go backwards and stumble and fall, and their name shall be blotted out, and God shall reward them according to all their abominations.

cause; it is because we were honest men and were determined to defend the lives of the saints at the expense of our own. I say unto you that those who have thus vilely treated us like Haman shall be hanged upon their own gallows, or in other words shall fall into their own gin and trap and ditch which they have prepared for us and shall go backward and stumble and fall, and their names shall be blotted out, and God shall reward them according to all their abominations.[14]

Though in Prison, Yet Hearts Not Faint

Joseph Smith Letter

Dear brethren, do not think that our hearts faint, as though some strange thing had happened unto us, for we have seen and been assured of all these things beforehand, and have an assurance of a better hope than that of our persecutors. Therefore God hath made broad our shoulders for the burden. We glory in our tribulation, because we know that God is with us, that He is our friend, and that He will save our souls. We do not care for them that can kill the body; they cannot harm our souls. We ask no favors at the hands of mobs, nor of the [p.124] world, nor of the devil, nor of his emissaries the dissenters, and those who love, and make, and swear falsehoods, to take away our lives. We have never dissembled, nor will we for the sake of our lives.

Dear brethren do not think that our hearts faint as though some strange thing had happened unto us for we have seen and been [p.300] assured of all these things beforehand, and have an assurance of a better hope than that of our persecutors. Therefore God has made our shoulders broad that we can bear it. We glory in our tribulation because we know that God is with us, that he is our friend and that he will save our souls. We do not care for those that kill the body they cannot harm our souls; we ask no favors at the hands of mobs nor of the world, nor of the devil nor of his emissaries the dissenters. We have never dissembled nor will we for the sake of our lives.

Forasmuch, then, as we know that we have been endeavoring with all our mind, might, and strength, to do the will of God, and all things whatsoever He has commanded us; and as to our light speeches, which may have escaped our lips from time to time, they have nothing to do with the fixed purposes of our hearts; therefore it sufficeth us to say, that our souls were vexed from day to day. We refer you to Isaiah, who considers those who make a man an offender for a word, and lay a snare

Forasmuch then as we know that we have been endeavoring with all our mights, minds, and strength to do the will of God and all things whatsoever he has commanded us. And as to our light speeches from time to time they have nothing to do with the fixed principle of our hearts. Therefore it sufficeth us to say that our souls were vexed from day to day. We refer you to Isaiah who considers those who make a man an offender for a word and lay a snare for them that reproveth in the gate. We believe

---

14. 16 December 1838, Letter to the Church in Caldwell County, Missouri, *JSP, D6*, 299. See also *PWJS*, 415–16.

for him that reproveth in the gate. We believe that the old Prophet verily told the truth: and we have no retraction to make. We have reproved in the gate, and men have laid snares for us. We have spoken words, and men have made us offenders. And notwithstanding all this, our minds are not yet darkened, but feel strong in the Lord. But behold the words of the Savior: "If the light which is in you become darkness, behold how great is that darkness." Look at the dissenters. Again, "If you were of the world the world would love its own."	the old prophet verily told the truth. We have no retraction to make, we have reproved in the gate and men have laid snares for us we have spoken words and men have made us offenders, and notwithstanding all this our minds are not darkened but feel strong in the Lord. But behold the words of the savior, if the light which is in you become darkness behold how great is that darkness. Look at the dissenters. And again if you were of the world the world would love its own[15]

* * *

Blessed Are the Persecuted

	Joseph Smith Letter
Perhaps our brethren will say, because we thus write, that we are offended at these characters. If we are, it is not for a word, neither because they reproved in the gate—but because they have been the means of shedding innocent blood. Are they not murderers then at heart? Are not their consciences seared as with a hot iron? We confess that we are offended; but the Savior said, "It must needs be that offenses come, but woe unto them by whom they come." And again, "Blessed are ye when men shall revile you, and persecute you, and shall say all manner of evil against you falsely for my sake; rejoice and be exceeding glad, for great is your reward in heaven, for so persecuted they the Prophets which were before you."	Perhaps our brethren may say because we thus write that we are offended at those characters, if we are, it is not for a word neither because they reproved in the gate. But because they have been the means of shedding innocent blood. Are they not murderers then at heart? Are not their consciences seared as with a hot iron? We confess that we are offended but the saviour said that offences must come but woe unto them by whom they come, and again blessed are ye when all men shall revile you and speak all manner of evil against you falsely for my sake, rejoice and be exceeding glad for great is your reward in heaven for so persecuted they the prophets which were before you.
Now, dear brethren, if any men ever had reason to claim this promise, we are the men; for we know that the world not only hate us, but they speak all manner of evil of us falsely, for no other reason than that we have been endeavoring to teach the fullness of the Gospel of Jesus Christ.	Now dear brethren if any men ever had reason to claim this promise we are the men, for we know that the world not only hates us but ~~but~~ speak all manner of evil of us falsely for no other reason than because we have been endeavoring to teach the fulness of the gospel of Jesus Christ
[p.125] After we were bartered away by Hinkle, and were taken into the militia camp,	after we were bartered away by Hinkle and were taken into the militia camp we had all

---

15. 16 December 1838, Letter to the Church in Caldwell County, Missouri, *JSP, D6*, 299–300. See also *PWJS*, 416–17.

we had all the evidence we could have asked for that the world hated us. If there were priests among them of all the different sects, they hated us, and that most cordially too. If there were generals, they hated us; if there were colonels, they hated us; and the soldiers, and officers of every kind, hated us; and the most profane, blasphemous, and drunkards; and whoremongers, hated us—they all hated us, most cordially. And now what did they hate us for? Purely because of the testimony of Jesus Christ. Was it because we were liars? We know that it has been so reported by some, but it has been reported falsely. Was it because we have committed treason against the government in Daviess county, or burglary, or larceny, or arson, or any other unlawful act in Daviess county? We know that we have been so reported by priests, and certain lawyers, and certain judges, who are the instigators, aiders, and abettors of a certain gang of murderers and robbers, who have been carrying on a scheme of mobocracy to uphold their priestcraft, against the Saints of the last days; and for a number of years have tried, by a well contemplated and premeditated scheme, to put down by physical power a system of religion that all the world, by their mutual attainments, and by any fair means whatever, were not able to resist.

the evidence we could have wished for that the world hated us and that most cordially too. If there were priests of all the different sects they hated us, if there were Generals they hated us, if there were Colonels they hated us, and the soldiers and officers of every kind hated us, and the most profane blasphemers and drunkards & whoremongers hated us, they all hated us most cordially. And now what did they hate us for, purely because of the testimony of Jesus Christ. Was it because we were liars? We know that it has been reported by some but it has been reported falsely Was it because we have **[p.303]** committed treason against the government in Daviess County or of burglary, or of larceny or arson, or any other unlawful act in Daviess county. We know that certain priests and certain lawyers and certain judges who are the instigators aiders and abettors of a certain gang of murderers and robbers who have been carrying on a scheme of mobocracy to uphold their priestcraft against the saints of the last days for a number of years and have tried by a well contemplated and premeditated scheme to put down by physical power a system of relig[i]on that all the world by all their mutual attainments and by any fair means whatever were not able to resist.[16]

Accused by False Witnesses

Hence mobbers were encouraged by priests and Levites, by the Pharisees, by the Sadducees, and Essenes, and Herodians, and the most worthless, abandoned, and debauched, lawless, and inhuman, and the most beastly set of men that the earth can boast of—and indeed a parallel cannot be found anywhere else—to gather together to steal, to plunder, to starve, and to exterminate, and burn the houses of the "Mormons."

Joseph Smith Letter

Hence, mobbers were encouraged by priests and Levites, by the Pharisees, Sadducees, and Essenees, and the Herodians, and the most ruthless, abandoned, and debauched, lawless inhuman and the most beastly set of men that the earth can boast of; and indeed a parallel cannot be found any where else; to gather together to steal to plunder to starve and to exterminate and burn the houses of the Mormons

---

16. 16 December 1838, Letter to the Church in Caldwell County, Missouri, *JSP, D6,* 302–3. See also *PWJS,* 417–18.

These are characters that, by their treasonable and overt acts, have desolated and laid waste Daviess county. These are the characters that would fain make all the world believe that we are guilty of the above named acts. But they represent us falsely; we stood in our own defense, and we believe that no man of us acted only in a just, a lawful, and a righteous retaliation against such marauders.[17]

We say unto you, that we have not committed treason, nor any other unlawful act in Daviess county. Was it for **[p.126]** murder in Ray county, against mob-militia; who was as a wolf in the first instance, hide and hair, teeth, legs and tail, who afterwards put on a militia sheep skin with the wool on; who could sally forth, in the day time, into the flock, and snarl and show his teeth, and scatter and devour the flock, and satiate himself upon his prey, and then sneak back into the bramble in order that he might conceal himself in his well tried skin with the wool on?

We are well aware that there is a certain set of priests and satellites, and mobbers that would fain make all the world believe that we were guilty of the doings of their howling wolf that made such havoc among the sheep, who, when he retreated, howled and bleated at such a desperate rate, that if one could have been there, he would have thought that all the wolves, whether wrapped up in sheep skins or in goat skins, or in some other skins, and in fine all the beasts of the forest, were awfully alarmed, and catching the scent of innocent blood, they sallied forth with one tremendous howl and crying of all sorts; and such a howling, and such a tremendous havoc never was known before; such inhumanity, and relentless cruelty and barbarity as were practiced against the Saints in Missouri can scarcely be found in the annals of history.

---

17. The portion of this letter that reads, "we stood in our own defense, and we believe that no man of us acted only in a just, a lawful, and a righteous retaliation against such marauders" is not found in the original letter, but was added in History, C-1, 870.

Now those characters if allowed to would make the world believe that we had committed murder, by making an attack upon this howling wolf, while the fact is we were at home and in our bed, and asleep, and knew nothing of that transaction any more than we know what is going on in China while we are within these walls. Therefore we say again unto you, we are innocent of these things, and they have represented us falsely.

Was it for committing adultery that we were assailed? We are aware that that false slander has gone abroad, for it has been reiterated in our ears. These are falsehoods also. Renegade "Mormon" dissenters are running through the world and spreading various foul and libelous reports against us, thinking thereby to gain the friendship of the world, because they know that we are not of the world, and that the world hates us; therefore they [the world] make a tool of these fellows [the dissenters]; and by them try to do all the injury they can, and after that they hate them worse than they do us, because they find them to be base traitors and sycophants.

[p.127] Such characters God hates; we cannot love them. The world hates them, and we sometimes think that the devil ought to be ashamed of them.

We have heard that it is reported by some, that some of us should have said, that we not only dedicated our property, but our families also to the Lord; and Satan, taking advantage of this, has perverted it into licentiousness, such as a community of wives, which is an abomination in the sight of God.

These are the characters that would make the world believe that we had committed murder by making an attack upon this howling wolf while we were at home and in our beds and asleep and knew nothing of that transaction any more than we know what is going on in China while we are within these walls. Therefore we say again unto you we are innocent of these things they have represented us falsely

Was it for committing adultery, we are aware that false slander has gone abroad for it has been reiterated in our <ears>. These are falsehoods also. [p.305] Renegadoes, mormon dissenters are running through the world and spreading various foul and libelous reports against us thinking thereby to gain the friendship of the world because they know that we are not of the world and that the world hates us; therefore they make a tool of these fellows by them they do all the injury they can and after that they hate them worse than they do us because they find them to be base traitors and sycophants.[18]

Consecrated Lives

Joseph Smith Letter

God Such characters God hates we cannot love them the world hates them and we sometimes think the devil ought to be ashamed of them.

We have heard that it has been reported by some that some of us should have said that we not only dedicated our property but our families also to the Lord, and satan taking advantage of this has transfigured it into lasciviousness such as a community of wives which is an abomination in the sight of God.

---

18. 16 December 1838, Letter to the Church in Caldwell County, Missouri, *JSP, D6*, 303–5. See also *PWJS*, 418–19.

When we consecrate our property to the Lord it is to administer to the wants of the poor and needy, for this is the law of God; it is not for the benefit of the rich, those who have no need; and when a man consecrates or dedicates his wife and children, he does not give them to his brother, or to his neighbor, for there is no such law: for the law of God is, Thou shalt not commit adultery. Thou shalt not covet thy neighbor's wife. He that looketh upon a woman to lust after her, has committed adultery already in his heart. Now for a man to consecrate his property, wife and children, to the Lord, is nothing more nor less than to feed the hungry, clothe the naked, visit the widow and fatherless, the sick and afflicted, and do all he can to administer to their relief in their afflictions, and for him and his house to serve the Lord. In order to do this, he and all his house must be virtuous, and must shun the very appearance of evil.

Now if any person has represented anything otherwise than what we now write, he or she is a liar, and has represented us falsely—and this is another manner of evil which is spoken against us falsely.

We have learned also since we have been prisoners, that many false and pernicious things, which were calculated to lead the Saints far astray and to do great injury, have been taught by Dr. Avard as coming from the Presidency, and we have reason to fear that many other designing and corrupt characters like unto himself, have been teaching many things which the Presidency never knew were being taught in the Church by anybody until after they were made prisoners. Had they known of such things they would have spurned them and their authors as they would the gates of hell. Thus we find that there have been frauds and secret abominations and evil works of darkness going on, leading the minds of the weak and unwary **[p.128]** into confusion and distraction, and all the time palming it

When we consecrate our property to the Lord it is to administer to the wants of the poor and needy for this is the law of God it is not for the purpose of the rich those who have no need and when a man consecrates or dedicates his wife and children he does not give them to his brother or to his neighbor for there is no such law for the law of God is thou shalt not commit adultery thou shalt not covet thy neighbor's wife. He that looketh upon a woman to lust after her has committed adultery already in his heart. Now for a man to consecrate his property and his wife & children to the Lord, is nothing more nor less than to feed the hungry, clothe the naked, visit the widow and the fatherless, the sick, and the afflicted, and do all he can to administer to their relief in their afflictions, and for him and his house to serve the Lord. In order to do this he and all his house must be virtuous and shun every appearance of evil.

Now if any person has represented any **[p.306]** thing other wise than what we now write he or she is a liar and have represented us falsely. And this is another manner of of evil which is spoken against us falsely.

We have learned also since we have been in prison that many false and pernicious things which were calculated to lead the saints far astray and to do great injury <have been taught by Dr. [Sampson] Avard> as coming from the Presidency taught by Dr Avard and we have reason to fear <that> many <other things> designing and corrupt characters like unto himself <have been teaching many things> which the presidency never knew of being taught in the church by any body untill after they were made prisoners, which if they had known of, they would have spurned them and their authors from them as they would the gates of hell. Thus we find that there has been frauds and secret abominations and evil works of darkness going on leading the minds of the weak and unwary into confusion and off upon the Presidency, while the Presidency were ignorant as well as innocent of those things which those persons were practicing in the Church in their name. Meantime the Presidency were attending to their own secular and family concerns, weighed down with sorrow, in debt, in poverty, in hunger, essaying to be fed, yet finding [i.e., supporting] themselves. They occasionally received deeds of charity, it is true; but these were inadequate to their subsistence; and because they received those deeds, they were envied and hated by those who professed to be their friends.

But notwithstanding we thus speak, we honor the Church, when we speak of the Church as a Church, for their liberality, kindness, patience, and long-suffering, and their continual kindness towards us.

* * *

distraction, and palming it all the time upon the presidency while mean time the presidency were ignorant as well as innocent of these things, which were practicing in the church in their name and were attending to their own family concerns, weighed down with sorrow, in debt, in poverty, in hunger assaying to be fed yet finding themselves receiving deeds of charity but inadequate to their subsistence, and because they received those deeds they were envied and hated by those who professed to be their friends

But notwithstanding **[p.307]** we thus speak we honor the church when we speak of the church, as a church, for their liberality, kindness, patience, and long suffering, and their continued kindness towards us.[19]

* * *

Willful Sin Unpardonable

Joseph Smith Letter

Again, if men sin wilfully after they have received the knowledge of the truth, there remaineth no more sacrifice for sin, but a certain fearful looking for of judgment and fiery indignation to come, which shall devour these adversaries. For he who despised Moses' law died without mercy under two or three witnesses. Of how much more severe punishment suppose ye, shall he be thought worthy, who hath sold his brother, and ye, shall he be thought worthy, who hath sold his brother, and denied the new and everlasting covenant by which he was sanctified, calling it an unholy thing, and doing despite to the Spirit of grace.

And again we say unto you, that inasmuch as there is virtue in us, and the Holy Priesthood has been conferred upon us—and the keys of the kingdom have not been taken from us, for verily thus saith the Lord, "Be of good cheer,

Again if we sin wilfully after we have received the knowledge of the truth, there remaineth no more sacrifice for sin, but a certain fearful looking <for> of judgement and fiery indignation to come which shall devour these adversaries. For he who despiseth Moses' law died without mercy under two or three witnesses of how much more severe punishment suppose ye shall he be thought worthy who hath sold his brother and denied the new and everlasting covenant by which he was **[p.309]** sanctified calling it an unholy thing and doing despite to the spirit of grace.

And again we say unto you that inasmuch as there be virtue in us and the holy priesthood hath been conferred upon us, and the keys of the kingdom hath not been taken from us, for verily thus saith the Lord be of good cheer for

---

19. 16 December 1838, Letter to the Church in Caldwell County, Missouri, *JSP, D6*, 305–7. See also *PWJS*, 419–21.

for the keys that I gave unto you are yet with you"—therefore we say unto you, dear brethren, in the name of the Lord Jesus Christ, we deliver these characters unto the buffetings of Satan until the day of redemption, that they may be dealt with according to their works; and from henceforth their works shall be made manifest.	the keys that I gave unto \<you\> are yet with you Therefore we say unto you dear brethren in the name of the Lord Jesus Christ, we deliver these characters unto the buffetings of satan untill the day of redemption that they may be dealt with according to their works and from henceforth their works shall be made manifest.[20]

A Word of Exhortation

	Joseph Smith Letter
And now dear and well beloved brethren—and when we say brethren, we mean those who have continued faithful in **[p.129]** Christ, men, women and children—we feel to exhort you in the name of the Lord Jesus, to be strong in the faith in the new and everlasting covenant, and nothing frightened at your enemies. For what has happened unto us is an evident token to them of damnation; but unto us, of salvation, and that of God. Therefore hold on even unto death; for "he that seeks to save his life shall lose it; and he that loses his life for my sake, and the Gospel's, shall find it," saith Jesus Christ.	And now dear and well beloved brethren and when we say brethren we mean those who have continued faithful in christ men, women, and children, we feel to exhort you in the name of the Lord Jesus, to be strong in the faith of the new and everlasting covenant, and nothing frightened at your enemies. For what has happened unto us is an evident token to them of damnation but unto us of salvation and that of God. Therefore hold on even unto death, for he that seeks to save his life shall ~~loose~~ lose it but he that loseth his life for my sake and the gospels shall find it sayeth Jesus Christ.
Brethren, from henceforth, let truth and righteousness prevail and abound in you; and in all things be temperate; abstain from drunkenness, and from swearing, and from all profane language, and from everything which is unrighteous or unholy; also from enmity, and hatred, and covetousness, and from every unholy desire. Be honest one with another, for it seems that some have come short of these things, and some have been uncharitable, and have manifested greediness because of their debts towards those who have been persecuted and dragged about with chains without cause, and imprisoned. Such characters God hates—and they shall have their turn of sorrow in the rolling of the great wheel, for it rolleth and none can hinder. Zion shall yet live, though she seem to be dead.	Brethren from henceforth let truth and righteousness prevail and abound in you and in all things be temperate, abstain from every appearance of evil, drunkenness, and profane language, and from every thing which is unrighteous or unholy; also from enmity, and hatred, and covetousness and from every unholy desires. Be honest one with another, for it seemeth that some have come short of these things, and some have been uncharitable & have manifested greediness because of their debts towards those who have been persecuted & dragged about with chains without cause and imprisoned. Such persons God hates and they shall have their turn of sorrow in the rolling of the great wheel for it rolleth and none can hinder. Zion shall yet live **[p.310]** though she seemeth to be dead.

---

20. 16 December 1838, Letter to the Church in Caldwell County, Missouri, *JSP, D6*, 308–9. See also *PWJS*, 421–22.

Remember that whatsoever measure you mete out to others, it shall be measured to you again. We say unto you, brethren, be not afraid of your adversaries; contend earnestly against mobs, and the unlawful works of dissenters and of darkness.	Remember that whatsoever measure you meet out to others it shall be measured to you again. We say unto you brethren be not afraid of your adversaries contend earnestly against mobs, and the unlawful works of dissenters and of darkness.
And the very God of peace shall be with you, and make a way for your escape from the adversary of souls. We commend you to God and the word of His grace, which is able to make us wise unto salvation. Amen. JOSEPH SMITH, JUN. —DHC 3:226-233.	And the very God of peace shall be with you and make a way for your escape from the adversary of your souls we commend you to God and the word of his grace which is able to make us wise unto salvation. Amen. Joseph Smith Jun.[21]

The Prophet's Epistle to the Church, Written in Liberty Prison, Clay County, Missouri, March 25, 1839

	Joseph Smith Letter
To the Church of Latter-day Saints at Quincy, Illinois, and scattered abroad, and to Bishop Partridge in particular;[22]	To the church of Latterday saints at Quincy Illinois and scattered abroad and to Bishop [Edward] Partridge in particular.
[p.130] Your humble servant, Joseph Smith, Jun., prisoner for the Lord Jesus Christ's sake, and for the Saints, taken and held by the power of mobocracy, under the exterminating reign of his excellency, the governor, Lilburn W. Boggs, in company with his fellow prisoners and beloved brethren, Caleb Baldwin, Lyman Wight, Hyrum Smith, and Alexander McRae, send unto you all greeting. May the grace of God the Father, and of our Lord and	your humble servant Joseph Smith Jr prisoner for the Lord Jesus Christ's sake and for the saints taken and held by the power of mobocracy under the exterminating reign of his excelancy the Governer Lilburn W. Boggs in company with his fellow prisoners and beloved Brethren Caleb Baldwin Lymon [Lyman] Wight. Hyram [Hyrum] Smith and Alexander McRae. Send unto you all greeting. May the grace of God the father and of our

---

21. 16 December 1838, Letter to the Church in Caldwell County, Missouri, *JSP, D6*, 309–10. See also *PWJS*, 422.

22. 20 March 1839, Joseph Smith et al., Letter to the Church and Edward Partridge, *JSP, D6*, 360–66. Also see *PWJS*, 430. Part of this letter is now found in section 121 of the Doctrine and Covenants. The original *TPJS* footnote reads: "The following important communication written by the Prophet and signed by all of his fellow prisoners, to the Church at large, and to Bishop Edward Partridge in particular, was written between the 20th and 25th of March. In the Prophet's history as published many years ago in current issues of the Deseret News and Millennial Star the communication is divided near the middle of it by reciting the few incidents happening between the 20th and 25th of March—the former being the date on which the letter was begun, the latter the date on which it was completed; but in this publication it is thought desirable that the letter be given without this division, and hence it appears under the date on which it was completed, viz., the 25th of March, 1839. The parts of the communication enclosed in brackets were regarded of such special value that they were taken from this communication, and placed in the Doctrine and Covenants and comprise sections 121, 122 and 123 of that work."

Savior Jesus Christ, rest upon you all, and abide with you forever. May knowledge be multiplied unto you by the mercy of God. And may faith and virtue, and knowledge and temperance, and patience and godliness, and brotherly kindness and charity be in you and abound, that you may not be barren in anything, nor unfruitful.

Lord and savior Jesus Christ rest upon you all and abide with you for ever. May knoledge be multiplied unto you by the [p.361] meorcy of God. And may faith and virtue and knoledge and temperance and patience and Godliness and Brotherly kindness and charity be in you and abound that you may not be baron in anything nor unfrutefull.[23]

The Sustaining Love of God

Joseph Smith Letter

For inasmuch as we know that the most of you are well acquainted with the wrongs and the high-handed injustice and cruelty that are practiced upon us; whereas we have been taken prisoners charged falsely with every kind of evil, and a strong guard, who continually watch day and night as indefatigable as the devil does in tempting and laying snares for the people of God.

Forasmuch as we know that the most of you are well acquainted with the rongs and the high toned injustice and cruelty that is practiced upon us whereas we have been taken prisoners charged falsly with evry kind of evil and thrown into prison inclosed with strong walls surrounded with a strong guard who continually watch day and knight as indefatigable as the devil is in tempting and laying snayers for the people of God.

Therefore, dearly beloved brethren, we are the more ready and willing to lay claim to your fellowship and love. For our circumstances are calculated to awaken our spirits to a sacred remembrance of everything, and we think that yours are also, and that nothing therefore can separate us from the love of God and fellowship one with another; and that every species of wickedness and cruelty practiced upon us will only tend to bind our hearts together and seal them together in love. We have no need to say to you that we are held in bonds without cause, neither is it needful that you say unto us. We are driven from [p.131] our homes and smitten without cause. We mutually understand that if the inhabitants of the state of Missouri had let the Saints alone, and had been as desirable of peace as they were, there would have been nothing but peace and quietude in the state unto this day; we should not have been in this hell, surrounded with demons (if not those who are damned, they are those who shall be damned) and where we are

Therefore dearly and beloved Brethren we are the more ready and willing to lay claim to your fellowship and love. For our curcumstances are calculated to awaken our spirits to a sacred rememberance of evry thing and we think that yours are also and that nothing therefore can seperate us from the love of God, and fellowship one with another and that evry species of wickedness and cruelty practised upon us will only tend to bind our harts together and seal them together in love we have no need to say to you that we are held in bonds without cause neither is it needfull that you say unto us we are driven from our homes and smitten without cause. We mutually unders[t]and that if the inhabitance of the state of Missouri had let the saints alone and had been as deserable of peace as they waer there would have been nothing but peace and quiatude [quietude] in this <State> unto this day we should not have been in this hell surrounded with demonds if not those who are damned, they are those who shall be damned and where we are compeled

---

23. 20 March 1839, Joseph Smith et al., Letter to the Church and Edward Partridge, *JSP, D6*, 360–61.

The Persecution of the Saints

Joseph Smith Letter

compelled to hear nothing but blasphemous oaths, and witness a scene of blasphemy, and drunkenness and hypocrisy, and debaucheries of every description.	to hear nothing but blasphemo[u]s oaths and witness a seen of blasphemy and drunkeness and hypocracy and debaucheries of evry description.[24]
And again the cries of orphans and widows would not have ascended up to God against them. Nor would innocent blood have stained the soil of Missouri. But oh! the unrelenting hand! The inhumanity and murderous disposition of this people! It shocks all nature; it beggars and defies all description; it is a tale of woe; a lamentable tale; yea a sorrowful tale; too much to tell; too much for contemplation; too much for human beings; it cannot be found among the heathens; it cannot be found among the nations where kings and tyrants are enthroned; it cannot be found among the savages of the wilderness; yea, and I think it cannot be found among the wild and ferocious beasts of the forest—that a man should be mangled for sport! women be robbed of all that they have—their last morsel for subsistence, and then be violated to gratify the hellish desires of the mob, and finally left to perish with their helpless offspring clinging around their necks.	And again the ~~cry~~ cries of orphans and widdows would <not> have assended up to God. the blood of inocent women and children yea and of men also would not have cried to God against them <it> would <not> have stained the soyl of Missouri. but oh! the unrelenting hand the inhumanity and murderous disposition of this people it shocks all nature it beggers and defies all discription. it is a tail [tale] of wo a lamentable tail yea a sorrifull tail too much to tell too **[p.362]** much for contemplation too much to think of for a moment too much for human beings it cannot be found among the hethans it cannot be found among the nations where Kings and tyrants are inthroned it cannot be found among the savages of the wilderness yea and I think it cannot be found among the wild and ferocious beasts of the forist that a man should be mangled for sport women be ~~violated~~ <rob[b]ed> of all that they have their last morsel for subsistance and then be violated to gratify the ~~hells~~ <hellish> desires of the mob and finally left to perish with their helpless of[f]spring clinging around their necks
But this is not all. After a man is dead, he must be dug up from his grave and mangled to pieces, for no other purpose than to gratify their spleen against the religion of God.	but this is not all after a man is dead he must be dug up from his grave and mangled to peaces for no other purpose than to gratify their splean against the religeon of god.
They practice these things upon the Saints, who have done them no wrong, who are innocent and virtuous; who loved the Lord their God, and were willing to forsake all things for	They practise <these> things upon the saints who have done them no rong who are inocent and virtuous who loved the Lord their god and were willing to forsaik all things for ~~his~~

---

24. 20 March 1839, Joseph Smith et al., Letter to the Church and Edward Partridge, *JSP, D6*, 361. Also see *PWJS*, 430–31.

Christ's sake. These things are awful to relate, but they are verily true. It must needs be that offenses come, but woe unto them by whom they come.

<Christ> sake these things are awfull to relait [relate] but they are verily true it must needs bee that offences come, but WO! to them by whom they come.[25]

A Righteous Appeal to Heaven

Joseph Smith Letter

[Oh God! where art Thou? And where is the pavilion that covereth Thy hiding place? How long shall Thy hand **[p.132]** be stayed, and Thine eye, yea Thy pure eye, behold from the eternal heavens, the wrongs of Thy people, and of Thy servants, and Thy ear be penetrated with their cries? Yea, O Lord, how long shall they suffer these wrongs and unlawful oppressions, before Thine heart shall be softened towards them?

O Lord God Almighty, Maker of Heaven, Earth and Seas, and of all things that in them are, and who controllest and subjectest the devil, and the dark and benighted dominion of Sheol! Stretch forth Thy hand, let Thine eye pierce; let Thy pavilion be taken up; let Thy hiding place no longer be covered; let Thine ear be inclined; let Thine heart be softened, and Thy bowels moved with compassion towards us; let Thine anger be kindled against our enemies; and in the fury of Thine heart, with Thy sword avenge us of our wrongs; remember Thy suffering Saints. O our God! and Thy servants will rejoice in Thy name forever.]

O God where art thou and where is the pavilion that covereth thy hiding place how long shall thy hand be stayed and thine eye yea thy pure eye behold from ~~from~~ the etearnal heavens the rongs of thy people and of thy servants and thine ear be penetrated with their cyes [cries] yea o Lord how long shall they suffer these rongs and unlawfull oppressions before thine hart shall be softened towards them and thy bowels be moved with compassion to-words them.

O Lord God almity maker of heaven earth and seas and of all things that in them is and who controleth and subjecteth the devil and the dark and benig[h]ted dominion of shayole. Streach forth thy hand let thine eye pierce let thy pavilion be taken up let thy hiding place no longer be covered let thine ear be inclined let thine hart be softened and thy bowels moved with **[p.363]** compassion toward us let thine anger be kindle against our enemi[e]s and in the fury of thine hart with thy sword avenge us of our rongs remember thy suffering saint oh our God and thy servants will rejoyce in thy name for ever.[26]

Perilous Times

Joseph Smith Letter

Dearly and beloved brethren, we see that perilous times have come, as was testified of. We may look, then, with most perfect assurance, for the fulfillment of all those things that have been written, and with more confidence than

Dearly and beloved Brethren we see that peralas [perilous] times have come as was testified of we may look then with most purfect asshurance for the roling in of all those things that have been written and with more

---

25. 20 March 1839, Joseph Smith et al., Letter to the Church and Edward Partridge, *JSP, D6*, 361–62. Also see *PWJS*, 431.

26. 20 March 1839, Joseph Smith et al., Letter to the Church and Edward Partridge, *JSP, D6*, 362–63. Also see *PWJS*, 431–32.

ever before, lift up our eyes to the luminary of day, and say in our hearts, Soon thou wilt veil thy blushing face. He that said "Let there be Light," and there was light, hath spoken this word. And again, Thou moon, thou dimmer light, thou luminary of night, shalt turn to blood.

We see that everything is being fulfilled; and that the time shall soon come when the Son of Man shall descend in the clouds of heaven. Our hearts do not shrink, neither are our spirits altogether broken by the grievous yoke which is put upon us. We know that God will have our oppressors in derision; that He will laugh at their calamity, and mock when their fear cometh.

O that we could be with you, brethren, and unbosom our feelings to you! We would tell, that we should have been liberated at the time Elder Rigdon was, on the writ of habeas corpus, had not our own lawyers interpreted the law, contrary [p.133] to what it reads, against us; which prevented us from introducing our evidence before the mock court.

They have done us much harm from the beginning. They have of late acknowledged that the law was misconstrued, and tantalized our feelings with it, and have entirely forsaken us, and have forfeited their oaths and their bonds; and we have a come-back on them, for they are co-workers with the mob.

confidence than ever before lift up our eyes to the luminary of day and say in our harts soon thou wilt vail thy blushing face he that said let there be light, and there was light hath spoken this word, and again thou moon thou dimmer light thou luminary of night shall trurn <turn> to blood

we see that evry thing is fulfilling and the time shall soon come when the son of man shall descend in the clouds of <heaven,> our harts do not shrink neither are our spirits altogether broken at the grievous yoak which is put upon us We know that God will have our oppressors in derision that he laf <will laugh> at their calamity and mock when their fear comith

oh that we could be with you Brethren and unbosome our feeling to you we would tell that we should have been at <liberated> the time Elder [Sidney] Rigdon was on the writ of habeas corpus had not our own lawyers interpreted the law contrary to what it reads against <us,> which prevented us from introducing our evidence before the mock court,

they have done us much harm <from> the begining they have of late acknoledged that the law was misconstrewed and tantalised our feelings with it and have intirally [entirely?] forsaken us and have forfeited their oaths and their bonds and we have a come back on them for they are co-workers with the mob.[27]

Change of Public Opinion

Joseph Smith Letter

As nigh as we can learn, the public mind has been for a long time turning in our favor, and the majority in now friendly; and the lawyers can no longer browbeat us by saying that this or that is a matter of public opinion, for public opinion is not willing to brook it; for it is

As nigh as we can learn the publick mind has been for a long time turning in our favor and the majority is now friendly [p.364] and the lawyers can no longer browbeat us by saying that this or that is a matter of publick oppinion for publick oppinion is not willing to

---

27. 20 March 1839, Joseph Smith et al., Letter to the Church and Edward Partridge, *JSP, D6*, 363. Also see *PWJS*, 432.

beginning to look with feelings of indignation against our oppressors, and to say that the "Mormons" were not in the fault in the least. We think that truth, honor, virtue and innocence will eventually come out triumphant. We should have taken a habeas corpus before the high judge and escaped the mob in a summary way; but unfortunately for us, the timber of the wall being very hard, our auger handles gave out, and hindered us longer than we expected; we applied to a friend, and a very slight incautious act gave rise to some suspicions, and before we could fully succeed, our plan was discovered; we had everything in readiness, but the last stone, and we could have made our escape in one minute, and should have succeeded admirably, had it not been for a little imprudence or over-anxiety on the part of our friend.

The sheriff and jailer did not blame us for our attempt; it was a fine breach, and cost the county a round sum; but public opinion says that we ought to have been permitted to have made our escape; that then the disgrace would have been on us, but now it must come on the state; that there cannot be any charge sustained against us; and that the conduct of the mob, the murders committed at Haun's Mills, and the exterminating order of the governor, and the one-sided, rascally proceedings of the legislature, have damned the state of Missouri to all eternity. I would just name also that General Atchison has proved himself as contemptible as any of them.

We have tried for a long time to get our lawyers to draw us some petitions to the supreme judges of this state, but they [p.134] utterly refused. We have examined the law, and drawn the petitions ourselves, and have obtained abundance of proof to counteract all the testimony that was against us, so that if the supreme judge does not grant us our liberty, he has to act without cause, contrary to honor, evidence, law or justice, sheerly to please the devil, but we hope better things and

brook it for it is beginning to look with feelings of indignation against our oppresors and to say that the mormons were not in the fault in the least we think that truth honor and virtue and inocence will eventually come out tryumphant we should have taken a habeas corpus before the high Judge and escaped the mob in a summerary way but unfortunatly for us the timber of the wall being verry hard our auger handles gave out and hindered us longer than we expected we applied to a friend and a verry slight uncautious act gave rise to some suspition and before we could fully succeed our plan was discovered we had evry thing in readiness but the last stone and we could have made our escape in one minute and should have succeeded admirably had it not been for a little imprudance or over anxiety on the part of our friend.

The sheriff and jailor did not blame us for our attempt it was a fine breach and cost the county a round sum but publick oppinion says that we ought to have been permitted to have made our escape that then the disgrace would have been on us, but now it must come on the state. that there cannot be any charge sustained against us and that the conduct of the mob, the murders committed at hawns mill, and the exterminating order of the Governer, and the one sided rascally proceedings of the Legislature has damned the state of Missouri to all eternity I would just name also that Gen[L.] [David R.] Atchison has proved himself to be as contemtible as any of them

we have tryed for a long time to [p.365] get our lawyers to draw us some petitions to the supream Judges of this state. but they uterly refused we have examined the law and drawn the petitions oursevs and have obtained abundance of proof to counter act all the testimony that was against us, so that if the supream Judge dose [does] <not grant> us our liberty he has got to act without cause contrary to honor evidence law or justice shearly to please the devil but we hope better things and trust

The Sympathy of Friends

| | Joseph Smith Letter |

We received some letters last evening,—one from Emma, one from Don C. Smith, and one from Bishop Partridge—all breathing a kind and consoling spirit. We were much gratified with their contents. We had been a long time without information; and when we read those letters they were to our souls as the gentle air is refreshing, but our joy was mingled with grief, because of the sufferings of the poor and much injured Saints. And we need not say to you that the floodgates of our hearts were lifted and our eyes were a fountain of tears, but those who have not been enclosed in the walls of prison without cause or provocation, can have but little idea how sweet the voice of a friend is; one token of friendship from any source whatever awakens and calls into action every sympathetic feeling; it brings up in an instant everything that is passed; it seizes the present with the avidity of lightning; it grasps after the future with the fierceness of a tiger; it moves the mind backward and forward, from on thing to another, until finally all enmity, malice and hatred, and past differences, misunderstandings and mismanagements are slain victorious at the feet of hope; and when the heart is sufficiently contrite, then the voice of inspiration steals along and whispers—

we received some letters last evening one from Emma one from Don C[arlos] Smith and one from Bishop Partridge all breathing a kind and consoling spirit we were much gratified with there contence [contents] we had been a long time without information and when we read those letters they were to our soles <souls> as the gentle air, <is> refreshing but our joy was mingled with greaf because of the suffering of the poor and much injured saints and we need not say to you that the flood gates of our harts were hoisted and our eyes were a fountain of tears but those who have not been inclosed in the walls of a prison without cause or provication can have but a little ideah how sweat [sweet] the voice of a friend is one token of friendship from any sorce whatever awakens and calles into action evry simpathetick feeling it brings up in an instant evry thing that is pas[s]ed it sesses [seizes?] the presant with a vivasity of lightning It grasps after the future with the fearsness [fierceness] of a tiger it rhetrogrades from one thing to an other untill finally all enmity malice and hatred and past diferances misunderstandings and mismanagements lie slain victoms at the feet of hope and when the hart is sufficiently contrite and <then> the voice of inspiration **[p.366]** steals along and whispers[29]

The Value of Tribulation

| | Joseph Smith Letter |

[My son, peace be unto thy soul; thine adversity and thine afflictions shall be but a small moment; and then if thou endure it well, God

my son pease be unto thy soul thine advirsity and thy afflictions shall be but a small moment and then if thou indure it well God shall

---

28. 20 March 1839, Joseph Smith et al., Letter to the Church and Edward Partridge, *JSP, D6,* 363–65. Also see *PWJS,* 432–33.

29. 20 March 1839, Joseph Smith et al., Letter to the Church and Edward Partridge, *JSP, D6,* 365–66. Also see *PWJS,* 433–34.

shall exalt thee on high; thou shalt triumph over all thy foes. Thy friends do stand by thee, and they shall hail thee again, with warm hearts and friendly hands; thou art not yet as Job; thy friends do not contend against thee, neither charge thee with transgression, as they did Job; and they who do charge thee with transgression, their hope shall be blasted [p.135] and their prospects shall melt away as the hoar frost melteth before the burning rays of the rising sun; and also that God hath set His hand and seal to change the times and seasons, and to blind their minds, that they may not understand His marvelous workings, that He may prove them also and take them in their own craftiness; also because their hearts are corrupted, and the things which they are willing to bring upon others, and love to have others suffer, may come upon themselves to the very uttermost; that they may be disappointed also; and their hopes may be cut off; and not many years hence, that they and their posterity shall be swept from under heaven, saith God, that not one of them is left to stand by the wall. Cursed are all those that shall lift up the heel against mine anointed, saith the Lord, and cry they have sinned when they have not sinned before me, saith the Lord, but have done that which was meet in mine eyes, and which I commanded them; but those who cry transgression do it because they are the servants of sin and are the children of disobedience themselves; and those who swear falsely against my servants, that they might bring them into bondage and death; wo unto them; because they have offended my little ones; they shall be severed from the ordinances of mine house; their basket shall not be full, and their houses and their barns shall perish, and they themselves shall be despised by those that flattered them; they shall not have right to the Priesthood, nor their posterity after them, from generation to generation; it had been better for them that a millstone had been hanged about their necks, and they drowned in the depth of the sea.

exalts the[e] on high thou shalt tryumph over all they foes thy friends do stand by the[e] and they shall hail the[e] again with warm harts and friendly hands thou art ~~yet~~ not yet as Job thy friends do not contend again[st] the[e] ~~the~~ neither charge the[e] with transgretion as they did Job and they <who> do ~~the~~ charge the[e] with transgretion there hope shall be blasted and there prospects shall melt away as the hory frost melteth before the burning rays of the rising sun and also that God hath set to his hand and seal to change the times and seasons and to blind their minds that they may not understand his marvilos workings that he may prove them also and take them in there own craftiness also because their harts are corrupt and the thing which they are willing to bring upon others and love to have others suffer may come upon them<selvs> to the verry utmost that they may be disappointed also and their hopes may be cut off and not many years hence that they and their pasterity shall be swept from under heaven saith God that not one of them is left to stand by the wall cursed are all those that shall lift up the heal against mine anointed saith the Lord and cry they have sin[n]ed when they have not sined before me saith the Lord but have done that which was meat in mine eyes and which I commanded them but those who cry transgresion do it becaus they are the servants of sin and are the children of disobediance themselvs and those who swear false against my servants that they might bring them unto bondage and death. Wo unto them because they have offended my little ones they shall be severed from the ordinances of mine house their basket shall not be full their houses and their barnes shall famish and they themselvs shall be dispised by those that flattered them they shall not have right to the priesthood nor their posterity after them from generation to generation it had been better for them that a millstone had been hanged about [p.367] their necks and they ~~having~~ drownd in the depth of the see

Wo unto all those that discomfort my people, and drive and murder, and testify against them, saith the Lord of Hosts; a generation of vipers shall not escape the damnation of hell. Behold mine eyes see and know all their works, and I have in reserve a swift judgment in the season thereof, for them all; for there is a time appointed for every man according as his work shall be.]

wo unto all those that discomfort my people and drive and murder and testify against them saith the Lord of host a generation of viper shall not escape the damnation of hell behold mine eyes seeth and knoweth all their works and I have in reserve a swift judgement in the season thereoff for them all for there is a time appointed ~~for~~ <to> evry man according ~~their~~ <as his> work shall be[30]

A Tried People

Joseph Smith Letter

And now, beloved brethren, we say unto you, that inasmuch as God hath said that He would have a tried people, that He would purge them as gold, now we think that this time He has chosen His own crucible, wherein we have been tried; **[p.136]** and we think if we get through with any degree of safety, and shall have kept the faith, that it will be a sign to this generation, altogether sufficient to leave them without excuse; and we think also, it will be a trial of our faith equal to that of Abraham, and that the ancients will not have whereof to boast over us in the day of judgment, as being called to pass through heavier afflictions; that we may hold an even weight in the balance with them; but now, after having suffered so great sacrifice and having passed through so great a season of sorrow, we trust that a ram may be caught in the thicket speedily, to relieve the sons and daughters of Abraham from their great anxiety, and to light up the lamp of salvation upon their countenances, that they may hold on now, after having gone so far unto everlasting life.

and now beloved Brethren we say unto [you?] that inasmuch as ~~good~~ <God> hath said that he would have a tried people that he would purge them as gold now we think that this time he has chosen his own crusible wherein we have been tryed and we think if we get through with any degree of safty and shall have kept the faith that it will be a sign to this generation all together sufficient to leave them without excuse and we think also that it will be a tryal of our faith equal to that of Abraham and that the antionts [ancients] will not have were off [whereof] to bo[a]st over us in the day of judgment as being called to pass through heavier afflictions that we may hold an even waight in the balances with them but now after having suffered so grate a sacrifis and having pased through so grate a scene of sorrow we trust that a Ram may be caught in the thicket speedily to releave the sons and daughters of Abraham from their ~~grate~~ <great> anxiety and to light up the lamp of salvation upon their countinances that they may hold ~~up~~ <on> now after having gone so far unto everlasting life.[31]

A Location for the Saints

Joseph Smith Letter

Now, brethren, concerning the places for the location of the Saints, we cannot counsel you

Now brethren conserning the places for the location of the saints we cannot counsyl you

---

30. 20 March 1839, Joseph Smith et al., Letter to the Church and Edward Partridge, *JSP, D6*, 366–67. See also *PWJS*, 434–35.

31. 20 March 1839, Joseph Smith et al., Letter to the Church and Edward Partridge, *JSP, D6*, 367. See also *PWJS*, 435.

as we could if we were present with you; and as to the things that were written heretofore, we did not consider them anything very binding, therefore we now say once for all, that we think it most proper that the general affairs of the Church, which are necessary to be considered, while your humble servant remains in bondage, should be transacted by a general conference of the most faithful and the most respectable of the authorities of the Church, and a minute of those transactions may be kept, and forwarded from time to time, to your humble servant; and if there should be any corrections by the word of the Lord, they shall be freely transmitted, and your humble servant will approve all things whatsoever is acceptable unto God. If anything should have been suggested by us, or any names mentioned, except by commandment, or thus saith the Lord, we do not consider it binding; therefore our hearts shall not be grieved if different arrangements should be entered into. Nevertheless we would suggest the propriety of being aware of an aspiring spirit, which spirit has oftentimes urged men forward to make foul speeches, and influence the Church to reject milder counsels, and has eventually been the means of bringing much death and sorrow upon the Church.

as we could if we were presant with you and <as> to the things that ware writen heartofore [heretofore] we did not concider them any thing verry binding therfore we now say once for all that we think it most proper that the general affairs of the **[p.368]** church which are nessisary to be concidered while your humble servant remains in bondage s[h]ould be transacted by a general conferance of the most faithfull and the most respictible of the authorities of the church and a minute of those transactions may be kept and fowarded from time to time to your humble servant and if there should be any corrections by the word ~~of the word of~~ the Lord they shall be f[r]eely transmitted and your humble servant will approve all ~~the~~ things what soever is acciptable unto God if any thing ~~thing~~ should have been sejusted [suggested] by us or any names mentioned ex[ce]pt by commandment or thus saith the Lord we do not concider it binding. therefore our harts shall not be greaved if diferant arraingments should be entered into ~~the~~ nevertheless we would sejest the propriety of being awar[e] of an aspiring spirit which spirit has oftentimes urged men fowards to make foul speaches and influaance the church ~~and~~ to reject milder councils and has eventually ~~by~~ <been> the means ~~been~~ of bringing much death and sorrow upon the church[32]

Beware of Pride

Joseph Smith Letter

[p.137] We would say, beware of pride also; for well and truly hath the wise man said, that pride goeth before destruction, and a haughty spirit before a fall. And again, outward appearance is not always a criterion by which to judge our fellow man; but the lips betray the haughty and overbearing imaginations of the heart; by his words and his deeds let him be judged. Flattery is also a deadly poison. A frank and open rebuke provoketh a good

we would say be awar of pride also for well and truly hath the wise man s[a]id that pride goeth before distruction and a haughty spirit before a fall / and Again outward appearance is not always a Criterean for us to Judge our fellow man but the lips betray the haughty and over barinng immginations of the heart, by his words ~~by~~ <and> his deeds let him be scan[n]ed flaterly also is a deadly poison ~~an~~ a frank an <a frank and> open Rebuke

---

32. 20 March 1839, Joseph Smith et al., Letter to the Church and Edward Partridge, *JSP, D6*, 368–69. See also *PWJS*, 435–36.

man to emulation; and in the hour of trouble he will be your best friend; but on the other hand, it will draw out all the corruptions of corrupt hearts, and lying and the poison of asps is under their tongues; and they do cause the pure in heart to be cast into prison, because they want them out of their way.

A fanciful and flowery and heated imagination beware of; because the things of God are of deep import; and time, and experience, and careful and ponderous and solemn thoughts can only find them out. Thy mind, O man! if thou wilt lead a soul unto salvation, must stretch as high as the utmost heavens, and search into and contemplate the darkest abyss, and the broad expanse of eternity—thou must commune with God. How much more dignified and noble are the thoughts of God, than the vain imaginations of the human heart! None but fools will trifle with the souls of men.

How vain and trifling have been our spirits, our conferences, our councils, our meetings, our private as well as public conversations—too low, too mean, too vulgar, too condescending for the dignified characters of the called and chosen of God, according to the purposes of His will, from before the foundation of the world! We are called to hold the keys of the mysteries of those things that have been kept hid from the foundation of the world until now. Some have tasted a little of these things, many of which are to be poured down from heaven upon the heads of babes; yea, upon the weak, obscure and despised ones of the earth. Therefore we beseech of you, brethren, that you bear with those who do not feel themselves more worthy than yourselves, while we exhort one another to a reformation with one and all, both old and young, teachers and taught, both high and low, rich and

provoketh a good man to Emulation and in the hour of trouble he will be your best friend, but on the other-hand it will draw out all the corruption of a corrupt heart And lying and the poison of asps shall be under their tongues and they do cause the pure in heart to be cast in to prison because they want them out of thare way,

A fanciful and flowely and heated immagination be aware of because the things of God Are of deep import and time and expeariance and car[e]ful and pondurous and solom though[ts] can only find them out, thy mind O Man, if thou wilt lead a soul unto salvation must streach [stretch] as high as the utmost Heavens, and ~~sink~~ sear[c]h in to and contemplate the ~~loest~~ <lowest> consideatins [considerations] of the darkest abyss, and Expand upon the broad considerations of Eternal Expance, he must commune with God. how much more dignifide and noble are the thoughts of God, than the vane imagination [p.369] of the human heart, none but fools, will triful [trifle], with the souls of men,

how vane and trifling, have ben our spirits, our Conferencs our Coun[c]ils our— ~~private~~ Meetings our pri[v]ate as well as public Conversations to low to mean to vulgar to condecending, for the dignifide Characters of the Cald and Chosen of God, according to the purposes of his ~~word~~ will from befo[re] the foundation of the world. to hold the keys, of the mistres [mysteries] of those things that have ben kept hid from the foundation untill now, ~~for~~ <of> which som have tasted a little and which many of them are to be pored down from heaven upon the heads of babes, yea the weak, obscure and dispizable ones of this earth. therefore We beseath of you bretheren, that ~~bare~~ <you bear> with those [w]ho do not feel themselves more worthey than yourselves, while we Exort one another, to a reffermation [reformation?], with one an all. both old and young. teachers and taugt both poor, bond and free, male and female; let honesty, and sobriety, and candor, and solemnity, and virtue, and pureness, and meekness, and sim[p.138]plicity crown our heads in every place; and in fine, become as little children, without malice, guile or hypocrisy.

high and low rich and poor—bond and free. Male and female. let honesty and sobriety, and cander and solemnity, and virtue, and pureness, and Meekness, and simplisity, Crown our heads in every place, and in fine becom as little Children without mallice guile or ~~high packrichy~~ Hypokrisy:[33]

Revelation of Eternal Truth

Joseph Smith Letter

And now, brethren, after your tribulations, if you do these things, and exercise fervent prayer and faith in the sight of God always, [He shall give unto you knowledge by His Holy Spirit, yea by the unspeakable gift of the Holy Ghost, that has not been revealed since the world was until now; which our forefathers have waited with anxious expectation to be revealed in the last times, which their minds were pointed to by the angels, as held in reserve for the fullness of their glory; a time to come in which nothing shall be withheld, whether there be one God or many Gods, they shall be manifest; all thrones and dominions, principalities and powers, shall be revealed and set forth upon all who have endured valiantly for the Gospel of Jesus Christ; and also if there be bounds set to the heavens, or to the seas; or to the dry land, or to the sun, moon or stars; all the times of their revolutions; all the appointed days, months and years, and all the days of their days, months and years, and all their glories, laws, and set times, shall be revealed, in the days of the dispensation of the fullness of times, according to that which was ordained in the midst of the Council of the Eternal God of all other Gods, before this world was, that should be reserved unto the finishing and the end thereof, when every man shall enter into His eternal presence, and into His immortal rest].

and now Bretheren after your tribulations if you do this— things, and exercise fervent prayer, and faith in the sight of God Always, he shall give unto you knowledge by his holy spirit yea by the unspeakable gift of the holy-Ghost that has not been revealed since the world was untill now which our fathers have wated with anxious expectation to be revealed in the last times which their minds were pointed to by the Angels as held in reserve for the fullness of their glory a time to come in the which nothing shall be with held whither there be one god or many god's they shall be manifest all thrones and dominions principalities and powers shall be revealed and set forth upon all who have indured valienty for the gospel of Jesus Christ and also if there be bounds set to the heavens or to the seas or to the dry land or to the sun moon or starrs all the times of their revolutions all their appointed days month and years and all the Days of their days, months and years and all their glories laws and set [p.370] times shall be reveald in the days of the dispensation of the fullness of times according to that which was ordaind in the midst of the councyl of the eternal God of all other Gods before this world was that should be reserved unto the finishing and the end thereoff ~~where~~ <when> evry man shall enter into his eternal presants and into his imortal rest[34]

---

33. 20 March 1839, Joseph Smith et al., Letter to the Church and Edward Partridge, *JSP, D6*, 368–69. Also see *PWJS*, 436–37.

34. 20 March 1839, Joseph Smith et al., Letter to the Church and Edward Partridge, *JSP, D6*, 369–70. Also see *PWJS*, 437.

Ignorance Retards the Church

But I beg leave to say unto you, brethren, that ignorance, superstition and bigotry placing itself where it ought not, is oftentimes in the way of the prosperity of this Church; like the torrent of rain from the mountains, that floods the most pure and crystal stream with mire, and dirt, and filthiness, and obscures everything that was clear before, and all rushes along in one general deluge; but time weathers tide; and notwithstanding we are rolled in the mire of the flood for the time being, the next surge peradventure, as time rolls on, may bring to us the fountain as clear as crystal, and as pure as snow; while the filthiness, flood-wood and rubbish is left and purged out by the way.

Joseph Smith Letter

but I beg leave to say unto you Brethren that ignorance supe[r]stition and bigotry placing itself where it ought not is often times in the way of the prosperity of this church like the torant of rain from the mountains that floods the most pure and christle stream with mire and dirt and filthyness and obscures evry thing that was clear before and all hurls along in one general deluge but time tethers <wethers> tide and notwithstanding we are roled in for the time being by the mire of the flood the next surge peradventure as time roles on may bring us to the fountain as clear as cristal and as pure as snow while all the filthiness flood wood and rubbish is left is left and purged out by the way.[35]

The Hand of the Lord Cannot Be Stayed

[p.139] [How long can rolling waters remain impure? What power shall stay the heavens? As well might man stretch forth his puny arm to stop the Missouri river in its decreed course, or to turn it up stream, as to hinder the Almighty from pouring down knowledge from heaven, upon the heads of the Latter-day Saints.]

What is Boggs or his murderous party, but wimbling willows upon the shore to catch the flood-wood? As well might we argue that water is not water, because the mountain torrents send down mire and roil the crystal stream, although afterwards render it more pure than before; or that fire is not fire, because it is of a quenchable nature, by pouring on the flood; as to say that our cause is down because renegades, liars, priests, thieves and murderers, who are all alike tenacious of their crafts and creeds, have poured down, from their spiritual wickedness in high places, and from their

Joseph Smith Letter

How long can rowling watters reamin impure what power shall stay the heavens as well might man streach forth his puny arm to stop the Missouri River in its decread cours or to turne it up stream as to hinder the Almighty from pooring down knoledge from <heaven> upon the heads of the Latter day saints

what is Boggs or his murderous party but wimbling willows upon the shore to catch the flood wood as will might we argue that watter is not watter because the the mountain torants send down mire and riles the cristle stream altho afterwords ren[d]ers it more pure than before Or that fire is not fire because it is of a quenchable nature by pooing [pouring] on the flood, as to say that our cause is down because runegadoes lyers preasts theavs and murderers who are all alike tenatious of their crafts and creeds have poord down from their spiritual wickednes in hig[h] places and from their strong holds of

---

35. 20 March 1839, Joseph Smith et al., Letter to the Church and Edward Partridge, *JSP, D6*, 370. See also *PWJS*, 437.

strongholds of the devil, a flood of dirt and mire and filthiness and vomit upon our heads.	the divin[e] a flud of dirt and mire and **[p.371]** filthiness and vomit upon our heads
No! God forbid. Hell may pour forth its rage like the burning lava of mount Vesuvius, or of Etna, or of the most terrible of the burning mountains; and yet shall "Mormonism" stand. Water, fire, truth and God are all realities. Truth is "Mormonism." God is the author of it. He is our shield. It is by Him we received our birth. It was by His voice that we were called to a dispensation of His Gospel in the beginning of the fullness of times. It was by Him we received the Book of Mormon; and it is by Him that we remain unto this day; and by Him we shall remain, if it shall be for our glory; and in His Almighty name we are determined to endure tribulation as good soldiers unto the end.	no God forbid. hell may poor forth its rage like the burning lavy [lava] of mount vesuvias or of Etna or of the most terible of the burning mountains and yet shall mormonism stand. watter, fire, truth, and god are all the same truth is mormonism God is the author of it he is our shield it is by him we received our birth, it was by his voice that we were called to ~~in~~ a dispensation of his gospel in the begining of the fullness of tim[e]s it was by him we received the book of mormon and it was by him that we remain unto this day and by him we shall remain if it shall be for our glory and in his almighty name we are determined to indure tribulation as good soldiers unto the end
But brethren, we shall continue to offer further reflections in our next epistle. You will learn by the time you have read this, and if you do not learn it, you may learn it, that walls and irons, doors and creaking hinges, and half-scared-to-death guards and jailers, grinning like some damned spirits, lest an innocent man should make his escape to bring to light the damnable deeds of a murderous mob, are calculated in their very nature to make the soul of an honest man feel stronger than the powers of hell.	but brethren we shall continue to offer further reflections in our next epistle you will learn by the time you have read this and if you do not learn it you may learn it that walls and \<iron\> doors \<and screaking hinges\> ~~is only calcu~~ and half scard to death Guards and jailors grining like some damned spirit lest an inocent man should make his escape to bring to light the damnible deeds of a murderous mob is cal[c]ulated in its verry nature to make the sole of an honist man feel stronger than the powers of hell.
But we must bring our epistle to a close. We send our **[p.140]** respects to fathers, mothers, wives and children, brothers and sisters; we hold them in the most sacred remembrance.	But we must bring our epistle to a close we send our respects to Fathers, Mothers, wives, and children, Brothers, and Sisters. we hold them in the most sacred rememberance
We feel to inquire after Elder Rigdon; if he has not forgotten us, it has not been signified to us by his writing. Brother George W. Robinson also; and Elder Cahoon, we remember him, but would like to jog his memory a little on the fable of the bear and the two friends who mutually agreed to stand by each other. And	~~I send this epistle to Emma that She may have the first parusal of it~~ we feel to inquire after Elder Rigdon if he has not forgotten us it has not been signified to us by his ~~pen~~ scrawl. Brother George W Robinson also and Elder [Reynolds] Cahoon we remember him but would like to jog his memory a little on the fable of the bair and the two friends who

perhaps it would not be amiss to mention uncle John [Smith], and various others. A word of consolation and a blessing would not come amiss from anybody, while we are being so closely whispered by the bear. But we feel to excuse everybody and everything, yea the more readily when we contemplate that we are in the hands of persons worse than a bear, for the bear would not prey upon a dead carcass.

Our respects and love and fellowship to all the virtuous Saints. We are your brethren and fellow-sufferers, and prisoners of Jesus Christ for the Gospel's sake, and for the hope of glory which is in us. Amen.

We continue to offer further reflections to Bishop Partridge, and to the Church of Jesus Christ of Latter-day Saints, whom we love with a fervent love, and do always bear them in mind in all our prayers to the throne of God.

It still seems to bear heavily on our minds that the Church would do well to secure to themselves the contract of the land, which is proposed to them by Mr. Isaac Galland, and to cultivate the friendly feelings of that gentleman, inasmuch as he shall prove himself to be a man of honor and a friend to humanity; also Isaac Van Allen, Esq., the attorney-general of Iowa Territory, and Governor Lucas, that peradventure such men may be wrought upon by the providence of God, to do good unto His people. We really think that Mr. Galland's letter breathes that kind of a spirit, if we may

mutually agreed to stand by each other and prehaps it would not be amis to mention Unkle John [Smith] and various others, a word of consolation and a blessing would **[p.372]** not come amiss from any body while we are being so closly whispered by the Bair but we feel to excuse evry body and evry thing. Yea the more readily when we contemplate that we are in the hands of a wors than a Bair for a the Bair would not pray upon a dead carcus.

Our respects and love and fellowship to all the virtious saints we are your Brethren and fellow sufferers and prisoners of Jesus Christ for the gospels sake and for the hope of glory which is in us. Amen.
Joseph Smith Jr
Hyrum Smith
Lyman Wight
Caleb Baldwin
Alexander. McRae.[36]

Continued Reflections

Joseph Smith Letter

We continue to offer further reflections to Bishop [Edward] Partridge and to the church of Jesus Christ of Latter day saints whom we love with a fervent love and do always bear them in mind in all our prayers to the throne of God.

It still seems to bear ~~heavy~~ heavily in our minds that the church would do ~~will~~ well to secure to themselves the contract of the Land which is proposed to them **[p.392]** by Mr. Isaac Galland and to cultivate the friendly feelings of that gentleman in as much ~~shall~~ as he shall prove himself to be a man of honor ~~humanity~~ and a friend to humanity. We really think that his letter breaths that kind of spirit if we can judge correctly. And Isaac Van Allen Esqr the attorney Genl of Iawa Territory that peradventure such men may be wrought upon by the providence of God to do good unto

---

36. 20 March 1839, Joseph Smith et al., Letter to the Church and Edward Partridge, *JSP, D6*, 370–72. See also *PWJS*, 437–39. Part of this letter is now found in section 121 of the Doctrine and Covenants.

judge correctly. Governor Lucas' also. We suggest the idea of praying fervently for all men who manifest any degree of sympathy for the suffering children of God.

We think that the United States Surveyor of the Iowa Territory may be of great benefit to the Church, if it be the will of God to this end; and righteousness should be manifested as the girdle of our loins.

his people. Governer [Robert] Lucas also. We suggest the ideah of praying fervantly for all men who manifest any degree of sympathy for the suffering children of God.

We think that peradventure the united States survayor of the Iowa Territory may be of grate benefeit to the church if it be the will of God to this end if ritiousness ~~shall~~ should be manifested as the girdle of our loins.[37]

Preparation Against the Wrath of God

Joseph Smith Letter

[p.141] It seems to be deeply impressed upon our minds that the Saints ought to lay hold of every door that shall seem to be opened unto them, to obtain foothold on the earth, and be making all the preparation that is within their power for the terrible storms that are now gathering in the heavens, "a day of clouds, with darkness and gloominess, and of thick darkness," as spoken of by the Prophets which cannot be now of a long time lingering, for there seems to be a whispering that the angels of heaven who have been entrusted with the counsel of these matters for the last days, have taken counsel together; and among the rest of the general affairs that have to be transacted in their honorable council, they have taken cognizance of the testimony of those who were murdered at Haun's Mills, and also those who were martyred with David W. Patten, and elsewhere, and have passed some decisions peradventure in favor of the Saints, and those who were called to suffer without cause.

It seems to be deeply impresed upon our minds that the saints ought to lay hold of evry door ~~shall~~ that shall seem to be opened ~~for~~ unto them to obtain foot hold on the Earth and be a ~~make~~ making all the preparation<s> that is within the power of posibles for the terible storms that are now gethering in the heavens with darkness and gloominess and thick darkness as spoken of by the prophets which cannot be now of a long time lingering for there seems to be a whispering that the angels of heaven who have been intrusted with the ~~council~~ counsel of these matters for the last days have taken ~~council~~ counsel together: and among the rest of the general affairs that have to be transacted in their honorable ~~council~~ counsel they have taken cognisance of the testimony of those who were murdered at Hawns Mills and also those who [p.393] were martered with D[avid] W. Patten. and else where and have passed some decisions peradventure in favour of the saints and those who were called to suffer without cause

These decisions will be made known in their time; and the council will take into consideration all those things that offend.

these decisions will be made known in there time and they will take into concideration all those things that offend.

We have a fervent desire that in your general conferences everything should be discussed

We have a fervant desire that in your general conferences that evry thing should be discused

---

37. Circa 22 March 1839, *JSP, D6*, 391–92. See also *PWJS*, 439. Portions of this letter are found in sections 121, 122, and 123 of the Doctrine and Covenants.

with a great deal of care and propriety, lest you grieve the Holy Spirit, which shall be poured out at all times upon your heads, when you are exercised with those principles of righteousness that are agreeable to the mind of God, and are properly affected one toward another, and are careful by all means to remember, those who are in bondage, and in heaviness, and in deep affliction for your sakes. And if there are any among you who aspire after their own aggrandizement, and seek their own opulence, while their brethren are groaning in poverty, and are under sore trials and temptations, they cannot be benefited by the intercession of the Holy Spirit, which maketh intercession for us day and night with groanings that cannot be uttered.

We ought at all times to be very careful that such highmindedness shall never have place in our hearts; but condescend to men of low estate, and with all long-suffering bear the infirmities of the weak.

with a grate deal of care and propriety lest you grieve the Holy Spirit which shall be poured out at all times upon your heads when you are exercised with those principals of ritiousness that are agreeable to the mind of God and are properly affected one toward an other and are carefull by all means to remember those <who> are in bondage and in heaviness and in deep affliction for your sakes and if there are any among you who aspire after their own aggrandisement and seek their own oppulance while thier brethren are groaning in poverty and are under sore trials and temptations they can not be benefeited by the intersesion of the Holy Spirit <which> maketh intersesion for us ~~daily~~ day and knight with groning that cannot be uttered.

We ought at all times to be verry carefull that such high mindedness never have place in our hearts but condesend to men of low estate and with all long suffering bear the infermities of the weak.[38]

Many Called But Few Chosen

Joseph Smith Letter

[p.142] [Behold, there are many called, but few are chosen. And why are they not chosen? Because their hearts are set so much upon the things of this world, and aspire to the honors of men, that they do not learn this one lesson—that the rights of the Priesthood are inseparably connected with the powers of heaven, and that the powers of heaven cannot be controlled nor handled only upon the principles of righteousness. That they may be conferred upon us, it is true; but when we undertake to cover our sins, or to gratify our pride, our vain ambition, or to exercise control, or dominion, or compulsion, upon the souls of the children of men, in any degree of unrighteousness, behold, the heavens withdraw themselves; the Spirit of the Lord is

Behold there are ma[n]y called but few are chosen. And why are they not chosen? Because their hearts are set so much upon the things of this world and aspire to the honors of men that they do not learn this one lesson that the rights of priesthood are inseperably connected with the powers of heaven and that the powers of heaven cannot be controled nor handled only upon the principals of rightiousness. That they may be confered upon us it is true but when we undertake to cover our sins or to gratify our pride or vain ambition or to exercise controle or dominion or compulsion upon the souls of the children of men in any degree of unritiousness behold the heavens withdraw themselves the spirit of the Lord is grieved and when it has withdrawn Amen to

---

38. Circa 22 March 1839, *JSP, D6*, 392–93. See also *PWJS*, 439–40. Portions of this letter are found in sections 121, 122, and 123 of the Doctrine and Covenants.

grieved; and when it is withdrawn, Amen to the Priesthood, or the authority of that man. Behold! ere he is aware, he is left unto himself, to kick against the pricks; to persecute the Saints, and to fight against God.

We have learned by sad experience that it is the nature and disposition of almost all men, as soon as they get a little authority, as they suppose, they will immediately begin to exercise unrighteous dominion. Hence many are called, but few are chosen.

the priesthood or the authority of that man behold ere he is aware he is left unto himself to kicken against the pricks to persecute the saints and to fight against God.

We have learned by sad experiance that it is the nature and disposition of almost all men as soon as they get a little authority as they suppose they will imediately begin to **[p.394]** [e]xercise unritious dominion. hence ma[n]y [are] called but few are ch[osen.][39]

The Priesthood Gentle and Long-suffering

Joseph Smith Letter

No power or influence can or ought to be maintained by virtue of the Priesthood, only by persuasion, by long-suffering, by gentleness, and meekness, and by love unfeigned; by kindness, and pure knowledge, which shall greatly enlarge the soul without hypocrisy, and without guile, reproving betimes with sharpness, when moved upon by the Holy Ghost, and then showing forth afterwards an increase of love toward him whom thou hast reproved, lest he esteem thee to be his enemy; that he may know that thy faithfulness is stronger than the cords of death; let thy bowels also be full of charity towards all men, and to the household of faith, and let virtue garnish thy thoughts unceasingly, then shall thy confidence wax strong in the presence of God, and the doctrine of the Priesthood shall distil upon thy soul as the dews from heaven. The Holy Ghost shall be thy constant companion, and thy sceptre an unchanging sceptre of righteousness and truth, and thy dominion shall **[p.143]** be an everlasting dominion, and without compulsory means it shall flow unto thee forever and ever.]

[The ends of the earth shall inquire after thy name, and fools shall have thee in derision,

[No power or in]f[luence] can or ought to be maintained by <[vi]rt[ue]> of the Priesthood only by persuasion by long suffering by gentleness and meekness and by love unfaigned by kindness by pure knowledge which shall greatly enlarge the soul without hypocrisy and without guile reproving be-times with sharpness when moved upon by the Holy Ghost and then showing forth afterwords an increas of love toward him whom thou hast reproved lest he esteem the[e] to be his enimy that he may know that thy faithfulness is stronger than the cords of death thy bowells also being full of charity towards all men and to the household of faith and virtue garnish thy thoughts unceasingly then shall thy confidence wax strong in the presants of God, and the doctrins of the Priesthood shall destill upon thy soul as the dews from heaven the Holy Ghost shall be thy constant companion and thy septer an unchanging septer of ritiousness and truth and thy dominion shall be an everlasting dominion and without compulsory means it shall flow [un]to thee for ever and ever.

The ends of the Earth shall [enq]uire after thy na[me] and fools shall have thee in deri[s]ion

---

39. Circa 22 March 1839, *JSP, D6*, 393–94. See also *PWJS*, 440–41. Portions of this letter are found in sections 121, 122, and 123 of the Doctrine and Covenants.

and hell shall rage against thee, while the pure in heart, and the wise, and the noble, and the virtuous, shall seek counsel, and authority and blessings constantly from under thy hand, and thy people shall never be turned against thee by the testimony of traitors; and although their influence shall cast thee into trouble, and into bars and walls, thou shalt be had in honor, and but for a small moment and thy voice shall be more terrible in the midst of thine enemies, than the fierce lion, because of thy righteousness; and thy God shall stand by thee forever and ever.

and hell shall rage against thee while the pure in heart and the wise and the noble and the virtious shall seek ~~council~~ counsel and authority and blessings constantly from under thy hand and thy people shall never be turned against thee by the testimony of traitors and although their influenance shall cast the[e] into trouble and into bars and walls thou shalt be had in honor and **[p.395]** but for a small moment and thy voice shall be more terable in the midst of thine enemies than the fierce Lion because of thy ritiousness and thy God shall stand by the[e] for ever and ever.[40]

Experience Through Suffering

Joseph Smith Letter

If thou art called to pass through tribulations; if thou art in perils among false brethren; if thou art in perils among robbers; if thou art in perils by land or by sea; if thou art accused with all manner of false accusations; if thine enemies fall upon thee; if they tear thee from the society of thy father and mother and brethren and sisters; and if with a drawn sword thine enemies tear thee from the bosom of thy wife, and of thine offspring, and thine elder son, although but six years of age, shall cling to thy garments, and shall say, My father, my father, why can't you stay with us? O, my father, what are the men going to do with you? and if then he shall be thrust from thee by the sword, and thou be dragged to prison, and thine enemies prowl around thee like wolves for the blood of the lamb; and if thou shouldest be cast into the pit, or into the hands of murderers, and the sentence of death passed upon thee; if thou be cast into the deep, if the billowing surge conspire against thee; if fierce winds become thine enemy; if the heavens gather blackness, and all the elements combine to hedge up the way; and above all, if the very jaws of hell shall gape open the mouth wide after thee, know

If thou art called to pass through tribulation. If thou art in perals among fals brethren. If thou art in perals amongst robbers. If thou art in perals by land or by sea. If thou art accused with all maner of fals accusations. If thine enimies fall upon the[e]. If they tear the[e] from the society of thy father and mother and brethren and Sisters. And if with a drawn sword thine enimies tear the[e] from the bosome of thy Wife and of thine offsprings and thine El[d]er son although but six years of age shall cling to thy garments and shall say my Father my Father why cant you stay with us Oh my Father what are the men going to do with you. And if then he shall be thrust from the[e] by the sword and thou be draged to prison and thine enimies prowl around the[e] like wolves for blood of the Lamb and if thou shouldest be cast into the pit or into the hands of murderers and the sentantce of death pased upon thee. If thou be cast into the deep. If the billowing surge conspire against thee. If fierce wind become thine enimy. If the heavens gether blackness and all the elements combine to hedge up the way and above all if the verry jaws of hell shall gap open her mouth wide after <thee> know thou my son that all these

---

40. Circa 22 March 1839, *JSP, D6*, 394–95. See also *PWJS*, 441. Portions of this letter are found in sections 121, 122, and 123 of the Doctrine and Covenants.

thou, my son, that all these things shall give thee experience, and shall be for thy good. The Son of Man hath descended below them all; art thou greater than he?

things shall give thee experiance and shall be for thy good. The son of man hath desended below them all art thou greater than he?[41]

Gathering of the Saints

Joseph Smith Letter

Therefore, hold on thy way, and the Priesthood shall remain with thee, for their bounds are set, they cannot pass. Thy [p.144] days are known, and thy years shall not be numbered less; therefore, fear not what man can do, for God shall be with you forever and ever.]

Therefore hold on thy way and the priesthood shall remain with thee for their bounds are set they cannot pass. Thee Thy days are known and thy years shall not be numbered less. therefore fear not what man can do for God shall be with you for ever and ever.

Now, brethren, I would suggest for the consideration of the conference, it being carefully and wisely understood by the council or conferences that our brethren scattered abroad, who understood the spirit of the gathering, that they fall into the places and refuge of safety that God shall open unto them, between Kirtland and Far West. Those from the east and from the west, and from far countries, let them fall in somewhere between those two boundaries, in the most safe and quiet places they can find; and let this be the present understanding, until God shall open a more effectual door for us for further considerations.

Now brethren I would suggest for the concidereration of the conference of its being carefully and wisely understood by the <counsel> or conferences that our brethren [p.396] scattered abroad who understand the spirit of the gethering that they fall into the places of refuge and saf[e]ty that God shall open unto them betwean Kirtland and Far West. Those from the East and from the West and from far country countries let them fall in some where betwean those two boundries in the most safe and quiet places they can find and let this be the presant understanding untill God shall open a more effectual door for us for further conciderations.

And again, we further suggest for the considerations of the Council, that there be no organization of large bodies upon common stock principles, in property, or of large companies of firms, until the Lord shall signify it in a proper manner, as it opens such a dreadful field for the avaricious, the indolent, and the corrupt hearted to prey upon the innocent and virtuous, and honest.

And again we further suggest for the concideration of the counsel that there be no organizations of large bodies upon common stock principals in property or of large companies of firms untill the Lord shall signify it in a proper manner as it opens such a dreafull [dreadful] field for the averishous and the indolent and corrupt hearted to pray upon the inocent and virtious and honist

We have reason to believe that many things were introduced among the Saints before God had signified the times; and notwithstanding

We have reason to believe that many things were introduced among the saints before God had signified the times and not withstanding

---

41. Circa 22 March 1839, *JSP, D6*, 395. See also *PWJS*, 441–42. Portions of this letter are found in sections 121, 122, and 123 of the Doctrine and Covenants.

the principles and plans may have been good, yet aspiring men, or in other words, men who had not the substance of godliness about them, perhaps undertook to handle edged tools. Children, you know, are fond of tools, while they are not yet able to use them.

Time and experience, however, are the only safe remedies against such evils. There are many teachers, but, perhaps, not many fathers. There are times coming when God will signify many things which are expedient for the well-being of the Saints; but the times have not yet come, but will come, as fast as there can be found place and reception for them.

the principles and plans may have <been> good yet aspiring men or in other word men <who> had not the substance of Godliness about them perhaps undertook to handle edg tools children you know are fond of tools while they are not yet able to use them.

Time and experiance however is the only safe remidy against such evils there are many teachers but perhaps not many [p.397] Fathers. There are times comming when God will signify many things which are expediant for the well being of the saints but the times have not yet come but will come as fast as there can be found place and reseptions for them.[42]

The Gathering of False Reports

Joseph Smith Letter

[And again, we would suggest for your consideration the propriety of all the Saints gathering up a knowledge of all the facts and sufferings and abuses put upon them by the people of this state; and also of all the property and amount of damages which they have sustained, both of character and personal [p.145] injuries, as well as real property; and also the names of all persons that have had a hand in their oppressions, as far as they can get hold of them and find them out; and perhaps a committee can be appointed to find out these things, and to take statements, and affidavits, and also to gather up the libelous publications that are afloat, and all that are in the magazines, and in the encyclopedias, and all the libelous histories that are published, and are writing, and by whom, and present the whole concatenation of diabolical rascality, and nefarious and murderous impositions that have been practiced upon this people, that we may not only publish to all the world, but present them to the heads of government in all their dark and hellish hue, as the last effort which is enjoined on us by our Heavenly

And again we would suggest for your concideration the propriety of all the saints gethering up the <a> knowledge of <all> the facts and suffering and abuses put upon them by the people of this state and also of all the property and amount of damages which they have sustained both of character and personal <Injuries as will as real property> property and also the names of all persons that have had a hand in their oppressions as far as they can get hold of them and find them out. and perhaps a committe can be appointed to find out these things and to take statements and affidafets and also to gether up the libilous publications that are afloat and all that are in the magazines and in the Insiclopedias [encyclopedias] and all the libillious history histories that are published and that <are> writing and by whom and present the whole concatination of diabolical rascality and nefarious and murderous impositions that have been practised upon this people that we may not only publish to all the world but present them to the heads of the government in all there dark and hellish hugh [hue?] as the last effort which is injoined on us by our heavenly.

---

42. Circa 22 March 1839, *JSP, D6*, 395–97. See also *PWJS*, 442–43. Portions of this letter are found in sections 121, 122, and 123 of the Doctrine and Covenants.

Father, before we can fully and completely claim that promise which shall call Him forth from His hiding place, and also that the whole nation may be left without excuse before He can send forth the power of His mighty arm.

Father before we can fully and completely claim that promise which shall call him forth from his hiding place and also the whole nation may be left without excuse before he can send forth the power of his mighty arm.[43]

A Duty to Wives and Children

Joseph Smith Letter

It is an imperative duty that we owe to God, to angels, with whom we shall be brought to stand, and also to ourselves, to our wives and children, who have been made to bow down with grief, sorrow, and care, under the most damning hand of murder, tyranny, and oppressions, supported and urged on and upheld by the influence of that spirit which has so strongly riveted the creeds of the fathers, who have inherited lies, upon the hearts of the children, and filled the world with confusion, and has been growing stronger and stronger, and is now the very main-spring of all corruption, and the whole earth groans under the weight of its iniquity.

It is an imperious duty that we owe to God to angels with whom we shall be brought to stand and also to ourselves to our wives and our children who have been made to bow down with grief sorrow and care under the most damning hand of murder tyranny and oppression supported and urged on and upheld by the influance of that spirit which hath so strongly rivited the creeds of the fathers **[p.398]** who have inherited lies upon the harts of the children and filled the world with confusion and has been growing stronger and stronger and is now the verry mein main spring of all corruption and the whole Earth grones under the wait of its iniquity.

It is an iron yoke, it is a strong band; they are the very hand-cuffs, and chains, and shackles, and fetters of hell.

it is an iron yoke it is a strong band they are the verry hand cuffs and chains and shackles and fetters of hell

Therefore it is an imperative duty that we owe, not only to our own wives and children, but to the widows and fatherless, whose husbands and fathers have been murdered under its iron hand; which dark and blackening deeds are enough to make hell itself shudder, and to stand aghast and pale, and the hands of the very devil to tremble and palsy. And also it is an imperative duty that we owe to all the rising generation, and to all the pure in heart, (for there are many yet on the earth among all sects, parties, and denominations, who are blinded by the subtle **[p.146]** craftiness of men, whereby they lie in wait to deceive, and who are only kept from the truth because they

Therefore it is an imperious duty that we owe not only to our own wives and children but to the widdows and fatherless whose husbands and fathers have been murdered under its iron hand which dark and blackning deeds are enough to make hell itself shudder and to stand aghast and pale and the hands of the verry devil tremble and palsy and also it is an imperious duty that we owe to all the rising generation and to all the pure in heart which there <are> many yet on the Earth among all sects parties and de[no]minations who are blinded by the suttle craftiness of men whereby they ly in wait to decieve and only kept from the truth because they know not where

---

43. Circa 22 March 1839, *JSP, D6*, 397. See also *PWJS*, 443. Portions of this letter are found in sections 121, 122, and 123 of the Doctrine and Covenants.

know not where to find it); therefore, that we should waste and wear out our lives in bringing to light all the hidden things of darkness, wherein we know them; and they are truly manifest from heaven.

These should then be attended to with great earnestness. Let no man count them as small things; for there is much which lieth in futurity, pertaining to the Saints, which depends upon these things. You know, brethren, that a very large ship is benefited very much by a very small helm in the time of a storm, by being kept workways with the wind and the waves.

Therefore, dearly beloved brethren, let us cheerfully do all things that lie in our power, and then may we stand still with the utmost assurance, to see the salvation of God, and for His arm to be revealed.]

Counsel Against Secrecies

And again, I would further suggest the impropriety of the organization of bands or companies, by covenant or oaths, by penalties or secrecies; but let the time past of our experience and sufferings by the wickedness of Doctor Avard suffice and let our covenant be that of the Everlasting Covenant, as is contained in the Holy Writ and the things that God hath revealed unto us. Pure friendship always becomes weakened the very moment you undertake to make it stronger by penal oaths and secrecy.

Your humble servant or servants, intend from henceforth to disapprobate everything that is not in accordance with the fullness of the Gospel of Jesus Christ, and is not of a bold, and frank, and upright nature. They will not hold their peace—as in times past when they see iniquity beginning to rear its head—for fear

to find it therefore that we should waist and ware out our lives in bringing to light all the hidden things of darkness wherein we know them and they are truly manifest from heaven.

These should then be attended to with greate earnestness let no man counts them as small things for there is much which lieth in futurity pertaining to the saint which depends upon these things you know brethren that a verry large ship is benefeited verry much by a verry small helm in the time of a storm by being kept work ways with the wind and the waves

Therefore dearly beloved ~~beloved~~ brethren let us cheerfully do all things <that> lieth in our power and then may we stand still with the utmost asurance to see the salvation of God and for his arm to be revealed.[44]

Joseph Smith Letter

And again I would further suggest the impropriety of the organization of bands or companies by covenant or oaths by penalties <or ~~secrecy~~ secrecies> but let the time past of our experiance and sufferings by the wickedness of Doctor [Sampson] Avard suffise and let our covenant be that [p.399] of the everlasting covenant as is contained in the Holy writ and the things that God hath revealed unto us. Pure friendship always becomes weakened the verry moment you undertake to make it stronger by penal oaths and secrecy.

Your humble servant or servants intend from henceforth to disapprobate every thing that is not in accordance with the fulness of the gospel of Jesus Christ and is not of a bold and frank and an upright nature they will not hold their peace as in times past when they see iniquity begining to rear its head for fear

---

44. Circa 22 March 1839, *JSP, D6*, 397–98. See also *PWJS*, 443–44. Portions of this letter are found in sections 121, 122, and 123 of the Doctrine and Covenants.

of traitors, or the consequences that shall follow by reproving those who creep in unawares, that they may get something with which to destroy the flock. We believe that the experience of the Saints in times past has been sufficient, that they will from henceforth be always ready to obey the truth without having men's persons in admiration because of advantage. It is expedient that we should be aware of such things; and we ought always to be aware of those prejudices which sometimes so strangely present themselves, and are so congenial **[p.147]** to human nature, against our friends, neighbors, and brethren of the world, who choose to differ from us in opinion and in matters of faith. Our religion is between us and our God. Their religion is between them and their God.

There is a love from God that should be exercised toward those of our faith, who walk uprightly, which is peculiar to itself, but it is without prejudice; it also gives scope to the mind, which enables us to conduct ourselves with greater liberality towards all that are not of our faith, than what they exercise towards one another. These principles approximate nearer to the mind of God, because it is like God, or Godlike.

of traitors or the concecuences that shall flow <follow> by reproving those who creap in unawares that they may get something to distroy the flock. We believe that the experiance of the saints in times past has been sufficient that they will from henceforth be always ready to obey the truth without having mens persons in admiration because of advantage it is expediant that we should be aware of such things. And we should ought always to be aware of those prejudices which sometimes so strangly presented themselves and are so congenial to human nature against our nieghbors friends and brethren of the world who choose to differ with us in opinion and in matters of faith. Our religeon is betwean us and our God. Their religeon is betwean them and their God.

There is a ty from God that should be exercised towards those of our faith who walk uprightly which is peculiar to itself but it is without prejudice but gives scope to the mind which inables us to conduct ourselves with grater liberality to-wards all others that are not of our faith than what they exercise towards one another these principals approximate nearer to the mind of God because it is like God or God like.[45]

The Principle of Religious Freedom

Joseph Smith Letter

Here is a principle also, which we are bound to be exercised with, that is, in common with all men, such as governments, and laws, and regulations in the civil concerns of life. This principle guarantees to all parties, sects, and denominations, and classes of religion, equal, coherent, and indefeasible rights; they are things that pertain to this life; therefore all are alike interested; they make our responsibilities one towards another in matters of corruptible things, while the former principles do not destroy the latter, but bind us stronger, and make our responsibilities not only

There is a principal also which we are bound to be exercised with that is in common with all men such as governments and laws and regulations in the civil conserns of life This principal guarentees to all parties sects and denominations and classes of religeon equal coherant and indefeasible rights they are things that pertain to this life therefore all are alike **[p.400]** interested they make our responcibilities one towards another in matters of corruptible things while the former principals do not distroy the latter but bind us stronger and make our responcibilities

---

45. Circa 22 March 1839, *JSP, D6*, 398–99. See also *PWJS*, 444–45. Portions of this letter are found in sections 121, 122, and 123 of the Doctrine and Covenants.

one to another, but unto God also. Hence we say, that the Constitution of the United States is a glorious standard; it is founded in the wisdom of God. It is a heavenly banner; it is to all those who are privileged with the sweets of liberty, like the cooling shades and refreshing waters of a great rock in a thirsty and weary land. It is like a great tree under whose branches men from every clime can be shielded from the burning rays of the sun.

We, brethren, are deprived of the protection of its glorious principles, by the cruelty of the cruel, by those who only look for the time being, for pasturage like the beasts of the field, only to fill themselves; and forget that the "Mormons," as well as the Presbyterians, and those of every other class and description, have equal rights to partake of the fruits of the great tree of our national liberty. But notwithstanding we see what we see, and feel what we feel, and know what we know, yet that fruit is no less precious and delicious to our taste; we cannot be weaned from the milk, neither can we be driven from the breast; [p.148] neither will we deny our religion because of the hand of oppression; but we will hold on until death.

We say that God is true; that the Constitution of the United States is true; that the Bible is true; that the Book of Mormon is true; that the Book of Covenants is true; that Christ is true; that the ministering angels sent forth from God are true, and that we know that we have an house not made with hands eternal in the heavens, whose builder and maker is God; a consolation which our oppressors cannot feel, when fortune, or fate, shall lay its iron hand on them as it has on us. Now, we ask, what is man? Remember, brethren, that time and chance happen to all men.

We shall continue our reflections in our next.

We subscribe ourselves, your sincere friends and brethren in the bonds of the everlasting

not only one to another but unto God also hence we say that the constitution of the unitid States is a glorious standard it is founded in the wisdom of God. it is a heavenly banner it is to all those who are privilaged with the sweats of its liberty like the cooling shades and refreshing watters of a greate rock in a thirsty and a weary land it is like a greate tree under whose branches men from evry clime can be shielded from the burning rays of an inclemant sun.

We bretheren are deprived of the protection of this glorious principal by the cruelty of the cruel by those who only look for the time being for pasterage like the beasts of the field only to fill themselves and forget that the mormons as well as the presbitarians and those of evry other class and description have equal rights to partake of the fruite of the greate tree of our national liberty but notwithstanding we see what we see and we feel what we feel and know what we know. Yet that fruite is no less presious and delisious to our taist we cannot be weaned from the milk neither can we be drawn from the breast neither will we deny our religeon because of the hand of opresion but we will hold on untill death

we say say that God is true that the constitution of the united States is true that the [p.401] bible is true that the book of mormon is true <that> the book <of> covenants are true that Christ is true that the ministering angels sent forth from God are true and that we know that we have an house not made with hands eternal in the heavens whose ~~building~~ builder and maker is God a consolation which our oppressors cannot feel when fortune or fate shall lay its iron hand on them as it has on us. Now we ask what is man? Remember brethren that time <and> chance hapeneth to all men.

We shall continue our reflections in our next.

We subscribe ourselves your sinsear [sincere] friends and brethe[r]en in the bonds of the

Gospel, prisoners of Jesus Christ, for the sake of the Gospel and the Saints.

everlasting gospel prisoners of Jesus Christ for the sake of the gospel and the saints.

We pronounce the blessings of heaven upon the heads of the Saints who seek to serve God with undivided hearts, in the name of Jesus Christ, Amen.
JOSEPH SMITH, JUN.,
HYRUM SMITH,
LYMAN WIGHT,
CALEB BALDWIN,
ALEXANDER McRAE.
—DHC 3:289-305.

We pronounce the blessing of heaven upon the heads of the saints who seek to serve God with an undevided hearts in the name of Jesus Christ Amen.
Joseph Smith Jr
Hyrum Smith
Lyman Wight
Caleb Baldwin
Alexander. McRae.[46]

The Prophet's Instruction on Various Doctrines

Wilford Woodruff's "Book of Revelations"[47]
On the doctrins of faith

Faith comes by hearing the word of god, through the testimony of the servants of God; that testimony is always attended by the Spirit of prophecy and revelation.

Faith comes by hearing the word of God through the testimony of the Servants of God that Testimony is always attended by the spirit of prophecy & Revelation.

Repentance

Repentance is a thing that cannot be trifled with every day. Daily transgression and daily repentance is not that which is pleasing in the sight of God.

Is a thing that cannot be trifled with every Day. Daily transgression & daily repentance is not that which is pleasing in the sight of God

Baptism

Baptism is a holy ordinance preparatory to the reception of the Holy Ghost; it is the channel and key by which the Holy Ghost will be administered.

Is a Holy ordinance preparatory to the reception of the Holy Ghost; It is the Channel & Key by which the Holy Ghost will be administered.

The Gift of the Holy Ghost by the laying on of hands, cannot be received through the medium of any other principle than the principle of righteousness, for if the proposals are not complied with, it is of no use, but withdraws.

The gift of the Holy Ghost by the laying of on of hands cannot be received through the medium of any other principle <u>than the principle of righteousness</u> for if the proposals are not complied with it is of no use but withdraws

---

46. Circa 22 March 1839, *JSP, D6*, 399–401. See also *PWJS*, 445–46. Portions of this letter are found in sections 121, 122, and 123 of the Doctrine and Covenants.

47. Among other entries, Wilford Woodruff's Book of Revelations "contains Wilford Woodruff's notes beginning in 1841 in Nauvoo recording Joseph Smith's sermons and instructions, interspersed with copies of revelations received by Joseph Smith as early as 1832." This description of the content and Wilford Woodruff's Book of Revelations in its entirety can be accessed in the Church History Catalog at catalog.churchofjesuschrist.org.

Tongues were given for the purpose of preaching among [p.149] those whose language is not understood; as on the day of Pentecost, etc., and it is not necessary for tongues to be taught to the Church particularly, for any man that has the Holy Ghost, can speak of the things of God in his own tongue as well as to speak in another; for faith comes not by signs, but by hearing the word of God.

Tongues Were given for the purpose of preaching among those whose language is not understood as on the day of Pentecost &c. & it is not necessary for tongues to be taught to the Church particularly, for any man that has the Holy Ghost can speak of the things of God in his own tongue as well as to speak in another. for faith comes not by signs but by hearing the word of God[48]

Doctrines of Resurrection and Election

Wilford Woodruff's "Book of Revelations"

The Doctrines of the Resurrection of the Dead and the Eternal Judgment are necessary to preach among the first principles of the Gospel of Jesus Christ.

The doctrin of the Resurrection of the Dead and Eternal judgment are necisary to preach among the first principles of the gospel of Jesus Christ

The Doctrine of Election. Peter exhorts us to make our calling and election sure. This is the sealing power spoken of by Paul in other places.

[p.524] The Doctrin of Election St Paul exhorts us to make our calling & Election shure. This is that Sealing Power spoken of by Paul in other places

"13. In whom ye also trusted, that after ye heard the word of truth, the Gospel of your salvation: in whom also after that ye believed, ye were sealed with that Holy Spirit of promise,

See Ephe Ist 13-14. vs

"14. Which is the earnest of our inheritance until the redemption of the purchased possession, unto the praise of His glory, that we may be sealed up unto the day of redemption."—Ephesians, 1st chapter.

This principle ought (in its proper place) to be taught, for God hath not revealed anything to Joseph, but what He will make known unto the Twelve, and even the least Saint may know all things as fast as he is able to bear them, for the day must come when no man need say to his neighbor, Know ye that Lord; for all shall

that we may be sealed up unto the day of redemption, this principle ought (in its proper place) to be taught for God hath not revealed any thing to Joseph but what he will make known unto the Twelve & even the least saint may know all things as fast as he is able to hear them for the day must come when no man need say to his neighbour know ye the Son

---

48. *JSP, D6*, 523. See also *WJS*, 3–4. This discourse was given between circa 26 June and circa 2 July 1839.

The Two Comforters

There are two Comforters spoken of. One is the Holy Ghost, the same as given on the day of Pentecost, and that all Saints receive after faith, repentance, and baptism. This first Comforter or Holy Ghost has no other effect than pure intelligence. It is more powerful in expanding the mind, enlightening the understanding, and storing the intellect with present knowledge, of a man who is of the literal seed of Abraham, than one that is a Gentile, though it may not have half as much visible effect upon the body; for as the Holy Ghost falls upon one of the literal seed of Abraham, it is calm and serene; and his whole soul and body are only exercised by the pure spirit of intelligence; while the effect of the Holy Ghost upon a Gentile, is to purge out the old blood, and make him actually of the seed of Abraham. That man that has none of the blood of Abraham (naturally) must have a new creation by the Holy Ghost. In such a case, there may be more of a powerful effect upon the body, and visible to the eye, than upon an Israelite, while the Israelite at first might be far before the Gentile in pure intelligence.

Wilford Woodruff's "Book of Revelations"

know Him (who remain) from the least to the greatest. How is this to be done? It is to be done by this sealing power, and the other Comforter spoken of, which will be manifest by revelation.

for all shall know him (who remain) from the least to the greatest How is this to be done. it is to be done by this sealing power & the other Comforter spoken of which will be manifest by Revelation.⁴⁹

There is two comforters spoken of, the first Comforter is the Holy Ghost the same as given on the day of Pentecost & that all Saints recieve after faith, Repentance, & Baptism. This first Comforter or Holy Ghost has no other affect than pure intelligence It is more powerful in expanding the mind enlightening the understanding & storeing the intellect with present Knowledge of a man who is of the litteral Seed of Abram that than one that is a gentile though it may not have half as much visible affect upon the body for as the Holy Ghost falls upon one of the literal seed of Abram it is caml [calm] & serene & his Whole soul & body are only exercised by the Pure spirit of Intelligence. While the affect of the Holy Ghost upon a gentile is to purge out the old blood & make him actually of the seed of Abram That man that has none of the blood of Abram (naturally) must have a new creation by the Holy Ghost in such a case there may be more of a powerful affect upon the body & visible to the eye than upon an Israelite while the Israelite at first might be far before the gentile in pure intelligence.⁵⁰

The Second Comforter

Wilford Woodruff's "Book of Revelations"

The other Comforter spoken of is a subject of great interest, and perhaps understood by few of this generation. After a person has faith in Christ, repents of his sins, and is baptized for the remission of his sins and receives the Holy Ghost, (by the laying on of hands), which is

The other Comforter spoken off is a subject of great interest & perhaps understood by few of this generation. After a person hath faith in Christ, repents of his Sins & is baptized for the remission of his Sins & recieves the Holy Ghost (by the laying on of hands,)

---

49. Circa 26 June and circa 2 July 1839, *JSP, D6*, 523–24. See also *WJS*, 4.
50. Circa 26 June and circa 2 July 1839, *JSP, D6*, 524. See also *WJS*, 4.

the first Comforter, then let him continue to humble himself before God, hungering and thirsting after righteousness, and living by every word of God, and the Lord will soon say unto him, Son, thou shalt be exalted.

When the Lord has thoroughly proved him, and finds that the man is determined to serve Him at all hazards, then the man will find his calling and his election made sure, then it will be his privilege to receive the other Comforter, which the Lord hath promised the Saints, as is recorded in the testimony of St. John, in the 14th chapter, from the 12th to the 27th verses.

Note the 16, 17, 18, 21, 23 verses:

"16. And I will pray the Father, and He shall give you another Comforter, that he may abide with you forever;

"17. Even the Spirit of Truth; whom the world cannot receive, because it seeth him not, neither knoweth him; but ye know him; for he dwelleth with you, and shall be in you.

"18. I will not leave you comfortless: I will come to you.* *

"21. He that hath my commandments, and keepeth them, he it is that loveth me: and he that loveth me shall be loved of my Father, and I will love him, and will manifest myself to him.

"23. …If a man love me, he will keep my word: and my Father will love him, and we will come unto him, and make our abode with him."

Now what is this other Comforter? It is no more nor less **[p.151]** than the Lord Jesus Christ Himself; and this is the sum and substance of the whole matter; that when any man obtains this last Comforter, he will have the personage of Jesus Christ to attend him, or appear unto him from time to time, and even

which is the first Comforter then let him continue to humble himself before God hungering & thirsting after righteousness & living by every word of God, & the Lord will soon say unto him Son thou shalt be exalted, &c.

When the Lord has thoroughly proved him & find that the man is determind to serve him at all hazard then the man will find his calling & Election made sure then it will be his privilege to recieve the other Comforter which the Lord hath promised the Saints as is recorded in the testimony of St. John in the XIV ch from the 12 to the 27 vers

note the 16-17-18-21:23 verses

Now what is this other Comforter is it is no more or less than the Lord Jesus Christ himself & this is the sum & substance of the whole matter that when any man obtains this last Comforter he will have the personage of Jesus Christ to attend him or appear unto him from time to time Even he will manifest the Father

He will manifest the Father unto him, and they will take up their abode with him, and the visions of the heavens will be opened unto him, and the Lord will teach him face to face, and he may have a perfect knowledge of the mysteries of the Kingdom of God; and this is the state and place the ancient Saints arrived at when they had such glorious visions—Isaiah, Ezekiel, John upon the Isle of Patmos, St. Paul in the three heavens, and all the Saints who held communion with the general assembly and Church of the Firstborn.

unto him & they will take up there abode with him & the visions of the heavens will be opened unto him & the Lord will teach him face to face & he may have a perfect knowledg of the mysteries of the kingdom of God. & this is the state & place where the ancient Saints arived at when they had such glorious visions. Isaiah Ezekiel, John upon the Isle of Patmos, St Paul in the third heavens & all the Saints, who held communion with the general assembly & Church of the first born &c.[51]

The Spirit of Revelation

Wilford Woodruff's "Book of Revelations"

The Spirit of Revelation is in connection with these blessings. A person may profit by noticing the first intimation of the spirit of revelation; for instance, when you feel pure intelligence flowing into you, it may give you sudden strokes of ideas, so that by noticing it, you may find it fulfilled the same day or soon; (i.e.,) those things that were presented unto your minds by the Spirit of God, will come to pass; and thus by learning the Spirit of God and understanding it, you may grow into the principle of revelation, until you become perfect in Christ Jesus.

The spirit of Revelation is in connexion with those blessings. **[p.526]** A person may profit by noticeing the first intimations of the spirit of revelation for Instance when you feel pure intelligence flowing unto you it may give you sudden stoks [strokes] of Ideas that by noticing it you may find it fulfilled the same day or soon ie those things that were presented unto your mind by the spirit of God will come to pass & thus by learning the Spirit of God & understanding it you may grow into the principle of Revelation untill you become perfe[c]ted in Christ Jesus.[52]

The Evangelist

Wilford Woodruff's "Book of Revelations"
An Evangelist

An Evangelist is a Patriarch, even the oldest man of the blood of Joseph or of the seed of Abraham. Wherever the Church of Christ is established in the earth, there should be a Patriarch for the benefit of the posterity of the Saints, as it was with Jacob in giving his patriarchal blessing unto his sons, etc. (June 27, 1839.) DHC 3:379-381.

Is a patriarch even the oldest man of the Blood of Joseph or of the seed of Abram whare ever the Church of Christ is established in the Earth there should be a Patriarch for the benefit of the posterity of the Saints, as it was with Jacob in given his patriarchal bles[s]ing unto his Sons &c.[53]

---

51. Circa 26 June and circa 2 July 1839, *JSP, D6*, 524–25. See also *WJS*, 5.
52. Circa 26 June and circa 2 July 1839, *JSP, D6*, 525–26. See also *WJS*, 5–6.
53. Circa 26 June and circa 2 July 1839, *JSP, D6*, 526. See also *WJS*, 6.

SECTION FOUR

1839–1842

SECTION FOUR

The Prophet's Address to the Twelve

[p.154] In the afternoon of Monday, July 2, 1839, the Prophet met with the Apostles and some of the Seventies who were about to depart on their mission to Great Britain in fulfilment of the revelation of the Lord, and instructed them. A synopsis of his remarks he placed in his journal and this is here reproduced in full as they are given in History of the Church.[1]

Beware of Pride

Wilford Woodruff's "Book of Revelations"

Ever keep in exercise the principle of mercy & be ready to forgive our brother on the first intimations of repentance & asking forgiveness, & should we [p.519] even forgive our brother or Even our Enemy before they repent or ask forgiveness our heavenly father would be equally as merciful unto us.

Again let the Twelve & all Saints be willing to confess all ~~there~~ their Sins & not keep back a part & let the twelve be humble & not be exalted & beware of pride & not seek to excell one above another but act for each others good & pray for one & another & honour ~~over~~ our brother or make honourable mention of his name & not backbite & devour our brother. why will not man learn wisdom by precept at this late agee of the world where we have such a cloud of witnesses & Examples before us & not be oblieged to learn by sad experianc [experience] every thing we know. must the new ones that are chosen to fill the places of those that are fallen of the quorum of the Twelve begin to exalt themselves untill they exalt themselves so high that they will soon tumble [p.520] over & have a great fall & go wallowing through the mud & mire & darkness Judas like to the buffatings of Satan as several of the

---

1. This introductory paragraph was authored by Joseph Fielding Smith.

quorum of the Twelve have done or will they learn wisdom & be wise. (O God give them wisdom & keep them humble I pray)

When the Twelve or any other witnesses stand before the Congragations of the Earth & they preach in the power & demonstratio[n] of the spirit of God & the people are asstonised [astonished] & confounded at the doctrin & say that that man has preached a powerful discours a great sermon then let that man or those men take care that they do not asscribe the glory unto themselves but be careful that they are humble & asscribe the praise & glory to God & the Lamb for it is by the power of the Holy Priesthood & Holy Ghost they have power thus to speak; what art thou O man but dust & from wholm dost thou receive thy power & blessing but from God[2]

Not Sent to Be Taught

Then, O ye Twelve! notice this Key, and be wise for Christ's sake, and your own soul's sake.

Ye are not sent out to be taught, but to teach. Let every word be seasoned with grace. Be vigilant; be sober. It is a day of warning, and not of many words. Act honestly before God and man. Beware of Gentile sophistry; such as bowing and scraping unto men in whom you have no confidence. Be honest, open, and frank in all your intercourse with mankind.

Wilford Woodruff's "Book of Revelations"

Then O ye Twelve <u>notice</u> this key & be wise for Christ-sake & your own sols sake

Ye are not sent out to be taught but to teach. let every word be seasoned with grace be vigilent be sober. it is a day of warning <|[exhorting[3]]|> & not of many words. act honest before God & man beware of gentile <u>Sophestry</u> such as bowing & scraping unto men in whom you have no confiden[c]e be honset open & frank, in all your intercourse with mankind[4]

Do Not Betray the Brethren

O ye Twelve! and all Saints! profit by this important Key—that in all your trials, troubles, temptations, afflictions, bonds, imprisonments and death, see to it, that you do not betray heaven;

Wilford Woodruff's "Book of Revelations"

O ye Twelve & all Saints profit by this important <u>Key</u> that in all your trials troubles, temptations; afflictions, bonds, imprisionments, & death see to it that you do not betray heaven,

---

2. 2 July 1839, *JSP, D6*, 518–20. Joseph Fielding Smith used History, C-1, 10, for *TPJS*.
3. In Woodruff's notes he inserted the word "exhorting," but using Pitman shorthand—hence the unique bracketing utilized here.
4. 2 July 1839, *JSP, D6*, 520.

that you do not betray Jesus Christ; that you do not betray the brethren; that you do not betray the revelations of God, whether in Bible, Book of Mormon, or Doctrine and Covenants, or any other that ever was or ever will be given and revealed unto man in this world or that which is to come. Yea, in all your kicking and flounderings, see to it that you do not this thing, lest innocent blood be found upon your skirts, and you go down to hell. All other sins are not to be compared to sinning against the Holy Ghost, and proving a traitor to the brethren.

that you do not betray Jesus Christ, that you do not betray your Brethren, that you do not betray the Revelations of God, whether in the Bible Book of Mormon or Doctrins & Covenants or any other that ever was or ever will be given & revealed unto man in this world or that which is to come, yea in all your kick[i]ng & **[p.521]** floundering see to it that you do not this thing lest innocent Blood be found in your skirts & you go down to hell. all other sins are not to be compared to sining against the Holy Ghost & proving a traitor to thy brethren [5]

A Key to Mysteries

Wilford Woodruff's "Book of Revelations"
(A final key delivered from Joseph in the following language.)

I will give you one of the Keys of the mysteries of the Kingdom. It is an eternal principle, that has existed with God from all eternity: That man who rises up to condemn other, finding fault with the Church, saying that they are out of the way, while he himself is righteous, then know assuredly, that that man is in the high road to apostasy; and if he does not **[p.157]** repent, will apostatize, as God lives. The principle is as correct as the one that Jesus put forth in saying that he who seeketh a sign is an adulterous person; and that principle is eternal, undeviating, and firm as the pillars of heaven; for whenever you see a man seeking after a sign, you may set it down that he is an adulterous man.

I will give you one of the keys of the mysteries of the kingdom. It is an Eternal principle that has existed with God from all Eternity that that man who rises up to condemn others & finding fault with the Church saying that they are out of the way while he himself is righteous, then know assuredly that that man is in the high road to apostacy & if he does not repent will apostatize as God live, the principle is as correct as the one that Jesus put forth in saying that that person he who seeketh after a sign is an adulterous person & that principle is <Eternal> undeviating & firm as the pillars of heaven for whenever you see a man seeking after a Sign you may set it down that he is an adulterous man. [6]

The Prophet on Priesthood

Willard Richards Pocket Companion[7]

The Priesthood was first given to Adam; he obtained the First Presidency, and held the keys of it from generation to generation. He obtained it in the Creation, before the world was

The Priesthood was. first given To Adam: he obtained to the first Presidency & held the Keys of it, from genration to Generation; he obtained it in the creation before the world

---

5. 2 July 1839, *JSP, D6*, 520–21.

6. 2 July 1839, *JSP, D6*, 521. Joseph Fielding Smith used History, C-1, 10 for *TPJS*.

7. Among other things, Richards's Pocket Companion consists of copies Richards made of revelations and teachings of Joseph Smith, "probably from a record brought to England by another member of the Twelve in early 1840 (possibly Wilford Woodruff)." Richards was not present to hear a number of the teachings delivered by Joseph Smith included in his record. Thus, in many cases, his Pocket Companion

formed, as in Genesis 1:26, 27, 28. He had dominion given him over every living creature. He is Michael the Archangel, spoken of in the Scriptures. Then to Noah, who is Gabriel: he stands next in authority to Adam in the Priesthood; he was called of God to this office, and was the father of all living in this day, and to him was given the dominion. These men held keys first on earth, and then in heaven.

was formed as in Gen. I, 26:28,— he had dominion given him over every living Creature. He is Michael, the Archangel, spoken of in the Scriptures,— Then to Noah who is Gabriel, he stands next in authority to **[p.543]** Adam in the Priesthood; he was called of God to this office & was the Father of all living in his day, & To him was Given the Dominion. These men held keys, first on earth, & then in Heaven.—⁸

Priesthood Everlasting

Willard Richards Pocket Companion

The Priesthood is an everlasting principle, and existed with God from eternity, and will to eternity, without beginning of days or end of years. The keys have to be brought from heaven whenever the Gospel is sent. When they are revealed from heaven, it is by Adam's authority.

The Priesthood is an everlasting principle & Existed with God from Eternity & will to Eternity, without beginning of days or end of years. The Keys have to be brought from heaven whenever the Gospel is sent.— When they are revealed from Heaven it is by Adams Authority.⁹

Adam the Oldest Man

Willard Richards Pocket Companion

Daniel in his seventh chapter speaks of the Ancient of days; he means the oldest man, our Father Adam, Michael, he will call his children together and hold a council with them to prepare them for the coming of the Son of Man. He (Adam) is the father of the human family, and presides over the spirits of all men, and all that have had the keys must stand before him in this grand council. This may take place before some of us leave this stage of action. The Son of Man stands before him, and there is given him glory and dominion. Adam delivers up his stewardship to Christ, that which was delivered to him as holding the keys of the universe, but retains his standing as head of the human family.

Dan VII Speaks of the Ancient of days, he means the oldest man, our Father Adam, Michael; he will call his children together. & hold a council with them. to prepare them for the coming of the Son of Man. He, (Adam) is the Father of the human family & presides over the Spirits of all men, & all that have had the Keys must Stand before him in this grand Council. This may take place before some of us leave this stage of action, The Son of Man Stands before him & there is given him glory & dominion.— Adam delivers up his stewardship to Christ, that which was deliverd to him as holding the Keys of the Universe, but retains his standing as head of the human family.¹⁰

---

would be considered a secondary source. This description of the content of Willard Richards Pocket Companion and the entire journal can be accessed at catalog.churchofjesuschrist.org. Portions of the Pocket Companion are available at josephsmithpapers.org.

8. Discourse given between circa 26 June and circa 4 August 1839, Joseph Smith, *JSP, D6*, 542–43. See also *WJS*, 8. Joseph Fielding Smith dates this entry 2 July 1839.

9. Circa 26 June to circa 4 August 1839, *JSP, D6*, 543. See also *WJS*, 8.

10. Circa 26 June to circa 4 August 1839, *JSP, D6*, 543. See also *WJS*, 8–9. Joseph Fielding Smith dates this entry 2 July 1839.

The Spirit of Man

[p.158] The spirit of man is not a created being;[11] it existed from eternity, and will exist to eternity. Anything created cannot be eternal; and earth, water, etc., had their existence in an elementary state, from eternity. Our Savior speaks of children and says, Their angels always stand before my Father. The Father called all spirits before Him at the creation of man, and organized them. He (Adam) is the head, and was told to multiply. The keys were first given to him, and by him to others. He will have to give an account of his stewardship, and they to him.

Willard Richards Pocket Companion

The Spirit of Man is not a created being; it existed from Eternity & will exist to Eternity. Any thing created cannot be Eternal & earth, water &c— all these had their existence in an elementary state from Eternity. Our Savior speaks of Children & Says their angels always stand before my father. The father called all spirits before him at the creation of Man & organized them. He (Adam) is the head. & was told to multiply. The Keys were <first> given to him, <& by him to others> he will have to give an account of his Stewardship, & they to him.[12]

Keys Given to Peter, James and John

The Priesthood is everlasting. The Savior, Moses, and Elias, gave the keys to Peter, James and John, on the mount, when they were transfigured before him. The Priesthood is everlasting—without beginning of days or end of years; without father, mother, etc. If there is no change of ordinances there is no change of Priesthood. Wherever the ordinances of the Gospel are administered, there is the Priesthood.

Willard Richards Pocket Companion

The Priesthood is everlasting. The Savior. Moses. & Elias— gave the Keys to Peter, James & John on the Mount when they were [p.544] transfigured before him. The Priesthood is everlasting. without biginning of days or end of years, without Father. Mother &c.— If there is no change of ordinances there is no change of Priesthood. Wherever the ordinances of the Gospel are adminesterd there is the priesthood.[13]

Descent of Priesthood

Willard Richards Pocket Companion

How have we come at the Priesthood in the last days? It came down, down, in regular succession. Peter, James, and John had it given to them and they gave it to others. Christ is the Great High Priest; Adam next. Paul speaks of the Church coming to an innumerable

How have we come at the Priesthood in the last days? ~~They~~ <It> came down, down in regular succession— Peter James & John had it given to them & they gave it up.— Christ is the Great High priest; Adam next.— Paul speaks of ~~an~~ the Church coming to an innu-

---

11. The original *TPJS* footnote reads: "In saying the spirit of man is not created the Prophet without any doubt had in mind the intelligence as explained in the *Doctrine and Covenants*, Sec. 93:29: 'Man was also the beginning with God. Intelligence, or the light of truth, was not created or made, neither indeed can be.' From this we gather that the intelligence in man was not created, but the Prophet taught very clearly that man is in very deed the offspring of God, and that the spirits of men were born in the spirit world the children of God. See Doctrine and Covenants 76:24."

12. Circa 26 June to circa 4 August 1839, *JSP, D6*, 543. See also *WJS*, 9.

13. Circa 26 June to circa 4 August 1839, *JSP, D6*, 543–44. See also *WJS*, 9.

company of angels—to God the Judge of all the spirits of just men made perfect; to Jesus the Mediator of the new covenant. (Hebrews 12:22-24.)

I saw Adam in the valley of Adam-ondi-Ahman. He called together his children and blessed them with a patriarchal blessing. The Lord appeared in their midst, and he (Adam) blessed them all, and foretold what should befall them to the latest generation.

[p.159] This is why Adam blessed his posterity; he wanted to bring them into the presence of God. They looked for a city, etc., "whose builder and maker is God." (Hebrews 11:10.) Moses sought to bring the children of Israel into the presence of God, through the power of the Priesthood, but he could not. In the first ages of the world they tried to establish the same thing; and there were Eliases raised up who tried to restore these very glories, but did not obtain them; but they prophesied of a day when this glory would be revealed. Paul spoke of the dispensation of the fullness of times, when God would gather together all things in one, etc.; and those men to whom these keys have been given, will have to be there; and they without us cannot be made perfect.

These men are in heaven, but their children are on the earth. Their bowels yearn over us. God sends down men for this reason. "And the Son of Man shall send forth His angels, and they shall gather out of His kingdom all things that give offense and them that do iniquity." (Matthew 13:41.) All these authoritative characters will come down and join hand in hand in bringing about this work.

merable company of Angels, to God the Judge of all, the spirits of Just men made perfect, to Jesus the mediator of the New Covenant. &c Heb XII, 2 3.

I saw Adam in the valley of Ah-dam ondi-ahman— he called together his children & blessed them with a Patriarchal blessing. The Lord appeared in their midst. & he (Adam) blessed them all & foretold what should befall them to the latest generation— See D.C. Sec III 28. 29 par.—

This is why Abraham blessd his posterity; he wanted to bring them into the presence of God. They looked for a city, &c,— Moses Sought to bring the children of Israel into the presence of God. through the power of the Priesthood, but he could not. In the first ages of the world they tried to establish the same thing— & there were Elias's raised up who tried to restore these very glories but did not obtain them. <but> (Enoch did for himself & those that were with them Him, but not for the world. J. T.[14]) They prophecied of a day when this Glory would be revealed.— Paul spoke of the Dispensation of the fulness of times. When [p.545] God would gather together all things in one &c <&>, Those men to whom these Keys have been given will have to be there (I.E. when Adam shall again assemble his children of the Priesthood, & christ be in their midst) the Ancient of Days come &c &c J. T.) And they without us could <cannot> not be made perfect.

These men are in heaven, but their children are on Earth. Their bowels yearn over us. God sends down men for this reason, Mat. 13.41. & the Son of man shall send forth his angels &c— All these authoritative characters will come down & join hands in hand in bringing about this work—[15]

---

14. Willard Richards was likely copying from an account originally written by John Taylor (J. T.).
15. Circa 26 June to circa 4 August 1839, *JSP, D6*, 544–45. See also *WJS*, 9–10.

We Cannot Be Perfect Without Our Dead

Willard Richards Pocket Companion

The Kingdom of God is like a grain of mustard seed. The mustard seed is small, but brings forth a large tree, and the fowls lodge in the branches. The fowls are the angels. Thus angels come down, combine together to gather their children, and gather them. We cannot be made perfect without them, nor they without us; when these things are done, the Son of Man will descend, the Ancient of Days sit; we may come to an innumerable company of angels, have communion with and receive instruction from them. Paul told about Moses' proceedings; spoke of the children of Israel being baptized. (1 Cor. 10:1-4.) He knew this, and that all the ordinances and blessings were in the Church. Paul had these things, and we may have the fowls of heaven lodge in the branches, etc.

The "Horn" made war with the Saints and overcame them, until the Ancient of Days came; judgment was given to the Saints of the Most High from the Ancient of Days; the time came that the Saints possessed the Kingdom. This not only makes us ministers here, but in eternity.

The kingdom of heaven is like a grain of mustard seed. the mustard seed is Small but brings forth a large tree. <and the fowls lodge in the branches> The fowls are the Angels. the Book of Mormon perhaps. these thus Angels come down combine together to gather their children, & gather them. We cannot be made perfect without them. nor they without us when these <things> are done the Son of man will descend. the ancient of Days sit.— We may come to an innumerable compa[n]y of Angels have communion with & rece[i]ve instruction from. <them.>— Paul told about Moses's proceedings. Spoke of the Children of Israel being baptized. &, he knew this. & that all the ordinances & blessings were in the church. Paul had these things; <&> we may have the fowls of heaven Lodge in the branches &c.

The horn made war with the saints, <&> overcame them &c, until the Ancient of Days came, judgment was given to the Saints of the Most High, from the Ancient of Days— the time came that the saints possessed the kingdom— this not only makes us ministers here but in Eternity.[16]

No Salvation Without Revelation

Willard Richards Pocket Companion

[p.160] Salvation cannot come without revelation; it is in vain for anyone to minister without it. No man is a minister of Jesus Christ without being a Prophet. No man can be a minister of Jesus Christ except he has the testimony of Jesus; and this is the spirit of prophecy. Whenever salvation has been administered, it has been by testimony. Men of the present time testify of heaven and hell, and have never seen either; and I will say that no man knows these things without this.

Salvation cannot come without Revelation, it is in vain for any one to minister without it. No man is a minister of Jesus Christ. without being a Prophet. No man can be the minister of Jesus Christ, except he has the testimony of Jesus & this is the Spirit of Prophesy. Whenever Sa[l]vation has been administered it has been by Testimony, Men of the present time testify of Heaven & of Hell, & [p.546] have never Seen either & I will say that no man knows these things without this.[17]

---

16. Circa 26 June to circa 4 August 1839, *JSP, D6*, 545. See also *WJS*, 10.
17. Circa 26 June to circa 4 August 1839, *JSP, D6*, 545–46. See also *WJS*, 10.

Signs of Second Coming Have Commenced

Men profess to prophesy. I will prophesy that the signs of the coming of the Son of man are already commenced. One pestilence will desolate after another. We shall soon have war and bloodshed. the moon will be turned to blood. I testify of these things, and that the coming of the Son of Man is nigh, even at your doors. If our souls and our bodies are not looking forth for the coming of the Son of Man; and after we are dead, if we are not looking forth, we shall be among those who are calling for the rocks to fall upon them.

Willard Richards Pocket Companion

Men profess to prophecy. I will prophecy that the signs of the coming of the Son of man are already commencd, one pestilence will dessolate after another. we shall soon have war & bloodshed. The Moon will be turned into blood, I testify of these things. & that the coming of the Son of Man is nigh even at your doors,— If our souls & our bodies are not looking forth for the coming of the Son of Man. & after we are dead if we are not looking forth. &c We shall be among those who are calling for the rocks to fall upon us &c—[18]

Hearts of Children Turn to Fathers

The hearts of the children of men will have to be turned to the fathers, and the fathers to the children, living or dead, to prepare them for the coming of the Son of Man. If Elijah did not come, the whole earth would be smitten.

There will be here and there a Stake [of Zion] for the gathering of the Saints. Some may have cried peace, but the Saints and the world will have little peace from henceforth. Let this not hinder us from going to the Stakes; for God has told us to flee, not dallying, or we shall be scattered, one here, and another there. There your children shall be blessed, and you in the midst of friends where you may be blessed. The Gospel net gathers of every kind.

I prophesy, that that man who tarries after he has an opportunity of going, will be afflicted by the devil. Wars are at hand; we must not delay; but are not required to sacrifice. We ought to have the building up of Zion as our greatest object. When wars come, we shall have to flee to Zion. The cry is to make haste. The last revelation says, Ye shall not **[p.161]** have

Willard Richards Pocket Companion

The hearts of the children of men will have to be turned to the fathers. & the fathers to the children, living or dead, to prepare them for the coming of the Son of Man. If Elijah did not come the whole earth would be Smitten.

There will be here & there a stake &c. <for the gathering of the saints> Some may have cried peace. but the Saints & the world will have little peace from henceforth. Let this not hinder us from going to the Stakes, for God has told us to flee not dallying. or we shall be scattered. one here, another there, There your children shall be blessed & you in the midst of friends where you may be blessed. &c The gospel net gathers of every kind,

I prophecy that that man who tarries after he has an opportunity of going will be afflicted by the Devil. Wars are at hand we must not delay, but are not required to sacrifice. We ought to have the building up of Zion as our greatest object.— when wars come we shall have to flee to Zion. The cry is to make haste. The last revelation says ye shall not have time to have

---

18. Circa 26 June to circa 4 August 1839, *JSP, D6*, 546. See also *WJS*, 10–11.

time to have gone over the earth, until these things come. It will come as did the cholera, war, fires, and earthquakes; one pestilence after another, until the Ancient of Days comes, then judgment will be given to the Saints.

gone over the Earth until these things come. It will come as did the Cholera. war. & fires burning Earthquake one pestilence after another &c ~~until~~ until the Ancient of Days come then judgment will be given to the Saints.[19]

No Peace But in Zion

Willard Richards Pocket Companion
[p.547] What~~so~~ever you may hear about me or Kirtland, take no notice of. for if it be a place of refuge the Devil will use his greatest efforts to trap the Saints. You must make yourselves acquainted with those men, who, like Daniel, pray three times a day to the house of the Lord.— Look to the Presidency ~~&c~~ <& rece[i]ve instruction>.— Every man who is afraid. covetous &c will be taken in a snare— The time is soon coming when no man will have any peace but in Zion & her Stakes.

Whatever you may hear about me or Kirtland, take no notice of it; for if it be a place of refuge, the devil will use his greatest efforts to trap the Saints. You must make yourselves acquainted with men who like Daniel pray three times a day toward the House of the Lord. Look to the Presidency and receive instruction. Every man who is afraid, covetous, will be taken in a snare. The time is soon coming, when no man will have any peace but in Zion and her stakes.

I saw men hunting the lives of their own sons, and brother murdering brother, women killing their own daughters, and daughters seeking the lives of their mothers. I saw armies arrayed against armies. I saw blood, desolation, fires. The Son of man has said that the mother shall be against the daughters, and the daughter against the mother. These things are at our doors. They will follow the Saints of God from city to city. Satan will rage, and the spirit of the devil is now enraged. I know not how soon these things will take place; but with a view of them, shall I cry peace? No; I will lift up my voice and testify of them. How long you will have good crops, and the famine be kept off, I do not know; when the fig tree leaves, know then that the summer is nigh at hand.

I saw men hunting the lives of their own sons, & brother murdering brother, women killing their own daughters & daughters seeking the lives of their mothers. I saw armies arrayed against armies I saw blood. desolations, & fires &c,— The Son of Man has said that the mother Shall be against the daughter, & the daughter against the mother &c, ~~&c.~~— These things are at our doors. They will follow the Saints of God from City to City— Satan will rage & The Spirit of the Devil is now enraged. ~~&c~~ I know not how soon these things will take place, and with a view of them shall I cry peace? NO! I will lift up my voice & testify of them. How long you will have good crops. & the famin be kept. <off> I do not know. when the fig tree leaves, know then that the summer is nig~~h~~t at hand.[20]

---

19. Circa 26 June to circa 4 August 1839, *JSP, D6*, 546. See also *WJS*, 11.
20. Circa 26 June to circa 4 August 1839, *JSP, D6*, 547. See also *WJS*, 11–12.

Try the Spirits

We may look for angels and receive their ministrations, but we are to try the spirits and prove them, for it is often the case that men make a mistake in regard to these things. God has so ordained that when He has communicated, no vision is to be taken but what you see by the seeing of the eye, or what you hear by the hearing of the ear. When you see a vision, pray for the interpretation; if you get not this, shut it up; there must be certainty in this matter. An open vision will manifest that which is more important. Lying spirits are going forth in the earth. There will be great manifestations of spirits, both false and true.

Willard Richards Pocket Companion

we may look for Angel[s] &c. <& receive their ministreting> but we are to try the Spirits & prove them <for> it is often the case that men. make a mistake in regard to these things. God has so ordained that when he has communicated, <by vision,> no vision is to be taken but what you see by the seeing of the eye or what you hear by the hearing of the ear— When you see a vision &c pray for the interpretation if you get not this, shut it up— There must be certainty. <in this matter> An open vision will manifest that which is more important. Lying Spirits are going forth in the Earth. [p.548] There will be great manifestation of Spirit both false & true. &c.[21]

Angels Do Not Have Wings

[p.162] Being born again, comes by the Spirit of God through ordinances. An angel of God never has wings. Some will say that they have seen a spirit; that he offered them his hand, but they did not touch it. This is a lie. First, it is contrary to the plan of God; a spirit cannot come but in glory; an angel has flesh and bones; we see not their glory. The devil may appear as an angel of light. Ask God to reveal it; if it be of the devil, he will flee from you; if of God, He will manifest Himself, or make it manifest. We may come to Jesus and ask Him; He will know all about it; if He comes to a little child, he will adapt himself to the language and capacity of a little child.

Not every spirit, or vision, or singing, is of God. The devil is an orator; he is powerful; he took our Savior on to a pinnacle of the Temple, and kept Him in the wilderness for forty days. The gift of discerning spirits will be given to the Presiding Elder. Pray for him that

Willard Richards Pocket Companion

Being born again comes by the Spirit of God through ordinances. An angel of God never has wings. Some will Say that they have seen a Spirit. that he offered them his hand. but they did not touch it. This is a lie. First it is contrary to the plan of God A spirit can not come but in glory. An angel has flesh and bones. we see not their glory. The devil may appear as an angel of light. Ask God to reveal it. if it be of the Devil. he it be will of flee from you. if of God he will manifest himself or make it manifest. we may come to Jesus <& ask him> he will know all about it.— If he comes to a little child, he will adapt himself to the <Language &> capacity of a little child—

There is no Gold nor silver &c, it is false, all is plain in heaven; every Spirit or vision or singing is not of God. The Devil is an orator, &c; he is powerful: he took our Savior onto a pinnacle of the temple; <&> kept him in the Wilderness for forty days. The gift of discerning Spirits will

---

21. Circa 26 June to circa 4 August 1839, *JSP, D6*, 547–48. See also *WJS*, 12.

he may have this gift. Speak not in the gift of tongues without understanding it, or without interpretation. The devil can speak in tongues; the adversary will come with his work; he can tempt all classes; can speak in English or Dutch. Let no one speak in tongues unless he interpret, except by the consent of the one who is placed to preside; then he may discern or interpret, or another may. Let us seek for the glory of Abraham, Noah, Adam, the Apostles, who have communion with [knowledge of] these things, and then we shall be among that number when Christ comes. (July 2, 1839.) DHC 3:383-392.

be given to the presiding Elder. pray for him &c. \<that he may have this gift\> Speak not in the gift of Tongues without understanding it, or without interpretation, The Devil can speak in Tongues. The Adversary will come with his work, he can tempt all classes Can speak in English or Dutch.— Let no one speak in tongues unless he interpret except by the consent of the one who is placed to preside, then he may discern or interpret or another may. Let us seek for the Glory of Abraham. Noah. Adam. the Apostles have communion with these things and then we shall be among that number when Christ comes.[22]

Saints Not to Escape Judgments

Joseph Smith's Journal

I explained concerning the coming of the Son of Man; also that it is a false idea that the Saints will escape all the judgments, whilst the wicked suffer; for all flesh is subject to suffer, and "the righteous shall hardly escape;" still many of the Saints will escape, for the just shall live by faith; yet many of the righteous shall fall a prey to disease, to pestilence, etc., by reason of the weakness of the flesh, and yet be saved in the Kingdom of God. So that it is an unhallowed principle to say that such and such have transgressed because they have been prayed upon by disease or death, for all flesh is subject to **[p.163]** death; and the Savior has said, "Judge not, lest ye be judged." (September 29, 1839.) DHC 4:11.

Explained concerning the coming of the son of Man &c that all will be raised to meet him but the righteous will remain with him in the cloud whilst all the proud and all that do wickedly will have to return to the earth, and suffer his vengeance which he will take upon them this is the second death &c &c Also that it is a false idea that the saints will escape all the judgements whilst the wicked suffer— for all flesh is subject to suffer— and "the righteous shall hardly escape" still many of the saints will escape— for the just shall live by faith— yet many of the righteous shall fall a prey to disease to pestilence &c and yet &c by reason of the weakness of the flesh and yet be saved in **[p.353]** the kingdom of God So that it is an unhallowed principle to say that such and such have transgressed because they have been preyed upon by disease or death for all flesh is subject to death and the Saviour has said, "Judge not "lest ye be judged".[23]

---

22. Circa 26 June to circa 4 August 1839, *JSP, D6*, 548. See also *WJS*, 12.
23. 29 September 1839, *JSP, J1*, 352–53.

Letter of the Prophet to Elders Hyde and Page—Palestine Mission Considered

	Joseph Smith's Letter
Nauvoo, Hancock County, Illinois	Nauvoo Hancock Co. Ills
May 14th, 1840	May 14th 1840

To Orson Hyde and John E. Page:
Dear Brethren: I am happy in being informed by your letter that your mission swells "larger and larger." It is a great and important mission, and one that is worthy those intelligences who surround the throne of Jehovah to be engaged in. Although it appears great at present, yet you have but just begun to realize the greatness, the extent and glory of the same. If there is anything calculated to interest the mind of the Saints, to awaken in them the finest sensibilities, and arouse them to enterprise and exertion, surely it is the great and precious promises made by our heavenly Father to the children of Abraham; and those engaged in seeking the outcasts of Israel, and the dispersed of Judah, cannot fail to enjoy the Spirit of the Lord and have the choicest blessings of heaven rest upon them in copious effusions.

Dear Bretheren
I am happy in being informed by your letter that your mission swells "larger and larger"; it is a great and important mission, and one that is worthy **[p.282]** of those inteligences who surround the throne of Jehovah to be ingaged in; Altho it appears great at present, yet you have but just begun to realize the greatness, the extent and glory of the same. If there is any thing calculated to interest the mind of the saints, to awaken in them the finest sensibilities; and arouse them to enterprise, and exertion, surely it is the great and precious promises, made by our heavenly Father to the children of Abraham; and those engaged in seeking the outcasts of Israel, and the dispersed of Judah, cannot fail to enjoy the Spirit of the Lord, and have the choisests blessings of Heaven rest upon them in copious effusions,[24]

A Blessing to the Covenant People

Brethren, you are in the pathway to eternal fame, and immortal glory; and inasmuch as you feel interested for the covenant people of the Lord, the God of their fathers shall bless you. Do not be discouraged on account of the greatness of the work; only be humble and faithful, and then you can say, "What art thou, O great mountain! before Zerebbabel shalt thou be brought down." He who scattered Israel has promised to gather them; therefore inasmuch as you are to be instrumental in this great work, He will endow you with power, wisdom, might and intelligence, and every qualification necessary; while your minds will expand wider and wider, until you can circumscribe the earth

Joseph Smith's Letter
Bretheren you are in the path way to Eternal Fame! and immortal Glory; and inasmuch as you feel interested for the covenant people of the Lord, the God of their Father shall bless you. Do not be discouraged on accou[n]t of the greatness of the work; only be humble, and faithful, and then you can say, "what art thou, O, great mountain, "before Zerubbable shalt thou be brought down" He who scattered Israel has promised to gather them; therefore, inasmuch as you are to be instrumental in this great work, he will endow you with power, wisdom, might, and inteligence; and every qualification necessary; while your minds will expand wider and wider, untill you can circumscribe

---

24. 14 May 1840, *JSP, D7*, 281–82.

and the heavens, reach forth into eternity, and contemplate the mighty acts of Jehovah in all their variety and glory.

the Earth, & the Heavens, and reach forth into eternity; contemplate the mighty acts of Jehovah, in all their variety & glory[25]

The Publication of Books

Joseph Smith's Letter

In answer to your inquiries respecting the translation and publication of the Book of Mormon, hymn book, history of the [p.164] Church, etc., I would say that I entirely approve of the same, and give my consent, with the exception of the hymn book, as a new edition, containing a greater variety of hymns, will be shortly published or printed in this place, which I think will be a standard work. As soon as it is printed, you shall have some sent to you, which you may get translated, and printed into any language you please.

In answer to your inquiries, respecting the translation and publication, of the Book of Mormon, Hymn Book, History of the church, &c, &c; I would say, that I entirely approve of the same; and give my consent, with the exception of the Hymn Book, as a new edition, containing a greater variety of Hymns, will be shortly published or printed in this place; which, I think will be a standard work [p.283] As soon as it is printed, you shall have some to you, which you may get translated, and printed into any language you please.

Should we not be able to send some to you, and there should be a great call for hymn books where you may be, then I should have no objection to your publishing the present one. Were you to publish the Book of Mormon, Doctrine and Covenants, or hymn book, I desire the copyright of the same to be secured in my name.

Should we not be able to send some to you, and there should be a great call for Hymns where you ~~are~~ may be; then I should have no objections to your publishing the present one. Were you to publish the Book of Mormon, Doctrine & Covenants, or Hymn Book; I desire the copy rights of the same to be secured in my name.

With respect to publishing any other work, either original or those which have been published before, you will be governed by circumstances; if you think necessary to do so, I shall have no objection whatever. It will be well to study plainness and simplicity in whatever you publish, "for my soul delighteth in plainness."

With respect to publishing any other work, either original, or those which have been published before, you will be governed by circumstances; if you think necessary to do so I shall have no objections whatever— It will be well to study plainness and simplicity in whatever you may publish "for my soul delighteth in pla[i]nness".[26]

The Duty of Seventies

Joseph Smith's Letter

I feel much pleased with the spirit of your letter—and be assured, dear brethren, of my hearty cooperation, and my prayers for your welfare and success. In answer to your inquiry

I feel much pleased with the spirit of your letter, and be assured, Dear Bretheren, of my hearty co-operation, and my prayers for your welfare and sucess. In answer to your enquiry

---

25. 14 May 1840, *JSP, D7*, 282.
26. 14 May 1840, *JSP, D7*, 282–83.

in a former letter, relative to the duty of the Seventies in regulating churches, etc., I say that the duties of the Seventies are more particularly to preach the Gospel, and build up churches, rather than regulate them, that a High Priest may take charge of them. If a High Priest should be remiss in his duty, and should lead, or suffer the Church to be led astray, depart from the ordinances of the Lord, then it is the duty of one of the Seventies, acting under the special direction of the Twelve, being duly commissioned by them with their delegated authority, to go to the Church, and if agreeable to a majority of the members of said Church, to proceed to regulate and put in order the same; otherwise, he can have no authority to act.
JOSEPH SMITH, JUN.
DHC 4:128-129.

in a former letter, relative to the duty of the seventies in regulating churches &c; I say that the duties of the seventies is, more particularly to preach the Gospel, & build up churches, rather than regulate them.— that a high priest may take charge of them. [p.284] If a high priest should be remiss in his duty, & should lead, or suffer the church to be led astray; depart from the ordinances of the Lord, then it is the duty of one of the seventies, acting under the special direction of the twelve—being duly commissioned by them with their delegated authority, to go that church and if agreeable to a majority of the members of said church to proceed to regulate and put in order the same— otherwise he can have no authority to act[27]

Trials Before High Council

Saturday, July 11, 1840.—The High Council met at my office, when I taught them principles relating to their duty as [p.165] a Council, and that they might be guided by the same in future, I ordered it to be recorded as follows: "That the Council should try no case without both parties being present, or having had an opportunity to be present; neither should they hear one person's complaint before his case is brought up for trial; neither should they suffer the character of any one to be exposed before the High Council without the person being present and ready to defend him or herself; that the minds of the councilors be not prejudiced for or against any one whose case they may possibly have to act upon." (July 11, 1840.) DHC 4:154.

High Council Minutes

July 11th 1842 1840. High Council of the Church of Jesus Christ of Latter Day Saints of Nauvoo Illinois met in Council at the office of Joseph Smith jr. [p.332] There was no buisness before the council President Joseph Smith jr was present, who taught the Councellors things relative to their duty in Council. and give the folloing following precedent for the Council to be guided by and ordered the same to be recorded to. wit— That the Council should try no case without both parties being present or having had an opportunity to be present. neither should they hear one parties complaint before his case is brought up for trial— neither should they suffer the character of any one to be exposed before the High Council without the person being present and ready to defend him or herself—that the minds of the Councellors be not prejudiced for or against any one whose case they may possibly have to act upon. Adjourned
Hosea Stout Clk Pro Tem[28]

---

27. 14 May 1840, *JSP, D7*, 283–84.
28. 11 July 1840, *JSP, D7*, 331–32.

The Prophet's Letter to William W. Phelps, Welcoming Him Back into the Church

Joseph Smith Letter

Nauvoo, Hancock County, Illinois
July 22, 1840

Nauvoo Hancock Co Ills
July 22nd. 1840

Dear Brother Phelps.—I must say that it is with no ordinary feelings I endeavor to write a few lines to you in answer to yours of the 29th ultimo; at the same time I am rejoiced at the privilege granted me.

You may in some measure realize what my feelings, as well as Elder Rigdon's and Brother Hyrum's were, when we read your letter—truly our hearts were melted into tenderness and compassion when we ascertained your resolves. I can assure you I feel a disposition to act on your case in a manner that will meet the approbation of Jehovah, (whose servant I am), and agreeable to the principles of truth and righteousness which have been revealed; and inasmuch as long-suffering, patience, and mercy have ever characterized the dealings of our heavenly Father towards the humble and patient, I feel disposed to copy the example, cherish the same principles, and by so doing be a savior of my fellow men.

It is true, that we have suffered much in consequence of your behavior—the cup of gall, already full enough for mortals to drink, was indeed filled to overflowing when you turned against us. One with whom we had oft taken sweet counsel together, and enjoyed many refreshing seasons from the Lord—"had it been an enemy, we could have borne it. In the day that thou stoodest on the other side, in the day when strangers carried away captive his forces, and foreigners entered into his gates, and cast lots upon Far West, even thou wast as one of them; but thou shouldest not have looked on the day of thy brother, in the day that he became a stranger, neither shouldst thou have spoken proudly in the day of distress."

Dear Brother [William W.] Phelps
I must say that it is with no ordinary feelings I endeavour to write a few lines to you in answer to yours of the 29th. Ultimo, at the same time I am rejoiced at the priveledge granted me.

You may in some measure realise what my feelings, as well as Elder [Sidney] Rigdon's & Bro Hyrum [Smith]'s were when we read your letter, truly our hearts were melted into tenderness and compassion when we assertated your resolves &c I can assure you I feel a disposition to act on your case in a manner that will meet the approbation of Jehovah (whose servant I am) and agreeably to the principles of truth and righteousness which have been revealed and inasmuch as long-suffering patience and mercy have ever characterized the dealings of our heavenly Father towards the humble and penitent, I feel disposed, to copy the example and cherish the same principles, by so doing be a savior of my fellow men

It is true, that we have suffered much in consequence of your behavior— the cup of gall already full enough for mortals to drink, was indeed filled to overflowing when you turned against us: One with whom we had oft taken sweet council together, and enjoyed many refreshing seasons from the **[p.347]** Lord "Had it been an enemy we could have borne it" ["]In the day that thou stoodest on the other side, in the day when Strangers carried away captive his forces, and foreigners entered into his gates, and cast lots upon Far West even thou wast as one of them. But thou shouldst not have looked on the day of thy brother, in the day that he became a stranger neither shouldst thou have spoken proudly in the day of distress"

However, the cup has been drunk, the will of our Father has been done, and we are yet alive, for which we thank the Lord. And having been delivered from the hands of wicked men by the mercy of our God, we say it is your privilege to be delivered from the powers of the adversary, be brought into the liberty of God's dear children, and again take your stand among the Saints of the Most High, and by diligence, humility, and love unfeigned, commend yourself to our God, and your God, and to the Church of Jesus Christ.	However the cup has been drunk, the will of our heavenly Father has been done, and we are yet alive for which we thank the Lord. And having been delivered from the hands of wicked men by the mercy of our God, we say it is your privilidge to be delivered from the power of the Adversary— be brought into the liberty of God's dear children, and again take your stand among the saints of the Most High, and by diligence humility and love unfeigned, commend yourself to our God and your God and to the church of Jesus Christ
Believing your confession to be real, and your repentance genuine, I shall be happy once again to give you the right hand of fellowship, and rejoice over the returning prodigal.	Believing your confession to be real and your repentance genuine, I shall be happy once again to give you the right hand of fellowship, and rejoice over the returning prodigal.
Your letter was read to the Saints last Sunday, and an expression of their feeling was taken, when it was unanimously Resolved, That W. W. Phelps should be received into fellowship.	Your letter was read to the saints last sunday and an expression of their feeling was taken, when it was unanimously resolved that W. W. Phelps should be received into fellowship.
"Come on, dear brother, since the war is past,	**[p.348]** "Come on dear Brother since the war is past,
For friends at first, are friends again at last."	For friends at first are friends again at last."
Yours as ever, JOSEPH SMITH, JUN., —DHC 4:162-164.	Yours as Ever Joseph Smith Jr[29]

Remarks On Priesthood

At the Conference, October, 1840

The Melchizedek Priesthood Holds All Authority

	Joseph Smith's Instruction on Priesthood
In order to investigate the subject of the Priesthood, so important to this, as well as every succeeding generation, I shall proceed to trace the subject as far a I possible can from the Old and New Testaments.	In order to investigate the subject <of the Priesthood> so important to this as well as every succeeding generation, I shall proceed to trace the subject as far as I possibly can from the Old and new Testaments.

---

29. 22 July 1840, *JSP, D7*, 346–48. See also *PWJS*, 509–10.

There are two Priesthoods spoken of in the Scriptures, viz., the Melchizedek and the Aaronic or Levitical. Although there are two Priesthoods, yet the Melchizedek Priesthood comprehends the Aaronic or Levitical Priesthood, and is the grand head, and holds the highest authority which pertains to the priesthood, and the keys of the Kingdom of God in all ages of the world to the latest posterity on the earth; and is the [p.167] channel through which all knowledge, doctrine, the plan of salvation and every important matter is revealed from heaven.

There are two priesthoods spoken of in the scriptures, viz, the Melchisadeck and the Aaronic or Levitical Altho there are two priesthoods, yet the Melchisadeck priesthood comprehends the Aaronic or Levitical priesthood and is the Grand head and holds the hig[h]est Authority which pertains to the priesthood— the keys of the Kingdom of God in all ages of the world to the latest [p.435] posterity on the earth— and is the channel through which all knowledge, doctrine, the plan of salvation and every important ~~matter~~ truth is revealed from heaven.

Its institution was prior to the "foundation of this earth, or the morning stars sang together, or the Sons of God shouted for joy," and is the highest and holiest Priesthood, and is after the order of the Son of God, and all other Priesthoods are only parts, ramifications, powers and blessings belonging to the same, and are held, controlled, and directed by it. It is the channel through which the Almighty commenced revealing His glory at the beginning of the creation of the earth, and through which He has continued to reveal Himself to the children of men to the present time, and through which He will make known his purposes to the end of time.

Its institution was prior to "the foundation of this earth or the morning stars sang together or the sons of God shouted for joy," ~~and~~ it is the highest and holiest priesthood and is after the order of the Son [of] God, and all other priesthoods are only parts, ramifications, powers and blessings belonging to the same and are held controlled and directed by it. It is the Channel through which the Almighty commenced revealing his glory at the beginning of the creation of this earth and through which he has continued to reveal himself to the children of men ~~and~~ to the present time and through which he will make known his purposes to the end of time—[30]

Adam the First Man

Joseph Smith's Instruction on Priesthood

Commencing with Adam, who was the first man,[31] who is spoken of in Daniel as being the "Ancient of Days," or in other words, the first and oldest of all, the great, grand progenitor of whom it is said in another place he is Michael, because he was the first and father of all, not only by progeny, but the first to hold the spiritual blessings, to whom was made known the plan of ordinances for the salvation of his

Commencing with Adam who was the first man ~~of~~ whom ~~it~~ is spoken of in Daniel as being "the Antient of days" or in other words the first and oldest of all, the great grand progenitor of whom it is said in another place he is michael because he was the first and father of all, not only by progeny, but he was the first to hold the spiritual blessings, ~~the plan~~ to whom was made known the plan of ordinances for

---

30. 5 October 1840, *JSP, D7*, 434–35. See also *WJS*, 38–39.

31. The original *TPJS* footnote reads: "The doctrine here taught by the Prophet that Adam was the first man, and because of that fact was named the 'Ancient of Days,' the 'oldest of all,' because he is the grand progenitor of the earth, is confirmed in several passages of scripture. In the D&C 84:16, the Lord says in speaking of the authority of Priesthood: 'And from Enoch to Abel, who was slain by the conspiracy of his brother, who received the priesthood by the commandments of God, by the hand of

posterity unto the end, and to whom Christ was first revealed, and through whom Christ has been revealed from henceforth. Adam holds the keys of the dispensation of the fullness of times; i.e., the dispensation of all the times have been and will be revealed through him from the beginning to Christ, and from Christ to the end of the dispen[p.168]sations that are to be revealed. "Having made known unto us the mystery of His will, according to His good pleasure which He that purposed in Himself; that in the dispensation of the fullness of times He might gather together in one all things in Christ, both which are in heaven, and which are on earth; even in Him." (Ephesians 1:9-10.)	the Salvation of his posterity unto the end, and to whom Christ was first revealed, and through whom christ has been revealed from heaven and will continue to be revealed from henceforth. Adam holds the keys of the dispensation of the fulness of times, i.e. the dispensation of all the times have been and will be revealed through him from the beginning to Christ and from Christ to the end of ~~oo~~ all ~~world~~ the dispensations that have to be reveald Ephesians I$^{st.}$ chap 9 & 10 verses. ["]Having made known unto us the mystery of his will, according to his good pleasure which he has purposed in himself that in the dispensation of the fulness of times he might gather together in one all things in Christ both which are in heaven and which are on earth in him"[32]

Ordinances Always the Same

	Joseph Smith's Instruction on Priesthood
Now the purpose in Himself in the winding up scene of the last dispensation is that all things pertaining to that dispensation should be conducted precisely in accordance with the preceding dispensations.	[p.436] Now the purpose in himself in the winding up scene of the last dispensation is, that all things pertaining to that dispensation should be conducted precisely in accordance with the preceding dispensations,
And again, God purposed in Himself that there should not be an eternal fullness until every dispensation should be fulfilled and gathered together in one, and that all things whatsoever, that should be gathered together in one in those dispensations unto the same fullness and eternal glory, should be in Christ Jesus; therefore He set the ordinances to be the same forever and ever, and set Adam to watch over them, to reveal them from heaven to man, or to send angels to reveal them. "Are they not all ministering spirits, sent forth to	And again, God purposed in himself that there should not be an eternal fulness until every dispensation should be fulfilled and gathered together in one and that all things whatsoever that should be gathered together in one in those dispensations unto the same fulness and eternal glory should be in Christ Jesus; therefore he set the ordinances to be the same for Ever and ever and set Adam to watch over them to reveal them from heaven to man or to send Angels to reveal them Heb I Chap. 16 verse, ["]Are they not all ministring spirits

---

his father Adam, who was the first man.' Again in the Book of Moses, 1:34: 'And the first man of all men, have I called Adam, which is many,' (i.e., that is the name means many, because he is the father of all.) In the same record (Moses 3:7) we also read: 'And I, the Lord God, formed man from the dust of the ground, and breathed into his nostrils the breath of life; and man became a living soul, the first flesh upon the earth, the first man also.' In the Prophet Joseph Smith's revision of the Scriptures where the genealogy of our Lord is given in Luke (v. 45) we find the following: 'And of Enos, and of Seth, and of Adam, who was formed of God, and the first man upon the earth.'"

32. 5 October 1840, *JSP, D7*, 435. See also *WJS*, 39.

minister for them who shall be heirs of salvation?" (Hebrews 1:14.)

sent forth to minister to those who shall be heirs of salvation."

These angels are under the direction of Michael or Adam, who acts under the direction of the Lord. From the above quotation we learn that Paul perfectly understood the purposes of God in relation to His connection with man, and that glorious and perfect order which He established in Himself, whereby he sent forth power, revelations, and glory.

These angels are under the direction of Michael or Adam who acts under the direction of Christ From the above quotation we learn that Paul perfectly understood the purpose of God in relation <to> his connexion with man, and that glorious and perfect order which he established in himself whereby he sent forth power revelations and glory.[33]

Adam Received Commandments from God

Joseph Smith's Instruction on Priesthood

God will not acknowledge that which He has not called, ordained, and chosen. In the beginning God called Adam by His own voice. "And the Lord called unto Adam and said unto him, Where art thou? And he said, I heard thy voice in the garden, and I was afraid because I was naked, and hid myself." (See Genesis 3:9-10.) Adam received commandments and instructions from God: this was the order from the beginning.

God will not acknowledge that which he has not called, ordained, and chosen. In the beginning God called Adam by his own voice See Genesis 3 Chap 9 & 10 verses. ["]And the Lord called unto Adam and said unto him where art thou, and he said I heard thy voice in the garden and I was afraid because I was naked and hid myself.["] Adam received commandments and instruction from God, this was the order from the begining:

That he received revelations, commandments and ordinances at the beginning is beyond the power of controversy; **[p.169]** else how did they begin to offer sacrifices to God in an acceptable manner? And if they offered sacrifices they must be authorized by ordination. We read Genesis 4:4, that Abel brought the firstlings of the flock and the fat thereof, and the Lord had respect to Abel and to his offering. And, again, "By faith Abel offered unto God a more excellent sacrifice than Cain, by which he obtained witness that he was righteous, God testifying of his gifts; and by it he being dead, yet speaketh." (Hebrews 11:4.) How doth he yet speak? Why he magnified the Priesthood which was conferred upon him, and dies a righteous man, and therefore has become an angel of God by receiving his body from the dead, holding still the

that he received revelations, Commandments, and ordinances at the begining is beyond the power of controversy, else, how did they begin to to offer sacrifices to God in an acceptable manner? **[p.437]** And if they offered sacrifices they must be authorized by ordination. We read in Gen 4th Chap. V.4 that ["]Abel brought of the firstlings of the flock and the fat thereof and the Lord had respect to Abel and to his offring.["] And again Heb 11 Chap 4 verse. ["]By Faith abel offered unto God a more excellent Sacrifice than Cain by which he obtained witness that he was righteous God testifying of his gifts and by it he being dead yet speaketh.["] How doth he yet speak? Why he magnified the priesthood which was confired [conferred] upon him and died a righteous man, and therefore has become a ~~righteous man~~ an angel of God by receiving his body from the dead,

---

33. 5 October 1840, *JSP, D7*, 436. See also *WJS*, 39–40.

keys of his dispensation; and was sent down from heaven unto Paul to minister consoling words, and to commit unto him a knowledge of the mysteries of godliness.

therefore holding still the keys of ~~held~~ his dispensation and was sent down from heaven unto paul to minister consoleing words & to comnin [communicate?] unto him a knowledge of the mysteries of Godliness

And if this was not the case, I would ask, how did Paul know so much about Abel, and why should he talk about his speaking after he was dead? Hence, that he spoke after he was dead must be by being sent down out of heaven to administer.

and if this was not the case I would ask how did paul know so much about ~~able~~ Abel and why should he talk about his speaking after he was dead. now that he spoke after he was dead must be, by being sent down out of heaven, to administer.[34]

Adam Holds the Keys of Presidency

Joseph Smith's Instruction on Priesthood

This, then, is the nature of the Priesthood; every man holding the Presidency of his dispensation, and one man holding the Presidency of them all, even Adam; and Adam receiving his Presidency and authority from the Lord, but cannot receive a fullness until Christ shall present the Kingdom to the Father, which shall be at the end of the last dispensation.

This then is the nature of the priesthood, every man holding the presidency of his dispensation and one man holding the presidency of them all even Adam. and Adam receiving his Presidency and Authority from Christ, but cannot receive a fulness untill Christ shall present, the Kingdom to the Father which shall be at the end of the last dispensation—[35]

Cain Cursed for Unrighteousness

Joseph Smith's Instruction on Priesthood

The power, glory and blessings of the Priesthood could not continue with those who received ordination only as their righteousness continued; for Cain also being authorized to offer sacrifice, but not offering it in righteousness, was cursed. It signifies, then, that the ordinances must be kept in the very way God has appointed; otherwise their Priesthood will prove a cursing instead of a blessing.

The power, Glory, and blessings of the Priesthood could not continue with those who received ordination only as their righteousness continued, for Cain also being Authorized to offer sacrifice but not offering it in righteousness, therefore he was cursed. It signifies then, that the ordinances must be kept in the very way God has appointed, otherwise their priesthood will prove a cursing instead of a blessing.[36]

The Mission of Enoch

Joseph Smith's Instruction on Priesthood

If Cain had fulfilled the law of righteousness as did Enoch, he could have walked with God all

If Cain had fulfilled the law of righteousness as did Enoch he could have walked with God all the

---

34. 5 October 1840, *JSP, D7*, 436–37. See also *WJS*, 40.
35. 5 October 1840, *JSP, D7*, 437. See also *WJS*, 40.
36. 5 October 1840, *JSP, D7*, 437. See also *WJS*, 40–41.

the days of his life, and **[p.170]** never failed of a blessing. "And Enoch walked with God after he begat Methuselah 300 years, and begat sons and daughters, and all the days of Enoch were 365 years; and Enoch walked with God, and he was not, for God took him." (Genesis 5:22-23.) Now this Enoch God reserved unto Himself, that he should not die at that time, and appointed unto him a ministry unto terrestrial bodies, of whom there has been but little revealed. He is reserved also unto the presidency of a dispensation, and more shall be said of him and terrestrial bodies in another treatise. He is a ministering angel, to minister to those who shall be heirs of salvation, and appeared unto Jude as Abel did unto Paul; therefore Jude spoke of him (14, 15 verses). And Enoch, the seventh from Adam, revealed these sayings: "Behold, the Lord cometh with ten thousand of His Saints."

Paul was also acquainted with this character, and received instructions from him. "By faith Enoch was translated, that he should not see death, and was not found, because God had translated him; for before his translation he had this testimony, that he pleased God; but without faith, it is impossible to please Him, for he that cometh to God must believe that He is, and that He is a revealer to those who diligently seek Him." (Hebrews 11:5-6.)

days of his life and never faild of a blessing. Gen [*blank*] ["]And Enoch walked with God after he begat Mathusalah 300 years and begat Sons and Daughters and all the days of Enoch were 365 years and Enoch walked with God and he was not for God took him.["] Now this Enoch God **[p.438]** reserved unto himself that he should not die <at> ~~and~~ that time and appointed unto him a ministry unto terrestrial bodies of whom there has been but little revealed, He is reserved also unto ~~a~~ the presidency of a dispensation— ~~of~~ and more shall be said of him and terrestrial bodies in another treaties [treatise] He is a ministring Angel to minister ~~for~~ to those who shall be heirs of salvation and appered unto Jude as Abel did unto paul. therefore Jude spoke of him 14 & 15 verses in Jude. ["]and Enoch the Seventh revealed these sayings. Behold the Lord cometh with ten thousand of his saints["]

Paul was also aquainted with this Character and received instructions from him. Heb 11 Chap. 5 ver. ["]By Faith Enoch was translated that he should not see death, and was not found because God had translated him for before his translation he had this testimony that he pleased God. But without faith it is impossible to please God, for he that cometh to God must believe that he is, and that he is a revealer to those who diligently seek him,["]——[37]

The Doctrine of Translation

Now the doctrine of translation is a power which belongs to this Priesthood. There are many things which belong to the powers of the Priesthood and the keys thereof, that have been kept hid from before the foundation of the world; they are hid from the wise and prudent to be revealed in the last times.

Many have supposed that the doctrine of translation was a doctrine whereby men were taken immediately into the presence of God,

Joseph Smith's Instruction on Priesthood

Now the doctrine of translation is a power which belongs to this priesthood, there are many things which belong to the powers of the priesthood and the keys thereof that have been kept hid from before the foundation of the world. they are hid from the wise and prudent to be revealed in the last times.

many may have supposed, that the— doctrine of translation was a doctrine whereby men were taken immediately into the presence of

---

37. 5 October 1840, *JSP, D7*, 437–38. See also *WJS*, 41.

and into an eternal fullness, but his is a mistaken idea. Their place of habitation is that of the terrestrial order, and a place prepared for such characters He held in reserve to be ministering angels unto many planets, and who as yet have not entered into so great a fullness as those who are resurrected from the dead, "Others were tortured, not accepting deliverance, that they might obtain a better resurrection." (See Hebrews 11:35.)

Now it was evident that there was a better resurrection, [p.171] or else God would not have revealed it unto Paul. Wherein then, can it be said a better resurrection. This distinction is made between the doctrine of the actual resurrection and translation: translation obtains deliverance from the tortures and sufferings of the body, but their existence will prolong as to the labors and toils of the ministry, before they can enter into so great a rest and glory.

On the other hand, those who were tortured, not accepting deliverance, received and immediate rest from their labors. "And I heard a voice from heaven, saying, Blessed are the dead who die in the Lord, for from henceforth they do rest from their labors and their works do follow them." (See Revelation 14:13.)

They rest from their labors for a long time, and yet their work is held in reserve for them, that they are permitted to do the same work, after they receive a resurrection for their bodies. But we shall leave this subject and the subject of the terrestrial bodies for another time, in order to treat upon them more fully.

The Keys of Priesthood

The next great, grand Patriarch [after Enoch] who held the keys of the Priesthood was Lamech. "And Lamech lived one hundred

God and into an Eternal fulness but this is a mistaken idea. There place of habitation is that of the terrestrial order and a [p.439] place prepared for such characters, he held in reserve to be ministring Angels Unto many planets, and who as yet have not entered into so great a fulness as those who are resurrected from the dead. See Heb 11 Chap part of the 35 verse "others were tortured not accepting deliverance that they might obtain a better resurrection["]

Now it was evident, that there was a better resurrection or else God would not have revealed it unto paul wherein then can it be said a better ressurrection? This distinction is made between the doctrine of the actual ressurrection and the doctrine of translation, the doctrine of translation obtains deliverance from the tortures and sufferings of the body but their existance will prolong as to their labors and toils of the ministry before they can enter in to so great a rest and glory,

but on the other hand those who were tortured not accepting deliverance received an immediate rest from their labors, See Rev [*blank*] ["]And I heard a voice from heaven saying blessed are the dead who die in the Lord for from henceforth they do rest from their labors and their works do follow them["]—

They rest from their labors for a long time and yet their work is held in reserve for them, that they are permitted to do the same works after they receive a ressurection for their bodies, but we shall leave this subject and the subject of the terrestrial bodies for another time in order to treat upon them more fully[38]

Joseph Smith's Instruction on Priesthood

The next great grand patriarch who held the keys of the priesthood was Lamech See Gen 5 Chap 28 & 29 verses— ["]And Lamech lived

---

38. 5 October 1840, *JSP, D7*, 438–39. See also *WJS*, 41–42.

and eighty-two years and begat a son, and he called his name Noah, saying, this same shall comfort us concerning our work and the toil of our hands because of the ground which the Lord has cursed." (See Genesis 5:28-29.) The Priesthood continued from Lamech to Noah: "And God said unto Noah, The end of all flesh is before me, for the earth is filled with violence through them and behold I will destroy them with the earth." (Genesis 6:13.)

Thus we behold the keys of this Priesthood consisted in obtaining the voice of Jehovah that He talked with him [Noah] in a familiar and friendly manner, that He continued to him the keys, the covenants, the power and the glory, with which He blessed Adam at the beginning; and the offering of sacrifice, which also shall be continued at the last time; for all the ordinances and duties that ever have been required by the Priesthood, under the directions and commandments of the Almighty in any of the dispensations, shall all be had in the last dispensation, therefore all things had under the authority of the Priesthood at any former period, shall be had again, bringing to pass the restoration spoken of by the mouth of all [p.172] the Holy Prophets; then shall the sons of Levi offer an acceptable offering to the Lord. "And he shall sit as a refiner and purifier of silver; and he shall purify the sons of Levi, and purge them as gold and silver, that they may offer unto the Lord." (See Malachi 3:3.)

182 years and begat a Son and he called his name Noah saying this same shall comfort us concerning our work and the toil of our hands because of the ground which the Lord has Curst.["] The priesthood continued from Lamech to Noah Gen 6 Chap 13 verse. ["] And God said unto Noah the end of all flesh is before me, for the earth is filled with violence through them, and behold I will destroy them with the earth,"

thus we behold the keys of this priesthood consisted in obtaining the voice of Jehovah that he talked with him in a familiare and friendly manner, that he continued to him the keys, the covenants, the power and the glory with which he blessed Adam at the beginning and the offring of [p.440] sacrifice which also shall be continued at the last time. for all the ordinances and duties that ever have been required by the priesthood under the directions and commandments of the Almighty in the last dispensation at the end thereof in any of the dispensations, shall all be had in the last dispensations— Therefore all things had under the Authority of the Priesthood At any former period shall be had again— bringing to pass the restoration spoken of by the mouth of all the Holy prophets— then <Malach 3— 3> shall the Sons of Levi offer unto the Lord an acceptable offering" then shall the sons of Levi offer an acceptable sacrifice to the Lord Se[e] Malichi 3 Chap— 3 & 4 ["]And he shall sit as a refiners fire and purifier of silver; and he shall purify the sons of Levi, and purge them as gold and silver, that they may offer unto the Lord["]]³⁹

Sacrifice to Be Part of Restoration

Joseph Smith's Instruction on Priesthood

It will be necessary here to make a few observations on the doctrine set forth in the above quotation, and it is generally supposed that sacrifice was entirely done away when the Great Sacrifice [i.e.,] the sacrifice of the Lord

It will be necessary here to make a few observations on the doctrine, set forth in the above quotation, As it is generally supposed that sacrifice was entirely done away, <when the great sacrif[ic]e was offered up—> and that

---

39. 5 October 1840, *JSP, D7*, 439–40. See also *WJS*, 42.

Jesus was offered up, and that there will be no necessity for the ordinance of sacrifice in future; but those who assert this are certainly not acquainted with the duties, privileges and authority of the Priesthood, or with the Prophets.

The offering of sacrifice has ever been connected and forms a part of the duties of the Priesthood. It began with the Priesthood, and will be continued until after the coming of Christ, from generation to generation. We frequently have mention made of the offering of sacrifice by the servants of the Most High in ancient days, prior to the law of Moses; which ordinances will be continued when the Priesthood is restored with all its authority, power and blessings.

there will be no necessity for the ordinance of sacrifice in future; but those who assert this, are certainly not aquainted with the duties, privileges and authority of the priesthood. <or with the prophets>

The offering of sacrifice is has ever been connected, and forms a part of the <duties of the> priesthood. It began which with the priesthood and will be continued untill after the coming of christ from generation to generation—— We frequently have mention made of the offering of Sacrifice by the servants of the most high in antient days prior to the law of moses, See [*blank*] which ordinances will be continued when the priesthood is restored with all its Authority power and blessings.[40]

The Mission of Elijah

Elijah was the last Prophet that held the keys of the Priesthood, and who will, before the last dispensation, restore the authority and deliver the keys of the Priesthood, in order that all the ordinances may be attended to in righteousness. It is true that the Savior had authority and power to bestow this blessing; but the sons of Levi were too prejudiced. "And I will send Elijah the Prophet before the great and terrible day of the Lord," etc., etc. Why send Elijah? Because he holds the keys of authority to administer in all the ordinances of the Priesthood; and without the authority is given, the ordinances could not be administered in righteousness.

It is a very prevalent opinion that the sacrifices which were offered were entirely consumed. This was not the case; if you read Leviticus 2:2-3, you will observe that the priests took a part as a memorial and offered it up before the Lord, while the remainder was kept for the maintenance of the priests; so [p.173] that the offerings and sacrifices

Joseph Smith's Instruction on Priesthood
Elijah was the last Prophet that held the keys of this priesthood, and who will, before the last dispensation, restore the Authority and delive[r] the keys of this priesthood in order that all the ordinan[c]es may be attended to in righteousness. <It is true that the Savior [p.441] had authority and power to bestow this blessing <but the Sons of Levi were too predjudi[ced]>> And I will send Elijah the prophet before the great and terrible day of the Lord &c &c. Why send Elijah because he holds the keys of the Authority to administer in all the ordinances of the priesthood and without the Authority is given the ordinances could not be administered in righteousness.

It is a very prevalent opinion that in the sacrifices <sacrifices> of <which> were offered were entirely consumed, this was not the case if you read Leviticus [*blank*] Chap [*blank*] Verses you will observe that the priests took a part as a memorial and offered it up before the Lord, while the remainder was kept for the benefit <maintenance> of the priests— So that the offerings

---

40. 5 October 1840, *JSP, D7*, 440. See also *WJS*, 43.

All Ordinances Restored

Joseph Smith's Instruction on Priesthood

are not all consumed upon the altar—but the blood is sprinkled, and the fat and certain other portions are consumed.	and sacrifices are not all consumed upon the Alter, but the blood is sprinkled and the fat and certain other portions are consumed [41]
These sacrifices, as well as every ordinance belonging to the Priesthood, will, when the Temple of the Lord shall be built, and the sons of Levi be purified, be fully restored and attended to in all their powers, ramifications, and blessings. This ever did and ever will exist when the powers of the Melchizedek Priesthood are sufficiently manifest; else how can the restitution of all things spoken of by the Holy Prophets be brought to pass? It is not to be understood that the law of Moses will be established again with all its rites and variety of ceremonies; this has never been spoken of by the prophets; but those things which existed prior to Moses' day, namely, sacrifice, will be continued.	These sacrifices as well as every ordinance belonging to the priesthood will when the temple of the Lord shall be built <and the sons [of] Levi be purified> be fully restored and attended to ~~then the Sons of Levi shall be purified~~. all their powers, raniffications [ramifications], and blessings— this ever ~~was~~ did and will ~~be~~ exist when the powers of the Melchisadc Priesthood are sufficiently manifest. else how can the restitution of all things spoken of by all the Holy prophets be brought to pass ~~be brought to pass~~, It is not to be understood that, the law of Moses will be ~~fully~~ established again with all its rights and <variety of ~~ceremonies~~> ceremonies <this has never been spoken off by the prophets> but those things which existed prior to Mose's day viz sacrifice, will be continued—
It may be asked by some, what necessity for sacrifice, since the Great Sacrifice was offered? In answer to which, if repentance, baptism, and faith existed prior to the days of Christ, what necessity for them since that time? The Priesthood has descended in a regular line from father to son, through their succeeding generations. (See Book of Doctrine and Covenants.) (October 5, 1840.) DHC 4:207-212.	It may be asked by some what necesssity for Sacrifice since the great Sacrifice was offered? In answer to which if Repentance Baptism and faith ~~were necessary to Salvation~~ <existed> prior to the days of christ what necessity for them since that time—— [p.442] The priesthood has descended in a regular line from Father to Son through their succeeding generations See Book of Doctrine & Covenants[42]

An Epistle of the Prophet to the Twelve

Joseph Smith Letter

To the Traveling High Council and Elders of the Church of Jesus Christ of Latter-day Saints in Great Britain:	[p.460] Nauvoo Hancock Co, Ills. Decr 15. 1840
Beloved Brethren.—May grace, mercy, and peace rest upon you from God the Father and	Beloved Brethren. May Grace, Mercy, and Peace rest upon you, from God the Father and

---

41. 5 October 1840, *JSP, D7*, 440–41. See also *WJS*, 43.
42. 5 October 1840, *JSP, D7*, 441–42. See also *WJS*, 43–44.

the Lord Jesus Christ. Having several communications lying before me from my brethren the Twelve, some of which ere this have merited a reply, but from the multiplicity of business which necessarily engages my attention, I have delayed communicating with you to the present time.

Be assured, beloved brethren, that I am no disinterested observer of the things which are transpiring on the face of the whole earth; and amidst the general movements which are in progress, none is of more importance than the glorious work in which you are now engaged; consequently I feel some anxiety on you account, that you may by your virtue, faith, [p.174] diligence and charity commend yourselves to one another, to the Church of Christ, and to your Father who is in heaven; by whose grace you have been called to so holy a calling; and be enabled to perform the great and responsible duties which rest upon you. And I can assure you, that from the information I have received, I feel satisfied that you have not been remiss in you duty; but that your diligence and faithfulness have been such as must secure you the smiles of that God whose servant you are, and also the good will of the Saints throughout the world.

the Lord Jesus Christ. Having several communications laying before me, from my Brethren the "Twelve" some of which have ere this merited a a reply, but <from> the multiplicity of business which necessarily engages my attention I have delayed [p.462[43]] communicating to them, to the present time.

Be assured, my beloved brethren, that I am no disinterested observer of the things which are transpiring on the face of the whole earth and amidst the general movements which are in progress, none is of more importance, than the glorious work in which you are now engaged, and consequently, I feel some anxiety on your account, that you may, by your virtue, faith, diligence, and charity, commend yourselves to one another, <to the Church of Christ> and <to> your Father which is in heaven, by whose grace you have been called to so holy a calling, and be enabled to perform the great and responsible duties which rest upon you. And I can assure you, that from the information I have received, I feel satisfied, that you have not been remiss, <in your duty> but that your diligence and faithfulness have been such, as must secure you the smiles of that God, whose servants you are, and the good will of the saints throughout the world.[44]

The Gospel in England

The spread of the Gospel throughout England is certainly pleasing; the contemplation of which cannot but afford feelings of no ordinary kind, in the bosom of those who have borne the heat and burden of the day; and who were its firm supporters and strenuous advocates in infancy, while surrounded with circumstances the most unpropitious, and its destruction threatened on all hands; like the

Joseph Smith Letter

The spread of truth throughout England is certainly pleasing; the contemplation of which, cannot but afford feelings of no ordinary kind in the bosoms of those who have had to bear the heat and burthen of the day, and who were its firm supporters, and strenuous advocates, in infancy, while surrounded with circumstances the most unpropitious, and its destruction threatened on all hands. But like

---

43. Page 461 is a graphic.
44. 15 December 1840, *JSP, D7*, 460, 462. See also *PWJS*, 516; "Extract from an Epistle to the Elders in England," *T&S* 2, no. 5 (1 January 1841): 258. The 19 October 1840 date provided by Joseph Fielding Smith (for this discourse) is in error. The original letter was dated 15 December 1840.

gallant bark that has braved the storm unhurt, spreads her canvas to the breeze, and nobly cuts her way through the yielding wave, more conscious than ever of the strength of her timbers, and the experience and capability of her captain, pilot, and crew.

It is likewise very satisfactory to my mind, that there has been such a good understanding between you, and that the Saints have so cheerfully hearkened to counsel, and vied with each other in this labor of love, and in the promotion of truth and righteousness. This is as it should be in the Church of Jesus Christ; unity is strength. "How pleasing it is for brethren to dwell together in unity!" Let the Saints of the Most High ever cultivate this principle, and the most glorious blessings must result, not only to them individually, but to the whole Church—the order of the kingdom will be maintained, its officers respected, and its requirements readily and cheerfully obeyed.

the gallant Bark, that has braved the storm unhurt, spreads her canvass to the breese, and nobly cuts her way through the yielding wave, more conscious than ever of the strength of her timbers and the experience and capabilities of her Captain, Pilate and crew.

It is likewise very satisfactory to <my> mind, that there has been such a good understanding existing between you, and that the saints have <so> cheerfully, hearkened to council and vied with each other in their labors of love; and in the promotion of truth and righteousness; this is as it should be in the church of Jesus Christ. Unity is strength. "How pleasant it is for brethren **[p.463]** to dwell together in Unity &c" Let the saints of the most high, ever cultivate this principle, and the most glorious blessings must result, not only to them individually but to the whole church— The order of the Kingdom will be maintained,— Its officers respected, and its requirements readily and cheerfully obeyed.[45]

Love a Characteristic of Deity

Joseph Smith Letter

Love is one of the chief characteristics of Deity, and ought to be manifested by those who aspire to be the sons of God. A man filled with the love of God, is not content with blessing his family alone, but ranges through the whole world, anxious to bless the whole human race. This has been your feeling, and **[p.175]** caused you to forego the pleasure of home, that you might be a blessing to others, who are candidates for immortality, but strangers to truth; and for so doing, I pray that heaven's choicest blessings may rest upon you.

Love is one of the leading characteristics of Deity, and ou[gh]t to be manifested by those who aspire to be the Sons of God. A man filled with the love of God, is not content with blessing his family alone, but ranges through the world, anxious to bless the whole of the human family. This has been your feelings and caused you to forego the pleasures of home, that you might be a blessing to others, who are candidates for immortality but and who were strangers to the principals of truth and for so doing I pray that Heaven's choicest blessings may rest upon you.

Being requested to give my advice respecting the propriety of your returning in the spring, I will do so willingly. I have reflected on the subject some time, and am of the opinion that it would be wisdom in you to make preparations

Being requested to give my advice respecting the propriety of your returning in the spring, I will do so willingly. I have reflected on the subject some time and am of the opinion that it would be wisdom in you to make preparations

---

45. 15 December 1840, *JSP, D7*, 462–63. See also *PWJS*, 516–17; *T&S* 2, no. 5 (1 January 1841): 258.

to leave the scene of your labors in the spring. Having carried the testimony to that land, and numbers having received it, the leaven can now spread without your being obliged to stay.	to leave the scene of your labors in the spring. Having carried the testimony to that land, and numbers having received it, consequently the leaven can now spread, without your being obliged to stay.
Another thing—there have been whisperings of the Spirit that there will be some agitations, excitements, and trouble in the land in which you are now laboring. I would therefore say, in the meantime be diligent: organize the churches, and let everyone stand in his proper place, so that those who cannot come with you in the spring, may not be left as sheep without a shepherd.	Another thing, there has been some whisperings of the spirit; that there will be some agitation, some excitement, and some trouble in the land in which you are now laboring. I would therefore say in the mean time be diligent, organize the churches and let every one stand in his proper place, so that those who cannot come with you in the spring may not be left as sheep without shepherds.[46]

A Place of Gathering

Joseph Smith Letter

I would likewise observe, that inasmuch as this place has been appointed for the gathering of the Saints, it is necessary that it should be attended to in the order that the Lord intends it should. To this end I would say, that as there are great numbers of the Saints in England who are extremely poor, and not accustomed to the farming business, who must have certain preparations made for them before they can support themselves in this country, therefore to prevent confusion and disappointment when they arrive here, let those men who are accustomed to make machinery, and those who can command capital, though it be small, come here as soon as convenient, and put up machinery, and make such other preparations as may be necessary, so that when the poor come on, they may have employment to come to. This place has advantages for manufacturing and commercial purposes, which but very few can boast of; and the establishing of cotton factories, foundries, potteries, etc., would be the means of bringing in wealth, and raising it to a very important elevation.	I would likewise observe, that inasmuch as this place has been appointed for the gathering of the saints, it is necessary that it should be attended to, in the order which the Lord intended it should; to this end I would say that as there are great numbers of the saints in England, who are extremely poor and **[p.464]** not accustomed to the farming business, who must have certain preparations made for them before they can support themselves in this country, therefore to prevent confusion and disappointment when they arrive here, let those men who are accustomed to making machinery and those who can command a capital even if it be but small, come here as soon as convenient and put up machinery and make such other preparations as may be necessary, so, that when the poor come on they may have employment to come to. This place has advantages for a manufacturing and commercial purposes which but very few can boast of; and by establishing Cotton Factories, Founderies, Potteries &c &c would be the means of bringing in wealth and raising it to a very important elevation.

---

46. 15 December 1840, *JSP, D7*, 463. See also *PWJS*, 517; *T&S* 2, no. 5 (1 January 1841): 258.

I need not occupy more space on this subject, as its reasonableness must be obvious to every mind.

I need not occupy more space on this subject as its reasonableness must be obvious to every mind.[47]

Printing of Books

Joseph Smith Letter

[p.176] In my former epistle I told you my mind respecting the printing of the Book of Mormon, hymn book, etc. I have been favored by receiving a hymn book from you, and as far as I have examined it, I highly approve of it, and think it to be a very valuable collection. I am informed that the Book of Mormon is likewise printed, which I am glad to hear, and should be pleased to hear that it was printed in all the different languages of the earth. You can use your own pleasure respecting the printing of the Doctrine and Covenants. If there is a great demand for it, I have no objections, but would rather encourage it.

In my former epistle I told you my mind respecting the printing of the Book of Mormon. Hymn Book &c &c— I have been favored by receiving a Hymn Book from you and as far as I have examined it I highly approve of it and think it to be a very valuable collection. I am informed that the Book of Mormon is likewise printed, which I am glad to hear, and should be pleased to hear that it was printed in all the different Languages of the earth. You can use your own pleasure respecting [p.465] printing the Book of Doctrine & Covenants, if there is a great demand for them, I have not any objections, but would rather encourage it.

I can say, that as far as I have been made acquainted with your movements, I am perfectly satisfied that they have been in wisdom; and I have no doubt but that the Spirit of the Lord has directed you, and this proves to my mind that you have been humble, and your desires have been for the salvation of your fellow men, and not for your own aggrandizement, and selfish interests. As long as the Saints manifest such a disposition, their counsels will be approved of, and their exertions crowned with success.

I am happy to say, that as far as I have been made acquainted with your movements, I have been perfectly satisfied that they have been in wisdom, and I have no doubt but the spirit of the Lord has directed you. and this proves to my mind that you have been humble, and your desires have been, for the salvation of your fellow man, and not your own aggrandizement and selfish interest. As long as the saints manifest such a disposition their councils will be approved of, and their exertions crowned with success.

There are many things of much importance, on which you ask counsel, but which I think you will be perfectly able to decide upon, as you are move conversant with the peculiar circumstances than I am; and I feel great confidence in your united wisdom; therefore you will excuse me for not entering into detail. If I should see anything that is wrong, I would take the privilege of making known my mind to you, and pointing out the evil.

There are many things of minor importance, on which you ask council, but which I think you will be perfectly able to decide upon as I you are more conversant with the peculiar circumstances than I ~~can~~ am, and I feel great confidence in your united wisdom, therefore you will excuse me for not entering into detail. If I should see any thing that was wrong, I should take the priviledge of making known my mind to you and pointing out the evil.

---

47. 15 December 1840, *JSP, D7*, 463–64. See also *PWJS*, 517; *T&S* 2, no. 5 (1 January 1841): 258–59.

If Elder Parley P. Pratt should wish to remain in England some time longer than the rest of the Twelve, he will feel himself at liberty to do so, as his family are with him, consequently his circumstances are somewhat different from the rest; and likewise it is necessary that someone should remain who is conversant with the rules and regulations of the Church, and continue the paper which is published. Consequently, taking all these things into consideration, I would not press it upon Brother Pratt to return in the spring.

If Elder Parley P Pratt should wish to remain in England, for some time longer than the rest of the Twelve, he will feel himself at liberty to do so; as he his family are with him Consequently his circumstances are somewhat [p.466] different to the rest, and likewise it is necessary that some one should remain who is conversant with the rules, regulations &c & of the church And continue the paper which is published; consequently taking all these things into consideration I would not press upon Brother Pratt to return in the spring.[48]

The Saints Prospering

Joseph Smith Letter

[p.177] I am happy to inform you that we are prospering in this place, and that the Saints are more healthy than formerly; and from the decrease of sickness this season, when compared with the last, I am led to the conclusion that this must eventually become a healthy place. There are at present about 3,000 inhabitants in Nauvoo, and numbers are flocking in daily. Several stakes have been set off in different parts of the country, which are in prosperous circumstances.

I am happy to inform you that we are prospering in this place, and that the saints are more healthy than formerly, and from the decrease of sickness this season, when compared with the last, I am led to the conclusion that this, must eventually become a healthy place. There are at present about 3000 inhabitants in Nauvoo, and numbers are flocking in daily; severeal stakes have been set off in different parts of the ~~country~~ county, which are in prospering circumstances.

Provisions are much lower than when you left. Flour is about $4 per barrel. Corn and potatoes about 25 cents per bushel; and other things in proportion. There has been a very plentiful harvest throughout the Union.

Provisions are much lower than when you left. Flour is worth about four dollars per barrel, corn ~~25~~ 20 cents per bushel; Pottatoes about 20 cents. and other things in about the same proportion. There has been a very plentiful harvest indeed, throughout the Union.[49]

The Temple

Joseph Smith Letter

You will observe, by the Times and Seasons, that we are about building a temple for the worship of our God in this place. Preparations are now making; every tenth day is devoted by the brethren for quarrying rock, etc. We have secured one of the most lovely situations for it

You will observe by the "Times & Season" that we are about building a Temple for the worship of our God in this place; preparations are now making, every tenth day is devoted by the brethren here, for quarrying rock &c &. we have secured one of the most lovely sites for

---

48. 15 December 1840, *JSP, D7*, 464–66. See also *PWJS*, 517–18; *T&S* 2, no. 5 (1 January 1841): 259.
49. 15 December 1840, *JSP, D7*, 466. See also *PWJS*, 518–19; *T&S* 2, no. 5 (1 January 1841): 259.

in this region of country. It is expected to be considerably larger than the one in Kirtland, and on a more magnificent scale, and which will undoubtedly attract the attention of the great men of the earth.	it that there is in this region of Country. It is expected to be considerably larger and on <a> [p.467] more magnificent scale than the one in Kirtland and which will undoubtedly attract the attention[n] of the great men of the <earth>
We have a bill before the legislature for the incorporation of the city of Nauvoo, and for the establishment of a seminary of learning, and other purposes, which I expect will pass in a short time.	We have a bill before the Legislature for the incorporation of the City of Nauvoo for the establishment of a Seminary and other purposes, which I expect will pass in a short time.⁵⁰

Death of Patriarch Joseph Smith

	Joseph Smith Letter
You will also receive intelligence of the death of my father; which event, although painful to the family and to the Church generally, yet the sealing testimony of the truth of the work of the Lord was indeed satisfactory. Brother Hyrum succeeds him as Patriarch of the Church, according to his last directions and benedictions.	You will also have received intelligence of the death of my Father, which event altho painful to the family and to the church generally, yet the sealing testimony of the truth of the work of the Lord was indeed satisfactory; the particulars of his death &c you will find in the Sepr number of the "Times and seasons" Brother Hyrum [Smith] succeeds him as patriarch of the Church, according to his last directions and benedictions.
Several persons of eminence and distinction in society have joined the Church and become obedient to the faith; and I am happy to inform you that the work is spreading very fast upon this continent. Some of the brethren are now in New Orleans, [p.178] and we expect a large gathering from the south. I have had the pleasure of welcoming about one hundred brethren who came with Brother Turley; the remainder I am informed stayed in Kirtland, not having means to get any further. I think that those who came here this fall, did not take the best possible route, or the least expensive. Most of the brethren have obtained employment of one kind or another, and appear tolerably well contented, and seem disposed to hearken to counsel.	Several persons of emminece [eminence] and distinction in society, have joined the Church, and become obedient to the faith, and I am happy to inform you that the work is spreading very fast on this continent, [p.468] some of the Brethren are now in New Orleans, and we expect to have a gathering from the South. I have had the pleasure of wel[c]oming about One hundred of the Brethren from England, who came with Elder [Theodore] Turley, the remainder I am informed stop[p]ed in Kirtland, not having means to get any further. I think ~~they can~~ those that came here did not take the best possible rout, or the least expensive. Most of the brethren have obtained employment of one kind or another and appear tolerably well contented and seem disposed to hearken to council.⁵¹

---

50. 15 December 1840, *JSP, D7*, 466–67. See also *PWJS*, 519; *T&S* 2, no. 5 (1 January 1841): 259–60.
51. 15 December 1840, *JSP, D7*, 467–68. See also *PWJS*, 519; *T&S* 2, no. 5 (1 January 1841): 260.

Spread of the Gospel

| | **Joseph Smith Letter** |

Brothers Robinson and Smith lately had a letter from Elders Kimball, Smith and Woodruff, which gave us information of the commencement of the work of the lord in the city of London, which I was glad to hear. I am likewise informed that elders have gone to Australia and to the East Indies. I feel desirous that every providential opening of the kind should be filled, and that you should, prior to your leaving England, send the Gospel into as many parts as you possibly can.

Beloved brethren, you must be aware in some measure of my feelings, when I contemplate the great work which is now rolling on, and the relationship which I sustain to it, while it is extending to distant lands, and thousands are embracing it. I realize in some measure my responsibility, and the need I have of support from above, and wisdom from on high, that I may be able to teach this people, which have now become a great people, the principles of righteousness, and lead them agreeably to the will of Heaven; so that they may be perfected, and prepared to meet the Lord Jesus Christ when He shall appear in great glory. Can I rely on your prayers to our heavenly Father on my behalf, and on all the prayers of all my brethren and sisters in England, (whom having not seen, yet I love), that I may be enabled to escape every stratagem of Satan, surmount every difficulty, and bring this people to the enjoyment of those blessings which are reserved for the righteous? I ask this at your hands in the name of the Lord Jesus Christ.

Let the Saints remember that great things depend on their individual exertion, and that they are called to be co-workers with us and the Holy Spirit in accomplishing the great work of the last days; and in consideration

Brothers Robinson & Smith lately had a letter from Elders [Heber C.] Kimball, [George A.] Smith & [Wilford] Woodruff in London which gave us information of the commencement of the work of the Lord in that City, which I was glad to hear. I am likewise informed the Elders have gone to Australia & to the East Indies I feel deserieous that every providential opening of that kind should be filled, and that you should prior to your leaving England, send the gospel into as many parts as you possibly can.

Beloved brethren, you must be aware in some measure of my feelings when I contemplate the great work which is now rolling on, and the relationship which I sustain to it; while it is extending to distant lands, and islands, and thousands are embracing it, I realize in some measure my responsibility and the **[p.469]** need I have of support from above, and wisdom from on high; that I may be able to teach this people, which have now become a great people, the principles of righteousness, and lead them agreeably to the will of heaven so that they may be perfected and prepared to meet the Lord Jesus Christ, when he shall appear. in great glory. Can I rely on your prayers to your heavenly Father in my behalf? and on the prayers of all my brethren & sisters in England? (whom having not seen yet I love) that I may be enabled to escape every stra[ta]gem of satan, surmount every difficulty, and bring this people, to the enjoyment of those blessings, which are reserved for the righteous I ask this at your and their hands in the name of Jesus Christ.

Let the saints remember that great things depend on their individual exertion, and that they are called to be co-workers with us and the holy spirit in accomplishing the great works of the last days, and in consideration of the extent, the blessings and glories of the same, let every selfish feeling be not only buried, but annihilated; and let love to God and man predom[p.179]inate, and reign triumphant in every mind, that their hearts may become like unto Enoch's of old, and comprehend all things, present, past and future, and come behind in no gift, waiting for the coming of the Lord Jesus Christ.

of the extent, the blessings, and the glories of the same let every selfish feeling be not only buried, but anihalated, and let love to God and man, predominate and reign triumphant in every mind, that their hearts may become like unto Enoch's of old so that they may comprehend all things, present, past, and future, and "come behind in no gift waiting for the coming of the Lord Jesus Christ".[52]

Saints to Live unto God

Joseph Smith Letter

The work in which we are unitedly engaged is one of no ordinary kind. The enemies we have to contend against are subtle and well skilled in maneuvering; it behooves us to be on the alert to concentrate our energies, and that the best feelings should exist in our midst; and then, by the help of the Almighty, we shall go on from victory to victory, and from conquest to conquest; our evil passions will be subdued, our prejudices depart; we shall find no room in our bosoms for hatred; vice will hide its deformed head, and we shall stand approved in the sight of heaven, and be acknowledged the sons of God.

The work in which we are unitedly engaged in, is one of no ordinary kind, the enemies we have to contend against are subtle and well skilled in manuvering, it behoves us then to be on the alert, to concentrate our energies, and that the best feelings should exists in our midst, and then by the help of the Almighty we shall go on from victory to victory and from conquest unto conquest, our evil passions will be subdued, our predjudices depart, we shall find no room in our bosoms for hatred, vice will hide its deformed head, and we shall stand approved in the sight of heaven and be acknowledged "the Sons of God"

Let us realize that we are not to live to ourselves, but to God; by so doing the greatest blessings will rest upon us both in time and in eternity.

Let us realize that we are not to live to ourselves but to God by so doing the greatest blessings will rest upon us both in time and in Eternity.[53]

Baptism for the Dead

Joseph Smith Letter

I presume the doctrine of "baptism for the dead" has ere this reached your ears, and may have raised some inquiries in your minds respecting the same. I cannot in this letter give you all the information you may desire on the subject; but aside from knowledge independent of the Bible, I would say that it was certainly practiced by the ancient churches; and St. Paul endeavors to prove the doctrine of the

I presume the doctrine of "Baptizm for the dead" has ere this reached your ears, and may have raised some inquiries in your mind respecting the same. I **[p.470]** cannot in this letter give you all the information you may desire on the subject, but aside from my knowledg[e] independant of the Bible, I would say, that this was certainly practiced by the antient churches And. St Paul endeavors

---

52. 15 December 1840, *JSP, D7*, 468–69. See also *PWJS*, 519–20; *T&S* 2, no. 5 (1 January 1841): 260.
53. 15 December 1840, *JSP, D7*, 469. See also *PWJS*, 520–21; *T&S* 2, no. 5 (1 January 1841): 260–61.

resurrection from the same, and says, "Else what shall they do which are baptized for the dead, if the dead rise not at all? Why are they then baptized for the dead?"

I first mentioned the doctrine in public when preaching the funeral sermon of Brother Seymour Brunson: and have since then given general instructions in the Church on the subject. The Saints have the privilege of being baptized for those of their relatives who are dead, whom they believe would have embraced the Gospel, if they had been privileged with hearing it, and who have received the Gospel in the spirit, through the instrumentality of those who have been commissioned to preach to them while in prison.

[p.180] Without enlarging on the subject, you will undoubtedly see its consistency and reasonableness; and it presents the Gospel of Christ in probably a more enlarged scale than some have imagined it. But as the performance of this rite is more particularly confined to this place, it will not be necessary to enter into particulars; at the same time I always feel glad to give all the information in my power, buy my space will not allow me to do it.

We had a letter from Elder Hyde, a few days ago, who is in New Jersey, and is expecting to leave for England as soon as Elder Page reaches him. He requested to know if converted Jews are to go to Jerusalem or to come to Zion. I therefore wish you to inform him that converted Jews must come here.

to prove the doctrine of the ressurrection from the same, and says "else what shall they do who are baptized for the dead["] &c &c.

I first mentioned the doctrine in public while preaching the funeral sermon of Bro [Seymour] Brunson, and have since then given general instructions to the Church on the subject. The saints have the priviledge of being baptized for those of their relatives who are dead, who they feel to believe would have embraced the gospel if they had been priviledged with hearing it, and who have received the gospel in the spirit through the instrumentality of those who may have been commissioned to preach to them while in the prison.

Without enlarging on the subject you will undoubtedly see its consistancy, and reasonableness, and presents the the gospel of Christ in probably a more enlarged scale than some have received it. But as the performance of this right is more particularly confined to this place it will not be necessary to enter into particulars, at the same time I allways feel glad to give all the information in my power, but my space will not allow me to do it.

[p.471] We had a letter from Elder [Orson] Hyde a few days ago, who is in New Jersey, and is expecting to leave for England as soon as Elder [John E.] Page reaches him. He requested to know in his letter if converted Jews are to go to Jerusalem or to come to Zion. I therefore wish you to inform him that converted Jews must come here. If Elder Hydes & Pages testimony to the Jews at Jerusalem should be received then they may know "that the set time hath come": I will write more particular instructions to them afterwards. Your Your families are well and generally in good spirits, and bear their privations with christian fortitude and patience. Brother [Willard] Richards' question respecting arriving in the spring is answered I shall be very happy to see him & his family & likewise Brother [Joseph] Fielding, tell him that Bro [Robert B.] Thompson is making preparations for his coming. With respect to the rout best to be taken I think you will be better able to <give> advise than myself. But I would not advise coming round by the lakes. And it would not be prudent to come via New Orleans in the sickly season. but in the spring or fall or winter might do.

Give my kind love to all the brethren and sisters, and tell them I should have been pleased to come over to England to see them, but I am afraid that I shall be under the necessity of remaining here for some time; therefore I give them a pressing invitation to come and see me.

Give my kind love to all the brethren, and sisters, and tell them I should have been pleased to have come over to England to see them, but I am afraid that I shall be under the necessity of remaining here for some time, therefore I give them a pressing invitation to come and see me.

I remain, dear brethren, your affectionately,
JOSEPH SMITH.
(Oct. 19, 1840.) DHC 4:226–232.

[p.472] I am Dr Brethren Yours, Affectionately
Joseph Smith
To the Travelling High Council and Elders of the Church of Jesus Christ of L.D.S. in Great Britain

Do not understand me to say that all the Elders are to come with you, as it will be necessary for some to stay. J.[54]

Description of Paul

Given by the Prophet Joseph, January 5, 1841, at the organization of a school of instruction: "He is about five feet high; very dark hair, dark complexion; dark skin; large Roman nose; sharp face; small black eyes, penetrating as eternity; round shoulders; a whining voice, except when elevated, and then it almost resembled the roaring of a lion. He was a good orator, active and diligent, always employing himself in doing good to his fellow man."

Joseph Smith Discourse
By Joseph, Jany. 5th, 1841, at the organization of a school of instruction. Description of Paul— He is about 5 foot high; very dark hair; dark complection; dark skin; large Roman nose; sharp face; small black eyes, penetrating as eternity; round shoulders; a whining voice, expt when elevated and then it almost resembles the roaring of a Lion. He was a good orator, but Doctor [John C.] Bennett is a superior orator, and like Paul is active and diligent, always, employing himself in doing good to his fellow men.[55]

---

54. 15 December 1840, *JSP, D7*, 469–72. See also *PWJS*, 521–22; "Extract from an Epistle to the Elders in England," *T&S* 2, no. 5 (1 January 1841): 258.
55. 5 January 1841, *JSP, D7*, 493. See also *WJS*, 59.

Different Degrees of the Priesthood of Melchizedek

"Answer to the question, Was the Priesthood of Melchizedek taken away when Moses died? All Priesthood is Melchizedek, but there are different portions or degrees of it. That portion which brought Moses to speak with God face to face was taken away; but that which brought the ministry **[p.181]** of angels remained. All the prophets had the Melchizedek Priesthood and were ordained by God himself."

Joseph Smith Discourse

By Joseph, January 5th, 1841. Answer to the question, was the Priesthood of Melchizedeck taken away when Moses died. **[p.494]** All priesthood is Melchizedeck; but there are different portions or degrees of it. That portion which brought Moses to speak with God face to face was taken away; but that which brought the ministry of angels remained. All the Prophets had the Melchizedeck Priesthood and was ordained by God himself.[56]

Elements Are Eternal

Joseph Smith Discourse

The world and earth are not synonymous terms. The world is the human family. This earth was organized or formed out of other planets which were broke up and remodelled and made into the one on which we live. The elements are eternal. That which has a beginning will surely have an end. Take a ring, it is without beginning or end; cut it for a beginning place, and at the same time you ~~will~~ have an ending place.

The elements are eternal. That which has a beginning will surely have an end; take a ring, it is without beginning or end—cut it for a beginning place and at the same time you have an ending place.

A key: Every principle proceeding from God is eternal and any principle which is not eternal is of the devil. The sun has no beginning or end; the rays which proceed from himself have no bounds, consequently are eternal.

A key, every principle proceeding from God is eternal, and any principle which is not eternal is of the Devil. The sun has no beginning or end; the rays which proceed from himself have no bounds, consequently are eternal.

So it is with God. If the soul of man had a beginning it will surely have an end. In the translation "without form and void" it should be read, empty and desolate. The word created should be formed, or organized.

So it is with God. If the soul of man had a beginning it will surely have an end. In the translation; "without form and void" it should read "empty and desolate" The word "created" should be formed or organized.[57]

---

56. 5 January 1841, *JSP, D7*, 493–94. See also *WJS*, 59.
57. 5 January 1841, *JSP, D7*, 494. See also *WJS*, 60.

Observation on the Sectarian God

"That which is without body, parts and passions is nothing. There is no other God in heaven but that God who has flesh and bones. John 5:26. As the Father hath life in himself, even so hath he given to the Son to have life in himself. God the Father took life unto himself precisely as Jesus did."

"The first step in salvation of man is the laws of eternal and self-existent principles. Spirits are eternal. At the first organization in heaven we were all present, and saw the Savior chosen and appointed and the plan of salvation made, and we sanctioned it.

"We came to this earth that we might have a body and present it pure before God in the celestial kingdom. The great principle of happiness consists in having a body. The devil has no body, and herein is his punishment. He is pleased when he can obtain the tabernacle of man, and when cast out by the Savior he asked to go into the herd of swine, showing that he would prefer a swine's body to having none.

"All beings who have bodies have power over those who have not. The devil has no power over us only as we permit him. The moment we revolt at anything which comes from God, the devil takes power. This earth will be rolled back into the presence of God, and crowned with celestial glory."

Joseph Smith Discourse

Observations on the Sectarian God. That which is without body or parts is nothing. There is no other God in heaven but that God who has flesh and bones. John 5— 26, "As the father hath life in himself, even so hath he given the son to have life in himself." God the father took life unto himself precisely as Jesus did.

The first step in the salvation of men is the laws of eternal and self-existent principles. Spirits are eternal. At **[p.495]** the first organization in heaven we were all present and saw the Savior chosen and appointed, and the plan of salvation made and we sanctioned it.

We came to this earth that we might have a body and present it pure before God in the Celestial Kingdom. The great principle of happiness consists in having a body. The Devil has no body, and herein is his punishment. He is pleased when he can obtain the tabernacle of man and when cast out by the Savior he asked to go into the herd of swine showing that he would prefer a swines body to having none.

All beings who have bodies have power over those who have not. The devil has no power over us only as we permit him; the moment we revolt at anything which comes from God the Devil takes power. This earth will be rolled back into the presence of God and crowned with Celestial Glory.[58]

---

58. 5 January 1841, *JSP, D7*, 494–95. See also *WJS*, 60.

Excerpts from a Proclamation of the
First Presidency to the Saints Scattered Abroad

* * *

Nauvoo

Times and Seasons

[p.182] The name of our City (Nauvoo) is of Hebrew origin, and signifies a beautiful situation, or place, carrying with it, also, the idea of rest; and is truly descriptive of the most delightful location. It is situated on the east bank of the Mississippi River, at the head of the Des Moines Rapids, in Hancock county, bounded on the east by an extensive prairie of surpassing beauty, and on the north, west and south, by the Mississippi. This place has been objected to by some on account of the sickness which has prevailed in summer months, but * * * all the eastern and southern portions of the City of Nauvoo, are as healthful as any other portions of the western country, to acclimatized citizens.

* * *

The name of our city (Nauvoo,) is of Hebrew origin, and signifies a beauti[p.274]ful situation, or place, carrying with it, also, the idea of *rest*; and is truly descriptive of this most delightful situation. It is situated on the eastern bank of the Mississippi river, at the head of the Des Moines Rapids, in Hancock County; bounded on the east by an extensive prairie of surpassing beauty, and on the north, west, and south, by the Mississippi. This place has been objected to by some, on account of the sickness which has prevailed in the summer months, but it is the opinion of Doctor Bennett,[59] a physician of great experience and medical knowledge, that Hancock Co., and all the eastern and southern portions of the City of Nauvoo, are as healthy as any other portions of the western country, (or the world, to acclimated citizens,) whilst the northwestern portion of the city has experienced much affliction from ague and fever, which, however, he thinks can be easily remedied by draining the sloughs on the adjacent islands in the Mississippi.

The population of the city is increasing with unparalleled rapidity, numbering more than 3,000 inhabitants. Every facility is afforded, in the city and adjacent country, in Hancock County, for the successful prosecution of the mechanical arts and the pleasing pursuits of agriculture. The waters of the Mississippi can be successfully used for manufacturing purposes to almost an unlimited extent.—DHC 4:268.

* * *

The population of our city is increasing with unparralled rapidity, numbering more than three thousand inhabitants. Every facility is afforded in the city and adjacent country, in Hancock County, for the successful prosecution of the mechanical arts, and the pleasing pursuits of agriculture. The waters of the Mississippi can be successfully used for manufactoring purposes, to an almost unlimited extent.[60]

---

59. "Dr. Bennett" has reference to John C. Bennett.
60. *T&S* 2, no. 6 (15 January 1841): 273–74. See also History, C-1.

The Temple

Times and Seasons

The Temple of the Lord is in process of erection here, where the Saints will come to worship the God of their fathers, according to the order of His house and the powers of the Holy Priesthood, and will be so constructed as to enable all the functions of the Priesthood to be duly exercised, and where instructions from the Most high will be received, and from this place go forth to distant lands. Let us then concentrate all our powers, under the provisions of our magna charta granted by the Illinois legislature, at the "City of Nauvoo" and surrounding country, and strive to emulate the action of the ancient covenant fathers and patriarchs, in those things which are of such vast importance to this and every succeeding generation.—DHC 4:269.

The Temple of the Lord is in progress of erection here, where the Saints will come to worship the God of their fathers, according to the order of his house, and the powers of the holy priesthood, and will be so constructed as to enable all the functions of the priesthood to be duly exercised, and where instructions from the Most High will be received, and from this place go forth to distant lands. Let us then concentrate all our powers, under the provisions of our *magna charta* granted by the Illinois Legislature, at the "City of Nauvoo," and surrounding country, and strive to emulate the actions of the ancient covenant fathers, and patriarchs, in those things, which are of such vast importance to this and every succeeding generation.[61]

* * *

The Gathering of Saints

Times and Seasons

[p.183] The greatest temporal and spiritual blessings which always come from faithfulness and concerted effort, never attended individual exertion or enterprise. The history of all past ages abundantly attests this fact. In addition to all temporal blessings, there is no other way for the Saints to be saved in these last days, [than by the gathering] as the concurrent testimony of all the holy prophets clearly proves, for it is written—"They shall come from the east, and be gathered from the west; the north shall give up, and the south shall keep not back." "The sons of God shall be gathered from afar, and his daughters from the ends of the earth."

The great profusion of temporal and spiritual blessings, which always flow from faithfulness and concerted effort, never attend individual exertion or enterprize. The history of all past ages abundantly attests this fact. In addition to all temporal blessings, there is no other way for the Saints to be saved in these last days, as the concurrent testimony of all the holy prophets clearly proves, for it is written—"They shall come from the east and be gathered from the west; the north shall give up, and the south shall keep not back"—"the sons of God shall be *gathered* from far, and his daughters from the ends of the earth:"

It is also the concurrent testimony of all the prophets, that this gathering together of all the Saints, must take place before the Lord comes to "take vengeance upon the ungodly,"

it is also the concurrent testimony of all the prophets, that this gathering together of all the Saints, must take place before the Lord comes to "take vengeance upon the ungodly,"

---

61. *T&S* 2, no. 6 (15 January 1841): 274. See also History, C-1, 1147.

Order of the Priesthood in Temple Building

The following instruction was given at the time of the laying of the corner stones of the Nauvoo Temple, April 6, 1841.[63]

	Joseph Smith's History
If the strict order of the Priesthood were carried out in the building of Temples, the first stone would be laid at the south-east corner, by the First Presidency of the Church. The south-west corner should be laid next. The third, or north-west corner next; and the fourth, or north-east corner last. The First Presidency should lay the south-east corner stone and dictate who are the proper persons to lay the other corner stones.	If the strict order of the Priesthood, were carried out in the building of Temples. The first stone will be laid at the South East Corner by the First Presidency of the Church; the South West Corner should be laid next, the Third or N.W. Corner next, and the fourth or N.E. corner the last. The first presidency should lay the S.E. Corner stone, and dictate who are the proper persons to lay the other Corner Stones.[64]
If a Temple is built at a distance, and the First Presidency are not present, then the Quorum of the Twelve Apostles are the persons to dictate the order for that Temple; and in the absence of the Twelve Apostles, then the Presidency of the Stake will lay the south-east corner stone; the Melchizedek Priesthood laying the corner stones on the east side of the Temple, and the Lesser Priesthood those on the west side.—DHC 4:331.	If a Temple is built at a distance, and the First Presidency are not present, then the Quorum of the Twelve Apostles are the persons to dictate the order for that Temple; and in the absence of the Twelve Apostles, then the Presidency of the Stake, will lay the South East Corner Stone; the Melchisedeck Priesthood laying the Corner Stones at the East side of the Temple; and the Lesser Priesthood, those on the West side.[65]

---

62. *T&S* 2, no. 6 (15 January 1841): 276. See also *JSP, D7*, 507. The "Proclamation, 15 January 1841" is reproduced in its entirely in *JSP, D7*, 498–508. While Joseph Fielding Smith dates this proclamation 8 January 1841, the *T&S* and *History of the Church* give the date as 15 January 1841.

63. This introductory paragraph was authored by Joseph Fielding Smith.

64. This paragraph comes from the original manuscript of History, C-1. However, it appears to have been inserted at a later date, as the handwriting does not match that of the main text for this entry.

65. 6 April 1841, History, C-1, 1186. See also *Star* 18, no. 30 (26 July 1856): 470–71.

Report of the First Presidency at the April Conference, 1841

Times and Seasons

[p.184] The Presidency of the Church of Jesus Christ of Latter-day Saints, feel great pleasure in assembling with the Saints at another general conference, under circumstances so auspicious and cheering; and with grateful hearts to Almighty God for His providential regard, they cordially unite with the Saints, on this occasion, in ascribing honor, glory, and blessing to His Holy name.

The Presidency of the Church of Jesus Christ of Latter Day Saints, feel great pleasure in assembling with the Saints at another general conference, under circumstances so auspicious and cheering; and with grateful hearts to Almighty God for his providential regard, they cordially unite with the Saints, on this occasion, in ascribing honor, and glory, and blessing to his holy name.

It is with unfeigned pleasure that they have to make known the steady and rapid increase of the Church in this state, the United States, and Europe. The anxiety to become acquainted with the principles of the Gospel, on every hand is intense, and the cry of "come over and help us," is reaching the Elders on the wings of every wind; while thousands who have heard the Gospel have become obedient thereto, and are rejoicing in its gifts and blessings. Prejudice, with its attendant train of evil, is giving way before the force of truth, whose benign rays are penetrating the nations afar off.

It is with unfeigned pleasure that they have to make known, the steady and rapid increase of the church in this State, the United States, and in Europe. The anxiety to become acquainted with the principles of the gospel, on every hand, is intense and the cry of, "come over and help us," is reaching the elders on the wings of every wind, while thousands who have heard the gospel, have become obedient thereto, and are rejoicing in its gifts and blessings.— Prejudice with its attendant train of evils, is giving way before the force of truth, whose benign rays are penetrating the nations afar off.[66]

Missionary Reports Satisfactory

Times and Seasons

The reports from the Twelve Apostles in Europe are very satisfactory, and state that the work continues to progress with unparalleled rapidity, and that the harvest is truly great. In the Eastern States the faithful laborers are successful, and many are flocking to the standard of truth. Nor is the South keeping back. Churches have been raised up in the Southern and Western States, and a very pressing invitation has been received from New Orleans, for some of the Elders to visit that city; which has been complied with. In our own state and immediate neighborhood, many are avowing

The reports from the Twelve in Europe are very satisfactory, and state that the work continues to progress with unparalleled rapidity and that the harvest is truly great. In the eastern states, the faithful laborers are successful, and many are flocking to the standard of truth. Nor is the south keeping back—churches have been raised up in the southern and western states, and a very pressing invitation has been received from New Orleans for some of the elders to visit that city, which has been complied with. In our own State and immediate neighborhood, many are avowing their attachment

---

66. *T&S* 2, no. 12 (15 April 1841): 384.

their attachment to the principles of our holy religion, and have become obedient to the faith.

Peace and prosperity attend us; and we have favor in the sight of God and virtuous men. The time was, when we were looked upon as deceivers, and that "Mormonism" would soon pass away, come to nought, and be forgotten. But the time has gone by when it is looked upon as a transient matter, or a bubble on the wave, and it is now taking a deep hold in the hearts and affections of all those, who are noble-minded enough to lay aside the prejudice of education, and investigate the subject with candor and honesty. The truth, like the sturdy **[p.185]** oak, has stood unhurt amid the contending elements, which have beat upon it with tremendous force. The floods have rolled, wave after wave, in quick succession, and have not swallowed it up. "They have lifted up their voice; but the Lord of Hosts is mightier than the mighty waves of the sea"; nor have the flames of persecution, with all the influence of mobs, been able to destroy it; but like Moses' bush, it has stood unconsumed, and now at this moment presents an important spectacle both to men and angels. Where can we turn our eyes to behold such another? We contemplate a people who have embraced a system of religion, unpopular, and the adherence to which has brought upon them repeated persecutions. A people who, for their love for God, and attachment to His cause, have suffered hunger, nakedness, perils, and almost every privation. A people who, for the sake of their religion, have had to mourn the premature death of parents, husbands, wives, and children. A people, who have preferred death to slavery and hypocrisy, and have honorably maintained their characters, and stood firm and immovable, in times that have tried men's souls. Stand fast, ye Saints of God, hold on a little while longer, and the storm of life will be past, and you will be rewarded by that God whose servants you are, and who will duly appreciate all your

to the principles of our holy religion, and have become obedient to the faith.

Peace and prosperity attend us; and we have favor in the sight of God and virtuous men. The time was, when we were looked upon as deceivers, and that Mormonism would soon pass away, come to nought, and be forgotten. But the time has gone by when it was looked upon as a trancient matter, or a bubble on the wave, and it is now taking a deep hold in the hearts and affections of all those who are noble minded enough to lay aside the prejudice of education, and investigate the subject with candor and honesty. The truth, like the sturdy oak, has stood unhurt amid the contending elements, which have beat upon it with tremendous force. The floods have rolled, wave after wave, in quick succession; and have not swallowed it up. "They have lifted up their voice, O Lord, the floods have lifted up their voice; but the Lord of Hosts is migh**[p.385]**tier than the mighty waves of the sea." Nor, have the flames of persecution, with all the influence of mobs, been able to destroy it; but like Moses' bush it has stood unconsumed, and now at this moment presents an important spectacle both to men and angels.—Where can we turn our eyes to behold such another? We contemplate a people who have embraced a system of religion unpopular, and the adherence to which has brought upon them repeated persecutions—a people who for their love of God and attachment to his cause, have suffered hunger, nakedness, perils, and almost every privation—a people, who, for the sake of their religion, have had to mourn the premature deaths of parents, husbands, wives, and children—a people who have prefered death to slavery and hypocracy, and have honorably maintained their characters, and stood firm and immovable, in times that have tried men's souls. Stand fast, ye Saints of God, hold on a little while longer, and the storms of life will be past, and you will be rewarded by that God whose servants you are, and who will

A Prayer for Continued Peace

Times and Seasons

But we hope that those scenes of blood and gore will never more occur, but that many, very many such scenes as the present will be witnessed by the saints, and that in the Temple, the foundation of which has been so happily laid, will the saints of the Most High continue to congregate from year to year, in peace and safety.

From the kind and generous feelings manifest, by the citizens of this State, since our sojourn among them, we may continue to expect the enjoyment of all the blessings of civil and religious liberty, guaranteed by the constitution. The citizens of Illinois have done themselves honor in throwing the mantle of the constitution over a persecuted and afflicted people; and have given evident proof, that they are not only in the enjoyment of the privileges of freemen themselves, but that they willingly and cheerfully extend that invaluable blessing to others, and that they freely award to faithfulness and virtue their due.

The proceedings of the Legislature in regard to the citizens of this place have been marked with philanthropy and benevolence; and they have laid us under great and lasting obligations, in granting us the several liberal charters we now enjoy, and by which we hope to prosper, until our City becomes the most splendid, our University the most learned, and our Legion the most effective, of any in the Union.[68]

---

67. *T&S* 2, no. 12 (15 April 1841): 384–85.
68. *T&S* 2, no. 12 (15 April 1841): 385.

Impoverished Saints

	Times and Seasons

In consequence of the impoverished condition of the Saints, the buildings which are in course of erection do not progress as fast as could be desired; but from the interest which is generally manifested by the Saints at large, we hope to accomplish much by a combination of effort, and a concentration of action, and erect the Temple and other public buildings, which we so much need for our mutual instruction and the education of our children.

From the reports which have been received, we may expect a large emigration this season. The proclamation which was sent, some time ago, to the churches abroad, has been responded to, and great numbers are making preparations to come and locate themselves in this city and vicinity.

From what we now witness, we are led to look forward with pleasing anticipation to the future, and soon expect to see the thousands of Israel flocking to this region in obedience to the heavenly command; numerous inhabitants—Saints—thickly studding the flowery and wide-spread prairies of Illinois; temples for the worship of our God erecting in various parts, and great peace resting upon Israel.

We would call the attention of the Saints more particularly to the building of the Temple, for on its speedy erection great blessings depend. The zeal which is manifested by the Saints in this city is, indeed, praiseworthy, and, we hope will be imitated by the Saints in the various stakes and branches of the Church, and that those who cannot contribute labor will bring their gold and their silver, their brass and their iron, with the pine tree, and box tree, to beautify the same.

In consequence of the impoverished condition of the saints, the buildings which are in progress of erection do not progress as fast as could be desired; but from the interest which is generally manifested by the saints at large, we hope to accomplish much by a combination of effort, and a concentration of action, and erect the Temple and other buildings, which we so much need for our mutual instruction and the education of our children.

From the reports which have been received, we may expect a large emigration this season. The proclamation which was sent some time ago to the churches abroad, has been responded to, and great numbers are making preparations to come and locate themselves in this city and vicinity.

From what we now witness, we are led to look forward with pleasing anticipation to the future, and soon expect to see the thousands of Israel flocking to this region, in obedience to the **[p.386]** heavenly command; numerous habitations of the saints thickly studding the flowery and wide spread prairies of Illinois; temples for the worship of our God erecting in various parts; and great peace resting upon Israel.

We would call the attention of the saints more particularly to the erection of the Temple, for on its speedy erection great blessings depend. The zeal which is manifested by the saints in this city is indeed praise worthy, and we hope will be imitated by the saints in the various stakes and branches of the church, and that those who cannot contribute labor, will bring their gold and their silver, their brass, and their iron, with the pine tree and box tree, to beautify the same.

[p.187] We are glad to hear of the organization of the different quorums in this city, and hope that their organization will be attended to in every stake and branch of the Church, for the Almighty is a lover of order and good government.	We are glad to hear of the organization of the different quorums in this city, and hope that the organization will be attended to in every stake and branch of the church, for the Almighty is a lover of order and good government.
From the faith and enterprise of the Saints generally, we feel greatly encouraged and cheerfully attend to the important duties devolving upon us, knowing that we not only have the approval of heaven, but also that our efforts for the establishment of Zion and the spread of truth, are cheerfully seconded by the thousands of Israel.	From the faith and enterprise of the saints generally, we feel greatly encouraged, and cheerfully attend to the important duties devolving upon us, knowing that we not only have the approval of Heaven, but that our efforts for the establishing of Zion and the spread of truth, are cheerfully seconded by the thousands of Israel.
In conclusion we would say, brethren, be faithful, let your love and moderation be known unto all men; be patient, be mindful to observe all the commandments of your Heavenly Father, and the God of all grace shall bless you. Even so. Amen.—DHC 4:336-339. JOSEPH SMITH, President ROBERT B. THOMPSON, Clerk.	In conclusion we would say, brethren, be faithful; let your love and moderation be known unto all men; be patient; be mindful to observe all the commandments of your heavenly Father; and the God of all grace shall bless you, even so, Amen. R[obert] B. THOMPSON, *Clerk*.[69]

* * *

The Prophet's Discourse on Gospel Principles

	Times and Seasons
	The indications of the morning promised a beautiful day. At 10 o'clock A. M. a large concourse of the saints assembled on the meeting ground and were addressed by Pres. Joseph Smith, who spoke at considerable length.[70]
At 10 o'clock a.m. [May 16, 1841], a large concourse of the Saints assembled on the meeting ground, and were addressed by President Joseph Smith, who spoke at considerable length.	

The Doctrine of Agency

	Times and Seasons
He commenced his observations by remarking that the kindness of our Heavenly Father called for our heartfelt gratitude. He then observed that Satan was generally blamed for the evils	He commenced his observations by remarking that the kindness of our Heavenly Father, called for our heartfelt gratitude. He then observed that satan was generally blamed

---

69. *T&S* 2, no. 12 (15 April 1841): 385–86.
70. *T&S* 2, no. 15 (1 June 1841): 429.

which we did, but if he was the cause of all our wickedness, men could not be condemned. The devil could not compel mankind to do evil; all was voluntary. Those who resisted the Spirit of God, would be liable to be led into temptation, and then the association of heaven would be withdrawn from those who refused to be made partakers of such great glory. God would not exert any compulsory means, and the devil could not; and such ideas as were entertained [on these subjects] by many were absurd. The creature was made subject to vanity, not willingly, but Christ subjected the same in hope—all are subjected to vanity while they travel through the crooked paths and difficulties which surrounded them. Where is the man that is free from vanity? None ever were perfect but Jesus: [p.188] and why was He perfect? Because He was the Son of God, and had the fullness of the Spirit, and greater power than any man. But notwithstanding their vanity, men look forward with hope (because they are "subjected in hope") to the time of their deliverance.	for the evils which we did, but if he was the cause of all our wickedness, men could not be condemned. The devil cannot compel mankind to evil, all was voluntary.— Those who resist the spirit of God, are liable to be led into temptation, and then the association of heaven is withdrawn from those who refuse to be made partakers of such great glory— God would not exert any compulsory means and the Devil could not; and such ideas as were entertained by many were absurd. The creature was made subject to vanity, not willingly, but Christ subjected the same in hope—we are all subject to vanity while we travel through the crooked paths, and difficulties which surround us. Where is the man that is free from vanity? None ever were [p.430] perfect but Jesus, and why was he perfect? because he was the son of God, and had the fulness of the Spirit, and greater power than any man.—But, notwithstanding our vanity, we look forward with hope, (because "we are subjected in hope,") to the time of our deliverance.[71]

The First Principles

Times and Seasons

The speaker then made some observations on the first principles of the Gospel, observing, that many of the Saints who had come from different states and nations had only a very superficial knowledge of these principles, not having heard them fully investigated.	He then made some observations on the first principles of the gospel, observing that many of the saints who had come from different States and Nations, had only a very superficial knowledge of these principles, not having heard them fully investigated.
He then briefly stated the principles of faith, repentance, and baptism for the remission of sins, these were believed by some of the righteous societies of the day, but the doctrine of laying on of hands for the gift of the Holy Ghost was discarded by them. The speaker then referred to the 6th chapter of Hebrews, 1st and 2nd verses, "Not laying again the foundation of repentance from dead works," &c., but of the doctrine of baptisms, laying	He then briefly stated the principles of faith, repentance, and baptism for the remission of sins, which were believed by some of the religious societies of the day, but the doctrine of laying on of hands for the gift of the holy ghost, was discarded by them. The speaker then referred them to the 6th chap. of Heb. 1. and 2. verses. "not laying again the foundation of repentance from dead works &c., but of the doctrines of baptism, laying on of hands, the resurrection

---

71. *T&S* 2, no. 15 (1 June 1841): 429–30.

on of hands, the resurrection, and eternal judgment, &c. That the doctrine of eternal judgment was perfectly understood by the Apostles, is evident from several passages of Scripture. Peter preached repentance and baptism for the remission of sins to the Jews who had been led to acts of violence and blood by their leaders; but to the rulers he said, "I wot that through ignorance ye did it, as did also your rulers" "Repent ye therefore, and be converted, that your sins may be blotted out, when the times of refreshing (redemption) shall come from the presence of the Lord, and He shall send Jesus Christ, which before was preached unto you," &c. The time of redemption here had reference to the time when Christ should come; then, and not till then, would their sins be blotted out. For Peter, speaking of him says, "David hath not yet ascended into heaven, for his sepulchre is with us to this day." His remains were then in the tomb. Now, we read that many bodies of the Saints arose at Christ's resurrection, probably all the Saints, but it seems that David did not. Why? Because he had been a murderer. If the ministers of religion had a proper understand [p.189] ing of the doctrine of eternal judgment, they would not be found attending the man who forfeited his life to the injured laws of his country, by shedding innocent blood; for such characters cannot be forgiven, until they have paid the last farthing. The prayers of all the ministers in the world can never close the gates of hell against a murderer.

and eternal judgment &c." The doctrine of eternal judgment was perfectly understood by the apostle, is evident from several passages of scripture. Peter preached repentance and baptism for the remission of sins to the Jews, who had been led to acts of violence and blood, by their leaders, but to the rulers he said, "I would that through ignorance ye did it, as did also *those ye ruled.*"—Repent, therefore, and be converted that your sins may be blotted out, when the times of refreshing (redemption), shall come from the presence of the Lord, for he shall send Jesus Christ, who before was preached unto you &c." The time of *redemption* here had reference to the time, when Christ should come; then and not till then would their sins be blotted out. Why? Because they were murderers, and no murderer hath eternal life. Even David, must wait for those times of refreshing, before he can come forth and his sins be blotted out; for Peter speaking of him says, "David hath not yet ascended into Heaven, for his sepulchre is with us to this day;' his remains were then in the tomb. Now we read that many bodies of the saints arose, at Christ's resurrection, probably all the saints, but it seems that David did not. Why? because he had been a murderer. If the ministers of religion had a proper understanding of the doctrine of eternal judgment, they would not be found attending the man who had forfeited his life to the injured laws of his country by shedding innocent blood; for such characters cannot be forgiven, until they have paid the last farthing. The prayers of all the ministers in the world could never close the gates of hell against a murderer.[72]

The Doctrine of Election

Times and Seasons

He then spoke on the subject of election, and read the 9th chapter of Romans, from which it was evident that the election there spoken of was pertaining to the flesh, and had reference to the seed of Abraham, according to the promise

The speaker then spoke on the subject of election, and read the 9th chap. in Romans, from which it was evident that the election there spoken of was pertaining to the flesh, and had reference to the seed of Abraham, according to

---

72. *T&S* 2, no. 15 (1 June 1841): 430.

God made to Abraham, saying, "In thee, and in thy seed, all the families of the earth shall be blessed." To them belonged the adoption and the covenants, &c. Paul said, when he saw their unbelief, "I wish myself accursed"—according to the flesh—not according to the spirit. Why did God say to Pharaoh, "For this cause have I raised thee up"? Because Pharaoh was a fit instrument—a wicked man, and had committed acts of cruelty of the most atrocious nature. The election of the promised seed still continues, and in the last day, they shall have the Priesthood restored unto them, and they shall be the "saviors on Mount Zion," the ministers of our God; if it were not for the remnant which was left, then might men now be as Sodom and Gomorrah. The whole of the chapter had reference to the Priesthood and the house of Israel; and unconditional election of individuals to eternal life was not taught by the Apostles. God did elect or predestinate, that all those who would be saved, should be saved in Christ Jesus, and through obedience to the Gospel; but He passes over no man's sins, but visits them with correction, and if His children will not repent of their sins He will discard them.

This is an imperfect sketch of a very interesting discourse, which occupied more than two hours in delivery, and was listened to with marked attention, by the vast assembly present. (May 16, 1841.) DHC 4:358-360.

the promise God made to Abraham, saying, "In thee and in thy seed all the families of the earth shall be blessed." To them belonged the adoption, and the covenants &c. Paul said, when he saw their unbelief I wish myself accursed—according to the flesh— not according to the spirit. Why did God say to Pharoah, "for this cause have I raised thee up?" Because Pharoah was a fit instrument—a wicked man, and had committed acts of cruelty of the most atrocious nature. The election of the promised seed still continues, and in the last days, they shall have the priesthood restored unto them, and they shall be the "Saviors on mount Zion" the "ministers of our God," if it were not for the remnant which was left, then might we be as Sodom and as Gomorrah. The whole of the chapter had refer ence to the priesthood and the house of Israel; and unconditional election of individuals to eternal life was not taught by the apostles. God did elect or predestinate, that all those who would be saved, should be saved in Christ Jesus; and through obedience to the gospel; but he passes over no man's sins, but visits them with correction, and if his children will not repent of their sins, he will discard them.

This is but a very imperfect sketch of a very interesting discourse, which occupied more than two hours in delivery, and was listened to with marked attention by the vast assembly present.[73]

Three Independent Principles

Joseph Smith Discourse

May 16, 1841. There are three independent principles; the Spirit of God, the spirit of man, and the spirit of the devil. All men have power to resist the devil.

There are three independant principles; the spirit of God. the spirit of Man. & the spirit of the Devil. All men have power to resist the Devil.

[p.190] They who have tabernacles, have power over those who have not. The doctrine of eternal judgment; Acts 2:41. Peter preached,

They who have Taber[n]acles have power over those who have not. The docterine of eternal judgement acts 2— 41 Peter preached repent

---

73. 16 May 1841, report on sermon given by Joseph Smith, in T&S 2, no. 15 (1 June 1841): 430. See also JSP, D8, 151–52.

Repent, and be baptized in the name of Jesus Christ, for the remission of sins, &c.; but in Acts 3:19 he says, Repent, and be converted, that your sins may be blotted out when the times of redemption shall come, and he shall send Jesus, &c.

& be baptised in the name of jesus Christ for the remision of sins &c but in act 3 12[74] he says repent and be converted that your sins my be ~~forgiven~~ blotted out when the times of <u>refreshing</u> \<redemption\> shall come & he shall send jesus &c remission of sins by baptisom was not to be preached to murderers.[75]

The Three Personages

Joseph Smith Discourse
By Joseph.

Everlasting covenant was made between three personages before the organization of this earth, and relates to their dispensation of things to men on the earth; these personages, according to Abraham's record, are called God the first, the Creator; God the second, the Redeemer; and God the third, the witness or Testator.—MSS

Everlasting covenant was made between three personages before the organization of this earth and relates to their dispensation of things to men on the earth. These personages according to Abrahams record **[p.11]** are \<called\> God the first, the Creator; God the second, the Redeemer; and God the third, the Witness or Testator.[76]

The Twelve Next to the First Presidency

Times and Seasons

President Joseph Smith now arriving, proceeded to state to the conference at considerable length, the object of their present meeting, and, in addition to what President Young had stated in the morning, said that the time had come when the Twelve should be called upon to stand in their place next to the First Presidency, and attend to the settling of immigrants and the business of the Church at the stakes, and assist to bear off the kingdom victoriously to the nations, and as they had been faithful, and had borne the burden in the heat of the day, that it was right that

President Joseph Smith now arriving proceeded to state to the conference at considerable length, the object of their present meeting, and in addition to what President Young had stated in the morning, said that the time had come when the twelve should be called upon to stand in their place next to the first presidency, and attend to the settling of emegrants and the business of the church at the **[p.522]** stakes, and assist to bear off the kingdom victorious to the nations; and as they had been faithful and had borne the burden in the heat of the day that it was right that they should

---

74. The correct reference is Acts 3:19.

75. 16 May 1841, *JSP, D8*, 153. In the original handwritten note (which is in the handwriting of an unknown scribe) the following appears at the end of this entry: "preasts in crisendom [Christendom] might pray for a murderer on the scaffold forever but could not avail so much as a gnat towards their forgiveness; there is no forgiveness for murderers they will have to wait untill the times of redemtion shall come and that in hell. Peter had the Keys of eternal Judgement & he saw David in hell & knew for what reason. & that David would have to remain there untill the reserrection, at the coming of Christ. Rommans 9 All election that can be found in the scriptures is according to the flesh and pertaining to the Preasthood." *JSP, D8*, 153.

76. Discourse, circa May 1841, as reported by WCJ, 10–11. See also *WJS*, 87–88n5.

they should have an opportunity of providing something for themselves and families, and at the same time relieve him, so that he might attend to the business of translating.

Moved, seconded and carried, that the conference approve of the instructions of President Smith in relation to the Twelve, and that they proceed accordingly to attend to the duties of their office. (Aug. 16, 1841.) DHC 4:403.

Trust in God When Sick

Sunday, Sept. 5, 1841. I preached to a large congregation at the stand, on the science and practice of medicine, desiring to persuade the Saints to trust in God when sick, and not in an arm of flesh, and live by faith and not by medicine, or poison; and when they were sick, and had called for the Elders to pray for them, and they were not healed, to use herbs and mild food.—DHC 4:413.

Items of Instruction

Baptism for the Dead

[p.191] President Joseph Smith, by request of the Twelve Apostles, gave instructions on the doctrine of baptism for the dead, which were listened to with intense interest by the large assembly. He presented baptism for the dead as the only way that men can appear as saviors on Mount Zion.

The proclamation of the first principles of the gospel was a means of salvation to men individually; and it was the truth, not men, that saved them; but men, by actively engaging in rites of salvation substitutionally became instrumental in bringing multitudes of their kindred into the kingdom of God.

Joseph Smith's History

Sunday 5. I preached to a large congregation at the Stand, on the Science and practice of Medicine, desiring to persuade the Saints to trust in God. when sick, and not in an arm of flesh, and live by faith and not by—medicine, or poison, and when they were sick, and had called for the Elders to pray for them, and they were not healed, to use herbs and mild food.[78]

have an opportunity of provididing something for themselves and families, and at the same time relieve him so that he might attend to the businesss of translating.

Motioned seconded and carried that the conference approve of the instructions of President Smith, in relation to the twelve, and that they proceed accordingly, to attend to the duties of their office.[77]

Times and Seasons

President Joseph Smith, by request of some of the Twelve, gave instructions on the doctrine of Baptism for the Dead; which was listened to with intense interest by the large assembly. The speaker presented "Baptism for the Dead' as the only way that men can appear as saviors on mount Zion.

The proclamation of the first principles of the gospel was a means of salvation to men individually, and it was the truth, not men that saved them; but men, by actively engaging in rites of salvation substitutionally, became instrumental in bringing multitudes of their kin into the kingdom of God.[79]

---

77. 16 August 1841 report of sermon given by Joseph Smith, in T&S 2, no. 21 (1 September 1841): 521–22.
78. 5 September 1841, History, C-1, 1225. See also WJS, 76.
79. T&S 2, no. 24 (15 October 1841): 577.

Angels and Ministering Spirits

He explained the difference between an angel and a ministering spirit; the one a resurrected or translated body, with its spirit ministering to embodied spirits—the other a disembodied spirit, visiting and ministering to disembodied spirits. Jesus Christ became a ministering spirit (while His body was lying in the sepulchre) to the spirits in prison, to fulfill an important part of His mission, without which He could not have perfected His work, or entered into His rest. After His resurrection He appeared as an angel to His disciples.

Translated bodies cannot enter into rest until they have undergone a change equivalent to death. Translated bodies are designed for future missions.

The angel that appeared to John on the Isle of Patmos was a translated or resurrected body [i.e., personage]. Jesus Christ went in body after His resurrection, to minister to resurrected bodies. There has been a chain of authority and power from Adam down to the present time.

The best way to obtain truth and wisdom is not to ask it from books, but to go to God in prayer, and obtain divine teaching. It is no more incredible that God should save the dead, than that he should raise the dead.

Times and Seasons

He explained a difference between an angel and a ministering spirit; the one a resurrected or translated body, with its spirit, ministering to embodied spirits—the other a disembodied spirit, visiting and ministering to disembodied spirits. Jesus Christ became a minestering spirit, while his body laying in the sepulchre, to the spirits in prison; to fulfil an important part of his mission, without which he could not have perfected his work or entered into his rest. After his resurrection, he appeared as an angel to his disciples &c.

Translated bodies cannot enter into rest until they have undergone a change equivalent to death. Translated bodies are designed for future missions.

The angel that appeared to John on the Isle of Patmos was a translated or resurrected body.— Jesus Christ went in body, after his resurrection, to minister to translated and resurrected bodies. There has been a chain of authority and power from Adam down to the present time.

The only way to obtain truth and wisdom, is not to ask it from books, but to go to God in prayer and obtain divine teaching. It is no more incredible that God should *save* the dead, than that he should *raise* the dead.[80]

Pardoning Mercy an Eternal Principle

There is never a time when the spirit is too old to approach God. All are within the reach of pardoning mercy, who have not committed the unpardonable sin, which hath no forgiveness, [p.192] neither in this world, nor in the world to come. There is a way to release the spirits of the dead; that is by the power and

Times and Seasons

There is never a time when the spirit is too old to approach God. All are within the reach of pardoning mercy, who have not committed the unpardonable sin, which hath no forgiveness, neither in this world, nor in the world to come. There is a way to release the spirit of the dead; that is, by the power and authority of

---

80. *T&S* 2, no. 24 (15 October 1841): 577.

authority of the Priesthood—by binding and loosing on earth. This doctrine appears glorious, inasmuch as it exhibits the greatness of divine compassion and benevolence in the extent of the plan of human salvation.

This glorious truth is well calculated to enlarge the understanding, and to sustain the soul under troubles, difficulties and distresses. For illustration, suppose the case of two men, brothers, equally intelligent, learned, virtuous and lovely, walking in uprightness and in all good conscience, so far as they have been able to discern duty from the muddy stream of tradition, or from the blotted page of the book of nature.

One dies and is buried, having never heard the Gospel of reconciliation; to the other the message of salvation is sent, he hears and embraces it, and is made the heir of eternal life. Shall the one become the partaker of glory and the other be consigned to hopeless perdition? Is there no chance for his escape? Sectarianism answers "none." Such an idea is worse than atheism. The truth shall break down and dash in pieces all such bigoted Pharisaism; the sects shall be sifted, the honest in heart brought out, and their priests left in the midst of their corruption.

the Priest [h]ood—by binding and loosing on earth **[p.578]** This doctrine appears glorious, inasmuch as it exhibits the greatness of divine compassion and benevolence in the extent of the plan of human salvation.

This glorious truth is well calculated to enlarge the understanding, and to sustain the soul under troubles, difficulties, and distresses. For illustration the speaker presented, by supposition, the case of too men, brothers, equally intelligent, learned, virtuous and lovely, walking in uprightness and in all good conscience, so far as they had been able to discern duty from the muddy stream of tradition, or from the blotted page of the book of nature.

One dies, and is buried, having never heard the gospel of reconciliation; to the other the message of salvation is sent, he hears and embraces it, and is made the heir of eternal life. Shall the one become a partaker of glory, and the other be consigned to hopeless perdition? Is there no chance for his escape? Sectarianism answers, "none! none!! none!!!" Such an idea is worse than atheism. The truth shall break down and dash in pieces all such bigoted Pharisaism; the sects shall be sifted, the honest in heart brought out and their priests left in the midst of their corruption.[81]

Sectarian Baptism

Times and Seasons

Many objections are urged against the Latter-day Saints for not admitting the validity of sectarian baptism, and for withholding fellowship from sectarian churches. Yet to do otherwise would be like putting new wine into old bottles, and putting old wine into new bottles. What! new revelations in the old churches? New revelations would knock out the bottom of their bottomless pit. New wine into old bottles! The bottles burst and the wine runs out! What! Sadducees in the new church! Old wine in new leathern bottles will leak through

The speaker then answered the objections urged against the Latter Day Saints for not admitting the validity of sectarian baptism, and for withholding fellowship from sectarian churches. It was like putting new wine into old bottles and putting old wine into new bottles. What, new revelations in the old churches! New revelatiens knock out the bottom of their bottomless pit. New wine into old bottles!—the bottles burst and the wine runs out. What, Sadducees in the new church! Old wine in new leathern bottles will leak through

---

81. *T&S* 2, no. 24 (15 October 1841): 577–78.

the pores and escape. So the Sadducee saints mock at authority, kick out of the traces, and run to the mountains of perdition, leaving the long echo of their braying behind them.	the pores and escape; so the Saddacee saints mock at authority, kick out of the traces, and run to the mountains of perdition, leaving the long echo of their braying behind them.
He then referred to the [lack of] charity of the sects, in denouncing all who disagree with them in opinion, and in joining in persecuting the Saints, who believe that even such may be saved, in this world and in the world to come (murderers and apostates excepted).	The speaker then contrasted the charity of the sects, in denouncing all who disagree with them in opinion, and in joining in persecuting the saints, with the faith of the saints, who believe that even such may be saved in this world and in the world to come, (murderers and apostates excepted.)[82]

Salvation for the Dead

Times and Seasons

[p.193] This doctrine presents in a clear light the wisdom and mercy of God in preparing an ordinance for the salvation of the dead, being baptized by proxy, their names recorded in heaven and they judged according to the deeds done in the body. This doctrine was the burden of the scriptures. Those Saints who neglect it in behalf of their deceased relatives, do it at the peril of their own salvation. The dispensation of the fullness of times will bring to light the things that have been revealed in all former dispensations; also other things that have not been before revealed. He shall send Elijah, the Prophet, &c., and restore all things in Christ.

This doctrine, he said, presented in a clear light, the wisdom and mercy of God, in preparing an ordinance for the salvation of the dead, being baptised by proxy, their names recorded in heaven. and they judged according to the deeds done in the body. This doctrine was the burden of the scriptures. Those saints who neglect it, in behalf of their deceased relatives, do it at the peril of their own salvation. The dispensation of the fulness of times will bring to light the things that have been revealed in all former dispensations, also other things that have not been before revealed. He shall send Elijah the prophet &c., and restore all things in Christ.

President Joseph Smith then announced: "There shall be no more baptisms for the dead, until the ordinance can be attended to in the Lord's House; and the Church shall not hold another General Conference, until they can meet in said house. For thus saith the Lord!"[83] (Oct. 3, 1841.) DHC 4:424-426.

The speaker then announced, "There shall be no more baptisms for the dead, until the ordinance can be attended to in the font of the Lord's House; and the church shall not hold another general conference, until they can meet in said house. *For thus saith the Lord!*"[84]

---

82. *T&S* 2, no. 24 (15 October 1841): 578.

83. The original *TPJS* footnote reads: "The reason for the commandment from the Lord discontinuing baptism for the dead in the Mississippi River is found in the fact that the font in the Nauvoo Temple had been prepared for these ordinances. It was only in the days of poverty and when there was no font in a Temple, that the Lord granted baptism for the dead outside of his holy house. November 8, 1841, the font in the Nauvoo Temple was dedicated and from that time forth until the exodus baptism for the dead in the Temple in Nauvoo was performed."

84. 3 October 1841 minutes of a conference held in Nauvoo, in *T&S* 2, no. 24 (15 October 1841): 578. See also *JSP, D8*, 300-302.

Do Not Accuse the Brethren

I charged the Saints not to follow the example of the adversary in accusing the brethren, and said, "If you do not accuse each other, God will not accuse you. If you have no accuser you will enter heaven, and if you will follow the revelations and instructions which God gives you through me, I will take you into heaven as my back load. If you will not accuse me, I will not accuse you. If you will throw a cloak of charity over my sins, I will over yours—for charity covereth a multitude of sins. What many people call sin is not sin; I do many things to break down superstition, and I will break it down"; I referred to the curse of Ham for laughing at Noah, while in his wine, but doing no harm. Noah was righteous man, and yet he drank wine and became intoxicated; the Lord did not forsake him in consequence thereof, for he retained all the power of his Priesthood, and when he was accused by Canaan, [p.194] he cursed him by the Priesthood which he held, and the Lord had respect to his word, and the Priesthood which he held, notwithstanding he was drunk, and the curse remains upon the posterity of Canaan until the present day. (November 7, 1841.) DHC 4:445-446.

Wilford Woodruff's Journal

Br Joseph then deliver[e]d unto us an edifying address showing us what temperance faith, virtue, charity & truth was[.] he also said if we did not accuse one another God would not accuse us & if we had no accuser we should enter heaven. he would take us there as his backload. if we would not accuse him he would not accuse us & if we would throw a cloak of charity over his sins he would over ours. for charity cover[e]d a multitude of Sins & what many people called sin was not sin & he did many things to break down superstition & he would break it down. he spoke of the curse of ham for laughing at Noah while in his wine but doing no harm.[85]

Perfection of the Book of Mormon

Sunday, 28.—I spent the day in the council with the Twelve Apostles at the house of President Young, conversing with them upon a variety of subjects. Brother Joseph Fielding was present, having been absent four years on a mission to England. I told the brethren that the Book of Mormon was the most correct of any book on earth, and the keystone of our religion, and a man would get nearer to God

Wilford Woodruff's Journal

28th Sunday I spent the day at B. Young in company with Joseph & the Twelve in conversing upon a variety of Subjects[,] it was an interesting day[.] Elder Joseph Fielding was present[.] he had been in England four years[.] we also saw a number of english Brethren Joseph Said the Book of Mormon was the most correct of any Book on earth & the key Stone of our religion & a man would

---

85. Discourse, 7 November 1841, in WWJ, 1:481. See also JSP, D8, 358–59.

by abiding by its precepts, than by any other book. (November 28, 1841.) DHC 4:461.

get nearer to God by abiding by its precepts than any other <Book>[86]

IMORTANT INSTRUCTIONS

Value of Chastisement

President Joseph arose and said: "Brother Kimball has given you a true explanation of the parable," and then read the parable of the vine and its branches, and explained it, and said, "If we keep the commandments of God, we should bring forth fruit and be the friends of God, and know what our Lord did.

"Some people say I am a fallen Prophet, because I do not bring forth more of the word of the Lord, Why do I not do it? Are we able to receive it? No! Not one in this room. He then chastened the congregation for their wickedness and unbelief, 'for whom the Lord loveth he chasteneth, and scourgeth every son and daughter whom he receiveth,' and if we do not receive chastisements then we are bastards and not sons."

On the subject of revelation, he said, a man would command his sons to dig potatoes and saddle his horse, but before he had done either he would tell him to do something else. This is all considered right; but as soon as the Lord gives a commandment and revokes that decree and commands something else, then the Prophet is considered fallen. Because we will not receive chastisement at the hands of the Prophets and Apostles, the Lord chastiseth us with sickness and death. Let not any man publish his own righteousness, for others can see that for him; sooner let him confess his sins, and then he will **[p.195]** be forgiven, and he will bring forth more fruit. When a corrupt man is chastised he gets angry and will not endure it. The reason we do not have the

Wilford Woodruff's Journal

Joseph the Seer arose & read a Chapter in the New Testament containing the parable of the vine & its branches & explained it much to our edification & said "if we kept the commandments of God we should bring forth fruit & be the friends of God & know what our Lord did.

"Some say Joseph is a fallen Prophet because he does not bring forth more of the word of the Lord[.]" "why does he not do it[?]" are we able to receive it[?] No (says he) not one in this room. He then chastized us for our wickedness & unbelief knowing that whom the Lord loveth he chasteneth & Scourgeth evry son & daughter whom He receiveth & if we do not receive chastizements then are we Bastards & not Sons.

On Revelation He said "A man would command his Son to dig potatoes, saddle his horse but before he had done either tell him to do sumthing els[e], this is all considerd right. "But as soon as the Lord gives a commandment & revokes that decree & commands sumthing els[e] then the prophet is consider[e]d fallen &c" Because we will not receive chastizment at the hand of the Prophet & Apostles the Lord chastizeth us with Sickeness & death. Let not any man Publish his own righteousness for others can do that for him." sooner let him confess his sins & then he will be forgiven & he will bring forth more fruit. When A man is chastized he gets angry & will not endure it. The reason we do not have the Secrets of the Lord revealed unto us is because we do

---

86. Remarks, 28 November 1841, *WWJ*, 1:484.
87. Discourse, 19 December 1841, *WWJ*, 1:486.

secrets of the Lord revealed unto us, is because we do not keep them but reveal them; we do not keep our own secrets, but reveal our difficulties to the world, even to our enemies, then how would we keep the secrets of the Lord? I can keep a secret till Doomsday. What greater love hath any man than that he lay down his life for his friend; then why not fight for our friend until we die? (December 19, 1841.) DHC 4:478-479.

not keep them but reveal them. We do not keep our own secrets but reveal our difficulties to the world even to our enemies[.] then how would we keep the secrets of the Lord[?] Joseph Says I can keep a secret till dooms day He spoke of love[.] what greater love hath any man than that he lay down his life for his friend[?] then why not fight for our friend untill we die[?] & many other things of interest was spoken[88]

The Gift of Tongues

Joseph Smith's Journal

Sunday, December 26, 1841.—The public meeting of the Saints was at my house this evening, and after Patriarch Hyrum Smith and Elder Brigham Young had spoken on the principles of faith, and the gifts of the Spirit, I read the 13th chapter of First Corinthians, also a part of the 14th chapter, and remarked that the gift of tongues was necessary in the Church; but that if Satan could not speak in tongues, he could tempt a dutchman, or any other nation, but the English for he can tempt the Englishman, for he has tempted me, and I am an Englishman; but the gift of tongues by the power of the Holy Ghost in the Church, is for the benefit of the servants of God to preach to unbelievers, as on the day of Pentecost. When devout men from every nation shall assemble to hear the things of God, let the Elders preach to them in their own mother tongue, whether it is German, French, Spanish or Irish, or any other, and let those interpret who understand the language spoken, in their own mother tongue, and this is what the Apostle meant in First Corinthians 14:27. (December 26, 1841.) DHC 4:485-486.

December 26th. The public meeting of the saints was at President Joseph Smiths house, on Sunday evening Dec 26th. and after Patriarch Hyram [Hyrum Smith] & Elder Brigham [Young] had spoken on the principles of faith and the gifts of the spirit. President Joseph read the 13th. chap of Ist corinthians and a part of the 14 chap, and remarked that the gift of Tongues was necessary in the church; <but> That if satan could not speak in tongues he could not tempt a Dutchman, or any other nation, but the English, for he can tempt the Englishman, for he has tempted me, & I am an Englishman; but the Gift of Tongues, by the power of the Holy Ghost, in the church, is for the benefit of the servants of God to preach to unbelievers, as on the days of Pentecost. when devout men from evry nation shall assemble to hear of the things of God. let the <elders> preach to them in their own Mother tongue. whither it is German, French, Spanish or Irish. or any other. & let those interpret who understand the ~~tongue~~ <Language> spoken. in their mother tongue. & this is what the Apostle meant. in Is[t] corinthians 14.27.[89]

---

88. Discourse, 19 December 1841, *WWJ*, 1:486. See also *JSP, D9*, 33–34.
89. 26 December 1841, *JSP, J2*, 18.

Announcement Respecting Work on the Temple

To the Brethren in Nauvoo City: Greeting.—

It is highly important for the forwarding of the Temple, that an equal distribution of labor should be made in relation to time; as a superabundance of hands one week, and none the next, tends to retard the progress of the work; therefore every brother is requested to be particular to labor on the day set apart for the same, in his ward; and to remember that he that sows sparingly, shall also reap sparingly, so that if the brethren want a plentiful [p.196] harvest, they will do well to be at the place of labor in good season in the morning, bringing all necessary tools, according to their occupation, and those who have teams bring them also, unless otherwise advised by the Temple Committee. Should any one be detained from his labor by unavoidable circumstances on the day appointed, let him labor the next day, or the first day possible.

N. B.—The captains of the respective wards are particularly requested to be at the place of labor on their respective days, and keep an accurate account of each man's work, and be ready to exhibit a list of the same when called for.

The heart of the Trustee is daily made to rejoice in the good feelings of the brethren, made manifest in their exertion to carry forward the work of the Lord, and rear His Temple; and it is hoped that neither planting, sowing, or reaping will hereafter be made to interfere with the regulations hinted at above.
JOSEPH SMITH,
Trustee in Trust.
(February 21, 1842.) DHC 4:517.

Times and Seasons
TO THE BRETHREN IN NAUVOO CITY, GREETING:—

It is highly important, for the forwarding of the Temple, that an equal distribution of labor should be made, in relation to time; as a superabundance of hands one week, and none the next, tends to retard the progress of the work; therefore, every brother is requested to be particular to labor on the day set apart for the same, in his ward; and to remember that he that sows sparingly shall also reap sparingly,—so that if the brethren want a plentiful harvest, they will do well to be at the place of labor in good season in the morning, bringing all necessary tools, according to their occupation; and those who have teams bring them also, unless otherwise advised by the temple committee. Should any one be detained from his labor by unavoidable circumstances, on the day appointed, let him labor the next day, or the first day possible.

N. B.—The captains of the respective wards are particularly requested to be at the place of labor on their respective days, and keep an accurate account of each man's work, and be ready to exhibit a list of the same when called for.

The heart of the trustee is daily made to rejoice in the good feelings of the brethren, made manifest in their exertion to carry forward the work of the Lord, and rear his temple; and it is hoped that neither planting, sowing or reaping will hereafter be made to interfere with the regulations hinted at above.
JOSEPH SMITH.
Trustee in Trust.[90]

---

90. *T&S* 3, no. 9 (1 March 1842): 715. Dated in History, C-1 as 21 February 1842.

The Prophet's Sermon on Life and Death; the Resurrection and the Salvation of Children

Wilford Woodruff's Journal

March 20[th] Sunday Sermon of Joseph the Seer

A large assembly of Saints gather together at an early hour to hear a discours[e] deliver[e]d upon the Subject of Baptism by Joseph the Seer, but as a young child was dead & his Corpes presented in the assembly it called forth many remarks from The speaker upon death & the resurrection which were in the highest degree interesting & his remarks upon Baptism was truly glorious to the believer in Jesus Christ[.] The following is a brief synopsis of some of the items presented in the discours[e][91]

President Smith read the 14th chapter of Revelation, and said—We have again the warning voice sounded in our midst, which shows the uncertainty of human life; and in my leisure moments I have meditated upon the subject, and asked the question, why it is that infants, innocent children, are taken away from us, especially those that seem to be the most intelligent and interesting. The strongest reasons that present themselves to my mind are these: This world is a very wicked world; and it is a proverb that the "world grows weaker and wiser"; if that is the case, the world grows more wicked and corrupt. In the earlier ages of the world a righteous man, and a man of God and of intelligence, had a better chance to do good, to be believed and received than at the present day; but in these days such a man is much opposed and persecuted by most of the inhabitants of the earth, and he has much sorrow to pass through here. The Lord takes many away even in infancy, that they may escape the envy of man, and the sorrows and evils of this present world; they were too pure, **[p.197]** too

The Speaker read the 14 ch Revelations, And sayes "we have again the warning voice sounded in our midst which shows the uncertainty of human life. And in my leasure moments I have meditated upon the subject, & asked the question Why is it that infant innocent Children are taken away from us, esspecially those that seem to be most intelligent beings[?]"

Answer "This world is a vary wicked world & it is a proverb that the world grow weaker & wiser, but if it is the case the world grows more wicked & corrupt. In the early ages of the world A richeous man & a man of God & intelligence had a better chance to do good to be received & believed than at the present day. but in these days such a man is much opposed & persecuted by most of the inhabitants of the earth & he has much sorrow to pass through. hence the Lord takes many away even in infancy that they may escape the envy of man, the sorrows & evils of this present world & they were two pure & to lovly to

---

91. Discourse, March 20, 1842, *WWJ*, 1:497.

lovely, to live on earth; therefore, if rightly considered, instead of mourning we have reason to rejoice as they are delivered from evil, and we shall soon have them again.

live on Earth. Therefore if rightly considered ~~we have~~, instead of morning we have reason to rejoice, as they are deliver[e]d from evil & we shall soon have them again.[92]

Do Not Procrastinate Repentance

Wilford Woodruff's Journal[93]

What chance is there for infidelity when we are parting with our friends almost daily? None at all. The infidel will grasp at every straw for help until death stares him in the face, and then his infidelity takes its flight, for the realities of the eternal world are resting upon him in mighty power; and when every earthly support and prop fails him, he then sensibly feels the eternal truths of the immortality of the soul. We should take warning and not wait for the death-bed to repent, as we see the infant taken away by death, so may the youth and middle-aged, as well as the infant be suddenly called into eternity. Let this, then, prove as a warning to all not to procrastinate repentance, or wait till a death-bed, for it is the will of God that man should repent and serve Him in health, and in the strength and power of his mind, in order to secure his blessing, and not wait until he is called to die.

What chance is their for infidelity when we are parting with our friends almost daily[?] none at all[.] The infidel will grasp at evry straw for help untill death stares him in the face & then his infidelity takes its flight for the realities of the eternal world are resting upon him in mighty power & when evry earthly support & prop fails him, he then sensibly feels the eternal truths of the immortality of the Soul.

***

(We should take warning & not wait for the death bed to repent.) As we se[e] the infant taken away by death, so may the youth & middle aged as well as the infant suddenly be called into eternity. Let this then prove as a warning to all not to procrastinate repentance or wait till a death bed, for it is the will of God that man should repent & serve him in health & in the Strength & power of his mind in order to secure his blessings & not wait untill he is called to die.[94]

Redemption of Little Children

Wilford Woodruff's Journal

The doctrine of baptizing children, or sprinkling them, or they must welter in hell, is a doctrine not true, not supported in Holy Writ, and is not consistent with the character of God. All children are redeemed by the

Also the doctrin of Baptizing Children or sprinkling them or they must welter in Hell is a doctrin not true not supported in Holy writ & is not consistant with the character of God[.] The moment that Children leave

---

92. Discourse, March 20, 1842, *WWJ*, 1:497. See also *JSP, D9*, 291.

93. The original *TPJS* version of this sermon is in a somewhat different order than that found in the original transcript of the discourse in Wilford Woodruff's journal. The version found in *TPJS* was taken from the edited *Times and Seasons* version of the sermon: "Sabbath Scene in Nauvoo," *T&S* 3, no. 12 (15 April 1842): 751–53. We have ordered the paragraphs here so as to match that found in the original *TPJS*.

94. Discourse, March 20, 1842, *WWJ*, 1:497. See also *JSP, D9*, 291–92.

blood of Jesus Christ, and the moment that children leave this world, they are taken to the bosom of Abraham. The only difference between the old and young dying is, one lives longer in heaven and eternal light and glory than the other, and is freed a little sooner from this miserable wicked world. Notwithstanding all this glory, we for a moment lose sight of it, and mourn the loss, but we do not mourn as those without hope.

this world they are taken to the bosom of Abraham[.] The ownly difference between the old & young dying is one lives longer in heaven & Eternal light & glory than the other & was freed a little sooner from this miserable wicked world[.] Notwithstanding all this glory we for a moment loose sight of it & mourn the loss but we do not mourn as those without hope.[95]

Decrees Fixed and Immovable

Wilford Woodruff's Journal

My intention was to have spoken on the subject of baptism, but having a case of death before us, I thought proper to refer to that subject. I will now, however, say a few words upon baptism, as I intended.

"My intention (says the speaker) was to have treated upon the subject of Baptism. But having a case of death before us, I thought it proper to refer to that subject. I will now however say a few words upon that subject <Baptism> as intended

God has made certain decrees which are fixed and immovable; for instance, God set the sun, the moon, and the stars **[p.198]** in the heavens, and gave them their laws, conditions and bounds, which they cannot pass, except by His commandments; they all move in perfect harmony in their sphere and order, and are as lights, wonders and signs unto us. The sea also has its bounds which it cannot pass. God has set many signs on the earth, as well as in the heavens for instance, the oak of the forest, the fruit of the tree, the herb of the field, all bear a sign that seed hath been planted there; for it is a decree of the Lord that every tree, plant, and herb bearing seed should bring forth of its kind, and cannot come forth after any other law or principle.[96] Upon the same principle do I contend that baptism is a sign ordained of God, for the believer in Christ to take upon himself in order to enter into the kingdom of God, "for except ye are born of water and of

God has made certain decreas which are fixed & unalterable. for instance God set the Sun, the moon, the Stars in the heavens, & given them their laws conditions, & bounds which they cannot pass except by his command. they all move in perfect harmony in there sphere & order & are as wonders, lights & signs unto us. The sea also has its bounds which it cannot pass. God has set many signs in the earth as well as in heaven[.] for instance the oaks of the **[p.498]** forest, the fruit of the tree, the herd of the field all bear a sign that seed hath been planted there. for it is a decree of the Lord that evry tree fruit or herb bearing seed should bring forth after its kind & cannot Come forth after any other law or principle. upon the same principle do I contend that Baptism is a sign, ordained of God for the believer in Christ to take upon himself in order to enter into the kingdom of God. "for except you are born of the water & the spirit you can-

---

95. Discourse, 20 March 1842, *WWJ*, 1:497. See also *JSP, D9*, 291–92.

96. The original *TPJS* footnote reads: "This very positive statement by the Prophet, that every tree, plant, and herb, and evidently every other creature, cannot produce except after its kind, is in harmony not only with the scriptures, but also with all known facts in the world."

the Spirit ye cannot enter into the Kingdom of God," said the Savior. It is a sign and a commandment which God has set for man to enter into His kingdom. Those who seek to enter in any other way will seek in vain; for God will not receive them, neither will the angels acknowledge their works as accepted, for they have not obeyed the ordinances, nor attended to the signs which God ordained for the salvation of man, to prepare him for, and give him a title to, a celestial glory; and God had decreed that all who will not obey His voice shall not escape the damnation of hell. What is the damnation of hell? To go with that society who have not obeyed His commands.

not enter into the kingdom of God, saith the Savior. as It is a sign or command which God hath set for man to enter into this ~~Kingdom of God~~ those who seek to enter in any other way will seek in vain, for God will not receive them neither will the angels acknowledge their works as as accepted, for they have not taken upon themselves those ordinances & signs which God ordained for man to receive in order to receive a celestial glory, & God has decreed that all ~~that~~ <who> will not obey his voice shall not escape the damnation of hell. what is the damnation of hell. to go with that society who have not obeyed his commands[97]

Baptism and the Gift of the Holy Ghost

Wilford Woodruff's Journal

Baptism is a sign to God, to angels, and to heaven that we do the will of God, and there is no other way beneath the heavens whereby God hath ordained for man to come to Him to be saved, and enter into the Kingdom of God, except faith in Jesus Christ, repentance, and baptism for the remission of sins, and any other course is in vain; then you have the promise of the gift of the Holy Ghost.

Baptism is a sign to God, to Angels, to heaven that we do the will of God & their is no other way beneath the heavens whareby God hath ordained for man to come ~~to God~~ & any other cource is in vain. God hath decreed & ordained that man should repent of all his sins & Be Baptized for the remission of his sins[.] then he can come to God in the name of Jesus Christ in faith. then we have the promise of the Holy Ghost

What is the sign of the healing of the sick? The laying on of hands is the sign or way marked out by James, and the custom of the ancient Saints as ordered by the Lord, and we **[p.199]** cannot obtain the blessings by pursuing any other course except the way marked out by the Lord. What if we should attempt to get the gift of the Holy Ghost through any other means except the signs of way which God hath appointed—would we obtain it? Certainly not; all other means would fail. The Lord says do so and so, and I will bless you.

what is the sign of the healing of the sick! the laying on of hands, is the sign or way marked out by James & the custom of the ancient saints as ordered by the Lord & we Should not obtain the blessing by persuing any other course except the way which God has mark[e]d out. What if we should attempt to get the Holy Ghost through any other means except the sign or way which God hath appointed. Should we obtain it[?] certainly not[.] all other means would fail[.] The Lord says do so & so[98]

---

97. Discourse, 20 March 1842, *WWJ*, 1:497–98. See also *JSP, D9*, 292–93.
98. Discourse, 20 March 1842, *WWJ*, 1:498. See also *JSP, D9*, 293.

Key Words of the Priesthood

	Wilford Woodruff's Journal
There are certain key words and signs belonging to the Priesthood which must be observed in order to obtain the blessing. The sign of Peter was to repent and be baptized for the remission of sins, with the promise of the gift of the Holy Ghost obtained.	their is certain key words & signs belonging to the priesthood which must[99] be observed in order to obtaine the Blessings The sign of Peter was, to repent & be baptized for the remission of Sins, with the promise of the gift of the Holy Ghost & in no other way is the gift of the Holy Ghost obtained.[100]

Difference Between the Holy Ghost and the Gift of the Holy Ghost

	Wilford Woodruff's Journal
There is a difference between the Holy Ghost and the gift of the Holy Ghost. Cornelius received the Holy Ghost before he was baptized, which was the convincing power of God unto him of the truth of the Gospel, but he could not receive the gift of the Holy Ghost until after he was baptized. Had he not taken this sign or ordinance upon him, the Holy Ghost which convinced him of the truth of God, would have left him. Until he obeyed these ordinances and received the gift of the Holy Ghost, by the laying on of hands, according to the order of God, he could not have healed the sick or commanded an evil spirit to come out of a man, and it obey him; for the spirits might say unto him, as they did to the sons of Sceva: "Paul we know and Jesus we know, but who are ye?" It mattereth not whether we live long or short on the earth after we come to a knowledge of these principles and obey them unto the end. I know that all men will be damned if they do not come in the way which He hath opened, and this is the way marked out by the word of the Lord.	Their is a difference between the Holy Ghost & the gift of the Holy Ghost. Cornelius received the Holy Ghost before he was Baptized which was the convincing power of God unto him of the truth of the gospel. but he could not receive the gift of the Holy Ghost untill after he was Baptized, & had he not taken this Sign or [or]dinances upon him the Holy Ghost which Convinced him of the truth of God would have left him untill he obeyed these ordinances & received the gift of the Holy Ghost by the laying on of hands according to the order of God[.] he could not have healed the sick or command an evil spirit to Come out of a man & it obey him for the spirit might say to him as he did to the sons of Scava Peter I know & Christ I know but who are ye[?] It matereth not whether we live long or short after we come to a knowledge of the principles & obey them. I know that all men will be damned if they do not come in the way which God has appointed[101]

---

99. *JSP, D9*, 293 renders this word as "much," but Wilford Woodruff's original handwritten journal clearly says "must."

100. Discourse, 20 March 1842, *WWJ*, 1:498. See also *JSP, D9*, 293.

101. Discourse, 20 March 1842, *WWJ*, 1:498. See also *JSP, D9*, 293–94.

The Universal Resurrection

	Wilford Woodruff's Journal

As concerning the resurrection, I will merely say that all men will come from the grave as they lie down, whether old or young; there will not be "added unto their stature one cubit," neither taken from it; all will be raised by the power of God, **[p.200]** having spirit in their bodies, and not blood. Children will be enthroned in the presence of God and the Lamb with bodies of the same stature[102] that they had on earth, having been redeemed by the blood of the Lamb; they will there enjoy the fullness of that light, glory and intelligence, which is prepared in the celestial kingdom. "Blessed are the dead who die in the Lord, for they rest from their labors and their works do follow them."

As Concerning the resurrection I will merly Say that all men will come from the grave as they lie down, whether old or young[.] their will not be added unto the[i]r stature one cubit neither taken from it, All being raised by the power of God having the spirit of God in their bodies & not Blood[.] Children will be enthroned in the presence of God & the Lamb with bodies of the same stature that were on earth. Having been redeemed by the Blood of the Lamb they will there enjoy a fulness of that light Glory & intelligence which is received **[p.499]** in the celestial kingdom of God[.] "Blessed are the dead who die in the Lord, for they rest from their labours & their works do follow them

The speaker, before closing, called upon the assembly before him to humble themselves in faith before God, and in mighty prayer and fasting to call upon the name of the Lord, until the elements were purified over our heads, and the earth sanctified under our feet, that the inhabitants of this city may escape the power of disease and pestilence, and the destroyer that rideth upon the face of the earth, and that the Holy Spirit of God may rest upon this vast multitude.

The speaker before closing called upon the vast assembly before him to humble themselves in faith before God, & in mighty Prayer & fasting to call upon his Holy name, untill the elements were purified over our heads & the earth Sanctified under our feet that the inhabitants of this City may escape the power of the disease, pestilence & destroyer that rideth upon the face of the earth & that the holy spirit of God may rest upon this vast multitude[103]

Baptisms Performed

	Wilford Woodruff's Journal

At the close of the meeting, President Smith said he should attend to the ordinance of Baptism in the river, near his house, at two o'clock, and at the appointed hour, the bank

A[t] the close of the meeting President Smith informed the congregation that he should attend to the ordinance of Baptism in the his ho river near his house at 2 o-clock[.] And at the

---

102. The original *TPJS* footnote reads: "In the Improvement Era for June, 1904, President Joseph F. Smith in an editorial on the Resurrection said: 'The body will come forth as it is laid to rest, for there is no growth or development in the grave. As it is laid down, so will it arise, and changes to perfection will come by the law of restitution. But the spirit will continue to expand and develop, and the body, after the resurrection will develop to the full stature of man.' This may be accepted as the doctrine of the Church in respect to the resurrection of children and their future development to the full stature of men and women; and it is alike conformable to that which will be regarded as both reasonable and desirable."

103. Discourse, 20 March 1842, *WWJ*, 1:498–99. See also *JSP, D9*, 294.

of the Mississippi was lined with a multitude of people, and President Joseph Smith went into the river and baptized eighty persons for the remission of their sins, and what added joy to the scene was the person baptized was M. L. D. Wasson, a nephew of Mrs. Emma Smith—the first of her kindred that has embraced the fullness of the Gospel.

At the close of this interesting scene, the administrator lifted up his hands towards heaven, and implored the blessing of God to rest upon the people; and truly the Spirit of God did rest upon the multitude, to the joy and consolation of our hearts.

[p.201] After baptism, the congregation again repaired to the grove, near the Temple, to attend to the ordinance of confirmation, and, notwithstanding President Smith had spoken in the open air to the people, about fifty of those baptized received their confirmation under his hands in the after part of the day. While this was progressing, great numbers were being baptized in the font for the dead. (March 20, 1842.) DHC 4:553-557.

appointed hour the Bank of the missisippi was lined with a multitude of people & President Joseph Smith went forth into the river & Baptized with his own hands about 80 persons for the remission of their sins & what added Joy to the seene the first person Baptized was Mr L[orenzo]. D. Wason a nephew of sister Emma Smith the first of her kindred that have embraced the fulness of the gospel.

At the close of this interesting seene the Administrator lifted up his hands towards heaven & implored the blessing of ~~heaven~~ <God> to rest upon the People, & truly the spirit of God did rest upon the multitude to the Joy & consolation of our harts.

After Baptism the Congregation again repaired to the grove near the Temple to attend to the ordinance of Confirmation & notwithstanding president Smith had spoken in the open air to the people & stood in the water & Baptized about 80 person[s] about 50 of those Baptized received their Confirmation under his hands in the after part of the day, & during the intermission of these meetings their was probably as many more Baptized & confirmed for their Dead relatives at the Font By the Twelve[.] And those who wish for further information Concerning the seenes of the Sabbath in Nauvoo or any other day in the week I would say to all such come & see W. Woodruff.[104]

Synopsis of the Prophet's Sermon on Baptism for the Dead

Wilford Woodruff's Journal

This was an interesting day. A large assembly met in the grove near the Temple. Brother Amasa Lyman addressed the people in a very interesting manner. He was followed by Joseph,

This was an interesting day. [p.500] A large assembly met in the grove near the Temple[.] Br Amisa Lyman addressed the assembly & made many interesting remarks.[105] He [Amasa

---

104. Discourse, 20 March 1842, *WWJ*, 1:499. See also *T&S* 3, no. 12 (15 April 1842): 752–53. Both Wilford Woodruff's Journal and the *Times and Seasons* article end a little differently than Joseph Fielding Smith's ending. The Wilford Woodruff's Journal version is used here. This portion of the discourse was not included in *JSP, D9*.

105. Discourse, 27 March 1842, *WWJ*, 1:499–500. This portion of the discourse was not included in *JSP, D9*.

the Seer, who made some highly edifying and instructive remarks concerning baptism for the dead, if the dead rise not at all, why are they then baptized for the dead?" If there is one word of the Lord that supports the doctrine of baptism for the dead, it is enough to establish it as a true doctrine. Again; if we can, by the authority of the Priesthood of the Son of God, baptize a man in the name of the Father, of the Son, and of the Holy Ghost, for the remission of sins, it is just as much our privilege to act as an agent, and be baptized for the remission of sins for and in behalf of our dead kindred, who have not heard the Gospel, or the fullness of it. (March 27, 1842.) DHC 4:568-569.

Lyman] was followed by Joseph the Seer who made some edifying remarks concerning Baptism for the dead, He said the Bible supported the doctrine, "why are ye Baptized for the dead if the dead rise not &c" if their is one word of the Lord that supports the doctrin it is enough to mik [make] it a true doctrin Again if we can baptize a man in the Name of the Father of the Son & of the Holy Ghost for the remission of sins it is Just as much our privilege to act as an agent & be baptized for the remission of sins for & in behalf of our dead kindred who have not herd the gospel or fulness of it[106]

Synopsis of the Prophet's Remarks to the Female Relief Society

Relief Society Minutes

President Joseph Smith arose. Spoke of the organization of the Female Relief Society; said he was deeply interested, that it might be built up to the Most High in an acceptable manner; that its rules must be observed; that none should be received into it but those who were worthy; proposed a close examination of every candidate; that the society was growing too fast. It should grow up by degrees, should commence with a few individuals, thus have a select society of the virtuous, and those who would walk circumspectly; commended them for their zeal, but said sometimes their zeal was not according to knowledge. One principle object of the institution was to purge [p.202] out iniquity; said they must be extremely careful in all their examinations, or the consequences would be serious.

Prest. J. Smith arose—spoke of the organization of the Society—said he was deeply interested that it might be built up to the Most High in an acceptable manner—that its rules must be observed— that none should be received into the Society but those who were worthy—propos'd that the Society go into a close examination of every candidate— that they were going too fast— that the Society should grow up by degrees— should commence with a few individuals— thus have a select Society of the virtuous and those who will walk circumspectly—commended them for their zeal but said sometimes their zeal was not according to knowledge— One principal object of the Institution, was to purge out iniquity— said they must be extremely careful in all their examinations or the consequences would be serious

All difficulties which might and would cross our way must be surmounted. Though the soul be tried, the heart faint, and the hands hang down, we must not retrace out steps; there must be decision of character, aside from sympathy. When instructed, we must obey that voice, observe the laws of the Kingdom of God,

Said all difficulties which might & would cross our way must be surmounted, though the soul be <u>tried</u>, the heart faint, and hands hang down—must not retrace our steps—that there must be decision of character aside from sympathy— that when instructed we must obey that voice, observe the [p.43] Constitution

---

106. Discourse, 27 March 1842, *WWJ*, 1:499–500. See also *JSP, D9*, 303.

that the blessings of heaven may rest down upon us. All must act in concert, or nothing can be done, and should move according to the ancient Priesthood; hence the Saints should be a select people, separate from all the evils of the world—choice, virtuous, and holy. The Lord was going to make of the Church of Jesus Christ a kingdom of Priests, a holy people, a chosen generation, as in Enoch's day, having all the gifts as illustrated to the Church in Paul's epistles and teachings to the churches in his day—that it is the privilege of each member to live long and enjoy health. He then blessed the Saints. (March 30, 1842.) DHC 4:570.

that the blessings of heaven may rest down upon us— all must act in concert or nothing can be done— that the Society should move according to the ancient Priesthood, hence there should be a select Society separate from all the evils of the world, choice, virtuou[s] and holy— Said he was going to make of this Society a kingdom of priests an in Enoch's day— as in Pauls day— that it is the privilege of each member to live long and enjoy health[107]

"Try the Spirits"

The Prophet's Editorial in the Times and Seasons

Recent occurrences that have transpired amongst us render it an imperative duty devolving upon me to say something in relation to the spirits by which men are actuated.

It is evident from the Apostles' writings, that many false spirits existed in their day, and had "gone forth into the world," and that it needed intelligence which God alone could impart to detect false spirits, and to prove what spirits were of God. The world in general have been grossly ignorant in regard to this one thing, and why should they be otherwise—for "the things of God knoweth no man, but the Spirit of God."

The Egyptians were not able to discover the difference between the miracles of Moses and those of the magicians until they came to be tested together; and if Moses had not appeared in their midst, they would unquestionably have thought that the miracles of the magicians were performed through the mighty power of God, for they were great miracles that were performed by them—a

Times and Seasons

Recent occurrences that have transpired amongst us render it an imperative duty devolving upon me to say something in relation to the Spirits by which men are actuated.

It is evident from the apostle's writings that many false spirits existed in their day, and had "gone forth into the world," and that it needed intelligence which God alone could impart to detect false spirits, and to prove what spirits were of God. The world in general have been grossly ignorant in regard to this one thing, and why should they be otherwise, "For no man knows the things of God, but by the Spirit of God."

The Egyptians were not able to discover the difference between the miracles of Moses, and those of the magicians until they came to be tested together; and if Moses had not appeared in their midst they would unquestionably have thought that the miracles of the magicians were performed through the mighty power of God; for they were great miracles that were performed by them: a

---

107. 31 March 1842, *RSM*, 42–43.

supernatural agency was developed, and great power manifested.

* * *

It would have been equally as difficult for us to tell by what [p.203] spirit the Apostles prophesied, or by what power the Apostles spoke and worked miracles. Who could have told whether the power of Simon, the sorcerer, was of God or of the devil?

There always did, in every age, seem to be a lack of intelligence pertaining to this subject. Spirits of all kinds have been manifested, in every age, and almost among all people.

If we go among the pagans, they have their spirits; the Mohammedans, the Jews, the Christians, the Indians—all have their spirits, all have a supernatural agency, and all contend that their spirits are of God. Who shall solve the mystery? "Try the spirits," says John, but who is to do it? The learned, the eloquent, the philosopher, the sage, the divine—all are ignorant. The heathens will boast of their gods, and of the great things that have been unfolded by their oracles. The Mussulman will boast of his Koran, and of the divine communications that his progenitors have received. The Jews have had numerous instances, both ancient and modern, among them of men who have professed to be inspired, and sent to bring about great events, and the Christian world has not been slow in making up the number.

"Try the spirits," but what by? Are we to try them by the creeds of men? What preposterous folly—what sheer ignorance—what madness! Try the motions and actions of an eternal being (for I contend that all spirits are such) by a thing that was conceived in ignorance, and brought forth in folly—a cobweb of yesterday! Angels would hide their faces,

supernatural agency was developed; and great power manifested.

* * *

It would have been equally as difficult for us to tell by what spirit the prophets prophesied, or by what power the apostles spoke, and worked miracles. Who could have told whether the power of Simon, the sorcerer was of God, or of the devil?

There always did in every age seem to be a lack of intelligence pertaining to this subject. Spirits of all kinds have been manifested, in every age and almost amongst all people:

if we go among the Pagans they have their spirits, the Mahommedans, the Jews, the Christians, the Indians; all have their spirits, all have a supernatural agency; and all contend that their spirits are of God. Who shall solve the mystery? "Try the spirits," says John, but who is to do it? The learned, the eloquent, the philosopher, the sage, the divine, all are ignorant. The Heathens will boast of their Gods, and of the great things that have been unfolded by their oracles. The Mussulman will boast of his Koran and of the divine communications that his progenitors have received, and are receiving, The Jews have had numerous instances both ancient and modern among them of men who have professed to be inspired and sent to bring about great events, and the Christian world has not been slow in making up the number.[108]

Ignorance of the Nature of Spirits

Times and Seasons

"Try the spirits;" but what by? are we to try them by the creeds of men? what preposterous folly, what sheer ignorance, what madness. Try the motions and actions of an eternal being, (for I contend that all spirits are such,) by a thing that was conceived in ignorance, and brought forth in folly.—a cobweb of yesterday. Angels would hide their faces, and devils

---

108. *T&S* 3, no. 11 (1 April 1842): 743.

and devils would be ashamed and insulted, and would say, "Paul we know, and Jesus we know, but who are ye?" Let each man of society make a creed and try evil spirits by it, and the devil would shake his sides; it is all that he would ask—all that he would desire. Yet many of them do this, and hence "many spirits are abroad in the world."

One great evil is, that men are ignorant of the nature of spirits; their power, laws, government, intelligence, etc., and imagine that when there is anything like power, revelation, or vision manifested, that it must be of God. Hence the Methodists, Presbyterians, and others frequently possess a spirit that will cause them to lie down, and during its operation, animation is frequently entirely suspended; they consider it to be the power [p.204] of God, and a glorious manifestation from God—a manifestation of what? Is there any intelligence communicated? Are the curtains of heaven withdrawn, or the purposes of God developed? Have they seen and conversed with an angel—or have the glories of futurity burst upon their view? No! but their body has been inanimate, the operation of their spirit suspended, and all the intelligence that can be obtained from them when they arise, is a shout of "glory," or "hallelujah," or some incoherent expression; but they have had "the power."

The Shaker will whirl around on his heel, impelled by a supernatural agency or spirit, and think that he is governed by the Spirit of God; and the Jumper will jump and enter into all kinds of extravagances. A Primitive Methodist will shout under the influence of that spirit, until he will rend the heavens with his cries; while the Quakers (or Friends) moved as they think, by the Spirit of God, will sit still and say nothing. Is God the author of all this? If not all of it, which does He recognize? Surely, such a heterogeneous mass of confusion never can enter into the kingdom of heaven.

---

109. *T&S* 3, no. 11 (1 April 1842): 744.

Discerning of Spirits by Power of Priesthood

Times and Seasons

Every one of these professes to be competent to try his neighbor's spirit, but no one can try his own, and what is the reason? Because they have not a key to unlock, no rule wherewith to measure, and no criterion whereby they can test it. Could any one tell the length, breadth or height of a building without a rule? Test the quality of metals without a criterion, or point out the movements of the planetary systems, without a knowledge of astronomy? Certainly not; and if such ignorance as this is manifested about a spirit of this kind, who can describe an angel of light? If Satan should appear as one in glory, who can tell his color, his signs, his appearance, his glory, or what is the manner of his manifestation? Who can detect the spirit of the French prophets with their revelations and their visions, and power of manifestations? Or who can point out the spirit of the Irvingites, with their apostles and prophets, and visions and tongues, and interpretations, etc. Or who can drag into daylight and develop the hidden mysteries of the false spirits that so frequently are made manifest among the Latter-day Saints? We answer that no man can do this without the Priesthood, and having a knowledge of the laws [p.205] by which spirits are governed; for as no man knows the things of God, but by the Spirit of God, so no man knows the spirit of the devil, and his power and influence, but by possessing intelligence which is more than human, and having unfolded through the medium of the Priesthood the mysteries operations of his devices; without knowing the angelic form, the sanctified look and gesture, and the zeal that is frequently manifested by him for the glory of God, together with the prophetic spirit, the gracious influence, the godly appearance, and the holy garb, which are so characteristic of his proceedings and his mysterious windings.

Every one of these professes to be competent to try his neighbor's spirit, but no one can try his own, and what is the reason? because they have not a key to unlock, no rule wherewith to measure, and no criterion whereby they can test it; could any one tell the length, breadth, or height of a building without a rule? test the quality of metals without a criterion, or point out the movements of the planetary system without a knowledge of astronomy? certainly not: and if such ignorance as this is manifested about a spirit of this kind who can describe an angel of light, if Satan should appear as one in glory? Who can tell his color, his signs, his appearance, his glory? or what is the manner of his manifestation? Who can detect the spirit of the French Prophets, with their revelations, and visions and power and manifestations? or who can point out the spirit of the Irvingites with their apostles, and prophets, and visions, and tongues, and interpretations, &c. &c.; or who can drag into day-light and develope the hidden mysteries of the false spirits that so frequently are made manifest among the Latter-Day Saints? We answer that no man can do this without the Priesthood, and having a knowledge of the laws by which spirits are governed; for as, "no man knows the things of God but by the spirit of God," so no man knows the spirit of the devil and his power and influence but by possessing intelligence which is more than human, and having unfolded through the medium of the Priesthood the mysterious operations of his devices: without knowing the angelic form, the sanctified look, and gesture, and the zeal that is frequently manifested by him for the glory of God:— together with the prophetic spirit, the gracious influence, the godly appearance, and the holy garb which is so characteristic of his proceedings, and his mysterious windings.

A man must have the discerning of spirits before he can drag into daylight this hellish influence and unfold it unto the world in all its soul-destroying, diabolical, and horrid colors; for nothing is a greater injury to the children of men than to be under the influence of a false spirit when they think they have the Spirit of God. Thousands have felt the influence of its terrible power and baneful effects. Long pilgrimages have been undertaken, penances endured, and pain, misery and ruin have followed in their train; nations have been convulsed, kingdoms overthrown, provinces laid waste, and blood, carnage and desolation are habiliments in which it has been clothed.

* * *

A man must have the discerning of spirits, before he can drag into daylight this hellish influence and unfold it unto the world in all its soul destroying, diabolical, and horrid colors: for nothing is a greater injury to the children of men than to be under the influence of a false spirit, when they think they have the spirit of God. Thousands have felt the influence of its terrible power, and baneful effects; long pilgrimages have been undertaken, penances endured, and pain, misery and ruin have followed in their train; nations have been convulsed, kingdoms overthrown, provinces laid waste, and blood, carnage and desolation are the habilaments in which it has been clothed.[110]

* * *

The Spirit of God the Spirit of Knowledge

Times and Seasons

As we have noticed before, the great difficulty lies in the ignorance of the nature of spirits, of the laws by which they are governed, and the signs by which they may be known; if it requires the Spirit of God to know the things of God; and the spirit of the devil can only be unmasked through that medium, then it follows as a natural consequence that unless some person or persons have a communication, or revelation from God, unfolding to them the operation of the spirit, they must eternally remain ignorant of these principles; for I contend that if one man cannot understand these things but by the Spirit of God, ten thousand men cannot; it is alike out of the reach of the wisdom of the learned, the tongue of the eloquent, the power of the mighty. And we shall at last have to come to this conclusion, whatever we may think of revelation, that without it we can neither know nor understand anything of God, or the devil; and however unwilling the world may be **[p.206]** to acknowledge this principle, it is evident from the multifarious creeds and

As we have noticed before, the great difficulty lays in the ignorance of the nature of spirits, of the laws by which they are governed, and the signs by which they may be known; if it requires the spirit of God, to know the things of God, and the spirit of the devil can only be unmasked through that medium, then it follows as a natural consequence that unless some person, or persons, have a communication or revelation from God, unfolding to them the operation of spirit, they must eternally remain ignorant of these principles:— for I contend that if one man cannot understand these things but by the spirit of God, ten thousand men cannot; it is alike out of the reach of the wisdom of the learned, the tongue of the eloquent, and the power of the mighty. And we shall at last have to come to this conclusion, whatever we may think of revelation, that without it we can neither know, nor understand any thing of God, or the devil; and however unwilling the world may be to acknowledge this principle, it is evident from the multifarious creeds and notions

---

110. *T&S* 3, no. 11 (1 April 1842): 744.

notions concerning this matter that they understand nothing of this principle, and it is equally as plain that without a divine communication they must remain in ignorance. The world always mistook false prophets for true ones, and those that were sent of God, they considered to be false prophets and hence they killed, stoned, punished and imprisoned the true prophets, and these had to hide themselves "in deserts and dens, and caves of the earth," and though the most honorable men of the earth, they banished them from their society as vagabonds, whilst they cherished, honored and supported knaves, vagabonds, hypocrites, impostors, and the basest of men.

The Gift of Discernment of Spirits

A man must have the discerning of spirits, as we before stated, to understand these things, and how is he to obtain this gift if there are no gifts of the Spirit? And how can these gifts be obtained without revelation? "Christ ascended into heaven, and gave gifts to men; and he gave some Apostles, and some Prophets, and some Evangelists, and some Pastors and Teachers." And how were Apostles, Prophets, Pastors, Teachers and Evangelists chosen? By prophecy (revelation) and by laying on of hands—by a divine communication, and a divinely appointed ordinance—through the medium of the Priesthood, organized according to the order of God, by divine appointment. The Apostles in ancient times held the keys of this Priesthood—of the mysteries of the Kingdom of God, and consequently were enabled to unlock and unravel all things pertaining to the government of the Church, the welfare of society, the future destiny of men, and the agency, power and influence of spirits; for they could control them at pleasure, bid them depart in the name of Jesus, and detect their mischievous and mysterious operations when trying to palm themselves upon

concerning this matter, that they understand nothing of this principle, and it is equally as plain that without a divine communication they must remain in ignorance. The world always mistook false prophets for true ones, and those that were sent of God they considered to be false prophets; and hence they killed, stoned, punished and imprisoned the true prophets, and they had to hide themselves "in deserts, and dens, and caves of the earth;" and although the most honorable men of the earth, they banished them from their society as vagabonds; whilst they cherished, honored, and supported knaves, vagabonds, hypocrites, imposters and the basest of men.[111]

Times and Seasons

A man must have the discerning of spirits as we before stated to understand these things, and how is he to obtain this gift if there are no gifts of the spirit? And how can these gifts be obtained without revelation?—"Christ ascended into heaven and gave gifts to men, . . . "and he gave some apostles, and some prophets, and some evangelists, and some pastors and teachers." And how were apostles, prophets, pastors, teachers, and evangelists chosen? by "prophesy (revelation) and by laying on of hands:"—by a divine communication, and a divinely appointed ordinance—through the medium of the priesthood, organized according to **[p.745]** the order of God, by divine appointment. The apostles in ancient times held the keys of this priesthood—of the mysteries of the kingdom of God, and consequently were enabled to unlock, and unravel all things pertaining to the government of the church, the welfare of society, the future destiny of men, and the agency, power, and influence of spirits; for they could control them at pleasure, bid them depart in the name of Jesus, and detect their mischievous and mysterious operations when trying to palm themselves

---

111. *T&S* 3, no. 11 (1 April 1842): 744.

the Church in a religious garb, and militate against the interest of the Church and spread truth. We read that they "cast out devils in the name of Jesus," and when a woman possessing the spirit of divination, cried before Paul and Silas, "these are the servants of the Most High God that show unto us the way of salvation," they detected the spirit. And although she spake favorably of them, Paul commanded the spirit come out of her, and saved themselves from the opprobrium **[p.207]** that might have been heaped upon their heads, through an alliance with her, in the development of her wicked principles, which they certainly would have been charged with, if they had not rebuked the evil spirit.

upon the church in a religious garb, and militate against the interest of the church, and the spread of truth—we read that they "cast out devils in the name of Jesus," and when a woman possessing the spirit of divination cried before Paul and Silas "these are the servants of the most High God that shew unto us the way of salvation:" they detected the spirit and although she spake favorably of them. Paul commanded the spirit to come out of her, and saved themselves from the opprobrium that might have been heaped upon their heads, through an alliance with her, in the development of her wicked principles:—which they certainly would have been charged with if they had not rebuked the evil spirit.[112]

The Gift Held by the Prophets

Times and Seasons

A power similar to this existed through the medium of the Priesthood in different ages. Moses could detect the magician's power, and show that he [himself] was God's servant—he knew when he was upon the mountain (through revelation) that Israel was engaged in idolatry; he could develop the sin of Korah, Dathan and Abiram, detect witches and wizards in their proceedings, and point out the true prophets of the Lord. Joshua knew how to detect the man who had stolen the wedge of gold and the Babylonish garment. Michaiah could point out the false spirit by which the four hundred prophets were governed; and if his advice had been taken, many lives would have been spared, (2 Chronicles 18) Elijah, Elisha, Isaiah, Jeremiah, Ezekiel, and many other prophets possessed this power. Our Savior, the Apostles, and even the members of the Church were endowed with this gift, for, says Paul, (1 Corinthians 12), "To one is given the gift of tongues, to another the interpretation of tongues, to another the working of miracles, to another prophecy, to another the discerning of spirits." All these proceeded

A power similar to this existed through the medium of the priesthood in different ages. Moses could detect the magicians' power and shew that he was God's servant, he knew when he was upon the mountain (through revelation,) that Israel was engaged in idolatry; he could develope the sin of Korah, Dathan, and Abiram, detect witches and wizards in their proceedings, and point out the true prophets of the Lord. Joshua knew how to detect the man who had stolen the wedge of gold and the Babylonish garment, Michaiah could point out the false spirit by which the four hundred prophets were governed; and if his advice had been taken, many lives would have been spared. 2, Chron. xviii, 18. Elijah, Elisha, Isaiah, Jeremiah, Ezekiel and many other prophets possessed this power. Our Saviour, the apostles, and even the members of the church were endowed with this gift, for says Paul 1, Cor. xiii, "to one is given the gift of tongues, to another the interpretation of tongues, to another the working of miracles, to another prophesy, to another *the discerning of spirits,*" all these proceeded from

---

112. *T&S* 3, no. 11 (1 April 1842): 744–45.

from the same Spirit of God, and were the gifts of God. The Ephesian church were enabled by this principle, "to try those that said they were apostles, and were not, and found them liars." (Revelation 2:2.)

the same spirit of God, and were the gifts of God. The Ephesian church were enabled by this principle "to try those that said they were apostles, and were not, and found them liars." Rev. ii, 2.[113]

Difference Between Body and Spirit

Times and Seasons

In tracing the thing to the foundation, and looking at it philosophically, we shall find a very material difference between the body and the spirit; the body is supposed to be organized matter, and the spirit, by many, is thought to be immaterial, without substance. With this latter statement we should beg leave to differ, and state the spirit is a substance; that it is material, but that it is more pure, elastic and refined matter than the body; that it existed before the body, can exist in the body; and will exist separate from the body, when the body will be mouldering in the dust; and will in the resurrection be again united with it.

In tracing the thing to the foundation, and looking at it philosophically we shall find a very material difference between the body and the spirit:—the body is supposed to be organized matter, and the spirit by many is thought to be immaterial, without substance. With this latter statement we should beg leave to differ—and state that spirit is a substance; that it is material, but that it is more pure, elastic, and refined matter than the body;— that it existed before the body, can exist in the body, and will exist separate from the body, when the body will be mouldering in the dust; and will in the resurrection be again united with it.[114]

Spirits Eternal

Times and Seasons

[p.208] Without attempting to describe this mysterious connection, and the laws that govern the body and the spirit of man, their relationship to each other, and the design of God in relation to the human body and spirit, I would just remark, that the spirits of men are eternal, that they are governed by the same Priesthood that Abraham, Melchizedek, and the Apostles were: that they are organized according to that Priesthood which is everlasting, "without beginning of days or end of years,"—that they all move in their respective spheres, and are governed by the law of God; that when they appear upon the earth they are in a probationary state, and are preparing, if righteous, for a future and greater glory; that the spirits of good men cannot interfere with the wicked beyond their

Without attempting to describe this mysterious connexion and the laws that govern the body and spirit of man; their relationship to each other, and the design of God in relation to the human body and spirit, I would just remark that the spirits of men are eternal, that they are governed by the same priesthood that Abraham, Melchizedec, and the apostles were; that they are organized according to that priesthood which is everlasting, "without beginning of days or end of years"—that they all move in their respective spheres, and are governed by the law of God;—that when they appear upon the earth they are in a probationary state, and are preparing if righteous, for a future and a greater glory:—that the spirits of good men cannot interfere with the wicked

---

113. *T&S* 3, no. 11 (1 April 1842): 745.
114. *T&S* 3, no. 11 (1 April 1842): 745.

Wicked Spirits Restricted in Power

It would seem also, that wicked spirits have their bounds, limits, and laws by which they are governed or controlled, and know their future destiny; hence, those that were in the maniac said to our Savior, "Art thou come to torment us before the time?" and when Satan presented himself before the Lord, among the sons of God, he said that he came "from going to and fro in the earth, and from wandering up and down in it;" and he is emphatically called the prince of the power of the air; and, it is very evident that they possess a power that none but those who have the Priesthood can control, as we have before adverted to, in the case of the sons of Sceva.

Having said so much upon the general principles, without referring to the peculiar situation, power, and influence of the magicians of Egypt, the wizards and witches of the Jews, the oracles of the heathen, their necromancers, soothsayers, and astrologers, the maniacs or those possessed of devils in the Apostles' days, we will notice, and try to detect (so far as we have the Scriptures for our aid) some few instances of the development of false spirits in more modern times, and in this our day.

Times and Seasons

It would seem also that wicked spirits have their bounds, limits, and laws by which they are governed or controlled, and know their future destiny; hence those that were in the maniac said to our Saviour, "art thou come to torment us before the time:"— and when Satan presented himself before the Lord among the sons of God, he said that he came "from going to and fro in the earth, and from wandering up and down in it;" and he is emphatically called the prince of the power of the air; and it is very evident that they possess a power that none but those who have the priesthood can control, as we have before adverted to in the case of the sons of Sceva.

Having said so much upon general principles without referring to the peculiar situation, power, and influence of, the magicians of Egypt, the wizards, and witches of the Jews, the oracles of the Heathen; their necromancers, soothsayers, and astrologers; the maniacs or those possessed of devils in the apostles' days, we will notice and try to detect (so far as we have the scriptures for our aid) some few instances of the developement of false spirits in more modern times, and in this our day.[116]

False Prophets

The "French Prophets" were possessed of a spirit that deceived; they existed in Vivaris and Dauphany, in great num[p.209]bers in the year 1688; there were many boys and girls from seven to twenty-five; they had strange fits, as

Times and Seasons

The "French Prophets," were possessed of a spirit that deceived; they existed in Vivaris, and Dauphiny in great numbers in the year 1688, there were many boys, and girls, from seven to twenty five; they had strange fits as in

---

115. *T&S* 3, no. 11 (1 April 1842): 745.
116. *T&S* 3, no. 11 (1 April 1842): 745.

in tremblings and faintings, which made them stretch out their legs and arms, as in a swoon; they remained awhile in trances, and coming out of them, uttered all that came in their mouths. [see Buck's Theological Dictionary]

Now God never had any prophets that acted in this way; there was nothing indecorous in the proceeding of the Lord's prophets in any age; neither had the apostles nor prophets in the apostles' day anything of this kind. Paul says, "Ye may all prophesy, one by one; and if anything be revealed to another let the first hold his peace, for the spirit of the prophets is subject to the prophets;" but here we find that the prophets are subject to the spirit, and falling down, have twitchings, tumblings, and faintings through the influence of that spirit, being entirely under its control. Paul says, "Let everything be done decently and in order," but here we find the greatest disorder and indecency in the conduct of both men and women, as above described. The same rule would apply to the fallings, twitchings, swoonings, shaking, and trances of many of our modern revivalists.

Johanna Southcott professed to be a prophetess, and wrote a book of prophecies in 1804, she became the founder of a people that are still extant. She was to bring forth, in a place appointed, a son, that was to be the Messiah, which thing has failed. Independent of this, however, where do we read of a woman that was the founder of a church, in the word of God? Paul told the women in his day, "To keep silence in the church, and that if they wished to know anything to ask their husbands at home;" he would not suffer a woman "to rule, or to usurp authority in the church;" but here we find a woman the founder of a church, the revelator and guide, the Alpha and Omega, contrary to all acknowledged rule, principle, and order.

Jemimah Wilkinson was another prophetess that figured largely in America, in the last century. She stated that she was taken sick and died, and that her soul went to heaven, where it still continues. Soon after, her body was reanimated with the spirit and power of Christ, upon which she set up as a public teacher, and declared that she had an immediate revelation. Now the Scriptures positively assert that "Christ is the first fruit, afterwards those that are Christ's at His **[p.210]** coming, then cometh the end." But Jemimah, according to her testimony, died, and rose again before the time mentioned in the Scriptures. The idea of her soul being in heaven while her body was [living] on earth, is also preposterous. When God breathed into man's nostrils, he became a living soul, before that he did not live, and when that was taken away his body died; and so did our Savior when the spirit left the body, nor did His body live until His spirit returned in the power of His resurrection. But Mrs. Wilkinson's soul [life] was in heaven, and her body without the soul [or life] on earth, living [without the soul, or] without life!

Jemimah Wilkinson, was another prophetess that figured largely in America in the last century. She stated that she was taken sick and died, and that her soul went to heaven where it still continues. Soon after her body was reanimated with the spirit and power of Christ. upon which she set up as a public teacher and declared she had an immediate revelation. Now the Scriptures positively assert that "Christ is the first fruit, afterwards *those that are Christs at his coming*; then cometh the end;" But Jemimah, according to her testimony died, and rose again before the time mentioned in the scriptures. The idea of her soul being in heaven while her body was on earth is also preposterous; when God breathed into man's nostrils he became a living soul, before that he did not live, and when that was taken away his body died; and so did our Saviour when the spirit left the body; nor did his body live until his spirit returned in the power of his resurrection: but Mrs. Wilkinson's soul, [life] was in heaven and her body without the soul [or life] on earth, living [without the soul, or] without life.[117]

Irvingites

Times and Seasons

The Irvingites are a people that have counterfeited the truth, perhaps the nearest of any of our modern sectarians. They commenced about ten years ago in the city of London, in England; they have churches formed in various parts of England and Scotland, and some few in Upper Canada. Mr. Irving, their founder, was a learned and talented minister of the Church of Scotland, he was a great logician, and a powerful orator, but withal wild and enthusiastic in his views. Moving in the higher circles, and possessing talent and zeal, placed him in a situation to become a conspicuous character, and to raise up a society similar to that which is called after his name.

The Irvingites, are a people that have counterfeited the truth perhaps the nearest of any of our modern sectarians; they commenced about ten years ago in the city of London in England. They have churches formed in various parts of England and Scotland and some few in Upper Canada. Mr. Irving their founder was a learned and talented minister of the church of Scotland; he was a great logician, and a powerful orator; but withal wild and enthusiastic in his views. Moving in the higher circles, and possessing talent and zeal, placed him in a situation to become a conspicuous character, and to raise up a society similar to that which is called after his name.

---

117. *T&S* 3, no. 11 (1 April 1842): 745–46.

The Irvingites have apostles, prophets, pastors, teachers, evangelists, and angels. They profess to have the gift of tongues, and the interpretation of tongues, and, in some few instances, to have the gift of healing.

The first prophetic spirit that was manifested was in some Misses Campbell that Mr. Irving met with, while on a journey in Scotland; they had [what is termed among their sect] "utterances," which were evidently of a supernatural agency. Mr. Irving, falling into the common error of considering all supernatural manifestations to be of God, took them to London with him, and introduced them into his church.

They were there honored as the prophetesses of God, and when they spoke, Mr. Irving or any of his ministers had to keep silence. They were peculiarly wrought upon before the congregation, and had strange utterances, uttered with an unnatural, shrill voice, and with thrilling intonations they frequently made use of a few broken, unconnected sentences, **[p.211]** that were ambiguous, incoherent, and incomprehensible; at other times they were more clearly understood. They would frequently cry out, "There is iniquity! There is iniquity!" And Mr. Irving has been led, under the influence of this charge, to fall down upon his knees before the public congregation, and to confess his sin, not knowing whether he had sinned, nor wherein, nor whether the thing referred to him or somebody else. During these operations, the bodies of the persons speaking were powerfully wrought upon, their countenances were distorted, they had frequent twitchings in their hands, and the whole system was powerfully convulsed at intervals: they sometimes, however, (it is supposed) spoke in correct tongues, and had true interpretations.

Under the influence of this spirit the church was organized by these women; apostles, prophets, etc., were soon called, and a systematic order of things introduced, as above mentioned. A Mr.

Baxter (afterwards one of their principal prophets) upon going into one of their meetings, says, "I saw a power manifested, and thought that was the power of God, and asked that it might fall upon me, and it did so, and I began to prophesy." Eight or nine years ago they had about sixty preachers going through the streets of London, testifying that London was to be the place where the "two witnesses" spoken of by John, were to prophesy; that (they the church and the spirit were the witnesses, and that at the end of three years and a half there was to be an earthquake and great destruction, and our Savior was to come. Their apostles were collected together at the appointed time watching the event, but Jesus did not come, and the prophecy was then ambiguously explained away. They frequently had signs given them by the spirit to prove to them that what was manifested to them should take place. Mr. Baxter related an impression that he had concerning a child. It was manifested to him that he should visit the child, and lay hands upon it, and that it should be healed; and to prove to him that this was of God, he should meet his brother in a certain place, who should speak unto him certain words. His brother addressed him precisely in the way and manner that the manifestation designated. The sign took place, but when he laid his hands upon the child it did not recover. I cannot vouch for the authority of the last statement, as Mr. Baxter at that time had left the Irvingites, but it is in accord[p.212]ance with many of their proceedings, and the thing never has been attempted to be denied.

Baxter (afterwards one of the principal prophets) upon going into one of their meetings, says, I saw a power manifested and thought that it was the power of God, and asked that it might fall upon me; it did so and I began to prophesy. Eight or nine years ago, they had about sixty preachers going through the streets of London, testifying that London was to be the place where the 'two witnesses,' spoken of by John was to prophesy: that (they) 'the church and the spirit' were the witnesses, and that at the end of three years and a half there was to be an earthquake and great destruction, and our saviour was to come. Their apostles were collected together at the appointed time watching the event; but Jesus did not come, and the prophesy was then ambiguously explained away. They frequently had signs given them by the spirit, to prove to them that what was manifested to them should take place. Mr. Baxter related an impression that he had concerning a child. It was manifested to him that he should visit the child, and lay hands upon it, and that it should be healed:— and to prove to him that this was of God, he should meet his brother in a certain place who should speak unto him certain words; his brother addressed him precisely in the way and manner that the manifestation designated; the sign took place,—but when he laid his hands on the child it did not recover. I cannot vouch for the authority of the last statement as Mr. Baxter at that time had left the Irvingites, but it is in accordance with many of their proceedings, and the thing never has been attempted to be denied.[118]

All This Is Wrong

Times and Seasons

It may be asked, where is there anything in all this that is wrong?

It may be asked where is there any thing in all this that is wrong?

First. The church was organized by women, and God placed in the Church (first apostles, secondarily prophets,) and not first women;

1st. The church was organized by women and 'God placed in the church *first apostles, secondarily prophets:*' and not *first women*; but Mr.

---

118. *T&S* 3, no. 11 (1 April 1842): 746.

but Mr. Irving placed in his church first women (secondarily apostles,) and the church was founded and organized by them. A woman has no right to found or organize a church—God never sent them to do it.

Second. Those women would speak in the midst of a meeting, and rebuke Mr. Irving or any of the church. Now the Scripture positively says, "Thou shalt not rebuke an Elder, but entreat him as a father;" not only this, but they frequently accused the brethren, thus placing themselves in the seat of Satan, who is emphatically called "the accuser of the brethren."

Third. Mr. Baxter received the spirit on asking for it, without attending to the ordinances, and began to prophesy, whereas the scriptural way of attaining the gift of the Holy Ghost is by baptism, and by laying on of hands.

Fourth. As we have stated in regard to others, the spirit of the prophets is subject to the prophets; but those prophets were subject to the spirits, the spirits controlling their bodies at pleasure.

But it may be asked how Mr. Baxter could get a sign from a second person? To this we would answer, that Mr. Baxter's brother was under the influence of the same spirit as himself, and being subject to that spirit he could be easily made to speak to Mr. Baxter whatever the spirit should dictate; but there was not power in the spirit to heal the child.

Satan May Give Manifestations in Tongues

Again it may be asked, how it was that they could speak in tongues if they were of the devil. We would answer that they could be made to speak in another tongue, as well as their own, as they were under the control of that spirit, and the devil can tempt the Hottentot,

---

Irving placed in his church first women; *secondarily apostles*; and the church was founded and organized by them. A woman has no right to found or organize a church; God never sent them to do it.

2nd. Those women would speak in the midst of a meeting and rebuke Mr. Irving, or any of the church: now the scripture positively says, 'thou shalt not rebuke an elder, but entreat him as a father;' not only this but they frequent[p.747]ly *accused* the brethren, thus placing themselves in the seat of satan who is emphatically called 'the *accuser* of the brethren.'

3rd. Mr. Baxter received the spirit on asking for it without attending to the ordinances, and began to prophecy, whereas the scriptural way of attaining the gift of the Holy Ghost is by baptism, and by laying on of hands.

4th. As we have stated in regard to others the spirit of the prophets, are subject to the prophets; but those prophets were subject to the spirits; the spirit controlling their bodies at pleasure.

But it may be asked how Mr. Baxter could get a sign from a second person! To this we would answer that Mr. Baxter's brother was under the influence of the same spirit as himself; and being subject to that spirit, he could be easily made to speak to Mr. Baxter whatever the spirit should dictate; but there was not power in the spirit to heal the child.[119]

Times and Seasons

Again it may be asked how it was that they could speak in tongues if they were of the devil? we would answer that they could be made to speak in another tongue as well as in their own as they were under the control of that spirit, and the devil can tempt the

---

119. *T&S* 3, no. 11 (1 April 1842): 746–47.

the Turk, the Jew, or any other nation; and if these men were under the influence of his spirit, [p.213] they of course could speak Hebrew, Latin, Greek, Italian, Dutch, or any other language that the devil knew.

Some will say, "try the spirits" by the word. "Every spirit that confesseth that Jesus Christ is come in the flesh is of God, and every spirit that confesseth not that Jesus Christ is come in the flesh is not of God." 1 John 4:2, 3. One of the Irvingites once quoted this passage whilst under the influence of a spirit, and then said, "I confess that Jesus Christ is come in the flesh." And yet these prophecies failed, their Messiah did not come; and the great things spoken of by them have fallen to the ground. What is the matter here? Did not the Apostle speak the truth? Certainly he did—but he spoke to a people who were under the penalty of death, the moment they embraced Christianity; and no one without a knowledge of the fact would confess it, and expose themselves to death, and this was consequently given as a criterion to the church or churches to which John wrote. But the devil on a certain occasion cried out, "I know thee, who thou art, the Holy One of God!" Here was a frank acknowledgment under other circumstances that "Jesus had come in the flesh." On another occasion the devil said, "Paul we know, and Jesus we know"—of course, "come in the flesh." No man nor sect of men without the regular constituted authorities, the Priesthood and discerning of spirits, can tell true from false spirits. This power they possessed in the Apostles' day, but it has departed from the world for ages.

Hottentot, the Turk, the Jew, or any other nation; and if these men were under the influence of his spirit they of course could speak Hebrew, Latin, Greek, Italian, Dutch, or any other Language that the devil knew.

Some will say 'try the spirits' by the word. 'Every spirit that confesseth that Jesus Christ is come in the flesh is of God: and every spirit that confesseth not that Jesus Christ is come in the flesh is not of God.' John iv, 2, 3. One of the Irvingites once quoted this passage whilst under the influence of a spirit, and then said, 'I confess that Jesus Christ is come in the flesh.' And yet these prophecies failed, their Messiah did not come; and the great things spoken of by them have fallen to the ground. What is the matter here? did not the apostle speak the truth? certainly he did—but he spoke to a people who were under the penalty of death, the moment they embraced christianity; and no one without a knowledge of the fact would confess it and expose themselves to death: and this was consequently given as a criterion to the church or churches to which John wrote. But the devil on a certain occasion cried out, 'I know thee who thou art the '*Holy one of God*' Here was a frank acknowledgement under other circumstances,—that '*Jesus* had come in the flesh.' On another occasion the devil said 'Paul we know, and *Jesus we know*;' of course come in *the flesh*. No man nor set of men without the regular constituted authorities, the priesthood and discerning of spirits can tell true, from false spirits. This power they possessed in the apostles' day, but it has departed from the world for ages.[120]

False Spirits in the Church

Times and Seasons

The Church of Jesus Christ of Latter-day Saints has also had its false spirits; and as it is made up of all those different sects professing every variety of opinion, and having been un-

The church of Jesus Christ of Latter-Day Saints have also had their false spirits; and as it is made up of all those different sects professing every variety of opinion, and having been

---

120. *T&S* 3, no. 11 (1 April 1842): 747.

der the influence of so many kinds of spirits, it is not to be wondered at if there should be found among us false spirits.

Soon after the Gospel was established in Kirtland, and during the absence of the authorities of the Church, many false spirits were introduced, many strange visions were seen, and wild, enthusiastic notions were entertained; men ran out of doors under the influence of this spirit, and some of them got upon the stumps of trees and shouted, and all kinds of extravagances were entered into by them; one man pursued a ball that he said he saw flying in the air, until he came to a precipice, when he jumped into the top of a tree, which saved his life; [p.214] and many ridiculous things were entered into, calculated to bring disgrace upon the Church of God, to cause the Spirit of God to be withdrawn, and to uproot and destroy those glorious principles which had been developed for the salvation of the human family. But when the authorities returned, the spirit was made manifest, those members that were exercised with it were tried for their fellowship, and those that would not repent and forsake it were cut off.

At a subsequent period a Shaker spirit was on the point of being introduced, and at another time the Methodist and Presbyterian falling down power, but the spirit was rebuked and put down, and those who would not submit to rule and good order were disfellowshiped. We have also had brethren and sisters who have had the gift of tongues falsely; they would speak in a muttering, unnatural voice, and their bodies be distorted like the Irvingites before alluded to; whereas, there is nothing unnatural in the Spirit of God. A circumstance of this kind took place in Upper Canada, but was rebuked by the presiding Elder; another, a woman near the same place, professed to have the discerning spirits, and began to accuse another sister of things that she was not guilty of, which she said she knew was so by the spirit, but was afterwards proven to be false; she placed herself in the capacity of the "accuser of the brethren," and no person through the discerning of spirits can bring a charge against another, they must be proven guilty by positive evidence, or they stand clear.

There have also been ministering angels in the Church which were of Satan appearing as an angel of light. A sister in the state of New York had a vision, who said it was told her that if she would go to a certain place in the woods, and angel would appear to her. She went at the appointed time, and saw a glorious personage descending, arrayed in white, with sandy colored hair; he commenced and told her to fear God, and said that her husband was called to do great things, but that he must not go more than one hundred miles from home, or he would not return; whereas God had called him to go to the ends of the earth, and he has since been more than one thousand miles from home, and is yet alive. Many true things were spoken by this personage, and many things that were false. How, it may be asked, was this known to be a bad angel? By the color of his hair; that is one of the signs that he can **[p.215]** be known by, and by his contradicting a former revelation.

We have also had brethren and sisters who have written revelations, and who have started forward to lead this Church. Such was a young boy in Kirtland, Isaac Russell, of Missouri, and Gladden Bishop, and Oliver Olney of Nauvoo. The boy is now living with his parents who have submitted to the laws of the Church. Mr. Russell stayed in Far West, from whence he was to go to the Rocky Mountains, led by three Nephites; but the Nephites never came, and his friends forsook him, all but some of the blood relations, who have since been nearly destroyed by the mob. Mr. Bishop was tried by the High Council, his papers examined, condemned and burned, and he cut off the Church. He acknowledged the justice

it,—but was afterwards proven to be false—she placed herself in the capacity of the 'accuser of the brethren'—and no person through the discerning of spirits can bring a charge against another, they must be proven guilty by positive evidence, or they stand clear.

There have also been ministering angels in the church which were of satan appearing as an angel of light:—A sister in the State of New York had a vision who said it was told her that if she would go to a certain place in the woods an angel would appear to her,—she went at the appointed time and saw a glorious personage descending arrayed in white, with sandy colored hair; he commenced and told her to fear God and said that her husband was called to do great things, but that he must not go more than one hundred miles from home or he would not return; whereas God had called him to go to the ends of the earth; and he has since been more than one thousand miles from home, and is yet alive. Many true things were spoken by this personage and many things that were false.—How it may be asked was this known to be a bad angel? by the color of his hair; that is one of the signs that he can be known by, and by his contradicting a former revelation.

We have also had brethren and sisters that have had written revelations, and have started forward to lead this church. Such was a young boy in Kirtland —Isaac Russell of Mo. and Gladdon Bishop, and Oliver Olney of Nauvoo. The boy is now living with his parents, who have submitted to the laws of the church Mr. Russell stayed in Far West, from whence he was to go to the Rocky mountains, led by three Nephites, but the Nephites never came **[p.748]** and his friends forsook him all but some of his blood relations, who have since been nearly destroyed by the mob. Mr. Bishop was tried by the high council his papers examined, condemned, and burned, and he cut off from the church; he acknowledged the justice of the decision, and said "that he now saw his error, for if the had been governed by the revelations given before, he might have known that no man was to write revelations for the Church, but Joseph Smith," and begged to be prayed for, and forgiven by the brethren. Mr. Olney has also been tried by the High Council and disfellowshiped, because he would not have his writings tested by the word of God; evidently proving that he loves darkness rather than light, because his deeds are evil.

of the decision and said "that he now saw his error; for if he had been governed by the revelations given before he might have known that no man was to write revelations for the church but Joseph Smith," and begged to be prayed for and forgiven by the brethren. Mr. Olney has also been tried by the high council, and disfellowshiped because he would not have his writings tested by the word of God; evidently proving that he loves darkness rather than light because his deeds are evil. Ed.[121]

Remarks of the Prophet at the Funeral of Ephraim Marks

Wilford Woodruff Journal

The Saints in Nauvoo assembled at the house of President Marks, at an early hour in the morning, to pay their last respects to the body of Ephraim Marks, son of President William Marks, who died on the evening of the 7th. A large procession formed and walked to the Grove, where a numerous congregation had assembled. President Joseph Smith spoke upon the occasion with much feeling and interest. Among his remarks he said, "It is a very solemn and awful time. I never felt more solemn; it calls to mind the death of my oldest brother, Alvin, who died in New York, and my youngest brother, Don Carlos Smith, who died in Nauvoo. It has been hard for me to live on earth and see these young men upon whom we have leaned for support and comfort taken from us in the midst of their youth. Yes, it has been hard to be reconciled to these things. I

The Saints in Nauvoo assembled at[122] the house of president Marks at an early hour in the morning to pay their last respeck to the Body of Ephraim Marks Son of President Marks who died on the evening of the 7[th][.] A large procession[123] formed two by two & walked to the grove[.] a large concorse assembled[124] President Joseph Smith spoke upon the occasion with much feelings & interest. among his remarks he said it is a vary solumn & awful time[.] I never felt more solumn[.] it calles to mind the death of my oldest Brother who died in New York & my Youngest Brother Carloss Smith who died in Nauvoo. It has been hard for me to live on earth & see those young men upon whome we have leaned upon as a support & comfort taken from us in the midst of their youth. yes it has been hard to be reconciled to these things[.] I have sometimes felt

---

121. *T&S* 3, no. 11 (1 April 1842): 747–48. Although Joseph Smith was the editor of the *Times and Seasons* at this time, some scholars have questioned whether he is the actual author of this article. (See, for example, Bruce A. Van Orden, *We'll Sing and We'll Shout—The Life and Times of W. W. Phelps* [Religious Studies Center, Brigham Young University, 2018], 342n49, 406; Jonathan Nevill, *Brought to Light*, 2nd ed. [Digital Legend, 2016], 41–81.) However, owing to the fact that Joseph began teaching members of the Twelve about the importance of discerning spirits at least as early as 27 June 1839, it may be best to be tentative about suggestions that Joseph was not the primary source for the teachings in this particular discourse. See Appendix D herein for information regarding the possibility that some individuals wrote and published articles in the Prophet's name.

122. This is one of many places where Wilford Woodruff wrote one word but then erased the original and changed the word to something else. In each case, we have followed his final wording.

123. The "r" and "c" were added to the misspelled word after the fact.

124. Discourse, 9 April 1842, *WWJ*, 1:501.

have sometimes thought that I should have felt more reconciled to have been called away myself if it had been the will of God; yet I know we ought to be still and know it is of God, [p.216] and be reconciled to His will; all is right. It will be but a short time before we shall all in like manner be called: it may be the case with me as well as you. Some have supposed that Brother Joseph could not die; but this is a mistake; it is true there have been times when I have had the promise of my life to accomplish such and such things, but, having now accomplished those things, I have not at present any lease of my life, I am as liable to die as other men.

I can say in my heart, that I have not done anything against Ephraim Marks that I am sorry for, and I would ask any of his companions if they have anything against him that they are sorry for, or that they would not like to meet and answer for at the bar of God, if so, let it prove as a warning to all to deal justly before God, and with all mankind, then we shall be clear in the day of judgment.

When we lose a near and dear friend, upon whom we have set our hearts, it should be a caution unto us not to set our affections too firmly upon others, knowing that they in like manner be taken from us. Our affections should be placed upon God and His work, more intensely than upon our fellow beings. (April 9, 1842.) DHC 4:587.

that I should have felt more reconciled to have been called myself if it could have been the will of God. yet I know we ought to be still & know it is of God & be reconciled[.] all is right[.] it will be but a short time before we shall all in like manner be called. [p.502] It may be the case with me as well as you[.] Some has supposed that Br Joseph could not die but this is a mistake[.] it is true their has been times when I have had the promise of my life to accomplish such & such things, but having accomplish those things I have not at present any lease of my life & am as liable to die as other men

I Can say in my heart that I have not done any thing against Ephraim Marks that I am Sorry for & I would ask any of his Companions if they have done any thing against him that they are Sorry for or that they would not like to meet at the bar of God[.] if so let it prove as a warning to all men to deal justly before God & with all men[.] then we shall be clear in the day of judgment

When we loose a near & dear friend upon whom we have set our hearts we can never feel the same afterwards knowing that if we set our hearts upon others they may in like manner be taken from us[.] President Smith made many other interesting remarks & left it for President Rigdon to Close[125]

Synopsis of Remarks of the Prophet—Reproof of all Wickedness

Wilford Woodruff Journal

Joseph the Seer arose in the power of God; reproved and rebuked wickedness before the people, in the name of the Lord God. He wished to say a few words to suit the condition of the general mass, and then said: I shall speak with authority of the Priesthood in the name of the Lord God, which shall prove a savor of life unto life, or of death unto death. Notwithstanding

Then Joseph the Seer arose in the power of God reproved & rebuked wickedness before the people in the name of the Lord God[.] He wished to say a few words to suit the Condition of the general mass[.] And I shall speak with authority of the priesthood in the name of the Lord God, which shall prove a savior of life unto life or of death unto death. Notwithstanding this

---

125. Discourse, 9 April 1842, *WWJ*, 1:501–2. See also *JSP, D9*, 346–347; *WJS*, 112–13.

this congregation profess to be Saints, yet I stand in the midst of all [kinds of] characters and classes of men. If you wish to go where God is, you must be like God, or possess the principles which God possesses, for if we are not drawing towards God in principles, we are going from Him and drawing towards the devil.

Yes, I am standing in the midst of all kinds of people.

Search your hearts, and see if you are like God. I have searched mine, and feel to repent of all my sins.

Congregation profess to be Saints yet I stand in the midst of all characters and classes of men[.] If you wish to go whare God is you must be like God or possess the principles which God possesses[.] for if we are not drawing towards God in principle we are going from him & drawing towards the devil.

yes I am standing in the midst of all kinds of people[.]

Search your hearts & see if you are like God. I have searched mine & feel to repent of all my sins.[126]

Men are Saved Through Obedience to Knowledge

Wilford Woodruff Journal

[p.217] We have thieves among us, adulterers, liars, hypocrites. If God should speak from heaven, he would command you not to steal, not to commit adultery, not to covet, nor deceive, but be faithful over a few things. As far as we degenerate from god, we descend to the devil and lose knowledge, and without knowledge we cannot be saved, and while our hearts are filled with evil, we are studying evil, there is no room in our hearts for good, or studying good. Is not God good? Then you be good; if He is faithful, then you be faithful. Add to your faith virtue, to virtue knowledge, and seek for every good thing.

The Church must be cleansed, and I proclaim against all iniquity. A man is saved no faster than he gets knowledge, for if he does not get knowledge, he will be brought into captivity by some evil power in the other world, as evil spirits will have more knowledge, and consequently more power than many men who are on the earth. Hence it needs revelation to assist us, and give us knowledge of the things of God.

What is the reason that the Priests of the day do not get revelation? They ask only to

we have theives among us Adulterers, liars, hypocritts. if God should speak from Heaven he would Command you not to Steal, not to commit Adultery, nor to covet, nor deceive but be faithful over a few things [p.503] As far as we degenerate from God we desend to the devil & looses knowledge & without knowledge we cannot be saved & while our hearts are filled with evil & we are studying evil their is no room in our hearts for good or studying good. is not God good. Yes[.] then you be good. if he is faithful then you be faithful[.] Add to your faith virtue, to virtue knowledge, & seek for evry good thing[.]

The Church must be cleansed & I proclaim against all iniquity. A man is saved no faster than he gets knowledge for if he does not get knowledge he will be brought into Captivity by some evil power in the other world as evil spirits will have more knowledge & Consequently more power than many men who are on the earth. hence it needs Revelation to assist us & give us knowledge of the things of God.

what is the reason that the Priest of the day do not get Revelation[?] They ask ownly to

---

126. 10 April 1842, *WWJ*, 1:502. See also *JSP, D9*, 351; *WJS*, 113.

consume it upon their lusts. Their hearts are corrupt, and they cloak their iniquity by saying there are no more revelations. But if any revelations are given of God, they are universally opposed by the priests and Christendom at large; for they reveal their wickedness and abominations. (April 10, 1842.) DHC 4:588.

Baptism for the Dead

The great designs of God in relation to the salvation of the human family, are very little understood by the professedly wise and intelligent generation in which we live. Various and conflicting are the opinions of men concerning the plan of salvation, the requisitions of the Almighty, the necessary preparations for heaven, the state and condition of departed spirits, and the happiness or misery that is consequent upon the practice of righteousness and iniquity according to their several notions of virtue and vice.

The Mussulman condemns the heathen, the Jew, and the Christian, and the whole world of mankind that reject his Koran, as infidels, and consigns the whole of them to perdition.

The Jew believes that the whole world that rejects his faith and are not circumcised, are Gentile dogs, and will be damned. The heathen is equally as tenacious about his principles, and the Christian consigns all to perdition who cannot bow to his creed, and submit to his *ipse dixit*.

Justice of the Great Lawgiver

But while one portion of the human race is judging and condemning the other without mercy, the Great Parent of the universe looks upon the whole human family with a

---

127. 10 April 1842, *WWJ*, 1:502–3. See also *JSP, D9*, 351–52; *WJS*, 113–14.
128. *T&S* 3, no. 12 (15 April 1842): 759.

fatherly care and paternal regard; He views them as His offspring, and without any of those contracted feelings that influence the children of men, causes "His sun to rise on the evil and on the good, and sendeth rain on the just and on the unjust." He holds the reins of judgment in His hands; He is a wise Lawgiver, and will judge all men, not according to the narrow, contracted notions of men, but, "according to the deeds done in the body whether they be good or evil," or whether these deeds were done in England, America, Spain, Turkey, or India. He will judge them, "not according to what they have not, but according to what they have," those who have lived without law, will be judged without law, and those who have a law, will be judged by that law. We need not doubt the wisdom and intelligence of the Great Jehovah; He will award judgment or mercy to all nations according to their several deserts, their means of obtaining intelligence, the laws by which they are governed, the facilities afforded them of obtaining correct information, and His inscrutable designs in relation to the human family; and when the designs of God shall be made manifest, and the curtain of futurity be withdrawn, we shall all of us eventually have to confess that the Judge of all the earth has done right.

fatherly care, and paternal regard; he views them as his offspring; and without any of those contracted feelings that influence the children of men, causes "*his sun* to rise on the evil and the good; and sends *his rain* on the just and unjust." He holds the reigns of judgment in his hands; he is a wise lawgiver, and will judge all men, [not according to the narrow contracted notions of men, but] "according to the deeds done in the body whether they be good or evil;" or whether these deeds were done in England, America, Spain, Turkey India: he will judge them "not according to what they have not, but according to what they have;" those who have lived without law, will be judged without law, and those who have a law, will be judged by that law; we need not doubt the wisdom and intelligence of the great Jehovah, he will award judgment or mercy to all nations according to their several deserts, their means of obtaining intelligence; the facilities afforded them of obtaining correct information; and his inscrutable designs in relation to the human family: and when the designs of God shall be made manifest, and the curtain of futurity be withdrawn, we shall all of us eventually have to confess, that the Judge of all the earth has done right.[129]

Christ Preached to Spirits in Prison

The situation of the Christian nations after death, is a subject that has called forth all the wisdom and talent of the philosopher and the divine, and it is an opinion which is generally received, that the destiny of man is irretrievably fixed at his death, and that he is made either eternally happy, or **[p.219]** eternally miserable; that if a man dies without a knowledge of God, he must be eternally damned, without any mitigation of his punishment, alleviation of his pain, or the most latent hope

Times and Seasons
The situation of the Christian nations after death is a subject that has called forth all the wisdom, and talent of the philosopher, and the divine; and it is an opinion which is generally received, that the destiny of man is irretrievably fixed at his death; and that he is made either eternally happy, or eternally miserable' that if a man dies without a knowledge of God, he must be eternally damned; without any mitigation of his punishment, alleviation of his pain or the most latent hope

---

129. *T&S* 3, no. 12 (15 April 1842): 759.

of a deliverance while endless ages shall roll along. However orthodox this principle may be, we shall find that it is at variance with the testimony of Holy Writ, for our Savior says, that all manner of sin and blasphemy shall be forgiven men wherewith they shall blaspheme; but the blasphemy against the Holy Ghost shall not be forgiven, neither in this world, nor in the world to come, evidently showing that there are sins which may be forgiven in the world to come, although the sin of blasphemy [against the Holy Ghost] cannot be forgiven. Peter, also, in speaking concerning our Savior, says, that "He went and preached unto the spirits in prison, which sometime were disobedient, when once the long-suffering of God waited in the days of Noah" (1 Peter 3:19, 20). Here then we have an account of our Savior preaching to the spirits in prison, to spirits that had been imprisoned from the days of Noah; and what did He preach to them? That they were to stay there? Certainly not! Let His own declaration testify. "He hath sent me to heal the brokenhearted, to preach deliverance to the captives, and recovering of sight of the blind, to set at liberty them that are bruised." (Luke 4:18.) Isaiah has it—"To bring out the prisoners from the prison, and them that sit in darkness from the prison house." (Isaiah 13:7.) It is very evident from this that he not only went to preach to them, but to deliver, or bring them out of the prison house. Isaiah, in testifying concerning the calamities that will overtake the inhabitants of the earth, says, "The earth shall reel to and fro like a drunkard, and shall be removed like a cottage; and the transgression thereof shall be heavy upon it; and it shall fall and not rise again. And it shall come to pass in that day, that the Lord shall punish the host of the high ones that are on high, and the kings of the earth upon the earth. And they shall be gathered together, as prisoners are gathered in the pit, and shall be shut up in the prison, and after many days shall they be visited." Thus we find that God will deal with all the human

of a deliverance while endless ages shall roll along. However orthodox this principle may be, we shall find that it is at variance with the testimony of holy writ; for our Saviour says that all manner of sin, and blasphemy shall be forgiven men wherewith they shall blaspheme; but the blasphemy against the Holy Ghost shall not be forgiven, neither in *this world*, nor in the *world to come*; evidently shewing that there are sins which may be forgiven in the *world to come*; although the sin of blasphemy cannot be forgiven. Peter also in speaking concerning our Saviour says, that "he went and preached unto **[p.760]** spirits in prison, which sometimes were disobedient, when once the long suffering of God waited in the days of Noah." 1 Pet. iii, 19, 20. Here then we have an account of our Saviour preaching to the spirits in prison; to spirits that had been imprisoned from the days of Noah; and what did he preach to them? that they were to stay there? certainly not; let his own declaration testify; "he hath sent me to heal the broken hearted, to preach deliverance to the captives, and recovering of sight to the blind, to set at liberty them that are bruised"—Luke iv, 18, Isaiah has it;—"*To bring out the prisoners from the prison*, and them that sit in darkness *from the prison house.*" Is. xlii, 7 It is very evident from this that he not only went to preach to them, but to deliver, or bring them *out of the prison house.* Isaiah in testifying concerning the calamities that will overtake the inhabitants of the earth says, "The earth shall reel to and fro like a drunkard; and shall be removed like a cottage; and the transgressions thereof shall be heavy upon it; and it shall fall and not rise again. And it shall come to pass in that day; that the Lord shall punish the hosts of the high ones that are on high, and the kings of the earth upon the earth. And they shall be gathered together as prisoners are gathered in the pit, and shall be *shut up in prison*, and after many days *shall they be visited.*" Thus we find that God will deal with all the human family equally, and that as the antediluvians had their day of visitation, so will those characters referred to by Isaiah, have their time of visitation and deliverance; after having been many days in prison.

family equally; and that as the antediluvians had their day of visitation; so will those characters referred to by Isaiah, have their time of visitation, and deliverance, after having been many days in prison.[130]

Plan of Salvation Before the World Was

Times and Seasons

[p.220] The great Jehovah contemplated the whole of the events connected with the earth, pertaining to the plan of salvation, before it rolled into existence, or ever "the morning stars sang together" for joy; the past, the present, and the future were and are, with Him, one eternal "now;" He knew of the fall of Adam, the iniquities of the antediluvians, of the depth of iniquity that would be connected with the human family, their weakness and strength, their power and glory, apostasies, their crimes, their righteousness and iniquity; He comprehended the fall of man, and his redemption; He knew the plan of salvation and pointed it out; He was acquainted with the situation of all nations and with their destiny; He ordered all things according to the council of His own will; He knows the situation of both the living and the dead, and has made ample provision for their redemption, according to their several circumstances, and the laws of the kingdom of God, whether in this world, or in the world to come.

The great Jehovah contemplated the whole of the events connected with the earth, pertaining to the plan of salvation, before it rolled into existence, or ever the "morning stars sung together for joy," the past, the present and the future, were, and are with him one eternal now; he knew of the fall of Adam, the iniquities of the antedeluvians, of the depth of iniquity that would be connected with the human family; their weakness and strength, their power and glory, apostacies, their crimes, their righteousness, and iniquity; he comprehended the fall of man, and their redemption; he knew the plan of salvation, and pointed it out; he was acquainted with the situation of all nations; and with their destiny; he ordered all things according to the council of his *own* will, he knows the situation of both the living, and the dead, and has made ample provision for their redemption, according to their several circumstances, and the laws of the kingdom of God, whether in this world, or in the world to come.[131]

False Doctrines in the World

Times and Seasons

The idea that some men form of the justice, judgment, and mercy of God, is too foolish for an intelligent man to think of: for instance, it is common for many of our orthodox preachers to suppose that if a man is not what they call converted, if he dies in that state he must remain eternally in hell without any hope. Infinite years in torment must he spend, and never, never, never have an end;

The idea that some men form of the justice, judgment, and mercy of God, is too foolish for an intelligent man to think of; for instance it is common for many of our orthodox preachers to suppose, that if a man is not what they call converted, if he dies in that state, he must remain eternally in hell without any hope:— "Infinite years in torment must he spend;" "And never, never, never, have an end." And

---

130. *T&S* 3, no. 12 (15 April 1842): 759–60.
131. *T&S* 3, no. 12 (15 April 1842): 760.

and yet this eternal misery is made frequently to rest upon the merest casualty. The breaking of a shoe-string, the tearing of a coat of those officiating, or the peculiar location in which a person lives, may be the means, indirectly of his damnation, or the cause of his not being saved. I will suppose a case which is not extraordinary: Two men, who have been equally wicked, who have neglected religion, are both of them taken sick at the same time; one of them has the good fortune to be visited by a praying man, and he gets converted a few minutes before he dies; the other sends for three different praying men, a tailor, a shoemaker, and a tinman; the tinman has a handle to solder to a can, the tailor has a buttonhole to work on some coat that he needed in a hurry, and the shoemaker has a patch to put on somebody's boot; **[p.221]** they none of them can go in time, the man dies, and goes to hell: one of these is exalted to Abraham's bosom, he sits down in the presence of God and enjoys eternal, uninterrupted happiness, while the other, equally as good as he, sinks to eternal damnation, irretrievable misery and hopeless despair, because a man had a boot mend, the button-hole of a coat to work, or a handle to solder on to a saucepan.

yet this eternal misery is made frequently to rest upon the merest casualty;—The breaking of a shoe string; the tearing of a coat, of those officiating; or the peculiar location in which a person lives, may be the means indirectly of his damnation: or the cause of his not being saved. I will suppose a case which is not extraordinary:—Two men who have been equally wicked, who have neglected religion, are both of them taken sick at the same time; one of them has the good fortune to be visited by a praying man, and he gets converted a few minutes before he dies; the other sends for three different praying men, a tailor, a shoemaker, and a tinman. The tinman has a handle to solder on to a can; the tailor has a button-hole to work on some coat that is needed in a hurry; and the shoemaker has a patch to put on somebody's boot; they none of them can go in time, the man dies and goes to hell: one of these is exalted to Abraham's bosom; he sits down in the presence of God, and enjoys eternal, uninterrupted happiness; while the other who was equally as good as him, sinks to eternal damnation; irretrievable misery, and hopeless despair; because a man had a boot to mend, the button hole of a coat to work, or a handle to solder on to a saucepan.[132]

Plans of Jehovah Just

Times and Seasons

The plans of Jehovah are not so unjust, the statements of holy writ so visionary, nor the plan of salvation for the human family so incompatible with common sense; at such proceedings God would frown with indignance, angels would hide their heads in shame, and every virtuous, intelligent man would recoil.

The plans of Jehovah are not so unjust; the statements of holy writ so visionary; nor the plan of salvation for the human family so incompatible with common sense; at such proceedings God would frown with indignance, angels would hide their heads in shame; and every virtuous intelligent man would recoil.

If human laws award to each man his deserts, and punish all delinquents according to their several crimes, surely the Lord will not be more cruel than man, for He is a wise legislator, and His laws are more equitable, His

If human laws award to each man his deserts, and punish all delinquents, according to their several crimes; surely the Lord will not be more cruel than man, for he is a wise legislator, and his laws are more equitable, his enactments

---

132. *T&S* 3, no. 12 (15 April 1842): 760.

enactment more just, and His decisions more perfect than those of man; and as man judges his fellow man by law, and punishes him according to the penalty of the law, so does God of heaven judge "according to the deed done in the body." To say that the heathens would be damned because they did not believe the gospel would be preposterous, and to say that the Jews would all be damned that do not believe in Jesus would be equally absurd; for "how can they believe on him of whom they have not heard, and how can they hear without a preacher, and how can he preach except he be sent;" consequently neither Jew nor heathen can be culpable for rejecting the conflicting opinions of sectarianism, nor for rejecting any testimony but that which is sent of God, for as the preacher cannot preach except he be sent, so the hearer cannot believe without he hear a "sent" preacher, and cannot be condemned for what he has not heard, and being without law, will have to be judged without law.

more just, and his decisions more perfect than those of man: and as man judges his fellow man by law, and punishes him according to the penalty of that law; so does the God of heaven judge "according to the deeds done in the body." To say that the heathen would be damned because they did not believe the gospel would be preposterous; and to say that the Jews would all be damned that do not believe in Jesus, would be equally absurd; for "how can they believe on him of whom they have not heard; and how can they hear without a preacher; and *how can he preach except he be sent;*" consequently neither Jew nor heathen, can be culpable for rejecting the conflicting opinions of sectarianism, nor for rejecting any testimony but that which is *sent* of God, for as the preacher cannot preach except he be sent, so the hearer cannot believe without he hear a sent preacher; and cannot be condemned for what he has not heard; and being without law will have to be judged without law.[133]

What of the Fathers?

Times and Seasons

When speaking about the blessings pertaining to the Gospel, and the consequences connected with disobedience to the requirements, we are frequently asked the question, what has become of our fathers? Will they all be damned for not obeying [p.222] the Gospel, when they never heard it? Certainly not. But they will possess the same privilege that we here enjoy, through the medium of the everlasting Priesthood, which not only administers on earth, but also in heaven, and the wise dispensations of the great Jehovah; hence those characters referred to by Isaiah will be visited by the Priesthood, and come out of their prison upon the same principle as those who were disobedient in the days of Noah were visited by our Savior [who possessed the everlasting Melchizedek Priesthood] and had the Gospel preached to

When speaking about the blessings pertaining to the gospel, and the consequences connected with disobedience to its requirements, we are frequently asked the question, what has become of our Fathers? will they all be damned for not obeying the gospel, when they never heard it? certainly not. But they will possess the same privilege that we here enjoy, through the medium of the *everlasting* priesthood, which not only administers on earth but in heaven, and the wise dispensations of the great Jehovah; hence those characters referred to by Isaiah will be visited by this priesthood, and come out of their prison, upon the same principle as those who were disobedient in the days of Noah, were visited by our Saviour, [who possessed the everlasting, Melchizedec priesthood,] and had the gospel preached to them, by him in [p.761] prison; and in order

---

133. *T&S* 3, no. 12 (15 April 1842): 760.

them by Him in prison; and in order that they might fulfill all the requisitions of God, living friends were baptized for their dead friends, and thus fulfilled the requirement of God, which says, "Except a man be born of water and of the Spirit, he cannot enter into the kingdom of God," they were baptized of course, not for themselves, but for their dead.

Chrysostum says that the Marchionites practiced baptism for their dead. "After a catechumen was dead, they had a living man under the bed of the deceased; then coming to the dead man, they asked him whether he would receive baptism, and he making no answer, the other answered for him, and said that he would be baptized in his stead; and so they baptized the living for the dead." The church of course at that time was degenerate, and the particular form might be incorrect, but the thing is sufficiently plain in the Scriptures, hence Paul, in speaking of the doctrine, says, "Else what shall they do which are baptized for the dead, if the dead rise not at all? Why are they then baptized for the dead?" (1 Cor. 15:29.)

that they might fulfil all the requisitions of God, their living friends were baptized for their dead friends, and thus fulfilled the requirements of God which says, "Except a man be born again of water, and of the spirit he can in no wise enter into the kingdom of heaven;" they were baptized of course, not for themselves, but for their dead.

Crysostum says that the Marchionites practiced baptism for the dead, "after a catechumen was dead they hid a living man under the bed of the deceased; then coming to the dead man they asked him whether he would receive baptism; and he making no answer, the other answered for him, and said that he would be baptized in his stead; and so they baptized the living for the dead." The church of course at that time was degenerate, and the particular form might be incorrect, but the thing is sufficiently plain in the scriptures, hence Paul in speaking of the doctrine says, "Else what shall they do who are baptized for the dead? If the dead rise not all, why are they then baptized for the dead?" 1 Cor. xv, 29.[134]

Responsibility of the Jews

Times and Seasons

Hence it was that so great a responsibility rested upon the generation in which our Savior lived, for, says he, "That upon you may come all the righteous blood shed upon the earth, from the blood of righteous Abel unto the blood of Zacharias, son of Barachias, whom ye slew between the temple and the altar. Verily I say unto you, all these things shall come upon this generation." (Matthew 23:35, 36.) Hence as they possessed greater privileges than any other generation, not only pertaining to themselves, but to their dead, their sin was greater, as they not only neglected their own salvation but **[p.223]** that of their progenitors, and hence their blood was required at their hands:

Hence it was that so great a responsibility rested upon the generation in which our Savior lived; for says he "That upon you may come all the righteous blood shed upon the earth from the blood of righteous Abel, unto the blood of Zacharias, son of Barachias whom ye slew between the temple and the altar. Verily I say unto you all these things shall come upon this generation," Matt. xxiii. 35, 36. Hence as they possessed greater privileges than any other generation, not only pertaining to themselves but to their dead, their sin was greater; as they not only neglected their own salvation but that of their progenitors, and hence their blood was required at their hands.[135]

---

134. *T&S* 3, no. 12 (15 April 1842): 760–61.
135. *T&S* 3, no. 12 (15 April 1842): 761.

Saviors on Mount Zion

Times and Seasons

And now as the great purposes of God are hastening to their accomplishment, and the things spoken of in the Prophets are fulfilling, as the kingdom of God is established on the earth, and the ancient order of things restored, the Lord has manifest to us this day and privilege, and we are commanded to be baptized for our dead, thus fulfilling the words of Obadiah, when speaking of the glory of the latter-day: "And saviors shall come up on Mount Zion to judge the remnant of Esau, and the kingdom shall be the Lord's." A view of these things reconciles the Scriptures of truth, justifies the ways of God to man, places the human family upon an equal footing, and harmonizes with every principle of righteousness, justice and truth. We will conclude with the words of Peter: "For the time past of our life may suffice us to have wrought the will of the Gentiles." "For, for this cause was the Gospel preached also to them that are dead, that they might be judged according to men in the flesh, but live according to God in the Spirit." (April 15, 1842.) DHC 4:595-599.	And now as the great purposes of God are hastening to their accomplishment and the things spoken of in the prophets are fulfilling, as the kingdom of God is established on the earth, and the ancient order of things restored, the Lord has manifested to us this duty and privilege, and we are commanded to be baptized for our dead thus fulfilling the words of Obadiah when speaking of the glory of the Latter Day. "And saviours shall come up upon Mount Zion to judge the remnant of Esau; and the kingdom shall be the Lords". A view of these things reconciles the scriptures of truth, justifies the ways of God to man; places the human family upon an equal footing, and harmonizes with every principle of righteousness, justice, and truth. We will conclude with the words of Peter: "For the time past of our life may suffice us to have wrought the will of the Gentiles" . . . . "For, for this cause was the gospel preached also to them that are dead, that they might be judged according to men in the flesh, but live according to God in the spirit."—ED.[136]

REMARKS OF THE PROPHET TO THE RELIEF SOCIETY

All Offices in Church Honorable

Relief Society Minutes

President Smith arose and called the attention of the meeting to the 12th chapter of Corinthians—"Now concerning spiritual gifts, I would not have you ignorant." Said that the passage in the third verse, which reads, "No man can say that Jesus is the Lord, but by the Holy Ghost," should be translated "no man can know that Jesus is the Lord, but by the Holy Ghost."	Prest. J. Smith arose and call'd the attention of the meeting to the 12th Chap. of 1st Cor. "Now concerning spiritual gifts" &c.— Said that the passage which reads "no man can say that Jesus is the the Christ <Lord> but by the holy ghost," should be translated, no man can know &c

---

136. *T&S* 3, no. 12 (15 April 1842): 761. Although Joseph Smith was the editor of the *Times and Seasons* at this time, some scholars have questioned whether he is the actual author of this article. See Appendix D herein for information regarding the possibility that some individuals wrote and published articles in the Prophet's name.

He continued to read the chapter, and give instructions respecting the different offices, and the necessity of every individual acting in the sphere allotted him or her, and filling the several offices to which they are appointed. He spoke of the disposition of many men to consider the lower offices in the Church dishonorable, and to look with jealous eyes upon the standing of others who are called to preside over them; that it was the folly and nonsense of the human heart for a person to be aspiring to other stations than those to which they are **[p.224]** appointed of God for them to occupy; that it was better for individuals to magnify their respective calling, and wait patiently till God shall say to them, "come up higher."

He said the reason of these remarks being made was, that some little foolish things were circulating in the society, against some sisters not doing right in laying hands on the sick. Said that if the people had common sympathies they would rejoice that the sick could be healed; that the time had not been before that these things could be in their proper order; that the Church is not fully organized, in its proper order, and cannot be, until the Temple is completed, where places will be provided for the administration of the ordinances of the Priesthood.

He continued to read the Chap. and give instructions respecting the different offices, and the necessity of every individual acting in the sphere allotted him or her; and filling the several offices to which they were appointed— Spoke of the disposition of man, to consider the lower offices in the church dishonorable and to look with jealous eyes upon the standing of others— that it was the nonsense of the human heart, for a person to be aspiring to other stations than appointed of God— that it was better for individuals to magnify their respective callings, and wait patiently till God shall say to them come up higher.

He said the reason of these remarks being made, was, that some little thing was circulating in the Society, that some persons were not going right in laying hands on the sick &c. Said if he had common sympathies, would rejoice that the sick could be heal'd: that the time had not been before, that these things could be in their proper order— that the church is not now organiz'd in its proper order, and cannot be until the Temple is completed———[137]

Gifts of the Gospel

Relief Society Minutes

President Smith continued the subject, by quoting the commission given to the ancient Apostles in Mark, 16th chapter, 15th, 16th, 17th, 18th verses, "Go ye into all the world, and preach the Gospel to every creature. He that believeth and is baptized shall be saved; but he that believeth not shall be damned. And these signs shall follow them that believe: In my name shall they cast out devils; they shall speak with new tongues; they shall take up serpents; and if they drink any deadly

Prest. Smith continued the subject by adverting to the commission **[p.55]** given to the ancient apostles "Go ye into all the world" &c.—

---

137. 28 April 1842, *RSM*, 54. See also *WWJ*, 1:520–21.

thing, it shall not hurt them; they shall lay hands on the sick, and they shall recover."

No matter who believeth, these signs, such as healing the sick, casting our devils, etc., should follow all that believe, whether male or female. He asked the Society if they could not see by this sweeping promise, that wherein they are ordained, if it is the privilege of those set apart to administer in that authority, which is conferred on them; and if the sisters should have faith to heal the sick, let all hold their tongues, and let everything roll on.

He said, if God has appointed him, and chosen him as an instrument to lead the Church, why not let him lead it through? Why stand in the way when he is appointed to do a thing? Who knows the mind of God? Does He not reveal things differently from what we expect? He remarked that he was continually rising, although he had everything bearing him down, standing in his way, and opposing; notwithstanding all this opposition, he always comes out right in the end.

Respecting females administering for the healing of the sick [p.225] he further remarked, there could be no evil in it, if God gave His sanction by healing; that there could be no more sin in any female laying hands on and praying for the sick, than in wetting the face with water; it is no sin for anybody to administer that has faith, or if the sick have faith to be healed by their administration.

He proved those that were disposed to find fault with the management of the concerns of the Church, saying God had called him to lead the Church, and he would lead it right; those that undertake to interfere will be ashamed when their own folly is made manifest; that he calculates to organize the Church in its proper order as soon as the Temple is completed.

no matter who believeth; these signs, such as healing the sick, casting out devils &c. should follow all that believe whether male or female. He ask'd the Society if they could not see by this sweeping stroke, that wherein they are ordaind, it is the privilege of those set apart to administer in that authority which is confer'd on them— and if the sisters should have faith to heal the sick, let all hold their tongues, and let every thing roll on.

He said, if God has appointed him, and chosen him as an instrument to lead the church, why not let him lead it through? Why stand in the way, when he is appointed to do a thing? Who knows the mind of God? Does he not reveal things differently from what we expect?— He remark'd that he was continually rising— altho' he had every thing bearing him down— standing in his way and opposing— after all he always comes out right in the end.

Respecting the female laying on hands, he further remark'd, there could be no devil in it if God gave his sanction by healing— that there could be no more sin in any female laying hands on the sick than in wetting the face with water— that it is no sin for any body to do it that has faith, or if the sick has faith to be heal'd by the administration.

He reprov'd those that were dispos'd to find fault with the management of concerns— saying if he undertook to lead the church he would lead it right— that he calculates to organize the church in proper order &c.[138]

---

138. 28 April 1842, *RSM*, 54–55. See also *WWJ*, 1:521.

Aspiring Men

Relief Society Minutes

President Smith continued by speaking of the difficulties he had to surmount ever since the commencement of the work, in consequence of aspiring men. "Great big Elders," as he called them, who caused him much trouble; to whom he had taught the things of the kingdom in private councils, they would then go forth into the world and proclaim the things he had taught them, as their own revelations; said the same aspiring disposition will be in this Society, and must be guarded against; that every person should stand, and act in the place appointed, and thus sanctify the Society and get it pure. He said he had been trampled under foot by aspiring Elders, for all were infected with that spirit; for instance, John E. Page and others had been aspiring; they could not be exalted, but must run away as though the care and authority of the Church were vested with them. He said he had a subtle devil to deal with, and could only curb him by being humble.	President Smith continued by speaking of the difficulties he had to surmount ever since the commencement of the work in consequence of aspiring men, "great big Elders" as he call'd them, who had caused him much trouble, whom he had taught in the private counsel; and they would go forth into the world and ploclaim [proclaim] the things he had taught them; as their own revelations— said the same aspiring disposition will be in this Society, and **[p.56]** must be guarded against— that every person should stand and act in the place appointed, and thus sanctify the Society and get it pure—He said he had been trampled underfoot by aspiring Elders, for all were infected with that spirit, for instance P.[arley] Pratt O.[rson] Pratt, O.[rson] Hyde and J.[ohn] Page had been aspiring— they could not be exalted but must run away as tho' the care and authority of the church were vested with them— he said we had a subtle devil to deal with, and could only curb him by being humble.[139]

The Prophet's Intimation of His Death

Relief Society Minutes

As he had this opportunity, he was going to instruct the ladies of this Society, and point out the way for them to conduct themselves, that they might act according to the will of God; that he did not know that he should have many opportunities of teaching them, as they were going to be left to themselves; they would not long have him to instruct them; that the Church would not have his instructions long, and the world would not be troubled with him a great while, and would not have his teachings [in person].	He said as he had this opportunity, he was going to instruct the Society and point out the way for them to conduct, that they might act according to the will of God— that he did not know as he should have many opportunities of teaching them— that they were going to be left to themselves,— they would not long have him to instruct them— that the church would not have his instruction long, and the world would not be troubled with him a great while, and would not have his teachings—

---

139. 28 April 1842, *RSM*, 55–56. See also *WWJ*, 1:521.

[p.226] He spoke of delivering the keys of the Priesthood to the Church, and said that the faithful members of the Relief Society should receive them with their husbands, that the Saints whose integrity has been tried and proved faithful, might know how to ask the Lord and receive an answer; for according to his prayers, God had appointed him elsewhere.

He exhorted the sisters always to concentrate their faith and prayers for, and place confidence in their husbands, whom God has appointed for them to honor, and in those faithful men whom God has placed at the head of the Church to lead His people; that we should arm and sustain them with our prayers; for the keys of the kingdom are about to be given to them, that they may be able to detect everything false; as well as to all the Elders who shall prove their integrity in due season.

He spoke of delivering the keys to this Society and to the church— that according to his prayers God had appointed him elsewhere

[p.57] He exhorted the sisters always to concentrate their faith and prayers for, and place confidence, in those whom God has appointed to honor, whom God has plac'd at the head to lead— that we should arm them with our prayers.— that the keys of the kingdom are about to be given to them, that they may be able to detect every thing false— as well as to the Elders.[140]

Corruption Not to Be Condoned

Relief Society Minutes

He said if one member becomes corrupt, and you know it, you must immediately put it away, or it will either injure or destroy the whole body. The sympathies of the heads of the Church have induced them to bear a long time with those who were corrupt until they are obliged to cut them off, lest all become contaminated; you must put down iniquity, and by your good examples, stimulate the Elders to good works; if you do right, there is no danger of your going too fast.

He said he did not care how fast we run in the path of virtue; resist evil, and there is no danger; God, men, and angels will not condemn those that resist everything that is evil, and devils cannot; as well might the devil seek to dethrone Jehovah, as overthrow an innocent soul that resists everything which is evil.

He said if one member becomes corrupt and you know it; you must immediately put it away. The sympathies of the heads of the church have induc'd them to bear with those that were corrupt; in consequence of which all become contaminated— you must put down iniquity and by your good example provoke the Elders to good works— if you do right, no danger of going too fast:

he said he did not care how fast we run in the path of virtue. Resist evil and there is no danger. God, men, angels, and devils can't condemn those that resist every thing that is evil— as well might the devil seek to dethrone Jehovah, as that soul that resists every thing that is evil.

---

140. 28 April 1842, *RSM*, 56–57. See also *WWJ*, 1:521–22.

This is a charitable Society, and according to your natures; it is natural for females to have feelings of charity and benevolence. You are now placed in a situation in which you can act according to those sympathies which God has planted in your bosoms.

Relief Society Minutes

The charitable Society— this is according to your natures— it is natural for females to have feelings of charity— you are now plac'd in a situatio[n] where you can act according to those sympathies which God has planted in your bosoms.[141]

To Dwell with God, the Soul Must Be Pure

Relief Society Minutes

If you live up to these principles, how great and glorious will be your reward in the celestial kingdom! If you live up to your privileges, the angels cannot be restrained from **[p.227]** being your associates. Females, if they are pure and innocent, can come in the presence of God; for what is more pleasing to God than innocence; you must be innocent, or you cannot come up before God; if we would come before God, we must keep ourselves pure, as He is pure.

If you live up to these principles how great and glorious!— if you live up to your privilege, the angels cannot be restrain'd from being your associates— females, if they are pure and innocent can come into the presence of God; for what is more pleasing to God than innocence; you must be innocent **[p.58]** or you cannot come up before God. If ye \<we\> would come before God let us be pure ourselves.[142]

The Devil's Power to Deceive

Relief Society Minutes

The devil has great power to deceive; he will so transform things as to make one gape at those who are doing the will of God. You need not be teasing your husbands because of their deeds, but let the weight of your innocence, kindness and affection be felt, which is more mighty than a millstone hung about the neck; not war, not jangle, not contradiction, or dispute, but meekness, love, purity—these are the things that should magnify you in the eyes of all good men. Achan [see Joshua 7] must be brought to light, iniquity must be purged out from the midst of the Saints; then the veil will be rent, and the blessings of heaven will flow down— they will roll down like the Mississippi river.

The devil has great power— he will so transform things as to make one gape at those who are doing the will of God— You need not be tearing men for their deeds, but let the weight of innocence be felt; which is more mighty than a millstone hung about the neck. Not war, not jangle, not contradiction, but meekness, love, purity, these are the things that should magnify us.— Achan must be brought to light— iniquity must be purged out— <u>then</u> the vail will be rent and the blessings of heaven will flow down— they will roll down like the Missisippi river.

If this Society listen to the counsel of the Almighty, through the heads of the Church, they shall have power to command queens in their midst.

This Society shall have power to command Queens in their midst—

---

141. 28 April 1842, *RSM*, 57. See also *WWJ*, 1:522.
142. 28 April 1842, *RSM*, 57–58. See also *WWJ*, 1:522.

I now deliver it as a prophecy, if the inhabitants of this state, with the people of the surrounding country, will turn unto the Lord with all their hearts, ten years will not roll around before the kings and queens of the earth will come unto Zion, and pay their respects to the leaders of this people; they shall come with their millions, and shall contribute of their abundance for the relief of the poor, and the building up and beautifying of Zion.

I now deliver it as a prophecy that before ten years shall roll round, the queens of the earth shall come and pay their respects to this Society— they shall come with their millions and shall contribute of their abundance for the relief of the poor— If you will be pure, nothing can hinder.

After this instruction, you will be responsible for your own sins; it is a desirable honor that you should so walk before our heavenly Father as to save yourselves; we are all responsible to God for the manner we improve the light and wisdom given by our Lord to enable us to save ourselves.

After this instruction, you will be responsible for your own sins. It is an honor to save ~~yourself~~ yourselves— all are responsible to save themselves.[143]

Beware of Self-Righteousness

Relief Society Minutes

President Smith continued reading from the above-mentioned chapter, and to give instructions respecting the order of God, as established in the Church, saying everyone should aspire only to magnify his own office and calling.

Pres.^t Smith, after reading from the above mentioned Chapter, continued to give instruction respecting the order of God, as established in the church; saying every one should aspire only to magnify his own office &c.——

[p.228] He then commenced reading the 13th chapter—"Though I speak with the tongues of men and angels, and have not charity, I am become as sounding brass, or a tinkling cymbal;" and said, don't be limited in your views with regard to your neighbor's virtue, but beware of self-righteousness, and be limited in the estimate of your own virtues, and not think yourselves more righteous than others; you must enlarge your souls towards each other, if you would do like Jesus, and carry your fellow-creatures to Abraham's bosom. He said he had manifested long-suffering, forbearance and patience towards the Church, and also to his enemies; and we must bear with each

He then commenc'd reading the 13th chapter, "Though I speak with the tongues of men" &c;

and said don't be limited in your views with regard to your neighbors' virtues, but be limited towards your own virtues; and not think yourselves more righteous than others; you must enlarge your souls toward others if yould [you would?] do like Jesus, and carry your fellow creatures to Abram's bosom. He said he had manifested long suffering and we must do so too——

---

143. 28 April 1842, *RSM*, 58. See also *WWJ*, 1:522.

other's failings, as an indulgent parent bears with the foibles of his children.

President Smith the read the 2nd verse— "Though I have the gift of prophecy, and understand all mysteries, and all knowledge; and though I have all faith, so that I could remove mountains, and have not charity, I am nothing." He then said, though a man should become mighty, do great things, overturn mountains, perform mighty works, and should then turn from his high station to do evil, to eat and drink with the drunken, all his former deeds would not save him, but he would go to destruction! As you increase in innocence and virtue, as you increase in goodness, let your hearts expand, let them be enlarged towards others; you must be long-suffering, and bear with the faults and errors of mankind.	Pres$^{t.}$ Smith then read, "Though I have the gift of prophecy" &c. He then said, though one should become mighty— do great things— overturn mountains &c and should then turn to eat and drink with the drunken; all former deeds would not save him— but he would go to destruction! As you increase in innocence and virtue, as you increase in goodness, let your hearts expand— let them be enlarged towards others— you must be longsuff'ring and bear with the faults and errors of mankind.
How precious are the souls of men! The female part of the community are apt to be contracted in their views. You must not be contracted, but you must be liberal in your feelings. Let this Society teach women how to behave towards their husbands, to treat them with mildness and affection. When a man is borne down with trouble, when he is perplexed with care and difficulty, if he can meet a smile instead of an argument or a murmur—if he can meet with mildness, it will calm down his soul and soothe his feelings; when the mind is going to despair, it needs a solace of affection and kindness.	How precious are the souls of men!— The female part of community are apt to be contracted in their views. You must not be contracted, but you must be liberal in your feelings. **[p.59]** Let this Society teach how to act towards husbands to treat them with mildness and affection. When a man is borne down with trouble— when he is perplex'd; if he can meet a smile, an argument— if he can meet with mildness, it will calm down his soul and soothe his feelings. When the mind is going to despair, it needs a solace.[144]

Instruction Through the Priesthood

Relief Society Minutes

You will receive instructions through the order of the Priesthood which God has established, through the medium of those appointed to lead, guide and direct the affairs of the Church in this last dispensation; and I now turn the key in **[p.229]** your behalf in the name of the Lord, and this Society shall	This Society is to get instruction thro' the order which God has established— thro' the medium of those appointed to lead— and I now turn the key to you in the name of God and this Society shall rejoice and knowledge and intelligence shall flow down from this time— this is the beginning of better days, to this Society

---

144. 28 April 1842, *RSM*, 58–59. See also *WWJ*, 1:522–23.

rejoice, and knowledge and intelligence shall flow down from this time henceforth; this is the beginning of better days to the poor and needy, who shall be made to rejoice and pour forth blessings on your heads.

When you go home, never give a cross or unkind word to your husbands, but let kindness, charity and love crown your works henceforward; don't envy the finery and fleeting show of sinners, for they are in a miserable situation; but as far as you can, have mercy on them, for in a short time God will destroy them, if they will not repent and turn unto him.

When you go home never give a cross word, but let kindness, charity and love, crown your works henceforward. Don't envy sinners— have mercy on them, God will destroy them.—

Let your labors be mostly confined to those around you, in the circle of your own acquaintance, as far as knowledge is concerned, it may extend to all the world; but your administering should be confined to the circle of your immediate acquaintance, and more especially to the members of the Relief Society. Those ordained to preside over and lead you, are authorized to appoint the different officers, as the circumstances shall require.

Let your labors be confin'd mostly to those around you in your own circle; as far as knowledge is concerned, it may extend to all the world, but your administrations, should be confin'd to the circle of your immediate acquaintance, and more especially to the members of the Society. Those ordain'd to lead the Society, are authoriz'd to appoint to different offices as the circumstances shall require.[145]

The Gift of Tongues

Relief Society Minutes

If you have a matter to reveal, let it be in your own tongue; do not indulge too much in the exercise of the gift of tongues, or the devil will take advantage of the innocent and unwary. You may speak in tongues for your own comfort, but I lay this down for a rule, that if anything is taught by the gift of tongues, it is not to be received for doctrine.

If any have a matter to reveal, let it be in your own tongue. Do not indulge too much in the gift of tongues, or the devil will take advantage of the innocent. You may speak in tongues for your comfort but I lay this down for a rule that if any thing is is taught by the gift of tongues, it is not to be received for doctrine.

President Smith then gave instruction respecting the propriety of females administering to the sick by the prayer of faith, the laying on of hands, or the anointing with oil; and said it was according to revelation that the sick should be nursed with herbs and mild food, and not by the hand of an enemy. Who are

Pres.^{t.} S. then offered instruction respecting the propriety of females administering to the sick by the laying on of hands— said it was according to revelation &c.

---

145. 28 April 1842, *RSM*, 59. See also *WWJ*, 1:523.

better qualified to administer than our faithful and zealous sisters, whose hearts are full of faith, tenderness, sympathy and compassion. No one. Said he was never placed in similar circumstances before, and never had given the same instruction; and closed his instructions by expressing his heartfelt satisfaction in improving this opportunity.

said he never was plac'd in similar circumstances, and never had given the same instruction. He clos'd his instructions by expressing his satisfaction in improving the opportunity. [p.61[146]]

The Spirit of the Lord was poured out in a very powerful manner, never to be forgotten by those present on this interesting occasion. (April 28, 1842.) DHC 4:602-607.

The spirit of the Lord was pour'd out in a very powerful manner, never to be forgotten by those present on that interesting occasion.[147]

THE TEMPLE

Diligence of the Saints in Building the Temple

Times and Seasons

This noble edifice is progressing with great rapidity; strenuous exertions are being made on every hand to facilitate its erection, and materials of all kinds are in a great state of forwardness, and by next fall we expect to see the building enclosed; if not the top stone raised with "shouting of grace—grace unto it." There have been frequently, during the winter, as many as one hundred hands quarrying rock, while at the same time multitudes of others have been engaged in hauling, and in other kinds of labor.

This noble edifice is progressing with great rapidity; strenuous exertions are being made on every hand to facilitate its erection, and materials of all kinds are in a great state of forwardness, and by next fall we expect to see the building enclosed; if not the top stone raised with "shouting of grace—grace, unto it." There have been frequently, during the winter, as many as one hundred hands quarrying rock, while at the same time multitudes of others have been engaged in hauling, and in other kinds of labor.

A company was formed last fall to go up to the pine country to purchase mills, and prepared and saw lumber for the Temple and the Nauvoo House, and the reports from them are very favorable: another company has started, this last week, to take their place and to relieve those that are already there: on their return they are to bring a very large raft of lumber, for the use of the above-named houses.

A company was formed last fall to go up to the pine country to purchase mills, and prepare and saw lumber for the Temple, and the Nauvoo House, and the reports from them are very favorable; another company has started this last week, to take their place, and to relieve those that are already there; on their return they are to bring a very large raft of lumber for the use of the above named houses.

While the busy multitudes have thus been engaged in their several vocations performing

While the busy multitudes have thus been engaged in their several avocations performing

---

146. Page 60 contains a photograph.
147. 28 April 1842, *RSM*, 59, 61. See also *WWJ*, 1:523.

their labor, and working one-tenth of their time, others have not been less forward in bringing in their tithings and consecrations for the same great object. Never since the foundation of this Church was laid, have we seen manifested a greater willingness to comply with the requisitions of Jehovah, a more ardent desire to do the will of God, more strenuous exertions used, or greater sacrifices made than there have been since the Lord said, "Let the Temple be built by the tithing of my people." It seemed as though the spirit of enterprise, philanthropy and obedience rested simultaneously upon old and young, and brethren and sisters, boys and girls, and even strangers, who were not in the Church, united with an unprecedented liberality in the accomplishment of this great work; nor could the widow, in many instances, be prevented, out of her scanty pittance from throwing in her two mites.

We feel at this time to tender to all, old and young, both in the Church and out of it, our unfeigned thanks for their unprecedented liberality, kindness, diligence, and obedience which they have so opportunely manifested on the present occasion. Not that we are personally or individually benefitted **[p.231]** in a pecuniary point of view, but when the brethren, as in this instance, show a unity of purpose and design, and all put their shoulder to the wheel, our care, labor, toil and anxiety is materially diminished, our yoke is made easy and our burden is light.

The Cause of God a Common Cause

The cause of God is one common cause, in which the Saints are alike all interested; we are all members of the one common body, and all partake of the same spirit, and are baptized into one baptism and possess alike the same glorious hope. The advancement of the cause of God and the building up of Zion is as much

---

148. *T&S* 3, no. 13 (2 May 1842): 775–76.

one man's business as another's. The only difference is, that one is called to fulfill one duty, and another another duty; "but if one member suffers, all the members suffer with it, and if one member in honored all the rest rejoice with it, and the eye cannot say to the ear, I have no need of thee, nor the head to the foot, I have no need of thee;" party feelings, separate interests, exclusive designs should be lost sight of in the one common cause, in the interest of the whole.

as much one man's business as another. The only difference is that one is called to fulfil one duty and another another duty; "but if one member suffers, all the members suffer with it, and if one member is honored all the rest rejoice with it, and the eye cannot say to the ear I have no need of thee, nor the head to the foot I have no need of thee; party feelings, separate interests, exclusive designs should be lost sight off in the one common cause, in the interest of the whole.[149]

All Things to Be Gathered in One

Times and Seasons

The building up of Zion is a cause that has interested the people of God in every age; it is a theme upon which prophets, priests and kings have dwelt with peculiar delight; they have looked forward with joyful anticipation to the day in which we live; and fired with heavenly and joyful anticipations they have sung and written and prophesied of this our day; but they died without the sight; we are the favored people that God has made choice of to bring about the Latter-day glory; it is left for us to see, participate in and help to roll forward the Latter-day glory, "the dispensation of the fulness of times, when God will gather together all things that are in heaven, and all things that are upon the earth," "even in one," when the Saints of God will be gathered in one from every nation, and kindred, and people, and tongue, when the Jews will be gathered together into one, the wicked will also be gathered together to be destroyed, as spoken of by the prophets; the Spirit of God will also dwell with His people, and be withdrawn from the rest of the nations, and all things whether in heaven or **[p.232]** on earth will be in one, even in Christ. The heavenly Priesthood will unite with the earthly, to bring about those great purposes; and whilst we are thus united in one common cause, to roll forth the kingdom of God, the heavenly

The building up of Zion is a cause that has interested the people of God in every age; it is a theme upon which prophets, priests, and kings have dwelt with peculiar delight; they have looked forward with joyful anticipation to the day in which we live; and fired with heavenly and joyful anticipations they have sung, and wrote, and prophesied of this our day;—but they died without the sight; we are the favored people that God has made choice of to bring about the Latter Day glory; it is left for us to see, participate in, and help to roll forward the Latter Day glory; "the dispensation of the fulness of times, when God will gather together all things that are in heaven, and all things that are upon the earth, even in one," when the saints of God will be gathered in one from every nation, and kindred, and people, and tongue, when the Jews will be gathered together into one, the wicked will also be gathered together to be destroyed, as spoken of by the prophets; the spirit of God will also dwell with his people, and be withdrawn from the rest of the nations, and all things whether in heaven or on earth will be in one, even in Christ. The heavenly priesthood will unite with the earthly, to bring about those great purposes; and whilst we are thus united in the one common cause to roll forth the kingdom of God, the Heavenly

---

149. *T&S* 3, no. 13 (2 May 1842): 776.

Priesthood are not idle spectators, the Spirit of God will be showered down from above, and it will dwell in our midst. The blessings of the Most High will rest upon our tabernacles, and our name will be handed down to future ages; our children will rise up and call us blessed; and generations yet unborn will dwell with peculiar delight upon the scenes that we have passed through, the privations that we have endured; the untiring zeal that we have manifested; the all but insurmountable difficulties that we have overcome in laying the foundation of a work that brought about the glory and blessing which they will realize; a work that God and angels have contemplated with delight for generations past; that fired the souls of the ancient patriarchs and prophets; a work that is destined to bring about the destruction of the powers of darkness, the renovation of the earth, the glory of God, and the salvation of the human family. (May 2, 1842.) DHC 4:608-610.

Priesthood are not idle spectators; the Spirit of God will be showered down from above, it will dwell in our midst. The blessings of the Most High will rest upon our tabernacles, and our name will be handed down to future ages; our children will rise up and call us blessed; and generations yet unborn will dwell with peculiar delight upon the scenes that we have passed through, the privations that we have endured; the untiring zeal that we have manifested; the insurmountable difficulties that we have overcome in laying the foundation of a work that brought about the glory and blessings which they will realize; a work that God and angels have contemplated with delight, for generations past; that fired the souls of the ancient patriarchs and prophets—a work that is destined to bring about the destruction of the powers of darkness, the renovation of the earth, the glory of God, and the salvation of the human family.—[Ed.[150]

A Catacomb of Mummies found in Kentucky

Times and Seasons

Had Mr. Ash in his researches consulted the Book of Mormon his problem would have been solved, and he would have found no difficulty in accounting for the mummies being found in the above mentioned case. The Book of Mormon gives an account of a number of the descendants of Israel coming to this continent; and it is well known that the art of embalming was known among the

Had Mr. Ash in his researches consulted the Book of Mormon his problem would have been solved, and he would have found no difficulty in accounting for the mummies being found in the above mentioned case.[151] The Book of Mormon gives an account of a number of the descendants of Israel coming to this continent; and it is well known that the art of embalming was known among the Hebrews,

---

150. *T&S* 3, no. 13 (2 May 1842): 776. While it isn't clear whether Joseph wrote this, some historians think that—at the very least—he may have approved it.

151. Preceding this section in the *Times and Seasons* is the following explanatory section—not included in the original *TPJS*: "Lexington, in Kentucky, stands nearly on the site of an ancient town, which was of great extent and magnificence, as is amply evinced by the wide range of its circumvalliatory works, and the quantity of ground it once occupied. There was connected with the antiquities of this place, a catacomb, formed in the bowels of the limestone rock, about fifteen feet below the surface of the earth, adjacent to the town of Lexington. . . .[F]igures were found to be mummies, preserved by the art of embalming, to as great a state of perfection as was known among the ancient Egyptians. . . . On this subject Mr. Ash has the following reflections: 'How these bodies were embalmed, how long preserved, by what nations, and from what people descended, no opinion can be formed, nor any calculation made, but what must result from speculative fancy and wild conjecture.'" *T&S* 3, no. 13 (2 May 1842): 781.

Hebrews, as well as among the Egyptians, although, perhaps, not so generally among the former, as among the latter people; and their method of embalming also might be different from that of the Egyptians. Jacob and Joseph were no doubt embalmed in the manner of the Egyptians, as they died in that country. (Gen. 50:2, 3, 26.) When our Savior was crucified his hasty burial obliged them only to wrap his body in linen with a hundred pounds of myrrh, aloes, and similar spices, (part of the ingredients of embalming) given by Nicodemus for the purpose; but Mary and other holy women had prepared ointment and spices for embalming it. (Matt. 27:59; Luke 23:56; John 19:39, 40.)

This art was no doubt transmitted from Jerusalem to this continent, by the before mentioned emigrants, which accounts for this finding of the mummies, and at the same time in another strong evidence of the authenticity of the Book of Mormon. (May 2, 1842.) T&S 3:781-782.

---

152. *T&S* 3, no. 13 (2 May 1842): 781–82.

SECTION FIVE

1842–1843

SECTION FIVE

Highest Order of Priesthood Revealed

Joseph Smith's History

[p.237] Wednesday, 4.—I spent the day in the upper part of the store, that is in my private office * * * in council with General James Adams, of Springfield, Patriarch Hyrum Smith, Bishops Newel K. Whitney and George Miller, and President Brigham Young and Elders Heber C. Kimball and Willard Richards, instructing them in the principles and order of the Priesthood, attending to washings, anointings, endowments and the communication of keys pertaining to the Aaronic Priesthood, and so on to the highest order of the Melchizedek Priesthood, setting forth the order pertaining to the Ancient of Days, and all those plans and principles by which any one is enabled to secure the fullness of those blessing which have been prepared for the Church of the Firstborn,

Wednesday 4 In council in the Presidents & General offices with Judge [James] Adams. Hyram [Hyrum] Smith Newel K. Whitney. William Marks, Wm Law. George Miller. Brigham Young. Heber C. Kimball & Willard Richards. [illegible] & giving certain instructions concerning the priesthood. [illegible] &c on the Aronic Priesthood to the first [illegible] continueing through the day.[1]

---

1. 4 May 1842, *JSP, J2*, 53–54. This stunted journal entry is the earliest source for this statement. However, Joseph Fielding Smith chose to draw on History, C-1, 1328–29 (which was compiled after the Prophet's death). That fleshed-out account reads as follows: "Wednesday 4 I spent the day in the upper part of the Store (I.E.) in my private office (so called, because in that room I kept my sacred writings, translated ancient records, and received revelations) and in my general business office or Lodge Room (I.E. where the Masonic fraternity met occasionally for want of a better place) In Council with General James Adams, of Springfield, Patriarch Hyrum Smith, Bishops Newel K. Whitney and George Miller, —— —— and Presidents Brigham Young, Heber C. Kimball and Willard Richards, instructing them in the principles and order of the Priesthood, attending to washings, anointings, endowments and the communication of Keys pertaining to the Aaronic Priesthood, and so on to the highest order of Melchisedec Priesthood, setting forth the order pertaining to the ancient of Days, and all those plans and principles, by which any one is enabled to secure the fulness of those blessings, which have been prepared for the Church of the first born, and come up and abide in the presence of the Eloheim in the Eternal worlds. In this Council was instituted the Ancient order of things for the first time in these last days. And the communications I made to this Council were of things Spiritual, and to be received only by the Spiritual minded: and there was nothing made known to these men, but what will be made known to all <the> Saints of the last days, so soon as they are prepared to receive, and a proper place is prepared to communicate them, even to the weakest of the Saints; therefore let the Saints be diligent in building the Temple, and all houses which they have been, or shall hereafter be commanded of God to build; and wait their time with patience, in all meekness, faith and perserverance unto the end, knowing assuredly that all these things referred to, in this Counsel, are always governed by the principle of Revelation." Under this entry, the Joseph Smith Papers offers this explanatory footnote: "Richards, who participated in the events of 4 May 1842, made the brief summary of JS's daylong temple instruction in this journal entry and also prepared the following description of the new endowment, which later became part of the JS multivolume manuscript history." What followed Richard's "brief summary" was the History entry used by Joseph Fielding Smith in this part of *TPJS*.

and come up and abide in the presence of the Eloheim in the eternal worlds. In this council was instituted the ancient order of things for the first time in these last days. And the communications I made to this council were of things spiritual, and to be received only by the spiritual minded: and there was nothing made known to these men but what will be made known to all the Saints of the last days, so soon as they are prepared to receive, and a proper place is prepared to communicate them, even to the weakest of the Saints; therefore let the Saints be diligent in building the Temple, and all houses which they have been, or shall hereafter be, commanded of God to build; and wait their time with patience in all meekness, faith, perseverance unto the end, knowing assuredly that all these things referred to in this council are always governed by the principle of revelation. (May 4, 1842.) DHC 5:1-2.

ADDRESS OF THE PROPHET TO THE RELIEF SOCIETY

Beware of Excessive Zeal

President Joseph Smith read the 14th chapter of Ezekiel—said the Lord had declared by the Prophet, that the people should each one stand for himself, and depend on no man or [p.238] men in that state of corruption of the Jewish church—that righteous persons could only deliver their own souls—applied it to the present state of the Church of Jesus Christ of Latter-day Saints—said if the people departed from the Lord, they must fall—that they were depending on the Prophet, hence were darkened in their minds, in consequence of neglecting the duties devolving upon themselves, envious towards the innocent, while they afflict the virtuous with their shafts of envy.

There is another error which opens for the adversary to enter. As females possess refined feelings and sensitiveness, they are also subject to overmuch zeal, which must ever prove dangerous, and cause them to be rigid in a religious

Relief Society Minutes

Prest. J. Smith rose, read the 14th Chap. of Ezekiel— said the Lord had declar'd by the prophet that the people should each one stand for himself and depend on no man or men in that state of corruption of the Jewish church— that righteous persons could only deliver their own souls— app[l]ied it to the present state of the church of Latter-Day Saints— said if the people departed from the Lord, they must fall— that they were depending on the prophet hence were darkened in their minds from neglect of themselves— envious toward the innocent, while they afflict the virtuous with their shafts of envy.

There is another error which opens a door for the adversary to enter. As females possess refin'd feelings and sensitivenes[s], they are also subject to an overmuch zeal which must ever prove dangerous, and cause them to be rigid

The Spirit of Forgiveness

capacity—[they] should be armed with mercy, notwithstanding the iniquity among us.

Said he had been instrumental in bringing iniquity to light—it was a melancholy thought and awful that so many should place themselves under the condemnation of the devil, and going to perdition. With deep feeling he said that they are fellow mortals, we loved them once, shall we not encourage them to reformation? We have not yet forgiven them seventy times seven, as our Savior directed; perhaps we have not forgiven them once. There is now a day of salvation to such as repent and reform;—and they who repent not should be cast out from this society; yet we should woo them to return to God, lest they escape not the damnation of hell! Where there is a mountain top, there is also a valley—we should act in all things on a proper medium to every immortal spirit. Notwithstanding the unworthy are among us, the virtuous should not, from self-importance, grieve and oppress needlessly, those unfortunate ones—even these should be encouraged to hereafter live to be honored by this society, who are the best portions of the community. Said he had two things to recommend to the members of this society, to put a double watch over the tongue; no organized body can exist without this at all. All organized bodies have their peculiar evils, weaknesses and difficulties, the object is to make those not so good reform and return to the path of virtue that they may be numbered with the good, and even hold the keys of power, which will influence to virtue and goodness—should chasten and reprove, [p.239] and keep it all in silence, not even mention them again; then you will be established in power, virtue, and holiness, and the wrath of God will be turned away.

in a religious capacity— should be arm'd with mercy notwithstanding the iniquity among us.[2]

Relief Society Minutes

Said he had been instrumental in bringing it to light— melancholy and awful that so many are under the condemnation of the devil & going to perdition. With deep feeling said that they are our fellows— we lov'd them once. Shall we not encourage them to reformation? We have not forgivn them seventy times— perhaps we have not forgiven them once. There is now a day of salvation to such as repent and reform— they [p.70] should be cast out from this Society, yet we should woo them to return to God lest they escape not the damnation of hell! When there is a mountain top there also is a vally— we should act in all things an a proper medium— to every immortal spirit. Notwithstanding the unworthy are among us, the virtuous should not from self-importance grieve and oppress needlessly those unfortunate ones, even these should be encourag'd to hereafter live to be honored by this Society who are the best portions of community. Said he had two things to recommend to the Society, to put a double watch over the tongue. No organiz'd body can exist without this at all. All organiz'd bodies have their peculiar evils, weaknesses and difficulties— the object is to make those not so good, equal with the good and ever hold the keys of pow'r which will influence to virtue and goodness. Should chasten and reprove and keep in it all in silence, not even mention them again, then you will be established in power, virtue and holiness and the wrath of God will be turn'd away.[3]

---

2. 26 May 1842, *RSM*, 69. See also *WJS*, 120.
3. 26 May 1842, *RSM*, 69–70. See also *WJS*, 120–21.

Guard the Tongue

	Relief Society Minutes

I have one request to make of the President and members of the society, that you search yourselves—the tongue is an unruly member—hold your tongues about things of no moment—a little tale will set the world on fire. At this time, the truth on the guilty should not be told openly, strange as this may seem, yet this is the policy. We must use precaution in bringing sinners to justice, lest in exposing these heinous sins we draw the indignation of a Gentile world upon us (and, to their imagination, justly too). It is necessary to hold an influence in the world, and thus spare ourselves an extermination; and also accomplish our end in spreading the Gospel, or holiness, in the earth. If we were brought to desolation, the disobedience would find no help. There are some who are obedient, yet men cannot steady the ark—my arm cannot do it—God must steady it. To the iniquitous show yourselves merciful.

I am advised by some of the heads of the Church to tell the Relief Society to be virtuous, but to save the Church from desolation and the sword; beware, be still, be prudent, repent, reform, but do it in a way not to destroy all around you. I do not want to cloak iniquity—all things contrary to the will of God, should be cast from us, but don't do more hurt than good, with your tongues—be pure in heart. Jesus designs to save the people out of their sins. Said Jesus, "Ye shall do the work, which ye see me do." These are the grand key words for the society to act upon. If I were not in your midst to aid and counsel you, the devil would overcome you. I want the innocent to go free—rather spare ten iniquitous among you, than condemn one innocent one. "Fret not thyself because of evildoers." God will see to it. (May 26, 1842.) DHC 5:19-21.

One request to the Prest. and Society, that you search yourselves— the tongue is an unruly member— hold your tongues about things of no moment,— a little tale will set the world on fire. At this time the truth on the guilty should not be told openly— Strange as this may seem, yet this is policy. We must use precaution in bringing sinners to justice lest in exposing their heinous sins, we draw the indignation of a gentile world upon us (and to their imagination[n] justly too) It is necessary to hold an influence in the world and thus spare ourselves an extermination; and also accomplish our end in spreading the gospel or holiness in the earth. If we were brought to desolation, the disobedient would find no help. There are some who are obedient yet men cannot steady the ark— my arm cannot do it— God must steady it. To the iniquitous show yourselves merciful.

I am advis'd by some of the heads of the church to tell the Relief Society to be virtuous— but to save the church from desolation and the sword beware, be still, be prudent. Repent, reform but do it in a way to not destroy all around you. I do not want to cloak iniquity— All things contrary to the will of God, should be cast from us, but dont do more hurt than good with your tongues— be pure in heart— Jesus designs to save the people out of their sins. **[p.71]** Said Jesus ye shall do the work which ye see me do— These are the grand key words for the Society to act upon. If I were not in your midst to aid and council you, the devil would overcome you. I want the innocent to go free— rather spare ten iniquitous among you than than condemn one innocent one. "Fret not thyself because of evil doers." God will see to it.[4]

---

4. 26 May 1842, *RSM*, 70–71. See also *WJS*, 121.

Minutes of Meeting of the Female Relief Society, At the Grove, Nauvoo, June 9, 1842 (Reported by Miss E. R. Snow)

The Principle of Mercy

President Joseph Smith opened the meeting by prayer, and then addressed the congregation on the design of the insti[p.240]tution. Said it is no matter how fast the society increases, if all the members are virtuous; that we must be as particular with regard to the character of members now, as when the society was first started; that sometimes persons wish to crowd themselves into a society of this kind when they do not intend to pursue the ways of purity and righteousness, as if the society would be a shelter to them in their iniquity.

He said that henceforth no person shall be admitted, but by presenting regular petitions, signed by two or three members in good standing in the society, and whoever comes in must be of good report.

* * *

Said he was going to preach mercy. Suppose that Jesus Christ and holy angels should object to us on frivolous things, what would become of us? We must be merciful to one another, and overlook small things.

* * *

Christ said he came to call sinners to repentance, to save them. Christ was condemned by the self-righteous Jews because He took sinners into His society; He took them upon the principle that they repented of their sins. It is the object of this society to reform persons, not to take those that are corrupt and foster them in their wickedness; but if they repent,

Relief Society Minutes

Prest J. Smith opened the meeting by pray'r and proceeded to address the congregation on the design of the Institution— said it is no matter how fast the Society increases if all are virtuous— that we must be as particular with regard to the character of members, as when the Society first started— that sometimes persons wished to put themselves into a Society of this kind, when they do not intend to pursue the ways of purity and righteousness, as if the Society would be a shelter to them in their iniquity.

Prest. S. said that henceforth no person shall be admitted but by presenting regular petitions signed by two or three members in good standing in the Society— whoever comes in must be of good report.[5]

* * *

said he was going to preach mercy Supposing that Jesus Christ and angels should object to us on frivolous things, what would become of us? We must be merciful and overlook small things.[6]

* * *

if one member suffer all feel it— by union of feeling we obtain pow'r with God. Christ said he came to call sinners to repentance and save them. Christ was condemn'd by the righteous jews because he took sinners into his society— he took them <up>on the principle that they repented of their sins. It is the object of this Society to reform persons, not to take those that are corrupt, but if they repent we are bound to take them and by kindness sanc-

---

5. 9 June 1842, *RSM*, 77. See also *WJS*, 122–23.
6. 9 June 1842, *RSM*, 78. See also *WJS*, 123.

we are bound to take them, and by kindness sanctify and cleanse them from all unrighteousness by our influence over people as the fear of being disfellowshiped by so goodly a society as this.

* * *

Nothing is so much calculated to lead people to forsake sin as to take them by the hand, and watch over them with tenderness. When persons manifest the least kindness and love to me, O what power it has over my mind, while the opposite course has a tendency to harrow up all the harsh feelings and depress the human mind.

tify and cleanse from all unrighteousness, by our influence in watching over them— nothing will have such influence over people, as the fear of being disfellowship'd by so goodly a Society as this.[7]

* * *

Nothing is so much calculated to lead people to forsake sin as to take them by the hand and watch over them with tenderness. When persons manifest the least kindness and love to me, O what pow'r it has over my mind, while the opposite course has a tendency to harrow up all the harsh feelings and depress the human mind.[8]

Satan Retards the Human Mind

Relief Society Minutes

It is one evidence that men are unacquainted with the principles of godliness to behold the contraction of affectionate feelings and lack of charity in the world. The power and glory of godliness is spread out on a broad principle to throw out the mantle of charity. God does not look on sin with allow[p.241]ance, but when men have sinned, there must be allowance made for them.

It is one evidence that men are unacquainted with the principle of godliness, to behold the contraction of feeling and lack of charity. The pow'r and glory of Godliness is spread out on a broad principle to throw out the mantle of charity. God does not look on sin with allowance, but when men have sin'd there must be allowance made for them.

All the religious world is boasting of righteousness; it is the doctrine of the devil to retard the human mind, and hinder our progress, by filling us with self-righteousness. The nearer we get to our heavenly Father, the more we are disposed to look with compassion on perishing souls; we feel that we want to take them upon our shoulders, and cast their sins behind our backs. My talk is intended for all this society; if you would have God have mercy on you, have mercy on one another.

* * *

All the religious world is boasting of righteousness— tis the doctrine of the devil to retard the human mind and retard our progress, by filling us with selfrighteousness— The nearer we get to our heavenly Father, the more are we dispos'd to look with compassion on perishing souls— to take them upon our shoulders and cast their sins behind our back. [*blank*] I am going to talk to all **[p.79]** this Society— if you would have God have mercy on you, have mercy on one another.

Prest. S. then refer'd them to the conduct of the Savior when he was taken and crucified &c.[9]

---

7. 9 June 1842, *RSM*, 78. See also *WJS*, 123.
8. 9 June 1842, *RSM*, 78. See also *WJS*, 123.
9. 9 June 1842, *RSM*, 78–79. See also *WJS*, 123–24.

Men Cannot Be Compelled into Kingdom

Relief Society Minutes

He then made a promise in the name of the Lord, saying that that soul who has righteousness enough to ask God in the secret place for life, every day of their lives, shall live to three score years and ten. We must walk uprightly all the day long. How glorious are the principles of righteousness! We are full of selfishness; the devil flatters us that we are very righteous, when we are feeding on the faults of others. We can only live by worshiping our God; all must do it for themselves; none can do it for another. How mild the Savior dealt with Peter, saying, "When thou art converted, strengthen thy brethren." At another time, He said to him, "Lovest thou me?" and having received Peter's reply, He said, "Feed my sheep." If the sisters loved the Lord, let them feed the sheep, and not destroy them. How oft have wise men and women sought to dictate Brother Joseph by saying, "O, if I were Brother Joseph I would do this and that;" but if they were in Brother Joseph's shoes they would find that men or women could not be compelled into the kingdom of God, but must be dealt with in longsuffering, and at last we shall save them. The way to keep all the Saints together, and keep the work rolling, is to wait with all long-suffering, till God shall bring such characters to justice. There should be no license for sin, but mercy should go hand in hand with reproof.

Sisters of the society, shall there be strife among you? I will not have it. You must repent, and get the love of God. Away with self-righteousness! The best measure or principle to bring the poor to repentance is to administer to their wants.

[p.242] The Ladies' Relief Society is not only to relieve the poor, but to save souls.

President Smith then said that he would give a lot of land to the society by deeding to the

He then made a promise in the name of the Lord saying, that soul that has righteousness enough to ask God in the secret place for life, every day of their lives shall live to three score years & ten— We must walk uprightly all day long— How glorious are the principles of righteousness! We are full of selfishness— the devil flatters us that we are very righteous, while we are feeding on the faults of others— We can only live by worshipping our God— all must do it for themselves— none can do it for another. How mild the Savior dealt with Peter, saying "when thou art converted, strengthen thy brethren"— at another time he said to him "lovest thou me? "Feed my sheep".— If the sisters love the Lord let them feed the sheep and not destroy them. How oft have wise men & women sought to dictate br. Joseph by saying "O if I were br. Joseph I would do this and that." But if they were in br. Joseph's shoes, they would find that men could not be compel'd into the kingdom of God, but must be dealt with in long suffring— and at last we shall save them. The way to keep all the saints together and keep the work rolling, is to wait with all long suffring till God shall bring such character to justice. There should be no license for sin, but mercy should go hand in hand with reproof.

Sisters of this Society, shall there be strife among you? I will not have it— you must repent and get the love of God. Away with selfrighteousness. The best measure or principle to bring the poor to repentance is to administer to their wants—

the Society is not only to relieve the poor, but to save souls.

Prest. S. then said that he would give a lot of land to the Society by deeding it to the treasurer, that the society may build houses for the poor. He also said he would give a house, frame not finished, and that Brother Cahoon will move it on to the aforesaid lot, and the society can pay him by giving orders on the store; that it was a good plan to set those to work who are owing widows, and thus make an offset, &c.—DHC 5:23-25.

Treasurer, that the Society may build houses for the poor. He also said he would give a house— frame not finished— said that br. [Reynolds] Cahoon will move it on to the aforesaid lot, and the Society can pay him by giving Orders on the Store— that it was a good plan to set those to work who are owing widows and thus make an offsett &c. &c.[10]

The Gift of the Holy Ghost

An Editorial in the "Times and Seasons," by the Prophet

Times and Seasons
GIFT OF THE HOLY GHOST.

Various and conflicting are the opinions of men in regard to the gift of the Holy Ghost. Some people have been in the habit of calling every supernatural manifestation the effects of the Spirit of God, whilst there are others that think there is no manifestation connected with it at all; and that it is nothing but a mere impulse of the mind, or an inward feeling, and that there is no such a thing as an outward manifestation.

Various and conflicting are the opinions of men in regard to the gift of the Holy Ghost. Some people have been in the habit of calling every supernatural manifestation, the effects of the spirit of God, whilst there are others that think their is no manifestation connected with it at all; and that it is *nothing* but a mere impulse of the mind, or an inward feeling, impression, or secret testimony or evidence which men possess, and that there is no such thing as an outward manifestation.

It is not to be wondered at that men should be ignorant, in a great measure, of the principles of salvation, and more especially of the nature, office, power, influence, gifts, and blessings of the gift of the Holy Ghost, when we consider that the human family have been enveloped in gross darkness and ignorance for many centuries past, without revelation, or any just criterion [by which] to arrive at a knowledge of the things of God, which can only be known by the Spirit of God. Hence it not infrequently occurs, that when the Elders of this Church preach to the inhabitants of the world, that if they obey the Gospel they shall receive the gift of the Holy Ghost, that the people expect to see some wonderful manifestation, some great display of power, or some extraordinary miracle performed; and it is often the case

It is not to be wondered at that men should be ignorant, in a great measure, of the principles of salvation, and more especially of the nature, office, power, influence, gifts and blessings of the Gift of the Holy Ghost; when we consider that the human family have been enveloped in gross darkness and ignorance for many centuries past without revelation, or any just criterion to arrive at a knowledge of the things of God, which can only be known by the spirit of God. Hence it not unfrequently occurs, that when the elders of this church preach to the inhabitants of the world, that if they obey the gospel they shall receive the gift of the Holy Ghost, that the people expect to see some wonderful manifestation; some great display of power, or some extraordinary miracle performed; and it is often the case

---

10. 9 June 1842, *RSM*, 79. See also *WJS*, 124.

that young members of this Church for want of better information, carry along with them their old notions of things, and sometimes fall into egregious errors. We have lately had some information concerning a few members that are in this dilemma, and for their information make a few remarks upon the subject.

that young members in this church, for want of better information, carry along with them their old notions of things and sometimes fall into eggregious errors. We have lately had some information concerning a few members that are in this dilema, and for their information make a few remarks upon the subject.[11]

Gifts of the Spirit

Times and Seasons

[p.243] We believe in the gift of the Holy Ghost being enjoyed now, as much as it was in the Apostles' days; we believe that it [the gift of the Holy Ghost] is necessary to make and to organize the Priesthood, that no man can be called to fill any office in the ministry without it; we also believe in prophecy, in tongues, in visions, and in revelations, in gifts, and in healings; and that these things cannot be enjoyed without the gift of the Holy Ghost. We believe that the Holy Ghost, and that holy men in these days speak by the same principle; we believe in its being a comforter and a witness bearer, that it brings things past to our remembrance, leads us into all truth, and shows us of things to come; we believe that "no man can know that Jesus is the Christ, but by the Holy Ghost." We believe in it [this gift of the Holy Ghost] in all its fullness, and power, and greatness, and glory; but whilst we do this, we believe in it rationally, consistently, and scripturally, and not according to the wild vagaries, foolish notions and traditions of men.

* * *

We believe in the gift of the Holy Ghost being enjoyed now, as much as it was in the apostles days;—we believe that it is necessary to make and to organize the priesthood; that no man can be called to fill any office in the ministry without it; we also believe in prophesy, in tongues, in visions, and in revelations, in gifts, and in healings; and that these things cannot be enjoyed without the gift of the Holy Ghost; we believe that holy men of old spake as they were moved by the Holy Ghost, and that holy men in these days speak by the same principle; we believe in its being a comforter and a witness bearer, "that it brings things past to our remembrance, leads us into all truth, and shews us of things to come:" we believe that "no man can know that Jesus is the Christ, but by the Holy Ghost." We believe in it in all its fullness, and power, and greatness, and glory: but whilst we do this we believe in it rationally, reasonably, consistently, and scripturally, and not according to the wild vagaries, foolish, notions and traditions of men.[12]

Diversity of Gifts

Times and Seasons

We believe that the Holy Ghost is imparted by the laying on of hands of those in authority, and that the gift of tongues, and also the gift of prophecy are gifts of the Spirit, and are obtained through that medium; but then to

We believe that the Holy Ghost is imparted by the laying on of hands of those in authority, and that the gift of tongues, and also the gift of prophecy, are gifts of the spirit, and are obtained through that medium; but then

---

11. *T&S* 3, no. 16 (15 June 1842): 823.
12. *T&S* 3, no. 16 (15 June 1842): 823.

say that men always prophesied and spoke in tongues when they had the imposition of hands, would be to state that which is untrue, contrary to the practice of the Apostles, and at variance with holy write; for Paul says, "To one is given the gift of tongues, to another the gift of prophecy, and to another the gift of healing;" and again: "Do all prophesy? do all speak with tongues? do all interpret?" evidently showing that all did not possess these several gifts; but that one received one gift, and another received another gift—all did not prophesy, all did not speak in tongues, all did not work miracles; but all did receive the gift of the Holy Ghost; sometimes they spake in tongues and prophesied in the Apostles' days, and sometimes they did not. The same is the case with us also in our administrations, while more frequently there is no manifestation at all, that is visible **[p.244]** to the surrounding multitude; this will appear plain when we consult the writings of the Apostles, and notice their proceedings in relation to this matter. Paul, in 1st Cor. 12, says, "Now concerning spiritual gifts, brethren, I would not have you ignorant;" it is evident from this, that some of them were ignorant in relation to these matters, or they would not need instruction.

The Gift of Prophecy

Again in chapter 14, he says, "Follow after charity and desire spiritual gifts, but rather that ye may prophesy." It is very evident from these Scriptures that many of them had not spiritual gifts, for if they had spiritual gifts where was the necessity of Paul telling them to follow after them, and it is evident that they did not all receive those gifts by the imposition of the hands; for they as a Church had been baptized and confirmed by the laying on of hands—and yet to a Church of this kind, under the immediate inspection and superintendency of the Apostles, it was necessary for

Times and Seasons

to say that men always prophesied and spoke in tongues when they had the imposition of hands, would be to state that which is untrue, contrary to the practice of the apostles, and at variance with holy writ; for Paul says, "to one is given the gift of tongues, to another the gift of prophecy, and to another the gift of healing"— and again, "do all prophecy? do all speak with tongues? do all interpret?" evidently shewing that all did not possess these several gifts; but that one received one gift and another received another gift—all did not prophecy; all did not speak in tongues; all did not work miracles; but all did receive the gift of the Holy Ghost; sometimes they spake in tongues and prophesied in the Apostles' days, and sometimes they did not.—The same in the case with us also in our admin**[p.824]**istrations, while more frequently there is no manifestation at all that is visible to the surrounding multitude; this will appear plain when we consult the writings of the apostles and notice their proceedings in relation to this matter. Paul, in 1 Cor. xii. says, "Now concerning spiritual gifts, brethren, I would not have you ignorant;" it is evident from this that some of them were ignorant in relation to these matters, or they would not need instruction.[13]

Again, in the xiv. chapter, he says "Follow after charity and *desire spiritual gifts*, but rather that ye may prophecy." It is very evident from these scriptures that many of them had not spiritual gifts, for if they had spiritual gifts where was the necessity of Paul telling them to follow after them! and it is as evident that they did not all receive those gifts by the imposition of hands, for they as a church had been baptized and confirmed by the laying on of hands—and yet to a church of this kind, under the immediate inspection and seperintendance of the apostles, it was necessary for

---

13. *T&S* 3, no. 16 (15 June 1842): 823–24.

Paul to say, "Follow after charity, and desire spiritual gifts, but rather that ye may prophesy," evidently showing that those gifts were in the Church, but not enjoyed by all in their outward manifestations.

Paul to say "*follow after charity and desire spiritual gifts*, but rather that ye may prophecy," evidently showing that those gifts were in the church but not enjoyed by all in their outward manifestations.

But suppose the gifts of the Spirit were immediately, upon the imposition of hands, enjoyed by all, in all their fulness and power, the skeptic would still be as far from receiving any testimony except upon a mere casualty as before, for all the gifts of the Spirit are not visible to the natural vision, or understanding of man; indeed very few of them are. We read that "Christ ascended into heaven and gave gifts unto men; and He gave some Apostles, and some Prophets, and some Evangelists, and some Pastors and Teachers." (Eph. 4.)

But supposing the gifts of the spirit were immediately, upon the imposition of hands, enjoyed by all, in all their fullness and power; the skeptic would still be as far from receiving any testimony except upon a mere casualty as before, for all the gifts of the spirit are not visible to the natural vision, or understanding of man; indeed very few of them are. We read that "Christ ascended into heaven and gave gifts unto men; and he gave some apostles, and some prophets, and some evangelists, and some pastors and teachers;" Eph. iv.[14]

The Church a Compact Body

Times and Seasons

The Church is a compact body composed of different members, and is strictly analogous to the human system, and Paul, after speaking of the different gifts, says, "Now ye are the body of Christ and members in particular; and God hath set some in the Church, first Apostles, secondarily Prophets, thirdly Teachers, after that miracles, then gifts of healing, helps, governments, diversities of tongues. Are all Teachers? Are all workers of miracles? Do all speak with tongues? Do all interpret?" It is evident that they do not; yet are they all [p.245] members of one body. All members of the natural body are not the eye, the ear, the head or the hand—yet the eye cannot say to the ear, I have no need of thee, nor the head to the foot, I have no need of thee; they are all so many component parts in the perfect machines—the one body; and if one member suffer, the whole of the members suffer with it; and if one member rejoice, all the rest are honored with it.

The church is a compact body composed of different members and is strictly analagous to the human system, and Paul after speaking of the different gifts says, "Now ye are the *body* of Christ and *each one* members in particular; and God hath set some in the church, first apostles, secondarily prophets, thirdly teachers, after that miracles, then gifts of healing, helps, governments, diversities of tongues. Are all apostles? are all prophets? are all teachers? are all workers of miracles? have all the gifts of healing? do all speak with tongues? do all interpret?" It is evident that they do not; yet are they all members of the one body; all members of the natural body, are not the eye, the ear, the head or the hand—yet the eye cannot say to the ear, I have no need of thee, nor the head to the foot, I have no need of thee; they are all so many component parts in the perfect machine—the one body;—and if one member suffer, the whole of the members suffer with it; and if one member rejoice all the rest are honored with it.

---

14. *T&S* 3, no. 16 (15 June 1842): 824.

These, then, are all gifts; they come from God; they are of God; they are all the gifts of the Holy Ghost; they are what Christ ascended into heaven to impart; and yet how few of them could be known by the generality of men. Peter and John were Apostles, yet the Jewish court scourged them as impostors. Paul was both an Apostle and prophet, yet they stoned him and put him into prison. The people knew nothing about it, although he had in his possession the gift of the Holy Ghost. Our Savior was "anointed with the oil of gladness above his fellows," yet so far from the people knowing Him, they said He was Beelzebub and crucified Him as an impostor. Who could point out a Pastor, a Teacher, or an Evangelist by their appearance, yet had they the gift of the Holy Ghost?

These then are all gifts; they come from God; they are of God; they are all the gifts of the Holy Ghost; they are what Christ ascended into heaven to impart; and yet how few of them could be known by the generality of men. Peter and John were apostles, yet the Jewish court scourged them as impostors. Paul was both an Apostle and prophet, yet they stoned him and put him into prison. The people knew nothing about it, although he had in possession the gift of the Holy Ghost. Our Savior was "anointed with the oil of gladness above his fellows," yet so far from the people knowing him, they said he was Beelzebub, and crucified him as an imposter. Who could point out a pastor, a teacher or an evangelist, by their appearance; yet had they the gift of the Holy Ghost.[15]

The World Cannot Know the Gifts of the Spirit

Times and Seasons

But to come to the other members of the Church, and examine the gifts as spoken of by Paul, and we shall find that the world can in general know nothing about them, and that there is but one or two that could be immediately known, if they were all poured out immediately upon the imposition of hands. In 1 Cor. 12, Paul says, "There are diversities of gifts yet the same spirit, and there are differences of administrations but the same Lord; and there are diversities of operations, but it is the same God which worketh all in all. But the manifestations of the Spirit is given unto every man to profit withal. For to one is given, by the Spirit, the word of wisdom, to another, the word of knowledge by the same Spirit; to another faith by the same Spirit; to another the working of miracles; to another prophecy; to another the discerning of spirits; to another divers kinds of tongues; to another the interpretation of tongues. But all these worketh that one and the selfsame spirit, dividing to each man severally as he will.

But to come to the other members of the church and examine the gifts as spoken of by Paul, and we shall find that the world can in general know nothing about them, and that there is but one or two that could be immediately known, if they were all poured out immediately upon the imposition of hands. 1 Cor. xii. Paul says, "There are diversities of gifts yet the same spirit; and there are differences of administrations, but the same Lord; and there are diversities of operations, but it is the same God which worketh all in all. But the manifestation of the spirit is given unto *every man* to profit withall. For to one is given, by the spirit, the *word of wisdom*; to another the *word of knowledge*, by the same spirit; to another *faith* by the same spirit; to another the *gifts of healing*, by the same spirit; to another the *working of miracles*; to another *prophecy*; to another *discerning of spirits*; to another *divers kinds of tongues*; to another the *interpretation of tongues*. But all these worketh that one and the self same spirit, dividing to each man severally as he will."[16]

---

15. *T&S* 3, no. 16 (15 June 1842): 824.
16. *T&S* 3, no. 16 (15 June 1842): 824.

The Things of God Known Only by the Spirit of God

[p.246] There are several gifts mentioned here, yet which of them all could be known by an observer at the imposition of hands? The word of wisdom, and the word of knowledge, are as much gifts as any other, yet if a person possessed both of these gifts, or received them by the imposition of hands, who would know it? Another might receive the gift of faith, and they would be as ignorant of it. Or suppose a man had the gift of healing or power to work miracles, that would not then be known; it would require time and circumstances to call these gifts into operation. Suppose a man had the discerning of spirits, who would be the wiser of it? Or if he had the interpretation of tongues, unless someone spoke in an unknown tongue, according to Paul's testimony, he would be a barbarian to those present. They would say that it was gibberish; and if he prophesied they would call it nonsense. The gift of tongues is the smallest gift perhaps of the whole, and yet it is one that is the most sought after.

So that according to the testimony of Scripture and the manifestations of the Spirit in ancient days, very little could be known about it by the surrounding multitude, except on some extraordinary occasion, as on the day of Pentecost.

The greatest, the best, and the most useful gifts would be known nothing about by an observer. It is the true that man might prophesy, which is a great gift, and one that Paul told the people—the Church—to seek after and to covet, rather than to speak in tongues;

but what does the world know about prophesying? Paul says that it "serveth only to those that believe." But does not the Scriptures say that they spake in tongues and prophesied? Yes; but who is it that writes these Scriptures? Not the men of the world or mere casual observers, but the Apostles—men who knew one gift from another, and of course were capable of writing about it; if we had the testimony of the Scribes and Pharisees concerning the outpouring of the Spirit on the day of Pentecost, they would have told us that it was no gift, but that the people were "drunken with new [p.247] wine," and we shall finally have to come to the same conclusion that Paul did—"No man knows the things of God but by the Spirit of God;" for with the great revelations of Paul when he was caught up into the third heaven and saw things that were not lawful to utter, no man was apprised of it until he mentioned it himself fourteen years after; and when John had the curtains of heaven withdrawn, and by vision looked through the dark vista of future ages, and contemplated events that should transpire throughout every subsequent period of time, until the final winding up scene—while he gazed upon the glories of the eternal world, saw an innumerable company of angels and heard the voice of God—it was in the Spirit, on the Lord's day, unnoticed and unobserved by the world.

* * *

what does the world know about prophesying? Paul says that it "serveth only to those that believe."—But does not the scriptures say that they spake in tongues and prophesied? Yes; but who is it that writes these scriptures? Not the men of the world or mere casual observers, but the Apostles—men who knew one gift from another, and of course were capable of writing about it; if we had the testimony of the scribes and pharisees concerning the outpouring of the spirit on the day of Pentacost, they would have told us that it was no gift, but that the people "were drunken with new wine," and we shall finally have to come to the same conclusion that Paul did, that "no man knows the things of God but by the spirit of God," for with the great revelations of Paul, when he was caught up into the third heaven and saw things that were not lawful to utter, no man was apprised of it until he mentioned it himself fourteen years after; and when John had the curtains of heaven withdrawn, and by vision looked through the dark vista of future ages, and contemplated events that should transpire throughout every subsequent period of time until the final winding up scene—while he gazed upon the glories of the eternal world, saw an innumerable company of angels and heard the voice of God—it was in the spirit on the Lord's day; unnoticed and unobserved by the world.[17]

* * *

The Necessity of Prayer

Times and Seasons

The Lord cannot always be known by the thunder of his voice, by the display of His glory or by the manifestation of His power, and those that are the most anxious to see these things, are the least prepared to meet them, and were the Lord to manifest His powers as He did to the children of Israel, such characters would be the first to say, "Let not the Lord speak any more, lest we His people die."

The Lord cannot always be known by the thunder of his voice; by the display of his glory, or by the manifestation of his power; and those that are the most anxious to see these things, are the least prepared to meet them; and were the Lord to manifest his power as he did to the children of Israel, such characters would be the first to say "let not the Lord speak any more, lest we his people die."

---

17. *T&S* 3, no. 16 (15 June 1842): 824–25.

We would say to the brethren, seek to know God in your closets, call upon him in the fields. Follow the directions of the Book of Mormon, and pray over, and for your families, your cattle, your flocks, your herds, your corn, and all things that you possess; ask the blessing of God upon all your labors, and everything that you engage in. Be virtuous and pure; be men of integrity and truth; keep the commandments of God; and then you will be able more perfectly to understand the difference between right and wrong—between the things of God and the things of men; and your path will be like that of the just, which shineth brighter and brighter unto the perfect day.

The True Use of Tongues

Be not so curious about tongues, do not speak in tongues except there be an interpreter present; the ultimate design of tongues is to speak to foreigners, and if persons are very anxious to display their intelligence, let them speak to such in **[p.248]** their own tongues. The gifts of God are all useful in their place, but when they are applied to that which God does not intend, they prove an injury, a snare and a curse instead of a blessing. We may some future time enter more fully into this subject, but shall let this suffice for the present. (June 15, 1842.) DHC 5:26-32.

Times and Seasons

Be not so curious about tongues, do not speak in tongues except there be an interpreter present; the ultimate design of tongues is to speak to foreigners, and if persons are very anxious to display their intelligence, let them speak to such in their own tongues. The gifts of God are all useful in their place, but when they are applied to that which God **[p.826]** does not intend, they prove an injury, a snare, and a curse instead of a blessing. We may at some future time, enter more fully into this subject; but shall let this suffice for the present.—ED.[19]

The Government of God

An Editorial by the Prophet on the Failure of Man-made Governments and the Right of God to Rule

The government of the Almighty has always been very dissimilar to the governments of men, whether we refer to His religious

Times and Seasons
THE GOVERNMENT OF GOD.

The government of the Almighty, has always been very dissimilar to the government of men; whether we refer to his religious

---

18. *T&S* 3, no. 16 (15 June 1842): 825.

19. *T&S* 3, no. 16 (15 June 1842): 825–26. Although Joseph Smith was the editor of the *Times and Seasons* at this time, some scholars have questioned whether he is the actual author of this article. See Appendix D for information regarding the possibility that some individuals wrote and published articles in the Prophet's name.

government, or to the government of nations. The government of God has always tended to promote peace, unity, harmony, strength, and happiness; while that of man has been productive of confusion, disorder, weakness, and misery.

Man's Government Brings Misery and Destruction

The greatest acts of the mighty men have been to depopulate nations and to overthrow kingdoms; and whilst they have exalted themselves and become glorious, it has been at the expense of the lives of the innocent, the blood of the oppressed, the moans of the widow, and the tears of the orphan.

Egypt, Babylon, Greece, Persia, Carthage, Rome—each was raised to dignity amidst the clash of arms and the din of war; and whilst their triumphant leaders led forth their victorious armies to glory and victory, their ears were saluted with the groans of the dying and the misery and distress of the human family; before them the earth was a paradise, and the behind them a desolate wilderness; their kingdoms were founded in carnage and bloodshed, and sustained by oppression, tyranny, and despotism. The designs of God, on the other hand, have been to promote the universal good of the universal world; to establish peace and good will among men; to promote the principles of eternal truth; to bring about a state of things that shall unite man to his fellow man; cause the world to "beat their swords into plowshares, and their spears into pruning hooks," make the nations of the earth dwell in peace, and to bring about the millennial glory, when "the earth shall yield its increase, resume its paradisean glory, and become as the garden of the Lord."

Times and Seasons

The greatest acts of the mighty men have been to depopulate nations, and to overthrow kingdoms; and whilst they have exalted themselves and become glorious, it has been at the expense of the lives of the innocent—the blood of the oppressed—the moans of the widow, and the tears of the orphan.

Egypt, Babylon, Greece, Persia, Carthage, Rome—each were raised to dignity amid the clash of arms, and the din of war; and whilst their triumphant leaders led forth their victorious armies to glory and victory, their ears were saluted with the groans of the dying, and the misery and distress of the human family;—before them the earth was a paradise, and behind them a desolate wilderness; their kingdoms were founded in carnage and bloodshed, and sustained by oppression, tyranny, and despotism. The designs of God, on the other hand, have been to promote the universal good, of the universal world;—to establish peace and good will among men;—to promote the principles of eternal truth;—to bring about a state of things that shall unite man to his fellow man—cause the world to "beat their swords into plow-shares, and their spears into pruning-hooks"—make the nations of the earth dwell in peace; and to bring about the millenial glory—when "the earth shall yield its increase, resume its paradisean glory, and become as the garden of the Lord."[21]

---

20. *T&S* 3, no. 18 (15 July 1842): 855.
21. *T&S* 3, no. 18 (15 July 1842): 855.

Failure of the Governments of Men

Times and Seasons

The great and wise of ancient days have failed in all their attempts to promote eternal power, peace and happiness. Their nations have crumbled to pieces; their thrones have been cast down in their turn, and their cities, and their mightiest works of art have been annihilated; or their dilapidated towers, or time-worn monuments have left us but feeble traces of their former magnificence and ancient grandeur. They proclaim as with a voice of thunder, those imperishable truths—that man's strength is weakness, his wisdom is folly, his glory is his shame.

Monarchial, aristocratical, and republican governments of their various kinds and grades, have, in their turn, been raised to dignity, and prostrated in the dust. The plans of the greatest politicians, the wisest senators, and most profound statesmen have been exploded; and the proceedings of the greatest chieftains, the bravest generals, and the wisest kings have fallen to the ground. Nation has succeeded nation, and we have inherited nothing but their folly. History records their puerile plans, their short-lived glory, their feeble intellect and their ignoble deeds.

The great and wise of ancient days have failed in all their attempts to promote eternal power, peace, and happiness. Their nations have crumbled to pieces; their thrones have been cast down in their turn; and their cities, and their mightiest works of art, have been annihilated; or their dilapidated towers, or time worn monuments have left us but feeble traits of their former magnificence, and ancient grandeur. They proclaim as with a voice of thunder, those imperishable truths—that man's **[p.856]** strength is weakness, his wisdom is folly, his glory is his shame.

Monarchical, aristocratic, and republican forms of government, of their various kinds and grades, have in their turn been raised to dignity and prostrated in the dust. The plans of the greatest politicians, the wisest senators, and most profound statesmen have been exploded; and the proceedings of the greatest chieftains, the bravest generals, and the wisest kings have fallen to the ground. Nation has succeeded nation, and we have inherited nothing but their folly. History records their puerile plans, their short lived glory, their feeble intellect, and their ignoble deeds.[22]

Has Man Increased in Intelligence?

Times and Seasons

Have we increased in knowledge or intelligence? Where is there a man that can step forth and alter the destiny of nations and promote the happiness of the world? Or where is there a kingdom or nation that can promote the universal happiness of its own subjects, or even their general well-being? Our nation, which possesses greater resources than any other, is rent, from center to circumference, with party strife, political intrigues, and sectional

Have we increased in knowledge or intelligence? where is there a man that can step forth and alter the destiny of nations, and promote the happiness of the world? Or where is there a kingdom or nation, that can promote the universal happiness of its own subjects, or even their general well being? Our nation, which possesses greater resources than any other, is rent from center to circumference, with party strife, political intrigue, and sectional interest;

---

22. *T&S* 3, no. 18 (15 July 1842): 855–56.

interest; our counselors are panic-stricken, our legislators are astonished, and our senators are confounded, our merchants are paralyzed, our tradesmen are disheartened, our mechanics out of employ, our farmers distressed, and our poor crying for bread, our banks are broken, our credit ruined, and our states overwhelmed in debt, yet we are, and have been in peace.

Man Not Able to Govern Himself

[p.250] What is the matter? Are we alone in this thing? Verily no. With all our evils we are better situated than any other nation. Let Egypt, Turkey, Spain, France, Italy, Portugal, Germany, England, China, or any other nation, speak, and tell the tale of their trouble, their perplexity, and distress, and we should find that their cup was full, and that they were preparing to drink the dregs of sorrow. England, that boasts of her literature, her science, commerce, etc., has her hands reeking with the blood of the innocent abroad, and she is saluted with the cries of the oppressed at home. Chartism, O'Connelism, and radicalism are gnawing her vitals at home; and Ireland, Scotland, Canada, and the east are threatening her destruction abroad. France is rent to the core, intrigue, treachery, and treason lurk in the dark, and murder, and assassination stalk forth at noonday. Turkey, once the dread of European nations, has been shorn of her strength, has dwindled into her dotage, and has been obliged to ask her allies to propose to her tributary terms of peace; and Russia and Egypt are each of them opening their jaws to devour her. Spain has been the theater of bloodshed, of misery and woe for years past. Syria is now convulsed with war and bloodshed. The great and powerful empire of China, which has for centuries resisted the attacks of barbarians, has become tributary to a foreign fee, her batteries thrown down, many of her cities destroyed, and her villages

our counsellors are panic struck, our legislators are astonished, and our senators are confounded; our merchants are paralized, our tradesmen are disheartened, our mechanics out of employ, our farmers distressed, and our poor crying for bread. Our banks are broken, our credit ruined, and our states overwhelmed in debt;—yet we are, and have been in peace.—[23]

Times and Seasons

What is the matter? Are we alone in this thing? Verily, no. With all our evils we are better situated than any other nation. Let Egypt, Turkey, Spain, France, Italy, Portugal, Germany, England, China, or any other nation speak, and tell the tale of their trouble—their perplexity, and distress, and we should find that their cup was full, and that they were preparing to drink the dregs of sorrow. England, that boasts of her literature, her science, commerce, &c., has her hands reeking with the blood of the innocent, abroad; and she is saluted with the cries of the oppressed, at home.—Chartism, O'Connelism and Radicalism are gnawing her vitals at home; and Ireland, Scotland, Canada, and the East, are threatening her destruction abroad. France is rent to the core—intrigue, treachery, and treason lurk in the dark; and murder, and assassination stalk forth at noonday. Turkey, once the glory of European nations, has been shorn of her strength—has dwindled into her dotage, and has been obliged to ask her allies to propose to her tributary terms of peace: and Russia, and Egypt are each of them opening their jaws to devour her. Spain has been the theatre of bloodshed, of misery and woe, for years past. Syria is now convulsed with war and bloodshed. The great and powerful empire of China, which has for centuries resisted the attacks of barbarians, has become tributary to a foreign foe; her batteries thrown down; many of her cities destroyed, and her villages

---

23. T&S 3, no. 18 (15 July 1842): 856.

deserted. We might mention the Easter Rajahs, the miseries and oppressions of the Irish; the convulsed state of Central America; the situation of Texas and Mexico; the state of Greece, Switzerland and Poland; nay, the world itself presents one great theater of misery, woe, and "distress of nations with perplexity." All, all, speak with a voice of thunder, that man is not able to govern himself, to legislate for himself, to protect himself, to promote his own good, nor the good of the world.

The Design of Jehovah

It has been the design of Jehovah, from the commencement of the world, and is His purpose now, to regulate the affairs of the world in His own time, to stand as a head of the universe, and take the reins of government in His own hand. When [p.251] that is done, judgment will be administered in righteousness; anarchy and confusion will be destroyed, and "nations will learn war no more." It is for want of this great governing principle, that all this confusion has existed; "for it is not in man that walketh, to direct his steps;" this we have fully shown.

If there was anything great or good in the world, it came from God. The construction of the first vessel was given to Noah, by revelation. The design of the ark was given by God, "a pattern of heavenly things." The learning of the Egyptians, and their knowledge of astronomy was no doubt taught them by Abraham and Joseph, as their records testify, who received it from the Lord. The art of working in brass, silver, gold, and precious stones, was taught by revelation, in the wilderness. The architectural designs of the Temple at Jerusalem, together with its ornaments and beauty, were given of God. Wisdom to govern the house of Israel was given to Solomon, and the Judges of Israel; and if he had always been their king,

Times and Seasons

It has been the design of Jehovah, from the commencement of the world, and is his purpose now, to regulate the affairs of the world in his own time; to stand as head of the universe, and take the reigns of government into his own hand. When that is done judgment will be administered in righteousness; anarchy and confusion will be destroyed, and "nations will learn war no more." It is for want of this great governing principle that all this confusion has existed; "for it is not in man that walketh to direct his steps;" this we have fully shewn.

If there was any thing great or good in the world it came from God. The construction of the first vessel was given to Noah, by revelation. The design of the ark was given by God, "a pattern of heavenly things." The learning of the Egyptians, and their knowledge of astronomy was no doubt taught them by Abraham and Joseph, as their records testify, who received it from the Lord. The art of working in brass, silver, gold, and precious stones, was taught by revelation, in the wilderness. The architectural designs of the Temple at Jerusalem, together with its ornament and beauty was given of God. Wisdom to govern the house of Israel was given to Solomon, and to the judges of Israel; and if he had always been their king,

---

24. *T&S* 3, no. 18 (15 July 1842): 856.

and they subject to his mandate, and obedient to his laws, they would still have been a great and mighty people—the rulers of the universe, and the wonder of the world.

Government Established by God

If Nebuchadnezzar, or Darius, or Cyrus, or any other king possessed knowledge or power, it was from the same source, as the Scriptures abundantly testify. If, then, God puts up one, and sets down another at His pleasure, and made instruments of kings, unknown to themselves, to fulfill His prophecies, how much more was he able, if man would have been subject to His mandate to regulate the affairs of this world, and promote peace and happiness among the human family!

The Lord has at various times commenced this kind of government, and tendered His services to the human family. He selected Enoch, whom He directed, and gave His law unto, and to the people who were with him; and when the world in general would not obey the commands of God, after walking with God, he translated Enoch and his church, and the Priesthood or government of heaven was taken away.

Abraham was guided in all his family affairs by the Lord; was conversed with by angels, and by the Lord; was told where to go, and when to stop; and prospered exceedingly in all that [p.252] he put his hand unto; it was because he and his family obeyed the counsel of the Lord.

When Egypt was under the superintendence of Joseph it prospered, because he was taught of God; when they oppressed the Israelites, destruction came upon them. When the children of Israel were chosen with Moses at their head, they were to be a peculiar people, among whom God should place His name;

Times and Seasons

If Nebuchadnezzar, or Darius, or Cyrus, or any other king possessed knowledge or power, it was from the same source, as the scriptures abundantly testify. If then, God puts up one, and sets down another, at his pleasure—and made instruments of kings, unknown to themselves, to fulfill his prophesies, how much more was he able, if man would have been subject to his mandate, to regu[p.857]late the affairs of this world, and promote peace and happiness among the human family.

The Lord has at various times commenced this kind of government, and tendered his services to the human family. He selected Enoch, whom he directed, and gave his law unto, and to the people who were with him; and when the world in general would not obey the commands of God, after walking with God, he translated Enoch and his church, and the priesthood or government of heaven, was taken away.

Abraham was guided in all his family affairs by the Lord; was told where to go, and when to stop; was conversed with by angels, and by the Lord; and prospered exceedingly in all that he put his hand unto; it was because he and his family obeyed the counsel of the Lord.—

When Egypt was under the superintendence of Joseph, it prospered, because he was taught of God; when they oppressed the Israelites destruction came upon them. When the children of Israel were chosen with Moses at their head, they were to be a peculiar people, among whom God should place his name:

---

25. *T&S* 3, no. 18 (15 July 1842): 856.

their motto was: "The Lord is our lawgiver; the Lord is our Judge; the Lord is our King; and He shall reign over us." While in this state they might truly say, "Happy is that people, whose God is the Lord." Their government was a theocracy; they had God to make their laws, and men chosen by Him to administer them; He was their God, and they were His people. Moses received the word of the Lord from God Himself; he was the mouth of God to Aaron, and Aaron taught the people, in both civil and ecclesiastical affairs; they were both one, there was no distinction; so will it be when the purposes of God shall be accomplished: when "the Lord shall be King over the whole earth" and "Jerusalem His throne." "The law shall go forth from Zion, and the word of the Lord from Jerusalem."

their motto was "The Lord is our lawgiver; the Lord is our judge; the Lord is our king, and he shall reign over us." While in this state they might truly say, "happy is that people whose God is the Lord." Their government was a theocracy; they had God to make their laws, and men chosen by him to administer them; he was their God, and they were his people. Moses received the word of the Lord from God himself; he was the mouth of God to Aaron, and Aaron taught the people in both civil and ecclesiastical affairs; they were both one; there was no distinction; so will it be when the purposes of God shall be accomplished; when "the Lord shall be king over the whole earth" and "Jerusalem his throne." "The law shall go forth from Zion, and the word of the Lord from Jerusalem."[26]

Universal Peace to Come from God

Times and Seasons

This is the only thing that can bring about the "restitution of all things spoken of by all the holy Prophets since the world was"—"the dispensation of the fullness of times, when God shall gather together all things in one." Other attempts to promote universal peace and happiness in the human family have proved abortive; every effort has failed; every plan and design has fallen to the ground; it needs the wisdom of God, the intelligence of God, and the power of God to accomplish this. The world has had a fair trial for six thousand years; the Lord will try the seventh thousand Himself; "He whose right it is, will possess the kingdom, and reign until He has put all things under His feet;" iniquity will hide its hoary head, Satan will be bound, and the works of darkness destroyed; righteousness will be put to the line, and judgment to the plummet, and "he that fears the Lord will alone be exalted in that day." To bring about this state of things, there must of necessity be great confusion among the nations of the earth; "distress

This is the only thing that can bring about the "restitution of all things, spoken of by all the holy prophets since the world was"—"the dispensation of the fulness of times, when GOD shall gather together all things in one." Other attempts to promote universal peace and happiness in the human family have proven abortive; every effort has failed; every plan and design has fallen to the ground; it needs the wisdom of God, the intelligence of God, and the power of God to accomplish this. The world has had a fair trial for six thousand years; the Lord will try the seventh thousand himself; "he whose right it is will possess the kingdom, and reign until he has put all things under his feet;" iniquity will hide its hoary head, Satan will be bound, and the works of darkness destroyed; righteousness will be put to the line, and judgment to the plummet, and "he that fears the Lord will alone be exalted in that day." To bring about this state of things there must of necessity be great confusion among the nations of the earth; "distress

---

26. *T&S* 3, no. 18 (15 July 1842): 856–57.

of nations with perplexity." Am I asked what is the cause of **[p.253]** the present distress? I would answer, "Shall there be evil in a city and the Lord hath not done it?"

Earth Now Groaning Under Corruption

Times and Seasons

The earth is groaning under corruption, oppression, tyranny and bloodshed; and God is coming out of His hiding place, as He said He would do, to vex the nations of the earth. Daniel, in his vision, saw convulsion upon convulsion; he "beheld till the thrones were cast down, and the Ancient of Days did sit;" and one was brought before him like unto the Son of Man; and all nations, kindred, tongues, and peoples, did serve and obey Him. It is for us to be righteous, that we may be wise and understand; for none of the wicked shall understand; but the wise shall understand, and they that turn many to righteousness shall shine as the stars for ever and ever.

The earth is groaning under corruption, oppression, tyranny, and bloodshed; and God is coming out of his hiding place, as he said that he would do, to vex the nations of the earth. Daniel, in his vision, saw convulsion upon convulsion; he "saw till thrones were cast down, and the ancient of days did sit; and one was brought before him like unto the Son of man; and all nations, kindreds, tongues, and people, did serve and obey him." It is for us to be righteous that we may be wise and understand, for "none of the wicked shall understand; but the wise shall understand, and they that turn many to righteousness, as the stars for ever and ever."[28]

It Behooves Us to Be Wise

Times and Seasons

As a Church and a people it behooves us to be wise, and to seek to know the will of God, and then be willing to do it; for "blessed is he that heareth the word of the Lord, and keepeth it," say the Scriptures. "Watch and pray always," says our Savior, "that ye may be accounted worthy to escape the things that are to come on the earth, and to stand before the Son of Man." If Enoch, Abraham, Moses, and the children of Israel, and all God's people were saved by keeping the commandments of God, we, if saved at all, shall be saved upon the same principle. As God governed Abraham, Isaac and Jacob as families, and the children of Israel as a nation; so we, as a Church, must be under His guidance if we are prospered, preserved, and sustained. Our only confidence can be in

As a church, and a people it behoves us to be wise, and to seek to know the will of God, and then be willing to *do it*; for "blessed is he that heareth the word of the Lord and keepeth it," says the scriptures. "Watch and pray always," says our Savior, "that ye may be accounted worthy to escape the things that are coming on the earth, and to stand before the Son of man." If Enoch, Abraham, Moses, the children of Israel, and all God's people were saved by keeping the commandments of God, we, if saved at all, shall be saved upon the same principle. As God governed Abraham, Isaac and Jacob, as families, and the children of Israel as a nation, so we, as a church, must be under his guidance if we are prospered, preserved, and sustained. Our only confidence can be in

---

27. *T&S* 3, no. 18 (15 July 1842): 857.
28. *T&S* 3, no. 18 (15 July 1842): 857.

God; our only wisdom obtained from Him; and He alone must be our protector and safeguard, spiritually and temporally, or we fall.

We have been chastened by the hand of God heretofore for not obeying His commands, although we never violated any human law, or transgressed any human precept; yet we have treated lightly His commands, and departed from His ordinances, and the Lord has chastened us sore, and we have felt His arm and kissed the rod; let us be wise in time to come and ever remember that "to obey is better than sacrifice, and to hearken than the fat of rams." The Lord has told us to [p.254] build the Temple and the Nauvoo House; and that command is as binding upon us as any other; and that man who engages not in these things is as much a transgressor as though he broke any other commandment; he is not a doer of God's will, not a fulfiller of His laws.

The Saints Subject to Divine Counsel

In regard to the building up of Zion, it has to be done by the counsel of Jehovah, by the revelations of heaven; and we should feel to say, "If the Lord go not with us, carry us not up hence." We would say to the Saints that come here, we have laid the foundation for the gathering of God's people to this place, and they expect that when the Saints do come, they will be under the counsel that God has appointed. The Twelve are set apart to counsel the Saints pertaining to this matter; and we expect that those who come here will send before them their wise men according to revelation; or if not practicable, be subject to the counsel that God has given, or they cannot receive an inheritance among the Saints, or be considered as God's people, and they will be dealt with as transgressors of the laws of God. We are trying here to gird up our loins, and purge from our midst the workers of iniquity; and we hope

God; our only wisdom obtained from him; and he alone must be our protector and safeguard, spiritually and temporally, or we fall.

We have been chastened by the hand of God heretofore for not obeying his commands, although we never violated any human law, or transgressed any human precept: yet we have treated lightly his commands, and departed from his ordinances, and the Lord has chastened us sore, and we have felt his arm, and kissed the rod: let us we wise in time to come, and ever remember that "to obey is better than sacrifice; and to hearken than the fat of rams." The Lord has told us to build the temple, and the Nauvoo House, and that command is as binding upon us as any other; and that man who engages not in these things is as much a transgressor as though he broke any other command—he is not [p.858] a doer of God's will, nor a fulfiller of his laws.²⁹

Times and Seasons

In regard to the building up of Zion it has to be done by the counsel of Jehovah; by the revelations of heaven, and we should feel to say "if the Lord go not with us, carry us not up hence." We would say to the saints that come here, we have laid the foundation for the gathering of God's people to this place, and expect that when the saints do come they will be under the counsel of those that God has appointed. The Twelve are set apart to counsel the saints pertaining to this matter: and we expect that those who come here will send before them their wise men according to revelation; or if not practicable, be subject to the counsel that God has given or they cannot receive an inheritance among the saints, or be considered as God's people; and they will be dealt with as transgressors of the laws of God; we are trying here to gird up our loins, and purge from our midst the workers of in-

---

29. *T&S* 3, no. 18 (15 July 1842): 857–58.

that when our brethren arrive from abroad, they will assist us to roll forth this good work, and to accomplish this great design that "Zion may be built up in righteousness; and all nations flock to her standard;" that as God's people, under His direction, and obedient to His law, we may grow up in righteousness and truth; that when His purposes shall be accomplished, we may receive an inheritance among those that are sanctified. (July 15, 1842.) DHC 5:61-66.

iquity; and we hope that when our brethren arrive from abroad, they will assist us to roll forth this good work, and to accomplish this great design; that "Zion may be built up in righteousness; and all nations flock to her standard;" that as God's people, under his direction, and obedient to his law, we may grow up in righteousness, and truth; that when his purposes shall be accomplished, we may receive an inheritance among those that are sanctified.—ED.[30]

Letter of the Prophet to Governor Carlin—Satisfied with the Governor's Attitude

Joseph Smith Letter
Nauvoo July 30th 1842
Esteemed Sir,

Esteemed Sir:—Your favor of the 27th instant per Brevet Major-General Wilson Law is before me. I cannot let this opportunity pass without tendering to you my warmest thanks for the friendly treatment my lady as well as those with her received at your hands during the late visit, and also for the friendly feelings breathed forth in your letter. Your Excellency [p.255] may be assured that they are duly appreciated by me, and shall be reciprocated.

Your favour of the 27th inst. pr Brevet Major Gen. Wilson Law is before me. I cannot let this opportunity pass without tendering to you my Warmest thanks for the friendly treatment my Lady as well as those with her received at your hands during the late visit, and also for the friendly feelings breathed [p.324] forth in your letter. Your Excellency may be assured that they are duly appreciated by me and shall ever be reciprocated.

I am perfectly satisfied with regard to the subject under consideration, and with your remarks. I shall consider myself and our citizens secure from harm under the broad canopy of the law under your administration. We look to you for protection in the event of any violence being used towards us, knowing that our innocence with regard to all the accusations in circulation will be duly evidenced before an enlightened public.

I am perfectly satisfied with regard to the subject under consideration and with your remarks. I shall consider myself and our citizens secure from harm under the broad canopy of the Law under your administration, We look to you for protection in the event of any voilence being used towards us knowing that our innocence with reguard to all the accusations in circulation will be duly evidenced before an enlightned public.

Any service we can do the state at any time will be cheerfully done, for our ambition is to be serviceable to our country.

Any service we can do the State at any time will be cheerfully done, for our ambition is to be serviceable to our Country.

---

30. *T&S* 3, no. 18 (15 July 1842): 858. Although Joseph Smith was the editor of the *Times and Seasons* at this time, some scholars have questioned whether he is the actual author of this article. See Appendix D for information regarding the possibility that some individuals wrote and published articles in the Prophet's name.

With sentiments of respect and esteem, I remain your humble servant.
JOSEPH SMITH.
DHC 5:83.

With sentiments of respect and esteem I remain your humble Servant
Joseph Smith[31]

Prophecy That the Saints Would Be Driven to Rocky Mountains

Joseph Smith History

Saturday, Aug. 6, 1842.—Passed over the river to Montrose, Iowa, in company with General Adams, Colonel Brewer, and others, and witnessed the installation of the officers of the Rising Sun Lodge Ancient York Masons, at Montrose by General James Adams, Deputy Grand-Master of Illinois. While the Deputy Grand-Master was engaged in giving the requisite instructions to the Master-elect, I had a conversation with a number of brethren in the shade of the building on the subject of our persecutions in Missouri and the constant annoyance which has followed us since we were driven from that state. I prophesied that the Saints would continue to suffer much affliction and would be driven to the Rocky Mountains, many would apostatize, others would be put to death by our persecutors or lose their lives in consequence of exposure to disease, and some of you will live to go and assist in making settlements and build cities and see the Saints become a mighty people in the midst of the Rocky Mountains. (Aug. 6, 1842.) DHC 5:85.

<6> Saturday 6. Passed over the River to Montrose Iowa, in Company with General [James] Adams —— Colonel Brewer and others, and witnessed the Installation of the officers of the Rising Sun Lodge of Ancient York Masons, at Montrose by General James Adams. Deputy Grand Master of Illinois. <while the Deputy Grand Master was engaged in giving the requisite instructions to the Master elect, I had a conversation with a number of brethren in the shade of the building on the subject of our persecutions in Missouri, and the constant annoyance which has followed us since we were driven from that State. I prophecied that the Saints would continue to suffer much affliction and would be driven to the Rocky Mountains, many would apostatize, others would be put to death by our Persecutors, or lose their lives in consequence of exposure or disease, and some of you will live to go, and assist in making settlements and build cities and see the Saints become a mighty people in the midst of the Rocky Mountains.>.[32]

---

31. 30 July 1842, *JPS, D10*, 323–24.
32. 6 August 1842, History, D-1, 1362. There is some question as to whether the specificity of this statement can be rightly attributed to Joseph Smith. Certainly, Joseph Smith had been talking about going to the Rocky Mountains as early as 1841; however, it is unclear whether by 1842 he had given this kind of specificity. Manuscript History, D-1 (which was begun by Thomas Bullock in April 1845) attributes to Joseph such specificity, but the recollection is written after the Prophet's death and may have simply been the remembrance of one of the historians. Of this, David Bitton wrote: "Two errors have been made regarding this Rocky Mountains prophecy. The first is to reject it out of hand as a later invention of the Utah Mormons. There is enough discussion of possible westward moves during the later Nauvoo period to think that Joseph Smith, in one of his prophetic moods, might well have said something of the sort. The second error, even more serious, is to seize upon these fragments as the basis for concluding that Joseph knew exactly what the future held in store for the Saints down to every last detail. Like the constitution-by-a-thread prophecy, the Rocky Mountains prophecy probably had a basis in an actual statement. The two prophecies are alike, too, in the fact that they were extremely popular later on when they served the needs of the Saints for encouragement." Davis Bitton, "Joseph Smith in the Mormon Folk Memory," in *Restoration Studies*, ed. Maurice L. Draper, vol. 1 (Herald Publishing House 1980), 85.

Happiness the Design of Existence

	Sangamo Journal[33]
Happiness is the object and design of our existence; and will be the end thereof, if we pursue the path that leads to it; and this path is virtue, uprightness, faithfulness, holiness, and [p.256] keeping all the commandments of God. But we cannot keep all the commandments without first knowing them, and we cannot expect to know all, or more than we now know unless we comply with or keep those we have already received. That which is wrong under one circumstance, may be, and often is, right under another.	Happiness is the object and design of our existence, and will be the end thereof if we pursue the path that leads to it; and this path is virtue, uprightness, faithfulness, holiness, and keeping ALL the commandments of God. But we cannot keep *all* the commandments without first *knowing* them, and we cannot expect to know *all*, or more than we *now* know, unless we *comply* with or keep those we have *already received*. That which is *wrong* under one circumstance, may be, and often is, *right* under another.
God said, "Thou shalt not kill;" at another time He said, "Thou shalt utterly destroy." This is the principle on which the government of heaven is conducted—by revelation adapted to the circumstances in which the children of the kingdom are placed. Whatever	God said, *Thou shalt not kill,*—at another time he said, *thou shalt utterly destroy*. This is the principle on which the government of heaven is conducted—by *revelation* adapted to the circumstances in which the children of the kingdom are placed. *Whatever God requires is*

---

33. Added to the Documentary History of the Church in the 1850s, this letter purportedly written from Joseph Smith to Nancy Rigdon is not extant. The "original" source is from an article by John C. Bennett attacking Joseph Smith and Mormonism, published in the *Sangamo Journal*. (See John C. Bennett, "Letters From Gen. Bennett," letter 6, in *Sangamo Journal* [19 August 1842]: 2.) A version of the letter was also included in John C. Bennett's *The History of the Saints: An Exposé of Joe Smith and Mormonism* (Leland and Whiting, 1842), 243–45. Although accepted by many LDS and non-LDS readers as a legitimate Joseph Smith document, there are many problems and unanswered questions relating to this "letter." In a detailed examination of the so-called "Happiness Letter," Gerrit Dirkmaat wrote that—despite the popularity of the statement—"it presents special problems of provenance and authenticity to historians. . . . In effect, historians cannot demonstrate with certainty that Joseph Smith wrote the letter." See Gerrit Dirkmaat, "Searching for 'Happiness': Joseph Smith's Alleged Authorship of the 1842 Letter to Nancy Rigdon," *The Journal of Mormon History* 42, no. 3 (July 2016): 98–99; see also pages 94–119. In a letter dated 27 August 1842 written to the editor of *The Wasp*, Sidney Rigdon wrote, "Dear Sir: I am fully authorized by my daughter, Nancy, to say to the public through the medium of your paper, that the letter which has appeared in the Sangamo Journal, making part of General Bennett's letters to said paper, purporting to have been written by Mr. Joseph Smith to her, was unauthorized by her, and that she never said to Gen. Bennett or any other person, that said letter was written by said Mr. Smith, nor in his hand writing, but by another person, and in another persons' hand writing. She further wishes me to say, that she never at any time authorized Gen. Bennett to use her name in the public papers, as he has done, which has been greatly to the wounding of her feelings, and she considers the obtruding of her name before the public in the manner in which it has been done, to say the least of it, is a flagrant violation of the rules of gallantry, and cannot avoid to insult her feelings, which she wishes the public to know. I would further state that Mr. Smith denied to me the authorship of that letter. SIDNEY RIGDON P. S. I wish the Sangamo Journal and all papers that have copied Bennett's letters to copy this also, as an act of justice to Miss Rigdon. S. R." *The Wasp* 1, no. 20 (3 September 1842): 3.

God requires is right, no matter what it is, although we may not see the reason thereof till long after the events transpire. If we seek first the kingdom of God, all good things will be added. So with Solomon: first he asked wisdom, and God gave it him, and with it every desire of his heart, even things which might be considered abominable to all who understand the order of heaven only in part, but which in reality were right because God gave and sanctioned by special revelation.

A parent may whip a child, and justly, too, because he stole an apple; whereas if the child had asked for the apple, and the parent had given it, the child would have eaten it with a better appetite; there would have been no stripes; all the pleasure of the apple would have been secured, all the misery of stealing lost.

right, NO MATTER WHAT IT IS, although we may not see the reason thereof till long after the events transpire. If we seek first the kingdom of God, all *good things* will be added. So with Solomon—first he asked wisdom, and God gave it him, and with it every DESIRE of his heart, even things which might be considered *abominable* to all who do not *understand* the order of heaven only in part, but which, in reality, were right, because God gave and sanctioned by *special revelatio*n.

A parent may whip a child, and justly too, because he stole an apple; whereas if the child had asked for the apple, and the parent had given it, the child would have eaten it with a better appetite, there would have been no stripes—all the pleasures of the apple would have been received, all the misery of stealing lost.[34]

Every Gift from God Is Just

Sangamo Journal

This principle will justly apply to all of God's dealings with His children. Everything that God gives us is lawful and right; and it is proper that we should enjoy His gifts and blessings whenever and wherever He is disposed to bestow; but is we should seize upon those same blessings and enjoyments without law, without revelation, without commandment, those blessings and enjoyments would prove cursings and vexations in the end, and we should have to lie down in sorrow and wailings of everlasting regret. But in obedience there is joy and peace unspotted, unalloyed; and as God has designed our happiness—and the happiness of all His creatures, he never has—He never will institute an ordinance or give a commandment to His people that is not calculated in its nature to promote that happiness which He has designed, and which will not end [p.257] in the greatest amount of good and glory to those who become the recipients of his law and ordinances. Blessings

This principle will justly apply to all of God's dealings with his children. Every thing that God gives us is *lawful and right*, and 'tis proper that we should *enjoy* his gifts and blessings *whenever and wherever* he is disposed to bestow; but if we should seize upon these same blessings and enjoyments without law, without *revelation*, without commandment, those blessings and enjoyments would prove cursings and vexations in the end, and we should have to lie down in sorrow and wailings of everlasting regret. But in obedience there is joy and peace unspotted, unalloyed, and as God has designed our happiness, the happiness of all his creatures, he never has, he never will, institue an ordinance, or give a commandment to his people that is not calculated in its nature to promote that happiness which he has designed, and which will not end in the greatest amount of good and glory to those who become the recipients of his laws and ordinances. Blessings offered, but rejected, are

---

34. *Sangamo Journal* (19 August, 1842): 2.

offered, but rejected, are no longer blessings, but become like the talent hid in the earth by the wicked and slothful servant; the proffered good returns to the giver; the blessing is bestowed on those who will receive and occupy; for unto him that hath shall be given, and he shall have abundantly, but unto him that hath not or will not receive, shall be taken away that which he hath, or might have had.

Be wise today; 'tis madness to defer;
Next day the fatal precedent may plead.
Thus on till wisdom is pushed out of time
Into eternity.

Men are Judged According to Their Deeds

Our heavenly Father is more liberal in His views, and boundless in His mercies and blessings, than we are ready to believe or receive; and, at the same time, is more terrible to the workers of iniquity, more awful in the executions of His punishments, and more ready to detect every false way, than we are apt to suppose Him to be. He will be inquired of by His children. He says, "Ask and ye shall receive, seek and ye shall find;" but, if you will take that which is not your own, or which I have not given you, you shall be rewarded according to your deeds; but no good thing will I withhold from them who walk uprightly before me, and do my will in all things—who will listen to my voice and to the voice of my servant whom I have sent; for I delight in those who seek diligently to know my precepts, and abide by the law of my kingdom; for all things shall be made known unto them in mine own due time, and in the end they shall have joy. (Aug. 27, 1842.) DHC 5:134-136.

no longer blessings, but become like the talent hid in the earth by the wicked and slothful servant–the proffered good returns to the giver, the blessing is bestowed on those who will *receive*, and *occupy*; for unto him that hath shall be given, and he shall have *abundantly*; but unto him that hath not, or will not receive, shall be taken away that which he hath, or might have had.

"*Be wise* TO-DAY, *'tis* MADNESS to *defer*, Next day the fatal precedent may plead; Thus on till wisdom is pushed out of time" into eternity.[35]

Sangamo Journal

Our heavenly father is more liberal in his views, and boundless in his mercies and blessings, than we are ready to believe or receive, and at the same time is more terrible to the workers of iniquity, more awful in the executions of his punishments, and more ready to detect every false *way* than we are apt to suppose him to be. He will be inquired of by his children—he says *ask* and ye SHALL RECEIVE, *seek* and ye SHALL find, but if ye will take that which is not your own, or which I *have not given you*, you shall be rewarded according to your deeds, but no good thing will I withold from them who walk uprightly before me, and do my will in *all things*, who will listen to *my voice*, and to TO THE VOICE OF MY SERVANT WHOM I HAVE SENT, for I delight in those who seek diligently to know my precepts, and abide by the laws of my Kingdom, for all things shall be made known unto them in mine own due time, and in the end they shall have joy.[36]

---

35. *Sangamo Journal* (19 August, 1842): 2.
36. *Sangamo Journal* (19 August, 1842): 3. See also 27 August 1842, History, D-1, Addenda, 3–4.

MINUTES OF THE FEMALE RELIEF SOCIETY'S MEETING—REMARKS OF THE PROPHET

The Church to Prevail Against All Evil Powers

Relief Society Minutes
August 31, 1842 • Wednesday
Sixteenth Meeting of the Society.
Grove, August 31st.

President Joseph Smith arose and said, "I am happy and thankful for the privilege of being present on this occasion. Great exertions have been made on the part of our enemies to carry me to Missouri and destroy my life; but the Lord has hedged up their way, and they have not, as yet, accomplished **[p.258]** their purpose. God has enabled me to keep out of their hands. I have warred a good warfare, insomuch as I have out-generalled or whipped out all Bennett's corrupt host.

My feelings at the present time are that, inasmuch as the Lord Almighty has preserved me until today, He will continue to preserve me, by the united faith and prayers of the Saints, until I have fully accomplished my mission in this life, and so firmly established the dispensation of the fullness of the priesthood in the last days, that all the powers of earth and hell can never prevail against it.

This constant persecution reminds me of the words of the Savior, when He said to the Pharisees, "Go ye, and tell that fox, Behold, I cast out devils, and I do cures today and tomorrow, and the third day I shall be perfected." I suspect that my Heavenly father has decreed that the Missourians shall not get me into their power; if they do, it will be because I do not keep out of their way.

I shall triumph over my enemies: I have begun to triumph over them at home, and I shall do it abroad. All those that rise up against me

Prest. Joseph Smith opened the meeting by addressing the Society. He commenced by expressing his happiness and thankfulness for the privilege of being present on the occasion. He said that great exertions had been made on the part of our enemies, but they had not accomplished their purpose— God had enabled him to keep out of their hands— he had war'd a good warfare **[p.93]** inasmuch as he had whip'd out all of [John C.] Bennett's host—

his feelings at the present time were, that inasmuch as the Lord Almighty had preserv'd him today.

He said it reminded him of the Savior, when he said to the pharisees, "Go ye and tell that fox, Behold I cast out devils, and I do cures today and tomorrow, and the third day I shall be perfected." &c. He said he expected the heavenly Father had decreed that the Missourians shall not get him— if they do, it will be because he does not keep out of the way.

Prest. S. continued by saying, I shall triumph over my enemies— I have begun to triumph over them at home and I shall do it abroad—

will surely feel the weight of their iniquity upon their own heads. Those that speak evil of me and the Saints are ignorant or abominable characters, and full of iniquity. All the fuss, and all the stir, and all the charges got up against me are like the jack-a-lantern, which cannot be found.

all those that rise up against me will feel the weight of their iniquity upon their own heads— those that speak evil are abominable characters— and full of iniquity— All the fuss and all the stir against me, is like the jack in the lantern, it cannot be found.[37]

No Man Without Fault

Relief Society Minutes

Although I do wrong, I do not the wrongs that I am charged with doing; the wrong that I do is through the frailty of human nature, like other men. No man lives without fault. Do you think that even Jesus, if He were here, would be without fault in your eyes? His enemies said all manner of evil against Him— they all watched for iniquity in Him. How easy it was for Jesus to call out all the iniquity of the hearts of those whom He was among!

Altho' I do wrong, I do not the wrongs that I am charg'd with doing— the wrong that I do is thro' the frailty of human nature like other men. No man lives without fault. Do you think that even Jesus, if he were here would be without fault in your eyes? Th[e]y said all manner of evil against him— they all watch'd for iniquity. How easy it was for Jesus to call out all the iniquity of the hearts of those whom he was among?[38]

Most Injury Comes from Little Evils

Relief Society Minutes

The servants of the Lord are required to guard against those things that are calculated to do the most evil. The little foxes spoil the vines— little evils do the most injury to the Church. If you have evil feelings, and speak of them to one another, it has a tendency to do mischief. These things [p.259] result in those evils which are calculated to cut the throats of the heads of the Church.

The servants of the Lord are required to guard against those thing[s] that are calculated to do the most evil— the little foxes spoil the vines— little evils do the most injury to the church. If you have evil feelings and speak of them to one an other, it has a tendency to do mischief— these things result in those evils which are calculated to cut the throats of the heads of the church.

When I do the best I can—when I am accomplishing the greatest good, then the most evils and wicked surmisings are got up against me. I would to God that you would be wise. I now counsel you, that if you know anything calculated to disturb the peace or injure the feelings of your brother or sister, hold your tongues and the least harm will be done.

When I do the best I can— when I am accomplishing the greatest good, then the most evils are got up against me. I would to God that you would be wise. I now counsel you, if you know any thing, hold your tongues, and the least harm will be done.

---

37. 31 August 1842, *RSM*, 92–93. See also *WJS*, 129–30.
38. 31 August 1842, *RSM*, 93. See also *WJS*, 130.

The Female Relief Society have taken a most active part in my welfare against my enemies, in petitioning to the governor in my behalf. These measures were all necessary. Do you not see that I foresaw what was coming, beforehand, by the spirit of prophecy? All these movements had an influence in my redemption from the hand of my enemies. If these measures had not been taken, more serious consequences would have resulted. I have come here to bless you. The Society have done well: their principles are to practice holiness. God loves you, and your prayers in my behalf shall avail much: let them not cease to ascend to god continually in my behalf.

The Female Relief Society has taken the the most active part in my welfare— against my enemies— in petitioning to the Governor— These measures were all necessary— Do you not see that I foresaw what was coming beforehand, by the spirit of prophesy?— All had an influence in my redemption from the hand of my enemies. If these measures had not been taken, more serious consequences would have resulted. **[p.94]** I have come here to bless you. The Society has done well— their principles are to practice holiness— God loves you and your prayers in my behalf shall avail much— Let them not cease to ascend to God in my behalf.[39]

Persistence of Wicked Men

Relief Society Minutes

The enemies of this people will never get weary of their persecution against the Church, until they are overcome. I expect they will array everything against me that is in their power to control, and that we shall have a long and tremendous warfare. He that will war the true Christian warfare against the corruptions of these last days will have wicked men and angels of devils, and all the infernal powers of darkness continually arrayed against him. When wicked and corrupt men oppose, it is a criterion to judge if a man is warring the Christian warfare. When all men speak evil of you falsely, blessed are ye. Shall a man be considered bad, when men speak evil of him? No. If a man stands and opposes the world of sin, he may expect to have all wicked and corrupt spirits arrayed against him. But it will be but a little season, and all these afflictions will be turned away from us, inasmuch as we are faithful, and are not overcome by these evils. By seeing the blessings of the endowment rolling on, and the kingdom increasing and spreading from sea to sea, we shall rejoice that we were not overcome by these foolish things.

The enemy will never get weary— I expect he will array every thing against me— I expect a tremendous warfare. He that will war the christian warfare will have the angels of devils and all the infernal powers of darkness continually array'd against him. When wicked and corrupt men oppose, it is a criterion to judge if a man is warring the christian warfare. When all men speak evil of you, blessed are ye &c. Shall a man be considered bad, when men speak evil of him? No: If a man stands and opposes the world of sin, he may expect all things array'd against him. But it will be but a little season and all these afflictions will be turn'd away from us inasmuch as we are faithful and are not overcome by these evils. By seeing the blessings of the endowment rolling on, and the kingdom increasing and spreading from sea to sea; we will rejoice that we were not overcome by these foolish things.[40]

---

39. 31 August 1842, *RSM*, 93–94. See also *WJS*, 130–31.
40. 31 August 1842, *RSM*, 94. See also *WJS*, 131.

Baptism for the Dead

Relief Society Minutes

[p.260] A few very important things have been manifested to me in my absence respecting the doctrine of baptism for the dead, which I shall communicate to the Saints next Sabbath, if nothing should occur to prevent me.

Prest. S. then remark'd that a few things had been manifested to him in his absence, respecting the baptisms for the dead, which he should communicate next sabbath if nothing should occur to prevent.

Prest. S. then address'd the throne of Grace.[42]

* * *

President Smith said, "I have one remark to make respecting the baptism for the dead to suffice for the time being, until I have opportunity to discuss the subject at greater length—all persons baptized for the dead must have a recorder present, that he may be an eyewitness to record and testify of the truth and validity of his record. It will be necessary, in the General Council, that these things be testified to by competent witnesses. Therefore let the recording and witnessing of baptisms for the dead be carefully attended to from this time forth. If there is any lack, it may be at the expense of our friends; they may not come forth."[41] (Aug. 31, 1842.) DHC 5:139-141.

Prest. S. said he had one remark to make respecting the baptism for the dead— to suffice for the time being, until he has opportunity to discuss the subject to greater length— that is, all persons baptiz'd for the dead must have a Recorder present, that he may be an eyewitness to testify of it. It will be necessary in the grand Council, that these things be testified— let it be attended to from this time, but if there is any lack it may be at the expense of our friends— they may not come forth &c.[43]

Persecution the Heritage of the Righteous

From an Editorial in the "Times and Seasons," by the Prophet

* * *

Times and Seasons
PERSECUTION OF THE PROPHETS.

Abel was slain for his righteousness, and how many more up to the flood is not of much consequence to us now. But if we believe in present revelation, as published in the "Times and Seasons" last spring, Abraham, the prophet of the Lord, was laid upon the iron bedstead for slaughter; and the book of Jasher, which has not been disproved as a bad author, says he was cast into the fire of the Chaldees. Moses, the man of God, who killed an Egyptian

Abel was slain for his righteousness, and how many more up to the flood is not of much consequence to us now. But if we believe in present revelation, as published in the Times and Seasons last spring, Abraham, the prophet of the Lord, was laid upon the iron bedstead for slaughter; and the book of Jasher, which has not been disproved as a bad author, says he was cast into the fire of the Chaldees. Moses, the man of God, who killed an Egyptian

---

41. The original *TPJS* footnote reads: "See D&C, Sections 127, 128."
42. 31 August 1842, *RSM*, 94. See also *WJS*, 131.
43. 31 August 1842, *RSM*, 95. See also *WJS*, 131.

persecutor of the children of Israel, was driven from his country and kindred. Elijah had to flee his country, for they sought his life,—and he was fed by ravens. Daniel was cast into a den of lions: Micah was fed on the bread of affliction; and Jeremiah was cast into the filthy hole under the Temple; and did these afflictions come upon these prophets of the Lord on account of transgression? No! It was the iron hand of persecution—like the chains of Missouri! And mark—when these old prophets suffered, the vengeance of God, in due time, followed and left the wicked opposers of the Lord's anointed like Sodom and Gomorrah; like the Egyptians; **[p.261]** like Jezebel, who was eaten by dongs; and like all Israel, which were led away captive, till the Lord had spent his fury upon them—even to this day.

Let us come into New Testament times—so many are ever praising the Lord and His apostles. We will commence with John the Baptist. When Herod's edict went forth to destroy the young children, John was about six months older than Jesus, and came under this hellish edict, and Zacharias caused his mother to take him into the mountains, where he was raised on locusts and wild honey. When his father refused to disclose his hiding place, and being the officiating high priest at the Temple that year, was slain by Herod's order, between the porch and the altar, as Jesus said. John's head was taken to Herod, the son of this infant murderer, in a charger—notwithstanding there was never a greater prophet born of a woman than him!

---

44. The concept that John the Baptist's father, Zachariah [Zacharias], was killed by Herod's order in the temple courtyard comes from the apocryphal Protevangelium of James 23:1–24:4. (See Wilhelm Schneemelcher, ed., *New Testament Apocrypha*, trasn. R. McL. Wilson, rev. ed., 2 vols. [Westminster John Knox Press, 2003], 1:436–37.) Yet, biblical scholars traditionally believe that the "Zechariah" mentioned in Luke 11:51 is not the father of John the Baptist but, instead, a different Zechariah (mentioned in 2 Chronicles 24). (See John W. Wright, "Zechariah," in David Noel Freedman, ed., *The Anchor Bible Dictionary*, 6 vols. [Doubleday, 1992], 6:1058–59.) By attributing this article in the *Times and Seasons* to Joseph Smith, the belief that "the blood of Zacharias, which perished between the altar and the temple" (found in Luke 11:51) refers to John the Baptist's father has become a common view among many Latter-day Saints. It can be found in the writings of Latter-day Saint leaders and scholars and has appeared in Sunday school and Church Educational System manuals. S. Kent Brown wrote, "At issue is whether Joseph Smith wrote that editorial. If he did, he would have put his prophetic stamp

Jesus, the Son of God was crucified with his hands and feet nailed to the wood!

* * *

Saints Come Through Tribulation

Times and Seasons

It is a shame to the Saints to talk of chastisements, and transgressions, when all the Saints before them, prophets and apostles, have had to come up through great tribulation; whether a Herod, a Nero, or a Boggs, causes the affliction, or the blood to be shed, is all the same—these murderers will have their reward! and the saints theirs. How many have had to wander in sheep skins and goat skins, and live in caves and dens of the mountains, because the world was unworthy of their society! And was transgression or chastisement connected with their seclusion from the enjoyment of society? No! But remember, brethren, he that offends one of the least of the Saints, would be better off with a millstone tied to his neck and he and the stone plunged into the depth of the sea! Remember that he that gives a cup of cold water in the name of a disciple, to one of the saints in prison, or secluded from friends by reason of vexatious law suits, intended for persecution, shall in no wise lose his reward.

Never, while the spirit of liberty, or the virtue of a saint, hold communion in the flesh, let us hear of those who profess to be governed by the law of God, and make their garments [p.262] clean in the blood of the Lamb, shrinking from the assistance of those who bear the ark of the Lord—in the hour of danger!

It is a shme to the saints to talk of chastisements, and transgressions, when all the Saints before them, prophets and apostles, have had to come up through great tribulation; whether a Herod, a Nero, or a Boggs, causes the affliction, or the blood to be shed, is all the same,—these murderers will have their reward! and the saints theirs. How many have had to wander in sheep skins and goat skins, and live in caves and dens of the mountains, because the world was unworthy of their society! And was transgression, or chastisement connected with ther seclusion from the enjoyment of society? No! But remember, brethren, he that offends one of the least of the saints, would be better off with a mill stone tied to his neck and he and the stone plunged into the depth of the sea! Remember that he that gives a cup of cold water in the name of a disciple, to one of the saints in prison, or secluded from friends by reason of vexatious law suits, intended for persecution, shall in no wise lose his reward.

Never, while the spirit of liberty, or the virtue of a saint, hold communion in the flesh, let us hear of those who profess to be governed by the law of God, and make their garments clean in the blood of the Lamb, *shrinking* from the assistance of those who bear the ark of the Lord—*in the hour of danger!*[46]

* * *

---

on the notion that the Zacharias noted in Luke 11:51 was John the Baptist's father. As a matter of fact, the evidence stands against Joseph Smith's authoring the editorial in the *Times and Seasons*." S. Kent Brown, "Zacharias and Elisabeth, Joseph and Mary," in *The Life and Teachings of Jesus: From Bethlehem to the Sermon on the Mount*, ed. Richard Neitzel Holzapfel and Thomas A. Wayment (Deseret Book, 2005), 96. For a detailed examination of this issue, see Lynne Hilton Wilson, "The Confusing Case of Zacharias," *Religious Educator* 14, no. 2 (2013): 107–23.

45. *T&S* 3, no. 21 (1 September 1842): 902.
46. *T&S* 3, no. 21 (1 September 1842): 903.

Baptism

Times and Seasons
BAPTISM.

Upon looking over the sacred pages of the Bible, searching into the prophets and sayings of the apostles, we find no subject so nearly connected with salvation, as that of *baptism*. In the first place, however, let us understand that the word *baptise* is derived from the Greek verb *baptiso*, and means to immense or overwhelm, and that sprinkle is from the Greek verb *rantiso*, and means to scatter on by particles; then we can treat the subject as one inseperably connected with our eternal welfare; and always bear in mind that it is one of the only methods by which we can obtain a remission of sins in this world, and be prepared to enter into the joys of our Lord in the world to come.

As it is well known that various opinions govern a large portion of the sectarian world as to this important ordinance of the gospel, it may not be amiss to introduce the commissions and commands of Jesus himself on the subject.—He said to the twelve, or rather eleven at the time: Go ye therefore, and teach all nations, *baptising* them in the name of the Father, and of the Son, and of the Holy Ghost: teaching them to observe all things whatsoever I have commanded you: Thus it is recorded by Matthew. In Mark we have these important words: Go ye into *all the world*, and preach the gospel to every *creature*. He that believeth and is *baptised* shall be saved, and he that believeth not shall be *damned*. And to show how the believers are to be known from the *unbelievers*, he continues and says: And these signs shall follow them that believe: in my name shall they cast out devils: they shall speak with new tongues: they shall take up serpents: and if they drink any deadly thing it shall not hurt them: they shall lay hands on the sick and they shall recover. And in

we find the finishing clause like this,—that it was necessary that Christ should die and rise the third day—that remission of sins should be preached in his name among all nations, beginning at Jerusalem. And ye are witnesses of these things.

Luke we find the finish[p.904]ing clause like this,—that it was necessary that Christ should die and rise the third day—that remission of sins should be preached in his name among all nations, beginning at Jerusalem. *And ye are witnesses of these things.*[47]

Witnesses

Times and Seasons

We will now examine the witnesses. As it will be recollected, they were to wait at Jerusalem till they were endowed [p.263] with power from on high and then go and teach all nations whatsoever the Lord had commanded them. As Peter held the keys of the kingdom, we will examine him first.

We will now examine the witnesses. As it will be recollected, they were to wait at Jerusalem till they were endowed with power from on high and then go and teach all nations whatsoever the Lord had commanded them. As Peter held the keys of the kingdom, we will examine him first.

Now on the day of Pentecost, when there was a marvelous display of the gifts, according to the promise in Mark, many were pricked in the heart, and said unto Peter, and to the rest of the Apostles. Men and brethren what shall we do? Peter said unto them: Repent, and be baptized every one of you in the name of Jesus Christ, for the remission of sins, and ye shall receive the gift of the Holy Ghost, etc.—Here one of the witnesses says in so many words, repent and be baptized. And we are of the opinion that Peter having been taught by the Lord, and commissioned by the Lord, and endowed by the Lord, would be about as correct a counselor, or ambassador as we or they could enquire of to know the right way to enter into the kingdom.

Now on the day of Pentecost, when there was a marvellous display of the gifts, according to the promise in Mark, many were pricked in the heart, and said unto Peter, and to the rest of the Apostles, men and brethren what shall we do? Peter said unto them: Repent, and be *baptised* every one of you in the name of Jesus Christ, for the remissioe of sins, and ye shall receive the gift of the Holy Ghost, &c.—Here one of the witnesses says in so many words, repent and be *baptised*. And we are of the opinion that Peter having been taught by the Lord, and commissioned by the Lord, and endowed by the Lord, would be about as correct a counsellor, or ambassador as we or they could enquire of to know the *right way* to enter into the kingdom.

Again, Luke in his record of the Acts of the Apostles, says: And it came to pass, that while Apollos was at Corinth, Paul having passed through the upper coasts, came to Ephesus; and finding certain disciples, he said unto them, Have ye received the Holy Ghost since ye believed? And they said unto him. We have not so much as heard whether there be any Holy Ghost. And he said unto them, Unto

Again, Luke in his record of the acts of the Apostles, says:—And it came to pass, that while Apollos was at Corinth, Paul having passed through the upper coasts, came to Ephesus; and finding certain disciples, he said unto them, have ye received the Holy Ghost since ye believed? And they said unto him, We have not so much as heard whether there be any Holy Ghost. And he said unto them,

---

47. *T&S* 3, no. 21 (1 September 1842): 903–4.

what then were ye baptized? And they said: unto John's baptism. Then said Paul, John verily baptized with the baptism of repentance, saying unto the people, that they should believe on him which should come after him, that is on Christ Jesus. When they heard this, they were baptized in the name of the Lord Jesus.—And when Paul had laid his hands upon them, the Holy Ghost came on them; and they spake with tongues, and prophesied.

From the above witnesses we are informed that baptism was the essential point on which they could receive the gift of the Holy Ghost. It seems from the reasoning above that some sectarian Jew had been baptizing like John, but had forgotten to inform them that there was one to follow by the name of Jesus Christ, to baptize with fire and the Holy Ghost:—which showed these converts that their first baptism was illegal, and when they heard this they were gladly baptized, and after hands were laid on them, they received the gifts, according to promise, and spake with tongues and prophesied.

* * *

The Apostle says the Gospel is the power of God unto salvation [p.264] unto them that believe; and also informs us that life and immortality were brought to light through the gospel; that the scripture, as Paul said to the Galatians, foreseeing that God would justify the heathen through faith, preached before the gospel unto Abraham: saying, In thee shall all nations be blessed.

Unto what then were ye baptised? And they said. unto John's baptism. Then said Paul, John verily baptised with the baptism of repentance, saying unto the people, That they should believe on him which should come after him, that is on Christ Jesus. When they heard this, they were baptised in the name of the Lord Jesus.—And when Paul had laid his hands upon them, the Holy Ghost came on them; and they spake with tongues, and prophecied.

From the above witnesses we are informed that *baptism* was the essential point on which they could receive the gift of the Holy Ghost. It seems from the reasoning above that some sectarian *Jew* had been baptising *like* John, but had forgotten to inform them that there was one to follow by the name of Jesus Christ, to baptise with fire and the Holy Ghost:—which showed these converts that their first baptism was *illegal,* and when they heard this they were gladly baptised, and after hands were laid on them, they received the gifts, according to promise, and spake with *tongues and prophecied.*

* * *

The Apostle says the gospel is the power of God unto salvation unto them that believe; and also informs us that life and immortality were brought to light through the gospel; that the scripture, as Paul said to the Galatians, foreseeing that God would justify the heathen through faith, preached before the *gospel* unto Abraham: saying, In thee shall all nations be blessed.[48]

Gospel Always the Same

Times and Seasons

Now taking it for granted that the scriptures say what they mean, and mean what they say, we have sufficient grounds to go on and prove from the Bible that the gospel has always been the same, and the officers to officiate, the same; and the signs and fruits resulting from

Now taking it for granted that the scriptures say what they mean, and mean what they say, we have sufficient grounds to go on and prove from the bible that the gossel has always been the same; the ordinances to fulfil its requirements, the same; and the officers to officiate,

---

48. *T&S* 3, no. 21 (1 September 1842): 904.

the promises, the same: therefore, as Noah was a preacher of righteousness he must have been baptized and ordained to the priesthood by the laying on of the hands, etc. For no man taketh this honor unto himself except he be called of God as was Aaron, and Aaron was baptized in the cloud and in the sea, together with all Israel, as is related by the Apostle in Corinthians. This position or fact, is witnessed in this manner: the covenant of circumcision made with Abraham, and practiced steadily up to the departing of Israel out of Egypt, was abandoned in the wilderness, forty years—and renewed by Joshua after he passed over Jordan, and encamped at Gilgal, where he made sharp knives and circumcised the whole male portion of the church.

* * *

Nicodemus came to Jesus by night, and said unto him, Rabbi, we know that thou art a teacher come from God: for no man can do these miracles that thou doest, except God be with him. Jesus answered and said unto him, Verily, verily, I say unto thee, Except a man be born again he cannot see the kingdom of God. Nicodemus saith unto him, How can a man be born when he is old? can he enter the second time into his mother's womb, and be born?—Jesus answered, Verily, verily, I say unto thee, Except a man be born of water, and of the Spirit, he cannot enter into the kingdom of God. This strong and positive answer of Jesus, as to water baptism, settles the question: If God is the same yesterday, today, and forever: it [p.265] is no wonder he is so positive in the great declaration: He that believes and is baptized shall be saved, and he that believes not shall be damned! There was no other name given under heaven, nor

the same; and the *signs* and *fruits* resulting from the promises, the same: therefore, as Noah was a *preacher* of righteousness he must have been *baptised* and ordained to the priesthood by the laying on of the hands, &c. For no man taketh this honor upon himself except he be called of God as was Aaron, and Aaron was baptised in the cloud and in the sea, together with all Israel, as is related by the Apostle in Corinthians. This position or fact, is witnessed in this manner: the covenant of circumcission made with Abraham, and practiced steadily up to the departing of Israel out of Egypt, was abandoned in the wilderness, forty years—and renewed by Joshua after he passed over Jordan, and encamped at Gilgal, where he made sharp knives and circumcised the whole male portion of the church.[49]

Man Must Be Born Again

Times and Seasons

Circumcision was merely a sign of the priesthood, given to Abraham: according to the words of Jesus to Nicodemus, a ruler of the Jews: The same came to Jesus by night, and said unto him, Rabbi, we know that thou art a teacher come from God: for no man can do these miracles that thou doest, except God be with him. Jesus answered and said unto him, Verily, verily, I say unto thee, except a man be born again he cannot see the kingdom of God. Nicodemus saith unto him, How can a man be born when he is old? can he enter the second [p.905] time into his mother's womb, and be born?—Jesus answered, Verily, verily, I say unto thee, Except a man be born of water, and of the Spirit, he cannot enter into the kingdom of God. This strong and positive answer of Jesus, as to water baptism, settles the question: If God is the same yesterday, to day, and forever; it is no wonder he is so positive in the great declaration: He that believes and is *baptised* shall be *saved*, and he that believes not shall be damned! There was no other name

---

49. *T&S* 3, no. 21 (1 September 1842): 904.

no other ordinance admitted, whereby men could be saved: No wonder the Apostle said, being "buried with him in baptism," ye shall rise from the dead! No wonder Paul had to arise and be baptized and wash away his sins: No wonder the angel told good old Cornelius that he must send for Peter to learn how to be saved: Peter could baptize, and angels could not, so long as there were legal officers in the flesh holding the keys of the kingdom, or the authority of the priesthood. There is one evidence still further on this point, and that is that Jesus himself when he appeared to Paul on his way to Damascus, did not inform him how he could be saved. He had set in the church first Apostles, and secondly prophets, for the work of the ministry, perfecting of the saints, etc.; and as the grand rule of heaven was that nothing should ever be done on earth without revealing the secret to his servants the prophets, agreeably to Amos 3:7, so Paul could not learn so much from the Lord relative to his duty in the common salvation of man, as he could from one of Christ's ambassadors called with the same heavenly calling of the lord, and endowed with the same power from on high—so that what they loosed on earth, should be loosed in heaven; and what they bound on earth should be bound in heaven: He, the Lord being a priest forever, after the order of Melchizedek, and the anointed Son of God, from before the foundation of the world, and they be begotten sons of Jesus though the gospel, to teach all nations—and lo I am with you always to the end of the world—that is—by the other comforter which the world cannot receive—for ye are the witnesses—having the testimony of Jesus which is the spirit of prophecy.

given under heaven, nor no other ordinance admitted, whereby men could be saved: No wonder the Apostle said, being "*buried* with him in *baptism*," ye shall rise from the dead! No wonder Paul had to arise and be baptised and wash away his sins: No wonder the angel told good old Cornelius that he must send for Peter to learn how to be saved: Peter could baptise, and angels could not, so long as there were legal officers in the flesh holding the keys of the kingdom, or the authority of the priesthood. There is one evidence still further on this point, and that is that Jesus himself when he appeared to Paul on his way to Damascus, did not inform him how he could be saved. He had set in the church firstly Apostles, and secondly prophets, for the work of the ministry, perfecting of the saints, &c.; and as the grand rule of heaven was that nothing should ever be done on earth without revealing the secret to his servants the prophets, agreeably to Amos 3: 7. so Paul could not learn so much from the Lord relative to his duty in the common salvation of man, as he could from one of Christ's ambassadors called with the same heavenly calling of the Lord, and endowed with the same power from on high—so that what they loosed on earth, should be loosed in heaven; and what they bound on earth should be bound in heaven: He, the Lord being a priest forever, after the order of Melchisedec, and the anointed son of God, from before the foundation of the world, and they the begotten sons of Jesus through the gospel, to teach all nations—*and lo I am with you always to the end of the world*—that is—by the other comforter which the world cannot receive—for ye are the witnesses—having the testimony of Jesus which is the spirit of prophecy.[50]

Necessity of Repentance

Times and Seasons

From what has already been introduced as testimony to prove that no man can be saved

From what has already been introduced as testimony to prove that no man can be saved

---

50. *T&S* 3, no. 21 (1 September 1842): 904–5.

without baptism, it will be seen and acknowledged that if there was sin among men, repentance was as necessary at one time or age of the world as another—and that other foundation can no man lay than that is laid, which is Jesus Christ. If, then, Abel was a righteous man he had to become so by keeping the commandments; if [p.266] Enoch was righteous enough to come into the presence of God, and walk with him, he must have become so by keeping his commandments, and so of every righteous person, whether it was Noah, a preacher of righteousness; Abraham, the father of the faithful; Jacob, the prevailer with God; Moses, the man who wrote of Christ, and brought forth the law by commandment, as a schoolmaster to bring men to Christ, or whether it was Jesus Christ himself, who had no need of repentance, having no sin, according to his solemn declaration to John:—now let me be baptized: for no man can enter the kingdom without obeying this ordinance: for thus it becometh us to fulfil ALL RIGHTEOUSNESS. Surely, then, if it became John and Jesus Christ, the Savior, to fulfil all righteousness to be baptized—so surely, then, it will become every other person that seeks the kingdom of heaven to go and do likewise; for he is the door, and if any person climbs up any other way, the same is a thief and a robber!

without baptism, it will be seen and acknowledged that if there was sin among men, repentance was as necessary at one time or age of the world as another—and that other foundation can no man lay than that is laid, which is Jesus Christ. If, then Abel was a righteous man he had to become so by keeping the commandments: if Enoch was righteous enough to come into the presence of God, and walk with him, he must have become so by keeping his commandments, and so of every righteous person, whether it was Noah, a preacher of righteousness; Abraham, the father of the faithful; Jacob, the prevailer with God; Moses, the man who wrote of Christ, and brought forth the law by commandment, as a school master to bring men to Christ, or whether it was Jesus Christ himself, who had no need of repentance, having did no sin; according to his solemn declaration to John:—*now let me be baptised:* for no man can enter the kingdom without obeying this ordinance: FOR THUS IT BECOMETH US TO FULFIL ALL RIGHTEOUSNESS. Surely, then, if it became John and Jesus Christ, the Saviour, to fulfil *all righteousness to be baptised*—so surely, then, it will become every other person that seeks the kingdom of heaven to go and do likewise; for he is the door, and if any person climbs up any other way, the same is a thief and a robber![51]

Baptism Required in All Ages

Times and Seasons

In the former ages of the world, before the Savior came in the flesh, "the saints" were baptized in the name of Jesus Christ to come, because there never was any other name whereby men could be saved; and after he came in the flesh and was crucified, risen from the dead and ascended into heaven, that they might be buried in baptism like him, and be raised in glory like him, that as there was but one Lord, one faith, one baptism, and one God

In the former ages of the world, before the Saviour came in the flesh, "the saints" were baptised in the name of Jesus Christ to come, because there never was any other name whereby men could be saved; and after he came in the flesh and was crucified, then *the saints* were baptised in the name of Jesus Christ, crucified, risen from the dead and ascended into heaven, that they might be buried in baptism like him, and be raised in glory like

---

51. *T&S* 3, no. 21 (1 September 1842): 905.

and father of us all, even so there was but one door to the mansions of bliss. Amen. (Sept. 1, 1842.) T&S 3:902-905.

him, that as there was but *one* Lord, *one* faith, *one* baptism, and *one* God and father of us all, even so there was but *one* door to the mansions of bliss. Amen.—ED.[52]

"FACTS ARE STUBBORN THINGS"

Greatness of the Jaredites and Nephites

Times and Seasons

From an extract from "Stephen's Incidents of Travel in Central America," it will be seen that the proof of the Nephites and Lamanites dwelling on this continent, according to the account in the Book of Mormon, is developing itself in a more satisfactory way than the most sanguine believer in that revelation could have anticipated. It certainly affords us a gratification that the world of mankind does not enjoy, to give publicity [p.267] to such important developments of the remains and ruins of those mighty people.

When we read in the Book of Mormon that Jared and his brother came on to this continent from the confusion and scattering at the Tower, and lived here more than a thousand years, and covered the whole continent from sea to sea, with towns and cities; and that Lehi went down by the Red Sea to the great Southern Ocean, and crossed over to this land, and landed a little south of the Isthmus of Darien, and improved the country according to the word of the Lord, as a branch of the house of Israel, and then read such a goodly traditionary account as the one below, we can not but think the Lord has a hand in bringing to pass his strange act, and proving the Book of Mormon true in the eyes of all the people. The extract below, comes as near the real fact,

From an extract from "Stephens' Incidents of Travel in Central America," it will be seen that the proof of the Nephites and Lamanites [p.922] dwelling on this continent, according to the account in the Book of Mormon, is developing itself in a more satisfactory way than the most sanguine believer in that revelation, could have anticipated. It certainly affords us a gratification that the world of mankind does not enjoy, to give publicity to such important developements of the remains and ruins of those mighty people.

When we read in the Book of Mormon that Jared and his brother came on to this continent from the confusion and scattering at the Tower, and lived here more than a thousand years, and covered the whole continent from sea to sea, with towns and cities; and that Lehi went down by the Red Sea to the great Southern Ocean, and crossed over to this land, and landed a little south of the Isthmus of Darien, and improved the country according to the word of the Lord, as a branch of the house of Israel, and then read such a goodly traditionary account, as the one below, we can not but think the Lord has a hand in bringing to pass his strange act, and proving the Book of Mormon true in the eyes of all the people. The extract below, comes as near the real fact,

---

52. *T&S* 3, no. 21 (1 September 1842): 905. Although Joseph Smith was the editor of the *Times and Seasons* at this time, and though this article was signed "ED," some scholars have questioned whether the Prophet was the actual author of the article. See Appendix D for information regarding the possibility that some individuals wrote and published articles in the Prophet's name. Curiously, the previous article from the same issue (titled "Persecution of the Prophets," and included in *TPJS*) was not signed. It is possible that, because it was unsigned, Joseph Fielding Smith simply assumed that Joseph Smith was its author.

as the four Evangelists do to the crucifixion of Jesus.—Surely "facts are stubborn things." It will be as it ever has been, the world will prove Joseph Smith a true prophet by circumstantial evidence, *in experiments*, as they did Moses and Elijah. Now read Stephens' story:

"According to Fuentes, the chronicler of the kingdom of Guatimala, the kings of Quinche and Cachiquel were descended from the Toltecan Indians, who, when they came into this country, *found it already inhabited by people of different nations.* According to the the manuscripts of Don Juan Torres, the grandson of the last king of the Quiches, which was in the possession of the lieutenant general appointed by Pedro de Alvarado, and which Fuentes says he obtained by means of Father Francis Vasques, the historian of the order of San Francis, *the Toltecas themselves descended from the house of Israel*, who were released by Moses from the tyranny of Pharaoh, and after crossing the Red Sea, fell into Idolatry. To avoid the reproofs of Moses or from fear of his inflicting upon them some chastisement, they separated from him and his brethren, and under the guidance of Tanub, their chief, passed from one continent to the other, to a place which they called the seven caverns, a part of the kingdom of Mexico, where they founded the celebrated city of Tula."[53]

Effects of Disobeying Counsel

Joseph Smith's Journal

Saturday 29th. About 10 o clock this morning president Joseph rode up and viewed the Temple. He expressed his satisfaction at the arrangements made and was pleased the progress made in that sacred edifice. After conversing with several of the brethren and shaking hands with numbers who were very

---

53. *T&S* 3, no. 22 (15 September 1842): 921–22. The name of the author of this article is not given, though Joseph was the editor of the periodical at this time. Joseph Fielding Smith appears to presume the Prophet Joseph is the author.

I returned home; but soon afterwards went over to the store, where a number of brethren and sister were assembled, who had arrived this morning from the neighborhood of New York, Long Island, etc. After Elders Taylor, Woodruff and Samuel Bennett had addressed the brethren and sisters, I spoke to them at considerable length, showing them the proper course to pursue, and how to act in regard to making purchases of land, etc.

I showed them that it was generally in consequence of the brethren disregarding or disobeying counsel that they became dissatisfied and murmured; and many when they arrived here, were dissatisfied with the conduct of some of the Saints, because everything was not done perfectly right, and they get angry, and thus the devil gets advantage over them to destroy them. I told them I was but a man, and they must not expect me to be perfect; if they expected perfection from me, I should expect it from them; but if they would bear with my infirmities and the infirmities of the brethren. I would likewise bear with their infirmities.

I told them it was likely I would have again to hide up in the woods, but they must not be discouraged, but build up the city, the Temple, etc. When my enemies take away my rights, I will bear it and keep out of the way; but if they take away your rights, I will fight for you. I blessed them and departed. (Oct. 29, 1842.) DHC 5:181.

much rejoiced to see their Prophet again, he returned home; but soon afterwards went over to the store where a number of brethren and sisters were assembled who had arrived this morning from the neighborhood of New York, Long Island &c. After E[lde]rs [John] Taylor, [Wilford] Woodruff and Samuel Bennett had addressed the brethren and sisters President Joseph spoke to them considerable, showing them the proper course to pursue and how to act in regard to making purchases of land &c.

He showed them that it was generally in consequence of the brethren disobeying or disregarding council, that they became dissatisfied and murmered; and many when they arrived here were dissatisfied with the conduct of some of the saints because every thing was not done perfectly right, and they get mad and thus the devil gets advantage over them to destroy them. He said he was but a man and they must not expect him to be perfect; if they expected perfection from him, he should expect it from them, but if they would bear with his infirmities and the infirmities of the brethren, he would likewise bear with their infirmities.

He said, it was [p.165] likely he would have again to hide up in the woods, but they must not be discouraged but roll on the city, the Temple &c. When his enemies took away his rights he would bear it and keep out of the way but "if they take away your rights I will fight for you." After speaking considerable and giving them council he blessed them and departed. The company appear to be in good spirits.[54]

The Rule of Christ in the Millennium

While in conversation at Judge Adams' during the evening, I said, Christ and the resurrected Saints will reign over the earth during the thousand years. They will not probably dwell upon the earth, but will visit it when

Joseph Smith's Journal
Joseph said to Judge Adams that christ & the Resurrected saints will reign over the earth, but not dwell on the earth visit it when go they please or when necessary to govern it. There will be wicked men <on> the earth during the

---

54. 29 October 1842, *JSP, J2*, 164–65.

they please, or when it is necessary to govern it. There will be wicked[55] men on the **[p.269]** earth during the thousand years. The heathen nations who will not come up to worship will be visited with the judgments of God, and must eventually be destroyed from the earth. (Dec. 30, 1842.) DHC 5:212.

If any person should ask me if I were a prophet, I should not deny it, as that would give me the lie; for, according to John, the testimony of Jesus is the spirit of prophecy; therefore, if I profess to be a witness or teacher, and have not the spirit of prophecy, which is the testimony 1000 years. The heathen nations who will not come up to worship will be destroyed.[56]

What Constitutes a Prophet?

Joseph Smith's History
This A.M. we had a pleasant interview with Mr. Butterfield, Judge Douglas, Senator Gillespie & others. pres. Joseph stated to Mr. Butterfield the prominent points of difference in sentiment between the Latter Day Saints & sectarian viz: the latter are all circumscribed by some peculiar creed which deprives its members of the right of believing anything not contained in it; whereas the Latter Day Saints have no creed, but are ready to believe all true principle existing, as they are made manifest from time to time. He said further, that if any person should ask him if he was a prophet he should not deny it. As to deny it would give him the lie & then shewed from the Revelations of John that any man who has the testimony of Jesus has the spirit of prophesy &c.[57]

---

55. The original *TPJS* footnote reads: "The Prophet's statement that there will be wicked men on the earth during the Millennium has caused considerable confusion in the minds of many who have read in the Scripture in many places that when Christ comes the earth shall be cleansed from its wickedness, and that the wicked shall not stand, but shall be consumed. See D&C 5:18–19, 29:8–10, 101:23–25; Isaiah 24:1–3; Malachi 4:1. The evil-minded inhabitants, those 'who love and make a lie' and are guilty of all manner of corruption, will be consumed and pass away when Christ comes. In using the term 'wicked men' in this instruction at the home of Judge Adams, the Prophet did so in the same sense in which the Lord uses it in the eighty-fourth section of the Doctrine and Covenants, 49–53. The Lord in this scripture speaks of those who have not received the Gospel as being under the bondage of sin, and hence 'wicked.' However, many of these people are honorable, clean living men, but they have not embraced the Gospel. The inhabitants of the terrestrial order will remain on the earth during the Millennium, and this class are without the Gospel ordinances. See D&C 76:73–76."

56. 30 December 1842, *JSP, J2*, 200.

57. Clayton, Nauvoo Journal, 1 January 1843, cited in James B. Allen, *Trials of Discipleship: The Story of William Clayton, A Mormon* (University of Illinois Press, 1987): 92–93. See also 1 January 1843, History, D-1, 1433. Joseph Fielding Smith dated this statement 30 December 1842. One source for this entry is 1 January 1843, *JSP, J2*, 206, which states: "Joseph explained the nature of a prophet. Spirit of Prophecy. which is the testimony of Jesus is necessary to constitute a witness or a preacher. or a prophet."

of Jesus, I must be a false witness; but if I be a true teacher and witness, I must possess the spirit of prophecy, and that constitutes a prophet; and any man who says he is a teacher or a preacher of righteousness, and denies the spirit of prophecy, is a liar, and the truth is not in him; and by this key false teachers and impostors may be detected. (Dec. 30, 1842.) DHC 5:215-216.[58]

Status of the Negro

At five went to Mr. Sollars' with Elders Hyde and Richards. Elder Hyde inquired the situation of the negro. I replied, they came into the world slaves, mentally and physically. Change their situation with the whites, and they would be like them. They have souls, and are subjects of salvation. Go into Cincinnati or any city, and find an educated negro, who rides in his carriage, and you will see a man who has risen by the powers of his own mind to his exalted state of respectability. The slaves in Washington are more refined than many in high places, and the black boys will take the shine off many of those they brush and wait on.

Elder Hyde remarked, "Put them on the level, and they will rise above me." I replied, if I raised you to be my equal, and then attempted to oppress you, would you not be indignant and try to rise above me, as did Oliver Cowdery, Peter Whit**[p.270]**mer, and many others, who said I was a fallen Prophet, and they were capable of leading the people, although I never attempted to oppress them, but had always been lifting them up? Had I anything to do with the negro, I would confine them by strict law to their own species, and put them on a national equalization.

Joseph Smith's Journal

5 <o clock> went to Mr Wm Sollars Mr Bridewood visited. in the eve Elder [Orson] Hyde was present. & after Supper asked what is the situation of the Negro? They come into the world slaves mentally & phy[s]ically. change their situation with the white & they would be like them. they have souls & are subjects of salvation go into cincinati— & find one— educated rid[e]s in his carriage he has risen by the power of his mind to his exal[te]d state. of r[e]spectability. Slaves in washington more refind than the presidents. boys will take the shine off those they brush & wait on.—

Says Elder Hyde put them on the level & they will rise above me.— Joseph[:] if I raised you to be my equal & then attempt to oppress you would you not be indignant, & Try to rise above me? did not— Oliver Cowd[e]ry & Peter Whitmer & ma[n]y others say I was fallen & they were cap[a]ble of Leading the people had I any thing to do with the negro— I would confine them to by strict Laws to their own Species put them on a national Equalization[59]

---

58. The portion (in the original *TPJS*) beginning with "Therefore if I profess to be a witness or teacher" and concluding with "false teachers and imposters may be detected" is not found in the original source, but was added later in 1 January 1843, History, D-1, 1433.

59. 2 January 1843, *JSP, J2*, 212.

Necessity of Faith

	Joseph Smith's Journal
Because faith is wanting, the fruits are. No man since the world was had faith without having something along with it. The ancients quenched the violence of fire, escaped the edge of the sword, women received their dead, etc. By faith the worlds were made. A man who has none of the gifts has no faith; and he deceives himself, if he supposes he has. Faith has been wanting, not only among the heathen, but in professed Christendom also, so that tongues, healings, prophecy, and prophets and apostles, and all the gifts and blessings have been wanting.	Because faith is wanting the fruits are not.— No man Since the world was ever had faith without having something along with it. The ancients quenched the violence of escaped the edged of the sword women recevd their Dead. &c by faith the worlds were made.— a man who has none of the gifts— has no faith he deceives himself if he supposes it. faith has been wanting not only **[p.213]** among the heathen but but professed Christedom also.— that Tongues. & heali[n]gs & prophecy. & prophets & apostles & all these gifts & blessings have been wanting.——Joseph spoke at great length, & edification. to the little co[mpany] <obje[c]tions being made to the prophets meeknss>— I am meek & lowly in hea[r]t I will personify Jesus for a moment to illustrate & you ~~inquiry~~ inquirers— Wo unto you ye Doctors Wo unto you ye scribes pharises & Hypocrits— You cannot find the place where I ever went that I found fault with their food their drink their house or their Lodging— no never, & this is what is meant & by the meekness & Lowliness of Jesus[60]
Some of the company thought I was not a very meek Prophet; so I told them: "I am meek and lowly in heart," and will personify Jesus for a moment, to illustrate the principle, and cried out with a loud voice, "Woe unto you, ye doctors; woe unto you, ye lawyers; woe unto you, ye scribes, Pharisees, and hypocrites!" But you cannot find the place where I ever went that I found fault with their food, their drink, their house, their lodgings; no, never; and this is what is meant by the meekness and lowliness of Jesus.	

False Reports

	Joseph Smith's Journal
Mr. Sollars stated that James Mullone, of Springfield, told him as follows:—"I have been to Nauvoo, and seen Joe Smith, the Prophet: he had a gray horse, and I asked him where he got it; and Joe said, "You see that white cloud." "Yes." "Well as it came along, I got the horse from that cloud." This is a fair specimen of the ten thousand foolish lies circulated by this generation to bring the truth and its advocates into disrepute.	Mr Sollars stated that James Mullone— carpenter, of Springfield told him he "had been to Nauvoo & seen Joe Smith the prophet. he had a grey horse & I asked him where he got it & the Prophet said, you see that white cloud? yes, well ~~it~~ as it come along I got the horse from that cloud" Joseph replied <u>it was a lie. I never told him so.</u>

---

60. 2 January 1843, *JSP, J2*, 212–13.

What is it that inspires professors of Christianity generally with a hope of salvation? It is that smooth, sophisticated influence of the devil, by which he deceives the whole world. But, said Mr. Sollars, "May I not repent and be baptized, and not pay any attention to dreams, visions, and other gifts of the [p.271] Spirit?" I replied: "Suppose I am traveling and am hungry, and meet with a man and tell him I am hungry, and he tells me to go yonder, there is a house of entertainment, go and knock, and you must conform to all the rules of the house, or you cannot satisfy your hunger; knock, call for food, sit down and eat;—and I go and knock, and ask for food, and sit down to the table, but do not eat, shall I satisfy my hunger? No. I must eat. The gifts are the food; and the graces of the Spirit are the gifts of the Spirit. When I first commenced this work and had got two or three individuals to believe, I went about thirty miles with Oliver Cowdery, to see them. We had only one horse between us. When we arrived, a mob of about one hundred men came upon us before we had time to eat, and chased us all night; and we arrived back again a little after daylight, having traveled about sixty miles in all, and without food. I have often traveled all night to see the brethren; and, when traveling to preach the Gospel among strangers, have frequently been turned away without food." (Jan. 2, 1843.) DHC 5:217-219.

<In referen[ce] to professors Generally.> what is it inspires us with a hope of Salvation? It is that smooth sophi[s]ticated influence of the Devil by which he deceives the whole world.— Mr. Sollars says may I not Repent & be baptizd & not pay any attention to dreams & visions. &c? Joseph said suppose I am Travilling. & I am hungry I meet a man & tell him I am hungry. he tells me to go yonder, there is a house for Entertainment, go knock, & you must conform to all the rules of the house or you cannot satisfy your hunger— knock call for food. & set down & eat.— & I go & knock— & ask for food & set down to the table— but do not eat shall I satisfy my hunger— No! I must Eat. the Gifts are the food.— The graces of the spirit are the Gifts of the spirit.—

Joseph[:] When I first commencd this work & had got 2 or 3 indiv[i]duals to believe I went about 30 miles with Oliver Cowdery— one horse between us to see them. When we arrivd a mob of a hundrd came upon us before we had time to eat. & chased us all night & we arrived back again about 60 miles in all. and without food a little after Day light.— —I have [p.214] often travelled all night to see the brethren. & often been turnd away without food;—[61]

The Kingdom of God

Wilford Woodruff's Journal
22ᵈ Sunday
President Joseph Smith deliver[e]d an interesting discourse at the Temple to ~~an inter~~ a large congregation[.] among other things he treated upon the kingdom of God & the baptism of John. He remarked[62] not set up on earth untill the day of pentecost & that John did

Some say the kingdom of God was not set up on the earth until the day of Pentecost, and

---

61. 2 January 1843, *JSP, J2*, 213-14.
62. 22 January 1843, *WWJ*, 1:530.

that John did not preach the baptism of repentance for the remission of sins. But I say, in the name of the Lord, that the kingdom of God was set up on the earth from the days of Adam to the present time, whenever there has been a righteous man on earth unto whom God revealed His word and gave power and authority to administer in His name. And where there is a priest of God—a minister who has power and authority from God to administer in the ordinances of the gospel and officiate in the priesthood of God—there is the kingdom of God. And, in consequence of rejecting the Gospel of Jesus Christ and the Prophets whom God hath sent, the judgments of God have rested upon people, the case with the cities of Sodom and Gomorrah, that were destroyed for rejecting the Prophets.

not preach the Baptism of repentance for the remission of sins[.] **[p.531]** But I say in the name of the Lord that the kingdom of God was set upon earth from the days of Adam to the present time whenever there has been a righteous man on earth unto whom God revealed his word & gave power & authority to administer in his name: And whare theire is a Priest of God, A minister who has power & Authority from God to administer in the ordinances of the Gospel & officiate in the Priesthood of God, theire is the kingdom of God & in consequence of rejecting the gospel of Jesus Christ & the Prophets whom God hath sent, the judgments of God hath rested upon people, cities & nations in various ages of the world, which was the case with the cities of Sodom & gomoroah who were destroyed for rejecting the Prophets.[63]

Where the Kingdom of God is Not, There is No Salvation

Wilford Woodruff's Journal

Now I will give my testimony. I care not for man. I speak boldly and faithfully and with authority. How is it **[p.272]** with the kingdom of God? Where did the kingdom of God begin? Where there is no kingdom of God there is no salvation. What constitutes the kingdom of God? Where there is a prophet, a priest, or a righteous man unto whom God gives His oracles; and where the oracles are not, there the kingdom of God is not.

Now I will give my testimony[.] I care not for man[.] I speak boldly & faithfully & with authority. How is it with the kingdom of God. whare did the kingdom of God begin. whare their is no kingdom of God their is no salvation. what constitutes the kingdom of God Whare there is a prophet, a priest, or a righteous man unto whom God gives his oracles there is the kingdom of God, & whare the oracles of God are not there the kingdom of God is not.

In these remarks, I have no allusion to the kingdoms of the earth. We will keep the laws of the land; we do not speak against them; we never have, and we can hardly make mention of the state of Missouri, of our persecutions there, but what the cry goes forth that we are guilty of larceny, burglary, arson, treason, murder, &c., &c., which is false. We speak of the kingdom of God on the earth, not the kingdoms of men.

In these remarks I have no allusion to the kingdoms of the earth. we will keep the Laws of the Land. we do not speak against them. we never have & we can hardly make mention of the State of Missouri of our persecutions there &c but what the cry goes forth that we are guilty of larceny, Bur[g]lary, arson treason & murder &c &c which is fals[e]. we speak of the kingdom of God on the earth not the kingdoms of men.[64]

---

63. 22 January 1843, *WWJ*, 1:530–31. See also *JSP, D11*, 357.
64. 22 January 1843, *WWJ*, 1:531. See also *JSP, D11*, 357–58.

Need of Revelation

Wilford Woodruff's Journal

The plea of many in this day is, that we have no right to receive revelations; but if we do not get revelations, we do not have the oracles of God; and if they have not the oracles of God, they are not the people of God. But say you, What will become of the world, or the various professors of religion who do not believe in revelation and the oracles of God as continued to His Church in all ages of the world, when He has a people on earth? I tell you, in the name of Jesus Christ, they will be damned; and when you get into the eternal world, you will find it will be so, they cannot escape the damnation of hell.

The plea of many in this day is that we have no right to receive revelations. But if we do not get revelations we do not have the oracles of God & if they have not the oracles of God they are not the people of God[.] But say you what will become of the world or the various professors of religion who do not believe in revelation & the oracles of God as Continued to his Church in all ages of the world when he has a people on earth. I Tell you in the name of Jesus Christ they will be damned & when you get into the eternal world you will find it to be so[.] they cannot escape the damnation of hell.[65]

John Held Keys of Aaronic Priesthood

Wilford Woodruff's Journal

As touching the Gospel and baptism that John preached, I would say that John came preaching the Gospel for the remission of sins; he had his authority from God, and the oracles of God were with him, and the kingdom of God for a season seemed to rest with John alone. The Lord promised Zacharias that he should have a son who was a descendant of Aaron, the Lord having promised that the priesthood should continue with Aaron and his seed throughout their generations. Let no man take this honor upon himself, except he be called of God, as was Aaron; and Aaron received his call by revelations. An angel of God also appeared unto Zacharias while in the Temple, and told him that he should have a son, whose name should be John, and he should be filled with the Holy [p.273] Ghost. Zacharias was a priest of God, and officiating in the Temple, and John was a priest after his father, and held the keys of the Aaronic Priesthood, and was called of god to preach the Gospel of the kingdom of God. The Jews,

As touching the gospel & Baptism that John preached I would say that John Came preaching the gospel for the remission of Sins[.] he had his authority from God & the oricles of God were with him & the kingdom of [God] for a season seemed to rest be with John alone. The Lord promised Zecheriah that he should have a son, which was a desendant of Aaron & the Lord promised that the priesthood should Continue with Aaron & his seed throughout their generations. Let No man take this honour upon himself except he be Called of God as was Aaron, & Aaron received his Call by Revelation. An angel of God Also appeared unto Zecheriah while in the Temple [and said] that he should have a son whose name should be John & he should be filled with the Holy Ghost[.] Zechariah was a priest of God & officiating in the Temple & John was a priest after his father & held the keys of the aronic priesthood & was Called of God to preache the Gospel & the kingdom of God & the Jews as a nation having departed from the Law of

---

65. 22 January 1843, *WWJ*, 1:531. See also *JSP, D11*, 358.

as a nation, having departed from the law of God and the Gospel of the Lord, prepared the way for transferring it to the Gentiles.

But, says one, the kingdom of God could not be set up in the days of John, for John said the kingdom was at hand. But I would ask if it could be any nearer to them than to be in the hands of John. The people need not wait for the days of Pentecost to find the kingdom of God, for John had it with him, and he came forth from the wilderness crying out, "Repent ye, for the kingdom of heaven is nigh at hand," as much as to say, "Out here I have got the kingdom of God, and you can get it, and I am coming after you; and if you don't receive it, you will be damned;" and the scriptures represent that all Jerusalem went out into John's baptism. There was a legal administrator, and those that were baptized were subjects for a king; and also the laws and oracles of God were there; therefore the kingdom of God was there; for no man could have better authority to administer than John; and our Savior submitted to that authority Himself, by being baptized by John; therefore the kingdom of God was set up on the earth, even in the days of John.

The Kingdom and Its Fruits

There is a difference between the kingdom of God and the fruits and blessings that flow from the kingdom; because there were more miracles, gifts, visions, healings, tongues, &c., in the days of Jesus Christ and His apostles, and on the day of Pentecost, than under John's administration, it does not prove by any means that John had not the kingdom of God, any more than it would that a woman had not a milkpan because she had not a pan of milk, for while the pan might be compared to the kingdom, the milk might be compared to the blessings of the kingdom.

God & the gospel the Lord prepared the way for transfering it to the gentiles.

But says one the kingdom of God Could not be set up in the days of John for John said the Kingdom was at hand[.] But I would ask if it could be any nearer to them than to be in the hands of John. the people need not wait for the days of Pentecost to find the kingdom of God for John had it with him, & he came forth from the wilderness crying out repent ye for the kingdom of heaven is at hand as much as to baul out here I have got the kingdom of God & I am coming after you. Ive got the kingdom of God & you can get it & I am Coming after you & if you dont receive it you will be damned & the Scriptures represent **[p.532]** that all Jerrusalem went out unto Johns Bapt<ism>[.] Here was a legal administrator, & those that were baptized were subjects for a king & also the laws & oracles of God were there[.] therefore the kingdom of God was there, for no man Could have better authority to Administer than John & our Savior submitted to that authority himself by being Baptized By John[.] therefore the kingdom of God was set up upon the earth even in the days of John.[66]

Wilford Woodruff's Journal

their is a difference between the kingdom of God & the fruits & blessings that flow from that kingdom becaus[e] their was more miracles, gifts, graces visions healings, tongues &c in the days of Jesus Christ & the Apostles, & on the day of pentecost than under Johns Administration. it does not prove by any means that John had not the kingdom of God; any more than it would that a woman had not a milk pan because she had not a pan of milk. for while the pan might be Compared to the kingdom the milk might be Compared to the blessings of the kingdom

---

66. 22 January 1843, *WWJ*, 1:531–32. See also *JSP, D11*, 358–60.

John was a priest after the order of Aaron, and had the keys of that priesthood, and came forth preaching repentance and baptism for the remission of sins, but at the same time cries out, "There cometh one mightier than I after me, the latchet of whose shoes I am not worthy to stoop down and [p.274] unloose," and Christ came according to the words of John, and He was greater than John, because He held the keys of the Melchizedek Priesthood and kingdom of God, and had before revealed the priesthood of Moses, yet Christ was baptized by John to fulfill all righteousness; and Jesus in His teachings says, "Upon this rock I will build my Church, and the gates of hell shall not prevail against it." What rock? Revelation.	John was a priest after the order of Aaron & had the keys of that priesthood & came forth preaching repentance & Baptism for the remission of sins but at the same time crys out there cometh one after me more mighter than I the latches of whose shoes I am not worthy to unlose, & christ came according to the words of John, & he was greater than John because he held the keys of Melchisedic Priesthood & the kingdom of God & had before revealed the priesthood to Moses. yet Christ was baptiz[e]d by John to fulfill all righteousness & Jesus in his teaching says upon this rock I will build my Church & the gates of hell shall not prevail against it[.] what rock. Revelation
Again he says, "Except a man be born of water and of the Spirit, he cannot enter into the kingdom of God;" and, "heaven and earth shall pass away, but my words shall not pass away." If a man is born of water and of the Spirit, he can get into the kingdom of God. It is evident the kingdom of God was on the earth, and John prepared subjects for the kingdom, by preaching the Gospel to them and baptizing them, and he prepared the way before the Savior, or came as a forerunner, and prepared subjects for the preaching of Christ; and Christ preached through Jerusalem on the same ground where John had preached; and when the apostles were raised up, they worked in Jerusalem, and Jesus commanded them to tarry there until they were endowed with power from on high. Had they not work to do in Jerusalem? They did work, and prepared a people for the Pentecost. The kingdom of God was with them before the day of Pentecost, as well as afterwards; and it was also with John, and he preached the same Gospel and baptism that Jesus and the apostles preached after him. The endowment was to prepare the disciples for their missions unto the world.	Again he says except ye are born of the water & the spirit ye Cannot inter into the kingdom of God, And though the heavens & earth should pass away my words shall not pass away[.] If a man is born of the water & the spirit he can get into the kingdom of God[.] it is evident the kingdom of God was on the earth & John prepared subject for kingdom by preaching the gospel to them & Baptising them & he prepared the way d~~oo~~ before the savior or came as a fore runner & prepared subject for the preaching of Christ, & &c Christ preached through Jerrusalem on the same ground whare John had preached & when the Apostles were raised up they worked in Jerrusalem & Jesus commanded them to tarry there untill they were endowed with power from on high[.] had they not work to do in Jerrusalem. they did work & prepared a people for the pentecost[.] The kingdom of God was with them before the day of pentecost as well as afterwords & it was also with John & he preached the same gospel & Baptism that Jesus & the Apostles preached after him The endowment was to prepare the desiples for their mission into the world.[67]

---

67. 22 January 1843, *WWJ*, 1:532. See also *JSP, D11*, 360–61.

Divine Authority Necessary to Make Ordinances Valid

Whenever men can find out the will of God and find an administrator legally authorized from God, there is the kingdom of God; but where these are not, the kingdom of God is not. All the ordinances, systems, and administrations on the earth are of no use to the children of men, unless they are ordained and authorized of God; for nothing will save a man but a legal administrator; for none others will be acknowledged either by God or angels.

I know what I say; I understand my mission and business. God Almighty is my shield; and what can man do if God is my friend? I shall not be sacrificed until my time comes; then I shall be offered freely. All flesh is as grass, and a governor [p.275] is no better than other men; when he dies he is but a bag of dust. I thank God for preserving me from my enemies; I have no enemies but for the truth's sake. I have no desire but to do all men good. I feel to pray for all men. We don't ask any people to throw away any good they have got; we only ask them to come and get more. What if all the world should embrace this Gospel? They would then see eye to eye, and the blessings of God would be poured out upon the people, which is the desire of my whole soul. Amen. (Jan. 22, 1843.) DHC 5:256-259.

Wilford Woodruff's Journal

whenever men can find out the will of God & find an Administrator legally authorized from God there is the kingdom of God[.] but whare these are not, the kingdom of God is not[.] All the ordinances Systems, & Administrations on the earth is of no use to the Children of men unless they are ordained & authorized of God for nothing will save a man but a legel Administrator for none others will be acknowledge either by God or Angels that

I know what I say. I understand my mishion & business[.] God Almighty is my shield & what Can man do if God is my friend[?] I shall not be sacrafised untill my time comes[.] then I shall be offered freely. all flesh is is as grass & a governor is no better than other men[.] when he dies he is but a bag of dung. I thank God for preserving me from my enemies[.] I have no enmity[.] I have no desire but to do all men good[.] I feel to pray for all men[.] we dont ask any people to throw away any good they have got[.] we ownly ask them to Come & get more[.] what if all the world should embrace this gospel[?] they would then see eye to eye & the blessings of God would Be poured out upon the people which is my whol[e] Soul Amen[68]

Politics

To the Editor of the Wasp:—

Dear Sir: I have, of late, had repeated solicitations to have something to do in relation to the political farce about dividing the county; but as my feelings revolt at the idea of having anything to do with politics, I have declined in every instance in having anything to do on

Joseph Smith Letter

To the Editor of the Wasp:—

DEAR SIR: I have, of late, had repeated solicitations to have something to do in relation to the political farce about dividing the county, but as my feelings revolt at the idea of having any thing to do with politics, I have declined in every instance in having any thing to do

---

68. 22 January 1843, *WWJ*, 1:532. See also *JSP, D11*, 361–62.

the subject. I think it would be well for politicians to regulate their own affairs. I wish to be let alone, that I may attend strictly to the spiritual welfare of the church.

Please insert the above and oblige.
JOSEPH SMITH.
Nauvoo, Jan. 23, 1843.—The Wasp, Jan. 28, 1843, page 3.[69]

on the subject. I think it would be well for politicians to regulate their own affairs. I wish to be let alone that I may attend strictly to the spiritual welfare of the Church.

Please insert and oblige.
JOSEPH SMITH.
Nauvoo, Jan. 23, 1843.[70]

The Greatness and Mission of John the Baptist

Joseph Smith's Journal

I rise to address you on the important subjct. of the Prodagal Son
2 Items I wish— to noticce Last sabbath.— 2 questions saying of Jesus concerning John. a greater prophet. than Jonh [John]. 2,— least in the kingdom of God Greater than he.— some so blind they wont see. I dont expect I can wo[r]k mira[c]les enough to open **[p.251]** greatest propht. what constitudd him.—— no prop[h]et, if do no miracles John did no miracles.— How is it John was considerd one of the Greatest of Prophe[t]s? 3 things

The question arose from the saying of Jesus— "Among those that are born of women there is not a greater prophet than John the Baptist; but he that is least in the kingdom of God is greater than he." How is it that John was considered one of the greatest prophets? His miracles could not have constituted his greatness.

First. He was entrusted with a divine mission of preparing the way before the face of the Lord. Whoever had such a trust committed to him before or since? No man.

1st he was trusted with a divine missoin [mission] of preparing the way before the face of the Lord.— [blank] Trust before or since? no man!—

Secondly. He was entrusted with the important mission, and it was required at his hands, to baptize the Son of Man. Whoever had the honor of doing that? Whoever had so great a privilege and glory? Whoever led the Son of God into the waters of baptism, and had the privilege of beholding the Holy Ghost descend in the form of a dove, or rather in the **[p.276]** sign of the dove, in witness of that administration? The sign of the dove was instituted before the creation of the world, a witness for the Holy Ghost, and the devil cannot come in the sign of a dove. The Holy Ghost is

2d He was trusted & it was reqird at his ha[n]ds to baptize the son of Man. who evr did that? who had so gr[e]at a privelige & glory?— son of God into the waters of baptism & beholding the Holy Ghost.— in <in the sign> the form of a dove.— [blank]— [blank] with the sign of the dove. institutd before the creation Devil could not come in sign of a dove.— Holy Gh[o]st is a personage in the form of a personage.— does not confine itself to form of a dove.— but in sign of a dove.— No man holds the book more sacred than I do.—

---

69. Joseph Fielding Smith lists this being located on page 3 of this issue of *The Wasp*. However, it is actually found on page 4.
70. Joseph Smith, "To the Editor of the Wasp," *The Wasp* 1, no. 39 (28 January 1843): 4.

a personage, and is in the form of a personage. It does not confine itself to the form of the dove, but in sign of the dove. The Holy Ghost cannot be transformed into a dove; but the sign of a dove was given to John to signify the truth of the deed, as the dove is an emblem or token of truth and innocence.

Thirdly. John, at that time, was the only legal administrator in the affairs of the kingdom there was then on the earth, and holding the keys of power. The Jews had to obey his instructions or be damned, by their own law; and Christ Himself fulfilled all righteousness in becoming obedient to the law which he had given to Moses on the mount, and thereby magnified it and made it honorable, instead of destroying it. The son of Zacharias wrested the keys, the kingdom, the power, the glory from the Jews, by the holy anointing and decree of heaven, and these three reasons constitute him the greatest prophet born of a woman.

3ᵈ. John at that time was the only legal admini[s]trator holding the keys of Power thr [there] was on Earth. the keys the kingdm the power the glory from the Jews son of Zachari[a]h by the holy anoi[n]ting decree of heaven these 3 constitutd him the greatest born of woman.[71]

Christ Considered Least in the Kingdom by Jews

Joseph Smith's Journal

Second question:—How was the least in the kingdom of heaven great than he?

He that is least. in the Kingdom is gre[a]ter than he?

In reply I asked—Whom did Jesus have reference to as being the least? Jesus was looked upon as having the least claim in God's kingdom, and [seemingly] was least entitled to their credulity as a prophet; as though He had said—"He that is considered the least among you is greater then John—that is I myself."

who did the Jesus have refere[n]ce to?— Jesus. was looked up[o]n as the having the least claim in all gods kingdom.—

He that is considerd the least among you. is greater than John! that is myself.—[72]

***

The Parables of Jesus and the Interpretation of the Scriptures

Joseph Smith's Journal

In reference to the prodigal son, I said it was a subject I had never dwelt upon; that it was understood by many to be one of the intricate subjects of the scriptures; and even the Elders

Prodigal Son.— when you have heard go & read your bible. if the things are not verily true.— great deal of speculation. Subjct I never dwelt upon.— understood by many—

---

71. 29 January 1843, *JSP, J2*, 250–51.
72. 29 January 1843, *JSP, J2*, 251.

of this Church have preached largely upon it, without having any rule of interpretation. What is the rule of interpretation? Just no interpretation at all. Understand it precisely as it reads. I have a key by which I understand the scriptures. I enquire, what was the question which drew out the answer, [p.277] or caused Jesus to utter the parable? It is not national; it does not refer to Abraham, Israel or the Gentiles, in a national capacity, as some suppose. To ascertain its meaning, we must dig up the root and ascertain what it was that drew the saying out of Jesus.

While Jesus was teaching the people, all the publicans and sinners drew near to hear Him; "and the Pharisees and scribes murmured, saying: This man receiveth sinners, and eateth with them." This is the keyword which unlocks the parable of the prodigal son. It was given to answer the murmurings and questions of the Sadducees and Pharisees, who were querying, finding fault, and saying, "How is it that this man as great as He pretends to be, eats with publicans and sinners?" Jesus was not put to it so, but He could have found something to illustrate His subject, if He had designed if for nation or nations; but He did not. It was for men in an individual capacity; and all straining on this point is a bubble. "This man receiveth sinners and eateth with them."

And he spake this parable unto them—"What man of you, having an hundred sheep, if he lose one of them doth not leave the ninety-and-nine in the wilderness, and go after that which is lost, until he find it? And when he hath found it, he layeth it on his shoulders, rejoicing. And when he cometh home, he calleth together his friends and neighbors, saying unto them, Rejoice with me; for I have found my sheep which was lost. I say unto you, that likewise joy shall be in heaven over one sinner that repenteth, more than over ninety-and-nine just persons which need no repentance." The hundred sheep represent one hundred

to to one of the intricate subjects.— Elders in this church preach.— no rule of interpretation.— what is the rule of interpretati[o]n? Just no [p.252] interpretati[o]n at all, understand precisely as it read.— I have Key by whi[c]h I understa[n]d the scripture—— I enqire what was the question whi[c]h drew out the answer.——

nati[o]nal. Ab[r]aham. &ᶜ as some suppose 1ˢᵗ· place dig up the root— what drew out the saying out of Jesus?

Pharises & scribes murmured? this man recevess [receives] sinners & eatheth with them. this is the key word.— to answer the murmuring & qustioning of Saducees & Pharisee how is it this man <is> as great as he pretends to be. & eat with publican & sinners.—— Jesus not put to it so but he could have found somthing if the had discerned it for nations.— Men in an individaul capacity. all straining on this point is a bubblee.—

***

this man reciveth sinners—

he spoke this parable.— what man of you having an hundrd. sheep <&ᶜ> 100 saducees & Pharisees If you pharisees & saduce[e]s are in the sheepfold. I have no mission for you sent to look up sheep that are lost will back him up.— & make joy in heaven— hunting after a few individuals Laying it on his Shoulder— one publican you despise.— [blank] one piece of Silver— the piece which was lost.—

Sadducees and Pharisees are in the sheepfold, I have no mission for you; I am sent to look up sheep that are lost; and when I have found them, I will back them up and make joy in heaven." This represents hunting after a few individuals, or one poor publican, which the Pharisees and Sadducees despised.

He also gave them the parable of the woman and her ten pieces of silver, and how she lost one, and searching diligently, found it again, which gave more joy among the friends and neighbors than the nine which were not lost; like I say unto you, there is joy in the presence of the angels of God over one sinner that repenteth, more than over ninety-and-nine just **[p.278]** persons that are so righteous; they will be damned anyhow; you cannot save them. (Jan. 29, 1843.) DHC 5:260-262.

Joy in presence of the angels over one sinner that repe[n]teth so rightous they will be damned any how you cannot save them. rain off f[r]om a gooses back—[73]

Scriptural Correction

"The Spirit maketh intercession for us with groanings which cannot be uttered." It would be better thus: "The Spirit maketh intercession for us with striving which cannot be expressed." (Feb. 2, 1843.) DHC 5:264.

Joseph Smith's Journal
The spirit maketh. intercession &c better &c, "The spirit maketh intercession for us with striving which cannot be exp[r]essed:["][74]

The Calling of a Prophet

Wednesday, Feb. 8.—This morning I read German and visited with a brother and sister from Michigan, who thought that "a prophet is always a prophet;" but I told them that a prophet was a prophet only when he was acting as such.—DHC 5:265.

Joseph Smith's Journal
Wednesday Feb. 8. Lesson in German. Visited with breth[r]en & Sisters from. Michigan "A Prophet is not always a Prophet" only when he is acting as such.[75]

---

73. 29 January 1843, *JSP, J2*, 251–52. This rough draft of the sermon recorded by Willard Richards is probably the original or earliest source. Joseph Fielding Smith likely used the version found in 29 January 1843, History, D-1, 1458–59, and perhaps portions of what appears to be a report of the sermon in *T&S* 4, no. 13 (15 May 1843): 200.

74. 2 February 1843, *JSP, J2*, 254.

75. 8 February 1843, *JSP, J2*, 256.

The Sign Seeker

| | **Joseph Smith's Journal** |

When I was preaching in Philadelphia, a Quaker called out for a sign. I told him to be still. After the sermon, he again asked for a sign. I told the congregation the man was an adulterer; that a wicked and adulterous generation seeketh after a sign; and that the Lord had said to me in a revelation, that any man who wanted a sign was an adulterous person. "It is true," cried one, "for I caught him in the very act," which the man afterwards confessed when he was baptized. (Feb. 9, 1843.) DHC 5:268.

when I was preaching in Philadelphia a quaker wanted a sign— I told him to be still. after sermon he wanted a sign. I told the congregati[o]n the man was an adulterer, "A wicked & adulterous geneatin [generation]." & the Lord to me in a revelation that any man who. wantd a sign was adulteros person.— "It is true said one for I caught him in the very act.— which he afterwards confessed when he was baptized[76]

Views of the Prophet on Constitutional Powers

Joseph Smith's Journal

Situated as we are, with a flood of immigration constantly pouring in upon us, I consider that it is not only prudential, but absolutely necessary to protect the inhabitants of this city from being imposed upon by a spurious currency. Many of our eastern and old country fiends are altogether unacquainted with the situation of the banks in this region of country; and as they generally bring specie with them, they are perpetually in danger of being gulled by speculators. Besides there is so much uncertainty in the solvency of the best of banks, that I think it much safer to go upon the hard money system altogether.[77] I have examined the Constitution upon this subject and find my doubts removed. The Constitution is not a law, but it empowers the people to make laws. For instance, the Con[p.279]stitution governs the land of Iowa, but it is not a law for the people. The Constitution tells us what shall not be a lawful tender. Article I, Section 10 declares that nothing else except gold and silver shall be lawful tender, this not saying

I have read the Constitution. & find my doubts. removed.— the constitution is not a law. but empowers the people to make laws.— constitution govern the lands of Iowa but is not a law for the people. constitution tells what shall not be lawful tender— Constitution section 10 this is not saying gold & silver shall be lawful tender— it only provid[e]s the states may make a law— to make gold and silver— lawful Tender. the Ligislature have ceded up

---

76. 9 February 1843, *JSP, J2*, 258.

77. The first paragraph in this section of *TPJS* does not appear in Joseph Smith's journal. The source of this paragraph is *The Wasp* 1, no. 45 (8 March 1843): 2. John Taylor was editor of *The Wasp* at this time, and may have been the author of the unsigned article.

that gold and silver shall be lawful tender. It only provides that the state may make a law to make gold and silver lawful tender.

I know of no state in the Union that has passed such a law; and I am sure that Illinois has not. The legislature has ceded up to us the privilege of enacting such laws as are not inconsistent with the Constitution of the United States and the state of Illinois; and we stand in the same relation to the state as the state does to the Union.

The clause referred to in the Constitution is for the legislature—it is not a law for the people. The different states, and even Congress itself, have passed many laws diametrically contrary to the Constitution of the United States.

The state of Illinois has passed a stay law making property a lawful tender for the payment of debts; and if we have no law on the subject we must be governed by it. Shall we be such fools as to be governed by its laws, which are unconstitutional? No! We will make a law for gold and silver; and then the state law ceases and we can collect our debts. Powers not delegated to the states or reserved from the states are constitutional. The Constitution acknowledges that the people have all power not reserved to itself. I am a lawyer; I am a big lawyer and comprehend heaven, earth and hell, to bring forth knowledge that shall cover up all lawyers, doctors and other big bodies. This is the doctrine of the Constitution, so help me God. The Constitution is not law to us, but it makes provision for us whereby we can make laws. Where it provides that no one shall be hindered from worshiping God according to his own conscience, is a law. No legislature can enact a law to prohibit it. The Constitution provides to regulate bodies of men and not individuals. (Feb. 25, 1843.) DHC 5:289-290.

to us the privilige of enacting laws we stand in the same relation as the state.—

This clause is for the Legislature, is not a law— for the people. diametrically contra[r]y to the constitution. this state have passed a **[p.278]** stay law. making it lawful <to> tender to property.

and if we creat[e] no law. we must be govend [governed] by them.— shall we be such fools as to abide their laws. which are unconstitutional? No. we will make a law for Gold & Silver then their law ceases & we can collect our debts.— "Powers not delegated to the states— or reservd fr[o]m the states" is constituti[o]nal, congress. or constitution acknowledgd that the people have all power not reserved to itself) <I am a Lawyer> I am big Lawyer. & comprehnd heavn earth & hell— to bring forth knowledge which shall cover up all Lawyers & doctors—) this is the doctrine of the constitution so help me God.— the constitution is not Law to us— but provision to make laws, Where it provides that no one shall not be hinderd from worshipping God acording to his own conscenc [conscience] is a law.— No legislatu[r]e can enact a law,— to prohibit constitution provid[e]s to regulate bodies of men not individuals[78]

---

78. 25 February 1843, *JSP, J2*, 277–78. Joseph Fielding Smith used the following as his source: 25 February 1843, History, D-1, 1484.

The "Sign" of the Son of Man

Sir:—Among the many signs of the times and other strange things which are continually agitating the minds of men, I notice a small speculation in the Chicago Express, upon the certificate of one Hyrum Redding, of Ogle county, Illinois, stating **[p.280]** that he has seen the sign of the Son of Man as foretold in the 24th chapter of Matthew.

The slanderous allusion of a "seraglio" like the Grand Turk, which the editor applies to me, he may take to himself, for, "out of the abundance of the heart the mouth speaketh." Every honest man who has visited the city of Nauvoo since it existed, can bear record of better things, and place me in the front ranks of those who are known to do good for the sake of goodness, and show all liars, hypocrites and abominable creatures that, while vice sinks them down to darkness and woe, virtue exalts me and the Saints to light and immortality.

The editor, as well as some others, "thinks that Joe Smith has his match at last," because Mr. Redding thinks that he has seen the sign of the Son of Man. But I shall use my right, and declare that, notwithstanding Mr. Redding may have seen a wonderful appearance in the clouds one morning about sunrise (which is nothing very uncommon in the winter season) he has not seen the sign of the Son of Man, as foretold by Jesus; neither has any man, nor will any man, until after the sun shall have been darkened and the moon bathed in blood; for the Lord hath not shown me any such sign; and as the prophet saith, so it must be—"Surely the Lord God will do nothing, but He revealeth His secret unto His servants the prophets." (See Amos 3:7.) Therefore, hear this, O earth: The Lord will not come to reign over the righteous, in this world, in 1843, nor until everything for the Bridegroom is ready.

Battle of Gog and Magog

The battle of Gog and Magog will be after the millennium. The remnant of all the nations that fight against Jerusalem were commanded to go up to Jerusalem to worship in the millennium. (March 4, 1843.) DHC 5:298.

Joseph Smith's Journal

The Battle of Gog and Magog is after the Millenium, The[y] were command[ed] to come up to Jerusalem to worship in the Millenium.—[80]

Giving Blessings a Tax on Strength

Elder Jedediah M. Grant enquired of me the cause of my turning pale and losing strength last night while blessing children. I told him that I saw that Lucifer would exert his influ[p.281]ence to destroy the children that I was blessing, and I strove with all the faith and spirit that I had to seal upon them a blessing that would secure their lives upon the earth; and so much virtue went out of me into the children, that I became weak, from which I have not yet recovered; and I referred to the case of the woman touching the hem of the garment of Jesus. (Luke, 8:43-48.) The virtue here referred to is the spirit of life; and a man who exercises great faith in administering to the sick, blessing little children, or confirming, is liable to become weakened. (March 14, 1843.) DHC 5:303.

Joseph Smith's History
14 March 1843 • Tuesday

<14> Elder J[edediah] M. Grant enquired of me the cause of my turning pale and losing strength last night while blessing children; I told him that I saw that Lucifer would exert his influence to destroy the children that I was blessing, and I strove with all the faith and spirit that I had, to seal upon them a blessing, that would secure their lives upon the Earth, and so much virtue went out of me into the children that I became weak, of which I have not yet recovered, and referred to the case of the woman touching the hem of the garment of Jesus, (Luke 8th chapter) The virtue here referred to, is the spirit of life, and a man who exercises great faith in administering to the sick, blessing little children, or confirming, is liable to become weakened.[81]

---

79. *T&S* 4, no. 8 (1 March 1843): 113. The journal entry for 28 February 1843 in *JSP, J2*, 279, reads, "notice in Chicago Express that Wm <Hiram> Redding had seen sign of the son of man.— wrote Editor of Times & Seasons. for No 8. vol 4 that Reding had not seen the sign of the son of man. and he would not come in [18]43— &c see times & Seasons."

80. 4 March 1843, *JSP, J2*, 297.

81. 14 March 1843, History, D-1, 1497.

SECTION SIX

1843–1844

SECTION SIX

A Prophecy

Joseph Smith's Journal

[p.185] I prophesied, in the name of the Lord Jesus Christ, that Orrin Porter Rockwell would get away honorably from the Missourians. (March 15, 1843.) DHC 5:305.

Joseph. prophecied in the name of the Lord Jesus Christ. that [Orrin] Porter Rockwell will get away from the Missourians,[1]

Proclamation

Joseph Smith's Journal

Saturday March 25, 1843 In the office at 8 o clock. heard a report from Hyrum [Smith] concerning theives, as given by Z. [[Wilson]] and directed. a proclamation to be published offering secur[i]ty to all who will divulge their secrets,—[2]

The Wasp
Proclamation

To the Citizens of Nauvoo:

To the Citizens of Nauvoo.

Whereas it appears, by the republication of the foregoing proceedings and declaration, that I have not altered my views on the subject of stealing: And

Whereas it appears by the re-publication of the foregoing proceedings, and declaration, that I have not altered my views on the subject of stealing:

Whereas it is reported that there now exists a band of desperadoes, bound by oaths of secrecy, under severe penalties in case any member of the combination divulges their plans of stealing and conveying properties from station to station, up and down the Mississippi and other routes: And

And whereas it is reported that there now exists a band of desperadoes, bound by oaths of secrecy, under severe penalties in case any member of the combination divulges their plans of stealing and conveying properties from station to station up and down the Mississippi, and other routes:

Whereas it is reported that the fear of the execution of the pains and penalties of their secret oath on their persons prevents some members of said secret association (who have, through falsehood and deceit, been drawn into their snares) from divulging the same to the legally constituted authorities of the land:

And whereas it is reported that the fear of the execution of the pains and penalties of their secret oath, on their persons, prevents some of the members of said secret association, (who have, through falsehood and deceit, been drawn into their snares,) from divulging the same to the legally Constituted authorities of the land:

---

1. 15 March 1843, *JSP, J2*, 309.
2. 25 March 1843, *JSP, J2*, 316.

Know ye, therefore, that I, Joseph Smith, mayor of the city of Nauvoo, will grant and insure protection against all personal mob violence to each and every citizen of this city who will freely and voluntarily come before me and truly make known the names of all such abominable characters as are engaged in said secret combination for stealing, or are accessory thereto, in any manner. And I would respectfully solicit the co-operation of all ministers of justice in this and the neighboring states to ferret out a band of thievish outlaws from our midst. Given under my hand at Nauvoo City, this 25th day of March, A.D., 1843.
JOSEPH SMITH,
Mayor of said City.
—DHC 5:310.

Know ye therefore, That I, Joseph Smith, Mayor of the City of Nauvoo, will grant and ensure protection against all personal mob violence, to each and every citizen of this city, who will freely and voluntarily come before me, and truly make known the names of all such abominable characters as are engaged in said secret combination for stealing, or are accessory thereto in any manner; and I would respectfully solicit the co-operation of all ministers of Justice, in this and the neighboring States, to ferret out a band of thievish outlaws from our midst
Given under my hand at Nauvoo City, this, 25th day of March, A.D. 1843
Joseph Smith,
Mayor of said City.[3]

The Prophet On the Second Coming of Christ

Remarks at the Conference of the Church

Joseph Smith's Journal

[p.286] The question has been asked, can a person not belonging to the Church bring a member before the high council for trial? I answer, No. If I had not actually got into this work and been called of God, I would back out. But I cannot back out: I have no doubt of the truth. Were I going to prophesy, I would say the end [of the world] would not come in 1844, 5, or 6, or in forty years. There are those of the rising generation who shall not taste death till Christ comes.

<The question has been asked> can a member not belonging to the chu[r]ch bring a member before the high council, for trial? I answer No! I ask no jurisdiction. <in religious matters> I merely give my opinion when asked. If there was any feelings at Naashville because I gave my opniones [opinions], there is no occasion for it. I only advice the breth[r]en to come from Iowa, & they may do as they please. <about coming.> If I had not actually got into this work, & been called of God, I would back out . . . but I cannot back out,— I have no doubt of the truth. were I going to prophecy. I would procpesy [prophesy] the end will not come in 1844. [p.338] or 5— or 6. or 40 years more there are those of the rising generation who shall not taste death till christ come.

I was once praying earnestly upon this subject, and a voice said unto me, "My son, if thou livest until thou art eighty-five years of age, thou

<I was once praying earnestly upon this subject. and a voice said unto me.> My son, if thou livest till thou art 85 years of age, thou

---

3. Joseph Smith, "Proclamation, to the Citizens of Nauvoo," *The Wasp* 1, no. 48 (29 March 1843): 4.

shalt see the face of the Son of Man." I was left to draw my own conclusions concerning this; and I took the liberty to conclude that if I did live to that time, He would make His appearance. But I do not say whether He will make His appearance or I shall go where He is. I prophesy in the name of the Lord God, and let it be written—the Son of Man will not come in the clouds of heaven till I am eighty-five years old. Then read the 14th chapter of Revelation, 6th and 7th verses—"And I saw another angel fly in the midst of heaven, having the everlasting gospel to preach unto them that dwell on the earth, and to every nation, and kindred, and tongue, and people, saying with a loud voice, Fear God and give glory to Him, for the our of His judgment is come." And Hosea, 6th chapter, After two days, etc.,—2,520 years; which brings it to 1890. The coming of the Son of Man never will be—never can be till the judgments spoken of for this hour are poured out: which judgments are commenced. Paul says, "Ye are the children of the light, and not of the darkness, that that day should overtake you as a thief in the night." It is not the design of the Almighty to come upon the earth and crush it and grind it to powder, but he will reveal it to His servants the prophets.

Judah must return, Jerusalem must be rebuilt, and the temple, and water come out from under the temple, and the waters of the Dead Sea be healed. It will take some time to rebuild the walls of the city and the temple, Etc.; and all this must be done before the Son of Man will make his appearance. There will be wars and rumors of wars, signs in the heavens **[p.287]** above and on the earth beneath, the sun turned into darkness and the moon to blood, earthquakes in divers places, the seas heaving beyond their bounds; then will appear one grand sign of the Son of Man in heaven. But

shalt see the face of the son of man. . . . <I was left to draw my own conclusions concerni[n]g this &,> I took the liberty to conclude that if I did live till that time J̶e̶s̶u̶s̶ <he> would make his appearance.— <but I do not say whether he <u>will</u> make his appeara[n]ce, or I shall go where he is.—> I prophecy in the name of the Lord God.— & let it be written. <that the> Son of Man will not come in the heavns till I am 85. years old 48 years hence or about 1890.— <then Red> 14 Rev— 6 verse another angel fly in the midst of heaven; for the <u>hour</u> of his Judgmnt is come.— to exterminati[o]n— from the commenceme[n]t. commence when angel commences preachi[n]g this. gospel <I day— 1000 years— >. 1000 year as I day.— 41. yrs 8 months.— only 6 years from the voice, saying, if thou live till thou art 85,— <years old &c> Hosea 6th chapter after 2 days &c, 2520 years which— bri[n]gs it to 1890.— [John] Taylor says 45 years according <to>— bible recokoning. the coming of the Son of man never will be, never can be till the judgm[en]ts spoken of for this <hour> are poured out, <which Jud[g]ments are commenced.—> Paul says ye are th[e] children of the light & not of the darkness, that that day should not overtake us as a theif in the night.— it is not the design of the Almighty to come upon the Earth & crush it, & grind it to powder.— he will reveal it to his servants the prophets.[4]

***

Jerusalem— <must be> rebuilt. <Judah return. must return> & the timple— water come out from under the temple— the <waters of the> dead sea be heald.— <it will take> some time to build the walls & the temple. &c & all <this must be done before—> **[p.339]** Son of Man <will make his appence [appearance]>. wars & rumours of wars. signs in the heavens above on the earth beneath— sun turnd into darkness. moon to blood. earthquakes in divers places, oceans heaving beyond their bounds.— <then> one grand sign of the Son of the son of man in heaven.— but what will

---

4. 6 April 1843, *JSP, J2*, 337–38.

what will the world do? They will say it is a planet, a comet, etc. But the Son of Man will come as the sign of the coming of the Son of Man, which will be as the light of the morning cometh out of the east, (April 6, 1843.) DHC 5:336-337.

the world. do? they will say it is a planet. a comet. &c— conseq[u]ently the son of man will come as the sign of coming of the son of man. <is> as the light of the morni[n]g cometh out of the East.—[5]

On Leaving Meetings Near the Close

Joseph Smith's Journal

President Joseph Smith stated that the business of the conference had closed, and the remainder would be devoted to instruction. It is an insult to a meeting for persons to leave just before its close. If they must go out, let them go half an hour before. No gentlemen will go out of a meeting just at closing. (April 7, 1843.) DHC 5:338-339.

President Joseph. statd that the business of the confernce had closed. & the rem[ai]nder of the confernce would be devoted to instruction— it is an insult to the meeting to have people run out of meeting <Just> before we close. if they must go let them go 1/2 an hour before. No Gentleman will go out of meeting Just at close.[6]

The Prophet Expounds the Scriptures[7]

The Beasts of John's Revelation

Joseph Smith sermon, reported by William Clayton and Willard Richards

The subject I intend to speak upon this morning is one that I have seldom touched upon since I commenced my ministry in the Church. It is a subject of great speculation, as well amongst the elders of this Church, as among the divines of the day: it is in relation to the beasts spoken of by John the Revelator. I have seldom spoken from the revelations; but as my subject is a constant source of speculation amongst the elders, causing a division of sentiment and opinion in relation to it, I

The subject whicch I shall sp[e]ak from <is>[8] [one] that I seldom have touched upon since I commenced— subj— of great spec[ulation] as well among the E[lde]rs & the divin[e]s—[9] the, beasts spoken of by John.— I have seldom spoken from <the revelati[o]ns>[10] Reason why is in consequence of a division of sentiment amongst Ers my object is to do away div[ision]. The knowledge of this thing is not very essential in relation to beasts heads figures &c—[11]

---

5. 6 April 1843, *JSP, J2*, 338–39.

6. 7 April 1843, *JSP, J2*, 341.

7. The version of this discourse used in the original *TPJS* came from History, D-1. A footnote in *WJS* states: "The accounts in *History of the Church* and *Teachings* are an amalgamation of reports taken by William Clayton and Willard Richards (Joseph Smith Diary)." *WJS*, 275n1. Additionally, both the Willard Richards version (found in *JSP, J2*, 345–49 and *WJS*, 187–89) and the William Clayton version (found in *JSP, D12*, 186–90 and *WJS*, 182–87) are reproduced in their entirety in Appendix A of this volume.

8. Discourse, 8 April 1843, reported by Willard Richards, *JSP, J2*, 345.

9. Discourse, 8 April 1843, reported by William Clayton, *JSP, D12*, 186.

10. Discourse, 8 April 1843, reported by Willard Richards, *JSP, J2*, 345.

11. Discourse, 8 April 1843, reported by William Clayton, *JSP, D12*, 186.

now do it in order that division and differences of opinion may be done away with, and not that correct knowledge on the subject is so much needed at the present time. It is not essential for the elders to have knowledge in relation to the meaning of beasts, and heads and horns, and other figures made use of in the revelations; still, it may be necessary, to prevent contention and division and do away with suspense. If we get puffed up by thinking that we have much knowledge, we are apt to get a contentious spirit, and correct knowledge is necessary to cast out that spirit.

knowledge is necessary to prevent division although it may puff up it does away suspince [suspense]—[12]

if we get to much puffed up— k[knowledge] is nec to do away cont—[13]

The Punishment of Suspense

Joseph Smith sermon, reported by William Clayton and Willard Richards

The evil of being puffed up with correct (though useless) knowledge is not so great as the evil of contention. Knowl[p.288]edge does away with darkness, suspense and doubt; for these cannot exist where knowledge is.

the k of being puffed up is not so great as the evil of contention... knowledge does away darkness suspense, doubt— for where k is there is no doubt &c,

There is no pain so awful as that of suspense. This is the punishment of the wicked; their doubt, anxiety and suspense cause weeping, wailing and gnashing of teeth.

no pain so awful as the pain of suspense— this is the condemnation of the wicked— doubt anxiety causes wailing

In knowledge there is power. God has more power than all other beings, because he has greater knowledge; and hence he knows how to subject all other beings to Him. He has power over all.

in k there is power— God has more power than all other beings because he has more k. he knows how to subject other beings[14] he has power— over all.[15]

I will endeavor to instruct you in relation to the meaning of the beasts and figures spoken of. I should not have called up the subject had it not been for this circumstance. Elder Pelatiah Brown, one of the wisest old heads we

Instruct you in relation to the beasts—[16]

sould not have called up this subject if it had not been for this old white head before.[17] Er [Pelatiah] Brown has been the cause one of the

---

12. Discourse, 8 April 1843, reported by Willard Richards, *JSP, J2*, 345.
13. Discourse, 8 April 1843, reported by William Clayton, *JSP, D12*, 186.
14. Discourse, 8 April 1843, reported by William Clayton, *JSP, D12*, 186.
15. Discourse, 8 April 1843, reported by Willard Richards, *JSP, J2*, 345.
16. Discourse, 8 April 1843, reported by William Clayton, *JSP, D12*, 186.
17. Discourse, 8 April 1843, reported by Willard Richards, *JSP, J2*, 345.

have among us, and whom I now see before me, has been preaching concerning the beast which was full of eyes before and behind; and for this he was hauled up for trial before the High Council.

* * *

The High Council undertook to censure and correct Elder Brown, because of his teachings in relation to the beasts. Whether they actually corrected him or not, I am a little doubtful, but don't care. Father Brown came to me to know what he should do about it. The subject particularly referred to was the four beasts and four-and-twenty elders mentioned in Rev. 5:8—"And when he had taken the book, the four beasts and four-and-twenty elders fell down before the Lamb, having every one of them harps, and golden vials full of odors, which are the prayers of saints."

Father Brown has been to work and confounded all Christendom by making out that the four beasts represented the different kingdoms of God on the earth. The wise men of the day could not do anything with him, and why should we find fault? Anything to whip sectarianism, to put down priestcraft, and bring the human family to a knowledge of the truth. A club is better than no weapon for a poor man to fight with.

Father Brown did whip sectarianism, and so far so good; but I could not help laughing at the idea of God making use of the figure of a beast to represent His kingdom on the earth, consisting of men, when He could as well have used a far more noble and consistent figure. What! the Lord made use of the figure of a creature of the brute creation to represent that which is much more noble, glorious, and

wisest old heads we have among us has been called up before the high c[ouncil] on account of the beast—[18]

* * *

they undertook to correct him there Whether they did or not I dont care[19] Er B came to me.

Rev 5.— four beasts & four & twenty Ers (8 verse)[20]

Father Brown had been to work & confounded all christendom, that these were figure John saw in heavn to represent the different kingdoms of God on earth.[21] wise men could not do any thing with him— any thing to whip sectarian & put down priestcraft— a club as is better than none for a poor man to firht [fight][22]

he put down sectarianism, & so far so good.— — but I could not help laughing that God should take a figure of a beast to repr[e]sent his kingdom consisting of <men>.[23] when he could have used a more noble figure what? make use of the figure of a meaner creature to rep a much glorious one— you mist it old man but the sec. did not know enough to detect him,

---

18. Discourse, 8 April 1843, reported by William Clayton, *JSP, D12*, 186.
19. Discourse, 8 April 1843, reported by Willard Richards, *JSP, J2*, 345.
20. Discourse, 8 April 1843, reported by William Clayton, *JSP, D12*, 187.
21. Discourse, 8 April 1843, reported by Willard Richards, *JSP, J2*, 345.
22. Discourse, 8 April 1843, reported by William Clayton, *JSP, D12*, 187.
23. Discourse, 8 April 1843, reported by Willard Richards, *JSP, J2*, 345.

important—the glories **[p.289]** and majesty of His kingdom? By taking a lesser figure to represent a greater, you missed it that time, old gentleman; but the sectarians did not know enough to detect you.

When God made use of the figure of a beast in visions to the prophets He did it to represent those kingdoms which had degenerated and become corrupt, savage and beast-like in their dispositions, even the degenerate kingdoms of the wicked world; but He never made use of the figure of a beast nor any of the brute kind to represent His kingdom.	When God made use of the figure of a beast to the prophets he did it to rep. that portion, who had degenerated— the k's of the [world].[24]

Daniel's Vision of Beasts

	Joseph Smith sermon, reported by William Clayton and Willard Richards
Daniel says (chap. 7, v. 16) when he saw the vision of the four beasts, "I came near unto one of them that stood by, and asked him the truth of all this, " the angel interpreted the vision to Daniel; but we find, by the interpretation that the figures of beasts had no allusion to the kingdom of God. You there see that the beasts are spoken of to represent the kingdoms of the world, the inhabitants whereof were beastly and abominable characters; they were murderers, corrupt, carnivorous, and brutal in their dispositions. The lion, the bear, the leopard, and the ten-horned beast represented the kingdoms of the world, says Daniel; for I refer to the prophets to qualify my observations which I make, so that the young elders who know so much, may not rise up like a flock of hornets and sting me. I want to keep out of such a wasp-nest.	Daniel says when he saw bear— angel interpreted— had no allusion to the k. of God— all the figure of beast rep. the k of the [world] beastly & abominable charcters— they were murderous corrupt carniverous in their dispositions.[25] Bear. Lion &c represe[n]ted the kingdoms. of the world, Says Daniel.[26] I refer to the prophets, to qualify my observations. to keep out of the wasp nests or young elders,[27] that the young Ers may not choke me like hornets.[28]

---

24. Discourse, 8 April 1843, reported by William Clayton, *JSP, D12*, 187.
25. Discourse, 8 April 1843, reported by William Clayton, *JSP, D12*, 187.
26. Discourse, 8 April 1843, reported by Willard Richards, *JSP, J2*, 345. See also *JSP, D12*, 191.
27. Discourse, 8 April 1843, reported by Willard Richards, *JSP, J2*, 345. See also *JSP, D12*, 191.
28. Discourse, 8 April 1843, reported by William Clayton, *JSP, D12*, 187. See also *WJS*, 184, which gives this as follows: ". . . so that the young Elders who know so much may not rise up and choke me like hornets." See also History, D-1, 1522.

John's Vision of Futurity

There is a grand difference and distinction between the visions and figures spoken of by the ancient prophets, and those spoken of in the revelations of John. The things which John saw had no allusion to the scenes of the days of Adam, Enoch, Abraham or Jesus, only so far as is plainly represented by John, and clearly set forth by him. John saw that only which was lying in futurity and which was shortly subject:

"The revelation of Jesus Christ, which God gave unto Him, to show unto his servants things which must shortly come to pass; and He sent and signified it by His angel unto His servant John: who bare record of the word of God, and of the testimony of Jesus Christ, and of all things that he saw. Blessed is he that readeth, and they that hear the words of his prophecy and keep those [p.290] things that are written therein: for the time is at hand." Also Rev. 4:1. "After this I looked, and, behold, a door was opened in heaven; and the first voice which I heard was as it were of a trumpet talking with me; which said, Come up hither, and I will show thee things which must be hereafter."[29]

The four beasts and twenty-four elders were out of every nation; for they sang a new song, saying, "Thou art worthy to take the book, and to open the seal thereof: for thou wast slain, and hast redeemed us to God by the blood out of every kindred, and tongue, and

Joseph Smith sermon, reported by William Clayton and Willard Richards

dif between the prophets & the Rev of John—[30]

The things John say saw had no allusion to the day of Adam Enoch Abraham or Jesus— only as clearly specified & set forth to John. I saw that that which was lying in futurity.[31]

4. beasts. & 24 Elders which was out of every nation— <it is> great stuffing, to stuff all nations into 4 beasts & 24 Elders[32]

---

29. This paragraph in *TPJS* comes from History, D-1, 1522.
30. Discourse, 8 April 1843, reported by William Clayton, *JSP, D12*, 187. History, D-1 (available only online) gives this as: "There is a grand difference and distinction between the <visions and> figure spoken of by the ancient prophets, and these spoken of in the Revelations of John." History, D-1, 1522. See also *WJS*, 185, which states: "There is a grand distinction between the actual meaning of the Prophets and the Present translation."
31. Willard Richards report, in *JSP, J2*, 345. See also *JSP, D12*, 191.
32. Willard Richards report, in *JSP, J2*, 346. See also *JSP, D12*, 191.

people, and nation." (See Rev. 5:9.) It would be great stuffing to crowd all nations into four beasts and twenty-four elders.

Now, I make this declaration, that those things which John saw in heaven had no allusion to anything that had been on the earth previous to that time, because they were the representation of "things which must shortly come to pass," and not of what has already transpired. John saw beasts that had to do with things on the earth, but not in past ages. The beasts which John saw had to devour the inhabitants of the earth in days to come. "And I saw when the Lamb opened one of the seals; and I heard, as it were the noise of thunder, one of the four beasts saying, come and see. And I saw, and beheld a white horse: and he that sat on him had a bow; and a crown was given unto him: and he went forth conquering, and to conquer. And when he had opened the second seal, I heard the second beast say, Come and see. And there went out another horse that was red: and power was given to him that sat thereon to take peace from the earth, and that they should kill one another; and there was given unto him a great sword." (Rev. 6:1, 2, 3, 4.) The book of Revelation is one of the plainest books God ever caused to be written.

The revelations do not give us to understand anything of the past in relation to the kingdom of God. What John saw and speaks of were things which he saw in heaven; those which Daniel saw were on and pertaining to the earth.

declaration— those things that John saw in h[eaven] had no allusion to any thing that had been on the earth because John saw what was to shortly come to pass— John saw beasts that had two do with things on the earth— but not in past ages The beast had to devour the inhabitants,[33]

Rev is one of the plain[e]st. books god ever caused to be written—[34]

The Rev. do not give us to any thing past in relation of the k of God— what John saw was in heaven— prophets on the earth—[35]

---

33. Discourse, 8 April 1843, reported by William Clayton, *JSP, D12*, 187. The online History, D-1 records this as: "Now I make this declaration, that those things which John saw in heaven, had no allusion to anything that had been on the earth previous to that time; because they were the representation of 'things which must shortly come to pass,' and not of what had already transpired. John saw beasts that had to do with things on the earth, but not in past ages: the beasts which John saw had to devour the inhabitants of the earth in days to come." History, D-1, 1523.

34. Willard Richards report, in *JSP, J2*, 346. See also *JSP, D12*, 191.

35. Discourse, 8 April 1843, reported by William Clayton, *JSP, D12*, 187–88. The online History, D-1 gives this as: "The revelations do not give us to understand anything of the past in relation to the kingdom of God. What John saw and speaks of were things which he saw in heaven, those which Daniel saw were on, and pertaining to the earth." History, D-1, 1523.

Exceptions to Bible Translations

I am now going to take exceptions to the present translation of the Bible in relation to these matters. Our latitude and longitude can be determined in the original Hebrew with far greater accuracy than in the English version. There is a **[p.291]** grand distinction between the actual meaning of the prophets and the present translation. The prophets do not declare that they saw a beast or beasts, but that they saw the image or figure of a beast. Daniel did not see an actual bear or a lion, but the images or figures of those beasts. The translation should have been rendered "image" instead of "beast," in every instance where beasts are mentioned by the prophets. But John saw the actual beast in heaven, showing to John that beasts did actually exist there, and not to represent figures of things on the earth. When the prophets speak of seeing beasts in their visions, they mean that they saw the images, they being types to represent certain things. At the same time they received the interpretation as to what those images or types were designed to represent.

I make this broad declaration, that whenever God gives a vision of an image, or beast, or figure of any kind, He always holds Himself responsible to give a revelation or interpretation of the meaning thereof, otherwise we are not responsible or accountable for our belief in it. Don't be afraid of being damned for not knowing the meaning of a vision or figure, if God has not given a revelation or interpretation of the subject.

Joseph Smith sermon, reported by William Clayton and Willard Richards

going to take exceptions to the translations—[36] <and> in Hebrew, <it> is a Latitude & Longitude compar[e]d with English version[37]

distinction pro[phets] do not declare the[y] saw beast but that they saw the image or figure of a beast. they did not see an actual bear or lion— should have been rendered image instead of beast in every instance— John saw the actual beast in heaven, to shew that that being did exist there. when p saw they were images types to represent & they received an interpretation.

I set it forth by this broad dec— where God ever gives a vision of an image &c he always holds himself responsible to give a Rev. or interpretation. otherwise we are not responsible—

dont be afraid of being damned for not knowing this where God has not given a Rev.

---

36. Discourse, 8 April 1843, reported by William Clayton, *JSP, D12*, 188. The online History, D-1 gives this as: "I am now going to take exceptions to the present translation of the bible in relation to these matters; our latitude and longitude can be determined in the original Hebrew with far greater accuracy than in the English version." History, D-1, 1523. See also *WJS*, 185.

37. Willard Richards report, in *JSP, J2*, 346. See also *JSP, D12*, 191.

John saw curious looking beasts in heaven; he saw every creature that was in heaven,—all the beasts, fowls and fish in heaven,—actually there, giving glory to God. How do you prove it? (See Rev. 5:13.) "And every creature which is in heaven, and on the earth, and under the earth, and such as are in the sea, and all that are in them, heard I saying, Blessing, and honor, and glory, and power, be unto Him that sitteth upon the throne, and unto the Lamb for ever and ever."

read Rev 5— 11— particularly verse 13, John saw curious looking beasts in heaven— saw every creature that was in heaven &c— all the beast foul fish in heaven— actually their giving glory to God.[38]

Varied Creatures in Heaven

Joseph Smith sermon, reported by William Clayton and Willard Richards

I suppose John saw beings there of a thousand forms, that had been saved from ten thousand times ten thousand earths like this,—strange beasts of which we have no conception: all might be seen in heaven. The grand secret

I suppose John saw beings there that had been saved from 10000 times 10000 earths like this— strange beasts— might be seen them in heaven.—

---

38. Discourse, 8 April 1843, reported by William Clayton, *JSP, D12*, 188. See also *WJS*, 185, which reads: "I am now going to take exception to the present translation of the bible in relation to these matters. There is a grand distinction between the actual meaning of the Prophets and the Present translation. The Prophets do not declare that the[y] saw a beast or beasts, but that the[y] saw the image or figure of a beast. They did not see an actual bear or Lion but the images or figures of those beasts. The translation should have been rendered 'image' instead of 'beast' in every instance where beasts are mentioned by the Prophets. But John saw the actual beast in heaven, to show to John and to the inhabitant that that being did actually exist there. When the Prophets speak of seeing beasts in their visions, they saw the images; the types to represent certain things and at the same time they received the interpretation as to what those images or types were designed to represent. I make this broad declaration, that where God ever gives a vision of an image, or beast or figure of any kind he always holds himself responsible to give a revelation or interpretation of the meaning thereof, otherwise we are not responsible or accountable for our belief in them it. Dont be afraid of being damned for not knowing the meaning of a vision or figure where God has not given a revelation or interpretation on the subject (He here read Rev. ch 5 v 11 to 13) John saw curious looking beasts in heaven, he saw every creature that was in heaven, all the beasts, fowls, & fish in heaven, actually there, giving glory to God." History, D-1, 1523, gives this as: "There is a grand distinction between the actual meaning of the prophets and the present translation. The prophets do not declare that the[y] saw a beast or beasts, but that the[y] saw the image or figure of a beast. They do did not see an actual bear or a Lion, but the images or figures of those beasts. The translation should have been rendered 'image' instead of 'beast' in every instance where beasts are mentioned by the prophets. But John saw the actual beast in heaven, to show to John and to those [two words illegible] that that being did actually exist there. When the prophets speak of seeing beasts in their visions, they saw the images; the types to represent certain things and at the same time they received the interpretation as to what those images or types were designed to represent. I make this broad declaration, that where God ever gives a vision of an image, or beast or figure of any kind he always holds himself responsible to give a revelation or interpretation of the meaning thereof, otherwise we are not responsible or accountable for our belief in it."

was to show John what there was in heaven. John learned that God glorified Himself by saving all that His hands had made, whether beasts, fowls, fishes or men; and He will glorify Himself with them.

Says one, "I cannot believe in the salvation of beasts." Any man who would tell you that this could not be, would tell you that the revelations are not true. John heard the words of [p.292] the beasts giving glory to God, and understood them. God who made the beasts could understand every language spoken by them. The four beasts were four of the most noble animals that had filled the measure of their creation, and had been saved from other worlds, because they were perfect: they were like angels in their sphere. We are not told where they came from, and I do not know; but they were seen and heard by John praising and glorifying God.

The popular religionists of the day tell us, forsooth, that the beasts spoken of in the Revelation represent kingdoms. Very well, on the same principle we can say that the twenty-four elders spoken of represent beasts; for they are all spoken of at the same time, and are represented as all uniting in the same acts of praise and devotion.

John learned that God glorified himself by saving all that his hands made—[39]

says one I cannot beleive in salvati[o]n of bea[s]ts.—[40] a man who would tell you that this could not be would tell you that the Revelation John heard the they said.

God could understand every languag they talked—[41]
the 4 beasts,

were angels there.

dont know where they came from;[42]

Darling religion says that the beasts represent kingdoms very well on the same principle the 24 Er represent beast—[43]

---

39. Discourse, 8 April 1843, reported by William Clayton, *JSP, D12*, 188. See also *WJS*, 185, which reads: "suppose John saw beings there, that had been saved from ten thousand times ten thousand earths like this, strange beasts of which we have no conception all might be seen in heaven. John learned that God glorified himself by saving all that his hands had made whether beasts, fowl fishes or man."
40. Willard Richards report, in *JSP, J2*, 346. See also *JSP, D12*, 192.
41. Discourse, 8 April 1843, reported by William Clayton, *JSP, D12*, 188. History, D-1, 1523, gives this as: "Any man who would tell you that this could not be, would tell you that the revelations are not true. John heard the words of the beasts giving glory to God, and understood them. God who made the beasts could understand every language spoken by them." History, D-1, 1523.
42. Willard Richards report, in *JSP, J2*, 346. See also *JSP, D12*, 192.
43. Discourse, 8 April 1843, reported by William Clayton, *JSP, D12*, 188. History, D-1, 1523, gives this as: "The popular religionists of the day tell us forsooth, that the beasts spoken of in the revelations represent kingdoms. Very well; on the same principle can we say, that the twenty-four elders spoken of represent beasts; for they are all spoken of at the same time, and represented as all uniting in the same acts of praise and devotion." See also *WJS*, 186.

This learned interpretation is all as flat as a pancake! "What do you use such vulgar expressions for, being a prophet?" Because the old women understand it—they make pancakes. Deacon Homespun said the earth was flat as a pancake, and ridiculed the science which proved to the contrary. The whole argument is flat, and I don't know of anything better to represent it. The world is full of technicalities and misrepresentation, which I calculate to overthrow, and speak of things as they actually exist.

It is all as flat as a pancake what do <you> use such flat & vulger <expressions. for> being a prophet? because the old women understa[n]d it, they make pancakes.—[44] said the ~~earth~~ <arg[ument]> was flat as a pan-cake—

calculate to overthrow the technicalities of the world. and speak of things as they actually exist.

Again, there is no revelation to prove that things do not exist in heaven as I have set forth, nor yet to show that the beasts meant anything but beasts; and we never can comprehend the things of God and of heaven, but by revelation. We may spiritualize and express opinions to all eternity; but that is no authority.

Again— there is no Rev. to prove[45] there is no revelation any where to shew that the beasts meant any thing but beasts[46] (& we never can comprehend) without Rev.)

if we spiritualize
no authority)[47]

Elders to Preach Repentance and Let Mysteries Alone

Joseph Smith sermon, reported by William Clayton and Willard Richards

Oh, ye elders of Israel, hearken to my voice; and when you are sent into the world to preach, tell those things you are sent to tell; preach and cry aloud, "Repent ye, for the

O ye Elders of Israel hearken to my voice & when ye are sent into the world to preach. tell those things you are sent to tell.[48] preach repent ye for the k. of h is at hand—[49] declare

---

44. Willard Richards report, in *JSP, J2*, 346. See also *JSP, D12*, 192.

45. Discourse, 8 April 1843, reported by William Clayton, *JSP, D12*, 188–89. History, D-1, 1523, gives this portion of the discourse as follows: "Deacon Homespun said the earth was flat as a pancake, and ridiculed science which proved to the contrary. The whole argument is flat, and I don't know of anything better to represent it. The world is full of technicalities and misrepresentation, which I calculate to overthrow, and speak of things as they actually are . . . Again there is no revelation to prove that things do not exist< in heaven> as I have set forth." See also *WJS*, 186.

46. Willard Richards report, in *JSP, J2*, 347. See also *JSP, D12*, 192.

47. Discourse, 8 April 1843, reported by William Clayton, *JSP, D12*, 189. History, D-1, 1523, gives this portion of the discourse as follows: "nor yet to show that the beasts meant anything but beasts, and we never can comprehend the things of God and of heaven but by revelation. We may spiritualize and express opinions to all eternity; but that is no authority." See also *WJS*, 186.

48. Willard Richards report, in *JSP, J2*, 347. See also *JSP, D12*, 192.

49. Discourse, 8 April 1843, reported by William Clayton, *JSP, D12*, 189. The online History, D-1 gives this portion of the discourse as follows: "O! ye elders of Israel, hearken to my voice; and when you are sent into the world to preach, tell those things you are sent to tell: preach and cry aloud, 'repent ye: for the kingdom of heaven is at hand— repent and believe the gospel.' Declare the first principles, and let mysteries alone, lest you be overthrown." History, D-1, 1523. See also *WJS*, 186.

kingdom of heaven is at hand; repent and believe the Gospel." Declare the first principles, and let mysteries alone, lest ye be overthrown. Never meddle with the visions of beasts and subjects you do not understand. Elder Brown, when you go to Palmyra, say nothing about the four beasts, but preach those things the Lord has told you to preach about—repentance and baptism for the remission of sins.

[p.293] He then read Rev. 13:1-8. John says, "And I saw one of his heads as it were wounded to death; and his deadly wound was healed; and all the world wondered after the beast." Some spiritualizers say the beast that received the wound was Nebuchadnezzar, some Constantine, some Mohammed, and others the Roman Catholic Church; but we will look at what John saw in relation to this beast. Now for the wasp's nest. The translators have used the term "dragon" for devil. Now it was a beast that John saw could not be Nebuchadnezzar. The beast John saw was an actual beast, and an actual intelligent being gives him his power, and his seat, and great authority. It was not to represent a beast in heaven: it was an angel in heaven who has power in the last days to do a work.

the first principles, & let mysteries alone lest you be overthrown.—[50] never meddle with the beasts & subjects you do not understand. Er Brown when you go to Palmyra[51] say nothi[n]g about the 4 B[e]asts[52] but preach those things the Lord has told you to preach about— repentance and baptism for the remission of sins.

He then read Rev. ch 13. v. 1-8. In v. 3. John says: 'And I saw one of his heads as it were wounded to death; and his deadly wound was healed; and all the world wondered after the beast.'[53] they say the beast that received the wound was nebuchadnezzar—[54] Constantine.— & the catholic[55]

what John saw in relation to this beast[56] now for the wasp nest.—[57]

they have used the term Devil for dragon—it was a beast that John saw in heaven— what was shortly to come to pass. the beast was an actual b to which power was to be given an intelligent being in heaven—[58]

it was not to rep[res]ent beast on heaven— it was an angel in heaven. who has power in the last days to do a work.———[59]

---

50. Willard Richards report, in *JSP, J2*, 347. See also *JSP, D12*, 192.

51. Discourse, 8 April 1843, reported by William Clayton, *JSP, D12*, 189. The online History, D-1 gives this portion of the discourse as follows: "Never meddle with the visions of beasts, and subjects you do not understand. Elder Peletiah Brown when you go to Palmyra." History, D-1, 1523. See also *WJS*, 186.

52. Willard Richards report, in *JSP, J2*, 347. See also *JSP, D12*, 192.

53. History, D-1, 1523.

54. Discourse, 8 April 1843, reported by William Clayton, *JSP, D12*, 189.

55. Willard Richards report, in *JSP, J2*, 347. See also *JSP, D12*, 192.

56. Discourse, 8 April 1843, reported by William Clayton, *JSP, D12*, 189.

57. Willard Richards report, in *JSP, J2*, 347. See also *JSP, D12*, 192.

58. Discourse, 8 April 1843, reported by William Clayton, *JSP, D12*, 189. The online History, D-1 gives this portion of the discourse as follows: "The translators have used the term 'dragon' for 'devil', Now it was a beast that John saw in heaven, and he was then speaking of 'things which must shortly come to pass' and consequently the beast that John saw could not be Nebuchadnezzar. The beast John saw was an actual beast and an actual intelligent being gives him his power and his seat and great authority,' It was not to represent a beast in heaven it was an angel in heaven who has power in the last days to do a work." History, D-1, 1523. See also *WJS*, 186.

59. Willard Richards report, in *JSP, J2*, 347. See also *JSP, D12*, 192.

"All the world wondered after the beast," Nebuchadnezzar and Constantine the Great not excepted. And if the beast was all the world, how could the world wonder after the beast? It must have been a wonderful beast to cause all human beings to wonder after it; and I will venture to say that when God allows the old devil to give power to the beast to destroy the inhabitants of the earth, all will wonder. Verse 4 reads, "And they worshiped the dragon which gave power unto the beast; and they worshiped the beast, saying. Who is like unto the beast? Who is able to make war with him?"

Some say it means the kingdom of the world. One thing is sure, it does not mean the kingdom of the Saints. Suppose we admit that it means the kingdoms of the world, what propriety would there be in saying, Who is able to make war with my great big self? If these spiritualized interpretations are true, the book contradicts itself in almost every verse. But they are not true.

There is a mistranslation of the word dragon in the second verse. The original word signifies the devil, and not dragon, as translated. In chapter 12, verse 9, it reads, "That old serpent, called the devil," and it ought to be translated devil in this case, and not dragon. It is sometimes

All the world wondered after the b and if the beast was the world how could the world wonder after the beast— nebucha & constantine not excepted— it must have been a been [beast] that the human beings wondered after. When God gives power to a beast to destroy all will wonder. Read verse 4—[60] 'And they worshipped the Dragon which gave power unto the beast; and they worshipped the beast saying, Who is like unto the beast? Who is able to make war with him?[']⁶¹

some say it means the k's of the [world] dont mean the k of the saints— suppose it means the k's of the [world] what propriety is there in saying who is able to make war with myself— If these interpretations are true the book contradicts itself in almost every verse— but they are not true.

There is a mistranslation— the original word means the devil instead of the dragon— verse 9 ch 12— That old serpent called the devil[62] & it is sometimes Apolyel.—[63]

---

60. Discourse, 8 April 1843, reported by William Clayton, *JSP, D12*, 189.

61. Discourse, 8 April 1843, reported by William Clayton, History, D-1, 1523. See also *WJS*, 187.

62. Discourse, 8 April 1843, reported by William Clayton, *JSP, D12*, 189–90. In the online History, D-1, this section is given as: "There is a mistranslation of the word dragon in the second verse— the original Hebrew word signifies the Devil, and not Dragon as translated. In ch. 12. v. 9. it reads 'that old serpent called the devil,' and it ought to be translated devil in this case, and not dragon. It is sometimes translated Appollyon. Everything that we have not a keyword to, we will take it as it leads. The beasts which John saw and speaks of as being in heaven were actually living in heaven, and were actually to have power given to them over the inhabitants of the earth, precisely according to the plain reading of the revelations. I give this as a key to the elders of Israel. The Independent Beast is a beast that dwells in heaven abstract from the human family; the beast that rose up out of the sea should be translated the image of a beast, as I have referred to in Daniel's vision." History, D-1, 1523. See also *WJS*, 186–87.

63. Willard Richards report, in *JSP, J2*, 347. See also *JSP, D12*, 192. "Apolyel" is a reference the Greek word "Apollyon," which means "destroyer" and refers to the "angel of the bottomless pit." See Revelation 9:11.

translated Apollyon. Everything that we have not a keyword to, we will take it as it reads. The beasts which John saw and speaks of being in heaven, were actually living in heaven, and were actually to have power given to them over the inhabitants of the earth, **[p.294]** precisely according to the plain reading of the revelations. I give this as a key to the elders of Israel. The independent beast is a beast that dwells in heaven, abstract [apart] from the human family. The beast that rose up out of the sea should be translated the image of a beast, as I have referred to it in Daniel's vision.

I have said more than I ever did before, except once at Ramus, and then up starts the little fellow (Charles Thompson) and stuffed me like a cock-turkey with the prophecies of Daniel, and crammed it down my throat with his finger. (April 8, 1843.) DHC 5:339-345.

every thing that we have not a key word to we will take it as it reads. The beasts were being[s] in h that were to have power

I give this as a key to the Ers—[64] independent beasts. abstract from the human family.—

I said more than I <ever> did before except once at Ramus. & then the little. <upstarts <fellows> stufferd me like a <cock>. cock turkey— <with the prop[h]ecies of Daniels—> and crammed it down my throat. with their fingerss—[65]

Remarks of the Prophet on the Death of Lorenzo D. Barnes

The Resurrection

Joseph Smith's Journal
Sunday morning April 16. 1843 Meeting at the Temple. A.M. 10. o ck Joseph read Bro [Parley P.] Pratts letters to the Editor of "T[imes] & Seasons" concrning the death of Lorenzo Barn[e]s. <& remarked he read it because it was so appropriate to all who had died in the faith.—> Almost all who have fallen in these last days, in the church, have fallen in a strange land, this is a strange land. to tho[s]e who have come from a distance. we should cultivate sympathy for the afflicted. among us. If there is a place on earth. where men should cultivate this spirit & pour in the oil & wine <in the bosom of the afflicted> it is this place. <and this spirit is manifest here—> and although he is a stranger <& afflicted.> when he arrives, he finds. a brother— & friend ready to administer to his necessities.—

Almost all who have fallen in these last days in the Church have fallen in a strange land. This is a strange land to those who have come from a distance. We should cultivate sympathy for the afflicted among us. If there is a place on earth where men should cultivate the spirit and pour in the oil and wine in the bosoms of the afflicted, it is in this place; and this spirit is manifest here; and although a stranger and afflicted when he arrives, he finds a brother and a friend ready to administer to his necessities.

---

64. Discourse, 8 April 1843, reported by William Clayton, *JSP, D12*, 189–90.
65. Willard Richards report, in *JSP, J2*, 347. See also *JSP, D12*, 192–93.

I would esteem it one of the greatest blessings, if I am to be afflicted in this world, to have my lot cast where I can find brothers and friends all around me. But this is not the thing I referred to: it is to have the privilege of having our dead buried on the land where God has appointed to gather His Saints together, and where there will be none but Saints, where they may have the privilege of laying their bodies where the Son of Man will make His appearance, and where they may hear the sound of the trump that shall call them forth to behold Him, that in the morn of the resurrection they may come forth in a body, and come up out of their graves and strike hands immediately in eternal glory and felicity, rather than be scattered thousands of miles apart. There is something good and sacred to me in this thing. The place where a man is buried is sacred to me. This subject is made mention of in the Book of Mormon and other scriptures. Even to the aborigines of this land, the burying places of their fathers are more sacred than anything else.

[p.295] When I heard of the death of our beloved Brother Barnes, it would not have affected me so much, if I had the opportunity of burying him in the land of Zion.

I believe those who have buried their friends here, their condition is enviable. Look at Jacob and Joseph in Egypt, how they required their friends to bury them in the tomb of their fathers. See the expense which attended the embalming and the going up of the great company to the burial.

It has always been considered a great calamity not to obtain an honorable burial: and one of the greatest curses the ancient prophets could put on any man, was that he should go without a burial.

I have said, Father, I desire to die here among the Saints. But if this is not Thy will, and I go

another remark, I would esteem it one of the greatest blessings, if I am to be afflicted in this world, to have my lot cast where I can find breth[r]en & friends all arou[n]d me, \<but\> this is not. \<thing. I referred to is \<it\> is\> to have [p.359] the privilige of having our dead buri[e]d on the land where god has appointd to gather his saints together,— & where there will be nothing but saints, where they may have the privelege of laying their bodies where \<the\> Son will make his appearance. & where they may hear the. sound of the trump that shall call them forth, to behold him, that in the morn of the resurrecti[o]n, they may come forth in a body. & come right up out of their graves. & strike hands \<immediately\> in eternal glory. \<& felicity rather\> than to be scattered thousands of miles apart. There is something good. & sacred to me— \<in this thing.\> the place where a man is buried has been sacred to me.— \<this subjct is made mention of—\> In Book of Mormon & Scripturs. & \<to\> the aborigines \<regard\> the burying places of the\<ir\> fathers as \<is\> more sacred that than any thing else.

When I. heard of the death of our beloved bro \<Barns it would not have affected me so much\> if I had the opp[o]rtunity of burying him in the land of Zion.

I beleive, those who have buried their friends here their condition is enviable. Look at Joseph in Egypt how he required his friends to bury him in the tomb of his fathers,— see the expence & great company & \<which attended the\> embalming. \<&c \<and\> the going up of the great company. to his burial.\>

It has always been considird a g[r]eat curse not to obtain an honorable buryal. \<& one of the gratest curses the anci[e]nt prophets could put on any one was. that he man should go without a burial.\>

I have said, father, I desire to be burid here, & before I go home, but if \<this is not thy will\>

hence and die, wilt Thou find some kind friend to bring my body back, and gather my friends who have fallen in foreign lands, and bring them up hither, that we may all lie together.

I will tell you what I want. If tomorrow I shall be called to lie in yonder tomb, in the morning of the resurrection let me strike hands with my father, and cry, "My father," and he will say, "My son, my son," as soon as the rock rends and before we come out of our graves.

And may we contemplate these thing so? Yes, if we learn how to live and how to die. When we lie down we contemplate how we may rise in the morning; and it is pleasing for friends to lie down together, locked in the arms of love, to sleep and wake in each other's embrace and renew their conversation.

not may I return, or find Some kind friend to bring me back, & gather my friends, who have fallen in foreign lands, & bring them up hither, that we may may all lie together.—

I will tell you what I want. if tomorrow I shall be calld to lay in yonder tombs. in the morning of the resurrecti[o]n, let me strike hand<s> with my father, & cry, my father, & he will say my son, my Son,— as soon as the rock rends. & before we come out of our graves.

& may we contemplate these things so? yes, if we learn how to live & how to die [*blank*]. when we lie down we contemplat how we may rise up in the morni[n]g and <it is> pleasing for friends to lie down together locked **[p.360]** in the arms of love, to sleep, & wake in each others embrace <& renew their conversation.>[66]

The Righteous to Have Joy in the Resurrection

Would you think it strange if I relate what I have seen in vision in relation to this interesting theme? Those who have died in Jesus Christ may expect to enter into all that fruition of joy when they come forth, which they possessed or anticipated here.

So plain was the vision, that I actually saw men, before they had ascended from the tomb, as though they were getting up slowly. They took each other by the hand and said to each other, "My father, my son, my mother, my daughter, my brother, my sister." And when the voice calls for the dead to arise, suppose I am laid by the side of my father, what would be the first joy of my heart? To meet my father, my mother, **[p.296]** my brother, my sister; and when they are by my side, I embrace them and they me.

It is my meditation all the day, and more than my meat and drink, to know how I shall make

Joseph Smith's Journal

would you think it strange that I relate what I have seen in vision in relation.— this intere[s]ting theme. Those who have died in Jesus christ, may expect to enter in to all that fruition of Joy when they come forth. which they have possessed here,

so plain was the vision I actually saw men, before they had ascend[e]d from the tomb, as though they were getti[n]g up slowly, they tooke each othe[r] by the hand & it was my father & my Son. my mother & my daughter. <my brother & my sister> & when the voice calls, suppose I am laid by the side of my fathe[r].— what would be the first Joy of my heart? where is my fathr. my mother. my sister. they are by my side <I embrace them. & they me.>

It is my meditati[o]n all the day & more than my meat & drink to know how I shall make

---

66. 16 April 1843, *JSP, J2*, 358–60.

the Saints of God comprehend the visions that roll like an overflowing surge before my mind.	the saints of God to comprehe[n]d the visions that roll like <an> overflowing surge; ~~to~~ <before> my ~~vision~~ <mind>.

* * *

All your losses will be made up to you in the resurrection, provided you continue faithful. By the vision of the Almighty I have seen it.	all your losses will be made up to you in the resurrecti[o]n provi[d]ed you continue faithful by the vision of the almighty I have seen it.—
More painful to me are the thoughts of annihilation than death. If I have no expectation of seeing my father, mother, brothers, sisters and friends again, my heart would burst in a moment, and I should go down to my grave.	more painful to me the thoughts of annihilation & than death. if I had no expectation of seeing my mother Broth[ers] &c Sisters & fri[e]nds again my heart would burst in a moment. & I should go down to my grave.
The expectation of seeing my friends in the morning of the resurrection cheers my soul and makes me bear up against the evils of life. It is like their taking a long journey, and on their return we meet them with increased joy.	The expectati[o]n of seeing my f[r]iends in the morni[n]g of the resurrection cheers my soul. and make be bear up aginst the evils of life. it ~~it~~ is like their taking a long journey. & on their return we meet them with increasd joy.
God has revealed His Son from the heavens and the doctrine of the resurrection also; and we have a knowledge that those we bury here God will bring up again, clothed upon and quickened by the Spirit of the great God; and what mattereth it whether we lay them down, or we lay down with them when we can keep them no longer? Let these truths sink down in our hearts, that we may even here begin to enjoy that which shall be in full hereafter.	God has reveald his son from the heavens. & the doctrine of the resurrection also. & we have a knowledge that those we bury here. God bring them up again. clothed upon, & quckend [quickened] by the spirit of the great god. & what mattereth it whether we lay them down, or we lay down with them. when we can ~~live~~ keep them no longer **[p.361]** then let them sink down; like a ship in the storm. the mighty anchor holds the storm so let those thuths [truths] sink down in our hearts. that we may even here begin to enjoy. that which shall be in full hereafter.
Hosanna, hosanna, hosanna to Almighty God, that rays of light begin to burst forth upon us even now. I cannot find words in which to express myself. I am not learned, but I have as good feelings as any man.	Hosanna. Hosanna. Hosanna, to Almighty god that rays of light begin to bu[r]st fo[r]th upon us even now. I cannot find words to express myself I am not learnd. but I have as good feelings as any man.
O that I had the language of the archangel to express my feelings once to my friends! But I never expect to in this life. When other rejoice, I rejoice; when they mourn, I mourn.	O that I had the the language of the archangel to express my feelings once to my frends. but I never expect to when othe[r]s regoice I regoice. when ~~I~~ they mourn I would mourn—

To Marcellus Bates let me administer comfort. You shall soon have the company of your companion in a world of glory, and the friends of Brother Barnes and all the Saints who are mourning. This has been a warning voice to us all to be sober and diligent and lay aside mirth, vanity and folly, and to be prepared to die tomorrow.

* * *

President Joseph Smith said: "As president of this house, I [p.297] forbid any man leaving just as we are going to close the meeting. He is no gentleman who will do it. I don't care who does it, even if it were the king of England. I forbid it. (April 16, 1843.) DHC 5:360-363.

to Marcellus Bates. let me admi[ni]ster comfort, you shall soon have the company of your companion in a wo[r]ld of glory— & the frends of Bro. Barns.— & all the saints who are mourning, this has been a warning voice to us all. to be sober— & diligent— & lay aside mirth & vanity. & folly.—— & be prepard to die tomorrow . . . (preached abo[u]t 2 hours)

* * *

Prop[he]t Joseph said as president of this house I forbid any man's leaving this house ju[s]t as we are going to close the meeting. he is no gentleman who will do it. I dont care who it comes from— if it were from the King of England. I forbid it.—⁶⁷

Salvation Through Knowledge

Wilford Woodruff's Journal

It is not wisdom that we should have all knowledge at once presented before us; but that we should have a little at a time; then we can comprehend it. President Smith then read the 2nd Epistle of Peter, 1st chapter, 16th to last verses, and dwelt upon the 19th verse with some remarks.

Add to your faith knowledge, etc. The principle of knowledge is the principle of salvation. This principle can be comprehended by the faithful and diligent; and every one that does not obtain knowledge sufficient to be saved will be condemned. The principle of salvation is given us through the knowledge of Jesus Christ.

It is not wisdom that we should have all knowledge at once presented before us but that we should have a little[.] then we can comprehend it. He then read the second epistle of Peter 1st ch 16 to last vers & dwelt upon the 19th vers with som remarks[.]

Ad to your faith knowledge &c. The principle of knowledge is the principle of Salvation[.] the Principle can be comprehended, for any one that cannot get knowledge to be saved will be damned. The Principl[e] of Salvation is given to us through the knowledge of Jesus Christ[.]⁶⁸

Salvation Is to Triumph over Enemies

Wilford Woodruff's Journal

Salvation is nothing more nor less than to triumph over all our enemies and put them under our feet. And when we have power to put all enemies under our feet in this world, and a knowledge to triumph over all evil spirits in the world to come, then we are saved, as in the

Salvation is nothing more or less than to triumph over all our enemies & put them under our feet & when we have power to put all enemies under our feet in this world & a knowledge to triumph over all evil spirits in the world to come then we are saved as in the

---

67. 16 April 1843, *JSP, J2*, 360–61.
68. 14 May 1843, *WWJ*, 1:540. See also *JSP, D12*, 302.

case of Jesus, who was to reign until He had put all enemies under His feet, and the last enemy was death.

case of Jesus[.] he was to reign untill he had put all enemies under his feet & the last enemy was death[69]

No Salvation Without a Tabernacle

Wilford Woodruff's Journal

Perhaps there are principles here that few men have thought of. No person can have this salvation except through a tabernacle.

Perhaps there are principle[s] here that few men have thought of. No ~~power~~ <person> can have this Salvation except through a tabernacle

Now, in this world, mankind are naturally selfish, ambitious and striving to excel one above another; yet some are willing to build up others as well as themselves. So in the other world there are a variety of spirits. Some seek to excel. And this was the case with Lucifer when he fell. He sought for things which were unlawful. Hence he was sent down, and it is said he drew many away with him; and the greatness of his punishment is that he shall not have a tabernacle. This is his punishment. So the devil, thinking to thwart the decree of God, by going up and down in the earth, seeking whom he **[p.298]** may destroy—any person that he can find that will yield to him, he will bind him, and take possession of the body and reign there, glorying in it mightily, not caring that he had got merely a stolen body; and by and by some one having authority will come along and cast him out and restore the tabernacle to its rightful owner. The devil steals a tabernacle because he has not one of his own: but if he steals one, he is always liable to be turned out of doors.

Now in this world mankind are naturly selfish, ambitious & striving to excell one above another ~~swhile~~ yet some are willing to build up others as well as themselves[.] so in the other world their is a variety of spirits[.] Some who seek to excell, & this was the case with the devil. when he fell he sought for things which were unlawful[.] hence he was cast down & it is said he drew away many with him & the greatness of his punishment is that he shall not have a tabernacle[.] this is his punishment. So the devil thinking to thwart the decree of God by going up & down in the earth seeking whome he may destroy any person that he can find that will yield to him he will bind <him> & take possession of the Body & reign there glorying in it mightily not thinking that he had got a stolen tabernacle & by & by some one of Authority will come along & cast him out & restore the tabernacle to his rightful owner[.] but the bevil steals a tabernacle because he has not one of his own[.] but if he steals one he is liable to be turned out of doors.[70]

Calling and Election

Wilford Woodruff's Journal

Now, there is some grand secret here, and keys to unlock the subject. Notwithstanding the apostle exhorts them to add to their faith, virtue, knowledge, temperance, etc., yet he exhorts them to make their calling and election

Now their is some grand secrett here & keys to unlock the subject[.] Notwithstanding the Apostle exhorts them to ~~make their Calling~~ Add to their faith, virtue, knowledge, temperance &c yet he exhorts them to make their

---

69. 14 May 1843, *WWJ*, 1:540. See also *JSP, D12*, 302.
70. 14 May 1843, *WWJ*, 1:540. See also *JSP, D12*, 302, 304.

sure. And though they had heard an audible voice from heaven bearing testimony that Jesus was the Son of God, yet he says we have a more sure word of prophecy, whereunto ye do well that ye take heed as unto a light shining in a dark place. Now, wherein could they have a more sure word of prophecy than to hear the voice of God saying, This is my beloved Son.

Now for the secret and grand key. Though they might hear the voice of God and know that Jesus was the Son of God, this would be no evidence that their election and calling was made sure, that they had part with Christ, and were joint heir with him. They then would want that more sure word of prophecy, that they were sealed in the heavens and had the promise of eternal life in the kingdom of God. Then, having this promise sealed unto them, it was an anchor to the soul, sure and steadfast. Though the thunders might roll and lightnings flash, and earthquakes bellow, and war gather thick around, yet this hope and knowledge would support the soul in every hour of trial, trouble and tribulation. Then knowledge through our Lord and Savior Jesus Christ is the grand key that unlocks the glories and mysteries of the kingdom of heaven.

Compare this principle once with Christendom at the present day, and where are they, with all their boasted religion, piety and sacredness while at the same time they are crying out against prophets, apostles, angels, revelations, prophesying and visions, etc. Why, they are just ripening for the damnation of hell. They will be damned, for they reject the most glorious principles of the Gospel of Jesus Christ and treat with disdain **[p.299]** and trample under foot the key that unlocks the heavens and puts in our possession the glories of the celestial world. Yes, I say, such will be damned, with all their professed godliness. Then I would exhort you to go on and

Calling & election shure & though they had herd the audible voice from heaven bearing testimony that Jesus was the son of God yet he says we have a more sure word of Prophecy whare unto ye do well that ye take heed as unto a light shining in a dark place. Now wharein could they have a more sure word of prophecy than to hear the voice of God saying this is my Beloved Son &c.

[p.541] Now for the Secret & grand [*drawing of a key*] key. though they might hear the voice of God & know that Jesus was the son of God this would be no evidence that their election & Calling & election was made shure that they had part with Christ & was a Joint heir with him. they then would want that more sure word of Prophecy that they were sealed in the heavens & had the promise of eternal live in the kingdom of God then having this promise sealed unto them it was as an anchor to the soul sure & steadfast[.] though the thunders might roll, & lightnings flash & earthquakes Bellow & war gather thick around yet this hope & knowledge would support the soul in evry hour of trial trouble & tribulation[.] Then knowledge through our Lord & savior Jesus Christ is the grand key [*drawing of a key*] that unlocks the glories & misteries of the kingdom of heaven

Compair this principle once with Christondom at the present day & whare are they with all their boasted religion piety & sacredness while at the same time they are crying out against Prophets Apostles, Angels Revelations Prophesyings, & visions &c. why they are Just ripening for the damnation of hell. they will be damned for they reject the most glorious principle of the gospel of Jesus Christ & treat with disdain & trample under foot the main key that unlocks the heavens & puts in our possession the glories of the celestial world. yes I say such will be damned with all their professed godliness. Then I would exhort you to go on & Continue to call upon continue to call upon God until you make your calling and election surer for yourselves, by obtaining this more sure word of prophecy, and wait patiently for the promise until you obtain it, etc.

God untill you make your Calling & election sure for yourselves by obtaining this more sure word of Prophesey & wait patiently for the promise untill you obtain it[.][71]

* * *

The Value of Aged Men in Counsel

Wilford Woodruff's Journal

The way to get along in any important matter is to gather unto yourselves wise men, experienced and aged men, to assist in council in all times of trouble. Handsome men are not apt to be wise and strong-minded men; but the strength of a strong-minded man will generally create course features, like the rough, strong bough of the oak. You will always discover in the first glance of a man, in the outlines of his features something of his mind.

Br Joseph made the following remarks[:] The way to get along in any important matters was to gather unto yourself wise men experienced & aged men to assist in Council in all times of trouble[.] handsome men are not oft wise & strong minded men but the Strength of a strong minded man will Create corse features like the rough & strong bough of the oak[.] you will always discover in the first glance of a man in the outlines of his features Sumthing of the mind of the man

* * *

A man can bear a heavy burden by practice and continuing to increase it. The inhabitants of this continent anciently were so constituted, and were so determined and persevering, either in righteousness or wickedness, that God visited them immediately either with great judgments or blessings. But the present generation, if they were going to battle, if they got any assistance from God, they would have to obtain it by faith. (May 14, 1843.) DHC 5:387-390.

A man can bear a heavy Burdhen by practice & Continueing to increase it[.] The inhabitants of this continant anciently were so constituted & were so determined & persevering either in righteousness or wickedness that God visited them immediately either **[p.542]** with great Judgments or Blessings[.] But the present generation if they were going to Battle if they Got any assistance from God would have to obtain it it By faith[72]

Meaning of Word Mormon

To the Editor of the *Times & Seasons*:

Times and Seasons

To the EDITOR of the TIMES & SEASONS.

Sir:—Through the medium of your paper, I wish to correct an error among men that profess to be learned, liberal and wise; and I do it the more cheerfully, because I hope sober-thinking and sound-reasoning people will sooner listen to the voice of truth, than be led

SIR:—Through the medium of your paper, I wish to correct an error among men that profess to be learned, liberal and wise; and I do it the more cheerfully, because I hope sober-thinking and sound-reasoning people will sooner listen to the voice of truth, than be led

---

71. 14 May 1843, *WWJ*, 1:540–41. See also *JSP, D12*, 304–5.
72. 14 May 1843, *WWJ*, 1:541–42.

astray by the vain pretentions of the self-wise. The error I speak of, is the definition of the word "MORMON." It has been stated that this word was derived from the Greek word *mormo*. This is not the case. There was no Greek or Latin upon the plates from which I, through the grace of God, translated the Book of Mormon. Let the language of that book speak for itself. On the 523d page, of the fourth edition, it reads: "And now behold we have written this record according to our knowledge in the characters, which are called among us the *Reformed Egyptian*, being handed down and altered by us, according to our manner of speech; and if our plates had been sufficiently large, we should have written in Hebrew: but the Hebrew hath been altered by us, also; and if we could have written in Hebrew, behold ye would have had no imperfection in our record, but the Lord knoweth the things which we have written, and also, that none other people knoweth our language; therefore he hath prepared means for the interpretation thereof."

Here then the subject is put to silence, for "*none other people knoweth our language*," therefore the Lord, and not man, had to interpret, after the people were all dead. And, as Paul said, "the world by wisdom know not God," so the world by speculation are destitute of revelation; and as God in his superior wisdom, has always given his saints, wherever he had any on the earth, the same spirit, and that spirit, as John says, is the true spirit of prophesy, which is the testimony of Jesus, I may safely say that the word Mormon stands independent of the learning and wisdom of this generation.—Before I give a definition, however, to the word, let me say that the Bible in its widest sense, means *good*; for the Savior says according to the gospel of John, "I am the *good* shepherd;" and it will not be beyond the common use of terms, to say that good is among the most important in use, and though known by various names in different languages, still its meaning is the same, and

opposition to "bad." We say from the Saxon, "good"; the Dane, "god"; the Goth, "goda"; the German, "gut"; the Dutch, "goed"; the Latin, "bonus"; the Greek, "kalos"; the Hebrew, "tob"; and the "Egyptian, "mon." Hence, with the addition of "more," or the contraction, "mor," we have the word "mormon"; which means, literally, "more good." were
Yours,
JOSEPH SMITH.
(May 15, 1843.) T&S 4:194.

is ever in opposition to *bad*. We say from the Saxon, *good*; the Dane, *god*; the Goth, *goda*; the German, *gut*; the Dutch, *goed*; the Latin, *bonus*; the Greek, *kalos*; the Hebrew, *tob*; and the Egyptian, *mon*. Hence, with the addition of *more*, or the contraction, *mor*, we have the word MORMON; which means, literally, *more good*.
Yours,
JOSEPH SMITH.[73]

Remarks of the Prophet at Ramus—Importance of the Eternity of the Marriage Covenant

Joseph Smith's History

Except a man and his wife enter into an everlasting covenant and be married for eternity, while in this probation, by [p.301] the power and authority of the Holy Priesthood, they will cease to increase when they die; that is, they will not have any children after the resurrection. But those who are married by the power and authority of the priesthood in this life, and continue without committing the sin against the Holy Ghost, will continue to increase and have children in the celestial glory. The unpardonable sin is to shed innocent blood, or be accessory thereto. All other sins will be visited with judgment in the flesh, and the spirit being delivered to the buffetings of Satan until the day of the Lord Jesus.

He said that ["]except a man and his wife enter into an everlasting covenant and be married for eternity while in this probation by the power and authority of the Holy priesthood they will cease to increase when they die (i e) they will not have any children in the resurrection, but those who are married by the power & authority of the priesthood in this life & continue without committing the sin against the Holy Ghost will continue to increase & have children in the celestial glory. The unpardonable sin is to shed innocent blood or be accessory thereto. All other sins will be visited with judgement in the flesh and the spirit being delivered to the buffetings of Satan untill the day of the Lord Jesus." I feel desirous to be united in an everlasting covenant to my wife and pray that it may soon be.

The way I know in whom to confide—God tells me in whom I may place confidence.

pres.t J. said that they way he knew in whom to confide. God told him in whom he might place confidence.[74]

The Celestial Glory

Joseph Smith's History

In the celestial glory there are three heavens or degrees; and in order to obtain the highest, a

He also said that in the celestial glory there was three heavens or degrees, and in order to

---

73. *T&S* 4, no. 13 (15 May 1843): 194.
74. Instruction, 16 May 1843, reported by William Clayton, *JSP, D12*, 308.

man must enter into this order of the priesthood [meaning the new and everlasting covenant of marriage]; and if he does not, he cannot obtain it. He may enter into the other, but that is the end of his kingdom: he cannot have an increase." (May 16, 1843.) DHC 5:391-2.

obtain the highest a man must enter into this order of the priesthood and if he dont he cant obtain it. He may enter into the other but that is the end of his kingdom he cannot have an increase.[75]

Salvation and Sure Word of Prophecy

William Clayton Journal

He shewed that knowledge is power & the man who has the most knowledge has the greatest power. Also that Salvation means a mans being placed beyond the power of all his enemies.

Salvation means a man's being placed beyond the power of all his enemies.

The more sure word of prophecy means a man's knowing that he is sealed up unto eternal life by revelation and the spirit of prophecy, through the power of the holy priesthood. It is impossible for a man to be saved in ignorance. Paul saw the third heavens, and I more. Peter penned the most sublime language of any of the apostles. (May 17, 1843.) DHC 5:392.

He said the more sure word of prophecy meant, a mans knowing that he was sealed up unto eternal life by revelation & the spirit of prophecy, through the power of the Holy priesthood. He also showed that it was impossible for a man to be saved in ignorance. Paul had seen the third heavens and I more. Peter penned the most sublime language of any of the apostles.[76]

God Breathed into Adam His Spirit

William Clayton Journal

The 7th verse of 2nd chapter of Genesis ought to read—God breathed into Adam his spirit

The 7th verse of c 2 of Genesis ought to read God breathed into Adam the his spirit or

---

75. Instruction, 16 May 1843, reported by William Clayton, *JSP, D12*, 308–9. See also D&C 131:1–4. An editorial note in *JSP, J3* states: "According to Clayton's record, the group stayed only fifteen minutes in Carthage before proceeding to Ramus, where JS taught Benjamin and Melissa LeBaron Johnson about eternal marriage: 'He said that except a man and his wife enter into an everlasting covenant and be married for eternity while in this probation by the power and authority of the Holy priesthood they will cease to increase when they die (i.e. they will not have any children in the resurrection), but those who are married by the power & authority of the priesthood in this life & continue without committing the sin against the Holy Ghost will continue to increase & have children in the celestial glory.' On 17 May, after a 'pleasure ride' through Fountain Green, Illinois, in the morning, JS preached from the first chapter of 2 Peter about knowledge, salvation, and 'the more sure word of prophecy.' Later in the day, following further discussion of eternal marriage, JS attended the Ramus city council meeting, 'rode out' with the Johnson family, and attended a lecture given by a Methodist preacher. JS 'offered some corrections' about Genesis 2:7 following the lecture and also taught that 'spirit' was a 'more fine or pure' form of matter than is discernable by natural means. JS and his party returned to Nauvoo on 18 May 1843. Portions of JS's teachings given on 16 and 17 May were later canonized." *JSP, J3*, 17–18.

76. Discourse, 17 May 1843, reported by William Clayton, *JSP, D12*, 310.

[i.e., Adam's spirit] or breath of life; but when the word "rauch" applies to Eve, it should be translated lives.

breath of life. but when the word "ruach" applies to Eve it should be translated lives.[77]

Eternal Duration of Matter

William Clayton Journal

Speaking of eternal duration of matter, I said: There is no such thing as immaterial matter. All spirit is [p.302] matter, but is more fine or pure, and can only be discerned by purer eyes. We cannot see it, but when our bodies are purified, we shall see that it is all matter. (May 17, 1843.) DHC 5:392-3.

Speaking of eternal duration of matter he said, There is no such thing as immaterial matter. All spirit is matter but is more fine or pure and can only be discerned by purer eyes We cant see it but when our bodies are purified we shall see that it is all matter.[78]

The Prophecy on the Head of Stephen A. Douglas

History Draft

The following brief account of the Prophet's visit with Judge Douglas while at Carthage is from the journal of William Clayton, who was present. For the fulfilment of this prophecy the reader is referred to the comments in the Documentary History of the Church, 5:395-398.

Dined with Judge Stephen A. Douglas, who is presiding at court. After dinner Judge Douglas requested President Joseph to give him a history of the Missouri persecutions, which he did in a very minute manner, for about three hours. He also gave a relation of his journey to Washington city, and his application in behalf of the Saints to Mr. Van Buren, the President of the United States, for redress and Mr. Van Buren's pusillanimous reply, "Gentlemen, your cause is just, but I can do nothing for you;" and the cold, unfeeling manner in which he was treated by most of the senators and representatives in relation to the subject, Clay saying, "You had better go to Oregon," and Calhoun shaking his head solemnly, saying, "It's a nice question—a critical question, but it will not do to agitate it."

Dined with Judge Stephen A Douglass [Douglas] who is presiding at Court "After dinner, Judge Douglass requested Pres.t Joseph to give him a history of the Missouri persecution, which he did in a very ~~lengthy &~~ minute manner, <for about 3 hours,> & <he> also <gave> a relation of his <journey to Washington <City> & his ~~interview with~~ application in behalf of the Saints, to> ~~visit with~~ M.r [Martin] Van Buren, the Pres.t of the U. S., ~~& the heads of the nation~~ <for redress;> and M.r Van Buren's ~~acknowledgment that~~ <pusilaminous ~~saying~~ reply "Gentlemen> your cause is just, but I can do nothing for you." <and the cold unfeeling manner in which he was treated by <most of> the Senators & Representatives, in relation to the subject— Henry Clay saying <"you had better> "Go to

---

77. Discourse, 17 May 1843, reported by William Clayton, *JSP, D12*, 312.
78. Discourse, 17 May 1843, reported by William Clayton, *JSP, D12*, 313. See also D&C 131:7–8.

Oregon", [John C.] Calhoun shaking his head solemnly, saying, "Its a nice question, a critical question, but it will not do to agitate it." ~~Cast as Chairman of the Committee~~

The judge listened with the greatest attention and spoke warmly in deprecation of the conduct of Governor Boggs and the authorities of Missouri, who had taken part in the extermination, and said that any people that would do as the mobs of Missouri had done ought to be brought to judgment: they ought to be punished.

President Smith, in concluding his remarks, said that if the government, which received into its coffers the money of citizens for its public lands, while its officials are rolling in luxury at the expense of its public treasury, cannot protect such citizens in their lives and property, it is an old granny anyhow; and I prophesy in the name of the Lord God of Israel, unless the United States redress the wrongs committed upon the Saints in the state of Missouri and punish the crimes committed by her officers that in a few years the government will be utterly overthrown and wasted, and there will not be so much as a potsherd left, for their wickedness in permitting the murder of men, women and children, and the wholesale plunder and **[p.303]** extermination of thousands of her citizens to go unpunished, thereby perpetrating a foul and corroding blot upon the fair fame of this great republic, the very thought of which would have caused the high-minded and patriotic framers of the Constitution of the United States to hide their faces with shame. Judge, you will aspire to the presidency of the United States; and if ever you turn your hand against me or the Latter-day Saints, you will feel the weight of the hand of the Almighty upon you; and you will live to see and know that I have testified the truth to you; for the conversation of this day will stick to you through life.

The Judge listened with the greatest attention, & <then> spoke warmly in deprecation of the conduct of Gov. [Lilburn W.] Boggs & the authorities of ~~the~~ Missouri, who had taken ~~a leading~~ part in the extermination. <& said that any people that would do as the mobs of Missouri have done ought to be brought to Judgment, they ought to be punished.>

In concluding his remarks Pres$^{t.}$ Smith said, I ~~prophecies~~ prophecy in the name of the Lord God of Israel, that unless the U S redress the wrongs committed upon the Saints, ~~by~~ <in> the State of Missouri, & punish the crimes committed by her officers, that in a few years the Government will be utterly overthrown & wasted, & there will not be so much as a Potsherd left, for their wickedness ~~at conniving at~~ <in permitting> the ~~Missouri~~ murder of men women & children, & the wholesale plunder & extermination of 1000^s of her citizens ~~thereby~~ to go unpunished; thereby perpetuating a foul & corroding blot upon the fair fame of this great Republic, the very ~~mention~~ <thought> of which, would have caused the <high minded & patriotic> framers of the Constitution <of the U. S.> to hide their faces with shame. Judge you will aspire to the Presidency of the U. S. & if ever you ~~left a~~ <turn your> hand against me or the L. D. S. you will feel the weight of the hand of the Almighty upon you; & you will live to see & know that I have testified the Truth to you ~~this day~~. for the conversation of this day will stick to you thru' life.

He [Judge Douglas] appeared very friendly, and acknowledged the truth and propriety of President Smith's remarks. (May 18, 1843.) DHC 5:393-394.

He appears very friendly & acknowledged the propriety of ~~my~~ <Pres.^t Smith's> remarks.^79

The Prophet's Discourse from 2 Peter, First Chapter—Reproof of Self-Righteousness

Joseph Smith's Journal

I do not know when I shall have the privilege of speaking in a house large enough to convene the people. I find my lungs are failing with continual preaching in the open air to large assemblies.

when I shall have the opportunity of speaki[n]g in a house I know not. I find my lungs failing— it has always been my fortune almost. to speak in the open air to large assemblies.

I do not think there have been many good men on the earth since the days of Adam; but there was one good man and his name was Jesus. Many persons think a prophet must be a great deal better than anybody else. Suppose I would condescend--yes, I will call it condescend, to be a great deal better than any of you, I would be raised up to the highest heaven; and who should I have to accompany me?

I have not an idea there has been a great many very good men since Adam. There ~~is~~ was one good— man Jesus.— <many think a propht must be a gre[a]t deal better than any body else.—> suppose I would condesc[e]nd. yes I will <call it> condesce[n]d, to be a great deal better than any of you. I would be raised up to the highe[s]t heaven and who should I have to accompany me.

I love that man better who swears a stream as long as my arm yet deals justice to his neighbors and mercifully deals his substance to the poor, than the long, smooth-faced hypocrite.

I love that man better who swears a stream as long as my arm, and administ[er]ing to the poor & divide[n]g his substance. than the long smoothed faced hypo[c]rites

I do not want you to think that I am very righteous, for I am not, God judges men according to the use they make of the light which He gives them.

I dont want you to think I am very righteous. for I am not very righteous.— God judgeth men according to the light he gives them.

"We have a more sure word of prophecy, whereunto you do well to take heed, as unto a light that shineth in a dark place. We were eyewitnesses of his majesty and heard the voice of his excellent glory." And what could be more sure? When He was transfigured on the mount, what could be more sure to them? Divines have been quarreling for ages about the meaning of this.

we have a more sure word of prophecy. whereunto you do well to take heed— as unto a light that shineth in a dark place we were eyewitnesses of his maje[s]ty and heard the voice of his excellent glory— &. what could be more sure? transfigu[re]d on the mou[n]t &c what could be more sure?— Divines have been quarreelig [quarreling] for ages about the meaning. of this.^80

---

79. History Draft (1 March–31 December 1843), 32a. See also History D-1, 1553.
80. 21 May 1843, *JSP, J3*, 20.

The Prophet's Characterization of Himself

[p.304] I am like a huge, rough stone rolling down from a high mountain; and the only polishing I get is when some corner gets rubbed off by coming in contact with something else, striking with accelerated force against religious bigotry, priest-craft, lawyer-craft, doctor-craft, lying editors, suborned judges and jurors, and the authority of perjured executives, backed by mobs, blasphemers, licentious and corrupt men and women—all hell knocking off a corner here and a corner there. Thus I will become a smooth and polished shaft in the quiver of the Almighty, who will give me dominion over all and every one of them, when their refuge of lies shall fail, and their hiding place shall be destroyed, while these smooth-polished stones with which I come in contact become marred.[81]

Joseph Smith's Journal

rough stone roling down hill.[82]

---

81. The source of this paragraph, attributed to Joseph Smith, is 21 May 1843, History, D-1, 1556, which reads: "I am like a <huge> rough stone rolling down <from> a <high> mountain, and the only polishing I get, is when some corner gets rubbed off by coming in contact with something else striking with accelerated force against Religious bigotry, Priestcraft, Lawyer craft, Doctor craft, Lying Editors suborned Judges and Jurors, and the authority of Perjured Executives, backed by Mobs, Blasphemers, Licentious and corrupt men and women; all hell knocking off a corner here and a corner there; thus, I <will> become a smooth and polished shaft in the quiver of the Almighty, who will give me dominion over all and every one of them, when their refuge of lies shall fail, and their hiding place shall be destroyed, while these smooth polished stones with which I come in contact, become marred." The editors of *The Words of Joseph Smith* wrote: "Because there is no source yet found to document the following words, apparently the Church historians, taking the words 'rough stone roling down a hill' as a clue that the Prophet was making a self-characterization, expanded this to read" as it appears in History, D-1. The editors of *The Words of Joseph Smith* continue, "Apparently the Church historians recalled that Joseph Smith on this or some other occasion made such an autobiographical statement. For whatever reason, they felt justified in inserting this long statement in order to round out the discourse prior to publication." *WJS*, 282n7.

The probability that Joseph Smith made such a statement is evident from an 1843 Brigham Young sermon (recorded by Wilford Woodruff in his journal). Brigham Young is purported to have said, "But we are rough Stones out of the mountain, & when we roll through the forest & nock the bark of[f] from the trees it does not hurt us even if we should get [a?] Cornor nocked of[f] occasionally[.] for the more they roll about & knock the Cornors of[f] the better we are[.] but if we were polished & smooth when we get the Cornors kakocked [knocked] of[f] it would deface us. This is the Case with Joseph Smith[.] he never professed to be a dressed smooth polished stone but was rough out of the mountain & has been rolling among the rocks & trees & has not hurt him at all[.] but he will be as smooth & polished in the end as any other Stone, while many that were so vary polished & smooth in the beginning get badly defaced and spoiled while they are rolling about." 9 September 1843, *WWJ*, 1:578.

82. 21 May 1843, *JSP, J3*, 20. This line, "rough stone rolling downhill" is the only part of this quote found in the journal recorded by Willard Richards. Richards recorded a similar note in his 11 June 1843

The Secrets of Peter's Writings

Joseph Smith's Journal

There are three grand secrets lying in this chapter, [2 Peter 1.] which no man can dig out, unless by the light of revelation, and which unlock the whole chapter as the things that are written are only hints of things which existed in the prophet's mind, which are not written concerning eternal glory.

3 grand secrets lying in this chapter which no man can dig out. which unlocks the whole chapter. what is writtn are only hints of things which ex[is]ted in the prophts mind. which are not written. concer[n]ing eternal glory.

I am going to take up this subject by virtue of the knowledge of God in me, which I have received from heaven. The opinions of men, so far as I am concerned, are to me as the crackling of thorns under the pot, or the whistling of the wind. I break the ground;

[p.21] I am going to take up this subj[e]ct by virtue of the knowledge of God in me.— which I have received fr[o]m heaven. the opinions of men. so far as I am ~~possessed~~ concerned. are to me as the crackling of the thorns under the pot. or the whistle[n]g of the wind, Columbus and the eggs.—[83]

Joseph Smith's History

I lead the way like Columbus when he was invited to a banquet where he was assigned the most honorable place at the table, and served with the ceremonials which were observed towards sovereigns. A shallow courtier present, who was meanly jealous of him, abruptly asked him whether he though that in case he had not discovered the Indies, there were not other men in Spain who would have been capable of the enterprise? Columbus made no reply, but took an egg and invited the company to make it stand on end. They all attempted it, but in vain; whereupon he struck it upon the table so as to break one end, and left it standing on the broken part, illustrating that when he had once shown the way to the new world nothing was easier than to follow it.

like Columbus when he was invited to a banquet, where he was assigned the most honorable place at table and served with the ceremonials which were observed towards Soverigns. A shallow Courtier present, who was meanly jealous of him, abruptly asked him whether he thought, that in case he had not discovered the Indies, there were not other men in Spain, who would have been capable of the enterprise? Columbus made no reply, but took an egg and invited the Company to make it stand on end. They all attempted it, but in vain, whereupon he struck it upon the table, so as to break one end, and left it standing on the broken part. illustrating that when he had once shewn the way, to the New world, nothing was easier than to follow it.[84]

---

entry: "I a rough stone. the sound of the hammer & chisel was never hea[r]d on me. nor never will be. I desire the learning & wisdom of heaven alone." *JSP, J3*, 31.

83. 21 May 1843, *JSP, J3*, 20–21.

84. Church historians expanded the brief journal entries made by Willard Richards, 21 May 1843, recorded in History, D-1, 1556.

Things Unlawful to Utter

Paul ascended into the third heavens, and he could un[p.305]derstand the three principal rounds of Jacob's ladder—the telestial, the terrestrial, and the celestial glories or kingdoms, where Paul saw and heard things which were not lawful for him to utter. I could explain a hundred fold more than I ever have of the glories of the kingdoms manifested to me in the vision, were I permitted, and were the people prepared to receive them.

The Lord deals with this people as a tender parent with a child, communicating light and intelligence and the knowledge of his ways as they can bear it. The inhabitants of the earth are asleep; they know not the day of their visitation. The Lord hath set the bow in the cloud for a sign that while it shall be seen, seed time and harvest, summer and winter shall not fail; but when it shall disappear woe to that generation, for behold the end cometh quickly.

Joseph Smith's History

"Paul ascended into the third Heavens and he could understand the three principal rounds of Jacob's Ladder, the Telestial, the Terrestrial and the Celestial glories or Kingdoms, where Paul saw and heard things which were not lawful for him to utter. I could explain a hundred fold more than I ever have, of the glories of the Kingdoms manifested to me in the vision, were I permitted, and were the people prepared to receive it,

the Lord deals with this people as a tender parent with a child, communicating light and intelligence and the knowledge of his ways, as they can hear it. <see below +> [*Insertion at bottom of page*] <+The Inhabitants of the Earth are asleep, they know not the day of their visitation. The Lord hath set the bow in the cloud for a sign that while it shall be seen, seed time and harvest, summer and winter shall not fail, but when it shall disappear, wo to that generation, for behold the end cometh quickly[85]

Calling and Election to Be Made Sure

Contend earnestly for the like precious faith with the Apostle Peter, "and add to your faith virtue," knowledge, temperance, patience, godliness, brotherly kindness, charity; "for if these things be in you, and abound, they make you that ye shall neither be barren nor unfruitful in the knowledge of our Lord Jesus Christ." Another point, after having all these qualifications, he lays this injunction upon the people "to make your calling and election sure." He is emphatic upon this subject—after adding all this virtue, knowledge, etc., "Make your calling and election sure." What is the

Joseph Smith's Journal

like precious faith with us . . . .— add to your faith virtue &c ...

another point after having all these qualifictins [qualifications] he lays this injutin [injunction].— but rather make your calling & election sure— after adding all. this. virtue knowledge &. make your cal[l]ing. &c Sure.—

---

85. From the brief three-word journal entry made by Willard Richards, "Ladder and rainbow," Church historians expanded them in 21 May 1843, History, D-1, 1556.

secret—the starting point? "According as His divine power hath given unto us all things that pertain unto life and godliness." How did he obtain all things? Through the knowledge of Him who hath called him. There could not anything be given, pertaining to life and godliness, without knowledge. Woe! woe! woe to Christendom!—especially the divines and priests if this be true.

Salvation is for a man to be saved from all his enemies; for until a man can triumph over death, he is not saved. A knowledge of the priesthood alone will do this.

what is the secret, the starting point. according as his divine power which hath given unto all things that pertain to life & godliness. how did he obtain all things?— th[r]ough the knowledge of him who hath calld him.— there could not any be given pertain[in]g to life & knowledge & godliness without knowledge wo wo wo to the Ch[r]istendom.— the divine & priests; &c— if this be true.

salvation. is for a man to be seve[r]ed from all his enemies.— until a man can triumph over death. he is not saved. knowlidge will do this.[86]

The Devil's Punishment

The spirits in the eternal world are like the spirits in this world. When those have come into this world and received **[p.306]** tabernacles, then died and again have risen and received glorified bodies, they will have an ascendancy over the spirits who have received no bodies, or kept not their first estate, like the devil. The punishment of the devil was that he should not have a habitation like men. The devil's retaliation is, he comes into this world, binds up men's bodies, and occupies them himself. When the authorities come along, they eject him from a stolen habitation.

The design of the great God in sending us into this world, and organizing us to prepare us for the eternal worlds, I shall keep in my own bosom at present.

We have no claim in our eternal compact, in relation to eternal things, unless our actions and contracts and all things tend to this. But after all this, you have got to make your calling and election sure. If this injunction would lie largely on those to whom it was spoken, how much more those of the present generation!

Joseph Smith's Journal

organization of spirits in the eternal world.— spirits in the eternal wo[r]ld are like spir[i]ts in this world. when those spirits have come into this visi[o]n & received grolifed [glorified] bodies. they will have an ascndeny [ascendency] over spir[i]ts who have no bodi[e]s. or kept not their fi[r]st state like the devil. Devils puni[s]hment. should not have a habitati[o]n. like othr men.— D[e]vils retaliation— come into this w[o]rld bind up mens bod[i]es. & occuppy himself.— authorities come along and eject him from a stolen habitation

design of the great God. in sending us into this world. and organize[n]g us **[p.22]** to prepare us for the Eternal world.— I shall keep in my own bosom.

we have no claim in our eternal compact. in relation to Eternal thi[n]gs unless our actions. & contracts & all thi[n]gs tend to this end.— after all this make your calling and election sure. if this injuncti[o]n would lay lageley [largely] on those to whom it was spoken. how much more those to who th[e]m of the 19. century.—

---

86. 21 May 1843, *JSP, J3*, 21.

1st key: Knowledge is the power of salvation. 2nd key: Make your calling and election sure. 3rd key: It is one thing to be on the mount and hear the excellent voice, etc., and another to hear the voice declare to you, You have a part and lot in that kingdom. (May 21, 1843.) DHC 5:401-403.

<1 Key> Knowledge in the power of Salvati[o]n. <2 Key> Make his calling and Election Sure. 3ᵈ— it is one thing to be on the mount. & hear the excellent voice &c &c and another <to hear the> voice de[c]lare to you you have a part & lot in that kingdom.—[87]

The Prophet on Forming Temperance Societies

Times and Seasons

Dear Brother:—In answer to yours of May 4th, concerning the Latter-day Saints forming a temperance society, we would say, as Paul said—"Be not unequally yoked with unbelievers, but contend for the faith once delivered to the Saints"; and as Peter advises, so say we,

Dear Brother,—In anwer to your's of May 4th concerning the Latter Day Saints forming a Temperance Society, we would say as Paul said:—Be not unequally yoked with unbelievers," but contend for the faith once delivered to the saints, and, as Peter advises, so say we:—

"Add to your knowledge, temperance." As Paul said he had to become all things to all men, that he might thereby save some, so must the elders of the last days do; and, being sent out to preach the Gospel and warn the world of the judgments to come, we are sure, when they teach as directed by the Spirit, according to the revelations of Jesus Christ, that they will preach the truth and prosper without complaint. Thus we have no new commandment to give, but admonish elders and members to live by every word that proceedeth forth from the mouth of God, lest they come short of the glory that is reserved for the faithful. (May 22, 1843.) DHC 5:404.

add to your knowledge temperance. As Paul said he had to become all things to all men, that he might thereby save some, so must the elders of the last days do, and, being sent out to preach the gospel, and warn the world of the judgments to come, we are sure, when they teach as directed by the Spirit, according to the revelations of Jesus Christ, that they will preach the truth, and prosper, without complaint. Thus we have no new commandment to give, but admonish elders and members to live by every word that proceedeth forth from the mouth of God, lest they come short of the glory that is reserved for the faithful.

W. RICHARDS Clerk.[88]

Righteous Judgments

Wilford Woodruff's Journal

[p.307] Brother Joseph then addressed the Twelve, and said that in all our counsels, especially while on trial of any one, we should see and observe all things appertaining to the subject, and discern the spirit by which either party was governed. We should be in a situation to understand every spirit and judge

Br Joseph then addressed the Twelve & said that in all our Councils esspecially while on trial of any one we should see & observe all things appertaining to the subject & disern the spirit by which either party was governed[.] we should be in a situation to understand evry spirit & Judge wrighteous

---

87. 21 May 1843, *JSP, J3*, 21–22.
88. *T&S* 4, no. 13 (15 May 1843): 199.

righteous judgment and not be asleep. We should keep order and not let the council be imposed upon by unruly conduct. The Saints need not think because I am familiar with them and am playful and cheerful, that I am ignorant of what is going on. Iniquity of any kind cannot be sustained in the Church, and it will not fare well where I am; for I am determined while I do lead the Church, to lead it right. (May 27, 1843.) DHC 5:411.

judgment & not be asleep[.] we should keep order & not let the Council be imposed upon by unruly Conduct[.] The Saints need not think because I am familiar with them & am playful & Cheerful that I am ignorant of what is going on[.] impu[r]ity cannot be retained in the Church of any kind & it will not fare well whare I am for I am determined while I do lead the Church to lead them right[89]

Testimony Concerning Brigham Young and Heber C. Kimball

Joseph Smith's History

Of the Twelve Apostles chosen in Kirtland, and ordained under the hands of Oliver Cowdery, David Whitmer and myself, there have been but two but what have lifted their heel against me—namely Brigham Young and Heber C. Kimball. (May 28, 1843.) DHC 5:412.

Of the first Twelve Apostles chosen in Kirtland and ordained under the hands of Oliver Cowdery, David Whitmer, and myself, there have been but two, but what have lifted their heel against me, namely Brigham Young and Heber C. Kimball.[90]

The Purpose of the Gathering of Israel

Joseph Smith's Journal & Wilford Woodruff's Journal[91]

A large assembly of the Saints met at the Temple stand. Hymn by the choir. Prayer by Elder Parley P. Pratt, and singing.

Sunday June 11. 1843. 10. A.M. at the temple Stand. Hymn by the Quire. Read 23 matthew. P[arley] P. Pratt Prayed. Singing.— Matt. 23.37. Subject presented me since I came in this house.——

President Joseph Smith remarked—"I am a rough stone. The sound of the hammer and chisel was never heard on me until the Lord took me in hand. I desire the learning and wisdom of heaven alone. I have not the least idea, if Christ should come to the earth and preach such rough things as He preached to the Jews, but that this generation would reject Him for being so rough."

I a rough stone. the sound of the hammer & chisel was never hea[r]d on me. nor never will be. I desire the learning & wisdom of heaven alone. Have not the least idea but if Christ should come and preach such rough thi[n]gs as he preahd [preached] to the Jews. but this generate[o]n would reject reject him for b[e]ing so rough. I never can find much to say in expou[n]ding a text.[92]

---

89. 27 May 1843, *WWJ*, 1:544. See also *JSP, D12*, 350–51.

90. 28 May 1843, History, D-1, 1563.

91. The original *TPJS* account of the 11 June 1843 sermon is an amalgamation of several journal versions and some later additions made by historians. Joseph Fielding Smith appears to have relied upon the version found in History, D-1. The full texts of both Willard Richards's and the Wilford Woodruff's accounts can be found in Appendix B of this volume. Both versions of the sermon below are dated 11 June 1843.

92. 11 June 1843, *JSP, J3*, 31.

He then took for his text the 37th verse of 23rd chapter of Matthew—"O Jerusalem, Jerusalem, thou that killest the prophets and stonest them which are sent unto thee; how often would I have gathered thy children together, even as a hen gathereth her chickens under her wings, and ye would not."

This subject was presented to me since I came to the stand. What was the object of gathering the Jews, or the people of [p.308] God in any age of the world? I can never find much to say in expounding a text. A man never has half so much fuss to unlock a door, if he has a key, as though he had not, and had to cut it open with his jack-knife.

The main object was to build unto the Lord a house whereby He could reveal unto His people the ordinances of His house and the glories of His kingdom, and teach the people the way of salvation; for there are certain ordinances and principles that, when they are taught and practiced, must be done in a place or house built for that purpose.

He took for the foundation of his discourse the words of Jesus to the Jews how oft would I have gatherd you togetherd as a hen gathereth her chickens under wings But ye would not &c.[93]

He then asked what was the object of gathering the Jews together or the people of God in any age of the world,[94] never is half so much fuss to unlock a door if you have a key an[d] wh[e]n you have not. or have to cut it out with a jack knife.—[95]

the main object was to build unto the Lord an house whereby he could reveal unto his people the ordinances of his house and glories of his kingdom & teach the peopl the ways of salvation for their are certain ordinances & principles that when they are taught and practized, must be done in a place or house built for that purpose[96]

Principles of the Gospel Never Change

Joseph Smith's Journal
O. Jerusalem &c.— whenc[e] arises the curse of Almighty God that was to be pourd out up[o]n the heads of the jews? That they would not be gathe[re]d! beca[u]se they would not let Ch[r]ist gather them. It was the design in the [p.32] cou[n]cils of heaven before the world was, that the pri[n]ciple & law of that pri[e]st-hood was predicated up[o]n the gathe[rin]g of the people in every age of the world. Jesus did every thing posible to gather the people. & th[e]y would not be gathered and he poured out curses up[o]n the[m] Ordinances were instituted in heavn

It was the design of the councils of heaven before the world was, that the principles and laws of the priesthood should be predicated upon the gathering of the people in every age of the world. Jesus did everything to gather the people, and they would not be gathered, and He therefore poured out curses upon them. Ordinances instituted in the heavens before the foundation of the world, in the

---

93. 11 June 1843, *WWJ*, 1:545.
94. 11 June 1843, *JSP, D12*, 385. See also *WWJ*, 1:545.
95. 11 June 1843, *JSP, J3*, 31.
96. 11 June 1843, *JSP, D12*, 385. See also *WWJ*, 1:545.

priesthood, for the salvation of men, are not to be altered or changed. All must be saved on the same principles.

before the f[o]undation of the world ~~of~~ in the pri[e]sthood. for the salvati[o]n of man. not be alterd. not to be changed.— all must be saved upon the same principle.[97]

Salvation for the Dead

Joseph Smith's Journal & Wilford Woodruff's Journal

It is for the same purpose that God gathers together His people in the last days, to build unto the Lord a house to prepare them for the ordinances and endowments, washings and anointings, etc. One of the ordinances of the house of the Lord is baptism for the dead. God decreed before the foundation of the world that the ordinances should be administered in a font prepared for the purpose in the house of the Lord. "This is only your opinion, sir," says the sectarian.

it is for the same purpose that God gathers together the people in the last <days> to build unto the Lord an house to prepare them for the ordinances & endowments washings & anointings &c one of the ordinances of the house of the Lord is Baptism for the dead. God decreed before the foundation of the world that that ordinance should be administered in **[p.546]** a house prepared for that purpose.[98] that is only your opin[i]on Sir— say sectarians.—[99]

* * *

If a man gets a fullness of the priesthood of God he has to get it in the same way that Jesus Christ obtained it, and that was by keeping all the commandments and obeying all the ordinances of the house of the Lord.

If a man gets the fulness of God he has to get [it] in the same way that Jesus Christ obtained it & that was by keeping all the ordinances of the house of the Lord.[100]

Where there is no change of priesthood, there is no change of ordinances, says Paul. If God has not changed the ordinances and the priesthood, howl, ye sectarians! If he has when and where has He revealed it? Have ye turned revelators? Then why deny revelation?

where there is no change of pri[e]sthood there is no change of ordina[n]ces says ~~peter~~ Paul, If God has not changed the ordinances & pri[e]sthood. howl ye sectarians. if he has where has he revealed it. have ye turnd revelators? then why deny it?[101]

[p.309] Many men will say, "I will never forsake you, but will stand by you at all times." But the moment you teach them some of the mysteries of the kingdom of God that are retained in the heavens and are to be revealed to the children of men when they are prepared for them they will be the first to stone you and put you to

Men will say I will never forsake you but will stand by you at all times[.] but the moment you teach them some of the mysteries of God that are retained in the heavens and are to be revealed to the children of men when they are prepared, They will be the first to stone you & put you to death. It was the same principle

---

97. 11 June 1843, *JSP, J3*, 31–32.
98. 11 June 1843, *WWJ*, 1:545–46. See also *JSP, D12*, 385.
99. 11 June 1843, *JSP, J3*, 32.
100. 11 June 1843, *WWJ*, 1:546. See also *JSP, D12*, 385.
101. 11 June 1843, *JSP, J3*, 32.

death. It was this same principle that crucified the Lord Jesus Christ, and will cause the people to kill the prophets in this generation.

that crusified the Lord Jesus Christ.[102] and will cause the people to kill the Prophets in this generation.[103]

Many things are insoluble to the children of men in the last days: for instance, that God should raise the dead, and forgetting that things have been hid from before the foundation of the world, which are to be revealed to babes in the last days.

men have thought many things insutabl [inscrutable] in the last days. that he should raise the dead. Things have been hid from before the foundation of the [world] to be reveald in to babes in the last days.—[104]

Some Men "Too Wise to Be Taught"

Joseph Smith's Journal

There are a great many wise men and women too in our midst who are too wise to be taught; therefore they must die in their ignorance, and in the resurrection they will find their mistake.

there are a great ma[n]y wise men & women to[o] in our midst to[o] wise to be taught. & they mu[s]t die in their ignoranc[e] and in the resurrection they will find their mistake.

Many seal up the door of heaven by saying, So far God may reveal and I will believe.

many seal up to the door of heaven by saying so far god may reveal I & I will believe.—

All men who become heirs of God and joint heirs with Jesus Christ will have to receive the fulness of the ordinances of his kingdom; and those who will not receive all the ordinances will come short of the fullness of that glory, if they do not lose the whole.

heirs of God. &c. upon the same laws ordinance &c of Jesus Ch[r]ist. & he who will not have it all will come short. of that glory if not of the whole.[105]

Paradise

Joseph Smith's Journal & Wilford Woodruff's Journal

I will say something about the spirits in prison. There has been much said by modern divines about the words of Jesus (when on the cross) to the thief, saying, "This day shalt thou be with me in paradise." King James' translators make it out to say paradise. But what is paradise? It is a modern word: it does not answer at all to the original word that Jesus made use

I will say something about the Spirits in prision. theire has been much said about the Sayings of Jesus on the cross to the thief saying this day thou shalt be with me in paradise. The commentators make or translators make it out to say Paradise[.] but what is Paradise[?] it is a modern word[.] it does not answer at all to the original that Jesus made

---

102. 11 June 1843, *WWJ*, 1:546. See also *JSP, D12*, 385.
103. This phrase "and will cause the people to kill the Prophets in this generation" was added later; see 11 June 1843, History, D-1, 1573.
104. 11 June 1843, *JSP, J3*, 32.
105. 11 June 1843, *JSP, J3*, 32.
106. 11 June 1843, *WWJ*, 1:546. See also *JSP, D12*, 385–86.

of. Find the original of the word paradise. You may as easily find a needle in a haymow. Here is a chance for battle, ye learned men. There is nothing in the original word in Greek from which this was taken that signifies paradise; but it was—This day thou shalt be with me in the world of spirits: then I will teach you all about it and answer your inquiries. And Peter says he went and preached to the world of spirits (spirits in prison, 1 Peter, 3rd chap. 19th verse), so that they who would receive it could have it answered by proxy by those who live on the earth, etc.

use of.[106] find the origin of Paradise. find a needle in a hay mow.— here is a chance for a battle ye lear[ne]d man,—[107] their is nothing in the original in any language that signifies Paradise[.] But it was this day I will be with thee in the world of spirits & will teach thee or answer thy inquiries. The thief on the Cross was to be with Jesus christ in the world of spirits[.] he did not say Paradise or heaven.[108] & Peter says he went & preachd to the wo[r]ld of spi[r]its. so that they wo[u]ld receive it could have it answerd by proxig [proxy] by those who live on the earth &c—[109]

Baptism for the Dead Taught in New Testament

Joseph Smith's Journal & Wilford Woodruff's Journal

[p.310] The doctrine of baptism for the dead is clearly shown in the New Testament; and if the doctrine is not good, then throw the New Testament away; but if it is the word of God, then let the doctrine be acknowledged; and it was the reason why Jesus said unto the Jews, "How oft would I have gathered thy children together, even as a hen gathereth her chickens under her wings, and ye would not!"—that they might attend to the ordinances of baptism for the dead as well as other ordinances of the priesthood, and receive revelations from heaven, and be perfected in the things of the kingdom of God—but they would not. This was the case on the day of Pentecost: those blessings were poured out on the disciples on that occasion. God ordained that He would save the dead, and would do it by gathering His people together.

The doctrin of Baptism for the dead is clearly shown in the new testament[.] & if the doctrin is not good then throw away the new testament[.] but if it is the word of God then let the doctrin be acknowledged & it was one reason why Jesus said how oft would I have gathered you (the Jews) together that they might attend to the ordinance of the baptism for the dead as well as the other ordinances, the Priesthood[,] Revelations &c. This was the case on the day of Pentecost[.] these Blessings were poured out upon the deciples, on that occasion.[110] God ordai[ne]d that he who would save his dead should do it by gath[er]ing togethr as with the [p.33] jews….[111]

---

107. 11 June 1843, *JSP, J3*, 33.
108. 11 June 1843, *WWJ*, 1:546. See also *JSP, D12*, 386.
109. 11 June 1843, *JSP, J3*, 33.
110. 11 June 1843, *WWJ*, 1:546. See also *JSP, D12*, 386.
111. 11 June 1843, *JSP, J3*, 32–33. It should be noted that the compilers of the history not only made an amalgamation of this discourse from several sources, but they also made it a practice to take lines from one part of the discourse and insert them in a later part of their amalgamation. While it is worth looking at the original discourse, as posted on the The Joseph Smith Papers website, we have tried here to match what the historians used with the specific sources they drew upon.

The World of Spirits

	Joseph Smith's Journal & Wilford Woodruff's Journal
It always has been when a man was sent of God with the priesthood and he began to preach the fullness of the gospel, that he was thrust out by his friends, who are already to butcher him if he teach things which they imagine to be wrong; and Jesus was crucified upon this principle.	It always has been when a man was sent of good [God] with the Preth[ood] [priesthood]. & he began to preach the fulness of the gospel. that was thut [thrust] out by his fri[e]nds.—— and they are ready to but[c]her him if he teach things which th[e]y had imagind to be wrong.— Jesus was crucifi[e]d upon this principle—
I will now turn linguist. There are many things in the Bible which do not, as they now stand, accord with the revelations of the Holy Ghost to me.	I will turn linguist. ma[n]y things in the bible. whi[c]h do not. as th[e]y now stand. accord with the revelati[o]n of th[e] holy Gho[s]t to me.—...
I will criticise a little further. There has been much said about the word hell, and the sectarian world have preached much about it, describing it to be a burning lake of fire and brimstone. But what is hell? It is another modern term, and is taken from hades. I'll hunt after hades as Pat did for the woodchuck.	criticese [criticize] a little further...[112] Their has been Also much said about the word Hell & the sectarian world have preached much about it[.][113] Hell.— modern term. bur[n]ing lake of fire and Brimstone.[114] but what is hell[.] It is another modern term[.] it is taken from hades[115] I will hunt after Hades as pat did for woodchu[c]k.[116]
Hades, the Greek, or Sheol, the Hebrew, these two significations mean a world of spirits. Hades, Sheol, paradise, spirits in prison, are all one: it is a world of spirits.	hades the greek or shaole, the (hebrew) & the true signification is a world of spirits. Hades shaole paradise, spirits in prison is all one[.] it is a world of spirits.
The righteous and the wicked all go to the same world of spirits until the resurrection. "I do not think so," says one. If you will go to my house any time, I will take my lexicon and prove it to you.	the righteous & the wicked all go to the same world of spirits[117] I dont ~~they~~ thi[n]k so says one. go to my hous[e]— I will take my lexi[c]on— &c—
The great misery of departed spirits in the world of spirits, where they go after death, is	a world of departed spir[i]ts. disembodi[e]d spir[i]ts all go.——— good bad & indif[fer]ent—

---

112. 11 June 1843, *JSP, J3*, 33.
113. 11 June 1843, *WWJ*, 1:546. See also *JSP, D12*, 386.
114. 11 June 1843, *JSP, J3*, 33.
115. 11 June 1843, *WWJ*, 1:546. See also *JSP, D12*, 386.
116. 11 June 1843, *JSP, J3*, 33.
117. 11 June 1843, *WWJ*, 1:546. See also *JSP, D12*, 386.

to know that they come short of the glory that others enjoy and that they might have enjoyed [p.311] themselves, and they are their own accusers. "But," says one, "I believe in one universal heaven and hell, where all go, and are all alike, and equally miserable or equally happy."

What! where all are huddled together—the honorable, virtuous, and murderers, and whoremongers, when it is written that they shall be judged according to the deeds done in the body? But St. Paul informs us of three glories and three heavens. Now, if the doctrine of the sectarian world, that there is but one heaven, is true, Paul, what do you tell that lie for, and say there are three? Jesus said unto His disciples, "In my Father's house are many mansions, if it were not so, I would have told you. I go to prepare a place for you, and I will come and receive you to myself, that where I am ye may be also."

"[spirits] misery in a world of spi[ri]ts is to know th[e]y came short of the glory othe[r]s enjoy—— th[e]y are their own accusers one universal heaven— & hell—[118] but says one I believe in one hell & one heaven[.] all are equally miserable or equally happy.[119] &c says one, honorable & virtuo[u]s. & whoremonger— all hudld together.— judged according to deeds done in the body——[120] but St Paul informs us of three glories & three heavens[.] he knew a man caught up to the third heavens,[121] Paul says caught up to 3ᵈ heaven, what tell that Lie for Paul.— [p.34] sun moon & stars— many mansions— all one say Sectarians.—[122] & Jesus said their were many mansions in my Fathers kingdom[123] if it were not so, I would have told you. I go to prepare a place for you, and I will come and receive you to myself that where I am ye may be also.[124]

Men of God Endowed with Wisdom

Any many may believe that Jesus Christ is the Son of God, and be happy in that belief, and yet not obey his commandments, and at last be cut down for disobedience to the Lord's righteous requirements.

Joseph Smith's Journal & Wilford Woodruff's Journal

Any man may believe Jesus Christ is good & be happy in it & yet not obey his commands & at last be cut down by his righteous commandments[.]

A man of God should be endowed with wisdom, knowledge, and understanding, in order to teach and lead the people of God. The sectarian priests are blind, and they lead the blind, and they will all fall into the ditch together. They build with hay, wood, and stubble, on the

A man of God should be endowed with all wisdom[,] knowledge & understanding in order to teach & lead people. The blind may lead the blind & both fall into the death together;[125] They build hay wood & stubble. build on the old revelati[o]ns— with[o]ut the

---

118. 11 June 1843, *JSP, J3*, 33.
119. 11 June 1843, *WWJ*, 1:546. See also *JSP, D12*, 386.
120. 11 June 1843, *JSP, J3*, 33.
121. 11 June 1843, *WWJ*, 1:546. See also *JSP, D12*, 386.
122. 11 June 1843, *JSP, J3*, 33–34.
123. 11 June 1843, *WWJ*, 1:546. See also *JSP, D12*, 386.
124. The phrase "if it were not so, I would have told you. I go to prepare a place for you, and I will come and receive you to myself that where I am ye may be also" was added later in 11 June 1843, History, D-1, 1574.
125. 11 June 1843, *WWJ*, 1:546. See also *JSP, D12*, 386.

old revelations, without the true priesthood or spirit of revelation. If I had time, I would dig into hell, hades, sheol, and tell what exists there.

spi[r]it of Revelati[o]n or Pr[i]esthood. if had time I would dig into Hell. Hades. Shaol.— & tell what exists.—[126]

The Doctrine of the Godhead

Joseph Smith's Journal & Wilford Woodruff's Journal

There is much said about God and the Godhead. The scriptures say there are Gods many and Lords many, but to us there is but one living and true God, and the heaven of heavens could not contain him; for he took the liberty to go into other heavens. The teachers of the day say that the Father is God, the Son is God, and the Holy Ghost is God, and they are all in one body and one God. Jesus prayed that those that the Father had given him out of the world might be made one in them, as they were one [one in spirit, in mind, in purpose]. If I were to testify that the Christian world were wrong on this point, my testimony would be true.

Their is much said concerning God[,] the Godhead &c[.] the scripture says their is Gods many & Lords many. the teachers of the day say that the father is God the Son is God & the Holy Ghost is God & that they are all in one body & one God[.] Jesus says or prays that those that the father had given him out of the world might be made one in us as we are one. but if they were to be stuffed into one person they would make a great God. If I were to testify that the world was wrong on this point it would be true[.][127]

[p.312] Peter and Stephen testify that they saw the Son of Man standing on the right hand of God. Any person that had seen the heavens opened knows that there are three personages in the heavens who hold the keys of power, and one presides over all.

Peter— Steph[e]n— saw the Son of Man saw the son of man standi[n]g on the right hand of God.— 3 personages— in heavn who hold the keys.— one to preside over all.[128] any person that has seen the heavens opened knows that their is three personages in the heavens holding the keys of power[.][129]

If any man attempts to refute what I am about to say, after I have made it plain, let him beware.

If any mans attempt to refute. what I am about to say after I have made it plain let him be accursd.[130]

The Son Does What the Father Did

Joseph Smith's Journal & Wilford Woodruff's Journal

As the Father hath power in Himself, so hath the Son power in Himself, to lay down His life and take it again, so He has a body of His

As the fathr hath power in himself so hath the son power in hims[e]lf to lay down his life.— the son doeth what he hath seen the fath[er]

---

126. 11 June 1843, *JSP, J3*, 34.
127. 11 June 1843, *WWJ*, 1:546. See also *JSP, D12*, 386.
128. 11 June 1843, *JSP, J3*, 34.
129. 11 June 1843, *WWJ*, 1:546. See also *JSP, D12*, 386–87.
130. 11 June 1843, *JSP, J3*, 34.

own. The Son doeth what He hath seen the Father do: then the Father hath some day laid down His life and taken it again; so he has a body of His own; each one will be in His own body; and yet the sectarian world believe the body of the Son is identical with the Father's.

Gods have an ascendancy over the angels, who are ministering servants. In the resurrection, some are raised to be angels, others are raised to become Gods.

These things are revealed in the most holy places in a Temple prepared for that purpose. Many of the sects cry out, "Oh, I have the testimony of Jesus; I have the spirit of God; but away with Joe Smith; he says he is a prophet; but there are to be no prophets or revelators in the last days." Stop, sir! The Revelator says that the testimony of Jesus is the spirit of prophecy; so by your own mouth you are condemned. But to the text. Why gather the people together in this place? For the same purpose that Jesus wanted to gather the Jews—to receive the ordinances, the blessings, and glories that God has in store for His Saints.

I will now ask this assembly and all the Saints if you will now build this house and receive the ordinances and blessings which God has in store for you; or will you not build unto the Lord this house, and let Him pass by and bestow these blessings upon another people? I pause for a reply. (June 11, 1843.) DHC 5:423-427.

do.— &c—— take his body & stuff it into the fathr.[131] then the father has some day laid down his body & taken it again[.] <So he has a bo[d?]y of his own> So has his Son a body of his own[.] So each one will be in their own body.[132] and yet the Sectarian world believe the body of the son, is stuffed into his Father's.[133]

gods have ~~over~~ an ascenden[c]y over the angels angels remain angels.— some are resurrected to become gods by such revelations as god gives in the mo[s]t holy place.— in his temple. let them who are owing tythig [tithing] pay it up.— & bring stone.—[134]

These things are revealed in the most holy place in a temple prepared for that purpose.[135] Many of the sects cry out O I have the testimony of Jesus. I have the spirit of God. But away with Jo Smith[.] he says he is a Prophet But their is to be no Prophets nor revelations in the last days; But stop sir the Revelator says that the testimony of Jesus is the spirit of Prophecy[.] So by your own mouth you are Condemned. But to the text[.] why gather the people together in this place[?] for the same purpose **[p.547]** that Jesus wanted to gather the Jews. to receive the ordinances, the blessings & the glories that God has in store for his Saints[.]

And I would now ask this assembly and all the Saints if they will now build this house & receive the ordinances & Blessings which God has in store for you, or will you not build unto the Lord this house & let him pass by & bestow these blessings upon another[?] I pause for a reply.[136]

---

131. 11 June 1843, *JSP, J3*, 34.
132. 11 June 1843, *WWJ*, 1:546. See also *JSP, D12*, 387.
133. The phrase "and yet the Sectarian world believe the body of the son, is stuffed into his Father's" was added later in 11 June 1843, History, D-1, 1575.
134. 11 June 1843, *JSP, J3*, 34.
135. The phrase "These things are revealed in the most holy place in a temple prepared for that purpose" was added later in 11 June 1843, History, D-1, 1575.
136. 11 June 1843, *WWJ*, 1:546–47. See also *JSP, D12*, 387.

The Cause of the Prophet's Success—Love for His Fellow Man

	Joseph Smith's Journal Sunday July 9th. 1843
Joseph remarked that all was well between him and the heavens; that he had no enmity against any one; and as the prayer of Jesus, or his pattern, so prayed Joseph—Father, forgive me my trespasses as I forgive those who trespass against me, for I freely forgive all men. If we would secure and cultivate the love of others, we must love others, even our enemies as well as friends.	Joseph remarced [remarked] that all was well between him and the heavens that he had no emnity against any one. and as the prayer of Jesus. or his pattern so prayed Joseph. Father forgive me my trespasses. as I forgive those who trespass. against me. for I freely forgive all men.——— if we would s[e]cure & cultivate the love of others we must love others. even our enemies— as well as friends
Sectarian priests cry out concerning me, and ask, "Why is it this babbler gains so many followers, and retains them?" I answer, It is because I possess the principle of love. All I can offer the world is a good heart and a good hand.	"why is it this babler gains so many followers. & retains them"? because I possess the principle of love, All I can offer the world a good heart & a good hand.
The Saints can testify whether I am willing to lay down my life for my brethren. If it has been demonstrated that I have been willing to die for a "Mormon," I am bold to declare before Heaven that I am just as ready to die in defending the rights of a Presbyterian, a Baptist, or a good man of any other denomination; for the same principle which would trample upon the rights of the Latter-day Saints would trample upon the rights of the Roman Catholics, or of any other denominations who may be unpopular and too weak to defend themselves.	Mormons can testify whether I am willing to lay down my life for a mormon; If it has been demonstrated that I ~~am~~ have been willing to die for a mormon I am bold to declare <befo[r]e heaven> that I <am> just as ready to die for a presbytiran. a baptist or any other denomination.——[137]

Love of Liberty

	Joseph Smith's Journal
It is a love of liberty which inspires my soul—civil and religious liberty to the whole of the human race. Love of liberty was diffused into my soul by my grandfathers while they dandled me on their knees; and shall I want friends? No.	It is a love of libe[r]ty which inspires my soul. civil and religious liberty— were diffused into my soul by my grandfathers. while they dandld me on their knees.— and shall I want friends? no!—

---

137. 9 July 1843, *JSP, J3*, 55. Joseph Fielding Smith used additions inserted in 9 July 1843, History, E-1, 1666.

The inquiry is frequently made of me. "Wherein do you differ from others in your religious views?" In reality and essence we do not differ so far in our religious views, but that we could all drink into one principle of love. One of the grand fundamental principles of "Mormonism" is to receive truth, let it come from whence it may.

We believe in the Great Elohim who sits enthroned in yonder heavens. So do the Presbyterians. If a skilful mechanic, in taking a welding heat, uses borax, alum, etc., and succeeds in welding together iron or steel more perfectly than any other mechanic, is he not deserving of praise? And if by the principles of truth I succeed in uniting men of all denominations in the bonds of love, shall I not have attained a good object?

If I esteem mankind to be in error, shall I bear them down? No. I will lift them up, and in their own way too, if I cannot persuade them my way is better; and I will not seek to compel any man to believe as I do, only by the force of reasoning, for truth will cut its own way. Do you believe in Jesus Christ and [p.314] the Gospel of salvation which he revealed? So do I. Christians should cease wrangling and contending with each other, and cultivate the principles of union and friendship in their midst; and they will do it before the millennium can be ushered in and Christ takes possession of His kingdom.

"Do you believe in the baptism of infants?" asks the Presbyterian. No. "Why?" Because it is nowhere written in the Bible. Circumcision is not baptism, neither was baptism instituted in the place of circumcision. Baptism is for remission of sins. Children have no sins. Jesus blessed them and said, "Do what you have seen me do." Children are all made alive in Christ, and those of riper years through faith and repentance.

"Where in do you differ from other[s] in your religious. views?"— In reality & essencce we do not differ so far in our religio[us] v[i]ews but that we could all dring [drink] into one principle of love one [of] the grand fundamental principles of Mormonism <is> to recievee thruth [truth] let it come from where it may.—

we beli[e]ve in the great Eloheem. who— sits enthrond in yonder heavens.— so do the presbyterisan. If as a skillful mechanic In taking a weldi[n]g heat I use a borax & allum. &c.— an[d] succe[e]d in welding you all together shall I not have attained a good object. [p.56]

if I esteem mankind to be in error shall I bear them down? no! I will will lift them up.— & in his own way if I cannot persuade him my way is better? & I will ask no man to believe as I do. Do you believe in Jesus Christ &c? So do I. christians should cultivate the frie[n]dship of each other. & will do it. [Christians should cease wrangling and contention with each other and cultivate the principles of union and friendship in their midst; and they will do it before the Millennuim can be ushered in, and Christ takes possession of his kingdom.]¹³⁸

"Do you believe in the baptism of infants."? says the presby[t]erian.— No.— "why". because it is no where written in the book circumcision is not Baptism. Baptism is for remission of sins.— childrn have no sins— he <Jesus> blessed them— do what you have seen me do— all made alive in christ. faith & repentance.—

---

138. The portion in brackets was added later in 9 July 1843, History, E-1, 1666.

So far we are agreed with other Christian denominations. They all preach faith and repentance. The gospel requires baptism by immersion for the remission of sins, which is the meaning of the word in the original language—namely, to bury or immerse.

we are agreed.— baptism. yes by imme[r]sion. the Hebrew is the root. to ~~by~~ bury immerse———[139]

Necessity of Ordinances

Joseph Smith's Journal

We ask the sects, Do you believe this? They answer, No. I believe in being converted. I believe in this tenaciously. So did the Apostle Peter and the disciples of Jesus. But I further believe in the gift of the Holy Ghost by the laying on of hands. Evidence by Peter's preaching on the day of Pentecost, Acts 2:38. You might as well baptize a bag of sand as a man, if not done in view of the remission of sins and getting of the Holy Ghost. Baptism by water is but half a baptism, and is good for nothing without the other half—that is, the baptism of the Holy Ghost.

The Savior says, "Except a man be born of water and of the Spirit, he cannot enter into the kingdom of God." Though we or an angel from heaven, preach any other gospel unto you than that which we have preached unto you, let him be accursed," according to Galatians 1:8. (July 9, 1843.) DHC 5:498-500.

Do you believe this no.— I believe in b[e]ing ~~convertd~~ converted.——— I believe in this tin-aceously [tenaciously]

Holy Ghost by laying on of hands Evidence. Peter on days of Pentecost; might as well be ~~be baptism~~ baptise a bag of sand as a man if not done in view of the getting of the Holy ghost.— baptism by water is but ½ a baptism.— & is good for nothi[n]g with[out] the other. the Holy Gho[s]t.— <I> am free to day— messenger has retur[n]ed with offers of peace. from the governor except a man be born again. of water <& of the spir[i]t> can in no wise enter into the Kingdom— Though we or an angel f[r]om heaven preach any othe[r] gospel.[140]

Discourse—Burden of the Prophet's Ministry—Friendship

Joseph Smith's Journal
Sunday July 23—P.M.

I commence my remarks by reading this text—Luke 16:16: "The law and the prophets were until John: since that time the kingdom of God is preached, and every man presseth into it."

I do not know that I shall be able to preach much; but, **[p.315]** with the faith of the

Law and prophets were until John &c ~~15~~ 16 luke. 16 v— Joseph prea[c]hed— introduction—

---

139. 9 July 1843, *JSP, J3*, 56.
140. 9 July 1843, *JSP, J3*, 56.

Saints, may say something instructive. It has gone abroad that I proclaimed myself no longer a prophet. I said it last Sabbath ironically: I supposed you would all understand. It was not that I would renounce the idea of being a prophet, but that I had no disposition to proclaim myself such. But I do say that I bear the testimony of Jesus, which is the spirit of prophecy.

There is no greater love than this, that a man lay down his life for his friends. I discover hundreds and thousands of my brethren ready to sacrifice their lives for me.

The burdens which roll upon me are very great. My persecutors allow me no rest, and I find that in the midst of business and care the spirit is willing, but the flesh is weak. Although I was called of my Heavenly Father to lay the foundation of this great work and kingdom in this dispensation, and testify of His revealed will to scattered Israel, I am subject to like passions as other men, like the prophets of olden times.

Notwithstanding my weaknesses, I am under the necessity of bearing the infirmities of others, who, when they get into difficulty, hang on to me tenaciously to get them out, and wish me to cover their faults. On the other hand, the same characters, when they discover a weakness in Brother Joseph, endeavor the blast his reputation, and publish it to all the world, and thereby aid my enemies in destroying the Saints. Although the law is given through me to the Church, I cannot be borne with a moment by such men. They are ready to destroy me for the least foible, and publish my imaginary failings from Dan to Beersheba, though they are too ignorant of the things of God, which have been revealed to me, to judge of my actions, motives or conduct, in any correct manner whatever.

It has gone ab[r]oad that I was no longer a prophet.— I said it Ironically. I suppos'd you would all understand. I was not that I would renounce the idea of being a prophet. but that I would renou[n]ce the idea of proclaim[i]ng myself such. and saying. that I bear the testimony of Jesus.

No greater love than that a man lay down his life for his finds [friends]. I discover 100^s & 1000^s ready to do it for me

In the midst of business— &— find the spirit willing but the flesh is weak subject to like passions with other men.—

although I am under the necessity of bearing the infirmities of other men. &c——

on the other hand the same characters when th[e]y discover a weakness in brothr Joseph. blast his character. &c— all that law. &c th[r]ough him to the church.— he cannot be borne with a moment.[141] Although the law is given through me to the church, I cannot be borne with a moment by such men. They are ready to destroy me for the least foible, and publish my imaginary failings from Dan to Beersheba though they are too ignorant of the things of God which have been revealed to me to judge of my actions, motives or conduct in any correct manner whatever.[142]

---

141. 23 July 1843, *JSP, J3*, 65.
142. History, E-1, 1680.

The only principle upon which they judge me is by comparing my acts with the foolish traditions of their fathers and nonsensical teachings of hireling priests, whose object and aim were to keep the people in ignorance for the sake of filthy lucre; or as the prophet says, to feed themselves, not the flock. Men often come to me with their troubles, and seek my will, crying, Oh, Brother Joseph, help me! But when I am in trouble few of them sympathize with me or extend to me relief. I believe in a principle of reciprocity, if we do live in a devilish and wicked world where men busy themselves in watching for iniquity, and lay snares for those who reprove in the gate.

men mouth my troubles. wh[e]n <I> have trouble they forget it all I beli[e]ve in a principle of reciprociprocity [reciprocity]— if we live in a devilish world— &c—[143]

Loyalty to Friends

Love Begets Love

Joseph Smith's Journal

[p.316] It is a time-honored adage that love begets love. Let us pour forth love—show forth our kindness unto all mankind, and the Lord will reward us with everlasting increase; cast our bread upon the waters and we shall receive it after many days, increased to a hundredfold. Friendship is like Brother Turley in his blacksmith shop welding iron to iron; it unites the human family with its happy influence.

I see no faults in the chirch.— let me be resurrected with the saints whethr to heaven or helll or any other good place— good society. what do we care if the soc[i]ety is good?—— dont care what an a character is if he's my frie[n]d.— a fri[e]nd a true [p.66] friend. & I will be a f[r]iend to him frie[n]dship is the grand fundamental prin[c]iple of Mormonism. to revolutin [revolutionize?] civilize the world.— pour forth love. fredship [friendship] like Bro Tulys [Theodore Turley's] Blacksmith shop.—

I do not dwell upon your faults, and you shall not upon mine. Charity, which is love, covereth a multitude of sins, and I have often covered up all the faults among you; but the prettiest thing is to have no faults at all. We should cultivate a meek, quiet and peaceable spirit.

I do not dwell upon you[r] faults. you shall not upon mine— after you have covered up all the faults among you— the prettyest thing is have no faults at all— meek. qui[e]t. &c—

Have the Presbyterians any truth? Yes. Have the Baptists, Methodists, etc., any truth? Yes. They all have a little truth mixed with error. We should gather all the good and true principles in the world and treasure them up, or we shall not come out true "Mormons."

Presbyteri[a]n or any truth. emb[ra]ce that. Baptist. Methodist. &c— get all the good in the world. come out a pure mormon.

---

143. 23 July 1843, *JSP, J3*, 65.

[p.317] Last Monday morning certain brethren came to me and said they could hardly consent to receive Hyrum as a prophet, and for me to resign. But I told them, "I only said it to try your faith; and it is strange, brethren, that you have been in the Church so long, and not yet understand the Melchizedek Priesthood."

* * *144

It is contrary to Governor Ford's oath of office, to send a man to Missouri, where he is proscribed in his religious opinions; for he is sworn to support the Constitution of the United States and also of this State, and these constitutions guarantee religious as well as civil liberty to all religious societies whatever. (July 23, 1843.) DHC 5:516-518.

Last monday morni[n]g cert[a]in men cam[e] to me— Bro Joseph Hyrm [Hyrum Smith] is no propht. he cant lead the chu[r]ch— you must lead the Chu[rc]h— if you resign…

Tis contrary to a Governors oath to send a man to MO. where he is prescribed in his religious opinions.—145

Proverbs of the Prophet Joseph Smith—1843

1st. Never exact of a friend in adversity what you would require in prosperity.

2nd. If a man prove himself to be honest in his deal, and an enemy come upon him wickedly, through fraud or false pretences and because he is stronger than he, maketh him his prisoner and spoil him with his goods, never say unto that man in the day of his adversity, pay me what thou owest, for if thou doest it, thou addest a deeper wound, and condemnation shall come upon thee and thy riches shall be justified in the days of thine adversity if they mock at thee.

3rd. Never afflict thy soul for what an enemy hath put it out of thy power to do, if thy desires are ever so just.

4th. Let thy hand never fail to hand out that that thou owest while it is yet within thy grasp

Document Written by Erastus H. Derby

1st Never exact of a friend in adversity what you would require in prosperity

2d If a man prove himsellfe to be honest in his deal, & an enemy come upon him wickedly, through fraud or false pretences and because he is Stronger than he maketh him his prisener and Spoil him with his goods never Say unto that man in the day of his adversity pay me what thou owest, for if though [thou] doest it though addest a deeper wound, and condemnation Shall come upon the[e], and the [thy] richus Shall be Justifyd in the days of thine adversity if they mock at the[e]

3d Never afflict thy Soul for what an Enemy hath put it out of thy power to do, if thy Desieres are ever so just

4th Let thy hand never fale to hand out that that though [thou] owest while it is yet within

---

144. The missing portion here is included beginning on page 318 of *TPJS*.
145. 23 July 1843, *JSP, J3*, 65–67. The version of this account Joseph Fielding Smith used in *TPJS* comes from 23 July 1843, History, E-1, 1679–81.

to do so, but when thy stocks fails, say to thy heart, be strong, and to thine anxieties cease, for man, what is he; he is but dung upon the earth and although he demand of thee the cattle of a thousand hills, he cannot possess himself of his own life. God made him and thee and gave all things in common.

5th. There is one thing under the sun which I have learned and that is that the righteousness of man is sin because it exacteth over much; nevertheless, the righteousness of God is just, because it exacteth nothing at all, but sendeth the rain on the just and the unjust, seed time and harvest, for all of which man is ungrateful. (1843.) MSS Historian's Office.

thy grasp to do so, but when thy Stock fails— say to thy heart, be Strong and to thine anxieties cease, for man what is he, he is but dong [dung] upon the Earth and all though he demand of the[e] the cattle of an thousand hills he cannot possess himselfe of his own Life God made him and thee and gave all things in common

5th There is one thing under the Sun which I have learned and that is that the ritcheousness of man is Sin, because it exacteth over much nevertheless the ritcheousness of God is Just because it exacteth nothing at all, but sendeth the rain on the Just and the unjust— Seed time and harvest for all of which man is ungrateful.[146]

Excerpts from a Sermon by President Joseph Smith

July 23rd, 1843. **Joseph Smith's Journal**

[p.318] Last Monday morning certain men came to me and said: "Brother Joseph, Hyrum is no prophet—he can't lead the church; you must lead the church. If you resign, all things will go wrong; you must not resign; if you do the church will be scattered." I felt curious and said: "Have we not learned the Priesthood after the order of Melchizedek, which includes both Prophets, Priests and Kings: see Rev. 1 Chap., 6th v., and I will advance your Prophet to a Priest, and then to a King—not to the Kingdoms of this earth, but of the Most High God. See Rev. 5 Chap., 10th v.—'Thou hast made us unto our God, Kings and Priests, and we shall reign on the earth.'"

If I should be exalted would there not be a great many of my enemies disappointed in Missouri, when they wake up and find themselves in hell, see what they might have obtained, and realize what they have lost by not listening to my voice, and obeying my instructions?

Last monday morni[n]g cert[a]in men cam[e] to me— Bro Joseph Hyrm [Hyrum Smith] is no propht. he cant lead the chu[r]ch— you must lead the Chu[rc]h— if you resign[147]

I. felt curious— & said— here we lea[r]n in a priesthood after th[e] order of Melchisedek— Propht priest & king— & I will adva[n]ce f[ro]m prophet to pri[e]st & then to King not to the kingdoms of this earth but of the most high god.

If I should would there be a great many disappoitd [disappointed] in MO [Missouri]?

---

146. "Proverbs of Joseph declared by Joseph Smith to Erastus H. Derby in 1843," Church History Library, MS 155, box 5, folder 17.

147. 23 July 1843, *JSP, J3*, 66.

Matt. 5 Chap., 17 and 18 v.—"Think not that I am come to destroy the law, or the prophets; I am not come to destroy but to fulfil. For verily I say unto you, till heaven and earth pass, one jot or one tittle shall in no wise pass from the law till all be fulfilled."

Law & prop[h]ets. &c—

And again, Matt. 11 Chap., 12 and 13 v.—"And from the days of John the Baptist, until now, the Kingdom of Heaven suffereth violence, and the violent take it by force. For all the prophets and the law prophesied until John." John held the Aaronic Priesthood, and was a legal administrator, and the forerunner of Christ, and came to prepare the way before him.

suffereth violenc[e] & the viol[e]nt taketh it by force—

Christ was the head of the Church, the chief corner stone, the spiritual rock upon which the church was built, and the gates of hell shall not prevail against it. He built up the Kingdom, chose Apostles, and ordained them to the Melchizedek Priesthood, giving them power to administer in the ordinances of the Gospel. John was a priest after the order of Aaron before Christ.

heavens and earth shall pass away. &c says christ. he was the rock &c——

See Exodus 30 Chap. 30 and 31 v.—"And thou shalt anoint Aaron and his sons, and consecrate them, that they may minister unto me in the priest's office. And thou shalt speak unto the children of Israel, saying, This shall be an holy anointing [p.319] oil unto me throughout your generations." Also Exodus 40 Chap., 15 v.—"And thou shalt anoint them as thou didst anoint their father (Aaron) that they may minister unto me in the priest's office; for their anointing shall surely be an everlasting Priesthood throughout their generations."

gave the law 30 Ex. 30.31.— and thou shalt anoint A[a]ron &c. last chap Ex 15.— and thou shalt anoint. them &c.—

Here is a little of law which must be fulfilled. The Levitical Priesthood is forever hereditary—fixed on the head of Aaron and his sons forever, and was in active operation down to Zacharias the father of John. Zacharias would have had no child had not God given him a son. He sent his angel to declare unto

a tittle of law which must be fulfilled.— provend hereditary.— fixed on the head of aron— down to Zachariahe— the father of John.— Zachariah had no child— <had not> god gave him a son? sent his angel to declare a son henc[e] John.

Zacharias that his wife Elizabeth should bear him a son, whose name was to be called John.

The keys of the Aaronic Priesthood were committed unto him, and he was as the voice of one crying in the wilderness saying: "Prepare ye the way of the Lord and make his paths straight."	with the keys.—— John king and— lawgiver
The Kingdom of heaven suffereth violence, etc.	The Kingdom of heavn suffereth violenc [violence] &—
The kingdom of heaven continueth in authority until John.	The kingdm of heavn continuith in auth[o]rity. ~~beareth suffereth violinc.~~ until John.
The authority taketh it by absolute power.	the authority taketh it by absolute power.
John having the power took the Kingdom by authority.	John having the power— took the kingdom by authority.—
How have you obtained all this great knowledge? By the gift of the Holy Ghost. Wrested the Kingdom from the Jews.	How do you know all this g[rea]t knowledge—? by the gift of the H.G. [Holy Ghost] arrested the kingdom fr[o]m the Jews
Of these stony Gentiles—these dogs—to raise up children unto Abraham.	of these stony Gentil[e]s these dogs to raise up childrn unto Abraham
The Savior said unto John, I must be baptized by you. Why so? To fulfil all righteousness. John refuses at first, but afterwards obeyed by administering the ordinance of baptism unto him, Jesus having no other legal administrator to apply to.	John I must be baptized by you. why to answer my decreess— John refusees— Jesus had no legal admin[is]trator before John.
There is no salvation between the two lids of the Bible without a legal administrator. Jesus was then the legal administrator, and ordained His Apostles.—MSS Historian's Office.	No Salvation between the two lids of the bible without a legal administrator[148]

---

148. 23 July 1843, *JSP, J3*, 66–67. These notes on the prophet's "remarks" were drawn from Willard Richard's third memorandum book which he kept in Nauvoo from 15 July 1843 to 29 February 1844. (This third volume was one of four volumes which constituted "President Joseph Smith's Journal.") The notes of the sermon were later expanded in History, E-1, which was compiled after the Saints had established themselves in what would become the territory of Utah, After History, E-1 was composed, segments of this specific sermon were crossed out and other lines inserted. At some point, another version of this sermon was written, though it is unknown who recorded that version of Joseph's funeral remarks. It was from this latter version of the sermon that Joseph Fielding Smith took the version found in *TPJS*. See *WJS*, 294n1; 23 July 1843, History, E-1, 1681.

The Prophet's Remarks at the Funeral of Judge Higbee[149]

Joseph Smith's Journal
Sunday Aug 13[th] 1843. Joseph P[d.] [preached] in relati[o]n [to] the death of Judge Higby [Elias Higbee]

Brethren and Sisters, you will find these words in 2 Peter 3:10, 11:—"But the day of the Lord will come as a thief in the night; in the which the heavens shall pass away with a great noise, and the elements shall melt with fervent heat, the earth also and the works that are therein shall be burned up.

2.[d] Peter 3.[d] C[hapter]. ++ 10. 11. v——— Text

[p.320] Seeing then that all these things shall be dissolved, what manner of persons ought ye to be in all holy conversation and godliness."

I am not like other men. My mind is continually occupied with the business of the day, and I have to depend entirely upon the living God for every thing I say on such occasions as these.

said he was not like other men his mind was continually occ[u]pied with the business of the day. and he had to depend entirely upon the living god for evrey thing he said on such occasions.

The great thing for us to know is to comprehend what God did institute before the foundation of the world. Who knows it?

The great thing for us to know is to comprehe[n]d what. God did institute before the fou[n]dation of the world.——— Who knows it?

It is the constitutional disposition of mankind to set up stakes and set bounds to the works and ways of the Almighty.
* * *

It is the constitutional disposition of mankind to set up stakes & set bou[n]ds to the works and ways of the Almighty. **[p.76]** we are calld this mourn thies mo[r]ning the death of a good man a great man & a m[i]ghty man—It is a Sol[e]mn idea that man has no hope of seeing a frie[n]d after he has lost him.

But I will give you a more painful thought. Suppose you have an idea of a resurrection, etc., and yet know nothing at all of the Gospel, nor comprehend one principle of the order of heaven, but find yourselves disappointed— yes, at last find yourselves disappointed in every hope or anticipation, when the decision goes forth from the lips of the Almighty.

but I will give you a more painful thought—the thought is simple and I never design to communicate no ideas but what are simple for to this end I am sent.— suppose we have an idea of a resurrection. &c &c and yet know nothing at all of the gospel and could not comprehend one principle of the order of heavn. but found yourselves disappo[i]nted. yes. at last

---

149. Elias Higbee died June 8, 1843.

Would not this be a greater disappointment—a more painful thought than annihilation?	find yourselves disappointed in evrey hope or antiicipation when decis[i]on goes forth from the lips of the Almighty at last. would not this be a gre[a]ter disappotmt [disappointment]. a more painful thought than annihilate[i]on
Had I inspiration, revelation, and lungs to communicate what my soul has contemplated in times past, there is not a soul in this congregation but would go to their homes and shut their mouths in everlasting silence on religion till they had learned something.	had I inspiartion [inspiration], Revelation & lungs to communicate what my soul has contemplated in times \<past\> there is not a soul in this congregation but would go to their hom[e]s & shut their mouths in everlasting silnece [silence] on religin, till. they had learnd somethi[n]g.
Why be so certain that you comprehend the things of God, when all things with you are so uncertain. You are welcome to all the knowledge and intelligence I can impart to you. I do not grudge the world all the religion they have got: they are welcome to all the knowledge they possess.	why be so certain that you comprehend the things of God. when all things with you are so uncertain. you are welcome to all the knowledge & I do not grudge the world of all the religion— the[y] have got. they are welc[o]me to all the knowledge th[e]y possess—
The sound saluted my ears—"Ye are come unto Mount Zion, and unto the city of the living God, the heavenly Jerusalem, and to an innumerable company of angels, to the general assembly and church of the firstborn, which are written in heaven, and to God the Judge of all, and to the spirits of just men made perfect, and to Jesus the Mediator of the new covenant" (Hebrew 12:22, 23, 24). What would it profit us to come unto the spirits of the just men, but to learn and come up to the standard of their knowledge?	the sound saluted my ears. we are come unto Mt. Zion. &c. what could propet [profit] us to come unto the spirits of Just met [men] but to learn. and come to the <u>knowledge</u> of spi[ri]ts of the Just.
Where has Judge Higbee gone?	Where has Judge Higby gone?—[150]

[p.321] Covenants of the Fathers Revealed

	Joseph Smith's Journal
Who is there that would not give all his goods to feed the poor, and pour out his gold and silver to the four winds, to go where Judge Higbee has gone?	who is there that would not give all his goods to feed the poor— & pour out his gold & silver. to the four winds. to come where Judge Higby has gone.—

---

150. 13 August 1843, *JSP, J3*, 75–76.

That which hath been hid from before the foundation of the world is revealed to babes and sucklings in the last days.

The world is reserved unto burning in the last days. He shall send Elijah the prophet, and he shall reveal the covenants of the fathers in relation to the children, and the covenants of the children in relation to the fathers.

Four destroying angels holding power over the four quarters of the earth until the servants of God are sealed in their foreheads, which signifies sealing the blessing upon their heads, meaning the everlasting covenant, thereby making their calling and election made sure. When a seal is put upon the father and mother, it secures their posterity, so that they cannot be lost, but will be saved by virtue of the covenant of their father and mother.

To the mourners I would say—Do as the husband and the father would instruct you, and you shall be reunited.

The speaker continued to teach the doctrine of election and the sealing powers and principles, and spoke of the doctrine of election with the seed of Abraham, and the sealing of blessings upon his posterity, and the sealing of the fathers and children, according to the declarations of the prophets. He then spoke of Judge Higbee in the world of spirits, and the blessings which he would obtain, and of the kind spirit and disposition of Judge Higbee while living; none of which was reported. (Aug. 13, 1843.) DHC 5:529-531.[151]

that which hath been hid from before the fo[u]ndations of the w[o]rld. [*illegible*] reveald to babes and sucklings in the last days.—

[p.77] The wo[r]ld is reserved unto burni[n]g in the last days—— he shall send Elijah the prophet . . . and he shall reveal the covenants of the fathrs <in relation> to the childrn,— <~~originally written~~=> ~~and the childrn~~ and the covena[n]ts of the childr[en] in relati[o]n to the fathrs.—

4 destroying angels holding power ove[r] the 4 qua[r]ters of the earth— u[n]til the the se[r]vants of God are seald in their foreheads.— what is that seal. shall I tell you? ~~know~~ No.— Doctrine Election.—— sealing. <of the sevats [servants] of our god> on ~~their~~ the top of their heads.— tis ~~the~~ not the cross as the catholi[c]s would have it. doctrine of Electi[o]n to Abraham was in the relation to the Lord.— A man wishes to be embraced in the covena[n]t of Abraham— a man Judge. Higby—— in world.— of spir[i]ts— is sealed unto the throne, & doctrine of Electi[o]n sealing the father & childrn together.

to the mou[r]ner. do as the husband and the father would inst[r]uct you. & you shall be reunited.—

I have been acquited [acquainted] with Judge Higby a long time & I Never knew a more tender heartd man. The president was much exhau[s]ted[152]

---

151. 13 August 1843, *JSP, J3*, 76–77.

152. The final paragraph of this section in the original *TPJS* comes from 13 August 1843, History, E-1, 1690.

The Priesthood

President Smith read the 7th Chap. Hebrews and said: Salem is designed for a Hebrew term. It should be Shiloam, which signifies righteousness and peace; as it is, it is nothing—neither Hebrew, Greek, Latin, French, nor any other language.

I say to all those who are disposed to set up stakes for the Almighty, You will come short of the glory of God.

To become a joint heir of the heirship of the Son, one must put away all his false traditions.

* * *

[p.322] If I have sinned, I have sinned outwardly; but surely I have contemplated the things of God.

Respecting the Melchizedek Priesthood, the sectarians never professed to have it; consequently they never could save any one, and would all be damned together. There was an Episcopal priest who said he had the priesthood of Aaron, but had not the priesthood of Melchizedek; and I bear testimony that I never have found the man who claimed the Priesthood of Melchizedek. The power of the Melchizedek Priesthood is to have the power of "endless lives"; for the everlasting covenant cannot be broken.

The law was given under Aaron for the purpose of pouring out judgments and destructions.

* * *

Joseph Smith's Journal

Read 7th. Hebrews.
Salem is designed for a hebrew term. it should be Shiloam . . . which signifies Righteousness & peace. as it is, it is nothing, neither Hebrew. Greek. Latin french. or any other

To all those who are dis-posd to say to set up stakes for the almighty— will come short of the glory of god.

To becom[e] a joint heir of the h[e]irship of the son he must put away all his tradition

I bear record this morning that all the combined powers of ea[r]th & hell shall not over come this ~~by~~ boy—

If I have sinned I have sinned outwardly—but surely I have contemplated the things of God.

[p.86] told an anecdote of the Episcopali[a]n pri[e]st— who said he had the pr[i]esthood of A[a]ron— but not of Melichsedch [Melchizedek]— and bore this testimony that I never have found the man who claimed the pri[e]sthood of Melchisideck.

The law was given under Aaron for the purpose of pouring out Jud[g]ments— and destructi[o]ns.

The sectarian world are going to hell.— by. 100? 1000? 1000 000?[153]

---

153. 27 August 1843, *JSP, J3*, 85–86.

Three Grand Orders

	Joseph Smith's Journal
There are three grand orders of priesthood referred to here.	3 grand orders of pri[e]sthood referred to there . . .

1st. The King of Shiloam (Salem) had power and authority over that of Abraham, holding the key and the power of endless life. Angels desire to look into it, but they have set up too many stakes. God cursed the children of Israel because they would not receive the last law from Moses.

Ist. King of Shiloam.— power & authority over that of Abraham holding the key of the power of endless life.—— angels desire to loock into it. but they have set up to many stakes. god cursed the chldrn [children] of Israel because they would not receive the last law from Moses.

The sacrifice required of Abraham in the offering up of Isaac, shows that if a man would attain to the keys of the kingdom of an endless life; he must sacrifice all things. When God offers a blessing or knowledge to a man, and he refuses to receive it, he will be damned. The Israelites prayed that God would speak to Moses and not to them; in consequence of which he cursed them with a carnal law.

by the offering of Isaac.— if a man would attain— he must sacrific[e] all to attain. to the keys of the kingdom of an endless life[154] when God offers a blessing or knowledge to a man and he refuses to receive it he will be damned.—mentioning the case of the Israelites praying that God would speak to Moses & not to them—in consequense of which he cursed them with a carnal law.[155]

What was the power of Melchizedek? 'Twas not the Priesthood of Aaron which administers in outward ordinances, and the offering of sacrifices. Those holding the fulness of the Melchizedek Priesthood are kings and priests of the Most High God, holding the keys of power and blessings. In fact, that Priesthood is a perfect law of theocracy, and stands as God to give laws to the people, administering endless lives to the sons and daughters of Adam.

what was the power of Melchisedick twas not. P[riesthood] of Aaron— &c— a king and a pri[e]st to the most high Good [God]. a perfect law of Theocracy— <holding keys of powe[r] & bless[in]gs> stood as God to give laws to the people. administer[i]ng endless lives to the sons and daughter[r]s of Adam, kingly powe[r]s. of ano[i]nting.—

Abraham says to Melchizedek, I believe all that thou hast taught me concerning the priesthood and the coming of the **[p.323]** Son of Man; so Melchizedek ordained Abraham and sent him away. Abraham rejoiced, saying, Now I have a priesthood.

Abram says Melchsidek.— away I have a pr[i]esthood.—[156]

---

154. 27 August 1843, *JSP, J3*, 86.
155. Discourse, 27 August 1843, reported by William Clayton, *JSP, D13*, 76.
156. 27 August 1843, *JSP, J3*, 86.

The Mission of Elijah

	Joseph Smith's Journal
Salvation could not come to the world without the mediation of Jesus Christ.	Salvation could not come to the world without the mediate[o]n of Jesus Christ.
How shall God come to the rescue of this generation? He will send Elijah the prophet. The law revealed to Moses in Horeb never was revealed to the children of Israel as a nation. Elijah shall reveal the covenants to seal the hearts of the father to the children, and the children to the fathers	how shall god come to the rescue of this generate[o]n. he shall send Elijah law reveald to moses in Horeb— never was reveald to th[e] C[hildren] of Israel and he shall reveal the coven[an]ts to seal the hea[r]ts of the fath[er]s to the childrn and teh [the] childrn to the fathe[r]s.—
The anointing and sealing is to be called, elected and made sure.	<anointing & sealing.—> calld elected and made sure
"Without father, without mother, without descent, having neither beginning of days nor end of life, but made like unto the Son of God, abideth a priest continually." The Melchizedek Priesthood holds the right from the eternal God, and not by descent from father and mother; and that priesthood is as eternal as God Himself, having neither beginning of days nor end of life.	[p.87] without father &c. a priesthood which holds the pr[i]esthood by right from the Eternal Gods.— and not by des[c]ent from father and mother
The 2nd Priesthood is Patriarchal authority. Go to and finish the temple, and God will fill it with power, and you will then receive more knowledge concerning this priesthood.	2ᵈ Pri[e]sthood. patriarchal authority f[i]nish that temple. and god will fill it with power.
The 3rd is what is called the Levitical Priesthood, consisting of priests to administer in outward ordinances, made without an oath; but the Priesthood of Melchizedek is by an oath and covenant.	3ᵈ Priesthood. Levitical ~~Prest~~ Pri[e]sts made without an oath but the Pr[i]esthood of Melchisedek is by oath and cov[e]nant.
The Holy Ghost is God's messenger to administer in all those priesthoods.	Holy Ghost.
Jesus Christ is the heir of this Kingdom—the Only Begotten of the Father according to the flesh, and holds the keys over all this world.	jesus christ—

Men have to suffer that they may come upon Mount Zion and be exalted above the heavens.

I know a man that has been caught up to the third heavens, and can say, with Paul, that we have seen and heard things that are not lawful to utter. (Aug. 27, 1843.) DHC 5:554-556.

men have to suffer that th[e]y might come up on Mt. Zion. exalted above the heavens——

I know a man— that has been caught up to the 3ᵈ heavns—¹⁵⁷

Instructions Respecting Plurality of Wives

Joseph Smith's Journal

In the afternoon, rode to show some of the brethren some land. Evening, at home, and walked up and **[p.324]** down the streets with my scribe. Gave instructions to try those persons who were preaching, teaching, or practicing the doctrine of plurality of wives; for, according to the law, I hold the keys of this power in the last days; for there is never but one on earth at a time on whom the power and its keys are conferred; and I have constantly said no man shall have but one wife at a time, unless the Lord directs otherwise. (Oct. 5, 1843.) DHC 6:46.

P.M rode on prairie to shew ~~the~~ Some brethren some land.— eve at home walked up and down st. with scribe.— and gave inst[r]uction to try those who were preaching teaching or ~~preaching~~ the doctrin of plurality of wives. on this Law. Joseph forbids it. and the practice ther[e]of— No man shall have but one wife¹⁵⁸

THE PROPHET'S REMARKS ON THE DEMISE OF JAMES ADAMS

How Salvation Is Acquired

Joseph Smith's Journal & Times and Seasons¹⁵⁹

All men know that they must die. And it is important that we should understand the reasons and causes of our exposure to the vicissitudes of life and of death, and the designs and purposes of God in our coming into the world, our suffering here, and our departure hence. What is the object of our coming into existence, then dying and falling away, to be here

All men know that all men must die.—¹⁶⁰ He spoke of the importance of our understanding the reasons and causes of our exposure to the vicissitudes of life, and of death; and the designs and purposes of God, in our coming into the world, our sufferings here, and our departure hence—¹⁶¹ What is the object of our coming into existence. then dying and

---

157. 27 August 1843, *JSP, J3*, 86–87.
158. 5 October 1843, *JSP, J3*, 107.
159. The sermon was given on 9 October 1843. References to this sermon found in *JSP, J3* are all dated 9 October 1843. The report of the sermon found in the *Times and Seasons* is dated 15 September 1843. The reason for a sermon given in October being published in a September periodical is that the publishing of the *Times and Seasons* was behind schedule, so the September issue did not appear until later in October.
160. 9 October 1843, *JSP, J3*, 109.
161. *T&S* 4, no. 21 (15 September 1843): 331.

no more? It is but reasonable to suppose that God would reveal something in reference to the matter, and it is a subject we ought to study more than any other. We ought to study it day and night, for the world is ignorant in reference to their true condition and relation. If we have any claim on our Heavenly Father for anything, it is for knowledge on this important subject. Could we read and comprehend all that has been written from the days of Adam, on the relation of man to God and angels in a future state, we should know very little about it. Reading the experience of others, or the revelation given to them, can never give us a comprehensive view of our condition and true relation to God. Knowledge of these things can only be obtained by experience through the ordinances of God set forth for that purpose. Could you gaze into heaven five minutes, you would know more than you would by reading all that ever was written on the subject.

We are only capable of comprehending that certain things exist, which we may acquire by certain fixed principles. If men would acquire salvation, they have got to be subject, before they leave this world, to certain rules and principles, which were fixed by an unalterable decree before the world was.

[p.325] The disappointment of hopes and expectations at the resurrection would be indescribably dreadful.

falling away to be here no more?[162] that it is but reasonable to suppose that God would reveal something in reference to the matter—[163] This is a subject we ought to study more than any other, which we ought to study day and night.—[164] the ignorance of the world in reference to their true condition, and relation.[165] If we have any claim on our heavenly father for any thing it is for knowledge on this important subject— could we read and comprehend all that has been writtn from the days of Adam on the relation of man to God & angels. and the spirits of just men in a future state. we should know very little about it.[166] Reading the experience of others, or the revelations given to them, can never give us a comprehensive view of our condition and true relation to God. Knowledge of these things, can only be obtained by experience in these things, through the ordinance of God set forth for that purpose.[167] could you gaze in heaven 5 minute. you would know more— than you possibly would can know by read[ing] all that ever was writtn on the subject. We are one only capable of comprehedig [comprehending] that certain things exist. which we may acquire by certain fixed principles— If men would acquire salvation they have got to be subj[e]ct to certain rules. & principle which were fixed by an unalterable dercee [decree] before the world was. before they leave this wo[r]ld.[168]

He remarked that the disappointment of hopes and expectations at the resurrection, would be indescribably dreadful.[169]

---

162. 9 October 1843, *JSP, J3*, 109.
163. *T&S* 4, no. 21 (15 September 1843): 331.
164. 9 October 1843, *JSP, J3*, 109.
165. *T&S* 4, no. 21 (15 September 1843): 331.
166. 9 October 1843, *JSP, J3*, 109.
167. *T&S* 4, no. 21 (15 September 1843): 331.
168. 9 October 1843, *JSP, J3*, 109.
169. *T&S* 4, no. 21 (15 September 1843): 331.

Angels and Spirits

| | **Joseph Smith's Journal & Times and Seasons** |

The organization of the spiritual and heavenly worlds, and of spiritual and heavenly beings, was agreeable to the most perfect order and harmony: their limits and bounds were fixed irrevocably, and voluntarily subscribed to in their heavenly estate by themselves, and were by our first parents subscribed to upon the earth. Hence the importance of embracing and subscribing to principles of eternal truth by all men upon the earth that expect eternal life.

That the organization of the spiritual and heavenly worlds, and of spiritual and heavenly beings, was agreeably to the most perfect order and harmony—that their limits and bounds were fixed irrevocably, and voluntarily subscribed to by themselves—subscribed to upon the earth—hence the importance of embracing and subscribing to principles of eternal truth.

I assure the Saints that truth, in reference to these matters, can and may be known through the revelations of God in the way of His ordinances, and in answer to prayer. The Hebrew Church "came unto the spirits of just men made perfect, and unto an innumerable company of angels, unto God the Father of all, and to Jesus Christ the Mediator of the new covenant." What did they learn by coming to the spirits of just men made perfect? Is it written? No. What they learned has not been and could not have been written. What object was gained by this communication with the spirit of the just? It was the established order of the kingdom of God: The keys of power and knowledge were with them to communicate to the Saints. Hence the importance of understanding the distinction between the spirits of the just and angels.

He assured the saints that truth in reference to these matters, can, and may be known, through the revelations of God in the way of his ordinances, and in answer to prayer. The Hebrew church "came unto the spirits of just men made perfect, and unto an innumerable company of angels, unto God the Father of all, and to Jesus Christ the Mediator of the New Covenant;"[170] what did they learn by coming to the spirits of just men made perfect? is it written. No![171] What object was gained by this communication with the spirits of the just, &c.? It was the established order of the kingdom of God—the keys of power and knowledge were with them to communicate to the saints—hence the importance of understanding the distinction between the spirits of the just, and angels.

Spirits can only be revealed in flaming fire and glory. Angels have advanced further, their light and glory being tabernacled; and hence they appear in bodily shape. The spirits of just men are made ministering servants to those who are sealed unto life eternal, and it is through them that the sealing power comes down.

Spirits can only be revealed in flaming fire, or glory. Angels have advanced farther—their light and glory being tabernacled, and hence appear in bodily shape.[172] The spir[i]ts of just men are made ministering servants to those who are sealed unto life eternal. & it is through them that the sealing power comes down—

---

170. *T&S* 4, no. 21 (15 September 1843): 331.
171. 9 October 1843, *JSP, J3*, 109.
172. *T&S* 4, no. 21 (15 September 1843): 331.

Patriarch Adams is now one of the spirits of the just men made perfect; and, if revealed now, must be revealed in fire; and the glory could not be endured. Jesus showed Himself to His disciples, and they thought it was His spirit, and they were afraid to approach His spirit. Angels have advanced higher in knowledge and power than spirits.

Concerning Brother James Adams, it should appear strange that so good and so great a man was hated. The deceased ought never to have had an enemy. But so it was. Wherever [p.326] light shone, it stirred up darkness. Truth and error, good and evil cannot be reconciled. Judge Adams had some enemies, but such a man ought not to have had one. I saw him first at Springfield, when on my way from Missouri to Washington. He sought me out when a stranger, took me to his home, encouraged and cheered me, and gave me money. He has been a most intimate friend. I anointed him to the patriarchal power—to receive the keys of knowledge and power, by revelation to himself. He has had revelations concerning his departure, and has gone to a more important work. When men are prepared, they are better off to go hence. Brother Adams has gone to open up a more effectual door for the dead. The spirits of the just are exalted to a greater and more glorious work; hence they are blessed in their departure to the world of spirits. Enveloped in flaming fire, they are not far from us, and know and understand our thoughts, feelings, and motions, and are often pained therewith.

Flesh and blood cannot go there; but flesh and bones quickened by the Spirit of God, can.

The spirit of Patriarch adams now is <now of> the spirits of the just men made [perfect?]— and if revealed now. must be revealed in fire. And the glory could not be endured— Jesus. shewed himself to his disciples and they thought it was his a his spirit. & they were afr[a]id to approach his spirit. Angels have advanced higher in knowledge & power than Spirits[173]

Concerning brother James Adams, he remarked, that it should appear strange that so good and so great a man was hated. The deceased ought never to have had an enemy. But so it was, wherever light shone, it stirred up darkness. Truth and error, good and evil, cannot be reconciled.[174] Judge Adams had some enemies, but such a man ought not to have had an enemy. I saw him first at springfield. when on my way from Mo [Missouri] [p.110] to Washington. he sought me out when a stranger. took me to his house. encoura[ge]d & cheered me & give me money—[175] Judge Adams had been a most intimate friend. He had anointed him to the Patriarchial power— to receive the keys of knowledge, and power, by revelation to himself. He had had revelations concerning his departure, and had gone to a more important work—[176] when men are prepared. they are better off to go hence.— Bro Adams has gone to open up a more effectual door for the dead.—[177] The spirits of the just are exalted to a greater and more glorious work—hence they are blessed in departing hence. Enveloped in flaming fire, they are not far from us, and know and understand our thoughts, feelings and motions, and are often pained therewith.[178]

Flesh and blood cannot go there but flesh and bones quickened by the Spirit of God can

---

173. 9 October 1843, *JSP, J3*, 109.
174. *T&S* 4, no. 21 (15 September 1843): 331.
175. 9 October 1843, *JSP, J3*, 109–10.
176. *T&S* 4, no. 21 (15 September 1843): 331.
177. 9 October 1843, *JSP, J3*, 110.
178. *T&S* 4, no. 21 (15 September 1843): 331.

If we would be sober and watch in fasting and prayer, God would turn away sickness from our midst.

Hasten the work in the Temple, renew your exertions to forward all the work of the last days, and walk before the Lord in soberness and righteousness. Let the Elders and Saints do away with lightmindedness, and be sober. (Oct. 9, 1843.) DHC 6:50-52.

If we would be sober. & watch in fasting and prayer. God would tu[r]n away sickness from our midst.

Hasten the work of the temple. and all the work of the Last Days. Let the elders & sai[n]ts do away light mi[n]dedness and be sober.—[179]

The Prophet on the Constitution of the United States and the Bible—Temporal Economics

Joseph Smith's Journal
Sunday Oct 15th 1843
Stand east end of the temple.

It is one of the first principles of my life, and one that I have cultivated from my childhood, having been taught it by my father, to allow every one that liberty of conscience. I am the greatest advocate of the Constitution of the United States there is on the earth. In my feelings I am always ready to die for the protection of the weak and oppressed in their just rights. The only fault I find with the Constitution is, it is not broad enough to cover the whole ground.

It is one of the first principles of my life. & one that I have cultivated from my childhood. having been taught it of my father. to allow eve[r]y one the libe[r]ty of conscience. I am the greatest advocate of the C[onstitution] of U.S. there is there on the earth. in my feeling <the> only fault I can find with it is it is not broad enough to cover the whole ground.

Although it provides that all men shall enjoy religious freedom, yet it does not provide the manner by which the freedom can be preserved, nor for the punishment of Government officers who refuse to protect the people in their religious [p.327] rights, or punish those mobs, states, or communities who interfere with the rights of the people on account of their religion. Its sentiments are good, but it provides no means of enforcing them. It has but this one fault. Under its provision, a man or a people who are able to protect themselves can get along well enough; but those who have the misfortune to be weak or unpopular are left to the merciless rage of popular fury.

[Although it provides that all men shall enjoy religious freedom, yet it does not provide the manner by which that freedom can be preserved, nor for the punishment of government officers who refuse to protect the people in their religious rights, or punish those mobs, states, or communities, who interfere with the rights of the people on account of their religion. Its sentiments are good, but it provides no means of enforcing them. It has but this one fault; under its provisions a man or a people who are able to protect themselves can get along well enough, but those who have the misfortune to be weak or unpopular, are left to the merciless rage of popular fury.

---

179. 9 October 1843, *JSP, J3*, 110.

The Constitution should contain a provision that every officer of the Government who should neglect or refuse to extend the protection guaranteed in the Constitution should be subject to capital punishment; and then the president of the United States would not say, "Your cause is just, but I can do nothing for you," a governor issue exterminating orders, or judges say, "The men ought to have the protection of law, but is won't please the mob; the men must die, anyhow, to satisfy the clamor of the rabble; they must be hung, or Missouri be damned to all eternity." Executive writs could be issued when they ought to be, and not be made instruments of cruelty to oppress the innocent, and persecute men whose religion is unpopular.

The Constitution should contain a provision, that every officer of the Government who should neglect or refuse to extend the protection guaranteed in the Constitution, should be subject to capital punishment, and then the President of the United States would not say 'your cause is just, but I can do nothing for you;' a Governor issue exterminating orders; or Judges say, 'the men ought to have the protection of law, but is won't please the mob; the men must die anyhow to satisfy the clamor of the rabble; they must be hung, or Missouri be damned to all eternity.' Executive writs could be issued when they ought to be, and not be made instruments of cruelty to oppress the innocent, and persecute men whose religion is unpopular.][180]

The Creeds of Men

Joseph Smith's Journal

I cannot believe in any of the creeds of the different denominations, because they all have some things in them I cannot subscribe to, though all of them have some truth. I want to come up into the presence of God, and learn all things; but the creeds set up stakes, and say, "Hitherto shalt thou come, and no further"; which I cannot subscribe to.

I cannot beleive in any of the creeds of the differ[re]nt denominati[o]n. because they all have some things in th[e]m I cannot subscribe to though all of them have some thuth [truth]. but I want to come up into the presence of Good [God] & learn all things. but the creeds set up stakes & say hitherto shalt thou come & no further.—which I cannot subscribe to.[181]

Errors in the Bible

Joseph Smith's Journal

I believe the Bible as it read when it came from the pen of the original writers. Ignorant translators, careless transcribers, or designing and corrupt priests have committed many errors. As it read, Gen. 6:6, "It repented the Lord that he had made man on the earth"; also, Num. 23:19, "God is not a man, that he should lie; neither the Son of man, that he should repent"; which I do not believe. But it ought to read, "It repented Noah that God made man." This I believe, and then the other

I beli[e]ve the bible, as it ought to be, as it came from the pen of the original writers. as it reads it repented the Lord that he had made man. and. also God is <not> a man that he should repent.— which I do not believe.— but it **[p. 188]** repented Noah. that God made man.— this I beli[e]ve. & then the other quotation stands fair.— if any man will prove to me by one passage of Holy writ. one item I beli[e]ve, to be false. I will renounc[e] it disclaim it far as I have promulged it.—

---

180. The portion in brackets comes from 15 October 1843, History, E-1, 1754.
181. 15 October 1843, *JSP, J3*, 113.

quotation stands fair. If any man will prove to me, by one passage of Holy Writ, one item I believe to be false, I will renounce and disclaim it as far as I promulgated it.

[p.328] The first principles of the Gospel, as I believe, are, faith, repentance, baptism for the remission of sins, with the promise of the Holy Ghost.

Look at Heb. 6:1 contradictions—"Therefore leaving the principles of the doctrine of Christ, let us go on unto perfection." If a man leaves the principles of the doctrine of Christ, how can he be saved in the principles? This is contradiction. I don't believe it. I will render it as it should be—"Therefore not leaving the principles of the doctrine of Christ, let us go on unto perfection, no laying again the foundation of repentance from dead works, and of faith toward God, of the doctrine of baptisms, and of laying on of hands, and of resurrection of the dead, and of eternal judgment."

The first principles of the gospel as I believe. first Faith. Repentance. Baptism for the remission of sins. with the promise of the Holy Ghost.

Heb 6th contradictions "Leaving the principles of the doctrine. of c[h]rist.["] if a man leave the principles of the doctrin of C[hrist] how can he be saved in the principles? a contradiction. I dont beli[e]ve it. I will render it. therefore not leaving the P[rinciples] of the doctrin of c[h]rist. &c. Resurrection of the dead & Eternal judgme[n]t.[182]

The Kingdom of God

Joseph Smith's Journal

It is one thing to see the kingdom of God, and another thing to enter into it. We must have a change of heart to see the kingdom of God, and subscribe the articles of adoption to enter therein.

one thing to see the kingdom. & another to be in it. must have a change of heart. to see the kingdom of Good [God]. & subs[c]ribe the articles of adoption to enter therein.

No man can receive the Holy Ghost without receiving revelations. The Holy Ghost is a revelator.

no man can <not> r[e]ceive the Holy Ghost without r[e]ceiving re[v]elations, The H. G. is a revelator.[183]

Punishments Await this Generation

Joseph Smith's Journal

I prophesy, in the name of the Lord God of Israel, anguish and wrath and tribulation and the withdrawing of the Spirit of God from the earth await this generation, until they are

I propecy [prophesy] in the name of the Lord God anguish & wrath & trembulity & tribulati[o]n and the withdrawi[n]g of the spi[r]it of God await this genratin [generation].

---

182. 15 October 1843, *JSP, J3*, 113–14.
183. 15 October 1843, *JSP, J3*, 114.

visited with utter desolation. This generation is as corrupt as the generation of the Jews that crucified Christ; and if He were here today, and should preach the same doctrine He did then, they would put Him to death. I defy all the world to destroy the work of God; and I prophesy they never will have power to kill me till my work is accomplished, and I am ready to die.

* * *

until they are visited with utter dissolution. this generation is as corrupt as the geneatin [generation] of the Jews that crucified Christ. and if he were here to day. & should preach the same doctrin he did then they <why> they would crufing [crucify] him. I defy all the world. & I prophecy they never will overthrow me till I get ready

* * *[184]

Temporal Economy—Care of the Poor

Joseph Smith's Journal

The temporal economy of this people should be to establish and encourage manufactures, and not to take usury for their money. I do not want to bind the poor here to starve. Go out into the country and into the neighboring cities, and get food, and gird up you loins, and be sober. When you get food, return, if you have a mind to.

the temporal economy of this peop[l]es should be to establish— manufating [manufacturing] and. not to take usurry for his mony I do not wa[n]t to bind the poor here and starve. go out in the county and get food. & <in> cities— and gird up your loins— &c— be sober. when you— get food retu[r]n if you have. a mind. to.—

[p.329] Some say it is better to give to the poor than build the Temple. The building of the Temple has sustained the poor who were driven from Missouri, and kept them from starving; and it has been the best means for this object which could be devised.

<some say> It is better, say some, to give the poor than build the temple.—the building of the temple. has kept the poor who were driven from Missou[r]i from starving. as has been the best means for this obj[e]ct which could be devised

Oh, all ye rich men of the Latter-day Saints from abroad, I would invite you bring up some of your money—your gold, your silver, and your precious things, and give to the Temple. We want iron, steel, spades, and quarrying and mechanical tools. It would be a good plan to get up a forge to manufacture iron, and bring in raw materials of every variety, and erect manufacturing establishments of all kinds, and surround the rapids with mills and machinery.

all ye rich men. of the Latter Day Saints.— from abroad I would invite to br[i]ng up some of their money. <and give to the temple.> we want Iron steell powdrs.—&c— a good plan to get up a forge. bring in raw materials. & manuutig [manufacturing] establishig establishme[n]t of all kinds.— surround the rapids—

I never stole the value of a pin's head, or a picayune in my life; and when you are hungry don't steal. Come to me, and I will feed you.

I never stone stole the value of a pins head or a picayune in my life. & when you are hungry dont steal.— come to me & I will feed you.—

---

184. 15 October 1843, *JSP, J3*, 114.

The secret of Masonry is to keep a secret. It is good economy to entertain strangers—to entertain sectarians. Come up to Nauvoo, ye sectarian priests of the everlasting Gospel, as they call it, and you shall have my pulpit all day.

Woe to ye rich men, who refuse to give to the poor, and then come and ask me for bread. Away with all your meanness, and be liberal. We need purging, purifying and cleansing. You that have little faith in your Elders when you are sick, get some little simple remedy in the first stages. If you send for a doctor at all, send in the first stages.

All ye doctors who are fools, not well read, and do not understand the human constitution, stop your practice. And all ye lawyers who have no business, only as you hatch it up, would to God you would go to work or run away! (Oct. 15, 1843.) DHC 6:56-59.

the secrets of masonry. is to keep a secret. it is good economy to entertain strager [strangers]. to entertain sectarians. come up ye sectarian pri[e]sts.— of the eve[r]lasting gospel, as th[e]y call it & they shall have my pulpit all day.

wo to ye rich men. give to the poor. & then come and ask me for bread. away with all your meanness & be liberal wee need purging. purify[y]ing & cleansing you have— little faith in your elders get some little simple remedy in the first stages— if you send for a Dr at all send in the first stages

all ye Drs.— who are fools not well read do not understand the human constitution. stop your practice.— Lawyers who have no business only as you hatch up. would to God you would go to work & <or> run away."[185]

Discourse: the Sealing Power in the Priesthood

Wilford Woodruff's Journal

There are many people assembled here today, and throughout the city, and from various parts of the world, who say that they have received to a certainty a portion of the knowledge from God, by revelation, in the way that He has ordained and pointed out.

I shall take the broad ground, then, that we have received **[p.330]** a portion of knowledge from God by immediate revelation, and from the same source we can receive all knowledge.

Their are many people assembled here to day & throughout this city, & from various parts of the world who say that they have rec[ei]ved to a certainty a portion of knowledge from God by revelation<n> in the way that he has ordained & pointed out[.]

I shall take the broad ground then that if we have or can receive a portion of knowledge from God by immediate revelation by the same source we can rece<i>ve all knowledge.[186]

The Sending of Elijah

Wilford Woodruff's Journal

What shall I talk about to-day? I know what Brother Cahoon wants me to speak about. He wants me to speak about the coming of Elijah

What shall I talk about today[?] I know what Br Cahoon wants me to speak about, he wants me to speak about the Comeing of Elijah in

---

185. 15 October 1843, *JSP, J3*,113–16.
186. 21 January 1844, *WWJ*, 1:604. See also *JSP, D14*, 105. Wilford Woodruff has this sermon dated 21 January 1844. Joseph Fielding Smith dates the sermon 20 January 1844.

in the last days. I can see it in his eye. I will speak upon that subject then.

The Bible says, "I will send you Elijah the Prophet before the coming of the great and dreadful day of the Lord; and he shall turn the heart of the fathers to the children, and the heart of the children to the fathers, lest I come and smite the earth with a curse."

Now, the word turn here should be translated bind, or seal. But what is the object of this important mission? or how is it to be fulfilled? The keys are to be delivered, the spirit of Elijah is to come, the Gospel to be established, the Saints of God gathered, Zion built up, and the Saints to come up as saviors on Mount Zion.

But how are they to become saviors on Mount Zion? By building their temples, erecting their baptismal fonts, and going forth and receiving all the ordinances, baptisms, confirmations, washings, anointings, ordinations and sealing powers upon their heads, in behalf of all their progenitors who are dead, and redeem them that they may come forth in the first resurrection and be exalted to thrones of glory with them; and herein is the chain that binds the hearts of the fathers to the children, and the children to the fathers, which fulfills the mission of Elijah. And I would to God that this temple was now done, that we might go into it, and go to work and improve our time, and make use of the seals while they are on earth.

Saints Have Not Much Time

The Saints have not too much time to save and redeem their dead, and gather together their living relatives, that they may be saved also, before the earth will be smitten, and the consumption decreed falls upon the world.

the last days[.] I can see it in his eye. I will speak upon that Subject then.

The Bible says "I will send you Elijah before the great & dredful day of the Lord Come that he shall turn the hearts of the fathers to the Children & the hearts of the children[n] to their fathers lest I come & smite the whole earth with a Curse."

Now the word turn here should be translated (bind or seal). But what is the object of this important mission or how is it to be fulfilled. The keys are to be deliver[e]d the spirit of Elijah is to come, The gospel to be esstablished the Saints of God gather[e]d, Zion built up, & the Saints to Come up as Saviors on mount Zion[.]

but how are they to become Saviors on Mount Zion[?] by building their temples erecting their Baptismal fonts & going forth & receiving all the ordinances, Baptisms, confirmations, washings anointings, ordinations, & sealing powers upon our heads in behalf of all our Progenitors who are <u>dead</u> & redeem them that they may come forth in the first resurrection & be exhalted to thrones of glory with us, & herein is the Chain that binds the hearts of the fathers to the Children & the Children to the Fathers which fulfills the mission of Elijah & I would to God that this temple was now done that we might go into it & go to work & improve our time & make use of the seals while they are on earth[187]

Wilford Woodruff's Journal
& the Saints have none to much time to save & redeem their dead, & gather together [p.605] their living relatives that they may be saved also, before the earth will be smitten & the consumption decreed falls upon the world

---

187. 21 January 1844, *WWJ*, 1:604. See also *JSP, D14*, 105–6.

I would advise all the Saints to go with their might and gather together all their living relatives to this place, that they may be sealed and saved, that they may be prepared against the day that the destroying angel goes forth; and if the whole **[p.331]** Church should go to with all their might to save their dead, seal their posterity, and gather their living friends, and spend none of their time in behalf of the world, they would hardly get through before night would come, when no man can work; and my only trouble at the present time is concerning ourselves, that the Saints will be divided, broken up, and scattered, before we get our salvation secure; for there are so many fools in the world for the devil to operate upon, it gives him the advantage oftentimes.

& I would advise all the Saints to go to with their might & gather together all their living relatives to this place that they may be sealed & saved that they may be prepared against the day that the destroying angel goes forth & if the whole Church should go to with all their might to save their dead seal their posterity & gather their living friends & spend none of their time in behalf of the world they would hardly get through before night would come when no man Could work & my ownly trouble at the present time is concerning ourselves that the Saints will be divided & broken up & scattered before we get our Salvation secure[.] for thei[r] is so many fools in the world for the devil to operate upon it gives him the advantage often times.[188]

All Ordinances Necessary

Wilford Woodruff's Journal

The question is frequently asked, "Can we not be saved without going through with all those ordinances? I would answer, No, not the fulness of salvation. Jesus said, There are many mansions in my Father's house, and I will go and prepare a place for you. House here named should have been translated kingdom; and any person who is exalted to the highest mansion has to abide a celestial law, and the whole law too.

The question is freequently asked can we not be saved without going through with all thes[e] ordinances &c[.] I would answer No not the fulness of Salvation. Jesus Said their was many mansions in his fathers house & he would go & prepare a place for them. House here named should have been translated (kingdom) & any person who is exhalted to the highest mansion has to abide a Celestial law & the whole law to[o].

But there has been a great difficulty in getting anything into the heads of this generation. It has been like splitting hemlock knots with a corn-dodger for a wedge, and a pumpkin for a beetle. Even the Saints are slow to understand.

But their has been a great difficulty in getting anything into the heads of this generation[.] it has been like splitting hemlock knots with a corn doger for a wedge & a pumpkin for a beetle; Even the Saints are slow to understand[.][189]

Unwillingness of Saints to Learn

Wilford Woodruff's Journal

I have tried for a number of years to get the minds of the Saints prepared to receive the things of God; but we frequently see some of

I have tried for a number of years to get the minds of the saints prepared to recieve the things of God, but we freequent<ly> see some

---

188. 21 January 1844, *WWJ*, 1:604–5. See also *JSP, D14*, 106.
189. 21 January 1844, *WWJ*, 1:605. See also *JSP, D14*, 106.

them, after suffering all they have for the work of God, will fly to pieces like glass as soon as anything comes that is contrary to their traditions: they cannot stand the fire at all. How many will be able to abide a celestial law, and go through and receive their exaltation, I am unable to say, as many are called, but few are chosen. (Jan. 20, 1844.) DHC 6:183-185.

of them after suffering all they have for the work of God will fly to peaces like glass as soon as any thing Comes that is Contrary to their traditions. they cannot stand the fire at all. How many will be able to abide a Celestial law & go through & recieve their exhaltation I am unable to Say but many are Called & few are Chosen[190]

Views of the Prophet on His Candidacy for President of the United States

Wilford Woodruff's Journal

I would not have suffered my name to have been used by my friends on anywise as President of the United States, or candidate for that office, if I and my friends could have had the privilege of enjoying our religious and civil rights as Amer[p.332]ican citizens, even those rights which the Constitution guarantees unto all her citizens alike. But this as a people we have been denied from the beginning. Persecution has rolled upon our heads from time to time, from portions of the United States, like peals of thunder, because of our religion; and no portion of the Government as yet has stepped forward for our relief. And in view of these things, I feel it to be my right and privilege to obtain what influence and power I can, lawfully, in the United States, for the protection of injured innocence; and if I lose my life in a good cause I am willing to be sacrificed on the altar of virtue, righteousness and truth, in maintaining the laws and Constitution of the United States, if need be, for the general good of mankind. (Feb. 8, 1844.) DHC 6:210-211.

I would not have suffered my name to have been used by my friends on any wise as president of the united States or Candidate for that office If I & my friends Could have had the privilege of enjoying our religious & civel rights as American Citizen even those rights which the Constitution guarantee unto all her Citizens alike[.] but this we as a people have been denied from the beginning[.] Persecution has rolled upon our heads from time to time from portions of the United States like peels of thunder because of our religion [p.609] & no portion of the government as yet has steped forward for our relief & under view of these things I feel it to be my right & privilege to obtain what influence & power I Can lawfully in the United States for the protection of injured innocence & If I loose my life in a good Cause I am willing to be sacrificed on the alter of virtue rightousness & truth, in maintaining the laws & constitution of the United States if need be for the general good of mankind.[191]

Western Movement for the Church Contemplated

Joseph Smith's Journal

I instructed the Twelve Apostles to send out a delegation and investigate the locations of California and Oregon, and hunt out a good location, where we can remove to after the

I instructed the 12 to send out a delegation— & investigate the Locations of Californnia & mex oregon & find a good Location where we can remove after the Temple is completed.—

---

190. 21 January 1844, *WWJ*, 1:605. See also *JSP, D14*, 106–7. Wilford Woodruff has this sermon dated 21 January 1844. Joseph Fielding Smith dates the sermon 20 January 1844.

191. 8 February 1844, *WWJ*, 1:608–9. See also D14, 158–59.

temple is completed, and where we can build a city in a day, and have a government of our own, get up into the mountains, where the devil cannot dig us out, and live in a healthful climate, where we can live as old as we have a mind to. (Feb. 20, 1844.) DHC 6:222.

& build a city in a day— and have a governme[n]t of our own—— in a hea[l]thy climate—[192]

To Gain Salvation the Laws of God Must Be Obeyed

I * * * spoke to the people, showing them that to get salvation we must not only do some things, but everything which God has commanded. Men may preach and practice everything except those things which God commands us to do, and will be damned at last. We may tithe mint and rue, and all manner of herbs, and still not obey and teach others to obey God in just what He tells us to do. It mattereth not whether the principle is popular or unpopular, I will always maintain a true principle, even if I stand alone in it. (Feb. 21, 1844.) DHC 6:223.

Joseph Smith's Journal & Wilford Woodruff's Journal
Wednesday— Feb 21— 1844 at. home.
Rev Mr De. Wolf. Churchman. Lectu[r]ed in the assembly room. in the eve. I attended & after sermon— at his request. spoke to the people to show [p.181] them that to get salvation we must not only do some things but every thing whi[c]h God had commandd [commanded] to get salvati[o]n.[193] Among other things Said that men may preach & practice evry thing except those things which God Commands us to do & will be damned at last[.] we may tithe rue[,] annis & Cummin & still not obey the Commandments of God[.] the object with me is to obey & teach others to obey God in just what he tells us to do[.] It mattereth not whether the principle is popular or unpopular. I will always maintain a true principl[e] even if I Stand alone in it[194]

The Western Exploring Equipment

Met with the Twelve in the assembly room concerning the Oregon and California Exploring Expedition; Hyrum and Sidney present. I told them I wanted an exploration of all that [p.333] mountain country. Perhaps it would be best to go direct to Santa Fe. "Send twenty-five men: let them preach the Gospel wherever they go. Let that man go that can raise $500, a good horse and mule, a double-barrel gun, one-barrel rifle, and the other smooth bore, a

Joseph Smith's Journal
Met with the 12 &c in assembly Room concerning the oregon Expedition.— I told th[e]m I wanted an exposition of all that count[r]y— Send 25 men. Let them preach the gospel wherever they go.— Let that man go that can raise $500. a horse or mule a double barrel gun— one rifled and one shot.— saddle bridle. P[ai]r 8 bar[reled] Pistols— Bowie knife—— &c— Appoint a leader Let him beat up for volunteers. I want

---

192. 20 February 1844, *JSP, J3*, 180.
193. 21 February 1844, *JSP, J3*, 180–81.
194. 21 February 1844, *WWJ*, 1:610. See also *JSP, D14*, 213.

saddle and bridle, a pair of revolving pistols, bowie-knife, and a good sabre. Appoint a leader, and let them beat up for volunteers. I want every man that goes to be a king and a priest. When he gets on the mountains, he may want to talk with his God; when with the savage nations have power to govern, &c. If we don't get volunteers, wait till after the election." (Feb. 23, 1844.) DHC 6:224.

every man that goes to be a King and pri[e]st. when he gets on the mountain he may wa[n]t to talk with his god.—— when with the savage nations have power to govern &c— if we dont get volutees [volunteers] wait till after the election.—[195]

A Prophecy of Deliverance of the Saints

I gave some important instructions, and prophesied that within five years we should be out of the power of our old enemies, whether they were apostates or of the world; and told the brethren to record it, that when it comes to pass they need not say they had forgotten the saying. (Feb. 25, 1844.) DHC 6:225.

Wilford Woodruff's Journal

President Joseph Smith Prophesyed that within five years we should be rid of our old enemies whether they were Apostates or of **[p.611]** the world & wished us to record it that when it comes to pass that we need not say we had forgotten the saying[196]

The Worthy to Receive Endowments

Joseph Smith's Journal[197]

In relation to those who give in property for the temple. We want them to bring it to the proper source, and to be careful into whose hands it comes, that it may be entered into the Church books, so that those whose names are found in the Church books shall have the first claim to receive their endowments in the temple. I intend to keep the door at the dedication myself, and not a man shall pass who has not paid his bonus.

Joseph— said in relation to thos[e] who give p[r]operty on the temple. be careful into <whose> hands it come into that it m[a]y be ente[re]d into the church books. that those whose names are found in the chu[r]ch book shall have the first claim. in that house.— I int[e]nd to keep the door at dedication myself: & not a man shall pass who had not paid his bonus[198]

Remarks on Political Matters

Joseph Smith's Journal & Wilford Woodruff's Journal

As to politics, I care but little about the presidential chair. I would not give half as much for

I do not care ½ so much about the Pres[idential] election as I do the office I have got

---

195. 23 February 1844, *JSP, J3*, 182.
196. 25 February 1844, *WWJ*, 1:610–11.
197. It appears that for 7 March 1844, Joseph Fielding Smith used 7 March 1844, History, E-1, 1913–14, which is an amalgamation of Wilford Woodruff's journal and Joseph Smith's journal. Both the *JSP, J3* and the *WWJ* versions of this entry are also dated 7 March 1844.
198. 7 March 1844, *JSP, J3*, 196.

the office of President of the United States as I would for the one I now hold as Lieutenant-General of the Nauvoo Legion.

We have as good a right to make a political party to gain power to defend ourselves, as for demagogues to make use of our religion to get power to destroy us. In other words, as the world has used the power of government to oppress and persecute us, it is right for us to use it for the protection of our [p.334] rights. We will whip the mob by getting up a candidate for President.

When I get hold of the Eastern papers, and see how popular I am, I am afraid myself that I shall be elected; but if I should be, I would not say, "Your cause is just, but I can do nothing for you."

What I have said in my views in relation to the annexation of Texas is with some unpopular; the people are opposed to it. Some of the Anti-Mormons are good fellows. I say it, however, in anticipation that they will repent. They object to Texas on account of slavery. Why, it is the very reason she ought to be received, so that we may watch over them; for, of the two evils, we should reject the greatest.

Governor Houston of Texas, says—"If you refuse to receive us into the United States, we must go to the British Government for protection."

This would certainly be bad policy for this nation; the British are now throughout the whole country, trying to bribe all they can; and the first thing they would do, if they got possession, would be to set the negroes and the Indians to fight, and they would use us up.

we have. as good a right to make a political party to gain power to [p.197] defend ourselves. as for mormons demagogu[e]s to make use of our religin to get power to destroy ours[e]lves.— we will whip the mob by getting up a presidnt.[199]

when I get hold of the eastern paper & see how popular I am I am afraid myself that I shall be elected. But if I should be I would not say that your Cause is just & I Could not do any thing for you.

what I said in relation to the annexation of texas is with some unpopular[.] the people are opposed to it.[200] the anti-Mormns— are good fellows—. I say it in anticipation th[e]y will repent obj[e]ct to Texas on acco[u]nt of slavery.— Tis the very reason why she should be r[e]ceived.——[201] in order to watch over them[.] of the greatest <two> evils we should reject the greatest.[202]

[Samuel] Houston. says ["]gentlmn if you refuse to receiv us we mu[s]t go to the British"[203]

this would Certainly be bad policy for this Nation[.] the British are now through out that whole Country trying to bribe all they can.[204] and the first thing th[e]y will do will be to set the negroes free & Indians & th[e]y will use us up—

---

199. 7 March 1844, *JSP, J3*, 196–97.
200. 7 March 1844, *WWJ*, 1:614. See also *JSP, D14*, 249.
201. 7 March 1844, *JSP, J3*, 197.
202. 7 March 1844, *WWJ*, 1:614. See also *JSP, D14*, 249.
203. 7 March 1844, *JSP, J3*, 197.
204. 7 March 1844, *WWJ*, 1:614. See also *JSP, D14*, 249.

British officers are now running all over Texas to establish British influence in that country.

It will be more honorable for us to receive Texas and set the negroes free, and use the negroes and Indians against our foes. Don't let Texas go, lest our mothers and the daughters of the land should laugh us in the teeth; and if these things are not so, God never spoke by any Prophet since the world began.

How much better it is for the nation to bear a little expense than to have the Indians and British upon us and destroy us all. We should grasp all the territory we can. I know much that I do not tell. I have had bribes offered me, but I have rejected them.

The government will not receive any advice or counsel from me: they are self-sufficient. But they must go to hell and work out their own salvation with fear and trembling.

The South holds the balance of power. By annexing Texas, I can do away with this evil. As soon as Texas was annexed, I would liberate the slaves in two or three States, indemnifying their owners, and send the negroes to Texas, and from Texas to Mexico, where all colors are alike. And **[p.335]** if that was not sufficient, I would call upon Canada, and annex it. (March 7, 1844.) DHC 6:243-244.

British officers running all over Texas to pick a quarrel with us.—

more honorable for us to receve th[e]m. & set the negroes free & use the ngoes [negroes] & indians— agint [against] our foes. dont let Texas go lest Our Mother & th[e] daughtrs of th[e] land. will laugh us in the teeth.— and if these things are not so— god never spoke ~~with~~ by any prophet sinc[e] the world began.—[205]

How much better it is to be to a little expens[e] than to have the indians & British upon us & destroy us all. we should grasp all the territory we can and I know much that I do not tell[.] I have had bribes offered me, but I have rejected them.

The government will not receive any thing from me. they are self sufficient. But they must go to Hell & work out their own salvation with fear & trembling.[206]

south hold the balanc[e] of power &c— by annexing Texas.— I can do away this evil—liberate 2 or 3 states. & if that was not suffic[ie]nt. call in Canida—— Send the negroes to Texas. fr[o]m Texas to mexico—where all colors are alike.—[207] as soon as texas was annexed I would liberate two or three States & pay them for their salves & let them go to Mexico whare they are mixed blacks &c[.] I would also receive Canida & Stand by them[208]

Discourses of the Prophet—Elias, Elijah, Messiah

Wilford Woodruff's Journal

There is difference between the spirit and office of Elias and Elijah. It is the spirit of Elias I wish first to speak of; and in order to come at the subject, I will bring some of the testimony from the Scripture and give my own.

Their is a differance between the spirit & office of Elias & Eligah[.] it is the spirit of Elias I wish first to speak of. And in order to Come at the subject I will bring some of the testimony from the scripture & give my own. in the first place suffice it to say I went into the

---

205. 7 March 1844, *JSP, J3*, 197.
206. 7 March 1844, *WWJ*, 1:614. See also *JSP, D14*, 249–50.
207. 7 March 1844, *JSP, J3*, 198.
208. 7 March 1844, *WWJ*, 1:614. See also *JSP, D14*, 250.

In the first place, suffice it to say, I went into the woods to inquire of the Lord, by prayer, His will concerning me, and I saw an angel, and he laid his hands upon my head, and ordained me to a Priest after the order of Aaron, and to hold the keys of this Priesthood, which office was to preach repentance and baptism for the remission of sins, and also to baptize. But I was informed that this office did not extend to the laying on of hands for the giving of the Holy Ghost; that that office was a greater work, and was to be given afterward; but that my ordination was a preparatory work, or a going before, which was the spirit of Elias; for the spirit of Elias was a going before to prepare the way for the greater, which was the case with John the baptist. He came crying through the wilderness, "Prepare ye the way of the Lord, make his paths straight." And they were informed, if they could receive it, it was the spirit of Elias; and John was very particular to tell the people, he was not that Light, but was sent to bear witness of that Light.

He told the people that his mission was to preach repentance and baptize with water; but it was He that should come after him that should baptize with fire and the Holy Ghost.

If he had been an impostor, he might have gone to work beyond his bounds, and undertook to have performed ordinances which did not belong to that office and calling, under the spirit of Elias.

woods to inquire of the Lord by prayer his will Concerning me, & I saw an angel & he laid his hands upon my head & ordained me to be a priest after the order of Aaron & to hold the keys of this priesthood which office was to preach repentance & Baptism for the remissio<n> of Sins & also to baptize[.] but [I] was informed that this office did not extend to the laying on of hands for the giving of the Holy Ghost that that office was a greater work & was to be given afterwards[.] but that my ordination was a preparetory work or a going before which was the spirit of Elias for the spirit of Elias was a going before to prepare the way for the greater, which was the Case with John the Baptist he came balling through the wilderness prepare ye the way of the Lord & make his paths strait & they were informed if they could receive it it was the spirit of Elias & John was vary particul[ar?] to tell the people He was not that light but was sent to bear witness of that light.

He told the people that his mission was to preach repentance & baptize with water, but it was he that Should Come after him that should baptise with fire & the Holy Ghost[.]

if he had been an imposture he might have gone to work beyound his bounds & undertook to have performed ordinances that did not belong to that office & calling under the spirit of Elias.[209]

Mission of Elias to Prepare the Way

Wilford Woodruff's Journal

The spirit of Elias is to prepare the way for a greater revelation of God, which is the Priesthood that Aaron was ordained unto. And when God sends a man into the world to prepare for a greater work, **[p.336]** holding the keys of the power of Elias, it was called the

The spirit of Elias is to prepare the way for a greater revelation of God which is the priesthood of Elias or the Priesthood that Aaron was ordained unto. And when God sends a man into the world to prepare for a greater work [he] holds the keys of the power of Elias[.] it

---

209. 10 March 1844, *WWJ*, 1:615. See also *JSP, D14*, 256–57.

doctrine of Elias, even from the early ages of the world.

John's mission was limited to preaching and baptizing; but what he did was legal; and when Jesus Christ came to any of John's disciples, He baptized them with fire and the Holy Ghost.

We find the Apostles endowed with greater power than John; their office was more under the spirit and power of Elijah than Elias.

In the case of Phillip when he went down to Samaria, when he was under the spirit of Elias, he baptized both men and women. When Peter and John heard of it, they went down and laid hands upon them, and thy received the Holy Ghost. This shows the distinction between the two powers.

When Paul came to certain disciples, he asked if they had received the Holy Ghost. They said, No. Who baptized you, then? We were baptized unto John's baptism. No, you were not baptized unto John's baptism, or you would have been baptized by John. And so Paul went and baptized them, for he knew what the true doctrine was, and he knew that John had not baptized them. And these principles are strange to me, that men who have read the Scriptures of the New Testament are so far from it.

What I want to impress upon your minds is the difference of power in the different parts of the Priesthood, so that when any man comes among you saying, "I have the spirit of Elias," you can know whether he be true or false; for any man that comes, having the spirit and power of Elias, he will not transcend his bounds.

John did not transcend his bounds, but faithfully performed that part belonging to his office; and every portion of the great building should be prepared right and assigned to its proper place; and it is necessary to know who

was called the doctrin of Elias even from the early ages of the world.

John's mission was limited to preaching & Baptizing but what he done was legal & when Jesus Christ Came to any of John's deciples He baptized them with fire & the Holy Ghost.

[p.616] we find the Apostles endowed with greater power than John[.] their office was more under the spirit & power of Elijah than Elias.

In the Case of Philip when he went down to Samaria <when> [he] was under the spirit of Elias[.] he baptised both men & women. when Peter & John herd of it they went down & lade hands on them & they received the Holy Ghost[.] this shows the distinction between the two powers.

when paul came to certain deciples He asked if they had received the Holy Ghost[.] they said no. who baptized you then[?] we were Baptized unto Johns Baptism No John did not baptized you for he did his work right, & so Paul went & baptized them for He knew what the true doctrin was & he knew that John Had not Baptised them, & these principles and [it] is strange to me that men who have red the scriptures of the New Testament are so far from it.

What I want to impress upon your minds is the difference of power in the different parts of the Priesthood, so that when any man comes among you saying I have the spirit of Elias you can know whether he be true or fals[e]. for any man that comes having the spirit & power of Elias he will not transend his bounds; John did not transend his bound but faithfully performed that part belonging to his office, and evry portion of the great building should be prepared right & assigned to its proper place, & it is necessary to know who holds the keys holds the keys of power, and who does not, or we may be likely to be deceived.

That person who holds the keys of Elias hath a preparatory work. But if I spend much more time in conversing about the spirit of Elias, I shall not have time to do justice to the spirit and power of Elijah.

This is the Elias spoken of in the last days, and here is the rock upon which many split, thinking the time was past in the days of John and Christ, and no more to be. But the **[p.337]** spirit of Elias was revealed to me, and I know it is true; therefore I speak with boldness, for I know verily my doctrine is true.

Mission of Elijah

Now for Elijah. The spirit, power, and calling of Elijah is, that ye have power to hold the key of the revelations, ordinances, oracles, powers and endowments of the fulness of the Melchizedek Priesthood and of the kingdom of God on the earth; and to receive, obtain, and perform all the ordinances belonging to the kingdom of God, even unto the turning of the hearts of the fathers unto the children, and the hearts of the children unto the fathers, even those who are in heaven.

Malachi says, "I will send you Elijah the prophet before the coming of the great and dreadful day of the Lord: and he shall turn the hearts of the fathers to the children, and the heart of the children to their fathers, lest I come and smite the earth with a curse."

Now, what I am after is the knowledge of God, and I take my own course to obtain it. What are we to understand by this in the last days?

In the days of Noah, God destroyed the world by a flood, and He has promised to destroy

of power & who dont or we may be likely to be deceived.

That person who holds the keys of Elias hath a preparitory work. But if I spend much more time in conversing about the spirit of Elias I shall not have time to do justice to the spirit & power of Elijah[.]

this is the Elias spoken of in the last days & here is the <u>rock</u> upon which many split thinking the time was past in the days of John & Christ & no more to be. but the spirit of Elias was revealed to me & I know it is true[.] therefore I speak with boldness for I know varily my doctr<in> is true.[210]

Wilford Woodruff's Journal

Now for Elijah, the spirit power & Calling of Elijah is that ye have power to hold the keys of the revelations ordinances, oricles powers & endowments of the fulness of the Melchezedek Priesthood & of the kingdom of God on the Earth & to recieve, obtain & perform all the ordinances belonging to the kingdom of God even unto the sealing of the hearts of the ~~hearts~~ fathers unto the Children & the hearts of the children unto the fathers even those who are in heaven.

Malachi says I will send Elijah before[e] the great and dredful day of the Lord come & He shall turn the hearts of the Fathers to the Children and the hearts of the Children to the Fathers lest I come & smite the earth with a curse.

Now what I am after is the knowledge of God & I take my own course to obtain it. what are we to under<stand> by this in the last days.

in the days of Noah God destroyed the world by a flood & has promised to destroy it by

---

210. 10 March 1844, *WWJ*, 1:615–16. See also *JSP, D14*, 257–58.

it by fire in the last days: but before it should take place, Elijah should first come and turn the hearts of the fathers to the children, &c.

Now comes the point. What is this office and work of Elijah? It is one of the greatest and most important subjects that God has revealed. He should send Elijah to seal the children to the fathers, and the fathers to the children.

fire in the last days[.] but before it took place Elijah should first Come & turn the hearts of the Fathers to the children &c.

now comes the point[.] what is this office & work of Elijah. it is one of the greatest & most important subjects that God has revealed. He should send Elijah to seal the children to the fathers & fathers to the Children.[211]

For the Living and the Dead

Wilford Woodruff's Journal

Now was this merely confined to the living, to settle difficulties with families on earth? By no means. It was a far greater work. Elijah! what would you do if you were here? Would you confine your work to the living alone? No: I would refer you to the Scriptures, where the subject is manifest: that is, without us, they could not be made perfect, nor we without them; the fathers without the children, nor the children without the fathers.

I wish you to understand this subject, for it is important; and if you receive it, this is the spirit of Elijah, that we **[p.338]** redeem our dead, and connect ourselves with our fathers which are in heaven, and seal up our dead to come forth in the first resurrection; and here we want the power of Elijah to seal those who dwell on earth to those who dwell in heaven. This is the power of Elijah and the keys of the kingdom of Jehovah.

now was this merely confined to the living to settle difficulties with families on earth. by no means. it was a far greater work[.] Elijah what would you do if you was here? would you ~~con=fine~~ <refer> <confine> your work to the living alone. No[.] I would ~~confine~~ <refer> you to the scriptures whare the subject is manifest. i.e. without us they could not be made perfect, nor we without them, the fathers without the Children nor the Children without the fathers.

I wish you to understand this subject for it is important & if you will recieve it this is the spirit of Elijah that we redeem our dead & connect ourselves with our fathers which are in heaven & seal up our dead to come forth in the first resurrection & here we want the power of <u>Elijah</u> to <u>seal those who dwell on earth to those which dwell in heaven</u>. this is the power of Elijah & the keys of the kingdom of Jehovah.[212]

Sealing on Earth and in Heaven

Wilford Woodruff's Journal

Let us suppose a case. Suppose the great God who dwells in heaven should reveal himself to Father Cutler here, by the opening heavens, and tell him, I offer up a decree that whatsoever you seal on earth with your decree, I will seal it in heaven; you have the power then; can

Let us suppose a case. suppose the great God who dwells in heaven should reveal himself to Father Cutler here by the opening heavens and tell him I offer up a decree that **[p.617]** whatsoever you seal on earth with your decree I will seal it in heaven. you have power then.

---

211. 10 March 1844, *WWJ*, 1:616. See also *JSP, D14*, 258–59.
212. 10 March 1844, *WWJ*, 1:616. See also *JSP, D14*, 259.

it be taken off? No. Then what you seal on earth, by the keys of Elijah, is sealed in heaven; and this is the power of Elijah, and this is the difference between the spirit and power of Elias and Elijah; for while the spirit of Elias is a forerunner, the power of Elijah is sufficient to make our calling and election sure; and the same doctrine, where we are exhorted to go on to perfection, not laying again the foundation of repentance from dead works, and of laying on of hands, resurrection of the dead, &c.

We cannot be perfect without the fathers, &c. We must have revelation from them, and we can see that the doctrine of revelation far transcends the doctrine of no revelation; for one truth revealed from heaven is worth all the sectarian notions in existence.

This spirit of Elijah was manifest in the days of the Apostles, in delivering certain ones to the buffetings of Satan, that they might be saved in the day of the Lord Jesus. They were sealed by the spirit of Elijah unto the damnation of hell until the day of the Lord, or revelation of Jesus Christ.

Here is the doctrine of election that the world has quarreled so much about; but they do not know anything about it.

Can it be taken of[f]? No. Then what you seal on earth by the keys of Elijah is sealed in heaven, & this is the power of Elijah, & this is the difference between the spirit & power of Elias and Elijah. for while the spirit of Elias is a fore runner the power of Elijah is sufficient to make our Calling & Election sure, & the same doctrin whare we are exhorted to go on unto perfection not laying again the foundation of repentance from dead works but of laying on of hands, resurrection of the dead &c[.]

we cannot be perfect without the fathers, &c. we must have revelations then & we can see that the doctrin of revelation as far transcends the doctrin of no revelation as knowledge is above ignorance[.] for one truth revealed from heaven is worth all the sectarian notions in exhistance.

This spirit of Elijah was manifest in the days of the Apostles in delivering certain ones to the buffitings of Satan that they may be saved in the day of the Lord Jesus. they were sealed by the spirit of Elijah unto the damnation of Hell untill the day of the Lord or revelation of Jesus Christ

Here is the doctrin of Election that the world have quarreled so much about, but they do not know any thing about it.[213]

Falling from Grace

Wilford Woodruff's Journal

The doctrine that the Presbyterians and Methodists have quarreled so much about-one in grace, always in grace, or falling away from grace, I will say a word about. They are both wrong. Truth takes a road between them both, for while the Presbyterian says: "Once in grace, you cannot fall"; the Methodist says: "You can have grace today, fall from it tomorrow, next day

The doctrin that the Prysbeterians & Methodist have quarreled so much about once in grace always in grace, or falling away from Grace I will say a word about. they are both wrong. truth takes a road between them both. for while the Presbyterian Says once in grace you cannot fall the Methodist says you can have grace to day, fall from it to morrow, next

---

213. 10 March 1844, *WWJ*, 1:616–17. See also *JSP, D14*, 259–60.

have grace again; and so follow on, changing [p.339] continually." But the doctrine of the Scriptures and the spirit of Elijah would show them both false, and take a road between them both; for, according to the Scripture, if men have received the good word of God, and tasted of the powers of the world to come, if they shall fall away, it is impossible to renew them again, seeing they have crucified the Son of God afresh, and put Him to an open shame; so there is a possibility of falling away; you could not be renewed again, and the power of Elijah cannot seal against this sin, for this is a reserve made in the seals and power of the Priesthood.

I will make every doctrine plain that I present, and it shall stand upon a firm basis, and I am at the defiance of the world, for I will take shelter under the broad cover of the wings of the work in which I am engaged. It matters not to me if all hell boils over; I regard it only as I would the crackling of the thorns under a pot.

Murderers Have No Forgiveness

A murderer, for instance, on that sheds innocent blood, cannot have forgiveness. David sought repentance at the hand of God carefully with tears, for the murder of Uriah; but he could only get it through hell; he got a promise that his soul should not be left in hell.

Although David was a king, he never did obtain the spirit and power of Elijah and the fullness of the Priesthood; and the Priesthood that he received, and the throne and kingdom of David is to be taken from him and given to another by the name of David in the last days, raised up out of his lineage.

Peter referred to the same subject on the day of Pentecost, but the multitude did not get the endowment that Peter had; but several

Wilford Woodruff's Journal

day have grace again & so follow it. but the doctrin of the scriptures & the spirit of Elijah would show them both fals[e] & take a road between them both. for according to the scriptures if a man has receive[d] the good word of God & tasted of the powers of the world to come if they shall fall away it is impossible to renew them again, seeing they have Crucified the son of God afresh & put him to an open ~~frame~~ shame. so their is a possibility of falling away[.] Yee could not be renewed again, & the power of Elijah Cannot seal against this sin, for this is a reserve made in the seals & power of the priesthood.

I will make evry doctrin plain that I present & it shall stand upon a firm bases[.] And I am at the defiance of the world for I will take shelter under the broad ~~shelter~~ <cover> of the wings of the work in which I am ingaged. it matters not to me if all hell boils over[.] I regard it ownly as I would the Crackling of <the> thorns under a pot[214]

A murderer, for instance, one that sheds innocent Blood cannot have forgiveness. David sought repentance at the hand of God Carefully with tears, but he could ownly get it through Hell. he got a promise that his Soul should not be left in Hell.

Although David was a king he never did obtain the spirit & power of Elijah & the fulness of the Priesthood, & the priesthood that he received & the throne & kingdom of David is to be taken from him & given to another by the name of David in the last days, raised up out of his linage.

Peter refered to the same subject on the day of pentecost, but the multitude did not get the endowment that Peter had[.] but several days

---

214. 10 March 1844, *WWJ*, 1:617. See also *JSP, D14*, 260.

days after, the people asked, "What shall we do?" Peter says, "I would ye had done it ignorantly," speaking of crucifying the Lord &c. He did not say to them, "Repent and be baptized for the remission of your sins"; but he said, "Repent ye therefore, and be converted, that your sins may be blotted out, when the times of refreshing shall come from the presence of the lord." (Acts 3:19.)

This is the case with murderers. They could not be baptized for the remission of sins, for they had shed innocent blood.

[p.340] Again: The doctrine or sealing power of Elijah is as follows:—If you have power to seal on earth and in heaven, then we should be wise. The first thing you do, go and seal on earth your sons and daughters unto yourself, and yourself unto your fathers in eternal glory, and go ahead, and not go back, but use a little wisdom, and seal all you can, and when you get to heaven tell your Father that what you seal on earth should be sealed in heaven, according to his promise. I will walk through the gate of heaven and claim what I seal, and those that follow me and my counsel.

The Lord once told me that what I asked for I should have. I have been afraid to ask God to kill my enemies, lest some of them should, peradventure, repent.

I asked a short time since for the Lord to deliver me out of the hands of the Governor of Missouri, and if it needs must be to accomplish it, to take him away; and the next news that came pouring down from there was, that Governor Reynolds had shot himself. And I would now say, Beware, O earth, how you fight against the Saints of God and shed innocent blood; for in the days of Elijah, his enemies came upon him, and fire was called down from heaven and destroyed them.

after the people asked what shall we do. Peter says I would ye had done it ignorantly speaking of crucifying the Lord &c. He did not say to them repent & be baptized for the remission of your sins but he said repent therefore & be converted that your sins may be blotted out when the times of refreshing shall come from the presence of the Lord. <u>Acts</u> III, 19[.]

this is the case with murderers[.] they could not be baptized for the remission of sins for they had shed innocent Blood.

Again the doctrin or sealing power of Elijah is as follows[:] if you have power to seal on earth & in heaven then we should be crafty. the first thing you do go & seal on earth your sons & daughters unto yourself & yourself unto your fathers in eternal glory, & go ahead and not go back, but use a little Craftiness & seal all you can; & when you get to heaven tell your father that what you seal on earth should be sealed in heaven[.] I will walk through the gate of heaven and Claim what I seal & those that follow me & my Council

[p.618] The Lord once told me that what I asked for I should have. I have been afraid to aske to ask God to kill my enemies lest some of them should peradventure should repent[.]

I asked a short time since for the Lord to deliver me out of the hands of the govornor of Missouri & if it must needs be to accomplish it to take him away, & the next news that came pouring down from their, was Govornor <u>Reynolds</u> <u>had</u> <u>shot</u> <u>himself</u>. and I would now say beware O earth how you fight against the saints of God & shed innocent Blood, for in the days of Elijah his enemies came upon him & fire was Called down from heaven & destroyed them.[215]

---

215. 10 March 1844, *WWJ*, 1:617–18. See also *JSP, D14*, 260–61.

Mission of Messiah

	Wilford Woodruff's Journal
The spirit of Elias is first, Elijah second, and Messiah last. Elias is a forerunner to prepare the way, and the spirit and power of Elijah is to come after, holding the keys of power, building the Temple to the capstone, placing the seals of the Melchizedek Priesthood upon the house of Israel, and making all things ready; then Messiah comes to His Temple, which is last of all.	the spirit of Elias is first, Elijah second, & Mesiah last. Elias is a fore runner to prepare the way, & the spirit & power of Elijah is to come after holding the keys of power build[i]ng the Temple to the cap stone, placing the seals of the Melchezedeck priesthood upon the house of Israel & making all things ready[.] then Mesiah comes to his Temple which is last of all.
Messiah is above the spirit and power of Elijah, for He made the world, and was the spiritual rock unto Moses in the wilderness. Elijah was to come and prepare the way and build up the kingdom before the coming of the great day of the Lord, although the spirit of Elias might begin it.	Mesiah is above the spirit & power of Elijah for he made the world & was that spiritual rock unto Moses in the wilderness. Elijah was to come & prepare the way & build up the kingdom before the coming of the great day of the Lord Although the spirit of Elias might begin it,
I have asked of the Lord concerning His coming; and while asking the Lord, He gave a sign and said, "In the days of Noah I set a bow in the heavens as a sign and token that in any year that the bow should be seen the Lord would not come; but there should be seed time and harvest during **[p.341]** that year: but whenever you see the bow withdrawn, it shall be a token that there shall be famine, pestilence, and great distress among the nations, and that the coming of the Messiah is not far distant.	I have asked of the Lord concerning his Coming & while asking, the Lord <◊◊◊> gave me a sign & said in the days of Noah I set a bow in the heavens as a sign & token that in any year that the bow should be seen the Lord would not come, but their should be seed time & harvest during that year. but whenever you see the bow withdraw, it shall be a token that their shall be famin[e] pestilence & great distress among the nations.
But I will take the responsibility upon myself to prophesy in the name of the Lord, that Christ will not come this year, as Father Miller has prophesied, for we have seen the bow; and I also prophesy, in the name of the Lord, that Christ will not come in forty years; and if God ever spoke by my mouth, He will not come in that length of time. Brethren, when you go home, write it down, that it may be remembered.	But I take the responsibility upon myself to prophesy in the name of the Lord, that Christ will not Come this year as Miller has prophecyed, for we have seen the bow. And I also Prophecy in the name of the Lord that Christ will not Come in forty years & if God ever spake by my mouth he will not come in that length of time, &

Jesus Christ never did reveal to any man the precise time that He would come. Go and read the Scriptures, and you cannot find anything that specifies the exact hour He would come; and all that say so are false teachers.

There are some important things concerning the office of the Messiah in the organization of the world, which I will speak of hereafter. May God Almighty bless you and pour out His Spirit upon you, is the prayer of your unworthy servant. Amen. (March 10, 1844.) DHC 6:249-254.

Jesus Christ never did reveal to any man the precise time that he would Come. go & read the scriptures & you cannot find any thing that specifies the exact <time> he would come & all that say so are fals[e] teachers.

Their are some important things concerning the office of the Mesiah in the organization of the world which I will speak of hereafter. May God Almighty bless you & pour out his spirit upon you is the prayer of your unworthy servant Amen[216]

The Power of Truth

President Joseph Smith again arose and said— In relation to the power over the minds of mankind which I hold, I would say, It is in consequence of the power of truth in the doctrines which I have been an instrument in the hands of God of presenting unto them, and not because of any compulsion on my part. I wish to ask if ever I got any of it unfairly? If I have not reproved you in the gate? I ask, Did I ever exercise any compulsion over any man? Did I not give him the liberty of disbelieving any doctrine I have preached, if he saw fit? Why do not my enemies strike a blow at the doctrine? They cannot do it: it is truth, and I defy all men to upset it. I am the voice of one crying in the wilderness, "Repent ye of your sins and prepare the way for the coming of the Son of Man; for the kingdom of God has come unto you, and henceforth the ax is laid unto the root of the tree; and every tree that bringeth not forth good fruit, God Almighty * * * shall hew it down and cast it into the fire." (March 24, 1844.) DHC 6:273.

Wilford Woodruff's Journal

President Joseph Smith again arose & said[217] In relation to the power over the minds of mankind which I hold, I would say it is in consequence of the power of truth in the doctrins which I have been an instrument in the hands of God of presenting unto them, & not because of any compulsion on my part. I will <to> ask if I ever got any of it unfair. If I have not reproved you in the gate. I ask did I ever exercise any compulsion over any man. did I not give him the liberty of disbelieveing any doctrin I have preached if he saw fit. why do not my enemies strike a blow at the doctrin. they cannot do it, it is truth. And I am as the voice of one crying in the wilderness repent of your sins & prepare the way for the Coming of the son of Man, for the kingdom of God has Come unto you and henceforth the ax is laid unto the root of the tree, and evry tree that bringeth not forth good fruit, God Almighty (and not Jo Smith) shall hew down & cast it into the fire.[218]

---

216. 10 March 1844, *WWJ*, 1:618. See also *JSP, D14*, 261–62.
217. 24 March 1844, *WWJ*, 1:621.
218. 24 March 1844, *WWJ*, 1:621. See also *JSP, D14*, 282.

"The King Follett Discourse"[219]

he Being and Kind of Being God Is; The Immortality of the Intelligence of Man By Joseph Smith the Prophet[220]

[p.342] President Joseph Smith delivered the following discourse before about twenty thousand Saints at the April conference of the Church, 1844, being the funeral sermon of Elder King Follett.[221] Reported by Willard Richards, Wilford Woodruff, Thomas Bullock and William Clayton. This discourse was first published in the *Times and Seasons* of August 15, 1844.[222]

Beloved Saints, I will call the attention of this congregation while I address you on the subject of the dead. The decease of our beloved brother, Elder King Follett, who was crushed in a well by the falling of a tub of rock, has more immediately led me to that subject. I

I now call the attention of this congregation while I addres you upon the subject of the dead[.] The case of our Beloved Brother King Follet, who was crushed to death in a well,[223] Joseph commenced speaking on the subject of the Dead— relative to the death of elder King

---

219. The version of the King Follett Discourse used by Joseph Fielding Smith for the original *TPJS* was an amalgated and sometimes reordered version of the Prophet's discourse. It will be included in that order in the parallel columns here, but the four journal versions of the discourse (from which the *TPJS* version was drawn) are reproduced in their original order in Appendix C.

220. The Willard Richards journal account of the 7 April 1844 King Follett Discourse is found in *JSP, J3*, 216–22. The version recorded by William Clayton and the one recorded by Thomas Bullock can both be found in *JSP, D14*, 316–33. Wilford Woodruff's account of the sermon is also dated 7 April 1844 and is found in *WWJ*, 1:626–31. By the end of 1844, this discourse had been published three times. An amalgamated version taken from the journals of Thomas Bullock and William Clayton was published in *Times and Seasons* 5, no. 15 (15 August 1844): 612–17. This was later republished in *Millennial Star* 5, no. 6 (November 1844): 87–93. It was also included in a publication by John Taylor called the *Voice of Truth*. The account of the King Follett Discourse found in Manuscript History of the Church was compiled in the mid-1850s by a member of the Church Historian's staff, Jonathan Grimshaw. The Grimshaw amalgamation was later published in *History of the Church*, vol. 6. Joseph Fielding Smith appears to have used this Manuscript History of the Church version found in *History*, E-1, 7 April 1844, 1968–79.

221. The King Follett Sermon was given by the Prophet Joseph Smith at the 7 April 1844 conference of the Church in Nauvoo, Illinois. The talk references King Follett, a friend of the prophet, who had been killed in an accident on March 9. Thus, while this talk is traditionally referred to as the King Follett Sermon or Discourse—and while it is often called the "funeral sermon" of King Follett—it should be understood that Joseph did not deliver these remarks at Follett's funeral but, instead, at a general conference weeks after Follett's death.

222. This introductory paragraph was authored by Joseph Fielding Smith.

223. Discourse, 7 April 1844, reported by Wilford Woodruff, *WWJ*, 1:628. See also *JSP, D14*, 336.

have been requested to speak by his friends and relatives, but inasmuch as there are a great many in this congregation who live in this city as well as elsewhere, who have lost friends, I feel disposed to speak on the subject in general, and offer you my ideas, so far as I have ability, and so far as I shall be inspired by the Holy Spirit to dwell on this subject.

Follet[t] to who who was crushed in a well. by the falling of a tub of rock on him.—[224] as well as many others who have lost friends will be had in mind this afternoon, & [I] shall speak upon the subject in general as far as I shall be inspired by the Holy spirit to treat upon the subject <it>.[225] I shall speak in gen[era]ˡ· & offe[r] you my ideas so far as I have ability & so far as I shall be insp[ire]ᵈ· by the H S. [Holy Spirit] to dwell on this subj[ec]ᵗ·[226]

I want your prayers and faith that I may have the instruction of Almighty God and the gift of the Holy Ghost, so that I may set forth things that are true and which can be easily comprehended by you, and that the testimony may carry conviction to your hearts and minds of the truth of what I shall say. Pray that the Lord may strengthen my lungs, stay the winds, and let the prayers of the Saints to heaven appear, that they may enter into the ears of the Lord of Sabaoth, for the effectual prayers of the righteous avail much. There is strength here, and I verily believe that your prayers will be heard.

want your prayers faith, the inspirati[o]n of Almighty God, the Gift of H. G. that I may set forth truth things that can easily be comprehended & will carry the testimony to your heart, pray that the L[ord] may strengthe[n] my lungs caml [calm] the wind that it may enter into the ear of the Ld of Sabaoth the fervent effectual prayer of righteo[u]s man availed[h] mach [much]— will speak in order to hold out.[227]

there is strength here & your prayers will be herd.[228]

Before I enter fully into the investigation of the subject which is lying before me, I wish to pave the way and bring up the subject from the beginning, that you may understand it. I will make a few preliminaries, in order that you may understand the subject when I come to it. I do not intend to please your ears with superfluity of words or oratory, or with much learning; but I intend to edify you with the simple truths from heaven.

Before enter[ring] fully into the investigate[o]n wish to pave the way— make a few prelim[in]aries— bring the subject from th[e] beginning in order that you may understand the subject when I come to it. Do not calculate to please your ears with superfluity of words oratory much learning, but edify you by the simple truths of heaven—[229]

---

224. Discourse, 7 April 1844, in *JSP, J3*, 217. See also *JSP, D14*, 333.
225. Discourse, 7 April 1844, reported by Wilford Woodruff, *WWJ*, 1:628. See also *JSP, D14*, 336. In the original handwritten journal page, someone has crossed out (at a later time) the words "the subject," and added the word "it" in their place. Whether Wilford or someone else did this is unclear.
226. Discourse, 7 April 1844, reported by Thomas Bullock, *JSP, D14*, 316.
227. Discourse, 7 April 1844, reported by William Clayton, *JSP, D14*, 328.
228. Discourse, 7 April 1844, reported by Wilford Woodruff, *WWJ*, 1:628. See also *JSP, D14*, 337.
229. Discourse, 7 April 1844, reported by William Clayton, *JSP, D14*, 328.

The Character of God

[p.343] In the first place, I wish to go back to the beginning—to the morn of creation. There is the starting point for us to look to, in order to understand and be fully acquainted with the mind, purposes and decrees of the Great Elohim, who sits in yonder heavens as he did at the creation of this world. It is necessary for us to have an understanding of God himself in the beginning. If we start right, it is easy to go right all the time; but if we start wrong, we may go wrong, and it be a hard matter to get right.

There are but a very few beings in the world who understand rightly the character of God. The great majority of mankind do not comprehend anything, either that which is past, or that which is to come, as it respects their relationship to God. They do not know, neither do they understand the nature of that relationship; and consequently they know but little above the brute beast, or more than to eat, drink and sleep. This is all man knows about God or his existence, unless it is given by the inspiration of the Almighty.

If a man learns nothing more than to eat, drink and sleep, and does not comprehend any of the designs of God, the beast comprehends the same things. It eats, drinks, sleeps, and knows nothing more about God; yet it knows as much as we, unless we are able to comprehend by the inspiration of Almighty God. If men do not comprehend the character of God, they do not comprehend themselves.

first place wish to go back to the beginning of creation,[230] to the morn of creation[231] then the starting point in order to fully aquianted [acquainted] with purposes decrees &c of the great Elohem that sits in the h. for us to take up begin[in]g at the creati[o]n necessary to understand something of God himself in the beginning. If we start right easy to go right all the time— start wrong hard matter to get right.[232]

there are very few who understand rightly the char[acter] of God— they do not comprehend any thing that is past or that which is to come[233] they do not know they do not understand their relationship to God. the world know no more than the brute beast, & they know no more than to eat drink and sleep & this is all man knows about God or his exhistance, except what is given by the inspiration of the Almighty. go then to the beginning that you may understand.[234]

If a man comprehends nothing more than to eat sleep and and not any more and what the designs of Jehova[h] what better than the beast it does the same thing— eats drink— sleep & comprehends present and knows as much as we unless we are able to com by the inspirati[o]n of A[lmighty] God.[235] If men do not compreh[e]nd the character of God they do not comprehe[n]d themselvs.[236] Go back

---

230. Discourse, 7 April 1844, reported by William Clayton, *JSP, D14*, 328.
231. Discourse, 7 April 1844, reported by Wilford Woodruff, *WWJ*, 1:628. See also *JSP, D14*, 337.
232. Discourse, 7 April 1844, reported by William Clayton, *JSP, D14*, 328.
233. Discourse, 7 April 1844, reported by Thomas Bullock, *JSP, D14*, 316.
234. Discourse, 7 April 1844, reported by Wilford Woodruff, *WWJ*, 1:628. See also *JSP, D14*, 337.
235. Discourse, 7 April 1844, reported by William Clayton, *JSP, D14*, 328.
236. Discourse, 7 April 1844, in *JSP, J3*, 217. See also *JSP, D14*, 333.

I want to go back to the beginning, and so lift your minds into a more lofty sphere and a more exalted understanding than what the human mind generally aspires to.

to begin[nin]g to lift you[r] minds into a more exalted standing than the human mind is wont—[237]

What Kind of Being Is God?

I want to ask this congregation, every man, woman and child, to answer the question in their own heart, what kind of a being God is? Ask yourselves; turn your thought into your hearts, and say if any of you have seen, heard, or communed with him. This is a question that may occupy your attention for a long time. I again repeat the question—What kind of a being is God? Does any man or woman know? Have any of you seen him, heard him, or communed with him? Here is the question that will, peradventure, from this [p.344] time henceforth occupy your attention. The Scriptures inform us that "This is life eternal that they might know thee, the only true God, and Jesus Christ whom thou hast sent."

I want to ask this cong[regation]: every man wom[an]: & child to ans[we]ʳ· the quest[io]ⁿ· in their own heart what kind of a being is God I ag[ai]ⁿ· rep[ea]ᵗ· the questⁿ· what kind of a being is God does any man or woman know have any of you seen, him heard him, communed with him, here is the questⁿ· that will peradventure from <this time> henceforth occupy your attentⁿ·— the Apos[tle]: says this is Eternal life to know God & J. C [Jesus Christ] who he has sent— that is etern[a]ˡ· life[238]

If any man does not know God, and inquires what kind of a being he is,—if he will search diligently his own heart—if the declaration of Jesus and the apostles be true, he will realize that he has not eternal life; for there can be eternal life on no other principle.

if any man enquire what kind of being is God. cast his mind to know— if the declarati[o]n of the ap[ostle] be true he will realize that he has not eternal life. There can be eternal life on no other prinicple—

My first object is to find out the character of the only wise and true God, and what kind of a being he is; and if I am so fortunate as to be the man to comprehend God, and explain or convey the principles to your hearts, so that the Spirit seals them upon you, then let every man and woman henceforth sit in silence, put their hands on their mouths, and never lift their hands or voices, or say anything against the man of God or the servants of God again.

1ˢᵗ of object to find the character of the only wise & true God[239]
if I am so fortunate as to comprehe[n]d and explain[240]
so that the spirit seal it upon you[r] hearts let every man and woman put his hand on his mouth & never say any thing against the man of God again but if I fail it becomes my duty to renounce all my pretensions to inspirati[o]ns &c[241]

---

237. Discourse, 7 April 1844, reported by William Clayton, *JSP, D14*, 328.
238. Discourse, 7 April 1844, reported by Thomas Bullock, *JSP, D14*, 317.
239. Discourse, 7 April 1844, reported by William Clayton, *JSP, D14*, 328.
240. Discourse, 7 April 1844, in *JSP, J3*, 217. See also *JSP, D14*, 333.
241. Discourse, 7 April 1844, reported by William Clayton, *JSP, D14*, 329.

But if I fail to do it, it becomes my duty to renounce all further pretensions to revelations and inspirations, or to be a prophet; and I should be like the rest of the world—a false teacher, be hailed as a friend, and no man would seek my life. But if all religious teachers were honest enough to renounce their pretensions to godliness when their ignorance of the knowledge of God is made manifest, they will all be as badly off as I am, at any rate; and you might as well take the lives of other false teachers as that of mine, if I am false. If any man is authorized to take away my life because he thinks and says I am a false teacher, then, upon the same principle, we should be justified in taking away the life of every false teacher, and where would be the end of blood? And who would not be the sufferer? [242]

or to be a prophet. I would be like the rest of the world,[s] fals[e] teachers & you would want to take my life.[243]
if all are pretension to ~~the~~ God they will all be as bad off as I am they will all say I ought to be d[amne]d[244]

But you might just as well take the lives of other fals[e] teach[ers?] as mine if I was fals[e].[245] if any man is auth[d.] to take away my life who say I am a false teacher so I sho[d.] have the same right to all false teacher & where wo[d.] be the end of the blood[246]

and who would not be the sufferer—[247]

The Privilege of Religious Freedom

But meddle not with any man for his religion: and all governments ought to permit every man to enjoy his religion unmolested. No man is authorized to take away life in consequence of difference of religion, which all laws and governments ought to tolerate and protect, right or wrong. Every man has a natural, and, in our country, a constitutional right to be a false prophet, as well as a true prophet. If I show, verily, that **[p.345]** I have the truth of God, and show that ninety-nine out of every hundred professing religious ministers are false teachers, having no authority, while they pretend to hold the keys of God's kingdom

But meddle not with any man for his religion. evry goverment ought to permit evry man to enjoy his religion.[248] no man is authorised to take away life in consequence of their religion all laws and government ought to tolerate whethe[r] right or wron[g][249] Every man has a right to be a false prophet. as well as a true prophet.—[250] If I show that I have the truth of God & $99/100$ are false teacher[s] while they pretend to hold the keys of God & go to killing them because &c would it not deluge the wo[r]ld in blood.[251]

---

242. The original *TPJS* footnote reads: "These remarks will be better understood, if it is remembered that about this time the storms of a renewed persecution were bursting upon the Prophet, and his life was threatened upon every side."

243. Discourse, 7 April 1844, reported by Wilford Woodruff, *WWJ*, 1:628. See also *JSP, D14*, 337.
244. Discourse, 7 April 1844, reported by Thomas Bullock, *JSP, D14*, 317.
245. Discourse, 7 April 1844, reported by Wilford Woodruff, *WWJ*, 1:628. See also *JSP, D14*, 337.
246. Discourse, 7 April 1844, reported by Thomas Bullock, *JSP, D14*, 317.
247. Discourse, 7 April 1844, reported by William Clayton, *JSP, D14*, 329.
248. Discourse, 7 April 1844, reported by Wilford Woodruff, *WWJ*, 1:628. See also *JSP, D14*, 337.
249. Discourse, 7 April 1844, reported by William Clayton, *JSP, D14*, 329.
250. Discourse, 7 April 1844, in *JSP, J3*, 217. See also *JSP, D14*, 334.
251. Discourse, 7 April 1844, reported by William Clayton, *JSP, D14*, 329.

on earth, and was to kill them because they are false teachers, it would deluge the whole world with blood.

I will prove that the world is wrong, by showing what God is. I am going to enquire after God; for I want you all to know him, and to be familiar with him; and if I am bringing you to a knowledge of him, all persecutions against me ought to cease. You will then know that I am his servant; for I speak as one having authority.

I will show the world is <w>rong by showing what God is. I am going to inquire after God so that you may know God, that persecution may cease Concerning me.[252] I am his serv[an]t for I speak as one hav[in]g. auth[orit]y. & not as a senr.[253]

God an Exalted Man

I will go back to the beginning before the world was, to show what kind of being God is. What sort of a being was God in the beginning? Open your ears and hear, all ye ends of the earth, for I am going to prove it to you by the Bible, and to tell you the designs of God in relation to the human race, and why He interferes with the affairs of man.

I go back to the beginning to show what kind of a being God was. I will tell you & hear it O Earth![254] I am going to prove it to you with the Bible & I am going to tell you the desns. of God to the human race & why he interferes with the affairs of man[255]

God himself was once as we are now, and is an exalted man, and sits enthroned in yonder heavens! That is the great secret. If the veil were rent today, and the great God who holds this world in its orbit, and who upholds all worlds and all things by his power, was to make himself visible,—I say, if you were to see him today, you would see him like a man in form—like yourselves in all the person, image, and very form as a man; for Adam was created in the very fashion, image and likeness of God, and received instruction from, and walked, talked and conversed with him, as one man talks and communes with another.

1st. God that sets enthroned is a man like one of yourselves— that is the great secret. If the vail was rent to day & the great god who holds this world in its sphere in its orbit— the planets— if you were to see him to day you would see him in all the person image very form of man.

for Adam was created in the very fashion of God. Adam received instruction walked talked as one man with another[r].[256]

---

252. Discourse, 7 April 1844, reported by Wilford Woodruff, *WWJ*, 1:628. See also *JSP, D14*, 337.
253. Discourse, 7 April 1844, reported by Thomas Bullock, *JSP, D14*, 317. The Joseph Smith Papers website states of the last word in this sentence ("senr."): "Possibly 'servt.', although JS's scriptural allusion suggests that the word should have been rendered as 'scribe'. (See Matthew 7:28–29; and Mark 1:22)." *JSP, D14*, 317n98.
254. Discourse, 7 April 1844, reported by Wilford Woodruff, *WWJ*, 1:629. See also *JSP, D14*, 337.
255. Discourse, 7 April 1844, reported by Thomas Bullock, *JSP, D14*, 317.
256. Discourse, 7 April 1844, reported by William Clayton, *JSP, D14*, 329.

In order to understand the subject of the dead, for consolation of those who mourn for the loss of their friends, it is necessary we should understand the character and being of God and how he came to be so; for I am going to tell you how God came to be God. We have imagined and supposed that God was God from all eternity. I will refute that idea, and take away the veil, so that you may see.

In order to understand the dead for the consolation of those that mourn, I want you to understand God and how he comes to be God. We suppose that God was God from eternity. I will refute that Idea, or I will do away or take away the veil so you may see.[257]

These are incomprehensible ideas to some, but they are simple. It is the first principle of the Gospel to know for a certainty the Character of God, and to know that we may converse with him as one man converses with another, and that **[p.346]** he was once a man like us; yea, that God himself, the Father of us all, dwelt on an earth, the same as Jesus Christ himself did; and I will show it from the Bible.

These are incompr[e]hensible to some but are the first principle of the gospel— to know that we may converse with him as one man with another[258]

he once was <a> man like us,[259]
God himself the father of us all dwelt on a Earth same as J C himself did & I will shew it from the Bible—[260]

Power of the Father and the Son

I wish I was in a suitable place to tell it, and that I had the trump of an archangel, so that I could tell the story in such a manner that persecution would cease for ever. What did Jesus say? (Mark it, Elder Rigdon!) The Scriptures inform us that Jesus said, As the Father hath power in Himself, even so hath the Son power—to do what? Why, what the Father did. The answer is obvious—in a manner to lay down His body and take it up again. Jesus, what are you going to do? To lay down my life as my Father did, and take it up again. Do we believe it? I you do not believe it, you do not believe the Bible.[263] The Scriptures say it, and I defy all the learning

And I wish I was in a suitable place to tell it[.][261] I wish I had the trump of an Arch An[gel][262] If I have the privilege could tell the story in such a manner as persecution would cease forever— Said Jesus (mark it Br Rigdn [Sidney Rigdon]) What did Jesus say— as the father ~~hath~~ had power in himself even so hath the son power. to do what why what the father did To lay down his body and took it up again. Jesus what are you going to do— to lay down my life as my father did that I might take it up again.[264]
do you believe it. if not, dont believe the bible.[265]
I defy all hell all learn[in]^{g.} wisdom & records of hell tog[ethe]^r to refute it

---

257. Discourse, 7 April 1844, reported by Wilford Woodruff, *WWJ*, 1:629. See also *JSP, D14*, 337.
258. Discourse, 7 April 1844, reported by William Clayton, *JSP, D14*, 329.
259. Discourse, 7 April 1844, reported by Wilford Woodruff, *WWJ*, 1:629. See also *JSP, D14*, 337.
260. Discourse, 7 April 1844, reported by Thomas Bullock, *JSP, D14*, 318.
261. Discourse, 7 April 1844, reported by Wilford Woodruff, *WWJ*, 1:629. See also *JSP, D14*, 337.
262. Discourse, 7 April 1844, reported by Thomas Bullock, *JSP, D14*, 318.
263. The original *TPJS* footnote reads: "The argument here made by the Prophet is very much strengthened by the following passage: 'The Son can do nothing of himself, but what he seeth the Father do; for what things soever he [the Father] doeth, these also doeth the Son likewise.' (St. John 5:19)."
264. Discourse, 7 April 1844, reported by William Clayton, *JSP, D14*, 329.
265. Discourse, 7 April 1844, reported by Wilford Woodruff, *WWJ*, 1:629. See also *JSP, D14*, 338.

and wisdom and all the combined powers of earth and hell together to refute it.

Here, then, is eternal life—to know the only wise and true God; and you have got to learn how to be Gods yourselves, and to be kings and priests to God, the same as all Gods have done before you,[266] namely, by going from one [p.347] small degree to another, and from a small capacity to a great one; from grace to grace, from exaltation to exaltation, until you attain to the resurrection of the dead, and are able to dwell in everlasting burnings, and to	here then is Et[erna][1] life to know the only wise & true God[267] You have got to learn how to be a god yourself in order to save you[r]self— to be priests & Kings as all Gods has done— by going from a small degree to another from exaltation to ex[altation]— till they are able to sit in glory as doth those who sit enthroned. I want you to know while God is being proclaimed that he is not trifling with you nor me.[268]

---

266. The original *TPJS* footnote reads:

Perhaps no passage in the Prophet's discourse has given more offense than the one here noted, and yet men are coming to think and feel the truth of what he said. Henry Drummond, for instance (following the Prophet by half a century), in his really great work, *Natural Law in the Spiritual World*, in the chapter on Growth, wherein he points out the difference between the merely moral man and one whose life has been touched by the spiritual power of God, and so received something that the merely moral man has not received, says: 'The end of salvation is perfection, the Christ-like mind, character and life. * * * Therefore the man who has within himself this great formative agent, Life [spiritual life] is nearer the end than the man who has morality alone. The latter can never reach perfection, the former must. For the life must develop out according to its type; and being a germ of the Christ-life, it must unfold into a Christ.' Joseph Smith's doctrine means no more than this.

Sir Oliver Lodge says much to the same effect in the following passage on 'Christianity and Science' (Hibbert's Journal, April, 1906):

It is orthodox, therefore, to maintain that Christ's birth was miraculous and his death portentous, that he continued in existence otherwise than as we men continue, that his very body rose and ascended into heaven—whatever that collection of words may mean. But I suggest that such an attempt at exceptional glorification of his body is a pious heresy—a heresy which misses the truth lying open to our eyes. His humanity is to be recognized as real and ordinary and thorough and complete; not in middle life alone; but at birth, and at death and after death. Whatever happened to him may happen to any one of us, provided we attain the appropriate altitude; an altitude which, whether within our individual reach or not, is assuredly within reach of humanity. That is what he urged again and again. 'Be born again.' 'Be ye perfect.' 'Ye are the sons of God.' 'My Father and your Father, my God and your God.' The uniqueness of the ordinary humanity of Christ is the first and patent truth, masked only by well-meaning and reverent superstition. But the second truth is greater than that—without it the first would be meaningless and useless,—if man alone, what gain have we? The world is full of men. What the world wants is a God. Behold the God!—[That is, the God, Jesus Christ.]

The divinity of Jesus is the truth which now requires to be reperceived, to be illumined afresh by new knowledge, to be cleansed and revivified by the wholesome flood of scepticism which has poured over it: it can be freed now from all trace of grovelling superstition; and can be recognized freely and enthusiastically: the divinity of Jesus, and [the divinity] of all other noble and saintly souls, insofar as they, too, have been inflamed by a spark of Deity—insofar as they, too, can be recognized as manifestations of the Divine.—Notes by Elder B. H. Roberts.

267. Discourse, 7 April 1844, reported by Thomas Bullock, *JSP, D14*, 318.
268. Discourse, 7 April 1844, reported by William Clayton, *JSP, D14*, 329–30.

sit in glory, as do those who sit enthroned in everlasting power. And I want you to know that God, in the last days, while certain individuals are proclaiming his name, is not trifling with you or me.

The Righteous to Dwell in Everlasting Burnings

These are the first principles of consolation. How consoling to the mourners when they are called to part with a husband, wife, father, mother, child, or dear relative, to know that, although the earthly tabernacle is laid down and dissolved, they shall rise again to dwell in everlasting burnings in immortal glory, not to sorrow, suffer, or die any more; but they shall be heirs of God and joint heirs with Jesus Christ. What is it? To inherit the same power, the same glory and the same exaltation, until you arrive at the station of a God, and ascend the throne of eternal power, the same as those who have gone before. What did Jesus do? Why; I do the things I saw my Father do when worlds come rolling into existence. My Father worked out his kingdom with fear and trembling, and I must do the same; and when I get my kingdom, I shall present it to my Father, so that he may obtain kingdom upon kingdom, [p.348] and it will exalt him in glory. He will then take a higher exaltation, and I will take his place, and thereby become exalted myself. So that Jesus treads in the tracks of his Father, and inherits what God did before; and God is thus glorified and exalted in the salvation and exaltation of all his children. It is plain beyond disputation, and you thus learn some of the first principles of the Gospel, about which so much hath been said.

When you climb up a ladder, you must begin at the bottom, and ascend step by step, until you arrive at the top; and so it is with the principles of the Gospel—you must begin

how consoling to the mourner when they are cal[le]$^{d.}$ to part with a wife mother father d[ea]$^{r.}$ relative to know that all Earthly taber[nacles] shall be dissolved that they shall be heirs of God & j[oin]$^{t.}$ h[ei]rs of J. C. to inherit the same powers exalt[atio]$^{n.}$ until you asc[en]$^{d.}$ the throne of Et$^{l.}$ power same as those who are gone bef[ore]^{269} What did Jesus do— why I do the things that I saw the father do when worlds came into existens— I saw the father work out a kingdom with fear & trembling & I can do the same & when I get my k[ingdom] work I will present to the father & it will exalt his glory and Jesus steps into his tracts to inherit what God did before This is some of the first principles of the gospel about which so much hath been—^{270}
when I do so to[o] I will give to the father which will add to his glory. He will take a Higher exhaltation & I will take his place and am also exhalted.^{271}

so that J treads in his tracks as he had gone before it is plain beyond comprehens[io]$^{n.}$ & you thus learn the first prin[ciples] of th[e] Gospel

when you climb a ladder you must begin at the bottom run[g] until you learn the last prin[ciple] of the Gospel for it is a great thing to learn Sal[vatio]$^{n.}$ beyond the grave & it is

---

269. Discourse, 7 April 1844, reported by Thomas Bullock, *JSP, D14*, 319.
270. Discourse, 7 April 1844, reported by William Clayton, *JSP, D14*, 330.
271. Discourse, 7 April 1844, reported by Wilford Woodruff, *WWJ*, 1:629. See also *JSP, D14*, 338.

with the first, and go on until you learn all the principles of exaltation. But it will be a great while after you have passed through the veil before you will have learned them. It is not all to be comprehended in this world; it will be a great work to learn our salvation and exaltation even beyond the grave. I suppose I am not allowed to go into an investigation of anything that is not contained in the Bible. If I do, I think there are so many over-wise men here, that they would cry "treason" and put me to death. So I will go to the old Bible and turn commentator today.

not all to be com[prehended] in this world I sup[pose] I am not all[owe]d. to go into investig^{n.} but what is cont[aine]d. in the Bible & I think there is so many wise men who wo^{d.} put me to death for treason I shall turn commentator to day—[272]

If I should say any thing but what was in the bible the Cry of treason would be herd[.] I will then go to the Bible.[273]

Meaning of the Hebrew Scriptures

I shall comment on the very first Hebrew word in the Bible; I will make a comment on the very first sentence of the history of the creation in the Bible—Berosheit. I want to analyze the word. Baith—in, by through, and everything else. Rosh—the head. Sheit—grammatical termination. When the inspired man wrote it, he did not put the baith there. An old Jew without any authority added the word; he thought it too bad to begin to talk about the head! It read first, "The head one of the Gods brought forth the Gods." That is the true meaning of the words. Baurau signifies to bring forth. If you do not believe it, you do not believe the learned man of God. Learned men can teach you no more than what I have told you. Thus the head God brought forth the Gods in the grand council.

I will go to the old Bible the very Berosheit. make a comme[n]t on the first sentence of the history of creation— Berosheit ~~Barau~~ want to annalize the word— Ba in by through in & every thing else— rosh— next— the head. sheet where do it come from— when they inspired man wrote it he did not put the Ba. ther[e]— Bu[t] a jew put it there. It read in the first— The head one of the Gods brought forth the Gods— is the true meaning— rosheit signifies to bring forth the Eloheim, Learned man cann[o]t learn any more than what I have told you— hence the head God brought forth the head God in the grand Council—[274]

I will transpose and simplify it in the English language. Oh, ye lawyers, ye doctors, and ye priests, who have persecuted me, I want to let you know that the Holy Ghost knows something as well as you do. The head God called together the Gods and sat in grand council to bring forth the world. The grand councilors sat at the head in yonder heavens

I want to bring it to English Oh ye lawyers ye doctors I want to let you know that the H G. [Holy Ghost] knows something as well as you do— the Head God called tog^{r.} the Gods & set in Grand Council &c when I say a lawyer I mean a lawyer of the Scrip[ture] I have done so hither to let the lawyers flutter & let every body laugh at them— some learned D[octo]^{r.}

---

272. Discourse, 7 April 1844, reported by Thomas Bullock, *JSP, D14*, 319.
273. Discourse, 7 April 1844, reported by Wilford Woodruff, *WWJ*, 1:629. See also *JSP, D14*, 338.
274. Discourse, 7 April 1844, reported by William Clayton, *JSP, D14*, 330.

and con[p.349]templated the creation of the worlds which were created at the time. When I say doctors and lawyers, I mean the doctors and lawyers of the Scriptures. I have done so[275] hitherto without explanation, to let the lawyers flutter and everybody laugh at them. Some learned doctors might take a notion to say the Scriptures say thus and so; and we might believe the Scriptures; they are not to be altered. But I am going to show you an error in them.

I have an old edition of the New Testament in the Latin, Hebrew, German and Greek languages. I have been reading the German, and find it to be the most [nearly] correct translation, and to correspond nearest to the revelations which God has given to me for the last fourteen years. It tells about Jacobus, the son of Zebedee. It means Jacob. In the English New Testament it is translated James. Now, if Jacob had the keys, you might talk about James through all eternity and never get the keys. In the 21st of the fourth chapter of Matthew, my old German edition gives the word Jacob instead of James.

The doctors (I mean doctors of law, no physic) say, "If you preach anything not according to the Bible, we will cry treason." How can we escape the damnation of hell, except God be with us and reveal to us? Men bind us with chains. The Latin says Jacob and the German says Jacob; here we have the testimony of four against one. I thank God that I have got this old book; but I thank him more for the gift of the Holy Ghost. I have got the oldest book in the world; but I [also] have the oldest book in my heart, even the gift of the Holy Ghost.

mi[gh]t. take a not[io]n. to say thus & so— & are not to be alt[ere]d. & I am going to shew you an error[276] When I say Doctr & Lawyer I mean the D & L of the scriptures some learned docter might say the scriptures say thus & so and we must believe the scriptures.[277]

[they] are not to be alt[ere]d. & I am going to shew you an error[278]

I have an old book in the Latin Greek Hebrew & German & I have been read[in]g. the Germ[an]: I find it to be the most correct that I have found & it corespends the nearest to the rev[elatio]ns. that I have given the last 14 y[ea]rs it tells about Iachaboa means Jacob— in the English James— & you may talk about James thro all Eternity in the 21 v[erse] of 4th. Mat[thew]: where it gives the test. that it is to Jacob—[279]

The Dr says (I mean Dr of Law not of physic) If you say any thing not according to the Bible we will cry treason. But if ye are not led by revelation how can ye escape the damnation of Hell. here we have the testimony of four[.] I have the oldest Book in the world & the Holy Ghost[.] I thank God for the old Book but more for the Holy Ghost.[280]

---

275. The original *TPJS* footnote reads: "i.e. Used the term 'lawyer' without explanation hitherto."
276. Discourse, 7 April 1844, reported by Thomas Bullock, *JSP, D14*, 320.
277. Discourse, 7 April 1844, reported by William Clayton, *JSP, D14*, 330.
278. Discourse, 7 April 1844, reported by Thomas Bullock, *JSP, D14*, 320. This appears to have been added to the sermon in *T&S* 5, no. 15 (15 August 1844): 614.
279. Discourse, 7 April 1844, reported by Thomas Bullock, *JSP, D14*, 320–21.
280. Discourse, 7 April 1844, reported by Wilford Woodruff, *WWJ*, 1:629. See also *JSP, D14*, 338.

I have all the four Testaments. Come here, ye learned men, and read, if you can. I should not have introduced this testimony, were it not to back up the word rosh—the head, the Father of the Gods. I should not have brought it up, only to show that I am right.

I have all the 4 Test[aments] come here ye learned men & read if you can I sho^d. not have bro^t. up this wod²⁸¹ ~~oot~~²⁸² only to shew that I am right²⁸³

A Council of the Gods

In the beginning, the head of the Gods called a council of the Gods; and they came together and concocted a plan to create the world and people it. When we begin to learn this **[p.350]** way, we begin to learn the only true God, and what kind of a being we have got to worship. Having a knowledge of God, we begin to know how to approach him, and how to ask so as to receive an answer. When we understand the character of God, and how to come to him, he begins to unfold the heavens to us, and to tell us all about it. When we are ready to come to him, he is ready to come to us.

In the begin[nin]g the head of the gods calld a coun[c]il of the Gods— and concoctd a scheme to create this world.—²⁸⁴ When we begin in this way ~~be~~ we begin to find out God— what kind a being we have got to worship— when we begin to know how to come to him he begins to come to us.²⁸⁵

Soon as we begin to understand the character of ~~the~~ Gods, he begin[s] to unfold th[e] heavns to us.—²⁸⁶
When we are ready to come to him he is ready to receive us.²⁸⁷

Now, I ask all who hear me, why the learned men who are preaching salvation, say that God created the heavens and the earth out of nothing? The reason is, that they are unlearned in the things of God, and have not the gift of the Holy Ghost; they account it blasphemy in any one to contradict their idea. If you tell them that God made the world out of something, they will call you a fool. But I am learned, and know more than all the world put together. The Holy Ghost does, anyhow, and He is within me, and comprehends more than all the world: and I will associate myself with Him.

now I ask all the learned men who hear me whe[the]^r. the learned me[n] who are preach[in]^g. Sal^n. say that God created the Heavens & the Earth out of nothing & the reason is that they are unlearned & I know more than all the world put tog^r. & if the H. G. in me com[prehends]: more than all the world I will associate with it—²⁸⁸

---

281. The entry "wod" most likely should read "word."
282. The entry "~~oot~~" mostly likely should read "~~but~~."
283. Discourse, 7 April 1844, reported by Thomas Bullock, *JSP, D14*, 321.
284. Discourse, 7 April 1844, *JSP, J3*, 218. See also *JSP, D14*, 334 (Willard Richards).
285. Discourse, 7 April 1844, reported by William Clayton, *JSP, D14*, 331.
286. Discourse, 7 April 1844, *JSP, J3*, 218. See also *JSP, D14*, 334 (Willard Richards).
287. Discourse, 7 April 1844, reported by William Clayton, *JSP, D14*, 331.
288. Discourse, 7 April 1844, reported by Thomas Bullock, *JSP, D14*, 321.

Meaning of the Word Create

You ask the learned doctors why they say the world was made out of nothing; and they will answer, "Doesn't the Bible say He created the world?" And they infer, from the word create, that it must have been made out of nothing. Now, the word create came from the baurau which does not mean to create out of nothing; it means to organize; the same as a man would organize materials and build a ship.[289] Hence, we [p.351] infer that God had materi-

you ask ~~they~~ them why they say dont the bible say he created the world & they infer that it must be out of nothing The word create came from the word Barau— dont mean so— it means to organize— same as a man would use to build a ship— hence we infer that God had materials to organize from— chaos— chaotic matter— element had an existence from the time he had. The pure pure principles of element are principles that never can be de-

---

289. The original *TPJS* footnote reads:

The view of the Prophet on this subject of creation is abundantly sustained by men of learning subsequent to his time. The Rev. Baden Powell, of Oxford University, for instance, writing for Kitto's *Cyclopaedia of Biblical Literature*, says: "The meaning of this word (create) has been commonly associated with the idea of 'making out of nothing.' But when we come to inquire more precisely into the subject, we can of course satisfy ourselves as to the meaning only from an examination of the original phrase." The learned professor then proceeds to say that three distinct Hebrew verbs are in different places employed with reference to the same divine act, and may be translated, respectively, "create," "make," "form or fashion." "Now," continues the Professor, "though each of these has its shade of distinction, yet the best critics understand them as so nearly synonymous that, at least in regard to the idea of making out of nothing, little or no foundation for that doctrine can be obtained from the first of these words." And, of course, if no foundation for the doctrine can be obtained from the first of these words—viz., the verb translated "create," then the chances are still less for there being any foundation for the doctrine of creation from nothing in the verb translated, "made," "formed," or "fashioned."

Professor Powell further says: "The idea of 'creation,' as meaning absolutely 'making out of nothing,' or calling into existence that which did not exist before, in the strictest sense of the term, is not a doctrine of scripture; but it has been held by many on the grounds of natural theology, as enhancing the ideas we form of the divine power, and more especially since the contrary must imply the belief in the eternity and self-existence of matter."

Dr. William Smith's great dictionary of the Bible (Hackett edition, 1894) has no article on the term "create" or "creation," but in the article "earth" we have reference to the subject, and really an implied explanation as to why this work contains no treatise on "create" or "creation." "The act of creation itself, as recorded in the first chapter of Genesis, is a subject beyond and above the experience of man; human language, derived, as it originally was, from the sensible and material world, fails to find an adequate term to describe the act; for our word 'create' and the Hebrew bara, though most appropriate to express the idea of an original creation, are yet applicable and must necessarily be applicable to other modes of creation; nor does the addition of such expressions as 'out of things that were not,' or 'not from things which appear,' contribute much to the force of the declaration. The absence of a term which shall describe exclusively an original creation is a necessary infirmity of language; as the events occurred but once, the corresponding term must, in order to be adequate, have been coined for the occasion and reserved for it alone, which would have been impossible."

The philosophers with equal emphasis sustain the contention of the Prophet. Herbert Spencer, in his *First Principles*, (1860), said:

"There was once universally current, a notion that things could vanish into absolute nothing, or arise out of absolute nothing. * * * The current theology, in its teachings respecting the beginning

als to organize the world out of chaos—chaotic matter, which is element, and in which dwells all the glory. Element had an existence from the time he had. The pure principles of element are principles which can never be [p.352] destroyed; they may be organized and re-organized, but not destroyed. They had no beginning, and can have no end.[290]

stroyed— they may be organized— and reorganized— but not destroyed.[291]

The Immortal Spirit

I have another subject to dwell upon, which is calculated to exalt man; but it is impossible for me to say much on this subject. I shall therefore just touch upon it, for time will not permit me to say all. It is associated with the subject of the resurrection of the dead,— namely, the soul—the mind of man—the im-

I have ano^r to dwell on & it is impossible for me to say much but to touch upon them— for time will not permit me to say all— so I must come to the res[urrectio]^n of the dead— the soul the im^m [immortal] Spirit oh <man says> God created in the begin^g the very idea lestens man in my idea— I dont bel[ieve] the

---

and end of the world, is clearly pervaded by it. * * * The gradual accumulation of experiences, has tended slowly to reverse this conviction; until now, the doctrine that matter is indestructible has become a commonplace. All the apparent proofs that something can come of nothing, a wider knowledge has one by one cancelled. The comet that is suddenly discovered in the heavens and nightly waxes larger, is proved not to be a newly-created body, but a body that was until lately beyond the range of vision. The cloud which in the course of a few minutes forms in the sky, consists not of substance that has begun to be, but of substance that previously existed in a more diffused and transparent form. And similarly with a crystal or precipitate in relation to the fluid depositing it. Conversely, the seeming annihilation of matter turn out, on closer observation, to be only changes of state. It is found that the evaporated water, though it has become invisible, may be brought by condensation to its original shape. The discharged fowling-piece gives evidence that though the gunpowder has disappeared, there have appeared in place of it certain gases which, in assuming a larger volume, have caused the explosion."

Fiske follows Spencer, of course, and in his *Cosmic Philosophy* sums up the matter in these words. "It is now unconceivable that a particle of matter should either come into existence, or lapse into non-existence."

Robert Kennedy Duncan (1905), in his *New Knowledge* says: "Governing matter in all its varied forms, there is one great fundamental law which up to this time has been ironclad in its character. This law, known as the law of the conservation of mass, states that no particle of matter, however small, may be created or destroyed. All the king's horses and all the king's men cannot destroy a pin's head. We may smash that pin's head, dissolve it in acid, burn it in the electric furnace, employ, in a word, every annihilating agency, and yet that pin's head persists in being. Again, it is as uncreatable as it is indestructible. In other words, we cannot create something out of nothing. The material must be furnished for every existent article. The sum of matter in the universe is x pounds,—and, while it may be carried through a myriad of forms, when all is said and done, it is just—x pounds.[']—Note by Elder B. H. Roberts.

290. The original *TPJS* footnote reads: "'The elements are eternal, and spirit and element inseparably connected receive a fullness of joy. * * * The elements are the tabernacle of God; yea, man is the tabernacle of God, even temples.' (D&C Sec. 93:33–35.)"

291. Discourse, 7 April 1844, reported by William Clayton, *JSP, D14*, 331.

mortal spirit.²⁹² Where did it come from? All learned men and doctors of divinity say that God created it in the beginning; but it is not so: the very idea lessens man in my estimation. I do not believe the doctrine; I know better. Hear it, all ye ends of the world; for God has told me so; and if you don't believe me, it will not make the truth without effect. I will make a man appear a fool before I get through; if he does not believe it. I am going to tell of things more noble.

We say that God himself is a self-existent being. Who told you so? It is correct enough; but how did it get into you heads? Who told you that man did not exist in like manner upon the same principles? Man does exist upon the same principles. God made a tabernacle and put a spirit into it, and **[p.353]** it became a living soul. (Refers to the old Bible.) How does it read in the Hebrew? It does not say in the Hebrew that God created the spirit of man. It says "God made man out of the earth and put into him Adam's spirit, and so became a living body."

The mind or the intelligence which man possesses is co-equal²⁹⁶ with God himself. I know

doct[rine]: hear it all ye Ends of the World for God has told me so I am going to tell of things more noble—²⁹³ they say God created it in the beginning— the idea lessens man in my estimation. Dont believe the doctrine— know better— God told me so. Make a man appear a fool before he gets through if he dont believe it.

We say that God was selfexistent— who told you so? its correct enough but how did it get into your heads— who told you that man did not exist upon the same principle (— refer to the bible) dont say so in the old Hebrew— God made man out of the earth and put into him his spirit and then it became a living body.²⁹⁴ (refers to the old Bible,) how does it read in the Hebrew? It dont say so in the Hebrew, it says God made man out of the earth, and put into him Adam's spirit, and so became a living body. ²⁹⁵

The mind of man— the intelligent part is coequal with God himself I know that my

---

292. The original *TPJS* footnote reads: "It appears to be very clear that the Prophet had in mind the intelligence, when he said 'the soul—the mind of man—the immortal spirit,' was not created or made, and he did not have reference to the spirit as a begotten child of God. It was the doctrine of the Prophet, and is of the Church, that the spirits of men are begotten sons and daughters of God. See the official statement of the First Presidency and the Council of the Twelve as published in the *Improvement Era*, August, 1916, under the caption, *The Father and The Son*. The passage in the Doctrine and Covenants on which this doctrine is based is found in Sec. 93:29–30, and is as follows: 'Man was in the beginning with God. Intelligence, or the light of truth, was not created or made, neither indeed can be.' See also the statements in following paragraphs."

293. Discourse, 7 April 1844, reported by Thomas Bullock, *JSP, D14*, 321–22.

294. Discourse, 7 April 1844, reported by William Clayton, *JSP, D14*, 331.

295. *T&S* 5, no. 15 (15 August 1844): 615.

296. The original *TPJS* footnote reads: "Undoubtedly the proper word here would be 'co-eternal,' not 'co-equal.' This illustrates the imperfection of the report made of the sermon. For surely the mind of man is not co-equal with God except in the matter of its eternity. It is the direct statement in the Book of Abraham—accepted by the Church as scripture—that there are differences in the intelligences that exist, that some are more intelligent than others; and that God is 'more intelligent than them all' (Book of Abraham, chap. 3). I believe that this means more than that God is more intelligent than any other one of the intelligences. It means that he is more intelligent than all of the other intelligences combined. His intelligence is greater than that of the mass, and that has led me to say in the second Year Book of the Seventies:—'It is this fact doubtless which makes this One, 'more intelligent than them all,' God. He

that my testimony is true; hence, when I talk to these mourners, what have they lost? Their relatives and friends are only separated from their bodies for a short season: their spirits which existed with God have left the tabernacle of clay only for a little moment, as it were; and they now exist in a place where they converse together the same as we do on the earth.

I am dwelling on the immortality of the spirit of man. Is it logical to say that the intelligence of spirits is immortal, and yet that it had a beginning? The intelligence of spirits had not beginning, neither will it have an end. That is good logic. That which has a beginning may have an end. There never was a time when there were not spirits; for they are co-equal [co-eternal] with our Father in heaven.

[p.354] I want to reason more on the spirit of man; for I am dwelling on the body and spirit of man—on the subject of the dead. I take my ring from my finger and liken it unto the mind of man—the immortal part, because it has no beginning. Suppose you cut it in two; then it has a beginning and an end; but join it again, and it continues one eternal round. So with the spirit of man. As the Lord liveth, if it had a beginning, it will have an end. All the fools and learned and wise men from the beginning of creation, who say that the spirit of man had a beginning, prove that it must have

testimony is true. hence when I talk to these mourners what have they lost— they are only separated from their bodies for a short season. but their spirit existed coequal with God and they now exist in a place where ~~he~~ they converse together as much as we do on the earth.[297]

I am dwelling on the immutibility of the spirit of man. is it logic to say the spirit of man had a begining & yet had no end. it does not have a begining or end.[298]

good logic— illustrated by his ring.[299]

their spirit existed coequal with God[300]

I want to reason more on the Spirit of Man for I am dwelling on the body of man on the subj[t.] of the dead— ~~the Sp of Man~~ I take my ring from my finger & liken it unto the mind of man the im[morta]$^{l.}$ Sp[irit]. Bec[ause] it has no begin[g.] suppose you cut it into but as the L[or]$^{d.}$ lives there wo$^{d.}$ be an end all the fools & wise men from the begin^{g} of creation who say that man had begin— they must have an end & then the doc[trine] of annihilit$^{n.}$ [annihilation] wo$^{d.}$ be true— but if I am right I mi$^{t.}$ with boldness proclaim from the house top that God never had power to create the Sp

---

is the All-Wise One! The All-Powerful One! What he tells other Intelligences to do must be precisely the wisest, fittest thing that they could anywhere or anyhow learn—the thing which it will always behoove them, with right loyal thankfulness, and nothing doubting, to do. There goes with this, too, the thought that this All-Wise One will be the Unselfish One, the All-Loving One, the One who desires that which is highest, and best; not for himself alone, but for all: and that will be best for him too. His glory, his power, his joy will be enhanced by the uplifting of all, by enlarging them; by increasing their joy, power, and glory. And because this All Intelligent One is all this, and does all this, the other Intelligences worship him, submit their judgments and their will to his judgment and his will. He knows, and can do that which is best; and this submission of the mind to the Most Intelligent, Wisest—wiser than all—is worship. This is the whole meaning of the doctrine and the life of the Christ expressed in—'Father, not my will but Thy will, be done.'—Note by Elder B. H. Roberts."

297. Discourse, 7 April 1844, reported by William Clayton, *JSP, D14*, 331.
298. Discourse, 7 April 1844, reported by Wilford Woodruff, *WWJ*, 1:630. See also *JSP, D14*, 339.
299. Discourse, 7 April 1844, reported by William Clayton, *JSP, D14*, 332.
300. Discourse, 7 April 1844, reported by William Clayton, *JSP, D14*, 331.

an end; and if that doctrine is true, then the doctrine of annihilation would be true. But if I am right, I might with boldness proclaim from the house-tops that God never had the power to create the spirit of man at all. God himself could not create himself.

of Man at all— ~~it is no~~ God himself co$^{d.}$ not create himself

Intelligence is eternal and exists upon a self-existent principle. It is a spirit[301] from age to age, and there is no creation about it. All the minds and spirits that God ever sent into the world are susceptible of enlargement.

intelligence is self existent it is a Sp from age to end & there is no creat^n ab^t it[302]

all mi[n]ds & spir[i]t God ever sent into the wo[r]ld are susceptible of enlargeme[n]t.—[303]

The Power to Advance in Knowledge

The first principles of man are self-existent with God. God himself, finding he was in the midst of spirits and glory, because he was more intelligent, saw proper to institute laws whereby the rest could have a privilege to advance like himself. The relationship we have with God places us in a situation to advance in knowledge. He has power to institute laws to instruct the weaker intelligences, that they may be exalted with himself, so that they might have one glory upon another, and all that knowledge, power, glory, and intelligence, which is requisite in order to save them in the world of spirits.[308]

the first principles of Man are self exist with God— that God himself finds himself in the midst of Sp[irits] & bec he saw proper to institute laws[304] whereby the rest could have a privilege to advance like himself.[305]

the relationship we have with God places us in a situation to advance in knowledge. God has power to institute laws to instruct the weaker intelligences that they may be exhalted with himself[.][306] that they mi^t have one glory upon another in all that knowledge power & glory & so took in hand to save the world of Sp:[307]

---

301. The original *TPJS* footnote reads: "'A spirit from age to age'—not 'spirit from age to age'; but 'a spirit,' that is, an entity, a person, an individual. This paragraph in the Prophet's remarks may well be taken as an interpretation of D&C, Sec. 93:29.—Note by Elder B. H. Roberts."
302. Discourse, 7 April 1844, reported by Thomas Bullock, *JSP, D14*, 322.
303. Discourse, 7 April 1844, in *JSP, J3*, 220. See also *JSP, D14*, 335.
304. Discourse, 7 April 1844, reported by Thomas Bullock, *JSP, D14*, 322–23.
305. Discourse, 7 April 1844, reported by William Clayton, *JSP, D14*, 332.
306. Discourse, 7 April 1844, reported by Wilford Woodruff, *WWJ*, 1:630. See also *JSP, D14*, 339.
307. Discourse, 7 April 1844, reported by Thomas Bullock, *JSP, D14*, 323.
308. The original *TPJS* footnote reads: "'Behold this is my work and my glory—to bring to pass the immortality and eternal life of man.'—(The Lord to Moses, Book of Moses, chap. 1;39; Pearl of Great Price)—that is, 'to bring to pass the immortality and eternal life of man,' as man. The passage has reference doubtless to man as composed of spirit and body—a proper 'soul' (see D&C Sec. 88:15–16)—'For the spirit and the body is the soul of man; and the resurrection of the dead is the redemption of the soul.' In other words, the 'work' and the 'glory' of God are achieved in bringing to pass the 'immortality and eternal life of man,' as man, in the eternal union of the spirit and body of man through the resurrection through the redemption of the soul. This brings into eternal union 'spirit and element' declared by the word of God to be essential to a fulness of joy—'The elements are eternal, and spirit

[p.355] This is good doctrine. It tastes good. I can taste the principles of eternal life, and so can you. They are given to my by the revelations of Jesus Christ; and I know that when I tell you these words of eternal life as they are given to me, you taste them, and I know that you believe them. You say honey is sweet, and so do I. I can also taste the spirit of eternal life. I know it is good; and when I tell you of these things which were given my by inspiration of the Holy Spirit, you are bound to receive them as sweet, and rejoice more and more.

this is good d doctrin. it taste good. I can taste the principles of eternal life. so can you. they are given to me by the revelations of Jesus Christ and I know you believe it.[309]

you say honey is Sweet & so do I. I can also taste the Sp of Eternal life I know it is good & when I tell you— of these things that we[r]e given me by Insp[iration] of the H S. you are bound to rece[ive] it as sweet & I rej[oice] more & more—[310]

The Relation of Man to God

I want to talk more of the relation of man to God. I will open your eyes in relation to your dead. All things whatsoever God in his infinite wisdom has seen fit and proper to reveal to us, while we are dwelling in mortality, in regard to our mortal bodies, are revealed to us in the abstract, and independent of affinity of this mortal tabernacle, but are revealed to our spirits precisely as though we had no bodies at all; and those revelations which will save our spirits will save our bodies. God reveals them to us in view of no eternal dissolution of the body, or tabernacle. Hence the responsibility, the awful responsibility, that rests upon us in relation to our dead; for all the spirits who have not obeyed the Gospel in the flesh must either obey it in the spirit or be damned. Solemn thought!—dreadful thought! Is there nothing to be done?—no preparation—no salvation for our fathers and friends who have died without having had the opportunity to

Mans rel[ation] to God &c s I will open your eyes in rel to your dead all things which God of his inf[inite] reason has seen fit to reveal to us in our mortal state in regard to our mortal bodies are rev[eale]d. to us[311] in the abstract & independant of affinity of this mo[r]tal tabernacle— but they are revealed as though we had no bodies at all— tho revealed to our spirits & those revelations must of necessity save our spirits with them. Hence the responsibility— the awful res. that rest upon us in relations to our dead— for all spirits who have not obeyed the gospel in the flesh must obey the gospel or be damned.[312]

solemn tho[t.] dreadful tho[t.] is there nothing to be done for those who have gone before us with[t.] obey[in]g the decrees of God wo[d.] to God that I had 40 days & nights— to tell

---

and element, inseparably connected, receive a fulness of joy; and when separated man cannot receive a fulness of joy' (D&C, Sec. 93). Also, 'Adam fell that men might be: and men are that they might have joy' (2 Nephi 2:25). Indeed, the whole purpose of God in bringing to pass the earth life of man is to inure to the welfare and enlargement of man as urged in the teaching of the Prophet in the paragraph above. God affects man only to his advantage. See also Seventy's Year Book No. 2, Lesson 2, note 6.— Note by Elder B. H. Roberts."

309. Discourse, 7 April 1844, reported by Wilford Woodruff, *WWJ*, 1:630. See also *JSP, D14*, 339.
310. Discourse, 7 April 1844, reported by Thomas Bullock, *JSP, D14*, 323.
311. Discourse, 7 April 1844, reported by Thomas Bullock, *JSP, D14*, 323.
312. Discourse, 7 April 1844, reported by William Clayton, *JSP, D14*, 332.
313. Discourse, 7 April 1844, reported by Thomas Bullock, *JSP, D14*, 323.

obey the decrees of the Son of Man? Would to God that I had forty days and nights in which to tell you all! I would let you know that I am not a "fallen prophet."[314]

you all to let you know I am not a fal[le]n prop[het]—[313]

Our Greatest Responsibility

[p.356] What promises are made in relation to the subject of the salvation of the dead? and what kind of characters are those who can be saved, although their bodies are mouldering and decaying in the grave? When his commandments teach us, it is in view of eternity; for we are looked upon by God as though we were in eternity. God dwells in eternity, and does not view things as we do.

what promises are made,[315]

what kind of beings can be saved although their bodies are mouldering in the dust. Whe[n] his commandments touch us it is in view of eternity.[316]

we are looked upon by God as though we were in Eternity—[317]

The greatest responsibility in this world that God has laid upon us is to seek after our dead. The Apostle says, "They without us cannot be made perfect;" (Hebrews 11:40) for it is necessary that the sealing power should be in our hands to seal our children and our dead for the fulness of the dispensation of times— a dispensation to meet the promises made by Jesus Christ before the foundation of the world for the salvation of man.

the greatest responsibility lade open us in this life, is in relation to our dead[.] Paul <said we> cannot be made perfect without us. for it is necessary that the seals are in our hands to seal our Children & our dead for the fulness of the dispensation of times, A dispensation to meet the promises made by Jesus Christ befor[e] the foundation of the world for the salvation of man.[318]

Now, I will speak of them. I will meet Paul half way. I say to you, Paul, you cannot be perfect without us. It is necessary that those who are going before and those who come after us should have salvation in common with us; and thus hath God made it obligatory upon

now I am speaking of them I say to you Paul, you cant be perfect with[t] us.— those that are gone before & those who came after must be made perfect— & God has made it obligatory to man— God said he shall send Elijah &c[319]

---

314. The original *TPJS* footnote reads: "Accusations were repeatedly being made about this time that President Smith was a fallen prophet. But when the mighty doctrines that in this discourse he is setting forth are taken into account, and the spiritual power with which he is delivering them is reckoned with, no more complete refutation of his being a fallen prophet could be made. The Prophet lived his life in crescendo. From small beginnings, it rose in breadth and power as he neared its close. As a teacher he reached the climax of his career in this discourse. After it there was but one thing more he could do— seal his testimony with his blood. This he did less than three months later. Such is not the manner of life of false prophets.—Note by Elder B. H. Roberts."

315. Discourse, 7 April 1844, reported by Wilford Woodruff, *WWJ*, 1:630. See also *JSP, D14*, 339.
316. Discourse, 7 April 1844, reported by William Clayton, *JSP, D14*, 332.
317. Discourse, 7 April 1844, in *JSP, J3*, 220. See also *JSP, D14*, 335.
318. Discourse, 7 April 1844, reported by Wilford Woodruff, *WWJ*, 1:630. See also *JSP, D14*, 339.
319. Discourse, 7 April 1844, reported by Thomas Bullock, *JSP, D14*, 323.

A Salvation for Men

I have a declaration to make as to the provisions which God hath made to suit the conditions of man—made from before the foundation of the world. What has Jesus said? All sin, and all blasphemies, and every transgression, except one, that man can be guilty of, may be forgiven; and there is a salvation for all men, either in this world or the world to come, who have not committed the unpardonable sin, there being a pro[p.357]vision either in this world or the world of spirits. Hence God hath made a provision that every spirit in the eternal world can be ferreted out and saved unless he has committed that unpardonable sin which cannot be remitted to him either in this world or the world of spirits. God has wrought out a salvation for all men, unless they have committed a certain sin; and every man who has a friend in the eternal world can save him, unless he has committed the unpardonable sin. And so you can see how far you can be a savior.

I have a decla[ratio]n to make as to the prov[isio]n. which God made from before the found[atio]n. of the world. what has J. s$^{d.}$ all sins & all blas[phemies] every trans[gression]: that man may be guilty of there is a Sal$^{n.}$ for him or in the world to come—[320]

Hence God hath made a provision that ev[e]ry spirit can be ferreted out in that world that has not sin'd the upardnabl [unpardonable] sin. wether in this world or in the world of spirits. Every man who has a friend in the eternal world who hath not committed the ~~eternal sin~~ unpardonable sin you can save him[321] God has wro[ugh]$^{t.}$ out sal$^{n.}$ for all men unless they have com$^{d.}$ a cert$^{n.}$ sin a friend who has got a friend in the world can save him unless he has com$^{d.}$ the unpard[onable] sin & so you can see how far you can be Savior[322]

The Unpardonable Sin

A man cannot commit the unpardonable sin after the dissolution of the body, and there is a way possible for escape. Knowledge saves a man; and in the world of spirits no man can be exalted but by knowledge. So long as a man will not give heed to the commandments, he must abide without salvation. If a man has

A man cannot commit the unpardonable sin after the dissoluti[o]n of the body there is a way for his escape knowledge saves a man and in the world of spirits a man cant be exalted but by his knowledge. So long as a man will not give heed to the commandme[n]ts he must abide without salvation[323]

---

320. Discourse, 7 April 1844, reported by Thomas Bullock, *JSP, D14*, 323.
321. Discourse, 7 April 1844, reported by William Clayton, *JSP, D14*, 332.
322. Discourse, 7 April 1844, reported by Thomas Bullock, *JSP, D14*, 323–24.
323. Discourse, 7 April 1844, reported by William Clayton, *JSP, D14*, 332–33.

knowledge, he can be saved; although, if he has been guilty of great sins, he will be punished for them. But when he consents to obey the Gospel, whether here or in the world of spirits, he is saved.

A man is his own tormenter and his own condemner. Hence the saying, They shall go into the lake that burns with fire and brimstone. The torment of disappointment in the mind of man is as exquisite as a lake burning with fire and brimstone. I say, so is the torment of man.

I know the Scriptures and understand them. I said, no man can commit the unpardonable sin after the dissolution of the body, nor in this life, until he receives the Holy Ghost but they must do it in this world. Hence the salvation of Jesus Christ was wrought out for all men, in order to triumph over the devil; for if it did not catch him in one place, it would in another; for he stood up as a Savior. All will suffer until they obey Christ himself.

The contention in heaven was—Jesus said there would be certain souls that would not be saved; and the devil said he could save them all, and laid his plans before the grand council, who gave their vote in favor of Jesus Christ. So the devil rose up in rebellion against God, and was cast down, with all who put up their heads for him. (Book of Moses—Pearl of Great Price, Chap. 4:1-4; Book of Abraham, Chap. 3:23-28.)

If a man has knowledge he can be saved. if he has been guilty of great sins he is punished for it. when he Consents to obey the gospel whether, Alive or dead, he is saved,[324]

A man is his own torment hence the saying they shall go into the lake that burns with fire &c or as exquisite as a lake &c so is the torment of a man—[325]

I know the Scriptures I understand them— no man can commit the unpardonable sin after the diss$^{n.}$ of the body but they must do it in this world—[326] untill He receives the Holy Ghost.[327] hence the Sal$^{n.}$ of J. C was wrought out for all men to triumph over the devil—[328] if it did not catch him in one place it would another—[329] All will suffer untill they obey Christ himself.[330]

The contenti[o]n in heaven was Jesus said there were certain men would not be saved the devil said he could save them. he rebelled against God and was thrust down.[331]

& all who put up their heads for him[332]

---

324. Discourse, 7 April 1844, reported by Wilford Woodruff, *WWJ*, 1;630.. See also *JSP, D14*, 339
325. Discourse, 7 April 1844, reported by William Clayton, *JSP, D14*, 333.
326. Discourse, 7 April 1844, reported by Thomas Bullock, *JSP, D14*, 324.
327. Discourse, 7 April 1844, reported by Wilford Woodruff, *WWJ*, 1;630. See also *JSP, D14*, 340.
328. Discourse, 7 April 1844, reported by Thomas Bullock, *JSP, D14*, 324.
329. Discourse, 7 April 1844, reported by William Clayton, *JSP, D14*, 333.
330. Discourse, 7 April 1844, reported by Wilford Woodruff, *WWJ*, 1;630. See also *JSP, D14*, 340.
331. Discourse, 7 April 1844, reported by William Clayton, *JSP, D14*, 333.
332. Discourse, 7 April 1844, reported by Thomas Bullock, *JSP, D14*, 324.

The Forgiveness of Sins

[p.358] All sins shall be forgiven, except the sin against the Holy Ghost; for Jesus will save all except the sons of perdition. What must a man do to commit the unpardonable sin? He must receive the Holy Ghost, have the heavens opened unto him, and know God, and then sin against Him. After a man has sinned against the Holy Ghost, there is no repentance for him.[333] He has got to say that the sun does not shine while he sees it; he has got to deny Jesus Christ when the heavens have been opened unto him, and to deny the plan of salvation with his eyes open to the truth of it; and from that time he begins to be an enemy. This is the case with many apostates of the Church of Jesus Christ of Latter-day Saints.

When a man begins to be an enemy to this work, he hunts me, he seeks to kill me, and never ceases to thirst for my blood. He gets the spirit of the devil—the same spirit that they had who crucified the Lord of Life—the same spirit that sins against the Holy Ghost. You cannot save such persons; you cannot bring them to repentance; they make open war, like the devil, and awful is the consequence.

I advise all of you to be careful what you do, or you may by-and-by find out that you have been deceived. Stay yourselves; do not give

all sin shall be forgiven except the sin ag.ᵗ the H. G.[334] Jesus Christ will save all except the sons of perdition. what must a man do to commit the unpardonable sin. they must receive the Holy Ghost, have the heavens opened unto them, & know God, & then sin against him.[335] After a man has sinned the sin against the H G. there is no repentance for him.[336] he has got to say that the Sun does not shine while he sees it he has got to deny J. C. when the heavens are open to him—[337] Got to de[n]y th[e] plan of Salvati[o]n. &c— with his eyes open.—[338] & from that time they begin to be enenmies like many of the apostates of The Church of J. C of L. D. S [Jesus Christ of Latter-day Saints]—

when a man begins to be an enemy he hunts him[339] they seek to kill me they thirst for my blood they never cease— he has got the same spirit that crucified Jesus[340] they have got the same spirit the devil had. you cannot save them. they make open war like the devil.[341]

awful is the consequence

Advise all to be careful what they do— you may by and by find out that you have been deceived[342] Stay all that hear, dont make any

---

333. The original *TPJS* footnote reads: "'For it is impossible for those who were once enlightened, and have tasted of the heavenly gift, and were made partakers of the Holy Ghost, and have tasted the good word of God, and the powers of the world to come, if they shall fall away, to renew them again unto repentance; seeing they crucify to themselves the Son of God afresh, and put him to an open shame' (Heb. 6:4–6). Those who sin against the light and knowledge of the Holy Ghost may be said to crucify more than the body of our Lord, they crucify the Spirit."
334. Discourse, 7 April 1844, reported by Thomas Bullock, *JSP, D14*, 324.
335. Discourse, 7 April 1844, reported by Wilford Woodruff, *WWJ*, 1:630. See also *JSP, D14*, 340.
336. Discourse, 7 April 1844, reported by William Clayton, *JSP, D14*, 333.
337. Discourse, 7 April 1844, reported by Thomas Bullock, *JSP, D14*, 324.
338. Discourse, 7 April 1844, in *JSP, J3*, 221. See also *JSP, D14*, 335.
339. Discourse, 7 April 1844, reported by Thomas Bullock, *JSP, D14*, 324.
340. Discourse, 7 April 1844, reported by William Clayton, *JSP, D14*, 333.
341. Discourse, 7 April 1844, reported by Wilford Woodruff, *WWJ*, 1:630. See also *JSP, D14*, 340.
342. Discourse, 7 April 1844, reported by William Clayton, *JSP, D14*, 333.

way; don't make any hasty moves, you may be saved. If a spirit of bitterness is in you, don't be in haste. You may say, that man is a sinner. Well, if he repents, he shall be forgiven. Be cautious: await. When you find a spirit that wants bloodshed—murder, the same is not of God, but is of the devil. Out of the abundance of the heart of man the mouth speaketh.

hasty mooves[.] you may be saved. if a spirit of Bitterness is in you, dont be in haste. Say you that man is a sinner. well if he repents he shall be forgiven.[343]

be cautious— await— when you find a Sp. wants bloodshed murder same is not of God but is of the devil out of the abundance of the heart man speaks—[344]

"In My Father's House"

The best men bring forth the best works. The man who tells you words of life is the man who can save you. I warn you against all evil characters who sin against the Holy Ghost; **[p.359]** for there is no redemption for them in this world nor in the world to come.

best man brings forth best works.[345]
the man that tells you words of life is the man that can save you— I warn you ag^t all evil characters <who sin ag^t. H. G.> for there is no redemp[tio]^n. for them in this world nor in the world to come[346]

I could go back and trace every subject of interest concerning the relationship of man to God, if I had time. I can enter into the mysteries; I can enter largely into the eternal worlds; for Jesus said, "In my Father's house are many mansions; if it were not so, I would have told you. I go to prepare a place for you" (John 14:2). Paul says, "There is one glory of the sun, and another glory of the moon, and another glory of the stars; for one star differeth from another star in glory. So also is the resurrection of the dead" (1 Cor. 15:41). What have we to console us in relation to the dead? We have reason to have the greatest hope and consolations for our dead of any people on the earth; for we have seen them walk worthily in our midst, and seen them sink asleep in the arms of Jesus; and those who have died in the faith are now in the celestial kingdom of God. And hence is the glory of the sun.

I could go back and trace evry subject of interest concerning the relationship of man to God if i had time.[347] I can enter into the mysteries— I can enter largely into the eternal worlds— for J. s^d. ~~where my~~ In my Fa^rs. mansion there are many mansions &c there is one glory of the moon Sun & Stars &c[348]

what have we to console us in relation to our dead. we have the greatest hope in relation to our dead of any people on earth[.] we have seen them walk worthy on earth and[349] & sink asleep in the arms of J.[350] and those who have died in the faith are now in the selestial [Celestial] kingdom of God.[351] & hence is the glory of the Sun—[352]

---

343. Discourse, 7 April 1844, reported by Wilford Woodruff, *WWJ*, 1:630. See also *JSP, D14*, 340.
344. Discourse, 7 April 1844, reported by Thomas Bullock, *JSP, D14*, 325.
345. Discourse, 7 April 1844, in *JSP, J3*, 221. See also *JSP, D14*, 335.
346. Discourse, 7 April 1844, reported by Thomas Bullock, *JSP, D14*, 325.
347. Discourse, 7 April 1844, reported by Wilford Woodruff, *WWJ*, 1:630. See also *JSP, D14*, 340.
348. Discourse, 7 April 1844, reported by Thomas Bullock, *JSP, D14*, 325.
349. Discourse, 7 April 1844, reported by Wilford Woodruff, *WWJ*, 1:630. See also *JSP, D14*, 340.
350. Discourse, 7 April 1844, reported by Thomas Bullock, *JSP, D14*, 325.
351. Discourse, 7 April 1844, reported by Wilford Woodruff, *WWJ*, 1:630. See also *JSP, D14*, 340.
352. Discourse, 7 April 1844, reported by Thomas Bullock, *JSP, D14*, 325.

Righteous Mourners Rejoice

You mourners have occasion to rejoice, speaking of the death of Elder King Follett; for your husband and father is gone to wait until the resurrection of the dead—until the perfection of the remainder; for at the resurrection your friend will rise in perfect felicity and go to celestial glory, while many must wait myriads of years before they can receive the like blessings; and your expectations and hopes are far above what man can conceive; for why has God revealed it to us?

I am authorized to say, by the authority of the Holy Ghost, that you have no occasion to fear; for he is gone to the home of the just. Don't mourn, don't weep. I know it by the testimony of the Holy Ghost that is within me; and you may wait for your friends to come forth to meet you in the morn of the celestial world.

Rejoice, O Israel! Your friends who have been murdered for the truth's sake in the persecutions shall triumph gloriously in the celestial world, while their murderers shall welter for ages in torment, even until they shall have paid the uttermost farthing. I say this for the benefit of strangers.

I have a father, brothers, children, and friends who have gone to a world of spirits. They are only absent for a moment. They are in the spirit, and we shall soon meet again. The time **[p.360]** will soon arrive when the trumpet shall sound. When we depart, we

you mourners have occ[asio]^n to rejoice for your husband has gone to wait until the res^n.[353] the perfection.— of the reunion.— the resurrecti[o]n of your frie[n]d in felicity[354] to go to the celestial glory, while their are many who[355] mu[s]t wait myr[i]ads of years befor they can receive the like blessi[n]gs.—[356] & your exp[ectatio]^n & hope are far above what man can conceive— for why God has rev^d to us—

I am auth^d to say by the auth^y of the H. G. that you have no occas^n to fear for he is gone to the home of the just— dont mourn dont weep— I know it by the test[imony] of the H. G. that is within me—[357] that you may wait for your friends to come forth to meet you in eternity in the morn of the celestial world.[358]

rejoice O Israel— your friends shall triumph gloriously—[359] those Saints who have been murdered in the persecution shall triumph in the Celestial world while their murderers shall dwell in torment untill they pay the utmost farthing.[360] I say for the benefit of strangers

I have a Fa^r Bro^r Friends who are gone to a world of Sp— they are absent for a mom[en]^t— they are in the Sp.[361]

the time will soon be gone, the trump will soon be blown.[362]

---

353. Discourse, 7 April 1844, reported by Thomas Bullock, *JSP, D14*, 325.
354. Discourse, 7 April 1844, in *JSP, J3*, 221. See also *JSP, D14*, 335.
355. Discourse, 7 April 1844, reported by Wilford Woodruff, *WWJ*, 1:630. See also *JSP, D14*, 340.
356. Discourse, 7 April 1844, in *JSP, J3*, 221. See also *JSP, D14*, 335.
357. Discourse, 7 April 1844, reported by Thomas Bullock, *JSP, D14*, 325.
358. Discourse, 7 April 1844, reported by Wilford Woodruff, *WWJ*, 1:631. See also *JSP, D14*, 340.
359. Discourse, 7 April 1844, reported by Thomas Bullock, *JSP, D14*, 325.
360. Discourse, 7 April 1844, reported by Wilford Woodruff, *WWJ*, 1:631. See also *JSP, D14*, 340.
361. Discourse, 7 April 1844, reported by Thomas Bullock, *JSP, D14*, 325.
362. Discourse, 7 April 1844, reported by Wilford Woodruff, *WWJ*, 1:631. See also *JSP, D14*, 340.

shall hail our mothers, fathers, friends, and all whom we love, who have fallen asleep in Jesus. There will be no fear of mobs, persecutions, or malicious lawsuits and arrests; but it will be an eternity of felicity.[363]

* * *

then shall we hail our Mo[the]ʳ· Faʳˢ· Friends & all no fear of mobs— &c but all an Eternity of felicity—

Mothers you shall have your Children for they shall have it— for their debt is paid there is no dam[natio]ⁿ awaits them for they are in the Spirits— as the Child dies so shall it rise from the de[a]d & be living in the burnᵍ· of God— it shall be the child as it was bef it died out of your arms children dwell & exercise power in the same form as they laid them down[364]

Shall mothrs have their Child[re]n? Yes. th[e]y shall have it with[o]ut price. redempt[io]n is paid possessing all the intelgen [intelligence] of a god. the child as it was before it died out of y[o]ur arm throne up[o]n thrones. Domin[ion] up[o]n domnins [dominions] just as you——[365]

A question[.] will Mothers have their Children in Eternity? yes, yes, you will have the Children, <But> as it falls so it will rise. It will never grow. It will be in its precise form as it fell in its mothers arms. Eternity is full of thrones upon which dwell thousands of Children reigning on thrones of glory not one cubit added to their Stature.[366]

Baptism

I will leave this subject here, and make a few remarks on the subject of baptism. The baptism of water, without the baptism of fire and

I will leave this subject here and make a few remarks upon Baptism.[367] the Bap[tism] of Water withᵗ· the B[aptism] of Fire & the

---

363. The original *TPJS* footnote reads: "The omitted paragraph indicated by the asterisks refers to the exaltation and power that will be wielded by children in the resurrection before attaining to the development of stature of men and women; but which developments will surely come to those who are raised from the dead as infants. It is quite evident that there was some imperfection in the report of the Prophet's remarks at this point, and hence the passage is omitted. Those who desire to investigate the matter more fully should consult the *Documentary History*, Vol. 4, pp. 556–7 and footnote. See also discourse of June 16, 1844, this volume."

364. Discourse, 7 April 1844, reported by Thomas Bullock, *JSP, D14*, 325.

365. Discourse, 7 April 1844, in *JSP, J3*, 221–22. See also *JSP, D14*, 335–36.

366. Discourse, 7 April 1844, reported by Wilford Woodruff, *WWJ*, 1:631. See also *JSP, D14*, 340.

367. Discourse, 7 April 1844, reported by Wilford Woodruff, *WWJ*, 1:631. See also *JSP, D14*, 340.

the Holy Ghost attending it, is of no use; they are necessarily and inseparably connected. An individual must be born of water and the Spirit in order to get into the kingdom of God. In the German, the text bears me out the same as the revelations which I have given and taught for the last fourteen years on that subject. I have the testimony to put in their teeth. My testimony has been true all the time. You will find it in the declaration of John the Baptist. (Reads from the German.) John says, "I baptize you with water, but when Jesus comes, who has the power (or keys), he shall administer the baptism of fire and the Holy Ghost." Where is now all the sectarian world? And if this testimony is true, they are all damned as clearly as anathema can do it. I know the text is true. I call upon all you Germans who know that it is true to say, Aye. (Loud shouts of "Aye.")

H G. att[endin]^g it are nec^{y368} Baptism of water fire & Holy Ghost. are insepa[r]ably— connected.—^{369} he must be born of W[ater] & Sp in order to get into the K of God— in the German text bears me out same as the rev^n which I have given for the 14 years— I have the test to put in their teeth that my test has been true all the time you will find it in the decla[ratio]n of John the Bap[tist] (reads from the German) John says I bap[tize] you with Water but when J comes who has the power he shall adm[inister] the bap of F & the H. G. G[rea]^t God now where is all the Sec^t [sectarian] world— & if this est [testimony] is true they are all d—d as clearly as any Anathama ever was— I know the text is true— I call upon all to say I— (shouts of I)

Alexander Campbell, how are you going to save people with water alone? For John said his baptism was good for nothing without the baptism of Jesus Christ. "Therefore, not leaving the principles of the doctrine of Christ, let us go on unto perfection; not laying again the foundation of repentance from dead works, and of faith toward God, of the doctrine of baptisms, and of laying on of hands, and of resurrection of the dead, and of eternal judgment. And this will we do, if God permit." (Heb. 6:1-3).

Alex[ander] Campbell— how are you going to save them with water— for John s^d his bap^m was nothing with^t the test bap of J. C.^{370} Leaving th[e] pincipls [principles] of doctrin of baptism &c—^{371}

[p.361] There is one God, one Father, one Jesus, one hope of our calling, one baptism.

* * *

Many talk of baptism not being essential to salvation; but this kind of teaching would lay the foundation of their damnation. I have the truth, and am at the defiance of the world to contradict me, if they can.

One God, Fa^r, Jesus, hope of, our Calling, one baptism—^{372}

Many talk of any baptism not being essential to salvation but this would lay the foundation of their damnation,^{373} I have the truth & I am at the defiance of the world to contradict

---

368. Discourse, 7 April 1844, reported by Thomas Bullock, *JSP, D14*, 325.
369. Discourse, 7 April 1844, in *JSP, J3*, 222. See also *JSP, D14*, 336.
370. Discourse, 7 April 1844, reported by Thomas Bullock, *JSP, D14*, 325–26.
371. Discourse, 7 April 1844, in *JSP, J3*, 222. See also *JSP, D14*, 336.
372. Discourse, 7 April 1844, reported by Thomas Bullock, *JSP, D14*, 326.
373. Discourse, 7 April 1844, reported by Wilford Woodruff, *WWJ*, 1:631. See also *JSP, D14*, 340.

I have now preached a little Latin, a little Hebrew, Greek, and German; and I have fulfilled all. I am not so big a fool as many have taken me to be. The Germans know that I read the German correctly.

I have preached Latin Hebrew Greek German & I have fulfilled all I am not so big a fool as many have taken me for— the Germans know that I read the German corect—[374]

A Call to Repentance

Hear it, all ye ends of the earth—all ye priests, all ye sinners, and all men. Repent! repent! Obey the Gospel. Turn to God; for your religion won't save you, and you will be damned. I do not say how long. There have been remarks made concerning all men being redeemed from hell; but I say that those who sin against the Holy Ghost cannot be forgiven in this world or in the world to come; they shall die the second death. Those who commit the unpardonable sin are doomed to Gnolom—to dwell in hell, worlds without end. As they concoct scenes of bloodshed in this world, so they shall rise to that resurrection which is as the lake of fire and brimstone. Some shall rise to the everlasting burnings of God; for God dwells in everlasting burnings, and some shall rise to the damnation of their own filthiness, which is as exquisite a torment as the lake of fire and brimstone.

hear it all ye Ends of the Earth— all ye Sinners Repent Repent turn to God for your rel[igio]n. wont save you & ye will be d^d but I do not say how along—[375]
There has also been remarks made concerning all men being redeemed from Hell, But I say that[376] those who Sin ag^t the H. G. cannot be forgiven in this world or in the world to come but they shall die the 2$^{nd.}$ death—[377] those who commit the unpdoabl [unpardonable] sin are doomd to Gnolom. without end.—[378] as they concoct scenes of bloodshed in this world so they shall rise to that resur^n which is as the lake of fire & brimstone— some shall rise to the everlasting burning of God [379] God dwells in everlasti[n]g burnings.——[380] some shall rise to the d^n of their own filthiness— same as the lake of fire & brimstone—

I have intended my remarks for all, both rich and poor, bond and free, great and small. I have no enmity against any man. I love you all; but I hate some of your deeds. I am your best friend, and if persons miss their mark it is their own fault. If I reprove a man, and he hates me, he is a fool; for I love all men, especially these my brethren and sisters.

I have int[ende]^d my remarks to all— to all rich & poor bond & free great & small I have no enmity agst any man— I love you all— I am their best friend & if persons miss their mark it is their own fault— if I reprove a man & he hate me he is a fool— for I love all men especially these my brethren & sisters—

I rejoice in hearing the testimony of my aged friends. You don't know me; you never knew my heart. No man knows my history. I cannot

I rejoice in hearing the test of my aged friend— you never knew my heart no man knows my hist[ory]— I can not do it I shall

---

374. Discourse, 7 April 1844, reported by Thomas Bullock, *JSP, D14*, 326
375. Discourse, 7 April 1844, reported by Thomas Bullock, *JSP, D14*, 326.
376. Discourse, 7 April 1844, reported by Wilford Woodruff, *WWJ*, 1:631. See also *JSP, D14*, 340.
377. Discourse, 7 April 1844, reported by Thomas Bullock, *JSP, D14*, 326.
378. Discourse, 7 April 1844, in *JSP, J3*, 222. See also *JSP, D14*, 336.
379. Discourse, 7 April 1844, reported by Thomas Bullock, *JSP, D14*, 326–27.
380. Discourse, 7 April 1844, in *JSP, J3*, 222. See also *JSP, D14*, 336.

tell it: I shall never undertake it. I don't blame any one for not believing my history. If I had not experienced what I have, I could not have believed it myself. I never did harm any man since I was born in the world. My voice is always for peace.

I cannot lie down until all my work is finished. I never [p.362] think any evil, nor do anything to the harm of my fellowman. When I am called by the trump of the archangel and weighed in the balance, you will all know me then. I add no more. God bless you all. Amen. (April 7, 1844.) T&S Aug. 15, 1844.

never undertake— if I had not experienced what I have I should not have known it myself— I never did harm any man since I have been born in the world— my voice is always for peace—

I cannot lie down until my work is finished— I never think evil nor think any thing to the harm of my fellow man— & when I am called at the trump & weighed in the balance you will know me then— I add no more God bless you [a]men—[381]

President Joseph Smith's Remarks—The Whole of America Zion—April Conference, 1844

President Joseph Smith said:—It is as impossible for me to continue the subject of yesterday as to raise the dead. My lungs are worn out. There is a time to all things, and I must wait. I will give it up, and leave the time to those who can make you hear, and I will continue the subject of my discourse some other time. I want to make a proclamation to the Elders. I wanted you to stay, in order that I might make this proclamation. You know very well that the Lord has led this Church by revelation. I have another revelation in relation

Various Journal Entries of Remarks Made by Joseph Smith[382]

President J Smith arose and said it is impossible to continue the subject that I spoke upon yesterday[383] as to raise the dead[384] my lungs are worn out—[385] time to do things must wait— give it up and leave the time to those who can make you hear— will do it some other time—[386] Yet I have a proclamation to make to the Elders[.][387] wanted you to stay in order I might make this proc. You know the L[or]d has lead the c[h]urch from [*illegible*[388]]; Has another rev[evlation] in rel[ation] to [*illegible*[389]] in the church[390]

---

381. Discourse, 7 April 1844, reported by Thomas Bullock, *JSP, D14*, 327.
382. The various entries below referencing the April 1844 conference are all dated 8 April 1844.
383. Discourse, 8 April 1844, reported by Wilford Woodruff, *WWJ*, 1:631. See also *JSP, D14*, 357.
384. Discourse, 8 April 1844, reported by Willliam Clayton, *JSP, D14*, 355.
385. Discourse, 8 April 1844, reported by Thomas Bullock, *JSP, D14*, 353.
386. Discourse, 8 April 1844, reported by Willliam Clayton, *JSP, D14*, 355.
387. Discourse, 8 April 1844, reported by Wilford Woodruff, *WWJ*, 1:631. See also *JSP, D14*, 357.
388. Thomas Bullock's notes from this discourse say that this illegible word (in the Clayton account of the discourse) is "revelation."
389. Joseph Fielding Smith decided that the illegible word here looked to him like "economy." However, Thomas Bullock's account of this discourse does not have the word "economy" in it, and Clayton's handwriting of this word is illegible. Apparently relying on Joseph Fielding Smith's rendering of the word, subsequent transcriptions of Clayton's notes have been rendered "economy," though that does not appear to be an accurate reading of the illegible word in the opinion of the editors of this volume.
390. Discourse, 8 April 1844, reported by Willliam Clayton, *JSP, D14*, 355.

to economy in the Church—a great, grand, and glorious revelation. I shall not be able to dwell as largely upon it now as at some other time; but I will give you the first principles. You know there has been great discussion in relation to Zion--where it is, and where the gathering of the dispensation is, and which I am now going to tell you. The prophets have spoken and written upon it; but I will make a proclamation that will cover a broader ground. *The whole of America is Zion itself from north to south, and is described by the Prophets, who declare that it is the Zion where the mountain of the Lord should be, and that it should be in the center of the land.* When Elders shall take up and examine the old prophecies in the Bible, they will see it.

a great grand & glorious rev[n].[391] Shall not be able as largely as some other time will give 1st prin[ciple]— has ben great discussion in rel to Zion— prophets— make a proc that will cover a broader gd— the whole Americ[a] is ~~then~~ Zion itself— from North to South— that is the Zion where the Mountain of the Ld shd be—[392] & is desc[ribe]d. by the Prophets that it sho[ul]d. be in the centre of the land.[393]

when Ers take up b◊ will[394] see it—[395]

Ordinances in the Temple

The declaration this morning is, that as soon as the Temple and baptismal font are prepared, we calculate to give the Elders of Israel their washings and anointings, and attend to those last and more impressive ordinances, without which we cannot obtain celestial thrones. But there must be a holy place prepared for that purpose. There was a proclamation made during the time that the foundation of the Temple was laid to that effect, and there are provisions made until the work is [p.363] completed, so that men may receive their endowments and

Various Journal Entries of Remarks Made by Joseph Smith

Dec[laration]— this morning[396] that as soon as the temple & B[aptismal] font is prep[are]d. & so as we can wash & anoint the El[ders] of Israel[397] when those last & most imp[ortan]t ordinances can be done[398] there must be a place prep[d] for that purpose—[399]

Prov[isions]— made during time of laying found[ation]— where men may rec[eive] endow[men]t to make K[ings] & P[ries]ts—

---

391. Discourse, 8 April 1844, reported by Thomas Bullock, *JSP, D14*, 354. 8 April 1844, *JSP, J3*, 223 states: "made a p[r]oclamation—— I have another great and grand Revelation—— great discussion where Zion is— The whole America is Zion that is th[e] Zion where the mountain of th[e] Lords house shall be. about the central part of N. & South America.—"

392. Discourse, 8 April 1844, reported by Willliam Clayton, *JSP, D14*, 355.

393. Discourse, 8 April 1844, reported by Thomas Bullock, *JSP, D14*, 354.

394. While the JSP and Joseph Fielding Smith have rendered this word as "will," the handwriting on this word is illegible, and context seems to have dictated why they have rendered this as "will."

395. Discourse, 8 April 1844, reported by Willliam Clayton, *JSP, D14*, 355.

396. Discourse, 8 April 1844, reported by Willliam Clayton, *JSP, D14*, 355.

397. Discourse, 8 April 1844, reported by Thomas Bullock, *JSP, D14*, 354.

398. Discourse, 8 April 1844, reported by Willliam Clayton, *JSP, D14*, 355.

399. Discourse, 8 April 1844, reported by Thomas Bullock, *JSP, D14*, 354.

be made kings and priests unto the Most High God, having nothing to do with temporal things, but their whole time will be taken up with things pertaining to the house of God. There must, however, be a place built expressly for that purpose, and for men to be baptized for their dead. It must be built in this central place; for every man who wishes to save his father, mother, brothers, sisters and friends, must go through all the ordinances for each one of them separately, the same as for himself, from baptism to ordination, washing and anointings, and receive all the keys and powers of the Priesthood, the same as for himself.

unto the Most H G. [High God] having nothin to do wi[t]h temporal things[400] but as all to do with the ho[use] of God— but there must be an express place built for that purpose & for men to be B[aptized] for their d[ea]d[401] G has provided for a house to be built where we can get a House that's the central place & where we can be baptized for dead[.][402] for every man who wishes to save th[eir] F[ather] & M[other]— B[rothers] S[isters] & F[riends][403] must go through all the ordinances for them the same as for yourselves;[404] from bap[tism] to ordination & end[owmen]t.[405] & all the protect[io]n. of the powers of the Priesthood sam[e] as for themselves—[406]

Stakes of Zion

Various Journal Entries of Remarks Made by Joseph Smith

I have received instructions from the Lord that from henceforth wherever Elders of Israel shall build up churches and branches unto the Lord throughout the States, there shall be a stake of Zion. In the great cities, as Boston, New York, &c., there shall be stakes. It is a glorious proclamation, and I reserved it to the last, and designed it to be understood that this work shall commence after the washings, anointings, and endowments have been performed here.

From henceforth I have rec[eived]— inst[ruction] from Ld that Ers shall build churches where ever they raise branches through the States then builds stakes— in the g[rea]t cities Boston &c there shall be stakes— reserved the pro[clamation] to the last. All this to be und[erstood] that this work shall commence after the washing anontg [anointing] & end[o]wment here

The Lord has an established law in relation to the matter: there must be a particular spot for the salvation of our dead. I verily believe there will be a place, and hence men who want to save their dead can come and bring their families, do their work by being baptized and attending to the other ordinances for their dead, and then may go back again to live and

The Ld has an est[ablished] law in relation to the matter. there must be a particular spot for the sal[vation] of our dead. I verily believ this will be the place. hense men who want to save their dead can come and bring their families do their work and return to live and wait tills the[y] go to receive their reward. Shall leave the rest for the brethren— tis my duty to teach

---

400. Discourse, 8 April 1844, reported by Willliam Clayton, *JSP, D14*, 355–56.
401. Discourse, 8 April 1844, reported by Thomas Bullock, *JSP, D14*, 354.
402. Discourse, 8 April 1844, reported by Willliam Clayton, *JSP, D14*, 356.
403. Discourse, 8 April 1844, reported by Thomas Bullock, *JSP, D14*, 354.
404. Discourse, 8 April 1844, reported by Wilford Woodruff, *WWJ*, 1:631. See also *JSP, D14*, 357.
405. Discourse, 8 April 1844, reported by Willliam Clayton, *JSP, D14*, 356.
406. Discourse, 8 April 1844, reported by Thomas Bullock, *JSP, D14*, 354.

wait till they go to receive their reward. I shall leave my brethren to enlarge on this subject; it is my duty to teach the doctrine. I would teach it more fully—the spirit is willing but the flesh is weak. God is not willing to let me gratify you; but I must teach the Elders, and they should teach you. God made Aaron to be the mouthpiece for the children of Israel, and He will make me be god to you in His stead, and the Elders to be mouth for me; and if you don't like it, you must lump it. I have been giving Elder Adams instruction in some principles to speak to you, and if he makes a mistake, I will get up and correct him. (April 8, 1844.) DHC 6:318-320.

the doctrine— sp[iri]t is willing flesh is weak. God is not willing to let me gratify you— but I must teach the Ers and they should teach you[.] He will make me to be God in your stead & they be mouth for me. Have be[e]n giving some inst[ruction] to Er [George J.] Adams to to speak to you & when he makes a mistake [I] will get up and correct him.[407]

President Joseph Smith's Address—Defense of His Prophetic Calling—Resurrection of the Dead—Fulness of Ordinances Necessary Both for the Living and Dead

Thomas Bullock Report of 12 May 1844
Discourse by Joseph Smith

[p.364] The Savior has the words of eternal life. Nothing else can profit us. There is no salvation in believing an evil report against our neighbor. I advise all to go on to perfection, and search deeper and deeper into the mysteries of Godliness. A man can do nothing for himself unless God direct him in the right way; and the Priesthood is for that purpose.

The Savior has the words of Eternal life— nothing else can profit us— there is no salvation in believing an evil against our neighbor— I advise all to go on to perfection and search deeper into the mysteries of Godliness— a man can do nothing for himself—

The last time I spoke on this stand it was on the resurrection of the dead, when I promised to continue my remarks upon that subject. Let us this very day begin anew, and now say, with all our hearts, we will forsake our sins and be righteous. I shall read the 24th chapter of Matthew, and give it a literal rendering and reading; and when it is rightly understood, it will be edifying.

the last time I spoke it was on the resurrection of the dead; when I promised to continue— I still feel a desire to say something on this subject— let us this very day begin anew. and now say we will be righteous— I shall read the 24th. ch of Matthew and give it a litteral rendering & reading, and when rightly understood will be edifying (he translated it from the German)

I thought the very oddity of its rendering would be edifying anyhow—"And it will be preached, the Gospel of the kingdom, in the whole world, to a witness over all people: and

I thought the very oddity of its rendering would be edifying any how— "And it will preached be; the Gospel of the Kingdom in the whole world, to a witness over all people,

---

407. Discourse, 8 April 1844, reported by Willliam Clayton, *JSP, D14*, 356.

then will the end come." I will now read it in German [which he did, and many Germans who were present said he translated it correctly].

Interpretation of Scripture

The Savior said when these tribulations should take place, it should be committed to a man who should be a witness over the whole world: the keys of knowledge, power and revelations should be revealed to a witness who should hold the testimony to the world. It has always been my province to dig up hidden mysteries—new things—for my hearers. Just at the time when some men think that I have no right to the keys of the Priesthood—just at that time I have the greater right. The Germans are an exalted people. The old German translators are the most nearly correct—most honest of any of the translators; and therefore I get testimony to bear me out in the revelations that I have preached for the last fourteen years. The old German, Latin, Greek and Hebrew translations all say it is true: they cannot be impeached, and therefore I am in good company.

All the testimony is that the Lord in the last days would commit the keys of the Priesthood to a witness over all people.

[p.365] Has the Gospel of the kingdom commenced in the last days? And will God take it from the man until He takes him Himself? I have read it precisely as the words flowed from the lips of Jesus Christ. John the Revelator saw an angel flying through the midst of heaven, having the everlasting Gospel to preach unto them that dwell on the earth.

The scripture is ready to be fulfilled when great wars, famines, pestilence, great distress, judgments, &c., are ready to be poured out on the inhabitants of the earth. John saw the

and then will the end come". I will now read it in German— (several persons said he translated it correct)[408]

Thomas Bullock Report of 12 May 1844 Discourse by Joseph Smith

the Savior said, when those tribulations should take place, it should be committed to a man, who should be a witness over the whole world, the keys of knowledge, power, and revelations, should be revealed to a witness who should hold the testimony to the world; it has always been my province to dig up hidden mysteries, new things, for my hearers— just at the time when some [p.480] men think that I have no right to the keys just at that time, I have the greatest right— the Germans are an exalted people, the old German translators is the most correct, most honest and therefore I get testimony to bear me out in the revelations that I have preached for the last 14 years— the old German, Latin, Greek and Hebrew all say it is true, they cannot be impeached, and I am in good company—

all the testimony is, that the Lord in the last days would commit the keys to a witness over all people—

has the Gospel of the Kingdom commenced in the last days, and will God take it from the man, until he takes him, himself, I have read it precisely as the words flowed from the lips of Jesus Christ— John the Revelator saw an angel flying thro' the midst of heaven, having the everlasting Gospel to preach unto them that dwell on the earth, &c.

the Scripture is ready to be fulfilled when great wars, famines, pestilence, judgments &c are ready to be poured out on the Inhabitants of the Earth— John saw the angel having the

---

408. Discourse, 12 May 1844, reported by Thomas Bullock, *JSP, D14*, 479.

angel having the holy Priesthood, who should preach the everlasting Gospel to all nations. God had an angel—a special messenger—ordained and prepared for that purpose in the last days. Woe, woe be to that man or set of men who lift up their hands against God and His witness in these last days: for they shall deceive almost the very chosen ones!

priesthood who should preach— God had an angel, ordained, & prepared for ~~the~~ that purpose in the last days— Woe! Woe! be to that man, or set of men, who lift up their hands against God and his Witness in these last days— for they shall deceive almost the very chosen ones—[409]

Eternal Judgment

My enemies say that I have been a true prophet. Why, I had rather be a fallen true prophet than a false prophet. When a man goes about prophesying, and commands men to obey his teachings, he must either be a true or false prophet. False prophets always arise to oppose the true prophets and they will prophesy so very near the truth that they will deceive almost the very chosen ones.

The doctrine of eternal judgments belongs to the first principles of the Gospel, in the last days. In relation to the kingdom of God, the devil always sets up his kingdom at the very same time in opposition to God. Every man who has a calling to minister to the inhabitants of the world was ordained to that very purpose in the Grand Council of heaven before this world was. I suppose I was ordained to this very office in that Grand Council. It is the testimony that I want that I am God's servant, and this people His people. The ancient prophets declared that in the last days the God of heaven should set up a kingdom which should never be destroyed, nor left to other people; and the very time that was calculated on, this people were struggling to bring it out. He that arms himself with gun, sword, or pistol, except in the defense of truth, will sometime be sorry for it. I never carry any weapon with me bigger than my penknife. When I was dragged before [p.366] the cannon and muskets in Missouri,

Thomas Bullock Report of 12 May 1844 Discourse by Joseph Smith

my enemies say I have been a true prophet— & I had rather be a fallen true prophet, than a false prophet; when a man goes about prophesying and commands men to obey him, he must be either a true or false prophet— false prophets always arise to oppose the true prophets, and will deceive almost the very chosen ones—

the doctrine of eternal judgments belong to the 1ˢᵗ principles of the Gospel in the last days— in relation to the Kingdom of God— the devil always sets up his [p.482] Kingdom at the very same time— every man who has a calling to the world, was ordained to that very purpose in the grand Council of Heaven— I suppose that I was ordained to this very office in that grand Council— it is the testimony that I want, that I am God's servant, and this people his people— in the last days the God of Heaven shall set up a Kingdom & the very time that was calculated on, this people was struggling to bring it out— he that arms himself with Gun, sword, or Pistol will some time be sorry for it— I never carry any thing bigger than my Pen Knife— when I was dragged before the Cannon and muskets in Missouri, I was unarmed, God will always protect me

---

409. Discourse, 12 May 1844, reported by Thomas Bullock, *JSP, D14*, 479–80.

I was unarmed. God will always protect me until my mission is fulfilled.

I calculate to be one of the instruments of setting up the kingdom of Daniel by the word of the Lord, and I intend to lay a foundation that will revolutionize the whole world. I once offered my life to the Missouri mob as a sacrifice for my people, and here I am. It will not be by sword or gun that this kingdom will roll on: the power of truth is such that all nations will be under the necessity of obeying the Gospel. The prediction is that army will be against army: it may be that the Saints will have to beat their ploughs into swords, for it will not do for men to sit down patiently and see their children destroyed.

I calculate to be one of the Instruments of setting up the Kingdom of Daniel, by the word of the Lord, and I intend to revolutionize the whole world— I once offered my life to the Missouri Mob as a sacrifice for my people— and here I am— it will not be by Sword or Gun that this Kingdom will roll on— all nations will be under the necessity of obeying the Gospel— the prediction is that army will be against army— it may be that the Saints will have to beat their Ploughs into Swords [p.483]it will not do for men to sit down and see their women destroyed patiently,[410]

The Resurrection

Thomas Bullock Report of 12 May 1844 Discourse by Joseph Smith

My text is on the resurrection of the dead, which you will find in the 14th chapter of John—"In my Father's house are many mansions." It should be—"In my Father's kingdom are many kingdoms," in order that ye may be heirs of God and joint-heirs with me. I do not believe the Methodist doctrine of sending honest men and noble-minded men to hell, along with the murderer and the adulterer. They may hurl all their hell and fiery billows upon me, for they will roll off me as fast as they come on. But I have an order of things to save the poor fellows at any rate, and get them saved; for I will send men to preach to them in prison and save them if I can.

my text is 14 John In my Fathers house are many mansions &c In my Father's Kingdom are many Kingdoms— in order that ye may be heirs of God and joint heirs with me— I do not believe the methodist doctrine of sending honest men, and noble minded men to hell, along with the murderer and adulterer— they may hurl all their hell and fiery billows upon me, for they will roll off me as fast as they come on— but I have an order of things to save the poor fellows at any rate, and get them saved for I will send men to preach to them in prison and save them if I can.[411]

Salvation for the Dead

Thomas Bullock Report of 12 May 1844 Discourse by Joseph Smith

There are mansions for those who obey a celestial law, and there are other mansions for those who come short of the law, every man

There are mansions for those who obey a Celestial law— & there are other mansions for those who come short of that law— every

---

410. Discourse, 12 May 1844, reported by Thomas Bullock, *JSP, D14*, 480, 482–83.
411. Discourse, 12 May 1844, reported by Thomas Bullock, *JSP, D14*, 483.

in his own order. There is baptism for those to exercise who are alive, and baptism for the dead who die without the knowledge of the Gospel.

I am going on in my progress for eternal life. It is not only necessary that you should be baptized for your dead, but you will have to go through all the ordinances for them, the same as you have gone through to save yourselves. There will be 144,000 saviors on Mount Zion, and with them an innumerable host that no man can number. Oh! I beseech you to go forward, go forward and make your calling and your election sure; and if any man preach any other Gospel than that which I have preached, he shall be cursed; and some of you who now hear [p.367] me shall see it, and know that I testify the truth concerning them.

man in his own order—[412] there is baptism &c for those who are alive, and baptism for the dead, all who died without the knowledge of the gospel

I am going on in my progress for eternal life— it is not only necessary that you should be baptised for your dead, but you will have to go thro' all the ordinances for them, same as you have to save yourself; there will be 144,000 and an innumerable host, that no man can number— Oh! go forward, go forward and make your calling and your election sure— and if any man preach any other gospel than that which I have preached, he shall be cursed, and some of you who now hear me, shall see it—[413]

The Resurrection Universal

Thomas Bullock Report of 12 May 1844 Discourse by Joseph Smith

In regard to the law of the Priesthood, there should be a place where all nations shall come up from time to time to receive their endowments; and the Lord has said this shall be the place for the baptisms for the dead. Every man that has been baptized and belongs to the kingdom has a right to be baptized for those who have gone before; and as soon as the law of the Gospel is obeyed here by their friends who act as proxy for them, the Lord has administrators there to set them free. A man may act as proxy for his own relatives; the ordinances of the world have thus been fulfilled by them, and we may be baptized for those whom we have much friendship for; but it must first be revealed to the man of God, lest we should run too far. "As in Adam all die, even so in Christ shall all be made alive;" all shall be raised from the dead. The Lamb of

in regard to the law of the Priesthood— there should be a place where [p.484] all nations shall come up from time to time to receive their endowments, and the Lord has said, this shall be the place for the baptism for the dead— every man that has been baptized and belongs to the Kingdom, has a right to be baptized for those who are gone before, and, as soon as the Law is obeyed here the Lord has administrators there, to set them free— a man may act as proxy for his own relatives— the ordination was laid out before the foundation of the world— those who we have much friendship for, it must be first revealed to man from God lest he should run too far— as in Adam all die, so in Christ shall all be made alive, all shall be raised from the dead— the Lamb of God hath brought to pass the resurrection so that all shall rise from the dead—

---

412. 12 May 1844, History F-1, 19.
413. Discourse, 12 May 1844, reported by Thomas Bullock, *JSP, D14*, 483.

God hath brought to pass the resurrection, so that all shall rise from the dead.

God Almighty Himself dwells in eternal fire; flesh and blood cannot go there, for all corruption is devoured by the fire. "Our God is a consuming fire." When our flesh is quickened by the Spirit, there will be no blood in this tabernacle. Some dwell in higher glory than others.

Those who have done wrong always have that wrong gnawing them. Immortality dwells in everlasting burnings. I will from time to time reveal to you the subjects that are revealed by the Holy Ghost to me. All the lies that are now hatched up against me are of the devil, and the influence of the devil and his servants will be used against the kingdom of God. The servants of God teach nothing but principles of eternal life, by their works ye shall know them. A good man will speak good things and holy principles, and an evil man evil things. I feel, in the name of the Lord, to rebuke all such bad principles, liars, &c., and I warn all of you to look out whom you are going after. I exhort you to give heed to all the virtue and the teachings which I have given you. All men who are immortal dwell in everlasting burnings. You cannot go anywhere but where God can find you out. All men are [p.368] born to die, and all men must rise; all must enter eternity.

In order for you to receive your children to yourselves you must have a promise—some ordinance; some blessing, in order to ascend above principalities, or else it may be an angel. They must rise just as they died; we can there hail our lovely infants with the same glory—the same loveliness in the celestial glory, where they all enjoy alike. They differ in stature, in size, the same glorious spirit gives them the likeness of glory and bloom; the old man with his silvery hairs will glory in bloom and beauty. No man can describe it to you—no man can write it.

God Almighty himself dwells in Eternal fire, flesh and blood cannot go there, all corruption is devoured by the fire— our God is a consuming fire— when our flesh is quickened by the Spirit, there will be no blood— some dwell in higher glory than others—

those who have done wrong, always have that wrong knawing them— Immortality dwells in everlasting burnings— I will from time to time reveal the subjects that are revealed to me— all the lies that are now hatched up are of the devil— & all the influence of the [p.485] devil will be used against the kingdom of God— the Servants of God teach nothing but eternal life— by their works ye shall know them— a good man will speak good things,— I feel in the name of the Lord, to rebuke all such bad principles, liars &c and look out who you are going after— I exhort you to give heed to all the virtue and the teachings which I have given you; you cannot go any where, but where God can find you out; all must rise, all must enter eternity—

in order for you to receive your children to yourself, you must have a promise, some ordinance some blessing— or else it may be an angel— they must rise just as they died— we can there hail our lovely infants with the same glory, the same loveliness in the Celestial glory where they all enjoy alike— they differ in stature, in size— the same glorious spirit gives them the likeness of glory and bloom— the old man with his silvery hairs will glory in bloom & beauty— no man can describe it to you—no man can write it—

When did I ever teach anything wrong from this stand? When was I ever confounded? I want to triumph in Israel before I depart hence and am no more seen. I never told you I was perfect; but there is no error in the revelations which I have taught. Must I, then, be thrown away as a thing of naught?

I enjoin for your consideration—add to your faith, virtue, love, &c. I say, in the name of the Lord, if these things are in you, you shall be fruitful. I testify that no man has power to reveal it but myself—things in heaven, in earth, and hell; and all shut your mouths for the future. I commend you all to God, that you may inherit all things; and may God add His blessing. Amen. (May 2, 1844.) DHC 6:363-367.

when did I ever teach any thing wrong from this stand? when was I ever confounded? I want to triumph in Israel before I depart hence and am no more seen— I never told you I was perfect— but there is no error in the revelations which I have taught— must I then be thrown away as a thing of nought?—

I enjoin for your consideration, add to your faith, virtue, love &c I testify that no man has power to reveal it, but myself, things in heaven, in earth and hell— and all shut your mouths for the future— I commend you all to God, that you may inherit all things— & may God add his blessing Amen.[414]

The Prophet's Dreams on Conditions of Apostates at Nauvoo

In the evening I attended meeting in the Seventies' Hall. George J. Adams preached and I made some observations afterwards, and related a dream which I had a short time since. I thought I was riding out in my carriage, and my guardian angel was along with me. We went past the Temple and had not gone much further before we espied two large snakes so fast locked together that neither of them had any power. I inquired of my guide what I was to understand by that. He answered, "Those snakes represent Dr. Foster and Chauncey L. Higbee. They are your enemies and desire to destroy you; but you see they are so fast locked together that they have no power of themselves to hurt you."

Joseph Smith's Remarks at Seventies Hall, 13 June 1844, from Various Journals

P M. attend meeti[n]g in 70's Hall J. G. [George J.] Adams Preahd [preached]— after which I made some observati[o]ns—[415] After he had done the P/ Prophet Arose and Stated the Reason why he did not speak he felt much oppressed But he would Relate a Dream that he had the night before Which was in Substance as follows <I> He was Riding out by the temple in his Carriage He thad not gone far Whith my gardian Angel along with me Which was Always the Case they had not gone far before they espeyed Two Large Snakes So fast Locked together that either of them had no power I then enquired of my guide what they meant He said, He Answered Them Snakes, that you see Represents Docter Foster and Cauncey Higbee they are your enemies and Desire to Destroy you But you see they are so fast Locked together that they have no power and Can do you no harm

---

414. Discourse, 12 May 1844, reported by Thomas Bullock, *JSP, D14*, 483-85.
415. 13 June 1844, *JSP, J3*, 281.

I then thought I was riding up Mulholland street, but my guardian angel was not along with me. On arriving at the prairie, I was overtaken [p.369] and seized by William and Wilson Law and others, saying, "Ah, ah! we have got you at last! We will secure you and put you in a safe place!" and, without any ceremony dragged me out of my carriage, tied my hands behind me, and threw me into a deep, dry pit, where I remained in a perfectly helpless condition, and they went away. While struggling to get out, I heard Wilson Law screaming for help hard by. I managed to unloose myself so as to make a spring, when I caught hold of some grass which grew at the edge of the pit.

I looked out of the pit and saw Wilson Law at a little distance attacked by ferocious wild beasts, and heard him cry out, "Oh Brother Joseph, come and save me!" I replied, "I cannot, for you have put me into this deep pit." On looking out another way, I saw William Law with outstretched tongue, blue in the face, and the green poison forced out of his mouth caused by the coiling of a large snake around his body. It had also grabbed him by the arm, a little above the elbow, ready to devour him. He cried out in the intensity of his agony, "Oh, Brother Joseph, Brother Joseph, come and save me, or I die!" I also replied to him, "I cannot, William; I would willingly, but you have tied me and put me in this pit, and I am powerless to help you or liberate myself." In a short time after my guide came and said aloud, "Joseph, Joseph, what are you doing there?" I replied, "My enemies fell upon me, bound me and threw me in." He then took me by the hand, and drew me out of the pit, set me free, and we went away rejoicing. (June 13, 1844.) DHC 6:461-462.

I He then Dreamt again that he I was Riding Up Mullholland Street But he I had not my Conducter along with him me As Allways was the case before this time. When he I Came to the edge of the Priare Who Should he I see Approaching him me But Wm and Wilson Law Saying "Ah" Ah" Ah" now we have got you at Last We will secure you and put you in a Safe place.
And Without any Ceremony Dragged Me out of my Carriage. And Led me to the Edge of the Wood W[h]ere they had prepared a Deep Pit for the Purpose They put <me> Down into it Then Turned and went Away
They had not been gone long, When I heard them Calling out withall their Might "Joseph "Joseph "Joseph" Come to our help I replied "You have put me into this Deep pit And I can not get out
I then mad[e] a spring And I Caught hold of the grass which was growing on the edge of the pit with my fingers and pulled myself up saw has i could see on the priare And at a Little Distance I there beheld that A large snake had twisted itself around Wilson Law and grabbed him by the arm A little above the elbow and was fast strangling him, A little further. I, saw That a great Bear had Laid hold of him William Law and was tearing him to peices At this time I heard my name Called, Joseph, Joseph, What in goodness are you Doing here I looked up and Saw my gardian Angel Coming <Bounding> over the fence, I said my enemies hath put me here He Said take hold of my hand I Did so He perked me out of the pit And said follow me And he Led me of[f] in an oppisite Direction
I then Awoke
This is the Dream
And the interpretation you can give for yourselves

Miles Romney A hearer[416]

---

416. Miles Romney Report, circa 1854–1856, [1]–[2], Historian's Office, Joseph Smith History Documents, circa 1839–1860, Church History Library, CR 100 396. See also *The Latter-day Saints' Millennial Star* 24, no. 3 (18 January 1862): 39–40, and *The Latter-day Saints' Millennial Star* 24, no. 4 (25 January 1862): 55 (a continuation from the previous issue). The *Latter-day Saints' Millennial Star*

Sermon by the Prophet—The Christian Godhead—Plurality of Gods

Meeting in the Grove, east of the Temple, June 16, 1844[417]

* * *

President Joseph Smith read the 3rd chapter of Revelation, and took for his text 1st chapter, 6th verse—"And hath made us kings and priests unto God and His Father: to Him be glory and dominion forever and ever. Amen."

It is altogether correct in the translation. Now, you know that of late some malicious and corrupt men have sprung up and apostatized from the Church of Jesus Christ of Latter-day Saints, and they declare that the Prophet believes in a plurality of Gods, and, lo and behold! we have discovered a very great secret, they cry—"The Prophet says there are many Gods, and this proves that he has fallen."

It has been my intention for a long time to take up this subject and lay it clearly before the people, and show what my faith is in relation to this interesting matter. I have contemplated the saying of Jesus (Luke 17th chapter, 26th verse)—"And as it was in the days of Noe, so shall it be also in the days of the Son of Man." And if it does rain, I'll preach this doctrine, for the truth shall be preached.

Thomas Bullock's Report of a Discourse by Joseph Smith

* * *

The Prophet read the 3rd. Rev. text 6th. v. & made us K[ings] & P[riests] unto God & his Fa[the]r. To him be glory & dom[inion] for evermore—

[p.268] It is altog[ethe]r correct in the translat[io]n.—now you know that of late some have sprung up & apostat[ized]: & they declare that Pro[phet] bel[ieves]: in a plurality of Gods— & lo behold a very great secret they cry

it has been my intent[io]n. to take up this subj[ec]t. & shew what my Faith is in the matter—I have contemplated the saying of Je[sus] as it was in the days of Noah so shall it be at his 2nd. coming & if it rains[418]

---

was a newspaper published in Great Britain from 1840 to 1970. Also, in a letter to Thomas Bullock, Dan Jones gives an account of the same or a similar dream related by Joseph Smith in the Carthage Jail: "He entertained us much by the recital of two dreams the which he had received not long before, one, In which he saw himself pitched into a dry well by Wm and Wilson Law who had previously tied his hands behind him; while struggling to get up and near the top he discovered Wilson tackled by a ferocious wild beast in an adjoining wood, crying for his help while nearer to him still was William with outstretched tongue; blue in the face, and the green poison forced out of his mouth by the coiling of a huge serpent around his body, relaxing its embrace occasionally and thereby enabling him to cry aloud 'Oh brother Joseph come and save me or I die.' To which he reply'd as he had done to a similar request from his brother Wilson, 'I cannot, for you have tied my hands behind me.' Ere long however his guide finding him there released and comforted the Prophet while the others met the just retribution of the demerit." Dan Jones letter, 20 January 1855, in Ronald D. Dennis, trans., "The Martyrdom of Joseph Smith and His Brother Hyrum by Dan Jones," *BYU Studies* 24, no. 1 (Winter 1984): 99.

417. This introductory sentence was authored by Joseph Fielding Smith.
418. Discourse, 16 June 1844-A, reported by Thomas Bullock, *JSP, D15*, 267–68.

Plurality of Gods

	Thomas Bullock's Report of a Discourse by Joseph Smith
I will preach on the plurality of Gods. I have selected this text for that express purpose. I wish to declare I have always and in all congregations when I have preach on the subject of the Deity, it has been the plurality of Gods. It has been preached by the Elders for fifteen years.	ill [I'll] preach—the plurality of Gods—I have selected this text I wish to declare I have allways—& in all congregat[ns.] when I have preached it has been the plurality of Gods it has been preachd 15 years—
I have always declared God to be a distinct personage, Jesus Christ a separate and distinct personage from God the Father, and the Holy Ghost was a distinct personage and a Spirit: and these three constitute three distinct personages and three Gods. If this is in accordance with the New Testament, lo and behold! we have three Gods anyhow, and they are plural; and who can contradict it?	I have always decl[are][d.] God to be a distinct personage—J.C. [Jesus Christ] a sep[arate]: & distinct pers from God the Fa[r.], the H.G [Holy Ghost] was a distinct personage & or Sp[irit] & these 3 constit[ute]. 3 distinct personages & 3 Gods—if this is in accordance with the New Test[ament]—lo <&> behold we have 3 Gods any how & they are plural any how—
Our text says, "And hath made us kings and priests unto God and His Father." The Apostles have discovered that there were Gods above, for John says God was the Father of our Lord Jesus Christ. My object was to preach the scriptures, and preach the doctrine they contain, there being a God above, the Father of our Lord Jesus Christ. I am bold to declare I have taught all the stronger doctrines publicly, and always teach stronger doctrines in public than in private.	our text says the apost[le] have disc[overe][d.] that there were Gods above—God was the Fa[r.] of our L[or][d.] J.C.—my object was to preach the Scrip[tures]—& preach the doctrine there being a God above the Fa[r.] of our L[d.] J.C.—I am bold to declare I have tau[t] all the strong doctrines publicly—& always stronger that [than?] what I preach in private—
John was one of the men, and apostles declare they were made kings and priests unto God, the Father of our Lord Jesus Christ. It reads just so in the Revelation, Hence the doctrine of a plurality of Gods is as prominent in the Bible as any other doctrine. It is all over the face of the Bible. It stands beyond the power of controversy. A wayfaring man, though a fool, need not err therein.	John was one of the men & the apos. declare they were made K. & P. unto God the Fa[r.] of our L[d.] J.C. it reads just so hence the doctrine of a plurality of Gods is as prominent in the Bible as any doctrine—it is all over the face of the Bible, it stands beyond the power of controversy—a wayfaring man tho a fool need not fail—
Paul says there are Gods many and Lords many. I want to set it forth in a plain and simple	Paul says there are Gods many & Lords many—I want to set it in a plain simple

manner; but to us there is but one God—that is pertaining to us; and he is in all and **[p.371]** through all. But if Joseph Smith says there are Gods many and Lords many, they cry, "Away with him! Crucify him! Crucify him!"

Mankind verily say that the Scriptures are with them. Search the Scriptures, for they testify of things that these apostates would gravely pronounce blasphemy. Paul, if Joseph Smith is a blasphemer, you are. I say there are Gods many and Lords many, but to us only one, and we are to be in subjection to that one, and no man can limit the bounds or the eternal existence of eternal time. Hath he beheld the eternal world, and is he authorized to say that there is only one God? He makes himself a fool if he thinks or says so, and there is an end of his career or progress in knowledge. He cannot obtain all knowledge, for he has sealed up the gate to it.

man[n]er—but to us there is but one God pertaining to us, in **[p.269]** all thro all,—but if J. Smith says there is Gods many & L$^{ds.}$ many they cry away with him crucify him

mankind verily say that the Scrip [i]s with them—Search the Scrip &c they testify of things that apostates wo[ul]^d blaspheme— Paul if Jo Smith is a blasphemer you are—I say there are Gods many & L$^{d<s>}$ many but to us only one & we are to be in subjec$^{tn.}$ to that one & no man can limit the bounds, or the eternal existence of eternal time—hath he beheld the et[erna]^l world, & is he auth[orize]^d to say that there is only God he makes himself a fool—& there is an end of his career in knowledge he cannot obt[ai]^n all knowledge for he has sealed up the Gate to [it?][419]

Scriptural Interpretation

Some say I do not interpret the Scripture the same as they do. They say it means the heathen's gods. Paul says there are Gods many and Lords many; and that makes a plurality of Gods, in spite of the whims of all men. Without a revelation, I am not going to give them the knowledge of the God of heaven. You know and I testify that Paul had no allusion to the heathen gods. I have it from God, and get over it if you can. I have a witness of the Holy Ghost, and a testimony that Paul had no allusion to the heathen gods in the text. I will show from the Hebrew Bible that I am correct, and the first word shows a plurality of Gods; and I want the apostates and learned men to come here and prove to the contrary, if they can. An unlearned boy must give you a little Hebrew. Berosheit baurau Eloheim ait aushamayeen vehau auraits, rendered by King

Thomas Bullock's Report of a Discourse by Joseph Smith

some say I do not interpret same as you—they say it means the heathen God— Paul says there are Gods many &c it makes a plurality of Gods any how—

with[ou]^t a rev[elatio]^n I am not going to give the God of Heaven to them any how—you know & I testify that Paul had no allusions to it—I have it from God & get over it if you can—I have a witness of the H.G—& a test[imony] that Paul had no allusion to the Heathen G. in the text— I will shew from the Heb. Bible & the 1$^{st.}$ word shews a plurality of Gods—& I want the apostate & learned men to come here—& prove to the contrary an unlearned boy must give you a little Hebrew—Berosheit &c In the **[p.270]** begin[ning]: rosheit— the head— it sho[ul]^d read the heads of—to organize the Gods—[420]

---

419. Discourse, 16 June 1844-A, reported by Thomas Bullock, *JSP, D15*, 268–69.
420. Discourse, 16 June 1844, reported by Thomas Bullock, *JSP, D15*, 269–70.

James' translators, "In the beginning God created the heaven and the earth." I want to analyze the word Berosheit. Rosh, the head; Sheit, a grammatical termination; the Baith was not originally put there when the inspired man wrote it, but it has been since added by an old Jew. Baurau signifies to bring forth; Eloheim is from the word Eloi, God, in the singular number; and by adding the word heim, it renders it Gods. It read first, "In the beginning he head of the Gods brought forth the Gods," or, as other have translated it, "The head of the Gods called the Gods together." I want to show a little learning as well as other fools. * * *

[p.372] The head God organized the heavens and the earth. I defy all the world to refute me. In the beginning the heads of the Gods organized the heavens and the earth. Now the learned priests and the people rage, and the heathen imagine a vain thing. If we pursue the Hebrew text further, it reads, "The head one of the Gods said, Let us make a man in our own image," I once asked a learned Jew, "If the Hebrew language compels us to render all words ending in heim in the plural, why not render the first Eloheim plural?" He replied, "That is the rule with few exceptions; but in this case it would ruin the Bible." He acknowledged I was right. I came here to investigate these things precisely as I believe them. Hear and judge for yourselves; and if you go away satisfied, well and good.

In the very beginning the Bible shows there is a plurality of Gods beyond the power of refutation. It is a great subject I am dwell-

Berosheit barau Eloheim ait aushamayeem vehau auraits rendered by the King James translators In the beginning God created the Heavens and the Earth[421] Berosheit ~~Barau~~ want to annalize the word— Ba in by through in & every thing else— rosh— next— the head. sheet where do it come from— when they inspired man wrote he did not put the Ba.ther[e]— Bu[t] a jew put it there.[422] Barau, signifies to bring forth.[423] Eloi, heam Eloi. God in sing[ular], heam, renders Gods[424] It read in the first— The head one of the Gods brought forth the Gods—[425] I want a little learning as well as other fools[426]

the head God— organized the heavens & the Earth— I defy all the learning in the world to refute me— In the begin the heads of the Gods organized the heavens & the Earth— now the learned Priest— the people rage—& the heathen imagine a vain thing— if we pursue the Heb further— it reads The Head one of the Gods said let us make man in our image I once asked a learned Jew once— if the Heb. language compels us to render all words ending in heam in the plural— why not render the first plural—he replied it would ruin the Bible— he acknowledged I was right, I came here to investigate these things precisely as I believe it—hear & judge for yourself— & if you go away satisfied— well & good—

in the very beginning there [p.271] is a plurality of Gods—beyond the power of refutation—it is a great subject I am dwelling

---

421. History F-1, 102.
422. Discourse, 7 April 1844, reported by William Clayton, *JPS, D14*, 330. *T&S* renders this: "I want to analyze the word; *baith*, in, by, through, in, and every thing else. *Rosh*, the head. *Sheit*, grammatical termination. When the inspired man wrote it, he did not put the *baith* there. A man, A Jew without any authority, thought it too bad to begin to talk about the *head*." *T&S* 5, no. 15 (15 Aug. 1844): 614.
423. *T&S* 5, no. 15 (15 Aug. 1844): 614.
424. Discourse, 16 June 1844, reported by Thomas Bullock, *JSP, D15*, 270.
425. Discourse, 7 April 1844, reported by William Clayton, *JPS, D14*, 330. Willard Richards rendered this: "The head one called the Gods together in grand coun[c]il—" Discourse, 7 April 1844, reported by Willard Richards, *JSP, D14*, 334.
426. Discourse, 16 June 1844, reported by Thomas Bullock, *JSP, D15*, 270.

ing on. The word Eloheim ought to be in the plural all the way through—Gods. The heads of the Gods appointed one God for us; and when you take [that] view of the subject, its sets one free to see all the beauty, holiness and perfection of the Gods. All I want is to get the simple, naked truth, and the whole truth.

Many men say there is one God; the Father, the Son and the Holy Ghost are only one God. I say that is a strange God anyhow—three in one, and one in three! It is a curious organization. "Father, I pray not for the world, but I pray for them which thou hast given me." "Holy Father, keep through Thine own name those whom thou hast given me, that they may be one as we are." All are to be crammed into one God, according to sectarianism. It would make the biggest God in all the world. He would be a wonderfully big God—he would be a giant or a monster. I want to read the text to you myself—"I am agreed with the Father and the Father is agreed with me, and we are agreed as one." The Greek shows that it should be agreed. "Father, I pray for them which Thou hast given me out of the world, and not for those alone, but for them also which shall believe on me through their word, that they all may be agreed, as Thou, Father, are with me, and I with Thee, that they also may be agreed with us," and all come to dwell in unity, and in all the glory and everlasting burnings of the **[p.373]** Gods; and then we shall see as we are seen, and be as our God and He as His Father. I want to reason a little on this subject. I learned it by translating the papyrus which is now in my house.

on—the word Eloiheam ought to be in the plural all the way thro—Gods—the heads of the Gods appointed one God for us—& when you take a view of the subject it sets one free to see all the beauty holiness & perfection of the God—all I want is to get the simple truth—naked & the whole truth—

men say there is one God—the Fa^r· Son & the H.G are only 1 God— it is a strange God any how 3 in 1. & 1 in 3. it is a curious thing any how—Fa^r· I pray not for the world but I pray for those that thou givest me &c &c

all are to be crammed into 1 God—it wo^d· make the biggest God in all the world—he is a wonderful big God—he would be a Giant I want to read the text to you myself—I am agreed with the Fa^r· & the Fa^r· is agreed with me & we are agreed as one—the Greek shews that is sho^d· be agreed—

Fa^r· I pray for them that thou hast given me out of the world &c &c

that they may be agreed & all come to dwell in unity & in all the Glory & Everlasting burn[in]^{gs} of God & then we shall see as we are seen & be as God—& be as the God of his Fa^r·—

I want to reason—I learned it by translating the papyrus now in my house—[427]

Abraham's Reasoning

Thomas Bullock's Report of a Discourse by Joseph Smith

I learned a testimony concerning Abraham, and he reasoned concerning the God of heaven. "In order to do that," said he, "suppose we have two

I learned a test. concerning **[p.272]** Abraham & he reasoned concern^g· the God of Heaven—in order to do that s[ai]^d· he— suppose we have

---

427. Discourse, 16 June 1844-A, reported by Thomas Bullock, *JSP, D15*, 269–71.

facts: that supposes another fact may exist—two men on the earth, one wiser than the other, would logically show that another who is wiser than the wisest may exist. Intelligences exist one above another, so that there is no end to them."

If Abraham reasoned thus—If Jesus Christ was the Son of God, and John discovered that God the Father of Jesus Christ had a Father, you may suppose that He had a Father also. Where was there ever a son without a father? And where was there ever a father without first being a son? Whenever did a tree or anything spring into existence without a progenitor? And everything comes in this way. Paul says that which is earthly is in the likeness of that which is heavenly, Hence if Jesus had a Father, can we not believe that He had a Father also? I despise the idea of being scared to death at such a doctrine, for the Bible is full of it.

I want you to pay particular attention to what I am saying. Jesus said that the Father wrought precisely in the same way as His Father had done before Him. As the Father had done before? He laid down His life, and took it up the same as His Father had done before. He did as He was sent, to lay down His life and take it up again; and then was committed unto Him the keys. I know it is good reasoning.

two facts that supposes that ano^r fact may exist two men on the earth— one wiser that the other— wo^d shew that an^r who is wiser than the wisest may exist— intelligences exist one above ano^r that there is no end to it—

if Abra[ham]: reasoned thus— if J.C was the Son of God & John disc^d that God the Fa^r of J.C had a fa^r
you may suppose that he had a Fa^r also— where was ther ever a Son with^t a Fa^r—
when ever did a tree or any thing spring into existence with^t a progenitor— & every thing comes in this way—Paul says that which is Earthyly is in likeness of that which is Heavenly— hence if J. had a Fa^r can we not believe that he had a Fa^r also— I despise the idea of being scared to death—

I want you all to pay part[icu]ar attent[io]^n. J. s^d as the Fa^r wrought precisely in the same way as his Fa^r had done bef[ore]— as the Fa^r had done bef— he laid down his life & took it up same as his Fa^r had done bef— he did as he was sent to lay down his life & take it up again— & was then committed unto him the keys &c I know it is good reasoning—[428]

The Church Being Purged

Thomas Bullock's Report of a Discourse by Joseph Smith

I have reason to think that the Church is being purged. I saw Satan fall from heaven, and the way they ran was a caution. All these are wonders and marvels in our eyes in these last days. So long as men are under the law of God, they have no fears—they do not scare themselves.

I have reason to think that the Church is being purged— I saw Satan fall from heaven— & the way they ran was a caution— all these are wonders & marvellous in our eyes in these last days— so long as men are under the law of God they have no fears, they do not scare themselves—

I want to stick to my text, to show that when men open their lips against these truths they do

I want to stick to my text to shew that when men open their lips— they do not injure me—

---

428. Discourse, 16 June 1844-A, reported by Thomas Bullock, *JSP, D15*, 271–72.

not injure me, but injure themselves. To the law and to the testimony, for these prin[p.374]ciples are poured out all over the Scriptures. When things that are of the greatest importance are passed over by the weak-minded men without even a thought, I want to see truth in all its bearings and hug it to my bosom. I believe all that God ever revealed, and I never hear of a man being damned for believing too much; but they are damned for unbelief.

They found fault with Jesus Christ because He said He was the Son of God, and made Himself equal with God. They say of me, like they did of the Apostles of old, that I must be put down. What did Jesus say? "Is it not written in your law, I said, Ye are Gods? If He called them Gods unto whom the word of God came, and the Scriptures cannot be broken, say ye of Him whom the Father hath sanctified and sent into the world, Thou blasphemest; because I said I am the Son of God?" It was through Him that they drank of the spiritual rock. Of course He would take the honor to Himself. Jesus, if they were called Gods unto whom the word of God came, why should it be thought blasphemy that I should say I am the Son of God?

but injure themselves— to the law & to the testimony— they are poured all over the Scrip

when things that are great are passed over with[t.] even a tho[t.] I want to see all in all its bearings & hug it to my bosom—

I bel. all that God ever rev[eale]^d. & I never hear of a man being d[amne]d for bel^g. too much but they are d—d for unbel[ief]:

[p. 273] they found fault with J.C. bec[ause] he s^d. he was the Son of God— & made himself equal with God—they say like the apos[tates]: of old I must be put down—what Je. says it is written in your law I said Ye are Gods— it was thro' him that they drink of the rock— of course he wo^d. take the honor to himself— J. if they were called Gods unto whom the word of God why sho^d. it be tho[t] incredible that I sho^d say I am the Son of God— oh apostates did ye never think of this bef: these are the quotations that the apostates take to the Scrip—they swear that they bel the Bible & the Book of Mormon &c & then you will get filth & slander & bogus makers plenty— & one of the Church members prophesied that Jo Smith sho^d. never preach any more— & yet I am now preach[in]^g—[429]

Eternal Glories

Thomas Bullock's Report of a Discourse by Joseph Smith

Go and read the vision in the Book of Covenants. There is clearly illustrated glory upon glory—one glory of the sun, another glory of the moon, and a glory of the stars; and as one star differeth from another star in glory, even so do they of the telestial world differ in glory, and every man who reigns in celestial glory is a God to his dominions. By the apostates admitting the testimony of the Doctrine and Covenants they damn them-

go & read the vision— there is glory & glory—Sun. Moon & Stars— & so do they differ in glory

& every man who reigns is a God— & the test of the Do[ctrine] & Cov[t] [Covenants] damns themselves—

---

429. Discourse, 16 June 1844-A, reported by Thomas Bullock, *JSP, D15*, 272–73.

selves. Paul, what do you say? They impeached Paul and all went and left him. Paul had seven churches, and they drove him off from among them; and yet they cannot do it by me. I rejoice in that. My testimony is good.	Paul what do you say— they impeachd Paul & all went & left him— Paul had 7 Churches & they drove him off from among them— & yet they cannot do it by me— I rej[oice] in that—my test. is Good—
Paul says, "There is one glory of the sun, and another glory of the moon, and another glory of the stars; for one star differeth from another star in glory. So also is the resurrection of the dead." They who obtain a glorious resurrection from the dead, are exalted far above principalities, powers, thrones, dominions and angels, and are expressly declared to be heirs of God and joint heirs with Jesus Christ, all having eternal power.	Paul— says there is one Glory of the Sun— the Moon & the Stars— & as one Star differs &c—

they are exalted far above princ[ipalities] thrones. dom[inions] & angels— & are expressly decl^d to be heirs of God & j[oin]^t heirs with J.C. [p.274] all hav[in]^g et^l power— |
| These Scriptures are a mixture of very strange doctrines [p.375] to the Christian world, who are blindly led by the blind. I will refer to another Scripture. "Now," says God, when He visited Moses in the bush, (Moses was a stammering sort of a boy like me) God said, "Thou shalt be a God unto the children of Israel." God said, "Thou shalt be a God unto Aaron, and he shall be thy spokesman." I believe those Gods that God reveals as Gods to be sons of God, and all can cry, "Abba, Father!" Sons of God who exalt themselves to be Gods, even from before the foundation of the world, and are the only Gods I have a reverence for. | the Scrips are a very strange doct[rine]— I have an^r Scrip— now says God when visited Moses in the Bush— Moses was a stutt[er]ing sort of a boy like me— God said thou shalt be a God unto the Children of Israel— God said thou shalt be a God unto Aaron & he shall be thy spokes[man] I bel. in these Gods that God reveals as Gods— to be Sons of God & all can cry Abba Father— Sons of God who exalt themselves to be Gods even from bef the foundat[io]^n of the world & are all the only Gods I have a reverence for— |
| John said he was a king. "And from Jesus Christ, who is the faithful witness, and the first begotten of the dead, and the Prince of the kings of the earth. Unto Him that loved us, and washed us from our sins in His own blood, and hath made us kings and priests unto God, and His Father; to him be glory and dominion forever and ever, Amen." Oh, Thou God who art King of kings and Lord of lords, the sectarian world, by their actions, declare, "We cannot believe Thee." | John s^d he was a K[ing].—J.C. who hath by his own blood made us K & P. to God—

oh thou God who art K. of K's & L^d of L^{ds}— we cannot bel. thee— |
| The old Catholic church traditions are worth more than all you have said. Here is a prin- | old Catholic Church is worth more than all— here is a princ[iple]: of logic— that men have |

ciple of logic that most men have no more sense than to adopt. I will illustrate it by an old apple tree. Here jumps off a branch and says, I am the true tree, and you are corrupt. If the whole tree is corrupt, are not its branches corrupt? If the Catholic religion is a false religion, how can any true religion come out of it? If the Catholic church is bad, how can any good thing come out of it? The character of the old churches have always been slandered by all apostates since the world began.

no more sense— I will illustrate an old apple tree— here jumps off a branch & says I am the true tree— & you are corrupt— if the whole tree is corrupt how can any true thing come out of it—

if Catholic is bad how can any good thing come out of it— the char[acte]$^{rs.}$ of the old ones have always been sland[ere]$^{d.}$ by all apos since the world began—[430]

The Lord Will Not Acknowledge Traitors

Thomas Bullock's Report of a Discourse by Joseph Smith

I testify again, as the Lord lives, God never will acknowledge any traitors or apostates. Any man who will betray the Catholics will betray you; and if he will betray me, he will betray you. All men are liars who say they are of the true Church without the revelations of Jesus Christ and the Priesthood of Melchizedek, which is after the order of the Son of God.

I testify again as God never will acknowledge any apost: any man who will betray the Catholics will betray you—& if he will betray one ano$^{r.}$ he will betray you— all men are liars who say that they are of the true—

It is in the order of heavenly things that God should always send a new dispensation into the world when men have apostatized from the truth and lost the priesthood, but when men come out and build upon other men's foundations, they do [p.376] it on their own responsibility, without authority from God; and when the floods come and the winds blow, their foundations will be found to be sand, and their whole fabric will crumble to dust.

God always sent a new dispensat[io]$^{n.}$ into the world—when men came out & build upon o^{r} [other] men's foundat$^{n.}$—[431] they do it on their own responsibility, without authority from God; and when the floods come and the winds blow their foundations will be found to be sand and their whole fabric will crumble to dust.[432]

Did I build on any other man's foundation? I have got all the truth which the Christian world possessed, and an independent revelation in the bargain, and God will bear me off triumphant. I will drop this subject. I wish I

did I build on ano$^{r.}$ mans found$^{n.}$ but my own—I have got all the truth & an indeped[en]$^{t.}$ rev$^{n.}$ in the bargain—& God will bear me off triumphant—I will drop this subj$^{t.}$ I wish I co[ul]$^{d.}$ speak for 3 or 4 hours it

---

430. Discourse, 16 June 1844-A, reported by Thomas Bullock, *JSP, D15*, 273–74.
431. Discourse, 16 June 1844-A, reported by Thomas Bullock, *JSP, D15*, 274.
432. History F-1, 105.

could speak for three or four hours; but it is not expedient on account of the rain; I would still go on, and show you proof upon proofs; all the Bible is equal in support of this doctrine, one part as another. (June 16, 1844.) DHC 6:473-479.

is not exped[ien]ᵗ· on acct. of the rain—I will still go on & shew you proof on proof, all the Bible is as equal one part as another[433]

The Prophet Predicts His Death

The following items of history in relation to the surrender of the Prophet and Patriarch and their brutal martyrdom, are of such interest that they are included in this record. These brethren with a number of the leading Elders met at dusk, Saturday, June 22, 1844, in the Prophet's upper room. When they were assembled the Prophet presented to them a letter from Governor Ford which he read for the purpose of seeking the counsel of his brethren. At this point the narrative begins.[434]

Manuscript History

"Brethren, here is a letter from the Governor, which I wish to have read." After it was read through Joseph remarked, "There is no mercy—no mercy here." Hyrum said, "No; just as sure as we fall into their hands we are dead men." Joseph replied, "Yes; what shall we do, Brother Hyrum?" He replied, "I don't know." All at once Joseph's countenance brightened up and he said, "The way is open. It is clear to my mind what to do. All they want is Hyrum and myself; then tell everybody to go about their business, and not to collect in groups, but to scatter about. There is no doubt they will come here and search for us. Let them search; they will not harm you in person or property, and not even a hair of your head. We will cross the river to-night, and go away to the west." He made a move to go out of the house to cross the river. When out of doors he told Butler and Hodge to take the Maid of Iowa, (in charge of Repsher) get it to the upper

Joseph remarked: "There is no mercy here—no mercy here." Hyrum said, "No; just as sure as we fall into their hands we are dead men." Joseph replied, "Yes; what shall we do, Brother Hyrum?" He replied, "I don't know." All at once Joseph's countenance brightened up and he said, "The way is open. It is clear to my mind what to do. All they want is Hyrum and myself; then tell everybody to go about their business, and not to collect in groups, but to scatter about. There is no doubt they will come here and search for us. Let them search; they will not harm you in person or property, and not even a hair of your head. We will cross the river tonight, and go away to the West." He made a move to go out of the house to cross the river. When out of doors he told Butler and Hodge to take the Maid of Iowa, (in charge of Repsher) get it to the upper landing,

---

433. Discourse, 16 June 1844-A, reported by Thomas Bullock, *JSP, D15,* 274.
434. This introductory paragraph was authored by Joseph Fielding Smith.

and put his and Hyrum's families and effects upon her; then go down the Mississippi and up the Ohio River to Portsmouth, where they should hear from them. He then took Hodge by the hand and said, "Now, Brother Hodge, let what will come, don't deny the faith, and all will be well."

"I told Stephen Markham that if I and Hyrum were ever **[p.377]** taken again we should be massacred, or I was not a prophet of God. I want Hyrum to live to avenge my blood, but he is determined not to leave me."

* * *

Saturday, June 22, 1844, about 9 p.m. Hyrum came out of the Mansion and gave his hands to Reynolds Cahoon, at the same time saying, "A company of men are seeking to kill my brother Joseph, and the Lord has warned him to flee to the Rocky Mountains to save his life. Good-by, Brother Cahoon, we shall see you again." In a few minutes afterwards Joseph came from his family. His tears were flowing fast. He held a handkerchief to his face, and followed after Brother Hyrum without uttering a word.

Late that night the Prophet and Patriarch were taken across the river by Orrin P. Rockwell preparatory to their start towards the Rocky Mountains.

Early the next morning other brethren joined them.

---

landing, and put his and Hyrum's families and effects upon her; then go down the Mississippi and up the Ohio River to Portsmouth, where they should hear from them. He then took Hodge by the hand and said, "Now, Brother Hodge, let what will come don't deny the faith, and all will be well."

"I told Stephen Markham that if I and Hyrum were ever taken again we should be massacred, or I was not a Prophet of God. I want Hyrum to live to avenge my blood, but he is determined not to leave me."

Saturday, June 22, 1844, about 9 p.m. Hyrum came out of the Mansion and gave his hands to Reynolds Cahoon, at the same time saying, "A company of men are seeking to kill my brother Joseph, and the Lord has warned him to flee to the Rocky Mountains to save his life. Good-by, Brother Cahoon, we shall see you again." In a few minutes afterwards Joseph came from his family. His tears were flowing fast. He held a handkerchief to his face, and followed after Brother Hyrum without uttering a word.

About midnight, Joseph, Hyrum, and Dr. Richards called for O. P. Rockwell at his lodgings, and all went up the river bank until they found Aaron Johnson's boat, which they got into, and started about 2 a.m. to cross the Mississippi river. O. P. Rockwell rowed the skiff, which was very leaky, so that it kept Joseph, Hyrum, and the Doctor busy baling out the water with their boots and shoes to prevent it from sinking.

Sunday, 23.— At daybreak arrived on the Iowa side of the river. Sent O. P. Rockwell back to Nauvoo with instructions to return the next night with horses for Joseph and Hyrum, pass them over the river in the night secretly, and be ready to start for the Great Basin in the Rocky Mountains.

That same morning a posse arrived in Nauvoo to arrest Joseph Smith, but they did not find him, but they did succeed in creating fear in the hearts of some of the timid.

Early in the morning a posse arrived in Nauvoo to arrest Joseph, but as they did not find him, they started back to Carthage immediately, leaving one man of the name of Yates behind them, who said to one of the brethren that Governor Ford designed that if Joseph and Hyrum were not given up, he would send his troops and guard the city until they were found, if it took three years to do it.

At one p.m. that day Orrin P. Rockwell, who had returned to Nauvoo, arrived with a letter from Emma Smith, requesting the Prophet to return to Nauvoo. The Prophet and Patriarch with Willard Richards were in a room where they had assembled provisions preparatory for their journey.

At 1 p.m., Emma sent over O. P. Rockwell requesting him to intreat of Joseph to come back. Reynolds Cahoon accompanied him with a letter which Emma had written to the same effect, and she insisted that Cahoon should persuade Joseph to come back and give himself up. When they went over they found Joseph, Hyrum, and Willard in a room by themselves, having flour and other provisions on the floor ready for packing. Reynolds Cahoon informed the Prophet what the troops intended to do and urged upon him to give himself up, inasmuch as the Governor had pledged his faith and the faith of the State to protect him while he underwent a legal and fair trial.[435]

Reynolds Cahoon informed the Prophet what the troops intended to do and urged upon him to give himself up, inasmuch as the Governor had pledged his faith and the faith of the state to protect him while he underwent a legal trial. The Prophet, however, knew that the word of the Governor was not to be received in good faith. At this point our narrative continues.

False Accusations

Manuscript History

Reynolds Cahoon, Lorenzo D. Wasson and Hiram Kimball accused Joseph of cowardice for wishing to leave the people, adding that their property would be destroyed, and they left without house or home. Like the fable,

R. Cahoon, L. D. Wasson, and Hiram Kimball accused Joseph of cowardice for wishing to leave the people, adding that their property would be destroyed, and they left without house or home. Like the fable, when the

---

435. 22 June 1844, History, F-1, 147–48. This is an amalgamated account drawing on a number of sources. For example, in a letter from Stephen Markham to Wilford Woodruff, we find: "I asked him how this thing was going to come out. he replied if the Brethern would Let him manage the Business; there should be no blood shed, but if not it would be the hardest Blow the Church ever had or would receive, that if he & Hyrum were ever taken again the[y] would be Massacred or he was not a prophet of God, he said he wanted to save Hyrum to avenge is Blood. he said that Hyrum was determined Not to leave him but die with him." Stephen Markham letter, 20 June 1856, Joseph Smith History Documents, 1839–1860, Church History Library, retrievable at history.lds.org/section/library.

when the wolves came the shepherd ran from the flock, and left the sheep to be devoured. To which Joseph replied: "If my life is of no value to my friends it is of none to myself."

Joseph said to Rockwell, "What shall I do?" Rockwell replied, "You are the oldest and ought to know best; and as you make your bed, I will lie with you." Joseph then turned to Hyrum, who was talking with Cahoon, and said, "Brother Hyrum, you are the oldest, what shall we do?" Hyrum said, "Let us go back and give ourselves up, and see the thing out." After studying a few moments, Joseph said, "If you go back I **[p.378]** will go with you, but we shall be butchered." Hyrum said, "No, no; let us go back and put our trust in God, and we shall not be harmed. The Lord is in it. If we live or have to die, we will be reconciled to our fate." After a short pause Joseph told Cahoon to request Captain Daniel C. Davis to have his boat ready at half-past five to cross them over the river. (June 23, 1844.) DHC 6:545-551.

wolves came the shepherd ran from the flock, and left the sheep to be devoured. To which Joseph replied—"If my life is of no value to my friends it is of none to myself."

Joseph said to Rockwell, "What shall I do?" Rockwell replied, "You are the oldest and ought to know best; and as you make your bed, I will lie with you." Joseph then turned to Hyrum, who was talking with Cahoon, and said, "Brother Hyrum, you are the oldest, what shall we do?" Hyrum said, "Let us go back and give ourselves up, and see the thing out." After studying a few moments, Joseph said, "If you go back I shall go with you, but we shall be butchered." Hyrum said, "No, no; let us go back and put our trust in God, and we shall not be harmed. The Lord is in it. If we live or have to die, we will be reconciled to our fate." After a short pause Joseph told Cahoon to request Captain Daniel C. Davies to have his boat ready by half-past five o'clock to cross them over the river.[436]

Letter: Joseph and Hyrum Smith to Governor Ford—Consenting to Go to Carthage

Bank of the River Mississippi,
Sunday, June 23rd, 1844, 2 p.m.

His Excellency Governor Ford:

Sir: I wrote you a long communication at 12 last night, expressive of my views of your Excellency's communication of yesterday. I thought your letter rather severe, but one of my friends has just come to me with an explanation from the captain of your posse which softened the subject matter of your communication, and gives us greater assurance of protection, and that your Excellency has succeeded in bringing in subjection the spirits which surround your Excellency to some extent. And I declare again the only objection I ever had or

Joseph Smith Letter to Thomas Ford

Bank of the River Missisippi
Sunday June 23d 1844. 2 P.M.

His Excellency Thomas Ford

Sir: I wrote you a long communication at 12 last night, expressive of my views of your Excellency's communication of yesterday. I thought your Letter rather severe, but one of my friends has just come to me with an explanation from the captain of your possie which softened the subject matter of your communication, and gives me us greater assurance of protection, and that your Excellency has succeeded in bringing in subjection the spirits, which surround your Excellency, to some extent. And I declare again the only objection I ever had or ever made

---

436. 23 June 1844, History, F-1, 147–48.

ever made on trial by my country at any time, was what I have made in my last letter—on account of assassins, and the reason I have to fear deathly consequences from their hands.

But from the explanation, I now offer to come to you at Carthage on the morrow, as early as shall be convenient for your posse to escort us into headquarters, provided we can have a fair trial, not be abused nor have my witnesses abused, and have all things done in due form of law, without partiality, and you may depend on my honor without the show of a great armed force to produce excitement in the minds of the timid.

We will meet your posse, if this letter is satisfactory, (if not, inform me) at or near the Mound, at or about two o'clock tomorrow afternoon, which will be as soon as we can get our witnesses and prepare for trial. We shall expect to take our witnesses with us, and not have to wait a subpoena or part at least, so as not to detain the proceedings, although we may want time for counsel.

[p.379] We remain most respectfully, your Excellency's humble servants,
JOSEPH SMITH,
HYRUM SMITH.
(June 23, 1844.) DHC 6:550.

to trial by my country at any time was what I have made in my last letter—on account of assassins, & [the] reason I have to fear deathly consequences from their hands.

But from the Explanation I now offer to come to you at Carthage on the morrow as early as shall be convenient for your possie to escort me us in to Head Quarters, provided I we can have a fair trial, <which we> not be abused, nor have my witnesses abused, and have all things done in due form of law, without partiality, and you may depend on my honour without the show of a great armed force to produce excitement in the minds of the timid.

We I will meet your possie <if this letter is satisfactory if not inform me> at or near the Mound at or about two oclock tomorrow afternoon, which will be as soon as we can get our witnesses & prepare for trial. We shall expect to take our witnesses with us and not have to wait a subpoena, or a part at least, so as not <to> detain the procedings, although we may want time for counsel.

We remain most Respectfully your Excellencys Humble servants
Joseph Smith
Hyrum Smith[437]

The Start for Carthage

Manuscript History

Joseph paused when they got to the Temple, and looked with admiration first on that, and then on the city, and remarked, "This is the loveliest place and the best people under the heavens; little do they know the trials that await them." As he passed out of the city, he called on Daniel H. Wells, Esq., who was unwell, and on parting he said, "Squire Wells, I wish you to cherish my memory, and not think me the worst man in the world either."

Joseph paused when they got to the Temple, and looked with admiration first on that, and then on the city, and remarked, "This is the loveliest place and the best people under the heavens; little do they know the trials that await them." As he passed out of the city, he called on Daniel H. Wells, Esq., who was unwell, and on parting he said, "Squire Wells, I wish you to cherish my memory, and not think me the worst man in the world either."

---

437. 23 June 1844, Joseph Smith letter to Thomas Ford, Church History Library, in *PWJS*, 617–18.

At ten minutes to 10 a.m. they arrived at Albert G. Fellows' farm, four miles west of Carthage, where they met Captain Dunn with a company of about sixty mounted militia, on seeing which Joseph said, "Do not be alarmed, brethren, for they cannot do more to you than the enemies of truth did to the ancient Saints—they can only kill the body." The company made a halt, when Joseph, Hyrum and several others went into Fellows' house with Captain Dunn, who presented an order from Governor Ford for all the state arms in possession of the Nauvoo Legion, which Joseph immediately countersigned.

At 10 minutes to 10 a.m. they arrived at Albert G. Fellows' farm, four miles west of Carthage, where they met Captain Dunn, with a company of about sixty mounted militia, on seeing which Joseph said, "Do not be alarmed, brethren, for they cannot do more to you than the enemies of truth did to the ancient Saints—they can only kill the body." The company made a halt, when Joseph, Hyrum and several others went into Fellows' house with Captain Dunn, who presented an order from Governor Ford for all the State arms in possession of the Nauvoo Legion, which Joseph immediately countersigned.[438]

Like a Lamb to the Slaughter

Manuscript History

Henry G. Sherwood went up to Joseph and said, "Brother Joseph, shall I return to Nauvoo and regulate about getting the arms and get the receipts for them?" Joseph inquired if he was under arrest, or expected to be arrested. Sherwood answered "No," when Joseph directed him to return ahead of the company, gather the arms and do as well as he could in all things. Joseph then said to the company who were with him, "I am going like a lamb to the slaughter, but I am calm as a summer's morning. I have a conscience void of offense toward God and toward all men. If they take my life I shall die an innocent man, and my blood shall cry from the ground for vengeance, and it shall be said of me, 'He was murdered in cold blood!'" He then said to

Henry G. Sherwood went up to Joseph and said, "Brother Joseph, shall I return to Nauvoo and regulate about getting the arms and get the receipts for them?" Joseph inquired if he was under arrest, or expected to be arrested. Sherwood answered "No," when Joseph directed him to return a-head of the company, gather the arms and do as well as he could in all things. Joseph then said to the company who were with him, "I am going like a lamb to the slaughter, but I am calm as a summer's morning. I have a conscience void of offense toward God and toward all men. If they take my life I shall die an innocent man, and my blood shall cry from the ground for vengeance, and it shall be said of me, 'He was murdered in cold blood!'" He then said to

---

438. 24 June 1844, History, F-1, 151. Manuscript History is derivative from other sources. For example, part of the above quote may have come from a letter to Thomas Bullock from Dan Jones. Jones wrote: "Monday 24th—(June 1844) the Prophet as he mounted his steed, and together with his brother Hyrum and some 30 or 40 more who chose to follow, they ascended the hill; when near the sacred spot-the Temple, he paused, he looked with admiration first on that, then on the City ere it receded from view in the flats below, and remarked, this is the loveliest place and the best people under the heavens, little do they know the trials that await them. While on the prairie we met some messengers previously sent to Carthage who had but just been liberated from prison. When within 4 miles of Carthage we met a company of horsemen commanded by Captain Dunn." Dan Jones letter to Thomas Bullock, 20 January 1855, in Dennis, "The Martyrdom of Joseph Smith," 96. Other information may have come from the 30 November 1854, Albert G. Fellows Report, Historian's Office.

Father Sherwood, "Go, and God bless you." Sherwood then rode swiftly as he could to Nauvoo. (June 24, 1844.) DHC 6:554-555.

Father Sherwood, "Go, and God bless you." Sherwood then rode swiftly as he could to Nauvoo.[439]

Joseph Smith to Governor Ford—Explaining His Return to Nauvoo

Joseph Smith Letter to Thomas Ford

[p.380] Four Miles West of Carthage Mound, Hancock County, Illinois, Monday, 10 o'clock

Four miles west of Carthage Mound Hancock Co. Ill. Joseph Smith, The Personal Writings of Monday 10 oclock

His Excellency Governor Ford:

His Excellency Gov Ford

Dear Sir:—On my way to Carthage to answer your request this morning, I here met Captain Dunn, who has here made known to me your orders to surrender the state arms in possession of the Nauvoo Legion, which command I shall comply with; and that the same may be done properly and without trouble to the state, I shall return with Captain Dunn to Nauvoo, see that the arms are put into his possession, and shall then return to headquarters in his company, when I shall most cheerfully submit to any requisition of the Governor or our state.

Dear Sir on my way to Carthage to answer your Request, this morning, I have met Capt Dunn who has made known to me your order to surrender the state arms in possession of the Nauvoo Legion, which demand I shall most cheerfully comply with, and that the same may be done properly and without trouble to the state - I shall return with Capt Dunn to Nauvoo, see that the arms are put in his possession, and shall then return to head quarters in his company, when I shall most cheerfully submit to any requisition of the Governor of our state

With all due respect to your Excellency, I remain you obedient servant.
JOSEPH SMITH.
(June 24, 1844.) DHC 6:556.

With all due respect to your Excellency I remain sir most Respectfully
your obt servant
Joseph Smith[440]

---

439. 24 June 1844, History, F-1, 151. George A. Smith assembled a number of the amalgamated discourses found in TPJS—such as the one reported here—from highly fragmented accounts of the Prophet's teachings. He explained, "I have filled all the reports of sermons by Prestident Joseph Smith and others from minutes or sketches taken at the time in long hand by Dr. Willard Richards, Wilford Woodruff, Thomas Bullock, William Clayton, Miss Eliza R. Snow &c. which was an immense labor, requiring the deepest thought and the closest application, as there were mostly only two or three words (about half written) to a sentence. The greatest care has been taken to convey the ideas in the prophet's style as near as possible." George A. Smith letter to Wilford Woodruff, 21 April 1856, Historian's Office, Historical Record Book, 218. George A. Smith created the well-known "lamb to the slaughter" quotation based on a number of sources he had access to (some of which are no longer extant), including a letter from John M. Bernhisel to George A. Smith, which included the following statement: "Joseph being still seated on his favorite horse, and the solemnities of eternity seemed to be resting upon his mind, and looking me full in the face, he said: 'I am going as a lamb to the slaughter, but I am as calm as a summer's morning; I have a conscience void of offense towards God and man, and I am not afraid to die.'" John M. Bernhisel letter to George A. Smith, 11 September 1854, Church History Library, accessed 14 October 2024, https://catalog.churchofjesuschrist.org/assets/47c43c48-b1b5-4830-bf18-366736687678/0/0.

440. 24 June 1844, Joseph Smith letter to Thomas Ford, Church History Library, in PWJS, 619.

On the Way to Carthage

The company (about fifteen) then started again for Carthage, and when opposite to the Masonic Hall, Joseph said, "Boys, if I don't come back, take care of yourselves; I am going like a lamb to the slaughter." When they passed his farm he took a good look at it, and after they had passed it, he turned round several times to look again, at which some of the company made remarks, when Joseph said: "If some of you had got such a farm and knew you would not see it any more, you would want to take a good look at it for the last time." When they got to the edge of the woods near Nauvoo, they met A. C. Hodge returning from Carthage, told him what his feelings were and said, "Brother Hyrum, you are now clear, and if it was my duty to counsel you, I would say, do not go another foot, for they say they will kill you, if you go to Carthage," but as other persons gathered around, nothing further was said. (June 24, 1844.) DHC 6:558.

Manuscript History

The company (about fifteen) then started again for Carthage, and when opposite to the Masonic Hall, Joseph said, "Boys, if I don't come back, take care of yourselves; I am going like a lamb to the slaughter." When they passed his farm he took a good look at it, and after they had passed it, he turned round several times to look again, at which some of the company made remarks, when Joseph said: "If some of you had got such a farm and knew you would not see it any more, you would want to take a good look at it for the last time." When they got to the edge of the woods near Nauvoo, they met A. C. Hodge returning from Carthage, told him what his feelings were and said, "Brother Hyrum, you are now clear, and if it was my duty to counsel you, I would say, do not go another foot, for they say they will kill you, if you go to Carthage," but as other persons gathered around, nothing further was said.[441]

The Prophet's Interview with Militia Officers

[p.381] Several of the officers of the troops in Carthage, and other gentlemen, curious to see the Prophet, visited Joseph in his room. General Smith asked them if there was anything in his appearance that indicated he was the desperate character his enemies represented him to be; and he asked them to give him their honest opinion on the subject. The reply was, "No, sir, your appearance would indicate the very contrary, General Smith; but we cannot see what is in your heart, neither can we tell what are your intentions." To which Joseph replied, "Very true, gentlemen, you cannot see what is in my heart, and you are therefore unable to judge me or my intentions; but I can see what is in your hearts, and will tell you

Manuscript History

Several of the officers of the troops in Carthage, and other gentlemen, curious to see the Prophet, and to gratify a propensity to see the elephant, visited Joseph in his room. General Smith asked them if there was anything in his appearance that indicated he was the desperate character his enemies represented him to be; and he asked them to give him their honest opinion on the subject. The reply was, "No, sir, your appearance would indicate the very contrary, General Smith; but we cannot see what is in your heart, neither can we tell what are your intentions." To which Joseph replied, "Very true, gentlemen, you cannot see what is in my heart, and you are therefore unable to judge me or my intentions; but I can see what

---

441. 24 June 1844, History, F-1, 153.

what I see. I can see that you thirst for blood, and nothing but my blood will satisfy you.

It is not for crime of any description that I and my brethren are thus continually persecuted and harassed by our enemies, but there are other motives, and some of them I have expressed, so far as relates to myself; and inasmuch as you and the people thirst for blood, I prophesy, in the name of the Lord, that you shall witness scenes of blood and sorrow to your entire satisfaction. Your souls shall be perfectly satiated with blood, and many of you who are now present shall have an opportunity to face the cannon's mouth from sources you think not of; and those people that desire this great evil upon me and my brethren, shall be filled with regret and sorrow because of the scenes of desolation and distress that awaits them. They shall seek for peace, and shall not be able to find it. Gentlemen, you will find what I have told you to be true." (June 25, 1844.) DHC 6:566.

is in your hearts, and will tell you what I see. I can see that you thirst for blood, and nothing but my blood will satisfy you.

It is not for crime of any description that I and my brethren are thus continually persecuted and harassed by our enemies, but there are other motives, and some of them I have expressed, so far as relates to myself; and inasmuch as you and the people thirst for blood, I prophesy, in the name of the Lord, that you shall witness scenes of blood and sorrow to your entire satisfaction. Your souls shall be perfectly satiated with blood, and many of you who are now present shall have an opportunity to face the cannon's mouth from sources you think not of; and those people that desire this great evil upon me and my brethren, shall be filled with regret and sorrow because of the scenes of desolation and distress that awaits them. They shall seek for peace, and shall not be able to find it. Gentlemen, you will find what I have told you to be true."[442]

---

442. 25 June 1844, History, F-1, 157–58. This history is an amalgamated text taken from several sources. One of the sources was a letter from Cyrus Wheelock to George A. Smith, 29 December 1854, JS Collection, Church History Library. An extract from that letter reads: "Quite a number of the above named gentlemen present, who seemed apparently much interested in the situation of the prisoners, —the circumstances referred to as near as I can remember is as follows, - Bro Joseph appealed to the gentlemen present, to know if he looked like a man guilty of the charge preferred against him by his enemies; said he, gentlemen, I wish you to speak freely, & unreservedly, as you feel, & tell me, do I look like the character I am judged to be, — is there anything in my countenance or appearance to justify the belief that I am a murderer, or a whoremonger, or guilty of treasonable designs against the government; or would my appearance in any way lead you to suppose that I was the enemy of mankind & good order, and government. Gentlemen, please to answer me truthfully as upon your honor— to this appeal; the gentleman who offered to take the lead in the conversation, and in whom his associates seemed to have confidence, replied in the following words, No Sir, General Smith – your appearance would indicate the very contrary. I can see nothing in your appearance to justify the gross charges that are everywhere proclaimed against you, — but, said he, we cannot see what is in your heart, and we're unable to fathom your purposes; and then quite abruptly altered his tone & sentiment and said, the freedom of the press must be maintained, and you and your party, have destroyed one in your city, which act has raised the indignation of the republican spirit against you, which will no doubt result in serious consequences; to which brother Joseph replied very true gentlemen you cannot see what is in my heart, and are therefore unable to judge me or my intentions, but, I can see what is in your heart, and will tell you what I see—I can see your thirst for blood, and nothing but my blood will satisfy you, tis not for crime of any description that I, and my brethren are thus continually persecuted, and involved in lawsuits, and continually harassed by our enemies, but there are other motives, and some of them I have expected so far as relates to myself, and inasmuch as you, & the people, thirst for blood, I prophesy, in the name of

Letter—Joseph Smith to Governor Ford—Soliciting an Interview

Carthage Jail, June 26, 1844,
Ten minutes past 8 a.m.

His Excellency Governor Ford:

Sir.—I would again solicit your Excellency for an interview having been much disappointed the past evening. I hope you will not deny me this privilege any longer than your public duties shall absolutely require.

We have been committed under a false mittimus, and [p.382] consequently the proceedings are illegal, and we desire the time may be hastened when all things shall be made right, and we relieved from this imprisonment.
Your servant,
JOSEPH SMITH.
P.S.—Please send an answer per bearer.
(June 26, 1844.) DHC 6:575.

Joseph Smith Letter to Thomas Ford
Carthage Jail, June 26th 1844
10. mi past 8. AM.

His Excellency, Gov. Ford.

Sir. I would again solicit your Excellency for an interview, having been much disappointed the past evening. I hope you will not deny me this privilige any longer than your public duties shall absolutely require-

We have been committed under a false mittimus, and consequently the proceedings are illegal, & we desire the time may be hastened when all things shall be made right, and we relieved from this imprisonment, Your Servt.
Joseph Smith

P.S. Please send an answer per bearer.

His Excelly Gov. Ford
Head Quarters Carthage.[443]

The Prophet's Premonition

At noon, June 26, 1844, Willard Richards, the recorder, made copies of orders from the Prophet to brethren in Nauvoo; while doing so—

Manuscript History
W[illard] Richards made copies of the orders of Joseph Smith as ~~Major~~ Mayor to Marshal John P. Greene, and as Lieutenant General to Major General Jonathan Dunham

—Joseph remarked, "I have had a good deal of anxiety about my safety since I left Nauvoo, which I never had before when I was under arrest. I could not help those feelings, and they

Joseph remarked, "I have had a good deal of anxiety about my safety since I left Nauvoo, which I never had before when I was under arrest. I could not help those feelings and they

the Lord, that you shall witness the scenes of blood and sorrow to your entire satisfaction, your soul shall be perfectly satiated with blood, and many of you who are now present, shall have an opportunity to face the cannon's mouth from sources you think not of, and the people that desire this great evil upon me, and my brethren, shall be filled with regret and sorrow, because of the scenes of destruction and distress that await them, they shall seek for peace, and shall not be able to find it, Gentlemen you'll find what I have told you to be true."

443. 26 June 1844, Joseph Smith letter to Thomas Ford, Church History Library, in *PWJS*, 624–25.

have depressed me." Most of the forenoon was spent by Dan Jones and Col. Stephen Markham in hewing with a pen-knife a warped door to get it on the latch, thus preparing to fortify the place against any attack.

The Prophet, Patriarch, and their friends took turns preaching to the guards, several of whom were relieved before their time was out, because they admitted they were convinced of the innocence of the prisoners. They frequently admitted they had been imposed upon, and more than once it was heard, "Let us go home, boys, for I will not fight any longer against these men."

During the day Hyrum encouraged Joseph to think that the Lord, for His Church's sake, would release him from prison. Joseph replied, "Could my brother, Hyrum, but be liberated, it would not matter so much about me. Poor Rigdon, I am glad he is gone to Pittsburg out of the way; were he to preside he would lead the Church to destruction in less than five years." (June 26, 1844.) DHC 6:592-593.

have depressed me." Most of the forenoon was spent by Dan Jones and Col. Stephen Markham in hewing with a penknife, a warped door to get it on the latch; thus preparing to fortify the place against any attack.[444]

A portion of us were alternately preaching to the guards, at which the Prophet, Patriarch and all took turns, and several were relieved before their time was out because they admitted they were proselyted to the belief of the innocency of the prisoners, which, rendered them incompetent of guarding! Frequently they admitted they had been imposed upon by the tales of the mob and more than once was it heard "Let us go home boys for I will not fight against these men." Hyrum showed an ardent devotion to the Prophet, every way encouraging him to believe that the Lord for His Church's sake would release him to their service, while Joseph reply'd, "Could my brother Hyrum be but liberated it would not matter so much about me; poor Rigdon, I am glad he has gone to Pittsburgh out of way, were he to preside, in less than five years he would lead the Church to destruction."[445]

The Ill Treatment of John Smith—5:30 p.m.

Manuscript History

Patriarch John Smith came from Macedonia to jail to see his nephews, Joseph and Hyrum. The road was thronged with mobbers. Three of them snapped their guns at him, and he was threatened by many others who recognized him. The guard at the jail refused him admittance.

Joseph saw him through the prison window, and said to [p.383] the guard, "Let the old gentleman come in, he is my uncle." The

Patriarch John Smith came from Macedonia to the Jail to see his Nephews Joseph and Hyrum; the road was thronged with mobbers; three of them snapped their guns at him, and he was threatened by many others who recognized him; the guard at the Jail refused him admittance.

Joseph saw him through the prison window, and said to the guard, "let the old gentleman come in, he is my uncle." The guard replied

---

444. 26 June 1844, History, F-1, 168.

445. The account found in *TPJS* appears to have been taken directly from the Manuscript History of the Church. However, these paragraphs come from a letter from Dan Jones to Thomas Bullock, 20 January 1855, Church History Library, cited in Dennis, "The Martyrdom of Joseph Smith," 99. Manuscript History of the Church was compiled using earlier writings such as this one by Dan Jones.

guard replied they did not care who the hell he was uncle to, he should not go in.

Joseph replied, "You will not hinder so old and infirm a man as he is from coming in," and then said, "Come in, uncle;" on which, after searching him closely the guard let him pass into the jail, where he remained about an hour. He asked Joseph if he thought he should again get out of the hands of his enemies, when he replied, "My brother Hyrum thinks I shall. I wish you would tell the brethren in Macedonia that they can see by this, that it has not been safe for me to visit them; and tell Almon W. Babbitt I want him to come and assist me as an attorney at my expected trial tomorrow before Captain R. F. Smith. (June 26, 1844.) DHC 6:597-598.

they did not care who the hell he was uncle to, he should not go in.

Joseph replied, "you will not hinder so old and infirm a man as he is from coming in;" and then said, "come in uncle"; on which, after searching him closely, the guard let him pass into the jail, where he remained about an hour. He asked Joseph if he thought he should again get out of the hands of his enemies, when he replied: "my brother Hyrum thinks I shall; I wish you would tell the brethren in Macedonia that they can see by this, that it has not been safe for me to visit them; and tell Almon W. Babbitt, I want him to come and assist me as an attorney at my expected trial tomorrow before Captain R. F. Smith"[446]

The Last Night in Jail

June 26, 1844, 9:15 p.m.—Elder John Taylor prayed. Willard Richards, John Taylor, John S. Fullmer, Stephen Markham and Dan Jones stayed with Joseph and Hyrum in the front room.

During the evening the Patriarch Hyrum Smith read and commented upon extracts from the Book of Mormon, on the imprisonment and deliverance of the servants of God for the Gospel's sake. Joseph bore a powerful testimony to the guards of the divine authenticity of the Book of Mormon, the restoration of the Gospel, the administration of angels, and that the kingdom of God was again established upon the earth, for the sake of which he was

Manuscript History

9 ¼ Elder John Taylor prayed. Willard Richards, John Taylor, John S. Fullmer, Stephen Markham and Dan Jones staid with Joseph and Hyrum in the front room.[447]

During the evening the Patriarch read and commented upon copious extracts from the Book of Mormon, the imprisonments and deliverance of the servants of God for the Gospels sake; Joseph bore a powerful-testimony to the guards of the divine authenticity of the Book of Mormon—the restoration of the Gospel, the administration of angels, and that the Kingdom of God was again upon the earth, for the sake of which he was at that time incar-

---

446. 26 June 1844, History, F-1, 171. This History, F-1 entry is an amalgamated text taken from several sources. One of the sources was John Smith Journal, 1846–1854, Church History Library. On page 70 is written: "When I got there it was surrounded with armed men they forbade my going any farther Joseph looked out the window overhead & said to the guard that is my unkle, let him come in, God Bless you unkle come in, the guard Replied I Don't care who in hell's unkle he is I am set here to guard & I will guard Joseph said come in unkle, come along, the guard searched me to see if I had a weapon but finding I had none let me pass."

447. 26 June 1844, History, F-1, 172.

then incarcerated in that prison, and not because he had violated any law of God or man.

They retired to rest late. Joseph and Hyrum occupied the only bedstead in the room, while their friends lay side by side on the mattresses on the floor. Dr. Richards sat up writing until his last candle left him in the dark. The report of a gun fired close by caused Joseph to rise, leave the bed, and lay himself on the floor, having Dan Jones on his left, and John S. Fullmer on his right.

Joseph laid out his right arm, and said to John S. Fullmer, "Lay your head on my arm for a pillow, Brother John;" and when all were quiet they conversed in a low tone about the prospects of their deliverance. Joseph gave expression to several presentiments that he had to die, and said, "I would like to see my family again," and "I would [p.384] to God that I could preach to the Saints in Nauvoo once more." Fullmer tried to rally his spirits, saying he thought he would often have that privilege, when Joseph thanked him for the remark and good feelings expressed to him.

Soon after Dr. Richards retired to the bed which Joseph had left, and when all were apparently fast asleep, Joseph whispered to Dan Jones, "Are you afraid to die?" Dan said, "Has that time come, think you? Engaged in such

cerated in that prison, and not because-he had violated any law of God or of man.[448]

They retired to rest late; Joseph and Hyrum occupied the only bedstead in the room, while their friends lay side by side on the mattrasses on the floor. Dr. Richards sat up writing until his last candle left him in the dark; the report of a gun fired close by, caused Joseph to arise, leave the bed, and lay himself on the floor, having Dan Jones on his left, -[Jones]- and John S. Fullmer on his right.

Joseph laid out his right arm, and said to John S. Fullmer, "lay your head on my arm for a pillow brother John;" and when all were quiet they conversed in a low tone about the prospects of their deliverance, Joseph gave expression to several presentiments that he had to die, and said, "I would like to see my family again;" and "I would to God that I could preach to the Saints in Nauvoo once more." Fullmer tried to rally his spirits, saying he thought he would often have that privilege; when Joseph thanked him for the remarks and good feelings expressed to him. -[Fullmer]-.[449]

soon after Dr. Richards retired to the bed and while I thought all, but myself and heaven asleep, Joseph asked in a whisper if I was afraid to die. "has that time come think you? Engaged in such a cause I do not think that

---

448. Dan Jones letter to Thomas Bullock, 20 January 1855, in Dennis, "The Martyrdom of Joseph Smith," 101.

449. John S. Fulmer letter to George A. Smith, 27 November 1854, Church History Library, accessed 30 September 2024, https://catalog.churchofjesuschrist.org/assets/e6f546b5-01d1-4278-a738-76e9de49713f/0/0. An excerpt of Fulmer's letter reads: "The rest of us laid down side by side upon something spread upon the floor. Brother Joseph and I laid together; he laid his right arm out for me to lay my head upon it, which I did—a privilege which I shall ever remember with joy and satisfaction—after the brethren were all quiet and seemed asleep, excepting myself, he talked with me a little about the prospects of his deliverance. He did not say he knew that he had to die—but he inferred as much, and finally said he, 'would like to see his family again,'—and he 'would to God that he could preach to the Saints once more in Nauvoo.' These expressions I shall never forget; they spoke so direct what was in his heart." See also John S. Fulmer, *Assassination of Joseph and Hyrum Smith, the Prophet and the patriarch of the Church of Jesus Christ of Latter-day Saints also, A condensed history of the expulsion of the saints from Nauvoo* (F. D. Richards, 1855), 5–40. It is likely that the source of this section of TPJS was 26 June 1844, History, F-1, 173.

a cause I do not think that death would have many terrors." Joseph replied, "You will yet see Wales, and fulfill the mission appointed to you before you die." (June 26, 1844—midnight.) DHC 6:600-601.

death would have many terrors," I replied. "You will see Wales and fulfill the mission appointed you ere you die"[450]

Elder John Taylor's Account of Governor Ford's and President Smith's Interview[451]

This account was written by John Taylor subsequent to the events here portrayed.

Account by John Taylor

The following report is by Elder John Taylor:—

Governor.—General Smith, I believe you have given me a general outline of the difficulties that have existed in the country, in the documents forwarded to me by Dr. Bernhisel and Mr. Taylor; but, unfortunately, there seems to be a discrepancy between your statements and those of your enemies. It is true that you are substantiated by evidence and affidavit, but for such an extraordinary excitement as that which is now in the country, there must be some cause, and I attribute the last outbreak to the destruction of the *Expositor*, and to your refusal to comply with the writ issued by Esq. Morrison. The press in the United States is looked upon as the great bulwark of American freedom, and its destruction in Nauvoo was represented and looked upon as a high-handed measure, and manifests to the people a disposition on your part to suppress the liberty of speech and of the press; this, with your refusal to comply with the requisition of a write, I conceive to be the principal cause of this difficulty, and you are, moreover, represented to me as turbulent and defiant of the laws and institutions of your country.

"Governor. General Smith, I believe you have given me a general outline of the difficulties that have existed in the country, in the documents forwarded to me by Dr. John Bernhisel and Mr. Taylor, but unfortunately there seems to be a great discrepency betweeen your statements and those of your enemies; it is true that you are substantiated by evidence and affidavit, but for such an extraordinary excitement as that which is now in the country, there must be some cause, and I attribute the last outbreak to the destruction of the Expositor, and to your refusal to comply with the writ issued by Esq. Thomas Morrison. The press in the United States is looked upon as the great bulwark of American freedom, and its destructon in Nauvoo was represented, and looked upon as a high-handed measure, and manifests to the people a disposition on your part, to suppress the liberty of speech and of the press; this, with your refusal to comply with the requisitions of a writ, I conceive to be the principal cause of this difficulty, and you are moreover represented to me as turbulent and defiant of the laws and institutions of your country.

Gen. Smith.—Governor Ford, you, sir, as Governor of this State, are aware of the prosecutions and persecutions that I have endured. You know well that our course has

"Gen. Smith. Governor Ford, you, Sir, as Governor of this state, are aware of the persecutions that I have endured. You know well that our course has been peaceable and

---

450. Dan Jones letter to Thomas Bullock, 20 January 1855, in Dennis, "The Martyrdom of Joseph Smith," 101.

451. Report by John Taylor, in History, F-1, Addenda, 3–8. See also Mark H. Taylor, comp. and ed., *Witness to the Martyrdom: John Taylor's Personal Account of the Last Days of the Prophet Joseph Smith* (Deseret Book, 1999), 67–77.

been peaceable and law-abiding, for I have furnished this State, ever **[p.385]** since our settlement here, with sufficient evidence of my pacific intentions, and those of the people with whom I am associated, by the endurance of every conceivable indignity and lawless outrage perpetrated upon me and upon this people since our settlement here, and you yourself know that I have kept you well posted in relation to all matters associated with the late difficulties. If you have not got some of my communications, it has not been my fault.

Agreeably to your orders, I assembled the Nauvoo Legion for the protection of Nauvoo and the surrounding country against an armed band of marauders, and ever since they have been mustered I have almost daily communicated with you in regard to all the leading events that have transpired; and whether in the capacity of mayor of the city, or lieutenant-general of the Nauvoo Legion, I have striven to preserve the peace and administer even-handed justice to all; but my motives are impugned, my acts are misconstrued, and I am grossly and wickedly misrepresented. I suppose I am indebted for my incarceration here to the oath of a worthless man that was arraigned before me and fined for abusing and maltreating his lame, helpless brother.

That I should be charged by you, sir, who know better, of acting contrary to law, is to me a matter of surprise. Was it the Mormons or our enemies who first commenced these difficulties? You know well it was not us; and when this turbulent, outrageous people commenced their insurrectionary movements, I made you acquainted with them, officially, asked your advice, and have followed strictly your counsel in every particular.

Who ordered out the Nauvoo Legion? I did, under your direction. For what purpose? To suppress these insurrectionary movements. It was at your instance, sir, that I issued a

"Agreeably to your orders, I assembled the Nauvoo Legion for the protection of Nauvoo and the surrounding country against an armed band of marauders; and ever since they have been mustered, I have almost daily communicated with you in regard to all the leading events that have transpired; and whether in the capacity of Mayor of the city, or Lieutenant-general of the Nauvoo Legion, I have striven, according to the best of my judgment to preserve the peace and to administer even-handed justice; but my motives are impugned, my acts are misconstrued, and I am grossly and wickedly misrepresented. I suppose I am indebted for my incarceration to the oath of a worthless man who was arraigned before me and fined for abusing and maltreating his lame, helpless brother.

That I should be charged by you, Sir, who know better, of acting contrary to law, is to me a matter of surprise. Was it the Mormons or our enemies who first commenced these difficulties? You know well it was not us, and when this turbulent, outrageous people commenced their insurrectionary movements I made you acquainted with them officially, and asked your advice, and have followed strictly your counsel in every particular.

Who ordered out the Nauvoo Legion?—I did, under your direction. For what purpose?— To suppress the insurrectionary movements. It was at your instance, Sir, that I issued a proclamation calling upon the Nauvoo Legion to be in readiness, at a moment's warning, to guard against the incursions of mobs, and gave an order to Jonathan Dunham, acting major-general, to that effect. Am I then to be charged for the acts of others; and because lawlessness and mobocracy abound, am I when carrying out your instructions, to be charged with not abiding the law? Why is it that I must be held accountable for other men's acts? If there is trouble in the country, neither I nor my people made it, and all that we have ever done, after **[p.386]** much endurance on our part, is to maintain and uphold the Constitution and institutions of our country, and to protect an injured, innocent, and persecuted people against misrule and mob violence. Concerning the destruction of the press to which you refer, men may differ somewhat in their opinions about it; but can it be supposed that after all the indignities to which we have been subjected outside, that this people could suffer a set of worthless vagabonds to come into our city, and right under our own eyes and protection, vilify and calumniate not only ourselves, but the character of our wives and daughters, as was impudently and unblushingly done in that infamous and filthy sheet? There is not a city in the United States that would have suffered such an indignity for twenty-four hours.

Our whole people were indignant, and loudly called upon our city authorities for redress of their grievances, which, if not attended to they themselves would have taken the matter into their own hands, and have summarily punished the audacious wretches, as they deserved.

The principles of equal rights that have been instilled into our bosoms from our cradles, as American citizens, forbid us submitting to every foul indignity, and succumbing and pandering to wretches so infamous as these. But, independent of this, the course that we pursued we considered to be strictly legal; for notwithstanding the insult we were anxious to be governed strictly by law, and therefore convened the City Council; and being desirous in our deliberations to abide law, summoned legal counsel to be present on the occasion.

Upon investigating the matter, we found that our City Charter gave us power to remove all nuisances; and, furthermore, upon consulting Blackstone upon what might be considered a nuisance, that distinguished lawyer, who is considered authority, I believe, in all our courts, states, among other things, that a libelous and filthy press may be considered a nuisance, and abated as such.

Here, then, one of the most eminent English barristers, whose works are considered standard with us, declares that a libelous press may be considered a nuisance; and our own charter, given us by the legislature of this State, gives us the power to remove nuisances; and by ordering that press abated as a nuisance, we conceived that we were acting strictly in [p.387] accordance with law. We made that order in our corporate capacity, and the City Marshal carried it out. It is possible there may have been some better way, but I must confess that I could not see it.

In relation to the writ served upon us, we were willing to abide the consequences of our own acts, but were unwilling, in answering a writ of that kind, to submit to illegal exactions sought to be imposed upon us under the pretense of law, when we knew they were in open violation of it. When that document was presented to me by Mr. Bettisworth, I offered, in the presence of more than 20 persons, to go to any other magistrate, either in our city or Appanoose, or any other place where we should be safe, but we all refused to put ourselves into the power of a mob.

What right had that constable to refuse our request? He had none according to law; for you know, Governor Ford, that the statute law in Illinois is, that the parties served with the writ shall go before him who issued it, or some other justice of the peace. Why, then, should we be dragged to Carthage, where the law does not compel us to go? Does not this look like many others of our prosecutions with which you are acquainted? And had we not a right to expect foul play?

This very act was a breach of law on his part—an assumption of power that did not belong to him, and an attempt, at least, to deprive us of our legal and constitutional rights and privileges. What could we do under the circumstances different from what we did do? We sued for, and obtained a writ of *habeas corpus* from the hands of Constable Bettisworth, and brought before and acquitted by the Municipal Court.

After our acquittal, in a conversation with Judge Thomas, although he considered the acts of the party illegal, he advised, that to satisfy the people, we had better go before another magistrate who was not in our Church.

In accordance with his advice we went before Esq. Wells, with whom you are well acquainted; both parties were present, witnesses were called on both sides, the case was fully investigated, and we were again dismissed.

And what is this intended desire to enforce the law, and these lying, base rumors put into circulation for, but to seek, through mob influence, under pretense of law, to make us [p.388] submit to requisitions that are contrary to law, and subversive of every principle of justice?

And when you, sir, required us to come out here, we came, not because it was legal, but because you required it of us, and we were desirous of showing to you and to all men that we shrunk not from the most rigid investigation of our acts.

We certainly did expect other treatment than to be immured in a jail at the instance of these men, and I think, from your plighted faith, we had a right to, after disbanding our own forces, and putting ourselves entirely in your hands; and now, after having fulfilled my part, sir, as a man and an American citizen, I call upon you, Governor Ford, and think I have a right to do so, to deliver us from this place, and rescue us from this outrage that is sought to be practiced upon us be a set of infamous scoundrels.

Gov. Ford.—But you have placed men under arrest, detained men as prisoners, and given passes to others, some of which I have seen.

John P. Green, City Marshall.—Perhaps I can explain. Since these difficulties have commenced, you are aware that we have been placed under very peculiar circumstances, our city has been placed under a very rigid police guard; in addition to this, frequent guards have been placed outside the city to prevent any sudden surprise, and those guards have questioned suspected or suspicious persons as to their business.

To strangers, in some instances, passes have been given, to prevent difficulty in passing those guards. It is some of those passes that you have seen. No person, sir, has been imprisoned without a legal cause in our city.

Gov.—Why did you not give a more speedy answer to the posse that I sent out?

Gen. Smith.—We had matters of importance to consult upon. Your letter showed anything but an amicable spirit. We have suffered immensely in Missouri from mobs, in loss of property, imprisonment, and otherwise.

It took some time for us to weigh duly these matters. We could not decide upon the matters of such importance immediately, and your posse were too hasty in returning. We were consulting for a large people, and vast interests were at stake.

We had been outrageously imposed upon, and knew not how far we could trust anyone; besides, a question necessarily arose, how shall we come? Your request was that we should come unarmed. It became a matter of serious importance to decide how far promises could be trusted, and how far we were safe from mob violence.

Geddes.—It certainly did look from all I have heard, from the general spirit of violence and mobocracy that here prevails, that it was not safe for you to come unprotected.

Gov.—I think that sufficient time was not allowed by the posse for you to consult and get ready. They were too hasty; but I suppose they found themselves bound by their orders. I think, too, there is great deal of truth in what you say, and your reasoning is plausible; yet, I must beg leave to differ from you in relation to the acts of the City Council. That council, in my opinion, had no right to act in a legislative capacity, and in that of the judiciary.

They should have passed a law in relation to the matter, and then the Municipal Court, upon complaint, could have removed it; but for the City Council to take upon themselves the law-making and the execution of the laws, in my opinion, was wrong; besides, these men ought to have had a hearing before their property was destroyed; to destroy it without was an infringement of their rights; besides, it is so contrary to the feelings of the America people to interfere with the press.

And furthermore, I cannot but think that it would have been more judicious for you to have gone with Mr. Bettisworth to Carthage, notwithstanding the law did not require it. Concerning your being in jail, I am sorry for that, I wish it had been otherwise. I hope you will soon be released, but I cannot interfere.

Joseph Smith.—Governor Ford, allow me, sir, to bring one thing to your mind, that you seem to have overlooked. You state that you think it would have been better for us to have submitted to the requisition of Constable Bettisworth, and to have gone to Carthage.

Do you not know, sir, that that writ was served at the instance of an anti-Mormon mob, who had passed resolutions and published them to the effect that they would exterminate the Mormon leaders; and are you not informed that Captain Anderson was not only threatened when coming to Nauvoo, but had a gun fired at his boat by this said mob at Warsaw, when **[p.390]** coming up to Nauvoo, and that this very thing was made use of as a means to get us into their hands, and we could not, without taking an armed force with us, go there without, according to their published declarations, going into the jaws of death?

To have taken a force would only have fanned the excitement, as they would have stated that we wanted to use intimidation, therefore we thought it the most judicious to avail ourselves of the protection of the law.

Gov.—I see, I see.

Joseph Smith.—Furthermore, in relation to the press, you say that you differ with me in opinion; be it so, the thing after all is a legal difficulty, and the courts I should judge competent to decide on the matter.

If our act was illegal, we are willing to meet it; and although I cannot see the distinction that you draw about the acts of the City Council, and what difference it could have made in point of fact, law, or justice, between the City Council's acting together or separate, or how much more legal it would have been for the

that, I wish it had been otherwise. I hope you will soon be released, but I cannot interfere.

"Joseph Smith. Governor Ford, allow me, sir, to bring one thing to your mind that you seem to have overlooked. You state that you think it would have been better for us to have submitted to the requisition of Constable Bettisworth, and to have gone to Carthage.

Do you not know, Sir, that that writ was served at the instance of an anti-Mormon mob, who had passed resolutions and published them to the effect that they would exterminate the Mormon leaders? And are you not informed that Captain Anderson was not only threatened, but had a gun fired at his boat by this said mob in Warsaw when coming up to Nauvoo, and that this very thing was made use of as a means to get us into their hands; and we could not, without taking an armed force with us, go there without, according to their published declarations, going into the jaws of death?

To have taken a force with us, would only have fanned the excitement, and they would have stated that we wanted to use intimidation; therefore, we thought it the most judicious to avail ourselves of the protection of law.

"Gov. I see, I see.

"Joseph Smith. Furthermore, in relation to the press, you say that you differ from me in opinion. Be it so, the thing, after all, is only a legal difficulty, and the courts, I should judge, are competent to decide on that matter.

If our act was illegal, we are willing to meet it and although I can not see the distinction that you draw about the acts of the City Council, and what difference it could have made in point of fact, law, or justice between the City Council's acting together or separate, or how much more legal it would have been for the

Municipal Court, who were a part of the City Council, to act separate, instead of with the councilors. Yet, if it is deemed that we did a wrong in destroying that press, we refuse not to pay for it. We are desirous to fulfill the law in every particular, and are responsible for our acts.

You say that the parties ought to have had a hearing. Had it been a civil suit, this of course would have been proper; but there was a flagrant violation of every principle of right, a nuisance, and it was abated on the same principle that any nuisance, stench, or putrified carcass would have been removed.

Our first step, therefore, was to stop the foul, noisome, filthy sheet, and then the next, in our opinion, would have been to have prosecuted the men for a breach of public decency.

And furthermore, again, let me say, Governor Ford, I shall look to you for our protection. I believe you are talking of going to Nauvoo; if you go, sir, I wish to go along. I refuse not to answer any law, but I do not consider myself safe here.

Gov.—I am in hopes that you will be acquitted; but if I go, I will certainly take you along. I do not, however, apprehend danger. I think you are perfectly safe, either here or anywhere else. I cannot, however, interfere with the law. I am placed in peculiar circumstances and seem to be blamed by all parties.

[p.391] *Joseph Smith.*—Governor Ford, I ask nothing but what is legal. I have a right to expect protection at least from you; for, independent of law, you have pledged your faith, and that of the State, for my protection, and I wish to go to Nauvoo.

Gov.—And you shall have protection, General Smith. I did not make this promise without consulting my officers, who all pledged their honor to its fulfillment. I do not know that I shall go tomorrow to Nauvoo, but if I do, I will take you along. (June 26, 1844.) DHC 6:579-585.

honor to its fulfilment. I do not know that I shall go tomorrow to Nauvoo, but if I do, I will take you along"[452]

Letter: Joseph Smith to Emma Smith—Prophet's Instruction as to Reception of the Governor

Carthage Jail, June 27th, 1844.
20 minutes past eight a.m.

Joseph Smith Letter to Emma Smith
Carthage Jail Jun. 27th 1844,
20.Past 8. AM.

Dear Emma.—The Governor continues his courtesies, and permits us to see our friends. We hear this morning that the Governor will not go down with his troops today to Nauvoo, as we anticipated last evening; but if he does come down with his troops you will be protected; and I want you to tell Brother Dunham to instruct the people to stay at home and attend to their own business, and let there be no groups or gathering together, unless by permission of the Governor, they are called together to receive communications from the Governor, which would please our people, but let the Governor direct.

Dear Emma The Gov continues his courtesies, and permits us to see our friends. We hear this morning that the Governor will not go down with his troops to day <(to Nauvoo)> as was anticipated last Evening but, if he does come down with his troops you will be protected, & I want you to tell Bro Dunham to instruct the people to stay at home and attend to [p.630] their own business and let there be no groups or gathering together unless by permission of the Gov- they are called together to receive communications from the Gov- which would please our people, but let the Gov. direct. –

Brother Dunham of course will obey the orders of the government officers, and render them the assistance they require. There is no danger of any extermination order. Should there be a mutiny among the troops (which we do not anticipate, excitement is abating) a part will remain loyal and stand for the defense of the state and our rights.

Bro Dunham of course, will obey the orders of the Government officers, and render them the assistance they require. There is no danger of any "exterminating order" Should there be a mutiny among the troops, (which we do not anticipate, excitement is abating,) a part will remain loyal, and stand for the defence of the state & our rights;

There is one principle which is eternal; it is the duty of all men to protect their lives and the lives of the household, whenever necessity requires, and no power has a right to forbid it,

There is one principle which is Eternal, it is the duty of all men to protect their lives from every and the lives of their households whenever occasion <necessity> requires. and no power has

---

452. Report by John Taylor, in History, F-1, Addenda, 3–8. See also Mark H. Taylor, *Witness to the Martyrdom:*, 67–77. John Taylor was with Joseph Smith in the Carthage Jail and was an eyewitness to the martyrdom. Taylor was contacted by Church historians during the 1850s as they were compiling that portion of the *History of the Church*. Taylor composed a draft of what has been referred to as the Martyrdom Manuscript, dated 23 August 1856, and sent it to the historian's office. According to Mark H. Taylor, the first complete copy of the manuscript to be published was in Richard F. Burton's *City of the Saints*, published in London in 1861.

should the last extreme arrive, but I anticipate no such extreme, but caution is the parent of safety.
JOSEPH SMITH.

P.S.—Dear Emma, I am very much resigned to my lot, knowing I am justified, and have done the best that could be done. Give my love to the children and all my friends, Mr. Brewer, and all who inquire after me: and as for treason, I know that I have not committed any, and they cannot prove **[p.392]** anything of the kind, so you need not have any fears that anything can happen to us on that account. May God bless you all. Amen. (June 27, 1844.) DHC 6:605.

a right to forbid~~id~~ it. ~~when worst~~ should the last extreme arrive,- but <u>I anticipate no such extreme</u>, - but caution is the parent of safety. - Joseph Smith

PS Dear Emma, I am very much resigned to my lot knowing I am Justified and have done the best that could be done give my love to the children and all my Friends Mr Brower and all who ~~in after~~ inquire after me and as for treason I know that I have not commited any and they cannot prove one apearance of any thing of the kind So you need not have any fears that any harme can happen to us on that score may God ~~bll~~ bless you all Amen

Joseph Smith[453]

Not Always Wise to Expose Evil

Thursday, a.m.—June 27, 1844.—

Said Joseph, "Our lives have already become jeopardized by revealing the wicked and bloodthirsty purposes of our enemies; and for the future we must cease to do so. All we have said about them is truth, but it is not always wise to relate all the truth. Even Jesus, the Son of God, had to refrain from doing so, and had to restrain His feelings many times for the safety of Himself and His followers, and had to conceal the righteous purposes of His heart in relation to many things pertaining to His Father's kingdom. When still a boy He had all the intelligence necessary to enable Him to rule and govern the kingdom of the Jews, and could reason with the wisest and most profound doctors of law and divinity, and make their theories and practice to appear like folly compared with the wisdom He possessed; but He was a boy only, and lacked physical strength even to defend His own person; and was subject to cold, to hunger and to death. So it is with the Church of Jesus Christ of Latter-day Saints; we have the revelation

Said Bro Joseph "Our lives have already become jeopardized, by revealing the wicked and blood thirsty purposes of our enemies, and for the future, we must cease to do so, all we have said about them is truth, but it is not always wise to relate such truth, Even Jesus the Son of God had to refrain from doing so, and to restrain his feelings many times, for the safety of [page 5] his own person and those of his followers, and had to conceal the righteous purposes of his heart in relation to many things pertaining to his Father's Kingdom; when quite a boy, he had all the intelligence necessary to rule & govern the Kingdom of the Jews, and could reason with the wisest and most-profound doctors, of law and divinity, and make their theories and practices to appear like folly, compared with the wisdom he possessed; but he was a boy only, and lacked physical strength, even to defend his own person, and was subject to cold, to hunger, and to death, so it is, said he, "with the Church of Jesus Christ of Latter-day Saints; we have the principles of revelation, &

---

453. 27 June 1844, Joseph Smith letter to Emma Smith, in *PWJS*, 629–30.

of Jesus, and the knowledge within us is sufficient to organize a righteous government upon the earth, and to give universal peace to all mankind, if they would receive it, but we lack the physical strength, as did our Savior when a child, to defend our principles, and we have a necessity to be afflicted, persecuted and smitten, and to bear it patiently until Jacob is of age, then he will take care of himself."

Wheelock took a list of witnesses' names that were wanted for the expected trial on Saturday. When the list was read over, a number of names were stricken out, among whom were Alpheus Cutler and Reynolds Cahoon, it being deemed by Brother Hyrum unnecessary for them to attend. Brother Joseph asked why they should not come. Hyrum answered, "They may be very good men, but they don't know enough to answer a question properly." Brother Joseph remarked, "That is sufficient reason."

The prisoners also sent many verbal messages to their families. They were so numerous that Dr. Richards proposed **[p.393]** writing them all down, fearing Wheelock might forget, but Brother Hyrum fastened his eyes upon him, and with a look of penetration said, "Brother Wheelock will remember all that we tell him, and he will never forget the occurrences of this day."

the knowledge within us, sufficient to organize a righteous government upon the earth, & to give universal peace to all mankind, if they will receive it, but," said he, "we lack the physical strength, as did our Saviour when a child, to enforce our principles, and we shall have of necessity, to be afflicted, persecuted & smitten, and to bear it patiently, until Jacob is of age, then he will take care of himself."454

Wheelock took a list of witnesses names that were wanted for the expected trial on Saturday. When the list was read over a number of names were stricken out, among whom were Alpheus Cutler and Reynolds Cahoon <others>, it being deemed <by bro Hyrum> unnecessary for them to attend.455
Bro Joseph asked the reason why they should not come, Hyrum's answer was in short, "they may be very good men, but they don't know enough to answer a question properly. Bro. Joseph remarked that that was a sufficient reason.456

The prisoners also sent many verbal messages to their families; they were so numerous that457 Dr. Richards proposed writing them all down, fearing I might forget; but, Bro Hyrum fastened his eyes upon me, with a look of penetration, that I think I shall never forget, said he, "Bro Wheelock will remember all that we tell him, & he will never forget the occurrences of this day"458

The Prophet's Dream

Joseph related the following dream which he had last night: I was back in Kirtland, Ohio, and thought I would take a walk out by myself, and view my old farm, which I found

The second dream I will relate as near as possible in his own words, said he, "I was back in Kirtland Ohio, & thought I would take a walk out by myself, and view my old farm, which

---

454. Cyrus Wheelock letter to George A. Smith, 29 December 1854, Church History Library. George A. Smith used this letter in compiling 27 June 1844, History, F-1.

455. 27 June 1844, History, F-1, 177.

456. Cyrus Wheelock letter to George A. Smith, 29 December 1854, Church History Library. George A. Smith used this letter in compiling 27 June 1844, History, F-1.

457. 27 June 1844, History, F-1, 177.

458. Cyrus Wheelock letter to George A. Smith, 29 December 1854, Church History Library. George A. Smith used this letter in compiling 27 June 1844, History, F-1, 177.

grown up with weeds and brambles, and altogether bearing evidence of neglect and want of culture. I went into the barn, which I found without floor or doors, with the weatherboarding off, and was altogether in keeping with the farm.

"While I viewed the desolation around me, and was contemplating how it might be recovered from the curse upon it, there came rushing into the barn a company of furious men, who commenced to pick a quarrel with me.

"The leader of the party ordered me to leave the barn and farm, stating it was none of mine, and that I must give up all hope of ever possessing it.

"I told him the farm was given me by the Church, and although I had not had any use of it for some time back, still I had not sold it, and according to righteous principles it belonged to me or the Church.

"He then grew furious and began to rail upon me, and threaten me, and said it never did belong to me nor to the Church.

"I then told him that I did not think it worth contending about, that I had no desire to live upon it in its present state, and if he thought he had a better right I would not quarrel with him about it but leave; but my assurance that I would not trouble him at present did not seem to satisfy him, as he seemed determined to quarrel with me, and threatened me with the destruction of my body.

"While he was thus engaged, pouring out his bitter words upon me, a rabble rushed in and nearly filled the barn, drew out their knives, and began to quarrel among themselves for the premises, and for a moment forgot me, at which time I took **[p.394]** the opportunity to walk out of the barn about up to my ankles in mud.

I found grown up with weeds & brambles, & altogether bearing evidence of neglect, & want of culture, I went into the barn, which I found without floor & doors, with the weather boarding off, & was altogether in keeping with the farm;

while I viewed the desolation around me, I was contemplating how it might be recovered from the curse upon it, there came rushing into the barn a company of furious men, who commenced to pick a quarrel with me,

the leader of the party ordered me to leave the barn & the farm, stating it was none of mine, and that I must give up all hope of ever possessing it.

I told him the farm was given me by the Church, and although I had not had any use of it for some time back still I had not sold it, and according to righteous principles belonged to me or to the Church,

he then grew furious & began to rail upon me, & threaten me, & said it never did belong to me, nor the Church,

I then told him that I did not think it worth contending about, that I had no desire to live upon it in its present state, & if he thought he had a better right I would not quarrel with him about it, but leave, but my assurance that I would not trouble him at present, did not seem to satisfy him, as he seemed determined to quarrel with me, & threatened me with the destruction of my body,

While he was thus engaged, pouring out his hostile & bitter words upon me, a rabble rushed in and nearly filled the barn, drew out their knives, and began to quarrel among themselves, In the premises, & for a moment forgot me, at which time I took the opportunity to walk out of the barn, about up to my ankles in the dirt,

"When I was a little distance from the barn, I heard them screeching and screaming in a very distressed manner, as it appeared they had engaged in a general fight with their knives. While they were thus engaged, the dream or vision ended."

Both Joseph and Hyrum bore a faithful testimony to the Latter-day work, and the coming forth of the Book of Mormon, and prophesied of the triumph of the Gospel over all the earth, exhorting the brethren present to faithfulness and persevering diligence in proclaiming the Gospel, building up the Temple, and performing all the duties connected with our holy religion.

Joseph dictated the following postscript to Emma:
Letter: Postscript

P.S.—20 minutes to 10.—I just learn that the Governor is about to disband his troops, all but a guard to protect us and the peace, and come himself to Nauvoo and deliver a speech to the people. This is right as I suppose.

He afterwards wrote a few lines with his own hand, which were not copied. (June 27, 1844.) DHC 6:608-611.

in a little distance from the barn I heard them screeching & screaming in a very distressed manner, as it appeared they had engaged in a general fight with their knives; while they were thus engaged the dream or vision ended." The above is the substance of those dreams and as near the words as I can possibly remember.[459]

Brothers Joseph & Hyrum bore a faithful testimony of the latter-day work, & the coming forth of the Book of Mormon, & prophecied of the final triumph of the Gospel over all the earth, exhorting us to faithfulness, & persevering diligence in proclaiming the Gospel, building up the Temple, & performing all the duties with our holy Religion.[460]

Joseph dictated the following postscript to Emma:—

P.S. 20 mi[n] to 10 - I just learn that the Govrnor is about to disband his troops, all but a guard to protect us and the peace, - and come himself to Nauvoo and deliver a speech to the people. This is right as I suppose.[461]

And afterwards wrote a few lines with his own hand, which were not copied.[462]

Letter: Joseph Smith to O. H. Browning—Engaging Browning as Legal Counsel

Carthage Jail, June 27th, 1844.
Lawyer Browning:—
Sir.—Myself and brother Hyrum are in jail on charge of treason, to come up for examination on Saturday morning, 29th inst., and we

Joseph Smith Letter to Orville Browning
Carthage Jail, June 27th 1844
Lawyer Browning.
Sir, Myself and brother Hyrum are in Jail on [a] charge of Treason, to come up for examination on Saturday morning 29th inst. and

---

459. Cyrus Wheelock letter to George A. Smith, 29 December 1854, Church History Library. George A. Smith used this letter in compiling 27 June 1844, History, F-1, 177–78.
460. Cyrus Wheelock letter to George A. Smith, 29 December 1854, Church History Library. George A. Smith used this letter in compiling 27 June 1844, History, F-1, 178.
461. Joseph Smith letter postscript to Emma Smith, 27 June 1844, Church History Library, in *PWJS*, 630.
462. 27 June 1844, History, F-1, 178.

request you professional services at that time, on our defense, without fail.
Most respectfully your servant,
JOSEPH SMITH.

P.S.—There is no cause of action, for we have not been guilty of any crime, neither is there any just cause of suspicion against us; but certain circumstances make your attendance very necessary.
J. S.
—DHC 6:613.

This account brings us up to the afternoon of the day of the martyrdom. At 1:30 p.m. on that day some of the visitors at the prison were forced to leave, and Joseph Smith, Hyrum [p.395] Smith, John Taylor and Willard Richards were left to themselves. At 3:15 after the change of guards, they, the guards, became more severe and threatening. About this time Elder Taylor sang—A Poor Wayfaring Man of Grief. When he finished the song the Prophet requested him to sing it again, which he did, reluctantly, as he did not feel like singing. At 4 p.m. Hyrum did some reading to his fellow prisoners. The guard was again changed, only eight men being stationed at the jail, the main body of the Carthage Greys were in camp a quarter of mile distant, on the public square.

At 5 p.m. the jailor, Mr. Stigall, suggested that the brethren return to the cell where

we request your professional services at that time, on our defence without fail,
Most Respectfully
Your Servt.
Joseph Smith
P.S. There is no ground <cause> of action, for we have not been guilty of any crime; neither is there any just cause of suspicion against us when facts are shown but certain circumstances make your attendance very necessary.
J.S.[463]

Joseph Smith's Journal & John Taylor Account

3.15— P.M. The guard have been more severe in their ope[r]ations— threat[e]ning among themselves or telling what they would do when the ~~was~~ <war> was over— one would sell his farm and move out of the state if Smith staid.—— Taylor sung. "poor way faring man of grief—" Hyrum read from Josephus[464] 4 P. M. The guard was again changed; only eight men being stationed at the jail, whilst the main body of the Carthage Greys were in camp about a quarter of a mile distant, on the public square.[465]

4.15— Joseph commen[ce]d conve[r]sing with the guard about [Joseph H.] Jackson Law &c— & Hyrum & Dr Richads— Convesd [conversed] some till 5-15:— 5-20— [George] Stigall— retur[ne]d from town

---

463. Joseph Smith letter to Orville Browning, 27 June 1844, Church History Library, in *PWJS*, 634–35.

464. 27 June 1844, *JSP, J3*, 326. The following comes from John Taylor's account: "I sang the following song, that had lately been introduced into Nauvoo, entitled, 'A Poor Wayfaring Man of Grief,' etc. The song is pathetic, and the tune quite plaintive, and was very much in accordance with our feelings at the time, for our spirits were all depressed, dull and gloomy, and surcharged with indefinite ominous forebodings. After a lapse of some time, Brother Hyrum requested me again to sing that song. I replied, 'Brother Hyrum, I do not feel like singing;' when he remarked, 'Oh, never mind; commence singing, and you will get the spirit of it.' At his request I did so." John Taylor Martyrdom Account, Church History Library, in Taylor, *Witness to the Martyrdom*, 84.

465. 27 June 1844, History, F-1, 181.

they would be safer. The Prophet turned to Dr. Richards and said, "If we go into the cell, will you go in with us?" The Doctor replied, "Brother Joseph, you did not ask me to cross the river with you—you did not ask me to come to jail with you—and do you think I would forsake you now? But I will tell you what I will do; if you are condemned to be hung for treason, I will be hung in your stead, and you shall go free." Joseph said, "You cannot." The Doctor said, "I will."

and said Markham was surrounded— by a mob & had gone to Nauvoo and suggested that th[e]y would be safer in the jail Joseph said after supper we will go in— stigall went out.— and Joseph said to Dr Richads— If we go in the jail will you go in with us.— D^r— answer[re]d— Bro Joseph you did not ask me to cross the river with you— you did not ask me to come to ca[r]thage.— you did not ask me to come to Jail with you— and do you think I would forsake you now.— But I will tell you what I will do— if you are condemnd to be hung for treason I will be hung. in your ~~place~~ stead & you shall go freee. Joseph you cannot.— D^r said I will.—[466]

It was but a short time following this that there was a rustling at the door of the prison, the mob had arrived and was bent on taking the lives of the prisoners, which, as we all know, they wickedly did. The account of this tragedy is not to be related here. The reader is referred to the full account of the awful and bloody deed as it is recorded in the Documentary History of the Church.

a little rustling at the outer door.— the cry sur[r]ender &— discharge of 3 or 4 arm— followd intently [instantly].— D^r glanced an eye by the curtain— ~~say~~ saw a 100 ar[m]ed men arou[n]d the door.—[467]

---

466. 27 June 1844, *JSP, J3*, 326–27.
467. 27 June 1844, *JSP, J3*, 327.

APPENDICES

APPENDIX A

Joseph Smith Sermon
April 8, 1843

Joseph Smith delivered this sermon at a conference held 8 April 1843. When it was included in the *History of Joseph Smith*, it was an amalgamated version drawing from the journals of Willard Richards and William Clayton. What follows are the unedited notes of the two scribes.

Willard Richards Account[1]

3 requ[e]sts. **[p.345]**

1st that all who have faith will pray Lord to calm the wind. for as it is now. I can not speak.

2 that the Lord will strength<en> my Lungs—

3ᵈ that I may have the Holy Ghost.

The subject whicch I shall sp[e]ak from <is> the, beasts spoken of by John.— I have seldom spoken from <the revelati[o]ns> & I do it now to do away division & not that the knowledge is so much needed.—

knowledge is necessary to prevent division although it may puff up it does away suspince [suspense]——

in knowledge is power, hence God knows how to subject all beings he has power— over all.

should not have called up this subject if it had not been for this old white head before. Father [Pelatiah] Brown.——— I did not like the old man being called up. <before the High council.>— for erring in doctrine.——— why I feel so good to have the privelige of thinki[n]g & believing as I please.

they undertook to correct him there Whether they did or not I dont care

Rev— 5 chap. 8 verse.—

Father Brown had been to work & confounded all christendom, that these were figure John saw in heavn to represent the different kingdoms of God on earth. he put

William Clayton Account[2]

I have three requests to make of the congregation the first is that all who have faith will exercise it, that the Lord may be willing to calm the wind. The next is, that I may have your prayers that the Lord may strengthen my lungs so that, I may be able to make you all hear. And the next is, that I may have the Holy Ghost to rest upon me so as to enable me to declare those things that are true.

The subject I intend to speak upon this morning is one that I have seldom touched upon since I commenced as an Elder of the Church. It is a subject of great speculation as well amongst the Elders of the church as amongst the divines of the day; it is in relation to the beast spoken of in Revelations. The reason why it has been a subject of speculation amongst the Elders, is in consequence of a division of sentiment and opinion in relation to it. My object is to do away with this difference of opinion. The knowledge of the subject is not very essential to the Elders. To have knowledge in relation to the meaning of beasts with seven and heads and ten horns and other figure made use of in the revelations is not very essential to the Elders. If we get puffed up by thinking that we have much knowledge, we are apt to get a contentious spirit, and knowledge is necessary to do away contention. The evil of being puffed up is not so great as the evil of contention. Knowledge does away darkness, supense and doubt, for where Knowledge is there is no

---

1. 8 April 1843, *JSP, J2*, 344–47.
2. 8 April 1843, *WJS*, 183–87. See also History D-1, 1522.

Richards

down sectarianism, & so far so good.—— but I could not help laughing that God should take a figure of a beast to repr[e]sent his kingdom consisting of <Men>. . . . To take a lesser figure to represnt a gr[e]ater, old white head you missed it that time. By figure of Beasts God represented the kingdoms of the world.— Bear. Lion &c represe[n]ted the kingdoms. of the world, Says Daniel. <for>

I refer to the prophets, to qualify my observations. to keep out of the wasp nests or young elders,

The things John say saw had no allusion to the day of Adam Enoch Abraham or Jesus— only as clearly specified & set forth to John. I saw that that which was lying in futurity. Rev I.I.— read <is> key to the whole subject [p.346] 4. beasts. & 24 Elders which was out of every nation— <it is> great stuffing, to stuff all nations into 4 beasts & 24 Elders things which <he> saw had no allusions to what had been.— but what must shortly come to pass.— Rev is one of the plain[e]st. books god ever caused to be written—

what John saw he saw in heaven— <that which the> the prophet Saw, in vision, <was> on earth, <and> in Hebrew, <it> is a Latitude & Longitude compar[e]d with English version

they saw figurs of beasts.— they why, Dani[e]l did not say <see> a lion & a bear. he saw an image like unto a bear:— in every place.— John saw. the actual beast itself. <it was> to let John know that beasts existed there & not to represent figurs of things on the Earth.—— <The> prophets always had interpretati[o]ns of the[i]r visions &c

God always holds himself respons[i]ble to give revelati[o]ns of his visions & <if> he does it not. we are not responsible.—

speculators need not fear they shall be condemnd. if God has given no Rev[elation]

How do you prove John saw visions Beasts in heaven? 5 <C[hapter]> II <v—>

Clayton

doubt nor suspense nor darkness. There is no pain so awful as the pain of suspense, this is the condemnation of the wicked; their doubt and anxiety and suspense causes weeping, wailing and gnashing of teeth. In knowledge there is power. God has more power than all other beings, because he has greater Knowledge, and hence he knows how to subject all other beings to him. I will endeavour to instruct you in relation to the meaning of the beasts and figures spoken of. Er (Pelatiah) Brown has been the cause of this subject being now presented before you. He, is one of the wisest old heads we have among us, has been called up before the High Council on account of the beast. The old man has preached concerning the beast which was full of eyes before and behind and for this he was hauled up for trial. I never thought it was right to call up a man and try him because he erred in doctrine, it looks too much like methodism and not like Latter day Saintism. Methodists have creeds [p.184] which a man must believe or be kicked out of their church. I want the liberty of believing as I please, it feels so good not to be tramelled. It dont prove that a man is not a good man, because he errs in doctrine. The High Council undertook to censure and correct Er Brown because of his teachings in relation to the beasts, and he came to me to know what he should do about it. The subject particularly referred to, was the four beasts and four and twenty Elders mentioned in Rev. ch 5 v. 8. The old man has confounded all Christendom by speaking out that the four beasts represented the Kingdom of God; the wise men of the day could not do any thing with him, and why should we find fault, anything to whip sectarianism and put down priestcraft; a club is better than no weapon for a poor man to fight with, but I could not keep laughing at the idea of God making use of the figure of a <u>beast</u> to represent the Kingdom of God on the earth, when he could as well have used a far more noble and consistent figure.

Richards

Revelation.— 13 verse every creature. which was in heaven and on the Earth

I John saw all beasts &c in heaven. for I expect he saw the beasts of <a> 1000 forms <from> 10,000 worlds like this.— the grand secret was to tell what was in heaven.— God will gratify himself with all these animals. . . .

says one I cannot beleive in salvati[o]n of bea[s]ts.— I suppose God could underst[a]nd the beasts &c, in certain worlds— the 4 beasts, were angels there. dont know where they came from; <they were inteligent> inteligent.—

<but my> Darling religion, says, <they> meant something beside beast.— then the 24 elders must mean something else:— 4 beasts meant Buonpart [Bonaparte] & Cyrus. &c— then the 24 elders ment the kingdoms of the Beasts.— It is all as flat as a pancake

what do <you> use such flat & vulger <expressions. for> being a prophet? because the old women understa[n]d it, they make pancakes.— the whole argument is flat, & I dont know of any thing bette[r] to repr[e]sent.— the argument.— [p347]

there is no revelation any where to shew that the beasts meant any thing but beasts

O ye Elders of Israel hearken to my voice & when ye are sent into the world to preach. tell those things you are sent to tell. declare the first principles, & let mysteries alone lest you be overthrown.—

Father Brown when you go to palmyrar [Palmyra] say nothi[n]g about the 4 B[e]asts Danl. ~~12~~ 13 . . . <C.> 2. verse— <some say> Deadly wound.— <means> Nebuchadnezzar.— Constantine.— & the catholic now for the wasp nest.— priests. & Dragon for Devil they have translated beast in heaven— it was not to rep[res]ent beast on heaven— it was an angel in heaven. who has power in the last days to do a work.—— all the world wonderd after the beast:— <&> <u>if the beast was all the world. how could the world wonderd after the beast?</u> When the old

Clayton

What? The Lord make use of the figure of a creature of the brute creation to represent that which is much more noble and important. The glories of his Kingdom? You missed it that time, old man, but the sectarians did not know enough to detect you.

When God made use of the figure of a beast in visions to the prophets, he did it to represent those Kingdoms who had degenerated and become corrupt—the Kingdoms of the world, but he never made use of the figure of a beast nor any of the brute kind to represent his kingdom. Daniel says when he saw the vision of the four beasts "I came near unto one of them that stood by, and asked him the truth of all this." The angel interpreted the vision to Daniel, but we find by the interpretation that the figures of beasts had no allusion to the Kingdom of God. You there see that the beasts are spoken of to represent the Kingdoms of the world the inhabitants whereof were beastly and abominable characters, they were murderous, corrupt, carnivourous and brutal in their dispositions. I make mention of the prophets to qualify my declaration which I am about to make so that the young Elders who know so much may not rise up and choke me like hornets, there is a grand difference and distinction between the visions and figures spoken of by the prophets and those spoken of in the Revelations of John. None of the things John saw had any allusion to the scenes of the days of Adam or of Enoch or of Abraham or Jesus, only as far as is plainly [p.185] represented by John and clearly set forth. John only saw that which was "shortly to come to pass" and that which was yet in futurity (He read Rev. ch. 1 v. 1) Now I make this declaration, that those things which John saw in heaven, had no allusion to any thing that had been on the earth, because John says "he saw what was shortly to come to pass" and not what had already transpired. John saw beasts that had to do with things on the earth, but not in past ages; the beasts which

Richards

devil shall give power to ~~to~~ the beast to do all his mighty work all the wo[r]ld will wonder—

who is able to make war with the beast? says the inhabita[n]ts of the earth.— if it means the kin[g]doms of the world it dont mean the kingdoms of the Saints.— who is able to make war with my gr[e]at big self.— The Dragon.— we may interpret it.— & it is sometimes Apolyel[3].— 9 verse 12 chap— key word.— independent beasts. abstract from the human family.— (25 minutes past 11. lungs faild— the wind blew briskly.)— I said more than I <ever> did before except once at Ramus. & then the little <~~upstarts~~ <fellows> stufferd me like a ~~cock~~>. cock turkey— <with the prop[h]ecies of Daniels—> and crammed it down my throat. with their fingerss—

Clayton

he saw had to devour the inhabitants of the earth in days to come. The revelations do not give us to understand any thing of the past in relation to the Kingdom of God. What John saw and speaks of were things which were in heaven, what the prophets saw and speak of where things pertaining to the earth. I am now going to take exception to the present translation of the bible in relation to these matters. There is a grand distinction between the actual meaning of the Prophets and the Present translation. The Prophets do <u>not</u> declare that the[y] saw a beast or beasts, but that the[y] saw the <u>image</u> or <u>figure</u> of a beast. They did not see an actual bear or Lion but the images or figures of those beasts. The translation should have been rendered "image" instead of "beast" in every instance where beasts are mentioned by the Prophets. But John saw the actual beast in heaven, to show to John and to the inhabitant that that being did actually exist there. When the Prophets speak of seeing beasts in their visions, they saw the images; the types to represent certain things and at the same time they received the interpretation as to what those images or types were designed to represent. I make this broad declaration, that where God ever gives a vision of an image, or beast or figure of any kind he always holds himself responsible to give a revelation or interpretation of the meaning thereof, otherwise we are not responsible or accountable for our belief in them it. Dont be afraid of being damned for not knowing the meaning of a vision or figure where God has not given a revelation or interpretation on the subject

(He here read Rev. ch 5 v 11 to 13) John saw curious looking beasts in heaven, he saw every creature that was in heaven, all the beasts, fowls, & fish in heaven, actually there, giving glory to God. I suppose John saw beings there, that had been saved from ten thousand times

---

3. "Apolyel" is a reference the Greek word "Apollyon," which means "destroyer" and refers to the "angel of the bottomless pit." See Revelation 9:11.

Richards

Clayton

ten thousand earths like this, strange beasts of which we have no conception all might be seen in heaven. John learned that God glorified himself by saving all that his hands had made whether beasts, fowl fishes or man. Any **[p.186]** man who would tell you that this could not be, would tell you that the revelations are not true. John heard the words of the beasts giving glory to God and understood them. God who made the beasts could understand every language spoken by them; The beasts were intelligent beings and were seen and heard by John praising and glorifying God.

The popular religionsts of the day say that the beasts spoken of in the revelations represent Kingdoms. Very well, on the same principle we can say that the twenty four Elders spoken of represent beasts, for they are all spoken of at the same time, and represented as all giving uniting in the same acts of praise and devotion. Deacon Homespun said the earth was flat as a pan cake, but science has proved to the contrary. The world is full of technicalities and misrepresentation, but I calculate to overthrow the technicalities of the world and speak of things as they actually exist. Again there is no revelation to prove that things do not exist in heaven as I have set forth, and we never can comprehend the things of God and of heaven but by revelation. We may spiritualize and express opinions to all eternity but that is no authority.

Ye Elders of Israel hearken to my voice and when ye are sent into the world to preach, preach and cry aloud "repent ye for the Kingdom of heaven is at hand repent and believe the gospel." Never meddle with the visions of beasts and subjects you do not understand. Er Brown when you go to Palmyra dont say any thing about the beast, but preach those things the Lord has told you to preach about, repentance and baptism for the remission of sins. \(He here read Rev. ch 13 v 1 to 8) The spiritualizers say the beast that received the wound was Nebuchadnezzar,

Richards	Clayton
	but we will look at what John saw in relation to this beast. The translators have used the term "dragon" for "devil". Now it was a beast that John saw in heaven, and he was then speaking of "things that were shortly to come to pass." and consequently the beast John saw could not be Nebuchadnezzar The beast John saw as spoken of in the 13th chapter was an actual beast to whom power was to be given. An actual intelligent being in heaven and this beast was to have power given him. John saw "one of the heads of the beast as it were wounded to death; and his deadly wound was healed; and all the world wondered after the beast," Nebuchadnezzar and Constantine the great not excepted; it must have been a wonderful [p.187] beast that all human beings wondered after it, and I will venture to say that when God gives power to the beast to destroy the inhabitants of the earth, all will wonder. Verse 4 reads "And they worshipped the dragon which gave power unto the beast; and they worshipped the beast saying, who is like unto the beast? who is able to make war with him? Some say it means the kingdom of the world. One thing is sure, it dont mean the kingdoms of the saints. Suppose we admit that it means the kingdoms of the world, what propriety would there be in saying, who is able to make war with myself. If these spiritualizing interpretations are true, the book contradicts itself in almost every verse, but they are not true. There is a mistranslation of the word dragon in the second verse. The original hebrew word signifies the devil and not dragon as translated. Read ch 12 v 9 it there reads "that, old serpent called the devil, and it, ought to be translated devil in this case and not dragon. Everything that we have not a key word to, we will take it as it reads. The beasts which John saw and speaks of as being in heaven were actually living in heaven, and were actually to have power given to them over the inhabitants of the earth precisely according to the plain reading of the revelations. I give this as a key to the Elders of Israel.

APPENDIX B

Joseph Smith Sermon
June 11, 1843

Joseph Smith delivered this sermon to a large group of Latter-day Saints assembled at the Nauvoo Temple site on 11 June 1843. The compilers of the *History of the Church* created an amalgamated version of this discourse, drawing on several sources and taking lines from one part of Joseph's remarks and inserting them (out of order) into a different part of the amalgamated version of the discourse—presumably with the intent of improving the readability of the sermon. Notes of the discourse, taken by Willard Richard and Wilford Woodruff, were the primary sources for the amalgamated version of the talk that Joseph Fielding Smith drew on for *Teachings of the Prophet Joseph Smith*.

Willard Richards Account[1]

Matt. 23. 37.

Subject presented me since I came in this house.——

I a rough stone. the sound of the hammer & chisel was never hea[r]d on me. nor never will be. I desire the learning & wisdom of heaven alone.

Have not the least idea but if Christ should come and preach such rough thi[n]gs as he preahd [preached] to the Jews. but this generati[o]n would reject reject him for b[e]ing so rough. I never can find much to say in expou[n]ding a text.

never is half so much fuss to unlock a door if you have a key an[d] wh[e]n you have not. or have to cut it out with a jack knife.—

O. Jerusalem &c.— whenc[e] arises the curse of Almighty God that was to be pourd out up[o]n the heads of the jews? That they would not be gathe[re]d! beca[u]se they would not let Ch[r]ist gather them. It was the design in the cou[n]cils of heaven before the world was. that the pri[n]ciple & law of that pri[e]sthood was predicated up[o]n the gathe[rin]g of the people in every age of the world. Jesus did every thing possible to gather the people. & th[e]y would not be gathered and he poured

Wilford Woodruff Account[2]

June 11[th] A large assembly of Saints met at the Temple & were addressed by president Joseph Smith[.] He took for the foundation of his discourse the words of Jesus to the Jews how oft would I have gatherd you togetherd as a hen gathereth her chickens under wings But ye would not &c.

He then asked what was the object of Gathering the Jews together or the people of God in any age of the world. the main object was to build unto the Lord an house whereby he Could reveal unto his people the ordinances of his house and glories of his kingdom & teach the peopl[e] the ways of salvation[.] for their are certain ordinances & principles that when they are taught and practized, must be done in a place or house built for that purpose[.] this was purposed in the mind of God before the world was & it was for this purpose that God designed to gather together the Jews oft but they would not[.] it is for the same purpose that God gathers together the people in the last <days> to build unto the Lord an house to prepare them for the ordinances & endowments washings & anointings &c one of the ordinances of the house of the Lord is Baptism for the dead.

---

1. Discourse, 11 June 1843-A, reported by Willard Richards, *JSP, D12*, 380–85.
2. 11 June 1843, *WWJ*, 1:545–47. See also *JSP, D12*, 385–87; *WJS*, 212–14.

Richards

out curses up[o]n the[m] Ordinances were instituted in hevan before the f[o]undation of the world of in the **[p.381]** pri[e]sthood. for the salvati[o]n of man. not be alterd. not to be changed.— all must be saved upon the same principle.

that is only your opin[i]on sir— say sectarians.— when a man will go to hell. it is more than my meat & drink to help them to do as they want to.

where there is no change of pri[e]sthood there is no change of ordina[n]ces says peter Paul, If God has not changed the ordinances & pri[e]sthood. howl ye sectarians. if he has where has he revealed it. have ye turnd revelators? then why deny it?

men have thought many things insutabl [inscrutable] in the last days. that he should raise the dead.

Things have been hid from before the foundation of the [world] to be reveald in to babes in the last days.—

there are a great ma[n]y wise men & women to[o] in our midst to[o] wise to be taught. & they mu[s]t die in their ignoranc[e] and in the resurrection they will find their mistake.

many seal up to the door of heaven by saying so far god may reveal I & I will believe.— heirs of God. &c. upon the same laws ordinance &c of Jesus Ch[r]ist. & he who will not have it all will come short. of that glory if not of the whole.

ordinnc [ordinance] of the baptism. god decreed before the fundatin [foundation] of the wo[r]ld that this baptism sho[u]ld be perfmd [performed] in a house prepard for the purpose.—

Spirits of prison. the Holy Gho[s]t rev[e]als it. Spi[r]its in the wo[r]ld of prison Spi[ri]ts.— which Jesus went to preach to. God ordaind that he who would save his dead should do it by gath[er]ing togethr as with the jews . . . — . . . It always has been when a man was sent of good [God] with **[p.382]** the Prethood [priesthood].

Woodruff

God decreed before the foundation of the world that that ordinance should be administered in **[p.546]** a house prepared for that purpose. If a man gets the fulness of God he has to get [it] in the same way that Jesus Christ obtained it & that was by keeping all the ordinances of the house of the Lord. Men will say I will never forsake you but will stand by you at all times[.] but the moment you teach them some of the mysteries of God that are retained in the heavens and are to be revealed to the children of men when they are prepared, They will be the first to stone you & put you to death. It was the same principle that crusified the Lord Jesus Christ. I will say something about the Spirits in prision. theire has been much said about the Sayings of Jesus on the cross to the thief saying this day thou shalt be with me in paradise. The commentators make or translators make it out to say Paradise[.] but what is Paradise[?] it is a modern word[.] it does not answer at all to the original that Jesus made use of. their is nothing in the original in any language that signifies Paradise[.] But it was this day I will be with thee in the world of spirits & will teach thee or answer thy inquiries. The thief on the Cross was to be with Jesus christ in the world of spirits[.] he did not say Paradise or heaven. The doctrin of Baptism for the dead is clearly shown in the new testament[.] & if the doctrin is not good then throw away the new testament[.] but if it is the word of God then let the doctrin be acknowledged & it was one reason why Jesus said how oft would I have gathered you (the Jews) together that they might attend to the ordinance of the baptism for the dead as well as the other ordinances, the Priesthood[,] Revelations &c. This was the case on the day of Pentecost[.] these Blessings were poured out upon the deciples, on that occasion.

Their has been Also much said about the word Hell & the sectarian world have preached much about it[.] but what is hell. It

Richards

& he began to preach the fulness of the gospel. that was thut [thrust] out by his fri[e]nds.—— and they are ready to but[c]her him if he teach things which th[e]y had imagind to be wrong.— Jesus was crucifi[e]d upon this principle—

I will turn linguist. ma[n]y things in the bible. whi[c]h do not. as th[e]y now stand. accord with the revelati[o]n of th[e] holy Gho[s]t to me.—

Par[a]dise. "this day thou sha[l]t be with me in paradise.["] Paradise. Modern word.— dont answer to the original word used by Jesus.—

find the origin of Paradise. find a needle in a hay mow.— here is a chance for a battle ye lear[ne]d man,— Said Jesus. for there is not time to invstigat [investigate] this m[a]tter. for this day I <You> will be with you me in the wor[l]d of Spi[ri]ts. & there I will teach you all about it.— & Peter says he went & preachd to the wo[r]ld of spi[r]its. so that they wo[u]ld receive it could have it answerd by proxig [proxy] by those who live on the earth &c—

gathe[re]d you for baptism for the dead washing anoitigs [anointings] &c.— say said. Jesus to Jews. At one time God obtaind a hou[s]e where Peter was endowd. &c on th[e] day of pentecost.— [blank] criticese [criticize] a little further Hell.— modern term. bur[n]ing lake of fire and Brimstone. I wou[l]d make you think I was climbing a ladder when I I was **[p.383]** climbing a rainbow.— who ever reveald it. God never did.— Hades. I will hunt after Hades as pat did for woodchu[c]k. Shaol— who are you? God reveals. means a world of spi[r]its.——— I dont they thi[n]k so says one. go to my hous[e]— I will take my lexi[c]on— &c—

a world of departed spir[i]ts. disembodi[e]d spir[i]ts all go.— good bad & indif[fer]ent— " [spirits] misery in a world of spi[ri]ts is to know th[e]y came short of the glory othe[r]s enjoy— th[e]y are their own accusers one universal heaven— & hell— &c says one,

Woodruff

is annother modern term[.] it is taken from <u>hades</u> the greek or <u>shaole</u>, the (hebrew) & the true signification is a world of spirits. Hades shaole paradise, spirits in prison is all one[.] it is a world of spirits. the righteous & the wicked all go to the same world of spirits

but says one I believe in one hell & one heaven[.] all are equally miserable or equally happy. but St Paul informs us of three glories & three heavens[.] he knew a man caught up to the third heavens, & Jesus said their were many mansions in my Fathers kingdom Any man may believe Jesus Christ is good & be happy in it & yet not obey his commands & at last be cut down by his righteous commandments[.] A man of God should be endowed with all wisdom[,] knowledge & understanding in order to teach & lead people. The blind may lead the blind & both fall into the death together;

Their is much said concerning God[,] the Godhead &c[.] the scripture says their is Gods many & Lords many. the teachers of the day say that the father is God the Son is God & the Holy Ghost is God & that they are all in one body & one God[.] Jesus says or prays that those that the father had given him out of the world might be made one in us as we are one. but if they were to be stuffed into one person they would make a great God. If I were to testify that the world was wrong on this point it would be true[.] Peter says that Jesus Christ sat on the right hand of God[.] any person that has seen the heavens opened knows that their is three personages in the heavens holding the keys of power[.] As the father hath power in himself so the Son hath power in himself[.] then the father has some day laid down his body & taken it again[.] <So he has a bo[d?]y of his own> So has his Son a body of his own[.] So each one will be in their own body.

Many of the sects cry out O I have the testimony of Jesus. I have the spirit of God. But

Richards

honorable & virtuo[u]s. & whoremonger— all hudld together.— judged according to deeds done in the body— shame— shame— thus we can [tithe] mint & annice & cumin and [make] long praye[r]s. but touch not the law, as Peter tells us.—

Paul says caught up to 3d heaven, what tell that Lie for Paul.—

   sun moon & stars—
   many mansions—
   all one say Sectarians.—

They build hay wood & stubble, build on the old revelati[o]ns— with[o]ut the spi[r]it of Revelati[o]n or Pr[i]esthood. if I had time I would dig into Hell. Hades. Shaol.— & tell what exists.—

Heaven of Heavens could not contain. him.— he took the liberty to go into other heavens.— I thought— **[p.384]**

Fathe[r]— Son & H. Gho[s]t. all stuck into one person.—— I pray for them. fathr that we may be one— all stuffed into one God—— a big God.

Peter— Steph[e]n— saw the Son of Man saw the son of man standi[n]g on the right hand of God.— 3 personages— in heavn who hold the keys.— one to preside over all.

If any mans attempt to refute. what I am about to say after I have made it plain let him be accursd. As the fathr hath power in himself so hath the son power in hims[e]lf to lay down his life.—

the son doeth what he hath seen the fath[er] do.— &c—— take his body & stuff it into the fathr.

gods have over an ascenden[c]y over the angels angels remain angels.— some are resurrected to become gods by such revelations as god gives in the mo[s]t holy place.— in his temple. let them who are owing tythig [tithing] pay it up.— & bring stone.— **[p.385]**

what did Judge Higby [Elias Higbee] [say?]— ["]if those who are owing would bring stone we could get the walls to the roof this fall as easy as to let it down—"

Woodruff

away with Jo Smith[.] he says he is a Prophet But their is to be no Prophets nor revelations in the last days; But stop sir the Revelator says that the testimony of Jesus is the spirit of Prophecy[.] So by your own mouth you are Condemned.

But to the text[.] why gather the people together in this place[?] for the same purpose **[p.547]** that Jesus wanted to gather the Jews. to receive the ordinances, the blessings & the glories that God has in store for his Saints[.] And I would now ask this assembly and all the Saints if they will now build this house & receive the ordinances & Blessings which God has in store for you, or will you not build unto the Lord this house & let him pass by & bestow these blessings upon another[?] I pause for a reply.

APPENDIX C

King Follett Discourse
April 7, 1844

Of the various recorded accounts of this famed discourse, historian Dean C. Jessee wrote: "One aspect of the editing process that required careful comparison and concentration was the fusing of texts where more than one report was made of an address. A prime example is the King Follett discourse delivered by Joseph Smith on 7 April 1844. Lasting a reported two and a quarter hours, the published discourse was derived by dovetailing the reports of four persons who heard the speech: Wilford Woodruff, Willard Richards, Thomas Bullock, and William Clayton. The original reports reveal the comparative ability of these men to record what they heard on that occasion."[1]

What follows are the unedited notes of these four scribes, from which the amalgamated discourse currently found in Joseph Fielding Smith's edition of the *Teachings of the Prophet Joseph Smith* was created.

---

1. Dean C. Jessee, "Priceless Words and Fallible Memories: Joseph Smith as Seen in the Effort to Preserve His Discourses," *BYU Studies Quarterly* 31, no. 2 (Spring 1991): 30. Jessee adds: "Assuming Joseph Smith spoke approximately one hundred words per minute on the average (with no loudspeaking system to amplify his voice, he would have spoken somewhat slowly), the entire speech would have contined about 13,500 words. The longest of the four reports is Thomas Bullock's 4,500-word summary, which represents about 25 percent of the total discourse. William Clayton's 2,800-word report represents about 17 percent of the original; Wilford Woodruff's 2,400 words, 14 percent; and Willard Richards's 900 words, about 5 percent of the original."

Thomas Bullock account[2]

The Prophet while I address you on the subject which <in the fore p[ar]t. of the Con[ference]> was contemp[late]d.— as the wind blows very hard it will be hardly possible for me to make you all hear it is of the greatest importance & the mo[st] solemn of any that co[ul]d. occupy our attent[io]n. & that is the subj[ect] of the dead or the dece[ase] of our bro[r.] Follit [King Follett] who was crushed to death in a well— & insomuch as there <are> a great many in this congre[gation] who live in this city & who have lost friend I shall speak in gen[era]l. & offe[r] you my ideas so far as I have ability & so far as I shall be insp[ire]d. by the H S. [Holy Spirit] to dwell on this subj[ec]t. I want your prayer, faith the instr[uctio]n. of Alm[ighty] God to say things that are true & shall carry the testimony to your hearts & pray that he may streng[then] my lungs— stay the winds— & let the pray[ers] of the Saints to heaven appear— for the prayers of the righteous avail much & I verily believe that your prayers shall be heard before I enter in the investig[atio]n. fully of the subj[t.] that is lying before us I wish to make a few preliminaries in order that you may understand when I come to it I do not calculate to please your ears with oratory with much lea[rni]ng but I calculate to edify you with simple truths from Heaven— I wish to go back to the begin[inig]: of creation— it is necessary to know the mind decree & ordina[tio]n. of the great Eloe [*Elōheem* or Elohim] begin[nin]g at the create[io]n. & it is nec[essar]y. for us to have an understand[in]g. of God in the begin[g.] if we start right it is very easy for us to go right all the time but if we start wrong it is hard to get right there are very few who understand rightly the char[acter] of God— they do not comprehend any thing that is past or

William Clayton account[3]

Pres[t] J. Smith called the intention of the con[ference] upon the subject contemplate[d] in the fore part of the con— as the wind blows hard it will be impossib[le] to make hear unless profound attention— Subject of the greatest importance, and most solemn that could occupy our attention the subject of the dead ben requested to speak on the subject on the decease of br[o] Follet [King Follett] who was crushed to death &c— I have ben requested to speak **[p.328]** by his friends & relatives & inasmuch as great many here in con.— who live in this City as well as elsewhere who have deceased friends feel dispose to speak on the subject in general— and offer my ideas as far as ability— & as far as inspired by H. G. [Holy Ghost] want your prayers <u>faith</u>, the inspirati[o]n of Almighty God, the Gift of H. G. that I may set forth truth things that can easily be comprehended & will carry the testimony to your heart pray that the L[ord] may strengthe[n] my lungs caml [calm] the wind that it may enter into the ear of the Ld of Sabaoth the fervent effectual prayer of righteo[u]s man availet[h] mach [much]—will speak in order to hold out. Before ente[ring] fully into the investigate[o]n wish to pave the way— make a few prelim[in]aries— bring the subject from th[e] beginning to order that you may understand the subject when I come to it. Do not calculate to please your ears with superfluity of words oratory much learning, but edify you by the simple truths of heaven— first place wish to go back to the beginning of creation, then the starting point in order to fully aquianted [acquainted] with purposes decrees &c of the great Elohem that sits in the h. for us to take up begin[in]g at the creati[o]n necessary to understand something of God himself in the beginning. If we start right easy

---

2. Discourse, 7 April 1844, as reported by Thomas Bullock, *JSP, D14*, 316–27.
3. Discourse, 7 April 1844, as reported by William Clayton, *JSP, D14*, 327–33.

Wilford Woodruff account[4]

3 oclok PM April Sunday 7[th] 1844

The following important edefying & interesting discourse was deliver[e]d by President Joseph Smith to about ~~twenty~~ <ten> thousand souls upon the subject of the death of Elder King Follet.

I now call the attention of this congregation while I addres you upon the subject of the dead[.] The case of our Beloved Brother King Follet, who was crushed to death in a well, as well as many others who have lost friends will be had in mind this afternoon, & [I] shall speak upon the subject in general as far as I shall be inspired by the Holy spirit to treat upon ~~the subject~~ <it>. I want the Prayers & faith of the Saints that I may have the Holy Ghost, that the testimony may carry conviction to your minds of the truth of what I shall say, & pray that the Lord may strengthen my lungs. there is strength here & your prayers will be herd. Before I enter upon an investigation of this subject, I wish to pave the way, and bring up the subject from the beginning that you may understand. I do not intend to please you with oritory but with the simple truths of heaven <to> Edify you. Go to the morn of creation to understand ~~of~~ the decrees of the Eloheem at the creation. It is necessary for us to have an understanding of God at the beginning. if we get a good start first we can go right, but if you start wrong you may go wrong. But few understand the Character of God. they do not know they do not understand their relationship to God. the world know no more than the brute beast, & they know no more than to eat drink and sleep & this is all man knows about God or his exhistance, except what is given by the inspiration of the Almighty. go then to the beginning that you may understand. I ask this

Willard Richards account[5]

3¼ P.M.— Joseph commenced speaking on the subject of the Dead— relative to the death of elder King Follet[t] ~~to~~ who who was crushed in a well. by the falling of a tub of rock on him.—

If men do not compreh[e]nd the character of God they do not comprehe[n]d themselvs. what kind of a being is God?— Eternal life to know God.— if man does not know God. has not Eternal life.— if I am so fortunate as to comprehe[n]d and explain the—— [blank] let eve[r]y one sit in silenc[e] and never lift your voice again[s]t the servants of God again.

Every man has a right to be a false prophet. as well as a true prophet.—

in the beginning. befor the world was.— Is a man like one of yourselves— sh[o]uld you see him to day. you would see a man in fashion and in form. Adam was formd in his likeness.——

[p.218] refute the Idea that God was God from all eternity— Jesus said as the father Had power in himself even so hath the son power to do what the fathr did.— Lay down his body. & take it up again—— you have got to learn how to make you[r]selves Gods Kings. Prie[s]ts.— &c— by going from a small to g[r]eat capacity. . . Till they are able to dwell in evelastig [everlasting] burni[n]g & everlasti[n]g power.—

how consoling when calld to part with a dear frie[n]ds. to know their ve[r]y being will rise to dwell in everlasti[n]g bunig [burning].— heirs of God. and ascend a throne as those who have gone before.— I saw the father work out his kingdom with fear & trembling.—— god is gra[ti]fied in <salvati[o]n> Exaltation— of his creati[o]ns &c—

not all to be comprehedd [comprehended] in this world—— the head.— the head one—

---

4. Discourse, 7 April 1844, as reported by Wilford Woodruff, *WWJ*, 1:628–31. See also *JSP, D14*, 336–40.
5. Discourse, 7 April 1844, as reported by Willard Richards, in *JSP, J3*, 217–22. See also *JSP, D14*, 333–36.
6. This introductory paragraph does not appear in *JSP, D14*.

Bullock

that which is to come & com: but little more than the brute beast if a man learns know nothing more than to eat, drink, sleep, & does not comprehend any of the des[ig]ns of God the Beast can the same thing eats drin[ks] [p.317] sleeps— noes [knows] nothing more & how are we to do it by no o[the]r way then the Insp[iratio]n of A[lmighty] God I want to go back to the begin & so get you into a more lofty sphere than what the human being generally understands I want to ask this cong[regation]: every man wom[an]: & child to ans[we]r. the quest[io]n. in their own heart what kind of a being is God I ag[ai]n. rep[ea]t. the questn. what kind of a being is God does any man or woman know have any of you seen, him heard him, communed with him, here is the questn. that will peradventure from <this time> henceforth occupy your attentn.— the Apos[tle]: says this is Eternal life to know God & J. C [Jesus Christ] who he has sent— that is etern[a]l. life if any man enquire what kind of a being is God if he will search deligently his own heart that unless he knows God he has no eternal life— my first object is to find out the character of the true God & if I sho[ul]d. be the man to com[prehend]: the God & I com: them to your heart let every man & woman henceforth shut their mouths & never say anything ag[ain]st. the man of God & If I do not do it I have no right to rev[elatio]n. inspn. if all are pretension to the God they will all be as bad off as I am they will all say I ought to be d[amne]d there is not a man or wom who wo[ul]d not breath[e] out an anathema on my head & some wod. feel auth[orize]d to take away my life— if any man is authd. to take away my life who say I am a false teacher so I shod. have the same right to all false teacher & where wod. be the end of the blood & there is no law in the heart of God that wod. allow any one to interfere with the rights of man every man has a right to be a false as well as a true prophet— if I shew verily

Clayton

to go right all the time— start wrong hard matter to get right. few beings in the world who understand the character of God and do not comprehend their own character— They cannot com[prehend] from the beginning no the end not the[i]r own relation and is but little above the beast. If a man comprehends nothing more than to eat sleep and and not any more and what the designs of Jehova[h] what better than the beast it does the same thing— eats drink sleep & comprehends present and knows as much as we unless we are able to com by the inspirati[o]n of A[lmighty] God. Go back to begin[nin]g to lift you[r] minds into a more exalted standing than the human mind is wont— want to ask this this congregate[o]n every man, wom[an], &c what kind of a being is God— ask yourselves I repeat the question what kind of a being is God. Any man or woman that kno[ws] any of you seen him? <u>heard him?</u> <u>communed with him?</u> Here a subject that will peradventure occupy you[r] attenti[o]n while you live— The apostle says this is eternal life "to know &c" that is eternal life if any man enquire what kind of being is God. cast his mind to know— if the declarati[o]n of the ap[ostle] be true he will realize that he has not eternal life. There can be eternal life on no other prinicple— Ist of object to find the character of the only wise & true God. [p.329]

If I comprehend so that the spirit seal it upon you[r] hearts let every man and woman put his hand on his mouth & never say any thing against the man of God again but if I fail it becomes my duty to renounce all my pretensions to inspirati[o]ns &c and if I should do so should I not be as bad as all the rest of the world. not a man would not br[e]ath anathema if they knew I was a false prophe[t] som[e] would take my life. If any man is authorised to take my life because I am a false teacher then upon th[e] sam[e] principle am <I> authorised to take the life of every false

Woodruff

Congregation what kind of a being is God? turn your thoughts in your hearts, & say have any of you seen or herd him or communed with him? this is a question that may occupy your attention[.] The scriptures inform us that this is eternal life to know the ownly wise God & Jesus Christ whome He has sent. If any inquire what kind of a being God is I would say If you dont know God you have not eternal life. go back & find out what kind of a being God is. If I am the man that shows you what kind of a being God is, then let evry man & woman sit in silence and never lift up his hand against me again. if I do not do it, I will not make any furth[er?] pretentions to inspiration or to be a prophet. I would be like the rest of the world,[s] fals[e] teachers & you would want to take my life. But you might just as well take the lives of other fals[e] teach[ers?] as mine if I was fals[e]. But meddle not with any man for his religion, evry goverment ought to permit evry man to enjoy his religion. I will show the world is <w>rong by showing what God is. I am going to inquire after God so that you may know God, that persecution may cease Concerning me. I go back to the beginning to show what kind of a being God was. I will tell you & hear it O Earth! God who sits in <u>yonder</u> <u>heavens</u> is a <u>man</u> <u>like</u> <u>yourselves</u>[.]

That GOD if you were to see him to day that holds the worlds you would see him like a man in form, like yourselves. Adam was made in his image and talked with him, <&> walked with him. In order to understand the dead for the consolation of those that mourn, I want you to understand God and how he comes to be God. We suppose that God was God from eternity. I will refute that Idea, or I will do away or take away the veil so you may see. It is the first principle to know that we may convers with him and that he once was <a> man like us, and the Father was once on an earth like us. And I wish I was in a suitable place to tell it[.] <u>The</u> <u>scriptures</u> <u>inform</u> <u>us</u> <u>mark</u> <u>it</u> that

Richards

The head one of the God, brought fo[r]th the Gods.—

D^r & Lawyer that have persecuted.—

The head one called the Gods together in grand coun[c]il— to bring fo[r]th the world.— Example of error as Yacob. <Ja[c]ob—> th[e] son of Zebedee— & James James the son of Zebede[e] 2̶ 4. mat. 21. Greek Hebrew. German. & Latin.— In the begin[nin]g the head of the gods calld a coun[c]il of the Gods— and concoctd a scheme to create this world.— Soon as we begin to understand the character of t̶h̶e̶ Gods, he begin to unfold th[e] heavns to us.—

Doctors say.— created the earth out of nothing.

Barau.— create.— it means to organized.— God had mat[er]ials to organ[i]ze the world.— Elements— nothing. can destroy. no beginni[n]g no end.——

[p.220] The soul. Doctor of Divin[i]ty. God created in the beginn[in]g— lessens the chara[c]ter of man.— dont believe it.—— who told you God was Self existnt? correct enough.— in hebrew put into him his spirit.— which was created before. Mind of man co-equal with God him[s]elf— frie[n]ds separated. for a small mom[en]t. from their spir[i]ts. coequal with God. and hold conversa[tion] when they are one with another.—

If man had a beginig [beginning] he must have an end.—— might proclaim. God never had power to create the spir[i]t of man at at all.

Intiignc [Intelligence] exist upon a self existe[n]t principle no creation about. it. all mi[n]ds & spir[i]t God ever sent into the wo[r]ld are susceptible of enlargeme[n]t.——

all things God has seen fit proper to r[e]veal i̶n̶ while dwelli[n]g in mortality. are reveald.— precisely the same— as though we were destitute of bodies.——

what will save our spi[r]its will save our bodies.—— our taberacls [tabernacles]——

Bullock

that I have the truth of God & shew that ninety nine of 100. are false prop[hets] it wo[d.] deluge the whole world with blood I want you all to know God to be familiar with him & if I can bring you to him all persecute[io]n. agst. me will cease & let you know that I am his serv[an]t for I speak as one hav[in]g. auth[orit]y. & not as a senr. open your ears & eyes all ye Ends of the Earth & hear & I am going to prove it to you with the Bible & I am going to tell you the desns. of God to the human race & why he interferes with the affairs of man God himself who sits enthroned in yonder **[p.318]** Heavens is a man like unto one of yourselves who holds this world in its orbit & upholds all things by his power if you were to see him to day you wod. see him a man for Adam was an man like in fashion & image like unto him Adam walkd. talked & com[mune]d. with him as one man talks & com[munes]: with ano[the]r. in order to speak for the consol[atio]n. of those who mourn for the loss of their friend it is necy. to understand the cha[racte]r. & being of God for I am going to tell you what sort of a being of God for he was God from the begin of all Eternity & if I do not refute it— truth is the touchstone they are the simple & first princ[ipes]: of truth to know for a certainty the char. of God that we may conv[erse] with him same as a man & God himself the father of us all dwelt on a Earth same as J C himself did & I will shew it from the Bible— I wish I had the trump of an Arch An[gel] I cod. tell the story in such a manner that pers[ecution]: shod. cease for ever— J[esus]: s[ai]d. as the Fa[the]r. hath power in himself ~~to do~~ even so hath the Son power to do what the Far. did that ansr. is obvious in a manne[r] to lay down his body & take it up— J— did as my Far. laid down his body & take it up agn. if you dont believe it you dont believe the Bib[le] the Scrip[ture] says & I defy all hell all learn[in]g. wisdom & records of hell tog[ethe]r to refute it here then is Et[erna]l life to know

Clayton

teache[r] and who would not be the sufferer— but no man is authorised to take away life in consequence of their religion all laws and government ought to tolerate whethe[r] right or wron[g] If I show that I have the truth of God & $^{99}/_{100}$ are false teacher[s] while they pretend to hold the keys of God & go to killing them because &c would it not deluge the wo[r]ld in blood. Want you should all [k]now God— be familiar— If I can get you to know I can bring to him, & if as you will cease to persecute me I speak in authority— What kind of a being was God in the beginning. hear all ye ends of th[e] earth, I am going to prove it by the bible & the relati[o]n the human family sustains with God. Ist. God that sets enthroned is a man like one of yourselves— that is the great secret. If the vail was rent to day & the great God who holds this world in its sphere in its orbit— the planets— if you were to see him to day you would see him in all the person image very form of man. for Adam was created in the very fashion of God. Adam received instruction walked talked as one man with another[r]. In order to understand the subject of the ded for the consolation of thos[e] wh[o] mourn for the loss of their friends necessary they should understand[d] Going to tell you how God came to be God. We have imagined that God was God from all eternity. These are incompr[e]hensible to some but are the first principle of the gospel— to know that we may converse with him as one man with another & that he was once as one of us and was on a planet as Jesus was in the flesh

If I have the privilege could tell the story in such a manner as persecution would cease forever— Said Jesus (mark it Br Rigdn [Sidney Rigdon]) What did Jesus say— as the father ~~hath~~ had power in himself even so hath the son power. to do what why what the father did To lay down his body and took it up again. Jesus what are you going to do— to lay down my life as my father did that I might take it up

Woodruff

Jesus Christ Said As the Father hath power in himself so hath the son power in himself to do what the Father did even to lay down my body & take it up again[.] do you believe it. if not, dont believe the bible. I defy all Hell and earth to refute it. And you have got to learn how to make yourselves God, king and priest, by going from a small Capacity to a great capacity to the resurrection of the dead to dwelling in everlasting burnings. I want you to know the first principle of this law. how consoling to the mourner when they part with a friend to know that though they lay down this body it will rise & dwell with everlasting burnings to be an heir of God & joint heir of <with> Jesus Christ enjoying the same rise exhaltation & glory untill you arive at the station of a God. what did Jesus Christ do. the same thing as I se[e] the Father do. see the father do what. work out a kingdom. when I do so to[o] I will give to the father which will add to his glory. He will take a Higher exhaltation & I will take his place and am also exhalted. These are the first principles of the gospel. It will take a long time after the grave to understand the whole[.] If I should say any thing but what was in the bible the Cry of treason would be herd[.] I will then go to the Bible.

Barasheet in the beginning. Analize the word in and through the head. an old Jew added the word Bath. it red the head one of the gods, broat forth the gods. I will transpose it in the english language. I want you to know & learn that the Holy Ghost knows sumthing. The grand Council set at the head and contemplated the creation of the world. some will say, the scriptures say so & so, but I will show you a text out of an old book Containing the four languages. the german is here. what does this text say. Yoakabeam, the son of Zebedee. the bible says James the son of Zebedee, but this says Jacob son of jebedee 21 ch 4[th] ver Matthew The Dr says (I mean Dr of Law not of physic) If you say any thing not according

Richards

for our spi[r]its— All spi[r]its— who have not obedye [obeyed] th[e] Gospel must be damnd.— Who have not obeyed th[e] decrees of son of man.

we are looked upon by God as though we were in Eternity— the greate[s]t responibity [responsibility] resting upon us is to look after our dead.— they without us cann[o]t be made perfct without us. meet Paul I/2 way.—

Hence the saying of Elijah.—

[p.221] God made provisio[n]s before th[e] world was— for every cr[e]ature in

all sin shall be forgivn in this world or world to com—— except one[.] Salvati[o]n for all men who have not committd a certan sin

can save ev[er]y man who has not committd th[e] unprdonbl [unpardonable] sin. cannot comm[i]t the unpdonbl [unpardonable] sin after th[e] decay dissolution of the body—— Knowledge save a man.—

no way f[o]r a man to come to undestadig [understanding] but giv his conse[n]t to th[e] comandmt [commandment]—— Damnd by mo[r]tification—— a lake as of fire of brimston[e]— as exquisite th[e] disappointme[n]t of the mind of man——

why? must commit the unpardon[a]ble sin in this wo[r]ld. will suffer in th[e] ete[r]nal world until he will be exalted.—

works of th[e] devil. the pl[a]ns th[e] devil laid to save th[e] wo[r]ld.—

Devil said he could save them all— Lot fell on Jesus.——

all sin &c fogen [forgiven] except the sin agai[n]st th[e] Holy Gh[o]st.— Got to de[n]y th[e] plan of Salvati[o]n. &c— with his eyes open.— Like ma[n]y of the apostates of chu[r]ch of the chu[r]ch of Jesus Christ.— of Lat[ter] Days

Let All be careful.— lest you be dec[e]ived. best men brings forth best works. to the mourne[r]s your f[r]iend has gone to wait. the perfection.— of the reunion.— the

Bullock

the only wise & true God you have got to learn how to be a God yourself & be a **[p.319]** K[ing]. & ~~God~~ Priest to God same as all have done by going from a small cap[acit]y to an[other]r. from grace to grace until the res[urrectio]n. ~~of~~ & sit in everlasting power as they who have gone before & God in the L D. [last days] while cert[ai]n. indivdls [individuals] are proclaim[in]g. his name is not trifling with us— how consoling to the mourner when they are cal[le]d. to part with a wife mother father d[ea]r. relative to know that all Earthly taber[nacles] shall be dissolved that they shall be heirs of God & j[oin]t. h[ei]rs of J. C. to inherit the same powers exalt[atio]n. until you asc[en]d. the throne of Etl. power same as those who are gone bef[ore] what J. did I do the things I saw my Far. do before worlds came roll[e]d nto existence I saw my Far. work out his K[ingdom] with fear & trembling & I must do the same when I shall give my K to the Far. so that he obt[ai]ns K roll[in]g. upon K. so that J treads in his tracks as he had gone before it is plain beyond comprehens[io]n. & you thus learn the first prin[ciples] of th[e] Gospel when you climb a ladder you must begin at the bottom run[g] until you learn the last prin[ciple] of the Gospel for it is a great thing to learn Sal[vatio]n. beyond the grave & it is not all to be com[prehended] in this world I sup[pose] I am not all[owe]d. to go into investign. but what is cont[aine]d. in the Bible & I think there is so many wise men who wod. put me to death for treason I shall turn commentator to day— I shall go to the first Hebrew word in the Bible the Ist. sen[tence]: In **[p.320]** the beginning— Berosheet— In by thro[ugh] & every thing else Roshed the head when the Inspd. man wrote it he did not put the Ist. pt. to it a man a Jew with[ou]t. any authy. tho[ugh]t. it too bad to begin to talk about the head of any man— "The Head one of the Gods brought forth the Gods" is the true mean[in]g. of the word— if you do not

Clayton

again. If you deny it you deny the bible I defy the records and wisdom & all the combined powers of earth and hell to refute it. You have got to learn how to be a god yourself in order to save you[r]self— to **[p.330]** be priests & Kings as all Gods has done— by going from a small degree to another from exaltation to ex[altation]— till they are able to sit in glory as doth those who sit enthroned. I want you to know while God is being proclaimed that he is not trifling with you nor me. Ist principles of consolation— how consoling to the mourner when calld to part with husband father wife child to know that those being shall rise in immortal glory to sorrow die nor suffer anymore. & not only that to contemplate the saying they shall be heirs of God &c— What is it— to inherit the same glory power & exal[ta]tion with those who are gone— before— What did Jesus do— why I do the things that I saw the father do when worlds came into existns— I saw the father work out a kingdom with fear & trembling & I can do the same & when I get my k[ingdom] work I will present to the father & it will exalt his glory and Jesus steps into his tracts to inherit what God did before This is some of the first principles of the gospel about which so much hath been— You have got to find the beginning of the history & go on till you have learned the last— will be a great while before you learn the last. It is not all to be compreh[ende]d in this world. I suppose that I am not allowed to go into an investigate[o]n of any thing that is not in the Bible— you would cry treason so many learned and wise men here

I will go to the old Bible the very Berosheit. make a comme[n]t on the first sentence of the history of creation— Berosheit ~~Barau~~ want to annalize the word— Ba in by through in & every thing else— rosh— next— the head. sheet where do it come from— when they inspired man wrote it he did not put the Ba. Ther[e]— Bu[t] a jew put it there. It read in

Woodruff

to the Bible we will cry treason. But if ye are not led by revelation how can ye escape the damnation of Hell. here we have the testimony of four[.] I have the oldest Book in the world & the Holy Ghost[.] I thank God for the old Book but more for the Holy Ghost. The Gods came together & concocked the plan of making the world & the inhabitants. having an knowledge of God we know how to Approach him & ask & he will answer. An other thing[.] the learned Dr Says the Lords made the world out of nothing. you tell them that God made the world out of sumthing, & they think you are a fool. But I am learned & know more than the whole world. the Holy Ghost does any how, & I will associate myself with it. Beaureau to organize the world out of Chaotic matter, element[.] they are principles that Cannot be disolved[.] they may be reorganized. Another subject which is Calculated to exhalt man I wish to speak of, The resurrection of the dead. The soul the mind of man, whare did it come from? The learned says God made it in the beginning, but it is not so. I know better. God has told me so. If you dont believe it, it wont make the truth without effect. God was a self exhisting being. man exhists upon the same principle. God made a tabernacle & put a spirit in it and it became a **[p.630]** Human soul. man exhisted in spirit & mind coequal with God himself. you who mourn the loss of friends are ownly seperated for a moment. the spirit is seperated for a little time[.] they are now conversant with each other as we are on the earth. I am dwelling on the immutibility of the spirit of man. is it logic to say the spirit of man had a begining & yet had no end. it does not have a begining or end. my ring is like the exhistance of man[.] it has no begining or end. if [I] Cut in to it [t]heir would be a begining & end. so with man[.] if it had a begining it will have an end. if I am right I might say God never had pow[er] to create the spirit of man. God him-

Richards

resurrecti[o]n of your frie[n]d in felicity while worlds mu[s]t wait myr[i]ads of years befor they can receive the like blessi[n]gs.— leave th[e] subject.— bless thoes [those] who have lost frie[n]ds. only gon for a few mome[n]ts.—

Shall mothrs have their Child[re]n? Yes. th[e]y shall have it with[o]ut price. redempt[io]n is paid possessing all the intelgen [intelligence] of a god. the child **[p.222]** as it was before it died out of y[o]ur arm throne up[o]n thrones. Domin[ion] up[o]n domnins [dominions] just as you———

Baptism of water fire & Holy Ghost. are in sepa[r]ably— connected.— found in th[e] Germ[a]n Bible to prove what I have taught for 14 years ab[o]ut baptism.— I baptize you with— water. but when Jesus comes having the keys— he shall baptize you with th[e] baptisms of fire & Holy ghost.———

Leaving th[e] pincipls [principles] of doctrin of baptism &c— one god. one bapti[s]m— &c one bapti[s]m— I.E. all three—

called upon all men. Pri[e]sts and all to repe[n]t and ob[e]y the gospel.— if th[e]y do not th[e]y will be damnd.— those who commit the unpdoabl [unpardonable] sin are doomd to Gnolom. without end.—

God dwells in everlasti[n]g burnings.———

Love all men but hate your deeds.—

You dont know me— you never will

I dont blame you for not believi[n]g my histo[r]y had I not expeind [experienced] ~~by~~ it could not believe it myself

5½ closed.— sung———

Bullock

believe it you do not believe the learned man of God— no man can tell you more than I do thus the H[ead] God bro[ugh]t· forth the Gods in the Head council— I want to bring it to English Oh ye lawyers ye doctors I want to let you know that the H G. [Holy Ghost] knows something as well as you do— the Head God called tog·r the Gods & set in Grand Council &c when I say a lawyer I mean a lawyer of the Scrip[ture]. I have done so hither to let the lawyers flutter & let every body laugh at them— some learned D[octo]r· mi[gh]t· take a not[io]n· to say thus & so— & are not to be alt[ere]d· & I am going to shew you an error I have an old book in the Latin Greek Hebrew & German & I have been read[in]g· the **[p.321]** Germ[an]: I find it to be the most correct that I have found & it corespends the nearest to the rev[elatio]ns· that I have given the last 14 y[ea]rs it tells about Iachaboa means Jacob— in the English James— & you may talk about James thro all Eternity in the 21 v[erse] of 4th· Mat[thew]: where it gives the test. that it is to Jacob— & how can we escape the d[amnatio]n· of hell with·t God reveal to us. ~~one~~ <Latin> says that Iachobus. means Jacob— Hebrew says means Jacob— Greek says ~~Jachem~~ <Jacob> German says Jacob thank God I have got this book & I thank him more for the gift of the H G. I have all the 4 Test[aments] come here ye learned men & read if you can I shod· not have brot· up this wod ~~ott~~ only to shew that I am right when we beg[in] to learn in this way we beg to learn the only true God & when we find to know how to come to him & he begins to unfold the heavens to us & tell us all ab[ou]t· it bef our prayers get to his ears ~~at the b0~~ now I ask all the learned men who hear me whe[the]r· the learned me[n] who are preach[in]g· Saln· say that God created the Heavens & the Earth out of nothing & the reason is that they are unlearned & I know more than all the world put togr· & if the H.

Clayton

the first— The head one of the Gods brought forth the Gods— is the true meaning— rosheit signifies to being forth the Eloheim, Learned man cann[o]t learn any more than what I have told you— hence the head God brought forth the head God in the grand Council— will simplify it in the English language. Ye learned Docters who have persecuted me I want to let you know that the H. G.

The grand councilers set in yonder heavens and contemplated the creation of the worlds that was created at that tim[e]. When I say Doctr & Lawyer I mean the D & L of the scriptures some learned docter might say the scriptures say thus & so and we must believe the scriptures. He referred to an old Book (N. T [New Testament]). in the Hebrew. Latin German & Greek— find it to be the most correct— find it to correspond with the revelati[o]ns I have **[p.331]** received— It tells about Yachaubon the son of Zebedee— means Jacob. the N. T. says James— now if Jacob had the keys you might talk about James and never get the keys. Mathew 4— 21 verse ~~in~~ it gives the word Jacob instead of James— how can we escape the damnati[o]n of hell unless God be with us— men bind us with chains— read from the Hebrew Yongacoub— Jacob.— Greek Ichabon— Jacob— ~~German~~ He has got the oldest book in the world— but he has got the oldest book in his heart. Latin Yacobin— Jacob too Should not have introduced this testimony were it not to back up the word rosh— The head father of the Gods. When we begin in this way ~~be~~ we begin to find out God— what kind a being we have got to worship— when we begin to know how to come to him he begins to come to us. When we are ready to come to him he is ready to receive us. Learned Docters tell us God created the heavens & earth out of nothing they account it blasphemy to contradict the idea— they will call you a fool— you ask them ~~they~~ them why they say dont the bible say he

Woodruff

self Could not Create himself. Intelligence is Eternal & it is self exhisting. All mind ~~that~~ is susseptible of improvement. the relationship we have with God places us in a situation to advance in knowledge. God has power to institute laws to instruct the weaker intelligences that they may be exhalted with himself[.] this is good ~~d~~ doctrin. it taste good. I can taste the principles of eternal life. so can you. they are given to me by the revelations of Jesus Christ and I know you believe it. All things <that> God sees fit to reveal to us in relation to us, reveals his commandments to our spirits, and in saving our spirits we save the body, the same as though we had no Body How comes the awful responsibility if in relation to our dead, if they do not be baptized they must be damned. (I wish I had 40 days to talk) what promises are made, what can be said if in the grave, God dwells in eternity, and he does not view things as we do. the greatest responsibility lade open us in this life, is in relation to our dead[.] Paul <said we> cannot be made perfect without us. for it is necessary that the seals are in our hands to seal our Children & our dead for the fulness of the dispensation of times, A dispensation to meet the promises made by Jesus Christ befor[e] the foundation of the world for the salvation of man. All sins and blasphemys were to be forgiven except the sin against the Holy Ghost. God has made provision for evry spirit in the eternal world, and the spirits of our friends should be searched out & saved. Any man that has a friend in eternity can save him if he has not committed the unpardonable sin. He cannot be damned through all eternity. their is a possibility for his escape in a little time. If a man has knowledge he can be saved. if he has been guilty of great sins he is punished for it. when he Consents to obey the gospel whether, Alive or dead, he is saved, his own mind damns him[.] I have no fear of hell fire that dont exhist. No man can Commit the unpardonable sin, untill He

Richards

Bullock

G. in me com[prehends]: more than all the world I will associate with it— what does Boro mean it means to organize same as you wo[d.] organize a Ship— God himself had materials to org[anise] the world out of chaos which is Element & in which dwells all the glory— that nothing can destroy they never can have an ending they exist eternally— I have ano[r.] to dwell on & it is impossible for me to say much but to touch upon them— for time will not permit me to say all— so I must come to the res[urrectio][n.] of the dead— the soul the im[m.] [immortal] Spirit oh <man says> God created in the begin[g.] the very idea lessens man in my idea— I dont bel[ive] the doct[rine]: hear it all ye Ends of the World for God has told me so I am going to tell of things more noble— we say that God himself is a self existing God, who told you so, how did it get it into your head who told you that man did not exist in like manner— how does it read in the Heb[rew] that God made man & put into <it> Adams Spirit & so became a living Spirit— the mind of man— the mind of man is as immortal as God himself— hence while I talk to these mourners— they are only separated from their bodies for a short period— their Spirits coexisted with God & now converse one another same as we do— does not this give you satisfact[io][n.] I want to reason more on the Spirit of Man for I am dwelling on the body of man on the subj[t.] of the dead— ~~the Sp of Man~~

I take my ring from my finger & liken it unto the mind of man the im[morta][l.] Sp[irit]. bec[ause] it has no begin[g.] suppose you cut it into but as the L[or][d] lives there wo[d.] be an end all the fools & wise men from the begin[g.] of creation who say that man had begin— they must have an end & then the doc[trine] of annihilit[n.] [annihilation] wo[d.] be true— but if I am right I mi[t.] with boldness proclaim from the house top that God never had power to create the Sp of man at all— ~~it is no~~ God

Clayton

created the world & they infer that it must be out of nothing The word create came from the word Barau— dont mean so— it means to organize— same as a man would use to build a ship— hence we infer that God had materials to organize from— chaos— chaotic matter— element had an existence from the time he had. The pure pure principles of element are principles that never can be destroyed— they may be organized— and reorganized— but not destroyed.

It is as[so]ciated with the subject in question the resurrection of the dead Another subject— the soul— the mind of man— they say God created it in the beginning— the idea lessens man in my estimation. Dont believe the doctrine— know better— God told me so. Make a man appear a fool before he gets through if he dont believe it.

We say that God was selfexistent— who told you so? its correct enough but how did it get into your heads— who told you that man did not exist upon the same principle (— refer to the bible) dont say so in the old Hebrew— God made man out of the earth and put into him his spirit and then it became a living body. The mind of man— the intelligent part is coequal with God himself I know that my testimony is true. hence when I talk to these mourners what have they lost— they are only separated from their bodies for a short season. but their spirit existed coequal with God and they now exist in a place where ~~he~~ they converse together as much as we do on the earth. Is it logic to **[p.332]** say that a spirit is immortal and yet have a beginning because if a spirit have a beginning it will have an end— good logic— illustrated by his ring. All the fools learned & wise men that comes and tells that man has a beginning proves that he must have an end, and if that doctrine is true then the doctrine of annihilation is true. But if I am right then I might be bold to say that God never did have power to create the

Woodruff

receives the Holy Ghost. All will suffer untill they obey Christ himself. even the devil said I am a savior and can save all, <he> rose up in rebelion against God and was cast down. Jesus Christ will save all except the sons of perdition. what must a man do to commit the unpardonable sin. they must receive the Holy Ghost, have the heavens opened unto them, & know God, & then sin against him. this is the case with many apostates in this Church. they never scease to try to hurt me. they have got the same spirit the devil had. you cannot save them. they make open war like the devil. Stay all that hear, dont make any hasty mooves[.] you may be saved. if a spirit of Bitterness is in you, dont be in haste. Say you that man is a sinner. well if he repents he shall be forgiven. I could go back and trace evry subject of interest concerning the relationship of man to God if i had time. their is many mansions in my fathers Kingdom. what have we to console us in relation to our dead. we have the greatest hope in relation to our dead of any people on earth[.] we have seen them walk worthy on earth and those who have died in the faith are now in the selestial [Celestial] kingdom of God. they have gone to await the resurrection of the dead, to go to the celestial glory, while their are many who die who will have to wait many years. But I am authorized to say to you **[p.631]** my friends in the name of the Lord, that you may wait for your friends to come forth to meet you in eternity in the morn of the celestial world. those Saints who have been murdered in the persecution shall triumph in the Celestial world while their murderers shall dwell in torment untill they pay the utmost farthing.

I have Fathers, Brothers, Children, that are gone to eternity soon to meet me. the time will soon be gone, the trump will soon be blown. A question[.] will Mothers have their Children in Eternity? yes, yes, you will have the Children, <But> as it falls so it will rise. It

Richards

Bullock

himself co^d. not create himself intelligence is self existent it is a Sp from age to end & there is no creat^n ab^t. it the first principles of man are self exist with God— that God himself finds himself **[p.323]** in the midst of Sp[irits] & bec he saw proper to institute laws for those who were in less intelligence that they mi^t. have one glory upon another in all that knowledge power & glory & so took in hand to save the world of Sp: you say honey is Sweet & so do I. I can also taste the Sp of Eternal life I know it is good & when I tell you— of these things that we[r]e given me by Insp[iration] of the H S. you are bound to rece[ive] it as sweet & I rej[oice] more & more— mans rel[ation] to God ~~& s~~ I will open your eyes in rel to your dead all things which God of his inf[inite] reason has seen fit to reveal to us in our mortal state in regard to our mortal bodies are rev[eale]^d. to us as if we had no bodies & those rev^ns. which will save our dead will save our bodies— & God reveals them to us in the view of no Eternal diss[olutio]^n. of the body— hence the awful responsibility tha[t] rests upon ~~our~~ us for our dead— for all the Spirits must either obey the Gospel or be d—d [damned] solemn tho^t. dreadful tho^t. is there nothing to be done for those who have gone before us with^t. obey[in]^g the decrees of God wo^d. to God that I had 40 days & nights— to tell you all to let you know I am not a fal[le]^n prop[het]— what kind of characters are those who can be saved altho their bodies are decaying in the grave— the greatest responsibility that God has laid upon us to seek after our dead— the apostle says they without us cant be perfect— now I am speaking of them I say to you Paul, you cant be perfect with^t. us.— those that are gone before & those who came after must be made perfect— & God has made it obligatory to man— God said he shall send Elijah &c I have a decla[ratio]n to make as to the prov[isio]^n. which God made from before the found[atio]^n. of the world. what has J. s^d. all

Clayton

spirit of man at all. He could not create himself— Intelligence exists upon a selfexistent principle— is a spirit from age to age & no creation about it— All the spirits that God ever sent into the world are susceptible of enlargement— That God himself— find himself in the midst of spirit and glory— because he was greater saw proper to institute laws whereby the rest could have a privilege to advance like himself. I know that when I tell you those words of eternal life that are given to me I know you taste it and I know you believe it. Wants to talk more of the relation of man to God— in relation to your dead. All things whatsoever God has seen proper to reveal to us while we are dwelling in mortality are revealed to us in the abstract & independant of affinity of this mo[r]tal tabernacle— but they are revealed as though we had no bodies at all— tho revealed to our spirits & those revelations must of necessity save our spirits with them. Hence the responsibility— the awful res. that rest upon us in relations to our dead— for all spirits— who have not obeyed the gospel in the flesh must obey the gospel or be damned. Is there no preparation— no salvation for our father & friends who have died and not obeyed the decrees of the son of man— Would to God I had 40 days & nights I would let you know that I am not a fallen prophet. what kind of beings can be saved although their bodies are mouldering in the dust. Whe[n] his commandments touch us it is in view of eternity. the greatest responsibility in this world is to seek after our dead— they without[t] us cannot be made perfect— It is necessary that those who come after us should have salvation in common with us— & thus hath God laid this upon the eves of the world hence the saying of Elijah Speak in relation to the provisions God hath made to suit the conditions of man. What hath Jesus said? All sins & all blasphemis every tran[s]gression except one there is a provision either in this world or

Woodruff

will never grow. It will be in its precise form as it fell in its mothers arms. Eternity is full of thrones upon which dwell thousands of Children reigning on thrones of glory not one cubit added to their Stature.

I will leave this subject here and make a few remarks upon Baptism. I will read a tex[t] in Jerman upon Baptism. John says I Baptise you with water But when Jesus Christ Comes He shall administer the baptism of fire & the Holy Ghost. John said his baptism was good for nothing without the Baptism of Jesus Christ. Many talk of any baptism not being essential to salvation but this would lay the foundation of their damnation. There has also been remarks made concerning all men being redeemed from Hell, But I say that any man who commits the unpardonable sin must dwell in hell worlds without end

Richards

Bullock

sins & all blas[phemies] every trans[gression]: that man may be guilty of there is a Sal^{n.} for him or in the world to come— every Sp in the Et[ernal]: world can be ferreted out & saved unless he has com[mitte]^{d.} that Sin which cant be rem[itte]^{d.} to him— that God has wro[ugh]^{t.} out sal^{n.} for all men unless they have com^{d.} a cert^{n.} sin a friend who has got a friend in the **[p.324]** world can save him unless he has com^{d.} the unpard[onable] sin & so you can see how far you can be Savior [*blank*] there is no thing that a man can commit the unpardonable sin after the dissⁿ of the body & there is a way possible for escape not partarly d—d— those that are with^{t.} wisdom until they get exalted to wisdom ~~so long as man will not give acc^{r.} of his sins~~ a sinner has his own mind & is in his own condemner ~~for the G. will~~ the torment of the mind of man is as exquisite as a lake burn[in]^{g.} with fire & brimstone— I know the Scriptures I understand them— no man can commit the unpardonable sin after the diss^{n.} of the body but they must do it in this world— hence the Sal^{n.} of J. C was wrought out for all men to triumph over the devil— for he stood up for a Savior— J. cont[ende]^{d.} that there wo^{d.} be cert^{n.} souls that wo^{d.} be condemnd & the d[evi]l s^{d.} he co^{d.} save them all— as the grand council gave in for J. C. so the d l fell & all who put up their heads for him all sin shall be forgiven except the sin ag^{t.} the H. G. he has got to say that the Sun does not shine while he sees it he has got to deny J. C. when the heavens are open to him— & from that time they begin to be enemies like many of the apostates of The Church of J. C of L. D. S. [Jesus Christ of Latter-day Saints]— when a man begins to be an enemy he hunts him— for he has the same Sp. that they had who cruc[ifie]^{d.} the Lord of life— the same Sp. that Sin ag^{t.} the H. G. I advise all to be careful what you do— stay— do not give **[p.325]** way— you may find that some one has laid a snare for you

Clayton

in the world of spirit. Hence God hath made a provision that ev[e]ry spirit can be ferreted out in that world that has not sin'd the upardnabl [unpardonable] sin. wether in this world or in the world of spirits. Every man who has a friend in the eternal world who hath not committed the ~~eternal sin~~ unpardonable sin you can save him. A man cannot commit the unpardonable sin after the dissoluti[o]n of the body there is a way for his escape **[p.333]**

knowledge saves a man and in the wold of spirits a man cant be exalted but by his knowledge. So long as a man will not give heed to the commandme[n]ts he must abide without salvation. A man is his own torment hence the saying they shall go into the lake that burns with fire &c or as exquisite as a lake &c so is the torment of a man— I said no man could commit the unpardonable sin after the dissolution of the body— hence the salvation that the saviour wrough[t] out for the salvation of a man if it did not catch him in one place it would another— The contenti[o]n in heaven was Jesus said there were certain men would not be saved the devil said he could save them. he rebelled against God and was thrust down. After a man has sinned the sin against the H G. there is no repentance for him. Hence like many of the apostates of the C of J. C. L. D. S. [Church of Jesus Christ of Latter-day Saints] they go to[o] far the spirit leaves them hence they seek to kill me they thirst for my blood they never cease— he has got the same spirit that crucified Jesus You cant renew them to repentance— awful is the consequence Advise all to be careful what they do— you may by and by find out that you have been deceived

He continued his discourse— & told of parents receiving their children. Concluded his remarks by Baptism

Woodruff	Richards

Bullock

be cautious— await— when you find a Sp. wants bloodshed murder same is not of God but is of the devil out of the abundance of the heart man speaks— the man that tells you words of life is the man that can save you— I warn you ag[t] all evil characters <who sin ag[t] H. G.> for there is no redemp[tio]n for them in this world nor in the world to come I can enter into the mysteries— I can enter largely into the eternal worlds— for J. s[d] ~~where my~~ In my Fa[rs] mansion there are many mansions &c there is one glory of the moon Sun & Stars &c we have the reason to have the greatest hope & consol[n] for our dead— for we have aided them in the I[st] princ[iples] for we have seen them walk in the midst— & sink asleep in the arms of J. & hence is the glory of the Sun— you mourners have occ[asio]n to rejoice for your husband has gone to wait until the res[n] & your exp[ectatio]n & hope are far above what man can conceive— for why God has rev[d] to us— & I am auth[d] to say by the auth[y] of the H. G. that you have no occas[n] to fear for he is gone to the home of the just— dont mourn dont weep— I know it by the test[imony] of the H. G. that is within me— rejoice O Israel— your friends shall triumph gloriously— while their murderers shall welter for years—— I say for the benefit of strangers I have a Fa[r] Bro[r] Friends who are gone to a world of Sp— they are absent for a mom[en]t— they are in the Sp. then shall we hail our Mo[the]r Fa[rs] Friends & all no fear of mobs— &c but all an Eternity of felicity— Mothers you shall have your Children for they shall have it— for their debt is paid there is no dam[natio]n awaits them for they are in the Spirits— as the Child dies so shall it rise from the de[a]d & be living in the burn[g] of God— it shall be the child as it was bef it died out of your arms children dwell & exercise power in the same form as they laid them down

    the Bap[tism] of Water with[t] the B[aptism] of Fire & the H G. att[endin]g it are nec[y] he

Clayton

Woodruff **Richards**

Bullock

must be born of W[ater] & Sp in order to get into the K of God— in the German text bears me out same as the rev[n.] which I have given **[p.326]** for the 14 years— I have the test to put in their teeth that my test has been true all the time you will find it in the decla[ratio]n of John the Bap[tist] (reads from the German) John says I bap[tize] you with Water but when J comes who has the power he shall adm[inister] the bap of F & the H. G. G[rea][t.] God now where is all the Sec[t.] [sectarian] world— & if this est [testimony] is true they are all d—d as clearly as any Anathema ever was— I know the text is true— I call upon all to say I— (shouts of I) Alex[ander] Campbell— how are you going to save them with water— for John s[d.] his bap[m.] was nothing with[t] the test bap of J. C. One God, Fa[r.], Jesus, hope of, our Calling, one baptism— all three bap make one I have the truth & I am at the defiance of the world to contradict I have preached Latin Hebrew Greek German & I have fulfilled all I am not so big a fool as many have taken me for— the Germans know that I read the German corect— hear it all ye Ends of the Earth— all ye Sinners Repent Repent turn to God for your rel[igio][n.] wont save you & ye will be d[d] but I do not say how along— but those who Sin ag[t.] the H. G. cannot be forgiven in this world or in the world to come but they shall die the 2[nd.] death— but as they concoct scenes of bloodshed in this world so they shall rise to that resur[n.] which is as the lake of fire & brimstone— some shall rise **[p.327]** to the everlasting burning of God & some shall rise to the d[n.] of their own filthiness— same as the lake of fire & brimstone— I have int[ende][d.] my remarks to all— to all rich & poor bond & free great & small I have no enmity ag[st] any man— I love you all— I am their best friend & if persons miss their mark it is their own fault— if I reprove a man & he hate me he is a fool— for I love all men especially these my brethren & sisters— I rejoice in hearing

Clayton

Woodruff	Richards

Bullock	Clayton
the test of my aged friend— you never knew my heart no man knows my hist[ory]— I can not do it I shall never undertake— if I had not experienced what I have I should not have known it myself— I never did harm any man since I have been born in the world— my voice is always for peace— I cannot lie down until my work is finished— I never think evil nor think any thing to the harm of my fellow man— & when I am called at the trump & weighed in the balance you will know me then— I add no more God bless you [a]men—	

APPENDIX D

Joseph Smith's Potential Ghostwriters

While Joseph Fielding Smith's *Teachings of the Prophet Joseph Smith* takes for granted that each of the discourses or teachings attributed to Joseph in that volume were indeed the actual words of the Prophet, not all historians are certain of this. Indeed, there is some evidence that at least a portion of the words attributed to the Prophet therein may have actually been ghostwritten on his behalf by close associates, possibly including John Taylor, Wilford Woodruff, Gustavis Hills, Benjamin Winchester, and William Wines Phelps.[1]

The degree to which any of these men were involved in ghostwriting for the Prophet is unclear.[2] However, some church historians believe that W. W. Phelps—a prominent figure in the early Church and a close associate of the Prophet Joseph—was the most common ghostwriter, particularly in the 1840s.[3]

As a young man, Phelps apprenticed with a printer—learning the trade in his teens.[4] Later he was involved in a number of writing, printing, and publishing ventures, including writing for the *Cortland Republican* (1815), penning a novel (1825), and running his own newspaper known as the *Ontario Phoenix* (1828).[5] These and other experiences prepared Phelps for the literary influence he would have on The Church of Jesus Christ of Latter-day Saints. After his conversion to the restored Gospel, Phelps not only served as a clerk and scribe to the Prophet Joseph, but he also "edited *The Evening and the Morning Star*, prepared and printed revelations

---

1. "Besides [John] Taylor and Phelps, at least nine other men are believed to have worked in the Nauvoo printing office at this time [i.e., March 1845]: Ariah Brower, Joseph Cain, George Q. Cannon, Matthias Cowley, Chauncey Jennings, Lyman Littlefield, William Rowley, Elias Smith, and William Taylor." Minutes, 22 March 1845, in Matthew J. Grow, Ronald K. Esplin, Mark Ashurst-McGee, Gerrit J. Dirkmaat, and Jeffrey D. Mahas, eds., *Council of Fifty, Minutes, March 1844–January 1846* (Church Historian's Press, 2016), 375n577.

2. Some of the men who worked in the printing office (at various times) most likely did some writing and editing (e.g., W. W. Phelps, George Q. Cannon, Lyman Littlefield, and Elias Smith). See *JSP, R2*, 699–707. Others may have simply been "printer's devils" who did much of the grunt work needed to produce the paper. The editors of the Council of Fifty Minutes point out that "editorial material in both papers [i.e., the *Times and Seasons* and the *Nauvoo Neighbor*] was often unattributed." See 22 March 1845, *JSP, AR*, 376, note 583. Consequently, it is very difficult to ascertain who wrote what. This applies to the numerous things published under Joseph Smith's name when he served as the editor of the *Times and Seasons*.

3. See, for example, Bruce A. Van Orden, *We'll Sing and We'll Shout—The Life and Times of W. W. Phelps* (Religious Studies Center, Brigham Young University, 2018), chapters 24 and 27; Michael Hicks, "Joseph Smith, W. W. Phelps, and the Poetic Paraphrase of 'The Vision,'" in *Journal of Mormon History* 20, no. 2 (Fall 1994): 64, 67–68, 72, 74, 77; Samuel Brown, "The Translator and the Ghostwriter: Joseph Smith and W. W. Phelps," in *Journal of Mormon History* 34: no. 1 (Winter 2008): 26–62; Richard Neitzel Holzapfel, "'Eternity Sketch'd in a Vision': The Poetic Version of Doctrine & Covenants 76," in *The Heavens Are Open: The 1992 Sperry Symposium on the Doctrine and Covenants and Church History* (Deseret Book, 1993), 142.

4. See Van Orden, *We'll Sing and We'll Shout*, 15.

5. See Van Orden, 15–18.

for the *Book of Commandments*, helped with the compilation of the *Doctrine and Covenants*, acted as scribe for Joseph Smith in translating the book of Abraham, and assisted Emma Smith in compiling and printing the Church's first hymnbook. William also wrote several hymns."[6] On 20 July 1831, the Prophet Joseph received a revelation regarding W. W. Phelps. In it, the Lord commanded: "And again, verily I say unto you, let my servant William W. Phelps be planted in this place [Missouri], and be established as a printer unto the church" (D&C 57:11). As a result of this revelation, the Prophet Joseph placed Phelps in an influential position—working at the print office—thereby enabling William to have potentially significant influence over what appeared in several Church periodicals of that era. It is during his tenure at the printing office in Nauvoo, and while involved in the compilation and writing of the Church's history, that Phelps is believed to have done at least some ghostwriting on behalf of Joseph Smith.[7]

One of the primary reasons that some scholars believe that Phelps wrote a number of things attributed to the Prophet is the stylistic similarities between Phelps's personal writings and certain things attributed to Joseph Smith.[8] For example, Sam Brown pointed out that the King Follett Discourse "demonstrates a dramatically different style" from Joseph's "political pieces"[9]—which Phelps is understood to have authored.[10] Similarly, in examining the poetic version of D&C 76—known as "The Answer: A Vision"—Michael Hicks pointed out: "We must . . . scrutinize the structure and diction of the poem. Does it ring true to Joseph's already established voice? . . . [D]id Joseph have both the occasion and the ability to write the poem? As it turns out, virtually all of the evidence in these matters weighs against Joseph Smith as the poem's author and points instead to W. W. Phelps."[11] In his recent biography of W. W. Phelps, Bruce Van Orden—perhaps the most outspoken supporter of the theory that Phelps was a frequent ghostwriter for the Prophet—stated, "Based on contemporary evidence, Joseph Smith was not an efficient writer. The literary style of his personal writings and recorded speeches does not match that of the newspaper editorials attributed to him."[12] A number of scholars have pointed out that Phelps had a distinct style when it came to rhetoric, the use of hyper-

---

6. Sydney Marie Hughes, "William W. Phelps," in *Encyclopedia of Latter-day Saint History*, Arnold K. Garr, Donald Q. Cannon, and Richard O. Cowan, eds. (Deseret Book, 2000), 917.

7. Dean C. Jessee wrote, "William W. Phelps . . . assisted in writing early revelations. . . . In 1843 he was assisting Willard Richards on Joseph Smith's History. His clerical efforts are evident in early manuscript revelations, the Egyptian alphabet, a manuscript of the Book of Abraham, patriarchal records, and the 1839 Joseph Smith History." Dean C. Jessee, "The Writing of Joseph Smith's History," *BYU Studies Quarterly* 11, no. 4 (1971): 446.

8. There are other reasons for the presumption that Phelps was Joseph's ghostwriter. One proffered by Bruce Van Orden had to do with the topics written about in the *Times and Seasons*. Van Orden wrote that Phelps's "ghostwriting began with Smith's first issue as 'editor' on February 15, 1842. That issue carried a lengthy article on the past and future of the Jews, a subject that had captivated Phelps's previous interest in *The Evening and the Morning Star* and *The Latter Day Saint's Messenger and Advocate*." Van Orden, *We'll Sing and We'll Shout*, 329. This argument seems rather conjectural. Certainly Phelps may have had topics he was enamored with. However, we also know that he was quite captivated by *anything* that fell from the lips of the Prophet. Thus, subjects Phelps gravitated toward may simply have been things he had heard Joseph Smith teach.

9. Brown, "The Translator and the Ghostwriter," 50–51.

10. See Hicks, "Joseph Smith, W. W. Phelps, and the Poetic Paraphrase of 'The Vision,'" 74; Bruce A. Van Orden, "William W. Phelps's Service as Joseph Smith's Political Clerk," *BYU Studies* 32, nos.1–2 (Winter–Spring 1991): 88–89; Brown, "The Translator and the Ghostwriter," 26, 61.

11. Hicks, "Joseph Smith, W. W. Phelps, and the Poetic Paraphrase of 'The Vision,'" 64.

12. Van Orden, *We'll Sing and We'll Shout*, 327.

bole, forcefulness, grammar, punctuation, spelling, paragraph length, and the use of foreign language terms in his writing—a style that did *not* match samples of Joseph Smith's known writings.[13] Comparing what we know Joseph *did* author to things attributed to him (but where authorship is uncertain), consistently leaves one with the impression that Joseph likely is *not* the author of at least *some* of the pieces published under his name.[14]

It is important to emphasize that while some historians are quite certain about Phelps's work as ghostwriter, not all feel as confident in the assertion—or regarding which pieces may have been ghostwritten. One must be tentative about conclusions drawn on this subject, at least until further evidence can be discovered.[15] Generally speaking, scholars are more sure about Phelps's influence on certain writings attributed to the Prophet, and less definite about it for others. Van Orden estimated that "W. W. Phelps may have ghostwritten more than twenty-five articles in the *Times and Seasons* in behalf of Joseph Smith during Smith's editorship."[16] While this is possible, it cannot be proven.

Among the documents that various historians have suggested might be either ghostwritten or heavily edited by W. W. Phelps (and possibly others) are the following:

- Joseph's political materials—particularly those published in John Taylor's *The Voice of Truth*.[17]
- Joseph Smith's two 1842 letters regarding baptism for the dead, found in D&C 127 and 128.[18]

---

13. See Holzapfel, "'Eternity Sketch'd in a Vision': The Poetic Version of Doctrine & Covenants 76," 142; Van Orden, *We'll Sing and We'll Shout*, 327, 329, 333: Brown, "The Translator and the Ghostwriter,", 50–51; Hicks, "Joseph Smith, W. W. Phelps, and the Poetic Paraphrase of 'The Vision,'" 64.

14. Bruce Van Orden argues, if one compares other possible ghostwriters for Joseph, one still finds that Phelps's style tends to most closely match the pieces in question. As an example of this, Van Orden wrote: "John Taylor . . . was a powerful speaker and missionary, but these roles do not necessarily translate into writing extensive editorials. Taylor's known writing to that point does not match the style of the 1842 editorials in the *Times and Seasons* attributed to Joseph Smith." Van Orden, *We'll Sing and We'll Shout*, 327.

15. As already noted, Bruce Van Orden is the most dogmatic on this subject, writing quite emphatically about both Phelps as a ghostwriter for Joseph, and also with certitude about which pieces Phelps supposedly ghostwrote. Van Orden explained his dogmatism by writing, "My in-depth study of the Nauvoo newspapers and the writing styles of W. W. Phelps, Joseph Smith, John Taylor, William Smith, and other potential contributors has led me to this conclusion." Van Orden, 337n1.

16. Van Orden, 329.

17. See Brown, "The Translator and the Ghostwriter," 26, 61; Van Orden, "William W. Phelps's Service as Joseph Smith's Political Clerk," 88–89; Hicks, "Joseph Smith, W. W. Phelps, and the Poetic Paraphrase of 'The Vision,'" 74.

18. Dean Jessee indicated Phelps's "clerical efforts are evident in early manuscript revelations." Jessee, "The Writing of Joseph Smith's History," 446. Van Orden conjectures that these letters by Joseph (which would eventually be canonized) "could have been added to or edited by Phelps, given their stylistics and their use of the Latin phrases *propria persona* [D&C 128:8] and *summum bonnum* [D&C 128:11]." Van Orden, *We'll Sing and We'll Shout*, 331. None of this is to say that Phelps is actually writing the revelations. Rather, it is our opinion that Joseph likely dictated the letters, as the originals are in Phelps's handwriting. The originals have very little punctuation—in all probability because Phelps would not have been able to punctuate as he recorded the dictation, not knowing in advance the content of the letters he was recording. Were Phelps the source of the original letters, he would have punctuated as he drafted them. However, he did not do so, which supports the argument that he was recording Joseph's dictation. The *Times and Seasons* version of the letters are properly punctuated, suggesting that Phelps likely took the dictation as Joseph gave it and then went back and cleaned up the letters prior to publishing them.

- "Baptism for the Dead," in *Times and Seasons* 3 (15 April 1842): 759–61.[19]
- "Gift of the Holy Ghost," in *Times and Seasons* 3 (15 June 1842): 823–26.[20]
- "The Government of God," in *Times and Seasons* 3 (15 July 1842): 855–58.[21]
- "Baptism," in *Times and Seasons* 3 (1 September 1842): 903–5.[22]
- The poem titled "The Answer: A Vision," in *Times and Seasons* 4 (1 February 1843): 81–85.[23]
- "Try the Spirits," in *Times and Seasons* 3 (1 April 1842): 202–15.[24]
- "Knowledge is Power," in *Times and Seasons* 3 (15 August 1842): 889–900.[25]
- "Correspondence. To the Editor of the Times and Seasons," in *Times and Seasons* 4 (15 May 1843): 194.[26]
- "Persecution of the Prophets," in *Times and Seasons* 3 (1 September 1842): 903–5.[27]

---

19. See Van Orden, 332, 404.

20. See Van Orden, 332.

21. See Van Orden, 332.

22. See Van Orden, 332.

23. See Van Orden, 333.

24. See Van Orden, 342n49, 406. Van Orden cites Jonathan Neville, who holds that "Joseph Smith was definitely not the actual author of 'Try the Spirits,' but…the piece was a combination of the writings or contributions of Benjamin Winchester, W. W. Phelps, and John Taylor." See Jonathan Nevill, *Brought to Light*, 2nd. ed. (Digital Legend, 2016), 41–81, cited in Van Orden, *We'll Sing and We'll Shout*, 342n50. Though Nevill and Van Orden seem quite dogmatic about "Try the Spirits" not being authored by Joseph, there is hesitancy in fully embracing their conclusion. We have, for example, two dates on which Joseph appears to have taught on this subject; 27 June 1839 and sometime between 26 June and 4 August of 1839. Most of the pieces Van Orden proposes Phelps wrote on behalf of Joseph Smith are articles written in the *Times and Seasons* and not the Prophet's public discourses. Indeed, the public discourses are often used to show how they differ from things published in periodicals under Joseph's name. See, for example, Brown, "The Translator and the Ghostwriter," 50–51. In the case of "Try the Spirits," it does make its way into the *Times and Seasons*—but not until almost three years after Joseph first taught on the subject. When Joseph gave his 27 June 1839 discourse on this subject, we know that that Wilford Woodruff took notes and then copied those notes into his "Book of Revelations" notebook almost immediately thereafter. See *JSP, D6*, 509. Thus, this strongly suggests that Joseph, rather than Phelps, Taylor, or Winchester, was the source for these ideas. Willard Richard's "Pocket Companion" version of this discourse is believed to have come from an account of the discourse given to him by John Taylor, Wilford Woodruff, or another apostle, upon their arrival in England in early 1840. While we know that Wilford Woodruff wrote his notes of the discourse in his "Book of Revelations" almost immediately, we also know "Woodruff also copied the discourse into his 1839 journal. In the journal account, which Woodruff apparently made sometime after he wrote his 'Book of Revelations' account, Woodruff expanded on and reorganized the content in the earlier account." "Significant differences between Woodruff's notebook and journal accounts" exist. See *JSP, D6*, 509. All of this is simply to say that, while some think Joseph is not the direct author of "Try the Spirits" (as it appeared in the *Times and Seasons* in April of 1842), it seems quite evident that he *was* the source of the doctrinal ideas contained in the public discourse, and likely for much of the language—regardless of whether Phelps, Taylor, Winchester, or Woodruff had influence editorially.

25. See Van Orden, *We'll Sing and We'll Shout*, 400.

26. See Brown, "The Translator and the Ghostwriter," 42–44; Van Orden, *We'll Sing and We'll Shout*, 335–36, 344n66.

27. Gerald E. Jones, "Apocryphal Literature and the Latter-day Saints," in *Apocryphal Writings and the Latter-day Saints*, C. Wilfred Griggs, ed. (BYU Religious Studies Center, 1986), 26.

- "A Friendly Hint to Missouri," in *Times and Seasons* 5 (15 March 1844): 473–74.[28]
- "Latter Day Saints," in I. D. Rupp, *He Pasa Ekklesia: An Original History of Religious Denominations at Present Existing in the United States* (Clyde, Williams & Co., 1844), 404–10.[29]
- "Proclamation," in *Nauvoo Neighbor* 2, no. 7 (12 June 1844): 2–3.[30]
- The "Articles and Covenants of the Church of Christ."[31]
- The Articles of Faith.[32]
- Various editorials published in *The Wasp* during the time that William Smith was its editor.[33]
- Some of Joseph's correspondences.[34]

While this list is hardly exhaustive, it is a representative sampling of some of the documents published under Joseph's name but possibly written or edited for him by someone else. Again, while we simply cannot say to what degree each of these various documents was actually written by someone other than the Prophet, historians generally feel that Joseph would have given permission for any ghostwriting done on his behalf, and likely supervised any such writing—most likely feeding his ghostwriters ideas from which they used to replicate the Prophet's teachings on a given subject.[35] It is quite possible that Joseph read and approved most of the written pieces prior to their actual publication.[36] On some documents attributed to the Prophet, we are quite certain they were ghostwritten (under Joseph's supervision and approval); on others, we can only conjecture. Had the positions published in his name run counter to the Prophet's views, he certainly would have made his concerns known—and likely would have required some kind of retraction or clarification. As he did neither, we can assume that he was comfortable with what was written in his name, and also that he placed great trust in those who wrote for him.[37]

---

28. See *JSP, J3*, 199n873.
29. See *JSP, H1*, 503–16.
30. See *JSP, J3*, 278n1262.
31. See Hicks, "Joseph Smith, W. W. Phelps, and the Poetic Paraphrase of 'The Vision,'" 67.
32. See Hicks, 67.
33. See Van Orden, *We'll Sing and We'll Shout*, 328, 333, 339n17.
34. See Brown, "The Translator and the Ghostwriter," 61; *JSP, H1*, 503.
35. See, for example, Holzapfel, "'Eternity Sketch'd in a Vision': The Poetic Version of Doctrine & Covenants 76," 142; Van Orden, *We'll Sing and We'll Shout*, xvi, 327, 329, 333, 341n39. Also, see our discussion of "Try the Spirits" in note 22 of this appendix. Also see *JSP, J3*, 28, 101, 112, 132, 152, 168, 171, 178–79, 185, 199, 278, where Joseph assigns Phelps to write on his behalf, and often gives him instruction regarding what to write.
36. See, for example, *JSP, J3*, 127–28, 138, 152, 171, 179n796, 199, 251, where Joseph reviews what has been written in his name.
37. In March of 1845, the minutes of the Council of Fifty meetings show that there was quite a bit of discussion about the editors of the Church's periodicals altering things submitted to them. Brigham Young is said to have "heard a complaint that allmost all the articles sent by individuals for publication are alterd in the office." 22 March 1845, *JSP, AR*, 369–70. "G. A. Smith . . . once wrote two peices for the papers and they were altered so as to destroy the sense and he did not feel satisfied. He has wrote none since." 22 March 1845, *JSP, AR*, 376. Almon "Babbit referred to some errors in the publication of the report of his speeches before the Legislature." 22 March 1845, *JSP, AR*, 377. "O. Hyde explained the reasons why he had complained about the papers. He referred to an article which he wrote showing the reason why we held an election after the repeal of the charters, which had been altered so as to change the sense." 22

Finally, we might ask why Joseph was comfortable having some items written on his behalf by various scribes, associates, or editors. There has been a fair amount of supposition on this matter. Most assume that Joseph's primary reason was his remarkably busy schedule, making it nearly impossible to have the time to sit down and pen word-for-word a polished doctrinal treatise—particularly at the rate that such were being published in the *Times and Seasons*.[38] One historian conjectured, "As fame, legal battles, and the growing population of the Church threatened to drain all of his time, literary delegation became crucial. The presence of his name on any document from his last years is not an answer but a question."[39] Another supposition put forth is that those running the printing office felt they could do so best if they didn't have the direct oversight of Joseph. One historian wrote, "[John] Taylor is said to have asked Joseph Smith not to be involved directly with the editing of the paper; this according to an 1860 statement by Heber C. Kimball to Wilford Woodruff."[40] (Apparently Joseph had expressed concern that things were not being proofread as carefully as they should be, and this was not necessarily well received.[41]) Finally, it has been claimed that Joseph employed ghostwriters as a means of

---

March 1845, *JSP, AR*, 373–74. W. W. Phelps responded to Hyde's concern, explaining that "he ordered Er Hydes article to be altered" because it was "his legal opinion that we are not yet legally notified of the repeal of our charters" as Hyde's article had erroneously suggested. See 22 March 1845, *JSP, AR*, 375. Some of the changes made to submissions were clearly because of typos in the submissions, or because some of the articles submitted were poorly written. W. W. Phelps explained that they had to make some changes, as "there are but few men who can write an article suitable for the printers." See 22 March 1845, *JSP, AR*, 370. See also pages 372–73. "The chairman [Brigham Young] made some remarks in reply, especially in regard to typographical errors, and showed that it was not brother Taylor or Phelps alone, who had to bear the responsibility of the paper but the ~~Twelve~~ Church and especially the authorities of the church. He wants brother Taylor to bear with the errors of the brethren and publish their articles unaltered." 22 March 1845, *JSP, AR*, 373. Though Brigham argued that the editors should not make changes to content of the submissions, Heber C. Kimball felt that editing *should* take place when necessary. According to William Clayton's notes of the March 22 meeting, Heber argued, "If he [Taylor] saw a piece presented for publication wherein the doctrines were incorrect he should be unwilling to have it published untill it was corrected." 22 March 1845, *JSP, AR*, 376. The point of all of this is simply to say that the editors working in the print shop definitely changed things that were submitted; sometimes mostly addressing stylistic issues, and other times changing the actual meaning or content of the submissions. However, just as those who had been edited cried "foul," surely the Prophet would have done the same if things were published under his name with which he did not agree with the content. (It doesn't appear that Joseph actually made submissions to the printing office, though he likely dictated pieces or assigned pieces to be written on his behalf.) Even though Joseph did not involve himself in the day-to-day operations of the print shop, as Heber C. Kimball noted, "President Smith when alive considered every thing in this place was under his own control." 22 March 1845, *JSP, AR*, 375.

38. See, for example, Hicks, "Joseph Smith, W. W. Phelps, and the Poetic Paraphrase of 'The Vision,'" 67–68; Van Orden, *We'll Sing and We'll Shout*, 335.

39. Hicks, "Joseph Smith, W. W. Phelps, and the Poetic Paraphrase of 'The Vision,'" 68.

40. Van Orden, *We'll Sing and We'll Shout*, 343n57. Van Orden cites David J. Whittaker, "The Book in Early Mormon Culture," *Journal of Mormon History* 23, no. 1 (Spring 1997): 15n36, where Whittaker states, "Although Joseph Smith was critical of John Taylor's proofreading, he urged, 'I believe you can do more good in the editorial department than preaching. You can write for thousands to read, while you can preach to but a few at a time.' Later, according to Heber C. Kimball, Joseph complained that Taylor as editor was reluctant to let Smith do anything with the paper."

41. See Whittaker, "The Book in Early Mormon Culture," 15. The 19 April 1843 entry in Joseph Smith's journal states of John Taylor, "We have no one else we can trust the paper with. & hardly with you. you suffer the paper to come out with so many mistakes." *JSP, J2*, 368.

refuting his critics, who often characterized him as an uneducated dullard. As the theory goes, using some of his educated associates, Joseph was enabled to ensure that things published in his name were well worded and carefully edited.[42] Of course, *all* of these are nothing more than theories. Joseph doesn't specifically state why he at times leaned on ghostwriters. All that we know is that he apparently occasionally did.

In the end, it is impossible to say exactly how many ghostwriters Joseph had, how many pieces attributed to him were actually written in part or completely by others, why he chose to sometimes use ghostwriters, or the degree to which he was involved in the compilation of those things published in his name. Perhaps the one thing we can say with some certainty is that articles published in the *Times and Season* under the moniker "ED" should not necessarily be presumed to be the actual words of the Prophet Joseph Smith. Beyond that, anything else on this subject is conjecture.

---

42. See Hicks, "Joseph Smith, W. W. Phelps, and the Poetic Paraphrase of 'The Vision,'" 72, 77; Brown, "The Translator and the Ghostwriter," 38–41; Van Orden, *We'll Sing and We'll Shout*, 335–36.

INDEX

A

Aaronic Priesthood, John held keys of, 353, 417
Abel
    the Lord speaks to, 70
    offered sacrifice, 69
Abraham
    Gospel preached to, 71
    planetary system revealed to, 492–93
    reasoning of, 492–93
    sacrifice required of, 423
Account, all men to give, 81
Accusations
    by false brethren, 499
    do not make, against the brethren, 250
Accusers and fault-finders, on road to apostasy, 198
Acts of men are recorded, 83
Adam (Michael)
    acts under direction of Jesus Christ, 214
    appointed to open the way of the world, 9
    first man, 213
    holds keys of presidency, 199, 216
    is Michael, the Ancient of Days, 199
    presides over spirits of all men, 200
    received commandments from God, 215
    stands next to Jesus Christ in holding keys, 200
Adam-ondi-Ahman, 154, 202
Adam's body made out of the earth and his spirit put into it, 464
Adams, James, remarks at death of, 425–26
"After its kind," 256
Aged men in council, 389
Agency, the doctrine of, 57, 241
America is Zion, 477
    the place of, 15
Ancient of Days. (See Adam.) 154, 200, 213
    order pertaining to the, 305
Angel, destroying, to follow after the preaching of the Gospel, 114
Angels
    do not have wings, 206
    four destroying, hold sway, 421
    in resurrection some are raised to be only, 409
    ministering spirits, 247
    of destruction will commence work before Gentiles are fully warned, 108
    to assist in establishing righteousness, 104
    to gather out of kingdom all things that offend, 126, 202
Angels and spirits, 427
Animals, kindness to, 85
Annihilation, painful and false thought, 385
Answers to questions, 150
Apostasy, unjust criticism leads to, 199
Apostates
    how re-admitted into the Church, 21
    snares of the evil one, 79
    dream of, in Nauvoo, 486
    who have known light cannot be renewed, 101, 446
Apostles
    address to, 197
    authority of, 132
    calling of, 89–90
    decisions of, 89–90
    epistle to, 221
    hold keys of ministry in the world, 89–90
    not sent to be taught, but to teach, 198
    Prophet's remarks to, 111
    stand next to First Presidency, 245
    traveling High Council, 89–90
    revelatory, 137
    vision of the, 134–35
Appeal, righteous, 165–66
Archangel, Adam is the, 135
Armies to be against armies, 205
Aspiring men hinder the work, 292
Assembly, solemn, 113
Atonement, through the blood of Christ, 69
Authority, divine
    necessary to make ordinances valid, 356
    of Apostles next to Presidency, 132

B

Backbite, do not, 197
Baptism, 343
    a burial, 343
    decree of God, 257
    essential to salvation, 9
    for the dead, 229, 246, 260, 336
    in water good for nothing without baptism of Holy Ghost, 412, 474

not to be performed for wives if husbands object, 108
of infants a false doctrine, 411
required in all ages, 344
sectarian, 248
a sign that we keep the commandments, 257

Baptist, John the, greatness of, 357
Barnes, Lorenzo D., remarks on death of, 382
Baurau, meaning of, 459, 490
Be like God, to go where He is, 281
Beasts, Daniel's vision of, 373
Beginning, Gospel ordinances from the, 71
Berosheit, meaning of, 459
Betrayal of brethren, a major sin, 198
Bible,
  errors in the, 429–30
  important parts taken from, 6
  shows handiwork of God, 67
  teaches nature and character of God, 456–57
  translations, exceptions to, 376
Bishop is a High Priest, 142
Blasphemy against Holy Ghost not forgiven, 284
Blessed are the persecuted, 157
Blessings for the faithful, 73
Blood
  cannot dwell in eternal fire, 485
  cannot go where righteousness dwells, 428
  innocent, on skirts of betrayers of the brethren, 199
Bloodshed in United States, predicted, 16
Bodies
  of the righteous to be fashioned after that of Christ, 77
  they who have obtained, have power over those who have not, 233, 244
  to be raised, 103–4
Body, earth life is that man may obtain a, 233
Body and spirit, difference between, 269
Book of Commandments, 27
  revelations and value of, 3
Book of Life, the Lamb's, 5
Book of Mormon
  and the parable of the mustard seed, 121–22
  copyright secured, 3
  essential to our religion, 85
  like parable of hidden treasure, 122
  perfection of the, 3
  printing of, 3
  title page, 3
Books, printing of, in England, 225
Born again of water, man must be, 342
Boys and the preaching of the Gospel, 52

Brown, Father, teachings of, 371
Browning, O. H., letter to, 523
Buffeting of Satan until redemption, 163
Burial, sacredness of, 383
Burnings, everlasting, God dwells in, 458

C

Cain
  authorized to offer sacrifice before his fall, 215–16
  cursed, 215–16
  sacrificed of, not accepted, 69
Called, many are, but few chosen, 180
Calling and election, 191, 387, 398
Calling of the Apostles, 89–90
Captivity through lack of knowledge of the things of God, 281
Carlin, Governor, letter to, 328
Carthage, on way to, 504
Cause of God a common one, 299
Celestial glory
  all who obtain fullness of, to be gods, 391–92, 494
  wisdom of, 133
  who may enter, 8–9
Celestial law, many will fail to obtain, 435
Ceremonies, revelation of, 138
Chance, universe not by, 66
Chaos, result of absence of law, 66
Character and attributes of God, 453–55
Charity, greatness of, 295
Charity, towards all men, 181
Chastened by hand of God, Saints have been, 327
Chastisement, the value of, 251
Children
  hearts of, turn to fathers, 203, 443
  not to be baptized if parents object, 107
  redemption of little, 255
  salvation of, 254
  to be obedient to parents, 107
  who die are heirs of the celestial kingdom, 135
Chosen, few are, 180
Christ
  coming of, 32, 448–49
  Great High Priest, 201
  Head of the Church, 417
  rule of, in Millennium, 347
  second coming, 368
  the resurrection, 73
Christian Godhead, the, 488
Christianity
  professors of, inspired by Satan, 351
  sleeping, 12

Church
  analogous to the human body, 315
  compact body, 315
  organization and Priesthood, 137
  parable of the, in the last days, 122
  retarded by ignorance, 176
  to be purged, 493
  to prevail against all evil, 333
Church of the Firstborn, 10, 420
Circumcision not baptism, 411
Comforter, the Second, 191
Comforters, two, 191
Commandments, Book of. (See Book of Commandments.)
Commandments, only those who keep, to end, saved, 75
Compulsion
  exercise of, contrary to righteousness, 449
  not found in kingdom of God, 311
Confusion among nations, 323
Consecrated lives, 160
Consecrated property, 160
Contention
  evils of, 51–52
  in heaven, what it was, 470
Constitution
  a glorious standard, 188
  remarks on the, 429
  views of the Prophet on, 361
Correction, scriptural, 360
Corruption
  earth now groaning under, 326
  not to be condoned, 293
Council of the Gods, 461
Councils
  order in, 82, 116
  high, duties of, 114
  trials, 210
Counsel
  and admonition, 50
  effects of disobeying, 346
  for the exiled Saints, 183
  Saints subject to the divine, 327
  value of aged men in, 389
Covenant
  blessing to the people of the, 204–5
  Melchizedek Priesthood is by, 424
  of Christ rejected by the Jews, 13–13
  of tithing, 84
  with the Gentiles, 13
  with the fathers, 105

Covenants
  fulfilling of, with Israel, 12
  of the fathers revealed, 420
  we approach the Lord through, 78
Cowdery, Oliver, blessing of, 44
Create, meaning of the word, 462
Creatures in heavens, varied, 377
Creeds of men, 430
Crown of righteousness obtained through suffering, 76
Cursed are those who fight against the Lord's anointed, 171

D

Damnation
  awaiting the rebellious in Christendom, 388
  of hell, 257, 445
Daniel's vision of beasts, 373
Darkness
  condemnation of the world is, 119
  prevails on the earth, 111
  spiritual, 55
Daughter will oppose mother in great conflict, 204–5
David, punishment of, 243, 446
Dead, baptism for the, 246, 249, 260, 336
  taught in the New Testament, 405
  when first taught, 229
Dead
  resurrection of the, 480
  righteous, often pained knowing our thoughts and acts, 428
  rise as they are laid away, 485–86
  Saints have not too much time to labor for, 434
  salvation for, 403, 478–79
  worked for by the living, 444–45
Death
  Joseph Smith predicts own, 496–97
  sermon on life and, 253
Deceive, the devil's power to, 294
Decrees of God immovable, 256
Deeds, every man judged by, 306
Denial of Christ, does violence to good judgment, 77
Desolation
  awaits the world, 205
  to cover the earth, 85
Destroying angels, four, 421
Destruction
  angels of, 108
  of Saints, threatened, 36
Devil
  as angel of light, 206

has no power over man only as man permits, 233
inspires professors of religion, 351
power of to deceive, 294
punishment of, 387
steals bodies and has to be cast out, 387
unfaithful men draw near to the, 281
Devil's punishment to be without a body, 233
Devils, doctrine of, 25, 130
Die, Joseph Smith ready to, for religious freedom, 410
Diligence, to things of God increases knowledge, 60
Discerning of spirits, 264, 266
Discourse on Elias, Elijah, and Messiah, 440
Disobedient
    to commandments of the Lord offer violence to the Supreme Intelligence, 63–64
    to the laws of God, to be punished, 61
Disobeying counsel, effects of, 346
Disputes, avoiding, 51–52
Diversity of gifts, 313
Divine authority, necessary to make ordinances valid, 356
Doctrines of Christ
    importance of, 101
    of Priesthood, shall distill upon the soul, 181
    false, in the world, 285
Douglas, Stephen A., prophecy to, 393
Dream of the Prophet Joseph Smith, 521
Dunn, Captain of the militia, 502
Dust, shake off from feet, 108
Duty of wives and children, 185

E

Earth
    body of Adam made out of the, 464
    darkness prevails on the, 111
    defiled, 14
    groaning under corruption, 326
    to be swept by righteousness, 104
    to reel, 85
    transfiguration of, 10
Earth-life is that man may obtain bodies, 232–33
Economy, temporal, 432
Editorial, "Try the spirits," 262
Elders, duties of, 93, 107
Election
    and calling, 191, 243, 387
    made sure, 398
Elements are eternal, 233
Elias
    man of like passions as other men, 110
    office of, 441
Elijah
    holds keys of Priesthood, 220, 443
    mission of, 220, 424, 443
    office and mission of, 443
    the coming of, 433–34
Eloheim, meaning of, 491
Embalming transmitted from Jerusalem to America, 302
End, who endure to, are saved, 74–75
Endowment in Kirtland, 113
Endowments
    first given in 1842, 306
    necessary, 113
    to be given in place prepared for them, 478–79
    worthy saints receive, 438
Endure to the end, to be saved, 74–75
Enemies, overcoming of, is salvation, 386
England, the Gospel in, 222
Enoch, the mission of, 216
Epistles
    excerpts from an, 55
    from the Presidency, 19
    from Liberty prison, 154
    of the Prophet to the Twelve, 221
    Proclamation from the Presidency, 234
    to the Elders, 97, 102–3, 117
    to the saints, 92
Eternal, all things from God are, 232–33
Eternal
    judgment, one of the first principles of the Gospel, 482
    life, 457
Eternal fire, the Lord dwells in, 485
Eternal glories, 494
Eternity of marriage covenants, 391
Ether saw day of Christ, 106
Evangelist is a Patriarch, 193
Everlasting burnings, God dwells in, 457
Evil
    blessed are ye when speak, against you, 156
    committed voluntarily because of agency, 242
    not always wise to expose, 520
Evils, little, create most injury, 334
Exaltation
    based upon obedience to fullness of celestial law, 435
    of God, 455
Excel, some seek to, 387
Exhortation, a word of, 163
Existence
    happiness the design of, 330

not the product of chance, 66
object of, 425–26
purpose of, 66
Expedition to Rocky Mountains contemplated, 436–37
Experience, comes through suffering, 181–82
Exquisiteness if torment of the wicked, 470
Eyes and see not, 119

F

Faith
comes by hearing word of God, 189
greater need for, now, 111
necessity of, 350
parting of the veil through perfect, 5
where there is no, it is a sin, 69
Faithful, to receive celestial rest, 64
Falling from grace, 445
False Christs and deceptions, 6
False doctrines in the world, 285
False prophets, 270
False reports, 160, 182, 350
False spirits in the Church, 276
Father and the Son
power of the, 456–57
separate Personages, 408–9
Fathers blessed by the work of the children, 287
Faultfinders and accusers of the brethren on road to apostasy, 199
Faults
of men should not be spoken of at their backs, 34–35
no man without, 334
Feet, washing of, for official members only, 112–13
Fellows, Albert G., Prophet stops at home of, 502
Fire, God dwells in eternal, 484
Firstborn, Church of the. (See Church of the Firstborn.)
First Presidency, report of, at conference, 1841, 237
First principles of the Gospel, 189, 242
Flattery, a deadly poison, 173–74
Flesh and blood
cannot dwell in eternal fire where God is, 485
cannot go to place where exalted spirits are, flesh and bones can, 428
Flesh, of the righteous when quickened will dwell in eternal fire, 485
Fools trifle with souls, 173–74
Ford, Governor Thomas, letter to, 500
Forgiveness
a requirement, 197
the principle of, 307
of sins, 471
withheld from murderers, 446
Follett, King
death of, 450
discourse on death of, 450
Free agency, given to every person, 9
French prophets, 270
Friends, sympathy of, 170
Friendship, one of the grand fundamental principles, 414
Fruits of the kingdom of God, 354
Fullmer, John S., in Carthage, 508
Futurists, John's vision of, 374

G

Gabriel is Noah, 200
Gate, the strait, 79
Gathering, 204
of all things in one, 300
of the elect, 103–4
of false reports, 184
of Israel, 85, 105, 115, 183, 224, 235–36
work of the, 127
Generation, punishment awaits this, 431
Gentile nations hardly warned before destruction comes, 108
Gentile sophistry, warning against, 198
Gentiles
covenant with, 13
who unto the unbelieving, 106
German New Testament, the most nearly correct, 460
Ghost, Holy. (See Holy Ghost.)
Gift of the Holy Ghost and Holy Ghost, difference between, 258
Gift of tongues, 252, 297
Gifts
from God are just, 331
of the Gospel, 290
of Spirit, cannot be received by the world, 316
Glories
degrees of, 9
different, 472
eternal, 494
Gnolom, the punishment of those who commit the unpardonable sin, 476
God
character of, 453
kind of being He is, 453
kingdom of, 351
increases as man obeys, 60

to go in presence of, must be like Him, 281
the sectarian, 233
Godhead, Doctrine of, 245, 408
Gods
 council of the, 461
 Eternal, of all, 175
 have ascendency over angels, 409
 plurality of, 488
Gog and Magog, battle of, 364
Good, the source of all, 68
Good men have been few on the earth since Adam, 395
Gospel
 duty of Elders in preaching the, 107
 first principles of the, 431
 the gifts of the, 290
 great duty is to preach the, 142
 in England, 222
 net gathers all kinds, 204
 know carried to nations, 57
 ordinances always the same, 214
 ordinances from the beginning, 71
 preached to Abraham, 71
 preaching of, 52
 principles of, discourse on, 241
 spread of the, 228
 to go to all nations, 482
 unchangeableness of, 341, 403
Government established by the Father, 324
Government of God, 319
 based on correct principles, 61
 essential to exaltation, 60
 requirements of, 60, 330
Government of man, 282
 brings confusion, 319
 departed from the Lord, 68
Governmental authority necessary, 58
Governments, ancient, have failed, 321, 324–25
Grace, falling from, 445
Grandin, Egbert B., printer of Book of Mormon, 3
Graves, sacredness of, 383
Green, John P., at Carthage, 515
Guilty bring suffering upon the righteous, 39

H

Hades, or hell, 406
Hand of Lord cannot be stayed, 176
Hands, laying on of, discarded by the world, 242
Happiness the design of existence, 330
Harmony in Kingdom of God through obedience, 63
Hearts of children turn to fathers, 204, 443

Heaven
 the Lord speaks from, 63
 kingdom of, in last days, 121–23
 laws of binding upon man, 61
 more than one, 6
 righteous appeal to, 167
 sealing on earth and in, 444–45
 varied creatures in, 377
Heirs
 in kingdom of God, 63–64
 of the celestial kingdom, all who die who would have received the Gospel with all their hearts, 134–35
Hell, what is damnation of, 257
Heritage of the righteous, persecution is the, 336
Higbee, Judge, funeral of, 419
High Councils. (See also Councils, High.)
 duties of, 93, 114
 trials before, 210
High Priests
 administer in spiritual things, 21
 duty of, 21
 not to be seventies, 139
Hodge, A. C., mentioned, 504
Holy Ghost, gift of, 257, 312
 cannot be received without revelation, 431
 constant companion of the righteous, 181
 gift of and difference, 258
 Messenger of the Father and the Son, 424
Holy Spirit of promise, 190
Hope in God, brings purity, 76
"Horn" to make war with the Saints, 203
House of God, order always the same in, 113
Howe's *Mormonism Unveiled*, 123
Humility required of those who hold the Priesthood, 198
Husbands, love of, for wives, 109
Hyde, Orson, letter to, on Palestine mission, 208

I

Ignorance
 impossible for a man to be saved in, of the Gospel, 392
 of nature of spirits manifestations, 262
 retards the Church, 176
Imagination, beware of a fanciful, 173–74
Immorality, the curse of, 55
Immortal spirit, the, 463
Immortality
 dwells in everlasting burnings, 485
 of the spirit, 465

Increase, the power of, confined to the celestial kingdom, 391–92
Independent principles, three, 244
Indians
  the government and the, 115
  of Israel, 15, 115
Infants, baptism of,
  false doctrine, 411
  taken at times through mercy, 254
Ingratitude of men, 404
Inhabitants of earth commence to waste away before conclusion of warning, 108
Inheritance of Zion, value of, 341
Iniquity, do not look for, 41
Injury, most, comes from little things, 334
"In My Father's House," 472
Instructions
  important, 87, 90
  order of, in the Church, 21
  various, on doctrine, 189
Intelligence
  has man increased in, 321
  is eternal, 464
  the Lord is a perfect, 65
  not created, 201, 465
  superior, given to those who obey the Gospel, 80
  some greater than others, 492–93
Intemperance
  evils of, 137
  in all things a curse, 55
Interpretations of scripture, 481
Irvingvites, the, 272
Israel
  gathering of, 115
  this continent made known in Book of Mormon as residence of, 116
  purpose of the gathering of, 401
  the covenants with, to be kept, 14

J

Jacob
  known as James in the English Bible, 460
  the inheritance of, 60
Jail, last night in Carthage, 508
James and John, with Peter, received keys of Priesthood, 201
Jaques, Vienna, letter to, 28
Jaredites and Nephites, greatness of, 345
Jehovah, designs of, to regulate the affairs of men in His due time, 323

Jerusalem
  the New, 105
  to be built, 369
  and Zion, 15
  the two, 117
Jesus. (See also Christ.)
  did things His Father did, 456
  is the Lord, no man can known except by the Holy Spirit, 289
  the Mediator, 10
  only perfect being, 242
  testimony of, brought imprisonment, 155
Jews
  considered Jesus the least in the kingdom, 357
  responsibility of the, 288
John the Baptist
  greatness of mission of, 357
  held keys of Aaronic Priesthood, 353, 417
  mission of, 442
John the Revelator, with Peter and James, received keys of Priesthood, 201
Jones, Dan, in Carthage, 507
Joshua, the Jew, teachings of, 128
Joy
  comes through knowledge of God, 60
  in resurrection for the righteous, 384
Judah to return before Christ comes, 369
Judgment
  eternal, 190, 482
  evils of hasty, 148
  of men according to their deeds, 332
  to be based on purity of heart, 82
  of God on mankind, 14
Judgments
  righteous, 400
  Saints not to escape the, 207
  threatening over Zion, 18
  to be poured out, 369
Just are the plans of Jehovah, 286
"Just men are made perfect," 427
Justice
  for all the human family, 283
  in each gift from God, 331
  of the Great Lawgiver, 282

K

Key words of the Priesthood, 285
Keys of Aaronic Priesthood held by John, 353
Keys of presidency held by Adam, 216
Keys of Priesthood, 218
  brought from heaven when Gospel is sent, 200

given to Peter, James, and John, 201
held by Adam, 214
right to the, 480
Keys to mysteries, revealed, 199
Kimball, Heber C., testimony concerning, 401
Kind, every plant, tree, etc., cannot come forth only after its, 256
Kindness
should never be forgotten, 35
to animals required of man, 85
King of kings, Christ is, 495
Kingdom
all things that offend to be gathered out of the, 202
angels to gather out all things that offend, 125–26
Christ considered the least in the, by the Jews, 358
of God, 9, 45, 50, 81, 113, 121, 134–36, 139, 149, 193, 203, 207, 213, 246, 256–57, 259, 261, 267, 285, 288–89, 300, 311, 331, 342, 351–57, 373, 375, 388, 403, 405, 412, 427, 431, 443, 449, 472, 475, 482, 485, 508, 530–32, 551
fruits of, 354
requirements of, 61
of Heaven, 74–75, 90, 92, 118, 121–27, 135, 203, 264, 288, 344, 354, 358, 380, 388, 417–18, 533
men cannot be compelled into the, 310
of Satan set up, 482
vision of the celestial, 133
what it is, 352
Kings and priests unto God, 78, 416, 423, 457, 479, 488–89, 495
Knowledge
condemnation of man without, 453
he who lacks, will be brought into captivity, 281
increase of, as man approaches God, 60
men saved through obedience to, 281
of God known only by Spirit, 317
of the Gospel unlocks the mysteries of the kingdom, 388
of the purpose of existence obtained through experience, 425–26, 467
power to advance in, 427, 466
salvation through, 386
through the Spirit of God, 265
to be given to babes, 12, 174, 404
consequences of unwillingness to obtain, 386, 435

L

Lamanites to be blessed, 105
Lamb and lion to dwell together when men set example, 86
Lamech held keys of Priesthood, 218
Lands in Zion not to be sold, 37, 41
Language, Christ adapts, to capacity, 206
Law, celestial
many will fail to obtain, 435, 483
of God binding on men, 58
Law, William, dream of the Prophet concerning, 486
Law of Moses added to Gospel, 72
Lawgiver, justice of the great, 282
Laws of God
essential to glory, 64
just and holy, 63
kingdom of God governed by, 65
superior to laws of man, 61
vs. laws of man, 56–81
of man imperfect, 61
why given, 64
Laying on of hands discarded by the world, 242
Least in the kingdom of God, Christ is considered by the Jews, 358
Leaven, the parable of the, 124
Letters
from Joseph Smith to exiled Saints in Missouri, 38
to Gov. Ford, 500
to Emma Smith, 519
to O. H. Browning, 523
to Saints from Liberty prison, 164
Levitical Priesthood
added because of transgression, 72
hereditary, 417
without oath, 424
Liberty Jail, letter written from, 154
Life
the mortal, is not all, 66
purpose of, 67
source of, 66
the Son laid down his, 408–9
Life and death, sermon on, 254
Light, who will not receive, shall lose, 118
Little evils create most injury, 334
Living to work for the dead, 444
Lord, hand of
cannot be stayed, 176
the day of, approaching, 55
Love, begets love, 414
a characteristic of Deity, 223
false Christ cannot deceive those with perfect, 5
for fellow men, the Prophet's, 108, 410

of God, the sustaining kind, 165
Saints admonished to love one another, 92
the greatest, is to lay down life for friends, 252, 413
perfect, a safeguard against falling from grace, 5
Loyalty to friends, 414
Lucifer, the fall of, 387
Lying spirits abroad, 206

M

Man
condemns himself, 470
enlightened as he approaches God, 60
government of, imperfect and failure, 320
has departed from the Lord's government, 68
laws of, imperfect, 61
made out of the earth and his spirit put into him in the beginning, 463
no change in, since the fall, 71
relationship of, to God, 467
salvation of, 469
spirit of in the beginning, 201
unable to create a system of government, and to govern, 68, 322
Man, Son of. (See also Christ.) 32, 125–26, 168, 183, 200–207, 326, 357, 363, 369–70, 383, 408, 423, 430, 449, 468, 488, 538, 545, 552
Many called, but few chosen, 79, 181, 436
Markham, Stephen, in Carthage, 507–8
Marks, Ephraim, funeral of, 279
Marriage, for eternity confined to the celestial kingdom, 391
Marriage supper, parable of the, 74–75
Matter, external duration of, 393
Maxims, the Prophet's, 35
Mediator, Jesus is the, 420, 427
Meetings, insult to leave near the close of, 370
Melchizedek Priesthood, 140, 221, 287, 305, 343, 355, 415–17, 422–24, 443, 496
greater than offices, 212, 305
held by all prophets, 232
is by oath and covenant, 424
what it is, 140
Members, how dealt with, 22
Men
aged, in council, 389
dependent upon the Lord, 81
have been but few good, on the earth since Adam, 395
should lose desire to destroy in order that enmity may cease, 85
stand before God to be judged, 78

wicked persistence of, 335
Mercy, eternal principle of, 247, 309
Messiah, mission and office of, 440, 448
Michael, is Adam the Ancient of Days, 45, 154, 200, 202–3, 205, 213, 305, 326
Militia officers, the Prophet interviews, 504–5
Millennial Harbinger, the, of A. Campbell, 123
Millenium
day of, coming, 32
rule of Christ in, 347
Mind, Satan retards the human, 310
Minutes of Relief Society meeting, 333
Mission of Elijah, 220, 424, 434, 443
Mission of John the Baptist, 357, 441
Mission of John, the Revelator, 106, 201
Missionary reports, 237–39
Missouri
soil of, stained by blood, 166
the Prophet's commandment to go to, 97
Mobbings, particulars concerning, to be gathered, 35
Mormon, Book of (See Book of Mormon.)
Mormon, meaning of the word, 389
Mormonism Unveiled, Howe's, 123
Moroni, resurrected person, 150
Moses, Law of, added to Gospel, 72
Mothers arrayed against daughters, 205
Motto, political, 147
Mountains, Rocky, prophecy that Saints would be driven to the, 329
Mountains to be laid low, when Christ comes, 10
Mount Zion, saviors on, 244, 246, 289, 434, 484
Mourners, rejoice when righteous, 473
Mummies
found in Egypt with records of Abraham, 301
found in Kentucky, 301
Murderers, have no forgiveness, 446
Mustard seed, parable of the, 122, 203
Mysteries
Elders to let alone all, 94, 379
key to, 199
keys of, revealed, 174
Mysteries of the kingdom, instructions on, 149

N

Nations to be broken as potter's vessel, 14
Nauvoo
growth of, 234
meaning of name of, 234
Negro, status of the, 349
Nephite altar, at Adam-ondi-Ahman, 154
Nephites and Jaredites, greatness of, 345

Net cast in the sea, parable of, 127
Noah
  appointed to save seed of every thing from the flood, 9
  is Gabriel, 200

O

Obedience
  to government necessary, 58
  to knowledge a saving principle, 281
  to ordinances essential, 256
Offices in the Priesthood, 141
Offices and powers, part of the Priesthood, 213
Offices in the Church, all are honorable, 289
Oldest man, Adam is the, 200
"Olive Leaf," revelation, 17
Opinion, change of public, 168
Ordained
  every man who administers in the Gospel was, in grand council in heaven for that work, 482
Order
  in Church, 91
  in House of God always the same, 112–13
Ordinances
  administered by Priesthood, 201
  all are required of each individual, 435
  always the same, 214
  divine authority necessary to make valid all, 356
  fulfillment of, 435
  necessary for exaltation, 113
  in the Temple, 478
  restoration of, 221
  special, 112
Ordination
  by voice of Church, 136
  evils of hasty, 50
Organization, Priesthood and Church, 137
Overcometh, he shall be clothed in white that, 77

P

Palestine mission, letters to Elders Hyde and Page, 205
Parables
  of the Church in the last days, 122
  of the leaven, 124
  of the mustard seed, 203
  of the net cast in the sea, 127
  of the pearl of great price, 126
  of the sower, 120
  of the tares, 121
  of the treasure hid in a field, 126
  of Jesus and interpretation, 358
  why Jesus spoke in, 119
Paradise, 404
Patriarch, an Evangelist is a, 193
Patriarchal authority, 424
Patriarchal Priesthood, right of Joseph Smith Sr. to the, 44–45
Patten, David W., labors of, 29
Paul, description of, 231
Peace
  only in Zion to be found, 205
  prayer for, 239
  to be taken from earth, 205
  universal, to come from God, 325
Pearl of great price, parable of the, 127
Peck, Hezekiah, letter to, 96
Pentecost, Peter's remarks on day of, 446
People, a tried, 172
Perdition, state of sons of, 25
Perfect
  Jesus only perfect being, 242
  we cannot be, without our righteous dead, 445
Perfection
  as man approached God he draws nearer to, 60
  awaits the faithful, 64
  comes through salvation of all who are worthy, 202
  for living, depends upon their work for the righteous dead, 468
  of the Book of Mormon, 250
Perilous times, 167
Persecuted, to be blessed, 157
Persecution
  of the Prophet continues, 413
  heritage of the righteous, 336
Persecutions
  predicted, 36
  of the Saints, 166
Personages, three in Godhead, 245
Persons, the Lord no respecter of, 78
Peter, James, and John receive keys of Priesthood, 201
Peter
  the Prophet's discourse on, 395
  writings of, 397
Phelps, W. W., letter to, 17, 211
Plan of salvation, from before the world, 285
Plans of Jehovah are just, 286
Plural marriage, 426
Plural wives, instruction on, 425
Plurality of gods, 488, 491–92

Political motto, 147
Politics, Prophet's views on, 356, 438
Poor, care of the, 432
Power of wicked spirits restricted, 270
Pratt, Parley P., to remain in England, 226
Prayer,
    for afflicted Saints, 42
    in Liberty prison, 167
    necessity of, 318
Preaching to the guards, 507
Premonition of Joseph Smith, 506
Pre-ordination of every man who is called to preach the Gospel, 482
Preparation required of all who seek perfection, 65
Preparatory work, the work of Elias, 442
Presidency, First, dissolved when president dies, 133
Presidency of the United States, Prophet's views on his candidacy for the, 437
Pride
    beware of, 197
    evils of, 173
Priests should not be idle, 94
Priesthood
    all prophets held Melchizedek, 232
    all who hold, should be qualified, 142
    Church organization and, 137
    degrees of, 232
    descent of from Adam, 201
    discourse on, 199–200
    doctrines of, shall distil upon soul, 181
    gentle and long-suffering, 181
    highest order of, 305
    instruction on, 199
    is everlasting, 200
    key words of, 258
    key held by Adam next to Jesus Christ, 201
    keys of, 218, 481
    Melchizedek, holds all authority, 212
    order of, in temple building, 236
    offices in the, 141
    releases the spirits of the dead, 248
    three grand orders, 423
Principle of religious freedom, 187
Principles
    the first, 431
    not eternal are from the devil, 232
    of the Gospel never change, 402
    three independent, 244
Prison, spirits in, preached to, 283
Prisoners, last moments of, in Carthage, 524–25
Proclamation, to citizens of Nauvoo, 367

Procrastination of repentance, danger of, 255
Promises
    obtained through diligence, 78
    to ancient Saints are not ours, 78
    of God, not to be trifled with, 86
    of salvation, given to ancient Saints, 78
Property, in Zion, how to be distributed, 23
Prophecy
    that Saints would be beyond enemies in five years, 438
    gift of, 314
    is the testimony of Jesus, 150
    Saints would be driven to Rocky Mountains, 329
    sure word of, 392
    testimony of Jesus is the spirit of, 409
    to Stephen A. Douglas, 393
Prophet
    calling of a, 360, 480
    what constitutes a, 348
Prophets
    had gift of discerning of spirits, 268
    false, 270
    men should rejoice because of, 10
    reveal the word and will of God, 10
    subject to same passions as other men, 110
Proverbs of the Prophet, 415
Punishment of the devil, 387
Punishment of suspense, 371
Pure
    have hope in God, 77
    soul must be, to dwell with God, 294
Purged, the Church to be, 493

Q–R

Questions answered, 149
Reason teaches there is a God, 67
Rebellious, the, to be cast out of the kingdom of God, 61
Rebuke, value of a righteous, 142
Records
    keeping of, 87
    made of acts of men, 83
    a protection against evil, 88
Redemption, plan of, 56
Reflections, 110, 178
Reincarnation, doctrine of devil, 130
Relief Society
    address to the, 261, 306
    minutes of, 333
Religious freedom
    principle of, 187

privilege of, 454
Repentance, 100
   call to, 476
   cannot come after a man has sinned against the Holy Ghost, 472
   Christ came to call sinners to, 309
   danger of procrastination of, 255
   Elders to preach, 379
   necessity of, 379
   thing that cannot be trifled with, 189
Reports
   false, 350
   gathering of, 184
Resolutions, draft of, 136
Respect of persons, none in sight of God, 78
Responsibility
   left upon parents who deny the Gospel to children, 108
   our greatest, 468
   of the Jews who rejected the Gospel, 288
Restitution of all things, 125, 300
Restoration of ordinances, 221
Resurrection, 73, 104, 382, 483
   at time of Christ, 243
   doctrine of, among first principles, 190
   joy for the righteous in, 384
   of the dead, 480, 484
   salvation of children in, 254
   sermon on, 254
   some raised to be angels only in the, 409
   universal, 259, 484
Revelation
   Holy Ghost not received without, 431
   how and by whom received, 140
   importance of, 84
   need of, 203, 353
   not given to be trifled with, 64, 73
   of eternal truth, 175
   of necessary ceremonies, 138
   of the salvation of, the dead who died without knowledge of the Gospel, 135
   of things kept hid from before the world was, 421
   on knowledge of existence limited, 425–26
   Prophet's fear to approach the Lord for, in trivial matter, 23
   to Brigham Young, 148
   to the twelve, 137
   when and why received, 23
Revelation and the Bible, 72
Revelation and commandments, value of, 3

Revelations
   do not betray, 198
   should be searched, 8
Rewards to be given to the obedient, 64
Richards, Willard, at Carthage, 508
Rigdon, Sidney, the Prophet's reflections concerning, 33
Righteous
   crown for the, 76
   not increasing, 56
   suffer with the guilty, 38
   to dwell in everlasting burnings, 458
   to inherit glory, 9
   mourners rejoice, 473
Righteous judgment, 400
Righteousness,
   to sweep the earth, 103
   of man, and the, of God, 416
Rockwell, Orrin P., a prophecy concerning, 367
Rocky Mountain expedition, contemplated, 436
Rocky Mountain prophecy, 329
Rocky Mountains, the Prophet starts for the, 498
Rosh, meaning of, 459
Rule of Christ in Millennium, 347

S

Sacredness of burial grounds, 383
Sacrifice
   law of, 69
   of Son of God, 57
   part of restoration, 219
   type of the, of Christ, 69
Safety, a place of, to be chosen, 183
Saints
   come through tribulation, 338
   gathering of, 183
   have not much time to save their dead, 434
   location for, sought, 172
   not to escape the judgment, 207
   persecution of, 66
   prayer for afflicted, 42
   suffering of, in Missouri, 31
   to live unto God, 229
   unwillingness of, to learn, 435
Salem (Shiloam)
   king of, held keys over Abraham, 423
   should be Shiloam, 422
Salvation
   gift of, 81
   how acquired, 425
   in celestial kingdom requires baptism, 9

in fulness based upon obedience to all the
    ordinances, 435
is overcoming all enemies, 386
meaning of, 392
no, without a legal administrator, 418
no, without revelation, 203
no, without a tabernacle, 387
not where kingdom of God is not, 352
plan of, before the world was, 285
to gain, all laws must be obeyed, 437
through knowledge, 386
Salvation for the dead, 403, 479, 483
Satan
    an orator, 206
    appearing as an angel of light, 278
    buffeting of, 391, 445
    has gift of tongues, 207
    kingdom of, set up, 124, 482
    power of, to deceive, 294
    punishment of, 399
    rage of, 205
Scepter, of righteousness unchanging, 181
Sceva, modern sons of, 123
Scourge, an overflowing, to come upon mankind, 16
Scriptural correction, 360
Scriptures
    blessed is he who keeps, 326
    contain will of God, 63, 68
    interpretation of, 481, 490
    knowledge of, revealed through faith and study, 8
    meaning of the Hebrew, 459
    revision of, 6
    to be searched, 8
Sealed in Lamb's book of life, through perfect love, 6
Sealing on earth and in heaven, 444
Sealing power
    all things should be perfect through the, 447
    keys of, held by Elijah, 445
Sealings, necessary for the family order to continue in eternity, 485
Seaton, editor, 11
Second Comforter, the, 191
Second Coming of Christ, signs of, have commenced, 204, 368
Sectarian baptism, 248
Sectarian God, observation on the, 233
Secret councils, condemned, 186
Self-righteousness
    beware of, 295
    reproof of, 395
Sermons
    by the Prophet, July 23, 1843, 416
    on life and death, 254
Serpents protected by the Prophet, 86
Servants of God will not have gone over nations before destruction comes, 108
Seventies
    calling of, 91
    duties of, 209
    High Priests not to be, 139
Sherwood, Henry G., conversation with, 502
Sick
    administering to by women, 290
    should have faith, 433
    should trust in God, 246
Sign of the Son of Man, 363
Sign seeking, 361
Signs
    God has set many, 257
    of second coming have commenced, 204
    set for government of all things, 267
Sin
    people to be free from, when Christ comes, 116
    sometimes brethren accused falsely of, 250
Sin, the unpardonable, 162, 332
    cannot be committed after death, 469
    cannot be committed until after the power of the Holy Ghost is given, 470
    enormity of, 199
Sins
    all Saints should confess their, 198
    forgiveness of, 471
Smith, Alvin, heir of celestial kingdom, 135
Smith, Hyrum
    blessing of, 46
    reads from Book of Mormon in Carthage, 508
Smith, John, at Carthage, 506
Smith, Joseph
    accused by false brethren, 499
    crosses the Mississippi on way west, 500
    dream of, 521
    interview with militia officers, 504
    predicts his own death, 497
    premonition of, 506
    characterization of himself, 396
    ready to lay down life for religious freedom of all men, 410
    letter to Gov. Ford, explaining return to Nauvoo, 503
Smith, Joseph Sr.
    blessing of, 44

death of, 227
Smith, Lucy, blessing of, 44
Smith, Samuel, blessing of, 48
Smith, William, blessing of, 48
Societies, temperance, 400
Solemn assembly, 113
Son and the Father, Separate personages, Son did what Father did, 408
Son of Man
  sign of the, 363
  soon to come, 168
Sons of God, faithful are, 77
Sophistry, Gentile, warning against, 198
Soul must be pure to dwell with God, 294
Souls, saving of, 94
Souls of men, only fools trifle with, 174
Southcott, Johanna, professed prophetess, 271
Sower, parable of the, 120
Spirit
  gifts of the, 313
  Holy, of promise, 190
  Lord breathed into Adam his (Adam's), 392
  (Intelligence) not created, 201
  of God, forsakes apostates, 79
Spirit and body, difference between, 269
Spirit of God
  power of knowledge of the, 266
  things of God known only by, 317
Spirit of Lord
  testimony of, 32
  withdrawn from inhabitants of earth, 14
Spirit of murder, is not of God, 472
Spirit of Revelation, what it is, 193
Spirits
  converse together, 465
  discerning of, by power of Priesthood, 265
  do not deceive if righteous, 206
  false, in the Church, 265, 276
  how discerned, 206
  ignorance of nature of, 263
  manifestations of, 206
  ministering, 247
  try the, 206, 262
  wicked restricted in power, 270
Spirits and angels, 427
Spirits in prison, Christ preached to the, 283
Spirits of Just, are exalted, 428
Spirits of men, were in the beginning, 201
Spirits of our dead, near us and often grieved by our acts, 428
Spiritual blessings to be received, 111

Spiritual darkness, condemnation of the world, 55, 119
Spring Hill, or Tower Hill, 154
Stakes for the Almighty, all who set up for, will fail, 422
Stakes of Zion, 479
Stewardship, all who hold, must give account of, 201
Strait gate, strive to enter, 79
Strength, giving blessing a tax on, 364
Subjects of little consequence should not be brought to the Lord, 23
Sufferers to obtain a crown of righteousness, 76
Suffering, experiences through, 182
Supper, the marriage, 74
Suspense, the punishment of, 371
Sympathy of friends, 170

T

Tabernacle, no salvation without a. (See body,), 387
Tares, parable of the, 121
Taught
  Elders not sent to be, 198
  some men too wise to be, 404
Taylor, John, 510
  at Carthage, 508
Telestial kingdom, who will enter, 9
Temperance societies, the Prophet on, 400
Temple building, order of the Priesthood in, 236
Temple, Holy, things revealed in the, 409
Temple, the Nauvoo, 226, 235, 253, 298
Temple ordinances, 478
  always the same, 112
Terrestrial bodies, ministering angels, 217
Testimony of Jesus, and bond, 155
Things too wonderful to utter, 398
Throne of God, how obtained, 77
Tithing, covenant of, 84
Tongue
  guarding the, 308
  the gift of, 27, 252, 297
  proper use of, 207
  Satan can speak in, 207
  Satan can give manifestations of, 275
  true and false, 319
  were given for purpose of preaching in languages not understood, 190
"Too wise to be taught," some men are, 404
Torment, man creates his own, 470
Tower Hill, or Adam-ondi-Ahman, 154
Traitors, the Lord will not acknowledge, 496

Transfiguration of the earth shown on the mount, 10
Transgression, daily
    displeasing in sight of God, 189
    man has cut himself off from God through, 68
    of Church members, 95
Translation, the doctrine of, 217
Translations of the Bible, exceptions to, 376
Transmigration, doctrine of devil, 130
Treasure hid in a field, parable of, 126
Trials before High Councils, 210
Tribulation
    in last days, 204
    Saints came through, 338
    value of, 170
Tried people, Saints to be a, 172
Trifle not with the promises of God, 86
Trifles, the Lord not to be approached on, 23
Truth
    eternal, 175
    the power of, 449
Truth and righteousness to sweep the earth, 103
Truth in sectarian churches, 414
"Try the spirits," 262
Twelve Apostles
    address to the, 197
    authority of, 132
    not sent to be taught, but to teach, 198
    remarks to the, 110
    stand next to the First Presidency, 245

U

Unfaithfulness of men, 404
United States to be scene of bloodshed, 16
Universal, the resurrection is, 484
Unjust condemnation sign of apostasy, 199
Unlawful to utter, things, 398
Unpardonable sin, 162, 469
    cannot be committed after death, 469
    cannot be committed by man until he has first received the Holy Ghost, 470
    the shedding of innocent blood, 391

V

Valleys to be exalted, mountains abased, 10
Value of tribulation, 170
Veil, parting of, through faith, 5
Vengeance, comes through ignoring word of the Lord, 64, 94
Vicious dispositions should be overcome, 86
Violence, offered to God when his teachings are ignored, 64

Vision of the Apostles, 135
Vision of beasts, Daniel's, 372–73
Vision of the celestial kingdom, 132–33
Vision of the glories, the Prophet's views on the, 7
Vision of futurity, John's, 374
Visions
    not always from God, 206
    personal, intended only for the individual and not for the Church, 21
Voice of the Church, officers sustained by, 136

W

War and bloodshed to come, 204
Warning
    to the unrighteous, 204
    of nations not finished before angels of destruction begin work, 108
Washing and anointing, part of the endowment, 305, 478
Washing of feet, 113
Wells, Daniel H., the Prophet's remarks to, 501
Western movement of the Church, contemplated, 436
Wheelock, Cyrus, obtains list of witnesses, 521
Wicked, destruction of, at the end of the world, 125
Wicked men, persistence of, 335
Wicked spirits, restricted power of, 270
Wickedness of men, 55–56
Wickedness to prevail in the world, 205
Willful sin unpardonable, 162
Wilkinson, Jemimah, 272
Wings, angels do not have, 206
Wisdom
    God the source of, 65
    should be sought by Saints, 326
Wisdom, Word of, 148
Wise
    it behooves us to be, 326
    some are too, to be taught, 404
Witnesses, accusation of false, 158
Witnesses of the doctrines of Christ, 340
Wives
    love of, for husbands, 109
    not to be baptized contrary to wished of their husbands, 108
    plural, 425
Wives and children, duty of, 185
Wo unto the unbelieving Gentiles, 106
Women
    not with authority to organize the Church, 275

and children not to be baptized if husbands and fathers object, 108
Word of the Lord is precious, 116
Word of Wisdom should be observed, 148
Work
    the Prophet to live until his, is finished, 477
    to be cut short, 6
World
    darkness the condemnation of the, 119
    deplorable condition of the, 56
    mysteries kept hid from, 174
    not increasing in righteousness, 56, 240
Wrath of God, preparation against, 179
Writing, sacred, given by revelation, 64

Y–Z

Young, Brigham
    appointment to preach to Lamanites, 92
    revelation to, 148
    testimony concerning, 401
Zeal, beware of excessive, 306
Zion
    all of America is, 477
    city of, in Missouri, 16
    in the center of the land, 98, 478
    freedom among rulers in, 26
    how Saints should prepare to go to, 22
    and Jerusalem, 15
    saviors on Mount, 289, 434, 484
    stakes of, 479
    to be built in righteousness, 328
    to be the only place at peace, 205
    to suffer affliction, 38
    a warning to inhabitants of, 16

Also available from
GREG KOFFORD BOOKS

The Annals of the Southern Mission: A Record of the History of the Settlement of Southern Utah

James Godson Bleak
Edited by Aaron McArthur and Reid L. Neilson

Hardcover, ISBN: 978-1-58958-652-9

James G. Bleak's *Annals of the Southern Mission* (1900–1907) number 2,266 loose and lined pages and represent the finest early history of Southern Utah stretching from its initial Mormon settlement in 1849 into the early years of the twentieth century.

Bleak submitted the first portion of the history, numbering over 500 pages, to the Church Historian's Office in April 1903. He submitted additional increments of the manuscript when he visited Salt Lake City, usually for general conferences. He delivered the final installment of his Annals to the Historian's Office in October 1907. The complete holograph manuscript has been in the continuous custody of the Church History Department (formerly the Church Historian's Office) ever since.

Carefully transcribed and annotated by Aaron McArthur and Reid L. Neilson, this important work provides a detailed historical, ecclesiastical, agricultural, governmental, and cultural record of Southern Utah in the latter half of the nineteenth century.

Praise for *The Annals of the Southern Mission*:

"Professional historians and lay readers will be inspired by this vivid account of the pioneer experiences mostly before statehood or modernization. Developing water systems, establishing schools, creating courts and laws, constructing civic and commercial building and homes, raising food and animals promoting the arts, and generating faith and community harmony in some forty villages in Southern Utah and nearby Nevada and Arizona are all captured by James G.. Bleak. We will all be indebted to Brandon Metcalf for the fine Introduction and to Aaron McArthur and Reid Nielson for their brilliant editing of this important and extensive document." —Douglas Alder, Professor Emeritus and Former President of Dixie College

The Lost 116 Pages: Reconstructing the Book of Mormon's Missing Stories

Don Bradley

Paperback, ISBN: 978-1-58958-760-1
Hardcover, ISBN: 978-1-58958-040-4

On a summer day in 1828, Book of Mormon scribe and witness Martin Harris was emptying drawers, upending furniture, and ripping apart mattresses as he desperately looked for a stack of papers he had sworn to God to protect. Those pages containing the only copy of the first three months of Joseph Smith's translation of the golden plates were forever lost, and the detailed stories they held forgotten over the ensuing years—until now.

In this highly anticipated work, author Don Bradley presents over a decade of historical and scriptural research to not only tell the story of the lost pages but to reconstruct many of the detailed stories written on them. Questions explored and answered include:

- Was the lost manuscript actually 116 pages?
- How did Mormon's abridgment of this period differ from the accounts in Nephi's small plates?
- Where did the brass plates and Laban's sword come from?
- How did Lehi's family and their descendants live the Law of Moses without the temple and Aaronic priesthood?
- How did the Liahona operate?
- Why is Joseph of Egypt emphasized so much in the Book of Mormon?
- How were the first Nephites similar to the very last?
- What message did God write on the temple wall for Aminadi to translate?
- How did the Jaredite interpreters come into the hands of the Nephite kings?
- Why was King Benjamin so beloved by his people?

Despite the likely demise of those pages to the sands of time, the answers to these questions and many more are now available for the first time in nearly two centuries in *The Lost 116 Pages: Reconstructing the Book of Mormon's Missing Stories*.

Joseph Smith's Polygamy, 3 Vols.

Brian Hales

Hardcover
Volume 1: History 978-1-58958-189-0
Volume 2: History 978-1-58958-548-5
Volume 3: Theology 978-1-58958-190-6

Perhaps the least understood part of Joseph Smith's life and teachings is his introduction of polygamy to the Saints in Nauvoo. Because of the persecution he knew it would bring, Joseph said little about it publicly and only taught it to his closest and most trusted friends and associates before his martyrdom.

In this three-volume work, Brian C. Hales provides the most comprehensive faithful examination of this much misunderstood period in LDS Church history. Drawing for the first time on every known account, Hales helps us understand the history and teachings surrounding this secretive practice and also addresses and corrects many of the numerous allegations and misrepresentations concerning it. Hales further discusses how polygamy was practiced during this time and why so many of the early Saints were willing to participate in it.

Joseph Smith's Polygamy is an essential resource in understanding this challenging and misunderstood practice of early Mormonism.

Praise for *Joseph Smith's Polygamy*:

"Brian Hales wants to face up to every question, every problem, every fear about plural marriage. His answers may not satisfy everyone, but he gives readers the relevant sources where answers, if they exist, are to be found. There has never been a more thorough examination of the polygamy idea." —Richard L. Bushman, author of *Joseph Smith: Rough Stone Rolling*

"Hales's massive and well documented three volume examination of the history and theology of Mormon plural marriage, as introduced and practiced during the life of Joseph Smith, will now be the standard against which all other treatments of this important subject will be measured." —Danel W. Bachman, author of "A Study of the Mormon Practice of Plural Marriage before the Death of Joseph Smith"

"This is My Doctrine": The Development of Mormon Theology

Charles R. Harrell

Hardcover, ISBN: 978-1-58958-103-6

The principal doctrines defining Mormonism today often bear little resemblance to those it started out with in the early 1830s. This book shows that these doctrines did not originate in a vacuum but were rather prompted and informed by the religious culture from which Mormonism arose. Early Mormons, like their early Christian and even earlier Israelite predecessors, brought with them their own varied culturally conditioned theological presuppositions (a process of convergence) and only later acquired a more distinctive theological outlook (a process of differentiation).

In this first-of-its-kind comprehensive treatment of the development of Mormon theology, Charles Harrell traces the history of Latter-day Saint doctrines from the times of the Old Testament to the present. He describes how Mormonism has carried on the tradition of the biblical authors, early Christians, and later Protestants in reinterpreting scripture to accommodate new theological ideas while attempting to uphold the integrity and authority of the scriptures. In the process, he probes three questions: How did Mormon doctrines develop? What are the scriptural underpinnings of these doctrines? And what do critical scholars make of these same scriptures? In this enlightening study, Harrell systematically peels back the doctrinal accretions of time to provide a fresh new look at Mormon theology.

"*This Is My Doctrine*" will provide those already versed in Mormonism's theological tradition with a new and richer perspective of Mormon theology. Those unacquainted with Mormonism will gain an appreciation for how Mormon theology fits into the larger Jewish and Christian theological traditions.

Jan Shipps: A Social and Intellectual Portrait: How a Methodist Girl from Hueytown, Alabama, Became an Acclaimed Mormon Studies Scholar

Gordon Shepherd and Gary Shepherd

Paperback, ISBN: 978-1-58958-767-0
Hardcover, ISBN: 978-1-58958-768-7

How did Jo Ann Barnett—a Methodist girl born and raised in Hueytown, Alabama, during the Great Depression and World War II—come to be Jan Shipps, a renowned non-Mormon historian and scholar of The Church of Jesus Christ of Latter-day Saints? In Jan Shipps: A Social and Intellectual Portrait, authors Gordon Shepherd and Gary Shepherd tell the story of how Shipps not only became an important and trusted authority in a field that was predominantly made up of Mormon men, but also the crucial role she played in legitimizing Mormon Studies as a credible academic field of study.

Praise for *Jan Shipps: A Social and Intellectual Portrait*:

"The person and work of Jan Shipps comprise one of the ten most important factors enabling Mormon Studies to eclipse its parochial past. Authors Gordon and Gary Shepherd have adroitly marshalled the tools of history and social science to lay bare how this unlikely event came to be. This is important reading for any who hope to understand Shipps or the emergence of the field in which she worked. Important also for any scholar feeling that the deck in a competitive academy is stacked against them." —Phil Barlow, Neal A. Maxwell Fellow at the Neal A. Maxwell Institute for Religious Scholarship at Brigham Young University.

"Jan Shipps deserves and the Shepherds are to be thanked for this celebration of her celebrated career. The authors rightly insist this is not a thorough treatment of Jan's life but rather an account of her role in the rise Mormon Studies in the late-twentieth century. It was a watershed time and Jan was a creator of and catalyst to much of the best scholarship which flowed from it. As such, there is much to learn here about Mormonism itself and those who studied it during this period." —Kathleen Flake, Richard Lyman Bushman Professor of Mormon Studies, University of Virginia

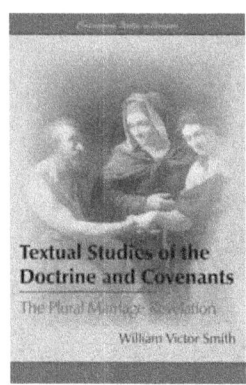

Textual Studies of the Doctrine and Covenants: The Plural Marriage Revelation

William Victor Smith

Paperback, ISBN: 978-1-58958-690-1
Hardcover, ISBN: 978-1-58958-691-8

Joseph Smith's July 12, 1843, revelation on plural marriage was the last of his formal written revelations and a transformational moment in Mormonism. While acting today as the basis for the doctrine of eternal nuclear families, the revelation came forth during a period of theological expansion as Smith was in the midst of introducing new temple rituals, radical doctrines on God and humanity, a restructured priesthood and ecclesiastical hierarchy, and, of course, the practice of plural marriage.

In this volume, author William V. Smith examines the text of this complicated and rough revelation to explore the motivation for its existence, how it reflects this dynamic theology of the Nauvoo period, and how the revelation was utilized and reinterpreted as Mormonism fully embraced and later abandoned polygamy.

Praise for *Textual Studies*:

"No Mormon text is as ritually important and as fundamentally mysterious as Doctrine and Covenants 132. William V. Smith's work is a fine example of what a serious-minded and meticulous blend of source and redaction critical methods can tell us about the revelations produced by Joseph Smith. This is a model of what the future of Mormon scriptural studies should be."
— Stephen C. Taysom, author of *Shakers, Mormons, and Religious Worlds: Conflicting Visions, Contested Boundaries*

Hearken, O Ye People: The Historical Setting of Joseph Smith's Ohio Revelations

Mark Lyman Staker

Hardcover, ISBN: 978-1-58958-113-5

2010 Best Book Award - John Whitmer Historical Association
2011 Best Book Award - Mormon History Association

More of Mormonism's canonized revelations originated in or near Kirtland than any other place. Yet many of the events connected with those revelations and their 1830s historical context have faded over time. Mark Staker reconstructs the cultural experiences by which Kirtland's Latter-day Saints made sense of the revelations Joseph Smith pronounced. This volume rebuilds that exciting decade using clues from numerous archives, privately held records, museum collections, and even the soil where early members planted corn and homes. From this vast array of sources he shapes a detailed narrative of weather, religious backgrounds, dialect differences, race relations, theological discussions, food preparation, frontier violence, astronomical phenomena, and myriad daily customs of nineteenth-century life. The result is a "from the ground up" experience that today's Latter-day Saints can all but walk into and touch.

Praise for *Hearken O Ye People*:

"I am not aware of a more deeply researched and richly contextualized study of any period of Mormon church history than Mark Staker's study of Mormons in Ohio. We learn about everything from the details of Alexander Campbell's views on priesthood authority to the road conditions and weather on the four Lamanite missionaries' journey from New York to Ohio. All the Ohio revelations and even the First Vision are made to pulse with new meaning. This book sets a new standard of in-depth research in Latter-day Saint history."
-Richard Bushman, author of *Joseph Smith: Rough Stone Rolling*

"To be well-informed, any student of Latter-day Saint history and doctrine must now be acquainted with the remarkable research of Mark Staker on the important history of the church in the Kirtland, Ohio, area."
-Neal A. Maxwell Institute, Brigham Young University

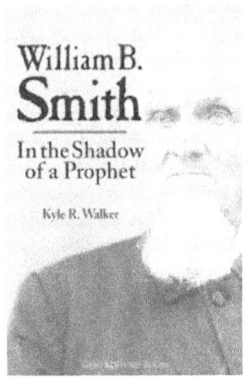

William B. Smith: In the Shadow of a Prophet

Kyle R. Walker

Paperback, ISBN: 978-1-58958-503-4

Younger brother of Joseph Smith, a member of the Quorum of the Twelve Apostles, and Church Patriarch for a time, William Smith had tumultuous yet devoted relationships with Joseph, his fellow members of the Twelve, and the LDS and RLDS (Community of Christ) churches. Walker's imposing biography examines not only William's complex life in detail, but also sheds additional light on the family dynamics of Joseph and Lucy Mack Smith, as well as the turbulent intersections between the LDS and RLDS churches. *William B. Smith: In the Shadow of a Prophet* is a vital contribution to Mormon history in both the LDS and RLDS traditions.

Praise for *William B. Smith*:

"Bullseye! Kyle Walker's biography of Joseph Smith Jr.'s lesser known younger brother William is right on target. It weaves a narrative that is searching, balanced, and comprehensive. Walker puts this former Mormon apostle solidly within a Smith family setting, and he hits the mark for anyone interested in Joseph Smith and his family. Walker's biography will become essential reading on leadership dynamics within Mormonism after Joseph Smith's death." — Mark Staker, author *Hearken, O Ye People: The Historical Setting of Joseph Smith's Ohio Revelations*

"This perceptive biography on William, the last remaining Smith brother, provides a thorough timeline of his life's journey and elucidates how his insatiable discontent eventually tempered the once irascible young man into a seasoned patriarch loved by those who knew him." — Erin B. Metcalfe, president (2014–15) John Whitmer Historical Association

"I suspect that this comprehensive treatment will serve as the definitive biography for years to come; it will certainly be difficult to improve upon." — Joe Steve Swick III, Association for Mormon Letters

www.ingramcontent.com/pod-product-compliance
Lightning Source LLC
Chambersburg PA
CBHW060344010526
44117CB00017B/2962